C0-BEG-273

Facets of European Modernism

Essays in honour of James McFarlane presented to him on his 65th birthday 12 December 1985

Edited by Janet Garton

Facets of European Modernism

Facets of European Modernism: Essays in honour of James McFarlane. Ed. Janet Garton. University of East Anglia, Norwich 1985.

ISBN 0-902171-14-3

The editor would like to thank the following institutions:

Munch Museum, Oslo, for permission to reproduce works by Edvard Munch in Carla Lathe: Edvard Munch and Modernism in the Berlin Art World 1892–1903

Rungstedlund Foundation, Denmark, and Random House, Inc., USA, for permission to quote from the Danish and English versions respectively of Karen Blixen's works in Elias Bredsdorff: Isak Dinesen v. Karen Blixen: **Seven Gothic Tales** and **Syv fantastiske Fortællinger**

Deutsches Theatermuseum, Munich, for permission to reproduce photographs from their archives in Elinor Shaffer: Christian Morgenstern and the Emergence of Modernism in the Berlin Theatre

The University of East Anglia, Norwich, for granting study leave to enable the editor to prepare the material for this volume

Printed by the University of East Anglia
Cover design by Richard Johnson

Foreword

In December 1985, James McFarlane – "Mac" – reaches the official retiring age for university professors. He comes to the end of a long and distinguished phase in his career, which began with a lectureship in German at the University of Newcastle, and led to a chair in European Literature at the newly founded University of East Anglia in the early 1960s. He was one of the founding fathers of the university, a central figure in the planning of its interdisciplinary structure and especially in the establishing of the School of European Studies, of which he became the first Dean in 1964. His skills as an administrator and his vision as a planner kept him involved at many levels in the development and growth of the university over the next two decades.

To his considerable number of friends and colleagues abroad, Mac is primarily an influential scholar and writer. His work on European and Scandinavian literature has won him an international reputation. He is particularly well known as the editor and main translator of the eight-volume standard edition of Ibsen in English, **The Oxford Ibsen**, and as co-editor with Malcolm Bradbury of the seminal work **Modernism.** In addition, he has produced a large number of scholarly articles and translations from Norwegian, including Knut Hamsun's novels **Pan** and **Wayfarers**. Since 1975 he has edited **Scandinavica**, the British journal of Scandinavian studies. His contribution to international scholarship has won him various distinguished awards: he is a member of the Norwegian Academy and the Danish Academy, and was in 1975 created a Knight Commander of the Royal Norwegian Order of St. Olaf.

Those who have the privilege of working closely with him, however, are as deeply impressed by his warmth and humanity as by his scholarship. Mac is a humanist in the fullest sense of the word. Generations of undergraduate and post-graduate students will remember him with gratitude as a wise and understanding teacher, whose standards were never less than exacting but whose judgments were always tempered with gentle and patient kindness. Colleagues who have worked with him on some of his many projects speak with affection of his unflagging enthusiasm and his generous openness to new ideas and suggestions. He is an unassuming and unselfish collaborator, never basking in the limelight but looking always to the advancement of his subject and the good of his colleagues, especially the many younger ones whose careers he has been influential in shaping.

There is, fortunately, no sign at all that Mac has any intention of curtailing his involvement in scholarly work following his official retirement. He will remain as editor of **Scandinavica**, and is, together with the editor of this volume, planning to embark upon an ambitious publishing enterprise, producing a series of books on Scandinavian literature and English translations of Scandinavian classics. In 1986 Norvik Press will issue its first publications. The project has already attracted considerable funding, and plans to make full use of modern word-processing technology – an area in which Mac has in recent years become an expert and a pioneer.

A number of Mac's friends, both former students and former and present colleagues, decided a few years ago that we should like to take this opportunity of his "official" retirement to show our appreciation and esteem by presenting him with a volume of essays on a subject which he has made his own. We have been joined by many people from around the world who have wished to add their congratulations and subscribe to the volume.

May we all wish you, Mac, many more fulfilling and productive years – for our sakes as much as for yours. We hope you like your book, which we present to you with gratitude and with love.

Janet

Contents

Tabula Gratulatoria

Asbjørn Aarseth
Åbo Akademi, Litteraturvetenskapliga institutionen
Gustav Albeck
Jenny Allison
A. Gerald Anderson
Stephen Archer

Michael Balfour
Oskar Bandle
Michael P. Barnes
Walter Baumgartner
John Bell
John Eric Bellquist
Aslaug and Edvard Beyer
Alan Birt
Alex Bolckmans
Harold and Margaret Borland
Malcolm Bradbury
Elias Bredsdorff
Nicholas Brooke
Karen Brookfield
J.W. Burrow
Wolfgang Butt
Dolores Buttry

Charlotte Carstairs
Christ's College Library, Cambridge
D.F.L. Chadd
David Charlton
Erik M. Christensen
Paul Christophersen
Ingrid Clareus
Gunnel Clark
August Closs
John Gordon Coates
Flemming Conrad
Eli and Mike Cook
Patricia Crampton
Vera Croghan
A.G. Cross

The Royal Danish Embassy
The Danish Cultural Institute, Edinburgh
Terence Dawson
E. Rodney Davey
Reidar Djupedal

Jørgen Egebak
Eiliv Eide
Bo Elbrønd-Bek
Bente and John Elsworth

Beatrice Fayl
Eric and Lorraine Fernie
Rolf Fjelde
Kjetil A. Flatin
John Fletcher
John Flower
Peter Foote
Leonard Forster
Malcolm Freegard
Wilhelm Friese
Nick and Sylvia Furness

Tom Geddes
Bernhard Glienke
Maurice Gravier
Ronald Gray
Vivian Mitchell Greene-Gantzberg
Valerie and Willi Guttsman

Otto Hageberg
Christine Hambro
Flora and Lars Hartveit
Ihab and Sally Hassan
Annegret Heitmann
George D. Hendry
Elizabeth Hill
Julian Hilton
Gladys Hird
Philip Holmes
Elsa and Ludvig Holm-Olsen
Eric Homberger
Lars Hulden

Faith and Niels Ingwersen
Toni Irvin

Barbro and Harry Järv
Niels Lyhne Jensen
Peter Johnson
Kirsten and Glyn Jones

Andrew F. Kennedy
Atle Kittang
H.K. Klein

Carla Lathe
Birgit and Åke Leander

Terje I. Leiren
Charles Leland
Åse Hiorth Lervik
Heinz Liebrecht
Elsa and Örjan Lindberger
Hans G. Lindkjølen
Leif Longum
Ivar Lunden

R.J. McClean
Tora and Leif Mæhle
Odd Martin Mæland
Frederick and Lise-Lone Marker
Eivor Martinus
Andras Masàt
Haydn Mason
Marshall Matson
Aslaug Groven Michaelsen
Josef B. Michl
P.M. Mitchell
Randi Langen Moen
Estelle Morgan
Irene V. Morris

Harald Næss
Walter W. Nelson
Rolf N. Nettum
Ingrid and Tor Neumann
Mary Kay Norseng
John Northam
The Royal Norwegian Embassy

Stewart P. Oakley
Kenneth H. Ober
Otto Oberholzer
Astrid E.J. Ogilvie
Birgitta Oglethorpe
Myles M.F. Oliver
Gavin Orton
John Osborne

Eirwen and Idris Parry
Fritz Paul
Timothy Penton
Kerstin Petersson
Karin Petherick
Siegbert Prawer
Göran Printz-Påhlson

Per Rand
Anna-Marie Ravn

Gerd Enno Rieger
Michael Robinson
Jytte and Gunner Roed
Elizabeth Rokkan
Helge Rønning
Oddveig Røsegg
Sven Hakon Rossel
Brian Rowley

Mary Sandbach
Kari Anne Rand Schmidt and Tom Schmidt
George C. Schoolfield
Irene Scobbie
Clive Scott
Henning Sehmsdorf
Monica Setterwall
Elinor Shaffer
Richard Sheppard
Leif Sjöberg
Kristian Smidt
Christopher Smith
Hassell Smith
Bodil Verhaegen Sommer
Mari and Daniel Soutine
Erich Speidel
Birgitta Steene
Thure Stenström
Richard N.M.C. Stephen
J.P. Stern
Torbjørn Støverud
Åsfrid Svensen
The Swedish Institute

Taylor Institution, Oxford
Frank and Jane Thistlethwaite
David Thomas
Birgitta and Laurie Thompson
Michael and Sybil Thompson
Grace Thornton
Egil Törnqvist
John Townsend

Universitetet i Bergen, Nordisk institutt
Universitetet i Odense, Nordisk institut
Universitetet i Oslo, Dept. of Scandinavian Languages and Literature
Universitetet i Trondheim, Nordisk institutt
University College Library, St David's, Lampeter
University of Cambridge, Modern and Medieval Languages Library
University of East Anglia Library
University of Leeds, Brotherton Library

University of London Institute of Germanic Studies
University of London Library
University of Newcastle upon Tyne, Dept. of German and Scandinavian Studies
University of Sheffield, Dept. of Germanic Studies
University of Washington Libraries

Amy van Marken
Einar A. Vannebo
Richard Beckman Vowles

Carla Waal
Peter David Walton
Stephen J. Walton
Albert Ward
Marie Wells
Geoff Williams
Simon Williams
Roy Wisbey
John and Kate Wood
Johan Wrede

Robin Young

The Final Year

It was the year when the abandoned cottage in the woods was sold for fire-wood.
The woodcutters came with their truck
and tore it down in three hours and a quarter
and even took with them the well-frame.
It was so small when they detached it from the well
that they did not bother to smash it
but put it up on the bed of the truck just as it was.
And there it sat, a little gray chest covered with moss.

When all was quiet again
the weasel came out of the old fireplace.
It summoned a cuckoo from the woods,
and the two of them held a devotional hour.
The cuckoo sang a cuckoo hymn.
By then everything was over:
Nothing after that was as it was before.
But still the summer sauntered forth,
loosening its grasses and garlands.

Harry Martinson
Translated from the Swedish
by William Jay Smith
and Leif Sjöberg

Anticipations of Modernism in the Age of Romanticism

Brian A. Rowley

The addressee of this volume has done pioneering work on the precise moment at which Modernist ideas and practice emerged.[1] The topic I am seeking to survey is a different but complementary one – that of the parallelism between Modernism and Romanticism, especially on the German side.

In a general way, this parallelism is a commonplace of literary history;[2] and there are also many references, in studies both of Romanticism and of Modernism, to particular parallels between the two. Nevertheless, it may still be useful to survey more systematically the ways in which Romanticism anticipated Modernism.

The simple chronological parallel between the two movements is itself of more than trivial importance. Romanticism established itself as the dominant literary movement in the 1790s, though with antecedents which go back some thirty years. Modernism, similarly, came to prominence in the 1890s – though in this case the cultural revolution took a little longer to establish itself – and here too there are antecedents going back to the 1860s. In each case, we must not overlook the influence of the turn of the century itself (B. & M., p.29): illogically perhaps, people expect years such as 1800 and 1900 to bring change, and this centennial expectation does itself help to bring about change – an effect that is apparent in Novalis's essay "Die Christenheit oder Europa". It will be intriguing to those, if any, of us who survive till then to see if this effect is repeated, though with a millenary emphasis, in the year 2000.

It has also not been overlooked that in each case the cultural movement was associated with decisive political change – Romanticism with the French Revolution,[3] Modernism with that decay of upper-class, "Edwardian" splendour which was uncovered by the First World War and ratified by the Russian Revolution. But, in a wider sense, Romanticism and Modernism marked a turning away from cultures which had become increasingly perceived as alien and alienating – cultures which were rational, practical, common-sense and, ultimately, materialist and monetarist. In this sense, Romanticism and Modernism are simply two examples – though two very important examples – of that oscillation between real and ideal, sense and sensibility, reason and imagination, which recurs in the history of human attitudes.

An important way of looking at both movements, then, is to see them as dissolving reasonable expectations, as dissecting our sensible, but not necessarily accurate, view of the solidity of experience; and as doing so somewhat ostentatiously, with the ethos of the avant garde (B. & M., p.194, cf. pp.24, 28). It is not surprising that Romantic writers were drawn to look below the surface appearance of the world, in view of what was going on in the natural sciences of their day (Hughes, pp.12–13). Lavoisier was laying the foundations of chemical analysis. More exciting was the early work on electricity, which was seen as providing a possible link between the physical and the psychological: the work of Galvani, for example, finds some curious echoes in Romantic writing, from the revival of Freya in "Klingsohrs Märchen" (**Heinrich von Ofterdingen**) to the creation of Frankenstein's monster in Mary Shelley's novel. Novalis himself made entries in his notebooks which suggest an incipient awareness of wave theory, and even of relativity.[4] More exciting still were the first faint stirrings of psychiatry and of depth psychology.[5] After a nineteenth century which was mainly concerned with practical function rather than with underlying essence, analysis returned with a vengeance at the end of the century, and the notion of surface solidity was finally exploded: in physics, with Einstein or Max Planck; in biology, with the beginnings of genetics in the work of Mendel; in psychology, notably with Freud and Jung; and in the new discipline of sociology (see Alan Bullock, in B. & M., pp.66–67).

It is easiest to recognize the new ethos of the work of art in Romanticism and Modernism in relation to formal features. The predecessors of each movement had tended to assume that content was what mattered, and that form was an agreeable adjunct: in the eighteenth century the emphasis had been placed on ideas, in the nineteenth century it was placed rather on objects. Hughes describes Romantic art as non-mimetic (p.61); whilst David Lodge suggests that both Romantic and Symbolist writings are metaphoric, in Jacobson's sense of the term, as opposed to the metonymic art of the Realists (in B. & M., pp.482–84). At the end of each century, the delights of form were rediscovered and, more especially, the attractions of formal innovations (B. & M., p.481). Writers became self-conscious about form, which previously had been seen, ideally, as transparent (B. & M., pp.393, 401, 425–26). A similar situation arose in the visual arts, where the abstract art of Modernism[6] is anticipated in the work of a painter such as Runge. Ludwig Tieck puts the following words into the mouth of Ludoviko, in **Franz Sternbalds Wanderungen**: "warum soll eben Inhalt den Inhalt eines Gedichts ausmachen?"[7] Similarly in Modernism; as Bradbury and McFarlane put it, the writings have "a quality of abstraction and highly conscious artifice, taking us behind familiar reality, breaking away from familiar functions of language and conventions of form" (p.24); and again: "art turns from realism and humanistic representation towards style, technique, and spatial form in pursuit of a deeper penetration of life" (p.25).

The emphasis in Romanticism was textural rather than structural and, within this, fell mainly on the aural aspects of language: rhythm and, more especially, tonal features, sounds. This is in line with the general Romantic view that music is the acme of the arts, because it is the one with the least element of content and the greatest element of form; it appeals, therefore, directly to the psyche, and not mediately through the intelligence. Tieck again:

Liebe denkt in süßen Tönen,
Denn Gedanken stehn zu fern . . .[8]

Tieck himself made great use of verbal sound, as of rhythmic ebb and flow, in his lyric verse; but Brentano was the great virtuoso of the Romantic movement in this dimension (Hughes, pp.88–89, following Enzensberger): sometimes with results that are more striking than convincing, as in "Wie sich auch die Zeit will wenden, enden",[9] or in "Wie wird mir?":

Wie wird mir? Wer wollte wohl weinen,
Wenn winkend aus wiegendem See
Süß sinnend die Sternelein scheinen,
Werd' heiter, weich' weiter du wildwundes Herz . . .

(I, p.244)

At its best, however, as in the contrast between the dark 'a' of past happiness now departed and the piercing 'ei' of present isolation and grief, in "Der Spinnerin Nachtlied" (I, p.131), or in the tonal evocation of evening stillness and sleep in "Hörst du wie die Brunnen rauschen" (I, p.252),[10] Brentano does succeed in exploring with a new intensity a resource of lyric art which his immediate predecessors had neglected. The new resource is even more successfully integrated by Eichendorff – who does not have the intoxicating enthusiasm of the pioneer – in poems such as "Sehnsucht"[11] or, more perfect still, "Mondnacht".[12]

Emphasis on the dimension of sound is equally apparent in many Modernist poets, as Robert Short brings out in his discussion of "phonetic poetry" in writers such as Marinetti, August Stramm or Richard Huelsenbeck (B. & M., p.298). Here, the tentative explorations of the Romantics are carried through to a – sometimes extreme – conclusion.

Although sound was the paramount formal resource for the Romantic poets, other formal aspects of language were also exploited. Rhythm and structure come together in the move away from the stanzaic form of much eighteenth-century poetry to the free verse which had been launched by Goethe and other poets of the Sturm und Drang, and which was further explored by Wordsworth, Hölderlin, Novalis, Tieck and others. Clive Scott has discussed the way in which these initiatives anticipate the veritable explosion of free-verse experimentation among Modernist poets (B. & M., p.350). It is only an apparent contradiction that there was also, especially from Novalis, Tieck and the English Romantics, a surge of interest in set forms, notably the sonnet;[13] for what free verse and the sonnet have in common is a conspicuous emphasis on the use of rhythm and structure to make meaning, in contradistinction to the continuation of a bland, imperceptible stanzaic norm. The widespread use of the sonnet, and of structures echoing the sonnet, in Modernism is illustrated by writers as different as Rimbaud and Rilke, Hopkins and Hofmannsthal, Owen and Trakl.

Concentration on sound, rhythm and structure is more effective in the small-scale vehicle of lyric poetry. Both in the lyric and in prose, however, the diction of Romantic writers also cultivates new dimensions: on the one hand, the language of feeling and intuition, and on the other, the even more creative language of the imagination, rich in imagery and symbolism – apparent, to take only a single example, in the way in which Novalis, in **Hymnen an die Nacht**, links together the experiences of love, religion, death, sleep and intoxication by an interlocking web of imagery – "Nacht", "Sonne", "Geliebte(r)", "Mohn", "Grab", "Hügel", "Schoß". This "belief in the regenerative function of language", as Hughes categorizes it (p.24), is one of the major links between Romanticism and Modernism – as is its concomitant, the notion of a linguistic crisis (B. & M., p.323). If Hofmannsthal is an example of this notion with a negative sign, Stefan George or James Joyce represent its more creative face. Wilhelm Emrich, too, has pointed out that the same preoccupation leads in Expressionism to an attempt to use language with an absolute immediacy of communication;[14] that is, once again, in the manner of music.

This preference for communication through form in the Romantic period is reflected not only in the differential emphasis on various aspects of language, but also in a spectrum shift between genres. The spotlight moves away from traditional drama, a genre which implies not only the physical presence of an audience, but also at least some community of expectation between writer and listener. Lyric poetry becomes the dominant form – and, whether we are talking of England, France or Germany, it is the lyric poets who spring to mind when we think of Romanticism. After the poetry, it is

Der blonde Eckbert or **Peter Schlemihl, Heinrich von Ofterdingen** or **Der goldne Topf, Der Sandmann** or **Frankenstein** which are the characteristic works of Romanticism. There is a preference for those forms of fiction which are not primarily concerned with representation – the **Märchen**, the **Bildungsroman**, and science fiction. Hughes has drawn attention to the absence of precise location in time and space in Romantic fiction – a good example would be Tiecke's **Der Runenberg**, where time is of no consequence, and space matters only in the symbolic separation of mountain and valley – and in this he sees foreshadowed a typical work of Modernist fiction, such as Kafka's **Das Schloß** (p.76). At the same time, external plot gives way to inner unity: in the **Bildungsroman**, for example in **Heinrich von Ofterdingen**, incidents are included because of their importance for Heinrich's self-awareness, not for their place in the plot. The same point is made about Modernist fiction by David Lodge (B. & M., p.481, cf. pp.393, 437, 453); and Michael Hollington identifies a more extreme form of the same phenomenon: "'Non-events' are distinctive features of Modernist writing" (B. & M., p.430). Such non-plots even become a feature of Modernist drama (B. & M., p.534). In Romanticism, the drama is very much an also-ran – except in the special case of France; and except in the equally special case of ironic comedy, where the Elizabethan interest in the mechanics of drama was revived by Ludwig Tieck, who created in **Der gestiefelte Kater** the first of a series of meta-dramas, delighting in their play with the illusion of drama itself. Both in Romanticism and in Modernism, writers tried to combine the fairy-tale with drama. Modernist examples given by McFarlane include Yeats, Maeterlinck and Strindberg (B. & M., p.563). There are precedents for this too in Tieck, not only in the ironic comedies such as **Der gestiefelte Kater**, but also in serious fairy-tale dramas such as **Leben und Tod der heiligen Genoveva**; even though we may say that the later writers followed Tieck's lead with greater finesse and, therefore, success.

These formal emphases and genre shifts represent, of course, a subjectivization, a making self-conscious of the manner of art. This is quite obvious in ironic comedy, where the person of "a dramatist" – not, of course, to be confused with "the author" – becomes a central part of the subject-matter, and his mode of operation is examined. In a more subtle way, the same is true of Romantic fiction: as is apparent in **Heinrich von Ofterdingen** when Heinrich is initiated into the art of story-telling by Klingsohr relating his own **Märchen** in Book I, Chapter 9; still more so in Chapter 5, when he looks into the book of his own life. In a different tone, but with the same preoccupation, the narrator of Brentano's **Kasperl und Annerl** distances himself from the role of writer; and the more unlikely events of Bertha's life, in **Der blonde Eckbert**, are told in her own narrative within the story. In **Godwi**, Brentano notoriously allows Godwi, having read the first volume of the story of his own life, to say to the narrator: "'Dies ist der Teich, in den ich Seite 146 im ersten Band falle.'" (II, p.307). These meta-fictions, and the many others in Romantic prose, were doubtless influenced by Goethe's ironization of Wilhelm's narrative of his own life, in the opening book of **Wilhelm Meisters Lehrjahre**, and his general play with levels of narration through the use of interpolation in the novel; and, behind Goethe again, by those fathers of the experimental novel, Diderot and Sterne, who were his mentors; and, behind these again, by Shakespeare, for example in **Hamlet** or **A Midsummer Night's Dream**.

Earlier writers on Romanticism treated these meta-fictions as simple illustrations of Friedrich Schlegel's views on irony – the so-called "Romantic Irony" – a view which has been persuasively refuted by Raymond Immerwahr.[15] Romantic practice has been followed by many Modernist writers: a predilection for meta-theatre is a familiar characteristic of Modernist drama, whether in Strindberg's **Dream Play** or in Pirandello's **Six Characters in Search of an Author** (B. & M., pp.509, 517–18, 567).

It is in any case a mistake to interpret Schlegel's theory narrowly as "the destruction of aesthetic illusion, to demonstrate artistic superiority", which is how Romantic Irony has sometimes been understood. Romantic theory, as set out by Friedrich Schlegel, implies something more than such trivial and local meta-fictions: it implies that whole works are informed by a frame of mind in which the author is exploring possibilities rather than operating within one of these possibilities: "The poem is no longer a finished statement, but an insight into a dynamically expanding range of possibilities" (Hughes, p.56). Hughes gives a specific Modernist parallel in Thomas Mann's fiction, from **Tonio Kröger** to **Doktor Faustus**. But the same openness is, of course, characteristic of many other Modernist works.

The subjectivization of the form of art, which I have just been discussing, is a reflection of that shift of attention from the outer to the inner world which characterizes both Romanticism and Modernism. As already stated, this is part of a pendulum swing in the history of human culture; but the two poles concerned are not, of course, selected at random. Whereas other species may occupy a world that is dominated by signals from outside, the human experience is defined by the dichotomy between outside world and self, object and subject. There are times in which, writers in whom, these two domains attain some kind of precarious balance – Goethe is an instructive example – but, for the most part, one or the other prevails; and Romanticism and Modernism are two high-points of the supremacy of the subject.[16]

However, this is not, as is often supposed, to be completely identified with the supremacy of feeling. It is true that both Romanticism and Modernism distrust and reject rationality; but this is because they perceive rationality as subordinating, indeed sacrificing the inner life of the spirit to rational demands which are ultimately demands of the outside world. It is an essential feature of this inner life that it preserves feeling, the affective life, but not at the expense of all else. Intellectuality is certainly contained within the inner life, as the reader of Novalis or Shelley, Joyce or Rilke will rapidly perceive. The "inner life" of Romanticism and Modernism is an inner life before the divorce between feeling and reason, as the personification of aspects of the psyche in human form which is at the heart of the plot of "Klingsohrs Märchen" makes clear. What is true, certainly, is that intellectual processes take place by intuition, stemming from this undivided personality, rather than from conscious processes of thought.

Bradbury and McFarlane have argued that the interpenetration of "reason and unreason, intellect and emotion, subjective and objective" is characteristic of Modernism and, by implication, may distinguish it from Romanticism (p.47). I am here arguing against that view or, at any rate, arguing that the difference is one of degree, not one of kind.

Not surprisingly then, this emphasis on the inner life shapes the subject-matter of Romantic and Modernist writing. It is not the outside world that makes up their subject-matter, but the inner world, or at best the reaction of the inner to the outer world (see B. & M., pp.196, 197, 393).

This is apparent already in the presentation of nature or, it might be better to say, landscape. The poets of the nineteenth century wrote objectively, in the sense that they wrote poems about objects, even though these object-poems – whether about beech trees or brimstone butterflies, North Sea mud-flats or Swiss lake-steamers – often symbolize and illuminate the inner world. But the Romantic nature-poet speaks rather of the relation between self and world (Hughes, p.5): sometimes directly, at its most extreme in the form of the pathetic fallacy of a poem like Lamartine's "Le lac", but at least indirectly, in a spiritualization of the landscape, which thus becomes a landscape of the soul, or of the beloved. So the "Heide" which Eichendorff's Taugenichts crosses to reach Rome is presented not only as a "heath", in the landscape sense, but also as a haunt of the "heathen";[17] and Heinrich's dream of plucking the Blue Flower, at the beginning of **Heinrich von Ofterdingen**, is set in a landscape which is erotic as well as topographical. Titles such as **The Map of Love**, or "The force that through the green fuse drives the flower", in Dylan Thomas, represent the last outpost in Modernism of this interpenetration of nature and landscape, on the one hand, and human experience, on the other.

This is not to say that the landscapes of Romanticism and of Modernism are identical. There is some overlap, certainly. Rilke or D.H. Lawrence were at home in the same world of bursting buds and falling leaves as Keats or Lamartine. But it may be objected that there is a cardinal difference: the pulsating, absorbing and yet repulsive world of the industrial city, which is such a central theme of Modernism (Richard Sheppard, in B. & M., p.383), appears to be absent from Romantic writing. In an obvious sense, this is true, and it is true because industrialization and even urbanization had made so little progress in the Romantic Age. In England, of course, industrialization started early: witness the first factory-made bridge across the River Severn, of 1786, which gave its name to the town of Ironbridge. In France and especially in Germany, the process was much slower in getting under way, and it is certainly doubtful if any of the German Romantics writing at the turn of the century had ever seen a factory. Even in England, however, industrialization had made so little headway when the Romantics were writing that almost every citizen could easily walk out into the country from his/her home or place of work, in a very short time. The evidence of Mrs Gaskell's **Mary Barton** makes it clear that this was still true as late as the 1840s, even in rapidly expanding industrial cities such as Manchester.

However, reactions to urbanization and industrialization are not entirely absent, even in the Romantic period. Blake's "dark Satanic Mills"[18] and Wordsworth's "Ships, towers, domes, theatres, and temples" and "very houses"[19] already adumbrate the elements of horror and delight which later characterize the Modernist image of the city. Moreover, though factories and even conurbations are not familiar features of Romantic writing, the attitudes to life which they represent certainly are. Eichendorff's contrast between:

Die Trägen, die zu Hause liegen,
Erquicket nicht das Morgenrot,
Sie wissen nur von Kinderwiegen,
Von Sorgen, Last und Not um Brot.

and:

Wem Gott will recht Gunst erweisen,
Den schickt er in die weite Welt;
Dem will er seine Wunder weisen
In Berg und Wald und Strom und Feld.[20]

is only one of the most famous of a range of similar statements, or implications, in German Romantic writing.

A particular feature of the affinity between man and nature is that moment of piercing perception in which some experience in the outside, natural world brings illumination to the experiencer. Such moments have come to be known, from their significance for James Joyce, for example in Stephen's experience in Dublin Bay, as "epiphanies", but they are by no means a monopoly of Joyce; they occur in writers as varied as Lawrence and Rilke, Hofmannsthal and Houseman. As Hughes has observed, however, they are also a feature of Romanticism (p.6, cf. p.61). The hero of **Aus dem Leben eines Taugenichts** experiences a whole series of such epiphanies, which for him are intimations of the divine – occasioned by "hieroglyphs", to use a favourite Romantic word. One of the most striking Romantic epiphanies is the experience of the bereaved lover who is the speaker in Novalis's **Hymnen an die Nacht**, at the grave of his beloved, in the third hymn.

As the **Hymnen an die Nacht** demonstrate, these Romantic epiphanies often take place at night. Night is one of the favourite aspects of nature for the Romantic writer, and this for a whole range of related reasons. It is a time when the natural world is at its most mysterious, seductive and/or threatening. It is a time when the diurnal demands of activity and work, the insistent clamourings of the outside world, are replaced by leisure to concentrate upon the self: in particular, the unconscious is freed from the constraints of rationality, and imagination can go free. It is a time associated with manifestations of the supernatural. It is a time of sleep, and therefore of dream: once again, a release of the imagination. It is a time analogous with death, that other great releaser. It is a time of love. All these attributes of night are perceived as interrelated by the Romantic writer – most strikingly, as we have seen, by Novalis in **Hymnen an die Nacht**. But night and its beauties and mysteries form a central theme of German Romantic poetry from Tieck and Brentano, who see it in a positive light, to Eichendorff and Mörike,[21] in whom it becomes more ambivalent. It is also a favourite setting in Romantic fiction, where the motif reaches a climax in the **Nachtwachen** of Bonaventura – a work which is clearly within the Romantic orbit, even if, as Linde Katritzky has recently argued,[22] its author turns out to have been Lichtenberg, a son of the Enlightenment. But in writers from Tieck and Brentano through Hoffmann and Mary Shelley to Eichendorff – as in the latter's fascinated repugnance for nocturnal experience in **Das Marmorbild**, to name only one example – night is a recurrent preoccupation, not to say obsession, of Romantic writing.

In relation to the motif of night, Modernist writing does not follow exactly its Romantic antecedents. There are certainly writers – Rilke and Lawrence are again obvious examples – for whom night is of paramount importance. But in many other writers, night is not a dominant motif, let alone an obsession. In some ways, perhaps, one might argue that the central place of night in the iconography of Romanticism is taken over by the motif of the city, which I have already discussed, and the motif of war, to which I shall return. To put it in another way: dream and nightmare have given way to day-dream and the nightmare of the everyday; and, in the course of this transformation, a predominantly positive accent has turned into something decidedly more negative. The depths of the unconscious turn out to be full of Dead Sea fruit. Or, as Mörike already expresses the disenchantment at the end of the Romantic movement itself:

Die goldnen Adern konnt' ich nirgend schauen,
Und um mich schüttert sehnsuchtvolles Grauen.[23]

If nature is an all-pervading dimension of the relationship between the self and the world in Romanticism, love follows close behind. And yet, there are some curious features of the Romantic representation of love. One of the most striking contrasts between Romantic and Realist writing is that, in the later movement, attention has shifted from love to marriage. Whether in **David Copperfield** or **Der Schimmelreiter, Madame Bovary** or **Anna Karenina, Middlemarch** or **Thérèse Raquin**, the focus is on the dynamics of marriage, or their absence. Will this relationship be harmonious? Will this choice of partner prove wise as well as wonderful? Might a better partner become available, even at the cost of great pain to one partner or to both? Marriage, and with it adultery, become central themes of fiction. But these themes are virtually absent from Romantic fiction, where "boy gets girl" is the end, not the beginning of the story. A second, though related, feature of Romantic love is the wanness – one might even say, the oneness – of the heroines. All these Berthas and Mathildes and Klaras and Biancas, with their blue eyes and golden hair, merge into one another and could almost be transposed between one story and the next: it is not entirely surprising that Nathanael, in Hoffmann's **Der Sandmann**, cannot distinguish between the real woman Klara, his fiancée, and the automaton Olympia! – This lack of individual characterization is connected with a third point, which aligns love with nature in Romantic writing: the women are not strongly differentiated because it is not so much the beloved herself that is important, as the emotional experience of love. The focus is on the lover, not the beloved; on the subjective, not the objective experience. A fourth dimension of the Romantic image of love, finally, is its preoccupation with the **dead** beloved: from Novalis to Lamartine, the death of the beloved is what creates a truly meaningful experience. Such a preference for communicating a sense of mourning occasioned by the loss of the beloved through death, as against exploring the experience of her continuing presence in marriage, is the final hallmark of the subjectivity of the Romantic view of love.

It is clear that such a view of love is not characteristic of Modernist literature. Lawrence is only the most obvious example of a Modernist approach which combines Realist concerns with the social, psychological and even physical dimensions of a continuing relationship, whether within marriage or outside it, with the emotional sensitivity and analytical subtlety of the Romantics. There are, however, a few Modernist works – of which Alain-Fournier's **Le grand Meaulnes** would be a cardinal example – which reflect closely the Romantic pattern of preoccupation with the expectation of love rather than its realization.

These perceptions of nature and of love demonstrate the pervasive subjectivity of Romantic writers. This quality is also reflected in the contemporary scientific awareness of the disintegration of outer reality, discussed earlier. In Romanticism, the most far-reaching consequence of this was for man's image of himself. The first decade of the nineteenth century saw the first tentative beginnings of the psychology of the unconscious (see note 5). The new ideas were explored discursively in the writings of the early psychologist G.H. Schubert, whose **Ansichten von der Nachtseite der Naturwissenschaft** appeared in 1808 (Hughes, pp.15–16). Such ideas had, however, already surfaced some time earlier within the first Romantic writings on aesthetic theory, which already contain a perception of the meaningfulness for artistic creativity of subconscious and unconscious, as exemplified by dreams. This was first clearly formulated, I believe, in Tieck's essay "Shakespeare's Behandlung des Wunderbaren", which originally appeared in 1793 as the preface to his adaptation of **The Tempest.**[24]

Many of the observations in this essay reveal a most surprising awareness for a writer in the 1790s who was, moreover, only just twenty years of age at the time: notably this passage on dreams as a model for the creative writer:

> Shakspeare, der so oft in seinen Stücken verräth, wie vertraut er mit den leisesten Regungen der menschlichen Seele sei, beobachtete sich auch wahrscheinlich in seinen Träumen, und wandte die hier gemachten Erfahrungen auf seine Gedichte an. Der Psychologe und der Dichter können ganz ohne Zweifel ihre Erfahrungen sehr erweitern, wenn sie dem Gange der Träume nachforschen: hier läßt sich gewiß oft der Grund entdecken, warum manche Ideencombinationen so heftig auf die Gemüther wirken; der Dichter kann hier am leichtesten bemerken, wie sich eine Menge von Vorstellungen an einander reihen, um eine wunderbare, unerwartete Wirkung hervorzubringen.[25]

Dreams certainly represented for the Romantics a major source of information about the life of the psyche.[26] In Romantic creative writing, dreams also play a substantial part. The earliest work by Tieck to have been published, **Die Sommernacht**, shows Shakespeare falling asleep and experiencing in dream form material which was later to form the basis of **A Midsummer Night's Dream**. Heinrich's dream of the Blue Flower, in the opening chapter of **Heinrich von Ofterdingen**, symbolically indicates the main lines on which his life was to develop. In **Die Bergwerke zu Falun**, Elis's dream, in the opening section, of the siren summons from below the surface of a frozen sea, articulates, though in transposed form, the main elements of the struggle between above and below, bourgeois and daemonic, which is to follow at Falun. These are only a few of the many Romantic dreams. Nor would it be correct to dismiss these dreams as merely predictive warnings, mysteriously inserted into the sleeper's awareness by some outside power, in the way that earlier ages had interpreted dreams. They **do** foreshadow the future, but this is because their elements are determined, not from outside, but by the make-up of the dreamer's own psyche, in the manner which Freud was later to explore in much greater detail in **Die Traumdeutung.**

But it is not only that actual dreams form a part of the subject-matter of Romantic writing. It is also that much of that writing does itself, and in its entirety, have the structure of a dream. Indeed, this accounts for the Romantic predilection for the **Märchen**, since the **Märchen** operates on the same principles of psychological symbolizing and free association as does the dream. This parallel has been explored in detail by Marianne Thalmann, in **Das Märchen und die Moderne** (see note 2). Moreover, **Märchen** and dream share many of the same mechanisms. **Déjà-vu** is one of these – the perception, often encountered in Romantic literature as in dream, that something has been seen or experienced before. Related to this is the notion of the "double" – the device, common in Romantic literature, for example in Hoffmann's **Die Elixiere des Teufels** or in Heine's poetry, of creating two characters who closely resemble one another. Though this device may sometimes have been used by Romantic – and other – writers for rather trivial motives – for instance, simply to create suspense which is later dispelled by some purely rational explanation such as "The doubles were really cousins" – it may also, more interestingly, reflect phenomena which have been identified by later psychologists, notably Freud, such as the duplication in dreams of people and situations which are psychically important to the dreamer, or the creation of split personalities as a form of psychic defence.

What happened in psychology in the Modernist period was that the intuitive insights of the Romantics were explored more analytically and more systematically by Freud, Jung and their followers.[27] The insights of these scientists also permeated the work of Modernist artists, notably towards the end of the period, in Surrealism. In earlier Modernist writers, dreams do not play so large a part as in the Romantics, but this is partly because they were seen as a worked-out resource. Their place was taken by other sources of material for analysis, especially the interior monologue. Its use by Schnitzler, in **Leutnant Gustl**, has been discussed by Franz Kuna, following Peter Stern (B. & M., pp.126–27). The interior monologue is a technique that was explored more fully outside German literature, crucially of course by James Joyce.

It is not possible to find in Romantic writing any very substantial use of the interior monologue, in the precise sense in which the term is used in relation to later fiction. But, as I have suggested, dreams themselves, and in a wider sense the dream-structure of the **Märchen**, are the equivalents of the interior monologue. There is also a set of devices which Romantic fiction was the first to employ and explore on any large scale, and which certainly can be seen as an anticipation of the interior monologue. These are the relativizing syntactical devices of the "as if" variety. Romantic fiction is characterized by the frequent use of formulae such as "Es war ihm, als ob . . .", or "Es schien ihm, daß . . ." – formulae by which the narrator withholds validation of the statements that follow (which may or may not be further coloured by the use of the subjunctive), leaving them only with the subjective validation of the character's own perception of his/her experience. The range, frequency and full significance of these formulae are, incidentally, a subject on which further research would be profitable, for the light it would throw not only on Romanticism, but also on the history and theory of narrative in general.

All these explorations of the psyche, in Romanticism and Modernism, represent important aspects of that "unleashing of the imaginative powers" of which Glyn Hughes speaks (p.5). They are part of an exploration of consciousness, more particularly of heightened consciousness (B. & M., p.47). This leads to a new concept of the hero, not as a man of action, but as a man – much less often, a woman – with a sensitive and heightened consciousness. Preoccupation with such heroes is already apparent in Goethe: Werther, Clavigo, Tasso, Wilhelm Meister are all variants of this basic type. In Goethe, however, the mode of existence of such characters is subject to question: Werther and Clavigo are destroyed, and damage others, by their personality; Tasso has to learn, in his confrontation with Antonio (who is seen much more sympathetically than Albert, the corresponding character in **Die Leiden des jungen Werthers**) to recognize and relativize himself; whilst Wilhelm Meister is made to abandon his artistic pretensions as an actor and to develop in other ways. This shift in Goethe's views brought opposition from the young Romantics who, whilst admiring Goethe's formal mastery, deprecated the import that this mastery is used to convey, as Novalis makes clear in the ambivalent comments on the **Lehrjahre** in his **Fragmente**. And so, the Romantic writers themselves created within Goethe's new sub-genre of the **Bildungsroman** a further subdivision, the **Künstlerroman**, and presented heroes who are painters, poets or musicians in a series of novels which runs from **Franz Sternbalds Wanderungen** and **Heinrich von Ofterdingen** to outriders like Mörike's **Maler Nolten** and even Keller's **Der grüne Heinrich**. The same is true of many of the shorter works of fiction and semi-fiction, from Wackenroder's "Berglinger" essays to Hoffmann's **Ritter Gluck, Die Jesuiterkirche in G.,** and **Das Fräulein von Scuderi,** a story in which the good artist, Scuderi, and the bad artist, Cardillac, are contrasted.

The same preoccupation with artistic consciousness and the artist appear in

Modernism. As John Fletcher and Malcolm Bradbury write, "The theme of the portrayed artist is a recurrent one in the Modernist novel . . . Proust's Marcel, Mann's Tonio Kröger, Joyce's Stephen Dedalus, Gide's Edouard are all 'portraits of the artist' . . ." (B. & M., p.404). Peter Stern explores the same point in greater detail in relation to Thomas Mann (B. & M., p.426). Doubtless, it can be shown that there are differences between the portrait of the artist in Romanticism and that in Modernism – the experiences which tend to shape Romantic artists are treated in a more "diagrammatic" way, whereas those of the Modernists are more differentiated and more sophisticated; but this does not outweigh the very real sense in which, in their preoccupation with the artist, the Romantics anticipated Modernism.

The concern with artists as a literary subject also leads, of course, to a concern with art. In Romantic fiction in particular, poems and even plays and stories are quoted and discussed; paintings are described, both as they come into being and in their final form; and, in particular, music is profusely described, by writers from Wackenroder to Hoffmann. Or rather: what happens is not precisely that it is described; but its effect upon the listener is conveyed, in line with the Romantic awareness, already discussed, of music as the supreme art-form – supreme, because it is the one which elicits the most direct emotional response (see Hughes, p.26). Concern with works of art, and especially works of music, is a well-recognized interest of Modernist fiction too: in Thomas Mann, for instance, whether in **Buddenbrooks** or in **Tristan** (see Peter Stern, in B. & M., p.427).

At this point, the wheel of my argument comes full circle, since the formal preoccupations of Romanticism and Modernism, and a favourite element in their subject-matter, coincide in music; and they do so because music stands for both movements as the supreme symbol of the sovereignty and autonomy of art. It is also music that can harmonize, can impose aesthetic meaning upon, a discordant world.

In this sense there is, paradoxically, a close connection between two apparently unrelated dimensions of Modernist literature, music and war. They represent respectively an extremely positive and an extremely negative response to contemporary reality. Richard Sheppard sees a connection between urbanization and warfare (B. & M., p.383), and it is a commonplace of criticism of Modernist poetry, and of much Modernist fiction and even drama, that it was decisively shaped by war. This is hardly surprising, since the First World War was not simply a continuation of the series of wars that had preceded it, but represented something different in kind – in the range of territories it affected, in the numbers of its victims, and in the violence of the injuries inflicted upon them by modern, industrialized equipment. The political, social and moral upheavals associated with the conflict added to the sense of disorientation which the First World War brought to Europe.

Despite the fact that, as Hughes has pointed out, the Romantics showed a somewhat surprising concern with contemporary events (p.4), the horrors of war were not a major theme for them. Indeed, in Germany the Wars of Liberation gave rise to a crop of patriotic war poetry, like that which flourished briefly in 1914. Nevertheless, there are already incipient signs in Romantic writers of the disenchantment with war which was to be the increasingly dominant mood of the future. The hero of Arnim's **Der tolle Invalide auf dem Fort Ratonneau** is an early example of the problems of war-wounded soldiers, and Heine's "Die Grenadiere" is at least ambivalent in its implications, as are many of Kleist's references to warfare, whether in **Penthesilea** or **Prinz Friedrich von Homburg, Die Marquise von O.** or **Die Hermannsschlacht**. In **Die Geschichte vom braven Kasperl und dem schönen Annerl**, Brentano too puts much of the blame for that false sense of honour which invades and destroys the characters' lives on the mistaken adoption of a military code which may have been suspect even in its original context. As with the city, then, the Romantic movement does begin to grapple with the Modernist theme of war, if only in a rather tentative way. A clearer step along the road to disenchantment is taken by Stendhal, in his ironization of Fabrice's attempts to find and take part in the battle of Waterloo, in **La chartreuse de Parme**.

More generally: the image of war was seen in Modernism as only the sharpest end of a general disenchantment caused by civilization and its discontents, to borrow Freud's title. And here, once again, there are parallels between the two movements. What Bradbury and McFarlane have called "a sense of the nihilistic disorder behind the ordered surface of life and reality" (p.393) – that is, the sense that the world we inhabit is not only lacking in solidity, as science was demonstrating, but is also deficient in meaning – was also present in Romantic writers, especially in those who succeeded the optimistic first wave of Romanticism represented by a Novalis or a Wordsworth (see Thalmann, p.106). The sense of disorder and disorientation is exemplified by the heroes of Tieck or Hoffmann, whose efforts to attain reality as they (confusedly and wrongly) perceive it lead them only further into disaster. It is exemplified, too, in the work of Kleist, whose work oscillates between the two poles of a rare intuitive perception of harmony and grace, exemplified by **Das Käthchen von Heilbronn**, and achieved only precariously by the central characters of **Die Marquise von O.** or **Prinz Friedrich von Homberg**, and a deep sense of alienation, experienced by the characters in **Michael Kohlhaas** or **Das Erdbeben in Chili**, as also to judge from his suicide, by Kleist himself. It is hardly surprising that modern critics have sensed an affinity between Kleist and the Existentialists.

But the work which gives the most powerful expression to existential despair is the **Nachtwachen** of Bonaventura (see Hughes, pp.28–29), in which the fictional device of a night watchman patrolling the town through the hours of darkness provides a perfect framework for the insights of the author, whoever he may have been, into the inadequacy of human beings and the insubstantiality of their hold upon the world. Such a work has many of the enigmatic, sardonic, and despairing qualities of the world-picture we associate with Modernism, especially with German Expressionism (Hughes, p.28). It would be foolish to claim that every aspect of Modernism is anticipated by Romanticism; it would be equally foolish to overlook the very considerable range and extent of these anticipations.

Notes

1. See J.W. McFarlane: "1871 and the Concept of Civilizational Change", paper read to the English Goethe Society, 14 March 1974; printed as "Cultural Conspiracy and Civilizational Change: Henrik Ibsen, Georg Brandes and the Modern European Mind", **Journal of European Studies**, 11 (1979), pp.155–73.

2. See the discussion in **Modernism 1890–1930**, edited by Malcolm Bradbury and J.W. McFarlane, Pelican Guides to European Literature (Harmondsworth, 1976), pp.46–47. (Later references to this volume are given in the text, abbreviated as "B. & M."). Marianne Thalmann: **Das Märchen und die Moderne**, second edition (Stuttgart etc., 1966), p.3, calls Romanticism "einen ersten Aufstand der Moderne".

3. See, for instance, G.T. Hughes: **Romantic German Literature** (London, 1979), p.7. Later references to this volume are given in the text as "Hughes" and page number.

4. See Hughes, p.78, and Wilhelm Emrich: "Romantik und modernes Bewußtsein", in his **Geist und Wiedergeist** (Frankfurt a.M., 1965), pp.246–52.

5. See Lionel Trilling: "Freud and Literature" (1940), reprinted in his **The Liberal Imagination** (New York, 1950), pp.34–57; and L.L. Whyte: **The Unconscious before Freud** (London, 1962).

6. See Emrich, pp.256–57.

7. Tieck: **Schriften** (Berlin, 1828–46), XVI, p.333.

8. Tieck: "Glosse", **Gedichte** (Berlin, 1841), p.198.

9. Brentano: **Werke**, edited by Friedhelm Kemp, I–IV (Munich, 1963–68), I, pp.123–24. This edition is henceforth cited by volume and page.

10. See B.A. Rowley: "An Analysis of Clemens Brentano's 'Hörst Du?'", **German Life & Letters**, 5 (1951–52), pp.188–90.

11. Eichendorff: **Werke in einem Band**, edited by Wolfdietrich Rasch (Munich, 1955), pp.30–31.

12. Eichendorff: **Werke**, pp.271–72.

13. See Walter Mönch: **Das Sonett: Gestalt und Geschichte** (Heidelberg, 1955), pp.169–264.

14. Emrich, p.256.

15. Raymond M. Immerwahr: **The Esthetic Intent of Tieck's Fantastic Comedy**, Washington University Studies, New Series, Language and Literature, 22 (Saint Louis, 1953).

16. See Hughes, p.10, on Fichte; cf. B. & M., pp.47, 369, 425, 428, 481.

17. See Oskar Seidlin: "Der Taugenichts ante portas. Interpretation einer Eichendorff-Stelle", **J. Engl. German. Philol.**, 52 (1953), pp.509–24; reprinted in **Aurora**, 16 (1956), pp.70–81.

18. Blake: "And did those feet in ancient time", **The Complete Writings**, edited by Geoffrey Keynes (London, 1966), p.481.

19. Wordsworth: **The Poetical Works**, edited by Thomas Hutchinson and revised by Ernest de Selincourt, new impression (London etc., 1942), p.269.

20. Eichendorff: **Werke**, p.10.

21. See B.A. Rowley: "A Long Day's Night: Ambivalent Imagery in Mörike's Lyric Poetry", **German Life & Letters**, 29 (1975–76), pp.109–22.

22. A.J. Dietlinde Katritzky: "Eine Untersuchung der Eigennamen in den Nachtwachen von Bonaventura und bei Georg Christoph Lichtenberg" (unpublished MA dissertation,

University of Florida, 1984); cf. her "Georg Christoph Lichtenberg, FRS", **Notes and Records of the Royal Society of London**, 39 (1984–85), pp.41–49 (pp.44–48).

23. From the second, cancelled stanza of the manuscript version of "Peregrina. I"; **Werke**, edited by Harry Maync (Leipzig & Wien, [1909]), I, p.467.

24. Tieck: "Ueber Shakspeare's Behandlung des Wunderbaren", in **Der Sturm** (Berlin & Leipzig, 1796), pp.1–43; reprinted in his **Kritische Schriften** (Leipzig, 1848–52), I, pp.35–74.

25. Tieck: **Kritische Schriften**, I, pp.43–44.

26. See Albert Béguin: **L'âme romantique et le rêve**, new edition (Paris, 1939).

27. See Trilling, passim, and Emrich, pp.238–39.

Christian Morgenstern and the Emergence of Modernism in the Berlin Theatre

E.S. Shaffer

In the summer of 1889 in Breslau Christian Morgenstern met Friedrich Kayssler, who was to be his lifelong friend. Kayssler later described his first encounter with Morgenstern. The portrait of the young Morgenstern is irresistible, and displays portents of the future poet, parodist, translator, cabaret artist, and visionary. Kayssler, a future actor, grasped at once the theatricality of the eighteen-year-old Morgenstern, the spell-binding quality of his poetic imagination, the sheer inventive humour and wit of the budding Modernist. Kayssler first saw him among a group of school friends in a house they had built themselves out of old crates, half ship's cabin, half pub:

> Einer der Hauptvorkämpfer des Volapük dieser Gruppe, gewisser Verdienste halber bereits mit einem Diplom ausgezeichnet, das in seiner Primanerbude im zweiten Stock oben eingerahmt hängt, ein Achtzehnjähriger, steht langbeinig aufgepflanzt vor den Reckstangenjünglingen und demonstriert ihnen seinen neuesten Entwurf: eine selbsterfundenene Sprache. Auf ein paar flatternden Heftseiten hält er die ersten Bruchteile eines imaginären Wörterbuchs in der Hand und verkündet die Urworte dieser noch nicht dagewesenen Sprache unter unauslöschlichem Gelächter.
>
> Er ist sehr schlank und groß, hat einen fast kleinen Kopf mit einer sehr hohen reinen Stirn und trägt einen gut sitzenden Anzug mit englischen Karos, um die ich ihn sofort sehnsüchtig beneide. Seine Augen sind tief und gut, aber auf ihrem Grunde schießt es hin und her von unerwarteten Listen und Einfällen, so daß keiner weiß, wessen er sich im nächsten Augenblick zu versehen hat. Er gilt als ausgemachter Dichter und unberechenbarer Kopf, im bürgerlichen Schulsinne als Freigeist. Man traut ihm viel zu in bezug auf Talente alle Art, aber auch Neckereien und Streiche, auf die man stets gefaßt sein muß. Sie kommen immer auf echt dichterische Weise, nämlich gegen alle Berechnung und Logik, darum treffen sie fast immer ins Schwarze; zuweilen können sie auch schmerzhaft sein, aber nur körperlich, und immer haben sie Humor, niemals Bosheit, nur List und Schlauheit im besten Indianersinne. Vielleicht hängt es damit irgendwie zusammen, daß ihn die Kameraden mit dem Namen des xenophontischen Feldherrn Bessos getauft haben, mit dem er sonst wirklich nichts zu tun hat. Man dichtet ihm gern eine Gefolgschaft an, und wenn wieder einmal etwas Unberechenbares in der Luft liegt, was sie seinen Einfällen zuschreiben möchten, so heißt es: ‚ὁ δὲ Βῆσσος καὶ οἱ ἀμφ' αὐτόν': "Bessos und die um ihn!"[1]

One of the leaders in the battle for Volapük [an artificial universal language of the type of Esperanto] in the group, a lad of eighteen years old, who for his efforts had already received a diploma which hung framed in his sixth-former's room above in the second storey, stood planted on his long legs in front of the young men of the horizontal bar [the apparatus of the gymnasium stood nearby] and demonstrated to them his latest invention: a language of his own creation. He held in his hand the first fragments of an imaginary dictionary, scribbled on several pages of a notebook, and revealed the original words of this language that had never before existed, amidst irrepressible laughter from his audience.

He is very slim and tall, with a head appearing almost small with a very high, fine forehead, and he is wearing a well-fitting suit with English revers, which I instantly envy him. His eyes are deep and good, but they dart here and there, full of unexpected mischief and sudden invention, so that no one knows whom his eye will light upon next. He is already accounted a fully-fledged poet and a clever head, in bourgeois school parlance, a freethinker. Much is expected of him, on the basis of his various talents, including, however, hoaxes and practical jokes, which one has to be on one's guard against at all times. They come always in true poetic fashion, flying in the face of all calculation and logic, and so strike the bull's eye almost without fail. Occasionally they can be painful, but only physically, and they always show humour, never malice, only cunning and subtlety in the best Indian fashion. Perhaps it is somehow connected with this that his comrades call him by the xenophontic name of general Bessos, with whom he otherwise has nothing in common. He is considered to have a large following, and when once again something incalculable is in the air which could be attributed to one of his inspirations, the cry goes up: ‚ὁ δὲ Βῆσσος καὶ οἱ ἀμφ' αὐτόν': "Bessos and his friends!"[2]

Here were the seeds of the **Galgenbrüderschaft**, the gallows brotherhood, the group of friends which, meeting in the mid-nineties in Berlin cafés, improvising songs and ceremonies around Morgenstern's linguistic inventions, was to have such a momentous significance for modern poetry, cabaret and intimate theatre.

Christian Morgenstern (1871–1914) is indeed best known and well beloved in Germany today as the author of the **Galgenlieder (Gallows Songs)**. These brilliant comic inventions, which represent the vein of lyric fantasy most familiar to English readers from the "nonsense verse" of Lewis Carroll and Edward Lear, transformed it into a modern experimentalism that bore fruit in Dada and Surrealism. His "gallows songs" range widely. They contain rueful, innocent yet eerie fantasy akin to Lear, especially in his imaginary bestiaries containing creatures such as the "Mondschaf" (Moon sheep) and the "Nachtwindhund" (Nightwind Hound):

Das Mondschaf

Das Mondschaf steht auf weiter Flur.
Es harrt und harrt der großen Schur.
Das Mondschaf.

Das Mondschaf rupft sich einen Halm
und geht dann heim auf seine Alm.
    Das Mondschaf.

Das Mondschaf spricht zu sich im Traum:
"Ich bin des Weltalls dunkler Raum".
    Das Mondschaf.

Das Mondschaf liegt am Morgen tot.
Sein Leib ist weiß, die Sonn'ist rot.
    Das Mondschaf.

The Moonsheep

The moonsheep stands upon the clearing.
He waits and waits to get his shearing.
    The moonsheep.

The moonsheep plucks himself a blade
returning to his alpine glade.
    The moonsheep.

The moonsheep murmurs in his dream:
'I am the cosmos' gloomy scheme'.
    The moonsheep.

The moonsheep, in the morn, lies dead.
His flesh is white, the sun is red.
    The moonsheep.[3]

They also rival the fey intellectual conundrums of Carroll, as in the following lines:

Das Lattenzaun

Es war einmal ein Lattenzaun,
mit Zwischenraum, hindurchzuschaun.

Ein Architekt, der dieses sah,
stand eines Abends plötzlich da,

und nahm den Zwischenraum heraus
und baute draus ein großes Haus.

Der Zaun indessen stand ganz dumm,
mit Latten ohne was herum.

The Picket Fence

There used to be a picket fence
with space to gaze from hence to thence.

An architect who saw this sight
approached it suddenly one night,

removed the spaces from the fence,
and built of them a residence.

The picket fence stood there dumbfounded
with pickets wholly unsurrounded.[4]

Moreover, German Romantic and folk traditions feed into his fantastic inventions, with their grotesque, often macabre and haunting presence in the midst of the apparently familiar, domestic world. Since the early essay of Leo Spitzer on his work, it has been taken as the type of "das Groteske" in modern German poetry.[5] He is also known for his later, more mystical lyrics, which have been compared to Hölderlin and to Rilke, which were written as his tubercular condition gradually worsened and he turned to the theosophy of Rudolph Steiner. More recently, his verbal inventiveness has been recognized as prefiguring Dada.[6] His poem "Das große Lalula", an incantation of sheer sound, is a very early example of sound poetry, as a fragment of it will demonstrate:

Kroklokwafzi? Seṁemeṁi!
Seiokrontro – prafriplo:
Bifzi, bafzi; hulaleṁi:
quasti basti bo . . .
Lalu, lalu lalu lalu la![7]

This is, of course, untranslatable; but Morgenstern characteristically supplied a mock "critical interpretation" of it in terms of an endgame at chess, in order to parody his own critics. Hugo Ball's phonic poems were anticipated by Morgenstern's "Fisches Nachtgesang" (Fish's Night Song), which a recent critic has declared is "composed of characters even more elemental than the sounds comprising the Zürich Dadaists' basic materials".[8]

Fisches Nachtgesang[9] | Fish's Night Song

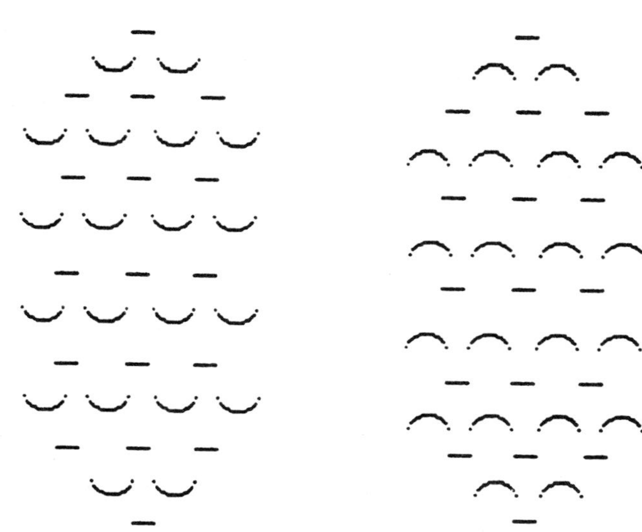

The "Fisches Nachtgesang" is unpronounceable (though Spitzer imagined the fish mouthing it rhythmically), but not, it seems, untranslatable, at least for Morgenstern; at the same time, the unspeakability of the translation, its negation of the metrical scansion, is a witty comment on all translation.

Much less well known than Morgenstern's poetry, however, is the role he played as a pioneer of the modern theatre. He was an important translator of Scandinavian Modernism, including Ibsen, Strindberg, Bjørnson, and Hamsun. He was a founder of the cabaret in Berlin, a writer and performer of his own poems, sketches, parodies, and short plays; and he was a close associate of Max Reinhardt, not only in the cabaret but as the editor of the periodical **Das Theater** (1903–1906), which did a great deal to forward the programme of Reinhardt's **Theater der Stile**, "Theatre of Styles", as it developed from cabaret into intimate theatre and then into the spectacular productions of the National Theatre, from 1905 under Reinhardt's direction. Even Morgenstern's later career, after his illness forced his retirement from the Berlin scene, was powerfully related to the theatre, for 1913 found him present at the première of Rudolph Steiner's first cycle of Mystery plays at the Goetheanum. Steiner's influence on the stage architecture, lighting, and body movement (eurhythmics) of the period has been noted in other contexts, but never related to Morgenstern's lifelong dramatic concerns. It is hard to account for this neglect; it may be that the continued popularity of the late Romantic stereotype of the young tubercular lyrical genius who threw veils of mysticism round his suffering and early death, that merciful death on the brink of the First World War, has hidden from view Morgenstern's irreverent experimentalism and his intense involvement with the new theatrical world.

Morgenstern as Translator of Scandinavian Modernism

Morgenstern's signal services to the reception of Scandinavian Modernism in Germany are surprisingly little remarked upon. His first and most straightforward role was as a translator of major writers. He translated Bjørnstjerne Bjørnson's poems and his play, **De Nygifte (The Newly Married Couple)**, as **Die Neuvermählten.** This play, written in 1865, is often rated as Bjørnson's and indeed Norway's first modern drama, for its depiction of the tensions among a handful of characters in a domestic, contemporary setting, and for containing at least in germ the role of the "liberated woman" that was to be so much further developed by Ibsen.[10] He also translated Strindberg's **Inferno** from Strindberg's French original on its first appearance in 1897.[11] He translated two plays by Knut Hamsun, in 1903 and 1910 respectively, the first two in a dramatic trilogy referred to as **Karenin.**[12] Hamsun's reputation in Germany had been made by the translation of **Sult (Hunger)**, in 1892, and his novels continued to be well received; his plays are little known, although they were performed at the time, these two in Morgenstern's translations.[13]

More important still, Morgenstern translated Ibsen's poems and his verse plays: **Catalina, The Feast at Solhaug (Gildet paa Solhaug), The Comedy of Love (Kjærlighedens Komedie), Brand, Peer Gynt,** and **When We Dead Awaken (Når vi døde vågner)**. His translations were commissioned for that great landmark, Ibsen's **Sämtliche Werke in deutscher Sprache**, edited by Georg Brandes, Julius Elias, and Paul Schlenther, and published in ten volumes in Berlin between 1898 and 1903. Morgenstern had met Schlenther in 1895, and from the beginning Schlenther had been enthusiastic about his work, written about it himself, and helped him place his early **feuilleton** pieces, with which he had eked out a living after the withdrawal of funds by his father and the collapse of his plans to take a degree in art history. The Ibsen translations were to give him financial security during the five years he spent on them.

This edition, still the standard German edition of Ibsen's works, was a consolidation of thirty years of Ibsen reception in Germany. As James McFarlane has written:

> . . . England was much later than Germany with her welcome. In the 1870s no fewer than six of Ibsen's plays had been translated into German, and indeed two of them, **Brand** and **Pillars of Society**, each appeared in three different translations; this as against one play (and a bit) in English, and none in French. By 1890 there were altogether 27 different German translations, covering 16 of the plays, plus also two separate translations of his poems; in England there were 7 translations of 5 of the plays; in France, two of the plays had been translated. Moreover, it is recorded that there were in one particular week in February 5 different companies in Berlin alone all performing **Pillars of Society.**[14]

The earliest phase of Ibsen reception in Germany had been accomplished by Ludwig Passarge, who had published the first translations of Ibsen's poems and plays, and the earliest partial edition, the **Gesammelte Werke**, in three volumes (Leipzig 1881), as well as the first book-length critical study of his work, which even today is a readable introduction to those of his plays that were then available.[15] Many others had been involved in the translation and staging of Ibsen in the interim, not least the editors of the 1898 edition. The social dramas had been instrumental in the 1880s in initiating and advancing the growth of German Naturalism. The decisive turning-point was the triumphant production of **Ghosts** in Berlin in 1889. In the same year **Papa Hamlet** by one "Bjarne P. Holmsen" appeared, "translated from the Norwegian by Dr Bruno Franzius", these being in fact the pseudonyms of Arno Holz and Johannes Schlaf. Afterwards known as Naturalist dramatists in their own right, the young German writers felt it necessary to make their way under cover of pseudo-translation of the already familiar Norwegian Naturalism, and the book was duly hailed by reviewers as "pessimistic", "gloomy" yet "gripping".[16] Gerhart Hauptmann had achieved success in the same year with **Vor Sonnenuntergang (Before Sundown)**, and produced a classic of German Naturalism in **Die Weber (The Weavers)**, by 1892. One of the first plays the young Morgenstern records seeing, while still in Breslau, was Hermann Sudermann's **Sodoms Ende**;[17] once in Berlin a steady diet of Naturalist drama was available.

Indeed, Berlin Naturalism was so well established that by the early 1890s a reaction against it set in. When Morgenstern arrived on the scene as a university student in 1894, the advanced literary and theatrical circles in which he quickly found himself (his friend Kayssler having preceded him was now a colleague of Max Reinhardt in the Deutsches Theater, under the direction of Otto Brahm, who had brought Reinhardt from Vienna) had long been deeply engaged in the struggle to gain a hearing for Naturalism. They were now preparing to move on. Morgenstern was to play a considerable role in the shift, through his sketches for the cabaret, where Naturalism became a major target, and through his own poetry of enacted verbal fantasy, Nietzschean **Spiel** and surreal perspectives. Thus he powerfully served the permanent establishment of the earlier phase of Modernism represented by Naturalism, while assisting at the initiation of its successors.

It may be in part for these reasons that Morgenstern's contributions as a translator of Ibsen have received less attention than they deserve. By hindsight at least, it appears that as the edition to which he contributed so much represents the consolidation of Ibsen's reputation as the leading modern dramatist, his revolutionary impact lay in the past, whereas Morgenstern's is now seen to have belonged to the future. Yet for Morgenstern himself the immersion in Ibsen was important for his self-definition, even if that constituted a clear distancing from Ibsen.

It was in 1897 that Schlenther approached Morgenstern with the proposal that he contribute to the new edition. Morgenstern set himself to learn Norwegian and produced his first translation, **Das Fest auf Solhaug**, with surprising celerity. He travelled to Norway, where he remained between May 1898 and September 1899, living near Christiania (Oslo), consulting with Ibsen on the translations, and finding time to travel in the north, with Ibsen's detailed instructions to guide him. The mountain landscapes moved him greatly; of a line of painters, and with a gift of his own in that direction, Morgenstern's response to the outer world played an ineffaceable if tenuous and surprising role in his primarily verbal inventiveness.

With Ibsen's encouragement, he got on rapidly. He left a vivid account, in letters and diary, of his meetings with Ibsen, who was often welcoming and expansive. His pleasure in Morgenstern's translations was often expressed, and by March they were conversing in Norwegian, and discussing in detail the productions of Ibsen's plays that he had seen.[18] He reported that in the winter of 1897 alone he had seen **Ghosts** five times. Although his task was to translate the poems and the verse plays, Ibsen was so pleased with the results that he requested the editors to invite Morgenstern to revise and improve the prose translations as well. He was also entrusted with the translation of Brandes' introduction. His translation of **The Comedy of Love** won immediate acclaim in both Norway and Germany, and was the first play to be put on by Max Reinhardt under his own name as director.

The only one of Ibsen's plays that was translated for the first time by Morgenstern was Ibsen's last, **When We Dead Awaken**. Ibsen particularly requested the editors that the translation should be done by Morgenstern, writing urgently to Julius Elias on 1 May 1899:

> Ich hege den lebhaften Wunsch, daß Herr Christian Morgenstern seinerzeit die Übersetzung meines neuen Stückes besorgen möge. Er ist ein höchst begabter, wirklicher Dichter . . . Außerdem ist er vollständig vertraut mit der norwegischen Sprache, ein Vorzug, den zu finden ich früher nicht bei vielen meiner deutschen Übersetzer das Glück hatte . . .[19]

> I cherish the strong wish that Mr Christian Morgenstern should look after the translation of my new play. He is a very highly talented poet, a true poet. In addition, he is fully at home in the Norwegian language, an advantage which I have not previously had the good fortune to find in many of my German translators . . .

Having returned to Berlin in the autumn of 1899, Morgenstern went to work on the new play, and with the aid of Elias, finished it in time to receive the first proofs by the end of November. The first performance followed shortly after. That Morgenstern's translations were done not merely for that literary monument for posterity, the **Gesamtausgabe**, but under pressure and for performance in the theatre, is vital for the understanding of his **theatralische Sendung**, his theatrical vocation.

If Morgenstern was not for the most part the first of Ibsen's translators, he has a claim to be considered the best. He brilliantly carried out the ambitious aim of the edition, which the editors stated as follows:

> Aber je mehr Henrik Ibsens Werk in deutscher Kunstempfindung Wurzel schlug, je mehr er der Unsere wurde, desto notwendiger wurde es, den deutschen Ausdruck so zu gestalten, wie ihn Henrik Ibsen vielleicht gewählt hätte wenn er nicht norwegisch, sondern deutsch geschrieben hätte.[20]

> But the more Henrik Ibsen's work put down roots in the German sensibility, the more he became one of our own, the more necessary did it become to formulate the German expression as Henrik Ibsen himself might have done, had he written not in Norwegian but in German.

Ibsen, then, had become an honorary German, and he must be seen to write in German. There was, of course, a good precedent for this complete incorporation of a writer into the national canon: the translation of Shakespeare by August Wilhelm Schlegel and Ludwig Tieck. The aim of full assimilation of Ibsen into the German sensibility was in no way a licence for free translation, imitation, or adaptation. On the contrary, it required the closest fidelity to the text, on the model of Schlegel's translations of the 1790s. Friedrich Gundolf has described the remarkable process of adoption of a foreign writer in **Shakespear und der deutsche Geist** (Shakespeare and the German Spirit). Given the assumption that there was an "affinity" between the writer and the nation adopting him as their own, it followed that the closer one came to the text the closer one would come to releasing and demonstrating its affinity with the German artistic sensibility. Once established, "affinity" justified and demanded "fidelity". Thus Morgenstern is never less than a faithful translator: he translated in verse, and nearly always line for line. Yet he produced a text that for the most part sounds wholly natural, wholly unforced in German; at his best, he produced German poetry of the first quality.

Morgenstern's Translation of **Peer Gynt**

To take just one example: Morgenstern excels in his translation of **Peer Gynt**. If the Shakespeare translations provided a model for assimilation, the process was furthered by the growing tendency to view Ibsen's verse plays, especially **Brand** and **Peer Gynt**, through the spectacles of **Faust**. This was natural and certainly not wholly unjustified, though much disputed. Ibsen himself, on the occasion of the first translation of **Peer Gynt**, had expressed his doubts to Passarge as to whether the character and habits of Norwegians would be understandable by a German audience.[21] Yet even Scandinavian critics who like Brandes resisted the identification of Brand and Peer with Faust, and insisted on the element of biting satire against Norway, accepted the high value placed on those plays through the analogy with **Faust**. Although Brandes wrote in his introduction to the **Sämtliche Werke** that to parallel Brand with Faust was "eine recht unverständige Auffassung",[22] "a complete misconstruction", he concurred with the German response in calling **Peer Gynt** "die Saft– und Kraftvollste von Ibsens sämtlichen Schöpfungen",[23] "the most vigorous and lively of all of Ibsen's creations". Putting aside any attempt at a parallel at the level of character, the analogy with **Faust** provided Morgenstern with a framework of vocabulary, verse forms, and a range of recognizable tones for the translation of important aspects of Ibsen's verse dramas. If no attempt was made to capture Ibsen's deliberate exploitation of the uncertain state of the evolving Norwegian language – indeed, Ibsen complained to Morgenstern of the editors' request that he smooth out the rough contrasts – it was an implicit aim of the editorial programme to display a German literary language that had achieved its evolution and arrived at maturity. If this was a distortion of Ibsen, it speeded his acceptance as an author of European stature, as Ibsen very well knew when he wrote to Brandes in 1872: "a victory in Germany, and you will be master of the situation at home!"[24] In a later speech he stressed the need to become a member of "the great Teutonic house".[25]

The resources of German Romantic poetry, both as incorporated in **Faust II** and as native to Morgenstern, are completely at his command and in place in **Peer Gynt**. He is a master of a folk ballad style, already transformed into the music of the nineteenth-century German **Lied**, and modified by the irony and the satiric edge of Heine. He deploys the shrewd peasant wit and the aphoristic power of the **Hauspostillien**, to be further developed by Brecht; he embraces with ease the inward soliloquies and the grotesque hilarity of Peer, already acclimatized in the **Hamlet** of the "great Teuton" Shakespeare; the folk fantasy with its macabre humour. Whatever help the **Walpurgisnacht** scene in **Faust** gave him, he is in his element in the Hall of the Troll King, the imaginary kingdom where humans may almost qualify as one-headed trolls. Morgenstern catches the elemental power of the charm and the riddle, and the pure abracadabra that he made his own (though Goethe's **West-östlicher Diwan** is a source at least as important as **Faust**). His gifts for the nonce-word and for sound poetry come to his aid in apparently insoluble cruces, and here Romantic witchery passes over into Modernism. Morgenstern's translation as a whole is a revelation of a play that sits very uneasily in its English translations, from the R. Farquharson Sharp and the William Archer versions (1906) almost contemporary with Morgenstern's, to Christopher Fry's version and the several more recent attempts (Michael Meyer, David Rudkin, Adrian Mitchell, Malcolm Griffiths).

To give just a few examples: The daydream of Peer of himself as emperor Morgenstern translates in a folk ballad style which ironizes not merely Peer's self-aggrandizement, but the aggrandizement of the form from Bürger through Goethe:

Nun bangt ihr! – Voran seinem Trosse
Reitet Peer Gynt auf goldhufigem Rosse.
Die Mähr' hat 'nen Federbusch zwischen den Ohren.
Selbst hat er Handschuh' und Säbel und Sporen.
Der Mantel ist lang und mit Tast ausgeschlagen.
Wacker sind die, die hinter ihm jagen
Er aber sitzt doch am strackssten zu Pferde,
Er aber strahlt doch am hellsten zur Erde.
Drunten die Leut' stehn, ein schwarzes Gewimmel,
Ziehen die Hüt' ab und gaffen gen Himmel.
Die Weiber verneigen sich. Alle gewahren
Kaiser Peer Gynt und seine Heerscharen.
Nickel und Silber, ein blankes Geriesel,
Streut er hinunter wie Hände voll Kiesel.
Allen im Dorf geht's von nun an zum Besten.
Peer Gynt sprengt quer übers Meer gen Westen.
Engellands Prinz steht und wartet am Strande;
Mit ihm alle Schönen von Engellande.
Engellands Kaiser und Engellands Barone
Steigen die Stufen herab vom Throne.
Der Kaiser nimmt seine Kron' ab und sagt –[26]

The original Norwegian runs as follows:

Ja, nu er hun bange. –
Peer Gynt rider først, og der følger ham mange.

Hesten har Sølvtopp og Guldsko fire.
Selv har han Handsker og Sabel og Slire.
Kaaben er sid og med Silke foret.
Gjilde er de, som ham følger i Sporet.
Ingen dog sidder saa stout paa Folen.
Ingen dog glittrer som ham imod Solen.
Nede staar Folk i Klynger langs Gjærdet,
løfter paa Hatten og glaner ivejret.
Kvinderne nejer sig. Alle kan kjende
Kejser Peer Gynt og hans tusende Svende.
Tolvskillingsstykker og blanke Marker
ned han som Smaasten paa Vejen sparker.
Rige som Grever blir alle i Byggden.
Peer Gynt rider tvers over Havet i Højden.
Engellands Prins staar paa Stranden og venter.
Det samme gjør alle Engellands Jenter.
Engellands Stormænd og Engellands Kejser,
der Peer rider frem, sig fra Højbordet rejser.
Kejseren letter paa Kronen og siger –[27]

The blank verse renderings in English completely miss the effect:

Well, she'll be in a fine state now!. . .
Peer Gynt at the head of a great procession,
His horse in a silver cap and gold shoes.

Himself with gauntlet, sabre and scabbard,
And a long cloak with a silk lining.[28]

Morgenstern lends Peer's threat to Solveig to transform himself into a troll and a werewolf just the right note of the sinister and the childish:

Du ich verwandel' mich in einen Troll!
Ich komme' an Dein Bett heut, wenn Mitternacht voll.
Hörst Du dann ein Geschab' und Gekratze,
So denk' nur nicht etwa, das wär' bloß die Katze.
Da komm' ich und trink' ich Dein Blut wie ein Mahr;
Und Dein Schwesterlein fress' ich mit Haut und mit Haar;
Ja, denn Du mußt wissen, ich bin Werwolf bei Nacht; –
Ich beiß' Dich in Lenden und Rücken und Mark –

(Jeg kan skabe mig om til et Trold!
Jeg skal komme for Sengen din inatt Klokken tolv.
Hører du nogen, som hvæser og fræser,
saa maa du ikke bilde dig ind det er Katten.
Det er mig, du! Jeg tapper din Blod i en Kopp;

og din vesle Syster, hende æder jeg opp;
ja, for du skal vide, jeg er Varulv om Natten; –
jeg skal bide dig over Lænder og Rygg –)

In the English versions, without the rhyme and the alliterative pairing, the incantatory power is lost. Here is Sharp:

I can turn myself into a troll!
I shall come and stand by your bed at midnight;
And if you hear something that's hissing and spitting,
Don't you suppose it's your cat you are hearing.
It is I! And I'll drain your life-blood out of you;
And your little sister – I'll eat her up,
For I turn to a were-wolf whenever the night falls,
Your loins and your back I'll bite all over –

The closest Fry can come is what appears to be an accidental internal rhyme in his blank verse medium:

I'll drain your blood
Into a cup, and as for your sister –
I'll gobble her up; I will, because
At night I'm a werewolf;[29]

Michael Meyer evidently noted this in Fry (or indeed in William Archer, who offers "I'll drain out your blood in a cup,/ And your little sister, I'll eat her up/") and converted it into an end-rhyme in the midst of his own otherwise unrhymed version of this passage:

Don't think it's the cat. It's me, my dear!
I'll be drawing your blood in a cup,
And your little sister, I'll gobble her up!
For at night I'm a werewolf. I'll bite you
All over your loins and your pretty back.[30]

Meyer repeats his borrowed rhyme in the very next scene (II,4), again in the midst of an unrhymed passage:

Look, now the old Bishop's clinking
His knife on his silver cup.
The captain has tossed back his bottle,
And broken the looking-glass up.

The palm for inadvertent rhymes in a prosaic medium is carried off by David Rudkin, in the same passage, from his truncated colloquial version:

It shattered the mirror but what does it matter.[31]

Morgenstern renders the same passage in abab rhyme and brings off a brilliant onomatopeia, which outdoes Ibsen himself:

Da messert die Plappertasche,
Der Propst, an sein Glas und girrt; –
Da schmeißt der Kap'tän seine Flasche,
Daß der Spiegel in Scherben zerklirrt. –

(Der hørte jeg Provsten klaske
med Knivsryggen mod sit Glas; –
der slængte Kaptejnen sin Flaske,
saa Spejlvæggen sprakk i Knas.)

Morgenstern's rendering of Act III scene 4 in which Peer and his mother rehearse the games they played when he was a child catches exactly the tone of intermingled wild romp, folk tale, and romantic ballad, as we would expect from the author of **Klein Irmchen** (Little Irma, his popular book of children's songs). Fry gives us a flat rendering, and with his dangling participle loses even the narrative thrust of the ballad form:

To the castle west of the moon
And the castle east of the sun,
To the Soria-Moria Castle
The road going up and down.
You made a driving-whip
From a stick we found in the cupboard.

William Archer offers a rhythmic version, which like his rendering of Anitra's song draws on a sing-song effect and a slightly archaic diction, aping but not attempting the rhyme the passage calls for, an effect belied by the clumsy, forced grammar of the last two lines:

To the castle west of the moon, and
    The castle east of the sun,
To Soria-Moria Castle
    The road ran both high and low.
A stick that we found in the closet,
    For a whip-shaft you made it serve.

Morgenstern gives us a quite different version that succeeds in linking the romantic balladry of the opening lines with the active imaginative conversion of the homely items of the house and farmyard that is the essence of the game:

Nach dem Schloß im Westen vom Monde
Und dem Schloß im Osten der Sonn',

Nach dem Soria-Moria-Schlosse
Ging's hurre-hop über die Diel',
Und 'ne alte Hühnerstallsprosse
Brauchst Du als Peitschenstiel.

Compare with Ibsen's original:

Til Slottet vestenfor Maane
og Slottet østenfor Sol,
till Soria-Moria-Slottet,
gik Vejen baade højt og lavt.
En Kjæpp, som vi fandt i Kottet,
du brugte til Svøbeskaft.

Morgenstern shows his quality not only in rendering the very varied individual passages, but in the way he controls and modulates the thematic references throughout the long text. Taking the central instance of the Troll ethic, we can see how **Faust** offered the German translator the possibility of conveying the more metaphysical dimensions of the play. In the celebrated speech comparing trolls and humans (II,6), the fine shade of difference is expressed in Fry's rendering as the difference between the human "To thine own self be true" and the troll adage "Be to thyself enough". Here the Shakespearean context of Polonius' speech of advice to Laertes is available in English to suggest how close the human version is, after all, to the trolls' version.[32] Michael Meyer offers a pungent if free rendering:

Men tell each other: 'Man, be thyself!'
But in here, among us trolls, we say:
'Be thyself – Jack!'

This works as more than a momentary play on "I'm all right, Jack", in that when Peer meets the Button Moulder and the Old Man it becomes important to prove he has always been Peer, himself; but instead, as the Old Man reminds him, he has followed the adage: "Be thyself – Jack." Not Peer. For an instant this takes on something of the revelatory force of "Je est un autre".

Morgenstern indulges in no such would-be pyrotechnics of vernacular grittiness (surely "Be yourself – Jack" would have been better). Not for him a statement like Meyer's: "Wherever I have had to choose between maintaining rhythm and using the most effective phrase, I have not hesitated to prefer the latter."[33] Rather he draws on the established relationship and familiar tones of Faust and Mephistopheles to convey the relationship of human being and troll. This is clearest in Peer's comments after hearing the funeral speech for the unknown dead man in Act V:

Sieh da, das nenn' ich noch Christentum!
Da war nichts, was einen peinlich berührte; –
Zumal dem: "Du selbst zu sein, sei dein Ruhm",
Zu dem am Schlusse die Predigt führte,
Auch an und für sich alles Lob gebührte.

Here the tone is unmistakably Faust's, in the famous scene in the Garden with Gretchen, whose anxious inquiries about his religious beliefs are fobbed off with evasive and humorous hypocrisy, echoing the accents of Mephistopheles, that shrewd worldling. Man and Mephistopheles, like Man and Troll, display their intimacy in secularized humbug. Thus, without identifying Peer with Faust, Morgenstern used the more darkly comedic aspects of **Faust** to create a **Peer Gynt** of its time, and presaging the Peter Stein production of 1971 in which Peer took on the tone and form of **Ubu Roi.**

Morgenstern's translation of **Peer Gynt** was not merely ensconced in the **Sämtliche Werke**, it was intended for the stage, and was used immediately for the Vienna production of 1901. This was a great success, indeed the first successful German language production. Morgenstern's version was thus vital to the movement towards verse drama in the theatre, already signalled by the emergence of Maeterlinck, the first professional productions of Shelley's **I Cenci** (never performed in its own time), the Celtic revival, and Lugné-Poe's symbolist productions of Ibsen in Paris.

It is not surprising that **Peer Gynt** has remained one of the most often played of Ibsen's works in Germany. If Morgenstern's translation helped make it so, it was overtaken by a grimly ironic fate. In 1914 **Peer Gynt** was performed at the Berlin Hoftheater in a new translation by Dieter Eckart. This version germanified Peer into a pseudo-Faustian folk hero, a type of "the nordic genius". Later taken up by the National Socialists, Eckart's was the popular version that held the stage until the end of the Second World War. Even recent works on the reception of Ibsen continue to devote attention to this translation at the expense of Morgenstern's.[34]

At the time of its first production the inferiority of Eckart's translation to Morgenstern's was perceived and expressed in the most vigorous terms by critics. Siegfried Jacobsohn, for example, complained that the falsification so often brought about by "operatic" presentations of the play had this time been perpetrated by sheer bad translation. He contrasts it to Morgenstern:

> Dank Christian Morgensterns vorbildlicher, aber freilich unnachahmlicher Verdichtungskraft beginnt das Stück mit dem Ausruf: "Peer, du lügst." Bei Eckart wird aus dem erleuchtenden Blitz eine Tranlampe, nämlich: "Hör auf! Ich habe genug! Was du sagst, ist Lug und Trug!"[35]

> Thanks to Christian Morgenstern's exemplary, but admittedly inimitable power of poetic compression, the play begins with the cry: "Peer, you're lying." In Eckart this revealing flash of lightning becomes a blubber lamp: "Be quiet! I've heard enough! What you say is lies and deception!"

Throughout, Jacobsohn points out, the translator displays "diese marklose Schwatzhaftigkeit", "this flabby garrulousness":

> Aus Ibsens schroffem, zerklüftetem, beißendem, abgründig vieldeutigem, blutendem und blütig reißendem Höhenwerk ist ein sanftes, zuckrig-schmalziges, überdeutliches, glatt und plattes, musikalisch aufgeschwemmtes Märchenvolksstück in Knallbonbonreimen geworden.[36]

> Out of Ibsen's abrupt, splintered, biting, precipitously ambiguous, bloody and

> bloodily rending work of high art, he has fashioned a soft, sugary and schmalzy, over-literal, smooth and flat, popular fairystory drowned in music and written in popgun rhyming couplets.

This clear and sharp perception of the superiority of Morgenstern's translation unfortunately could not stem the tide of history which overwhelmed both art and criticism.

The doctrine of "affinity" of the author to be translated with the literary and cultural sensibilities of the "target" audience patently needs to be handled with care. If "affinity" demands "fidelity", it does not require identification of the translator with his author. Indeed, a degree of distancing may be necessary for a sophisticated awareness of the nature and extent of "affinity". Morgenstern often expressed his reservations about Ibsen. They represent both the state of Ibsen reception – the urge felt to push beyond Ibsen – and, still more, Morgenstern's own inclinations and gifts as a poet. He often expressed his impatience, his distaste, above all, his sense of oppression during his long subjugation to Ibsen's mode of being and the letter of his text.

As he wrote to Efraim Frisch from Arosa:

> . . . Die "Gedichte" Ibsens liegen schwer auf mir; ich möchte endlich frei sein und soll immer noch diese fremde Welt mit mir herumschleppen, der ich mich oft aufs bitterste feind fühle. Ibsen ist in der Tat der persönliche Ausdruck jenes "Grauenvollen", wovon er schreibt; er zieht an und stösst ab. Wie aber spricht das Eisen zum Magneten? Ich hasse den am meisten, der anzieht, doch nicht festzuhalten weiß. Und noch ein anderes Wort Nietzsches geht mir durch den Kopf, seit ich vor kurzem wieder einmal den "Solness" las und dabei beinahe etwas wie Ekel empfand: Ein Haufe Krankheiten, der durch den Geist in die Welt hinaus greift.[37]

> Ibsen's "Poems" weigh heavily on me; I want finally to be free and must still carry this alien world around with me to which I often feel bitterly hostile. Ibsen is in fact the incarnation of that "Horrible" that he writes of; he attracts and repels. What does the iron say to the magnet? I hate that most which attracts but does not know how to retain. And another saying of Nietzsche's has been going through my head, since I recently reread "Solness" and experienced something almost like disgust: A heap of diseases, which through the spirit reaches out into the world.

When he had finally finished his translations of Ibsen, he noted epigrammatically:

> Der Tag im Hausbuch rot gemacht,
> da ich dich endlich über-dacht.[38]

> A red-letter day in my diary,
> When I papered you over finally.

However, even in the case of Ibsen's poems, which went most against his grain while he was translating them, time restored him to a juster appreciation of them. In 1903 he wrote to Ibsen asking his permission to dedicate a collection of his own poems to him, and after Ibsen's death he published the collection, **Sprüche**, dedicated to Ibsen as "Henrik dem dreizehnten", "Henry the Thirteenth". His long-standing interest in the brief aphoristic form (which he had found in his most admired models, Goethe, Novalis, and Nietzsche) had been tempered in practice by Ibsen's hardness. The opening poem of the collection refers directly to his experience with Ibsen, and provides an epitaph to the "servitude and grandeur" of the poet's apprenticeship in translation:

Ich riss des Herzens Furchen auf:
Da säten Wind und Sonnenschein
ihr Korn hinein;
da schoss es auf
aus rotem Grund
und wuchs mit zuckendem Purpurmund
zum Licht hinauf.

Alles Leben steht aus Messers Schneide.
Gleite aus und du ertrinkst in Leide.

Dulde, trage.
Bessere Tage
werden kommen.
Alles muss frommen
denen, die fest sind.
Herz, altes Kind,
dulde, trage.

Gib, gib und immer wieder gib der Welt,
und lass'sie, was sie mag, dir wiedergeben;
tu alles für, erwarte nichts vom Leben, –
genug, gibt es sich selbst dir zum Entgelt.[39]

I broke my heart's furrows open:
The wind and the sun sowed then
their seed within;
there it shot up
from the red earth
and grew with quivering scarlet mouth
up to the light.

All life stands on knife's edge.
Slip, and you drown in grief.

Be still, endure.
A better cure
comes without fail.
All shall avail
those who stand fast.
Heart, child of your past,
Be still, endure.

Give, give to the world, never spare expense,
and let it give back whatever it may;
expect nothing from life, do all for the day, –
enough, it gives you itself in recompense.

Morgenstern and the Cabaret

Morgenstern's involvement with the theatre was not confined to the translation of dramatic works, nor to the productions of his translations on the stage. During the time he was translating Ibsen the literary and satirical cabaret, already a feature of the Paris avant-garde, established itself in Berlin, in Ernst von Wolzogen's Überbrettl in 1900, and in 1901 in the "Schall und Rauch" cabaret associated with the name of Max Reinhardt. Morgenstern was in demand for both cabarets; indeed, his founding role in cabaret goes back much earlier, to the prototypical informal meetings of writers, actors, and artists in cafés round the city. Reinhardt's group of actors, "Die Brille", The Spectacles (including Friedrich Kayssler and Martin Zickel) is often named as the immediate source of the "Schall und Rauch", and related to a tradition of theatre parody leading back to Nestroy,[40] but one of the first groups to take on a new and distinctive character was Morgenstern's **Galgenbrüderschaft**, Gallows Brotherhood, which began to take form from 1894.

Morgenstern and the Galgenbrüderschaft

The Gallows Brotherhood contained the seeds of the cabaret; as one of its members, Georg Hirschfeld, wrote:

> Was ist aus dem holden Unsinn geworden? Nun, immerhin wenn man es recht betrachtet, Reinhardts "Brille", "Schall und Rauch", Kleines, Neues, Deutsches Theater. Der Galgenberg aber lebt in seinen Liedern fort.[41]
>
> What evolved from this blessed nonsense? Rightly considered, nothing less than Reinhardt's "Brille", "Schall und Rauch" cabaret, Little Theatre, New Theatre, and National Theatre. But the Gallows Hill lives on in his [Morgenstern's] songs.

In short, not only the cabaret in its various forms, but also the intimate theatre and Reinhardt's later theatre, indeed his stunning career as a director of international fame and influence, grew from this germ. But the germ of the idea is still visible in the **Gallows Songs.**

Morgenstern himself described the beginning of the joke:

> Die ersten, noch den neunziger Jahren entstammenden Galgenliedern entstanden für einen lustigen Kreis, der sich auf einem Ausflug nach Werder bei Potsdam, allwo noch heute ein sogenannte "Galgenberg" gezeigt wird, wie das so die Laune gibt, mit diesem Namen schmücken zu müssen meinte. Aus dem Namen erwuchs alsdann das Weitere, denn man wollte sich doch, war man schon nun einmal eine so benannte Vereinigung, auch das Gehörige dazu denken und vorstellen.[42]

> The earliest Gallows Songs, going back to the Nineties, came into being for a jolly circle that went on an excursion to Werder near Potsdam, where even today a so-called 'Gallows Hill' stands, which so set the mood that the group agreed they must deck themselves out in the title. Out of the name sprung the rest, for as we were already a society bearing the name, we wanted to carry out everything appropriate to it.

The friends began to meet as a society; they adopted roles, to which belonged certain props, and they evolved an elaborate ceremony. In Hirschfeld's account, the poems came first, and then musical accompaniments devised by his brother Julius, which the whole group sang together:

> Unsere Versammlungslokal lag zwar in keiner höllischen Gegend (ich glaube, die Charlottenstrasse war's), aber wenn wir beisammen sassen und unsere Lieder sangen – O Gott. . .[43]

> Our meeting place lay in no particularly hellish region (I believe it was Charlotte Street), but when we sat together and sang our songs – O God . . .

Morgenstern brought the poems scribbled in pencil on slips of paper, Julius Hirschfeld sat down at the piano and improvised tunes. The roles emerged: Morgenstern himself presided over the meetings of the Gallows Brotherhood with a rusty antique sword, and was known as Rabenaas (Gallows Bird); Julius was dubbed Schuhu, Georg was Vereckerle, Kayssler was Gurgeljochem, another friend Unselm, and the music was inspired by "the spirit of Sophie, the executioner's girl friend". Sentences were pronounced and written in red ink on parchment, and the executions carried out in darkened rooms with artful lighting.

Not only the fixed roles of the various members of the company were developed; Morgenstern's poems peopled the room with the Moon sheep, the conversing worms, the ravens and the owls, the Twelve-elf, and the fish with the unsounded song, or "Schnapp-Hymnus", as Spitzer was to call it. Somewhat more disturbing to the other patrons were the exotic sounds of "Das große Lalula". As their meetings turned more and more into ceremonies and performances, they were sometimes asked to leave the premises, and took their peripatetic theatre to another café.

Thus when the first collection of **Gallows Songs** was published in 1905, they had already a decade of private and public performance behind them. The decisive turning point had taken place, and came to public notice in the cabarets just after the turn of the century; the immediate popularity of the **Gallows Songs** from their publication marked general acceptance of the post-Naturalist phase of Modernism. As Hirschfeld put it:

> Galgenberg? – Es war ein Einfall, ein ganz privater Witz und doch ein geistiger Wendepunkt, der unübersehbare Folgen hatte. "Naturalisten" schwenkten ab und ließen die Macht der Phantastik in ihre Gedankenwelt. Schon siegte auf der Bühne das Märchen (der Erfolg der "Versunkenen Glocke" ereignete sich damals) – wir aber gingen viel weiter . . .[44]

> The Gallows Hill? – It was a caprice, a wholly private joke and nevertheless an intellectual turning-point which had unforeseeable consequences. "Naturalists" did an about-turn and let the power of fantasy into their mental world. Already the fairytale was victorious on the stage (the success of the "Sunken Bell" came at that time) – but we went much further . . .

It was in the theatre, then, that the "intellectual turning-point" was first marked. Reinhardt himself although not one of the founding members of the Gallows Brotherhood was well acquainted with its members and entered into the spirit of the thing. As Reinhardt wrote to Morgenstern, arranging to meet him after the performance of Hauptmann's **Die Weber**, in which he was appearing:

Berlin, 21 März 1897

Lieber Danton,

auch ich möchte, bevor ich Sie guillotinieren lasse, gerne mit Ihnen beisammen sein. Morgen ist jedoch ein angestrengter Tag, nachmittags bin ich aufreizender Weber Ansorge und abends versöhnender Pfarrer. Ich bin deshalb später fertig. Aber um halb elf abends, längstens elf Uhr, bin ich in **Amerika**, bar aller Begleitung und werde mich freuen, Sie drüben zu begrüßen. Später spielen wir wohl Domino um Menschenköpfe. Hoch die "Kaiserkrone", hoch der "Kaiserhof", hoch das "Monopol".

Ihr

Robespierre[45]

Berlin 4 March 1897

Dear Danton,

I too would like to be together with you before I have you guillotined. Tomorrow is a hectic day, though, in the afternoon I play insurrectionary Weaver Ansorge and in the evening reconciling pastor. So I finish later. But at half past ten, at the latest eleven, I'll be in "America", without company, and will be delighted to see you there. Later we shall play at dominoes for men's heads. Up the "Kaiser's Crown", up the "Kaiser's Court", up the "Monopoly".

Your

Robespierre

Reinhardt alludes not only to the sport of the Gallows Brotherhood, but to Büchner's play, **Dantons Tod (Danton's Death)**, which he would direct in its first German production in 1907, after a long struggle with the censors. The connection between the execution game, the modern drama, and the political censorship was not fortuitous.

It was not Reinhardt but Ernst von Wolzogen, however, who first opened the Berlin cabaret and began to perform Morgenstern's songs and dramatic sketches publicly. The Überbrettl took place in a hired theatre seating 650, larger than the informal café-style cabaret. It featured not only songs and short sketches, such as Morgenstern's parodies of the well-known Berlin theatre critic, Alfred Kerr (which always brought down the house), but plays and operettas: the first night included a part of Arthur Schnitzler's **Anatol**, a pantomime Pierrot play, a shadow play by Detlev von Liliencron, and opening the second half, Morgenstern's one-act parody of d'Annunzio, **Il Pranzo** (Lunchtime). The rest of the second half was taken up with Otto Julius Bierbaum's operetta play, **Der Lustige Ehemann (The Merry Husband)**.

Von Wolzogen wrote to Morgenstern, who was unable to attend the opening owing to illness, to describe their success, and in particular the good reception of Morgenstern's own pieces, and the plans to include further pieces in future performances:

Berlin, 20 Januar 1901

Lieber Meister Morgenstern!

Wir haben einen glänzenden Erfolg gehabt! Es war win gemütlicher, höchst animierter Abend, der 18. Januar. Die Zeitungen waren fast ausnahmslos des Lobes voll und nun dürfen wir auch mit guter Zuversicht auf den Bestand und den materiellen Erfolg der Sache rechnen. Leider wurde der Tenor krank, so daß Ihr "Anmutiger Vertrag" wegfiel. Aber das "Mahl" wirkte prächtig, und besonders meine Einleitungsconference, in der ich Ihre szenischen Anweisungen und die Charakteristik der Personen zum besten gab, wirkte außerordentlich erheiternd. Stürmische Heiterkeit entfesselte Ihre Kerrkritik, die freilich wohl nur bei dem literarischen Publikum der Première volles Verständnis fand. Sie wirkte um so mehr, als Kerr mit dem Vortrag eigener Dichtungen auf dem Zettel stand, hernach aber zurücktrat, weil ihm die Zensur das meiste gestrichen hatte, und nun ahnungslos unter den Zuschauern saß. Ob er es übel genommen hat, weiß ich nicht. Bis jetzt hat er noch nicht reagiert.

Ich möchte gern die "Dame von Minime" demnächst herausbringen – aber die Zensur nimmt Ärgernis an dem Bett! Ich werde nächster Tage noch einmal aufs Präsidium gehen und die hohen Herren von den tiefen ethischen Qualitäten Ihres Scherzes zu überzeugen versuchen.

Ich habe jetzt auch einige Ihrer Galgenlieder in der Hirschfeld'schen Vertonung erhalten und hoffe einiges davon bald herauszubringen.

Mit schönsten Gruß und herzlichem Dank für ihre fleißige Mitwirkung bin ich

Ihr sehr ergebener Ernst Frh.v. Wolzogen[46]

Berlin, 20 January 1901

Dear Maestro Morgenstern!

We have had a brilliant success! It was a cheerful, highly animated evening, the 18th of January. The newspapers were almost without exception full of praise and now we can also depend with confidence on the durability and the financial success of the thing. Unfortunately the tenor was ill, so that your "Gracious Request" had to be omitted. But the "Lunch" worked wonderfully, and especially my introduction, in which I did my best to present your stage directions and description of the dramatis personae, had an extraordinarily hilarious effect. Stormy applause was unleashed by your Kerr critique, which admittedly could only have been fully understood by the literary public of the opening night. It worked all the more because Kerr was on the programme to read his own poems, but afterwards withdrew, because the censors had cut him most, and he sat there helpless among the spectators. Whether he has taken it amiss, I don't know. So far I've heard nothing from him.

I'd very much like to bring out the "Lady from Minime" next – but the censors take umbrage at the bed! I'll go down to headquarters again in the next few days and try to persuade the powers that be of the profoundly ethical qualities of your joke.

I have also now got some of your Gallows Songs in Hirschfeld's settings and I hope to bring out something from them soon.

With warmest greetings and heartfelt thanks for your energetic co-operation, I remain

Yours faithfully Ernst Freiherr von Wolzogen

Morgenstern's "Mahl", a parody of the extreme aestheticism of Gabriele d'Annunzio, is a one-act play which takes about twenty minutes in performance.[47] The scene-settings and characterizations with which von Wolzogen regaled the audience are elaborately **fin-de-siècle.**

Another of Morgenstern's short plays was first performed at the Überbrettl, and in 1907 was used as the title piece of a collection of his sketches and parodies: **Egon und Emilie**. This is a particularly incisive example of his ability to use parody to break through to a new Modernist style. It is not surprising, after his intense personal struggle with Ibsen, that the play is a parody of **Nora**, that is, of Ibsen's **A Doll's House.** A great deal of controversy had arisen over it, especially in Berlin, where in 1896 it had been performed not with Nora's radical slamming of the door behind her as she leaves the family home, but with a reconciliation scene between her and Torwald. Morgenstern restores the original intention of a decisive break between the wife and husband, but projects it out of the realm of Naturalist social document into the new realm of self-reflexive comment on the dramatic form itself, in the manner of a later play that has become the hallmark of the style, Pirandello's **Six Characters in Search of an Author** (1921). It is also an early example of the cabaret's anti-bourgeois satire, of the kind developed in Brecht's early short play. **Die Kleinbürgerhochzeit (The Petit-bourgeois Marriage)**. Morgenstern's political edge characteristically displayed itself in a witty transcendence of the whole philistine life-style. Thus in **Egon und Emilie** the marriage is annulled before it takes place, and with it the drama itself: Egon steadfastly refuses to speak to his fiancée, who carries on an increasingly desperate monologue, employing every strategem to obtain a response, until finally she denounces him for denying her a role, and flees from the stage.[48] There can be no more bourgeois social drama.

Egon and Emily

Emily *(drawing Egon by the hand into the room):*
Come in! So, come in here, my beloved Egon! Oh how happy I am, how happy your Emily is!

Egon *(sits on the sofa and says nothing)*

Emily: Have you no words for our happiness? But surely – *(she stops)*

Egon *(remains silent)*

Emily: O you are still angry with me! It's true, isn't it, my Egon, you are still cross with me!

Egon *(is silent)*

Emily *(sitting on the bench near the chimney corner):*
I should have known it! I should have foreseen it! O how miserable I am! What a fool I am! But my God, all is not lost, – is it, Egon *(she springs up, in mounting fear)* – is it, Egon –?

Egon *(remains silent)*

Emily: Oh, I entreat you! Only say a word, just one single tiny word!

Egon *(remains silent)*

Emily *(by the round table)*
Yes, by the eternal God, – is it something so enormous that I ask, no, beg for,

plead for! I am not asking for your pardon or your understanding, no, not by a long way, for that we still have five acts' time; but give me some point of contact, surely you won't deny me some kind of reply –

Egon *(remains silent)*

Emily *(at the window):*
Egon! Egon!! Egon!!!

Egon *(remains silent)*

Emily *(going to him):*
Do you know, you vile man, that this means my death? That I can never become a character – on account of your mad silence? That now I have to leave this stage again, go out into the nameless nothingness, without having played, without having lived?

(She looks at her watch and waits a full minute)
No answer, not one single inarticulate grunt, not even a look! Stone, stone, ice. Cruel man, you have murdered my role, unnatural man, you are here strangling a family drama in its swaddling clothes. . . He is silent, he remains dumb, I am going. So then, fall again, curtain, almost before you have been raised; so go then, you beloved audience, go home. You have seen that I did my utmost. All for nothing. This monster doesn't want any drama, he wants his peace. Farewell *(exits).*

Egon *(rises):*
Quite right, I want my peace, I don't want any family drama. For your sake, dear spectators, should I place myself entirely at the disposal of this waterfall of a woman? For the sake of your beautiful eyes, should I get involved in an endless dialogue with her? I haven't the slightest intention of doing so. Now go home and come to the realization that today for the first time in your life you have seen on the stage a genuinely rational man, a man who does not merely pay lip service to the old proverb "Speech is silver, silence is golden", but fearlessly follows it, Farewell *(exits).*

Most popular of all were the **Galgenlieder.** Von Wolzogen put them on with the musical accompaniments devised by Hirschfeld. When the "Schall und Rauch" cabaret tried to retrieve them for their own use, von Wolzogen refused to hand them over, claiming they were lost. Angry correspondence ensued, and the Reinhardt men never had a good word for von Wolzogen.

Although in the annals of cabaret the Überbrettl tends to be deprecated, Morgenstern, in his editorial "Notices" in the periodical **Das Theater**, later described ironically the **Variété** show into which it deteriorated, and mourned for the old Überbrettl:

Das "Überbrettl" hat glücklicherweise als Wort wie als Sache abgewirtschaftet. Aber daß das, was wir Leute Variété nennen, nicht doch noch einmal menschenwürdiger werden könnte, keine moralische, aber eine ästhetische

Anstalt zum Vergnügen erwachsener Menschen – diesen thörichten Gedanken will und kann ich noch immer nicht aufgeben.[49]

The "Überbrettl" has happily as word and as fact gone out of business. But that what we call Variété could not once again become worthier of the human race, not a moral, but an aesthetic establishment for the pleasure of grown-ups – this foolish thought I will not nor can I ever give up.

Morgenstern and the "Schall und Rauch" Cabaret

If Morgenstern contributed signally to the success of the Überbrettl, he was even more closely associated with the "Schall und Rauch" cabaret that opened in 1901. "Schall und Rauch" is an allusion to the renowned passage in **Faust** in which Gretchen catechizes Faust about his religious beliefs, and he shrugs off the inquiry with an evasion: "Name ist Schall und Rauch", or "What's in a name?". For Morgenstern, as we have seen, this was related to Peer Gynt's hypocrisy. "Schall" and "Rauch" literally mean "noise" and "smoke", appropriate enough to the cabaret, but best translated perhaps as "sound and fury signifying nothing". Thus the cabaret's name – like its logo – cunningly refers both to the ordinary conditions inside a café, and to the theatrical player who "struts and frets his hour upon the stage", as well as conveying a whiff of the devil who stands behind Faust's equivocations. The programme for the opening night (fig.1) displays an unmistakably mephistophelean head wreathed in smoke.[50]

Again his own sketches figured prominently in the programmes. Morgenstern was benefited by the cabaret, in that some of the proceeds went to pay for one of his sojourns in a sanatorium in Switzerland; but he was an active instigator and a collaborator throughout.[51] Indeed, his excited correspondence with Kayssler shows that it was the prospects opened by the cabaret that brought Morgenstern back to Berlin and out of the solitude of his Ibsen translations.

Kayssler kept Morgenstern abreast of what was happening in Berlin, outlining the plans for the cabaret, soliciting Morgenstern's contributions and his presence, reporting on their reception. On 27 January 1901 he sent a programme of the opening night and a sheaf of favourable notices: "Du wirst selber herauslesen, daß diese Zeitungsseelen hier mal wie vergnügte Menschen reden. . ."[52] ("As you'll see for yourself, these journalistic souls here sound like contented men for once. . ."). If only Morgenstern were with them:

. . . Dich könnten wir gerade brauchen. Diesmal kamen Deine Sachen zu spät; wir denken das nächste Mal an die Szene vom "Gesellschafter". "Schluck und Jau" waren auch sehr schön, aber wir stehen ratlos vor den vielen Personen und Masken. Fällt Dir nicht etwas ein an schlagender Parodie, was dem Carlos an Farbe nahe kommt? Aber es müßte natürlich was ganz andres sein, nicht wieder Schiller. Hast Du denn nicht noch irgendeine Maeterlincksache, kurz und ulkig? Zu schade, daß wir die "Krankenstube" nicht mehr erwischt haben.[53]

We have need of you just now. Your pieces arrived too late this time; we plan to do the scene from "Party-goer" next time. "Bite and Sup" would be very good too, but we're stymied by the numbers of characters and masks. Have you an idea for a hard-hitting parody in the manner of the "Carlos" [Reinhardt's parody of Schiller's **Don Carlos**]? But it would have to be something quite different, of course, not Schiller again. Haven't you still got one of your Maeterlinck pieces, short and larky? It's too bad we couldn't find the "Sickroom".

In fact, the opening performance had included a piece by Morgenstern: **Die Jongleuse**, The Lady Juggler (fig.2).[54] This piece uses the circus motifs of the Paris cabaret, most familiar in the German-speaking milieu perhaps through Wedekind, especially his mime play, **Die Kaiserin von Neufundland**, (**The Empress from Newfoundland**), and later the **Lulu** trilogy.[55] Shocking and incisively comic at their inception, these motifs became a cliché by the time of Max Ophüls' film **Lola Montez.**[56] Some of them were renewed again in Peter Stein's 1971 **Peer Gynt**, which imported the tactics of the early cabaret into the verse drama, revivifying and telescoping the history of modern drama just as Morgenstern had in his own work faithfully inscribed the continuity between Faust and Peer, while initiating the decisive break that made Peer a grotesque Ubu-like contra-Faust. The cabaret scene of the satiric tour round the naked, tattoo'd body of Germany epitomizes the power of this imagery.[57] An element in the transformation was Morgenstern's own drafted play, **Weltkobold**, in which the world appears as a game, a farce (**Narrensposse**) of God; the world is the fantasy of an all-powerful rogue.

A few days later Kayssler wrote again to describe the plans to open another theatre, to prepare for the day two years hence when Otto Brahm was scheduled to resign from the directorship of the Deutsches Theater and both Reinhardt and Kayssler expected to have to find other engagements as actors. He points out that Morgenstern himself had stressed the distinction between intimate and grand theatre:

Wir werden keine historischen Tragödien spielen können, wohl aber ausser Einaktern Ibsen, Strindberg. Du selbst sprachst seiner Zeit von einer zukünftigen Scheidung zwischen Intimen und Großem Theater. Hier ist sie. Wir fangen mit dem Intimen an. Ob das Große daraus wird, liegt in unserer Hand.[58]

We shan't be able to play any historical tragedies, but we can do Ibsen, Strindberg, as well as one-acters. You yourself spoke in the past of the future distinction between intimate and grand theatre. Here it is. We're beginning with the intimate. Whether the grand will come out of it is up to us.

As the news came in of the success of his plays, sketches, and poems in the cabarets, Morgenstern was amused to think that they were now hailed as the latest novelty, when in fact he had written, and indeed published some of them long ago. He wrote playfully to another friend:

Schallundrauchst Du nicht auch etwas? Da Du den elf Scharfrichtern glücklich durchgebrannt bist? Das Drama in einem Satz ist wirklich gut. Meine Drämchen etc. wollen noch immer nicht verlegt werden. Und so kommts, daß das Publikum – worauf ja allerdings **sehr** viel ankommt! – zuletzt meint, man machte die "Mode" mit, während man sie längst vorgemacht hat.[59]

SCHALL UND RAUCH

UNTER DEN LINDEN 44

Eröffnungs-Vorstellung

Mittwoch, den 9. October 1901

Fig. 1. Illustration from the programme for the opening night of **Schall und Rauch**, 9 October 1901.

PROGRAMM.

I. PROLOG. Nach dem Englischen des Shakespeare von Friedrich Kayssler.

Erster Narr . . . . Richard Leopold.
Zweiter Narr . . . . Ferdinand Kurth.
Dritter Narr . . . . Heinrich Liebmann.
Der Geist . . . . Josef Dill.
Polonius . . . . Victor Arnold.

II. NARRENLIED von Alice Berend. Musik von Hugo Koppel.
Ernst Grinzenberger.

III. KULTUR-KARRIKATUREN.

DIE DEKADENTEN. Nach einer Idee von G. K. Hardenberg (Der „Jugend" entnommen.)

Der Sanfte . . . . Alfred Kühne.
Der Cholerische . . . . Ferdinand Kurth.

DER DEUTSCHE JÜNGLING von Robert Eysler. Musik von Gustav Lazarus.

DIE DICHTERSCHULE von Victor Ottmann (Der „Jugend" entnommen.)

Lehrer . . . . Victor Arnold.
Schuler . . . . Richard Leopold.

IV. TRAGÖDIE von H. Heine. Musik von Schumann.
LIEBESGARTEN von R. Reinick. Musik von Schumann.
Franz und Magda von Dulong.

5 Minuten Pause.

V. DIE GEFANGENE. Ein Dialog von O. G. Friedrich.
Die Gefangene . . . . Luise Kayssler.

VI. DIE JONGLEUSE von Chr. Morgenstern. Musik von Bogumil Zepler.
LA DERNIÈRE. Gavotte von Fénicienne Varques. Musik von Lucienne Delormes.
HINTERM DEICH von Gustav Falke. Musik von Kurth Schindler.
Mira Gotmar.

VII. ZAHNWEH, Komisch-tragisches Duett von R. Genée

Doctor . . . . Ernst Grinzenberger.
Patient . . . . Constanze Zinner.

VIII.

Rex.

Alte Mär' ohne Worte von Richard Vallentin.

Der König . . . . Josef Dill.
Die Geliebte . . . . Maria Eisenhut.
SEIN Diener . . . . Victor Arnold.
Der Koch . . . . Hanns Wassmann.
Der Priester . . . . Alfred Kühne.
Der fahrende Sänger . . . . . . Richard Leopold.
Der Feldherr . . . . Ernst Grinzenberger.
Ein Bedienter . . . . Ferdinand Kurth.

Zeitlos. — Ort nach Wahl.

Fig.2. Programme for the opening night of Schall und Rauch.

Fig.3. Stage sketch by Edvard Munch for Ibsen's **Ghosts**, Berlin, 8 November 1906. *Deutsches Teatermuseum*, Munich.

Fig. 4. Photograph of Shakespeare's **A Midsummer Night's Dream**, Berlin 1906. *Deutsches Teatermuseum*, Munich.

> Aren't you Noise-and-smoking too? Now that you've fired up The Eleven Executioners [the Munich cabaret] so successfully? The play in one phrase is really good. My playlets etc. refuse to lie down. And so it comes to pass that the public – on whose coming so much depends! – at last imagines that I am following the "fashion", whereas I set the fashion long in advance.

Some of the sketches he had indeed published during his early days in Berlin. One, for example, from **Der Zuschauer** in 1894, was **Epigo und Decadentia. Ein Satirisches Märchen** (Epigo and Decadentia. A Satirical Fairytale). This is the tale of two uncharming twins who each believes that he or she is the long-lost child of the king. They arrange a drama competition, instead of a revolution, to enable the people to judge who is the rightful heir. Epigo's contribution is a weighty historical drama, **Assaph und Debora, oder: Schuld und Sühne. Iambentragödie in fünf Akten** (Assaph and Deborah, or: Guilt and Repentance. An Iambic Tragedy in five Acts). The model is Hebbel's tragedy **Judith**, based on the Biblical story of Judith and Holofernes, or Sudermann's **Sodoms Ende**, which Morgenstern had admired in his Breslau days.

Decadentia's contributions to the drama competition are two pieces that were later plucked out for performance in the cabaret, and later still published as separate items, under different titles:

Ich.
Du.
Er!
Sie. . .?
Es –
Wir?
Ihr?
Sie!. . .

She got no further; Epigo's supporters shouted furiously that it was a lot of nonsense and completely incomprehensible, while her own supporters insisted just as fanatically that they had understood the profound sense of the poem down to its subtlest detail.

"Erklären, erklären!" rief das Volk. Ohne Bedenken willfahrte sie.
"Ich, Du-: Ein Ehepaar, nicht wahr?
Er-: Ein Hausfreund.
Sie?-: Die Gattin zwischen zwei Feuern. Was wird sie tun?
Es-: Das Dämonische, das Heranschleichende.
Wir?-: Bleiben wir Mann und Weib beieinander?
Ihr?-: Oder gehst du, Weib, mit ihm?
Sie!-: Da gehen sie hin, die beiden. Ende."

"Explain, explain!"
cried the people. She replied instantly:
"I, you-: a married couple, of course.
He-: a family friend.

She. . .?-: the wife between two fires. What will she do?
It-: the demonic, the approaching Fatality.
We?-: Do we, husband and wife, stay together?
You?-: Or, woman, do you go away with him?
They!-: Then they go, the two of them.
The End[60]

Decadentia's second offering – and her entries win the plaudits of the people – is a Naturalist drama: **Knochenfraß**, or **Bonestew**, subtitled "Naturalistische Handlung vom Ende der 80er Jahre (Berliner Schule)", "Fragment"; ("Naturalistic drama of the end of the 1880s", a "Fragment"). As in the d'Annunzio parody, the stage setting dominates the drama, and sums up the style; here, indeed, the scene itself ("scene two"), the fragment of the Berlin dialect, is just three lines. The date is part of the polemic indicating that this is an outmoded style, although Hauptmann was at the height of his popularity at the time Morgenstern first wrote the parody, which antedates by half a dozen years Reinhardt's more famous Hauptmann parody, the second version of **Don Carlos; Karle. Ein Diebskomödie (Carl. A Thief's Comedy)**. This latter was the most effective of the parodies of Schiller in four styles, or the so-called "Tetralogie der Stilarten": the first, in the grandiose manner of the Deutsches Theater with Director Otto Brahm's wife as an over-statuesque Prinzessin; the second, the Naturalistic version, with a superb characterization of Carl as the neurasthenic "modern young man", certainly a parody of the original model, Ibsen's Oswald in **Ghosts**, as much as of Hauptmann's imitations; the third, of Maeterlinck, which may also owe something to Morgenstern's earlier Maeterlinck parodies, referred to by Kayssler; the fourth, in Überbrettl style. Karle is described as follows, in a parody of Hauptmann's detailed, often unplayably unvisual notes:

Anmerkung für den Schauspieler

Karle, Neurastheniker, 21 Jahre alt, durch und durch verwachsen, auf dem rechten Auge etwas weitsichtig, zwerchfellleidend. Er hat das moderne, nervöse Reißen im Antlitz, leidet an habitueller Verstopfung und besitzt Plattfüße und einen Kahlkopf von hydrocephaler Formation. Die käsige Blässe seines Gesichtes ist mit roten Pickeln besternt. Grünlichschillernde Augen, krankhaft sinnliche Lippen und große, weiße, lasterhafte Hände. Er spricht stoßweise und abgerissen und zwar durch die Nase. Sein Ton klingt, als ob er Baumwolle in der Nase hätte. Er pfeift auf alles. Nur manchmal ludert es unheimlich in ihm auf. Im übrigen spaziert er auf der Grenze zwischen Genie und Wahnsinn. Hinter den Ohren ist eine gewisse Feuchtigkeit bemerkbar. Er ist die Reinkultur eines modernen, jungen Mannes.[61]

Note to the Actor

Carl, a neurotic twenty-one year old, a thoroughly deformed figure, with a cross-eye on the right, and suffering from epileptic fits. He has the twitching face of the true modern, suffers from chronic constipation and has flat feet and a bald head of hydrocephalic type. The cheesy pallor of his face is scarred with red acne. Greenish glimmering eyes, sickly sensual lips and great, white, vice-ridden hands. He speaks in fragmented, abrupt bursts and through his nose. He sounds as if he had cottonwool up his nose. He doesn't give a damn for anything. Only sometimes there is a flash of lewdness from deep within. For the rest he walks the knife-edge between genius and madness. There is a certain dampness noticeable behind his ears. He is the purest specimen of the modern young man.

The setting for Morgenstern's **Knochenfraß** consists of a minutely described low-life interior replete with cracked and peeling walls, a rusty undervest hanging on a hook, and in the corner on the right "a moaning shapeless mass" wrapped "in the rags of a Turkish shawl", from which an ashen face has just worked its way out. "Durch die dicke Dämmerung dunstet ein grünlich-schleimiges Lallen." ("Through the thick gloom wafts a greenish-slimy babble.") "Ein Weib in Lumpen trampst herein." ("A woman in rags tramps in.") "Mitte Vierziger. Fett. Kolporteuse-Manieren." ("Middle forties. Fat. Manners of a fish-wife".)

The fragment of "scene two" ensues:

Nabend! *(Schnubbert in die Alkohol-Atmosphäre. Geht nach hinten, stößt mit dem linken Fuß ärgerlich nach dem türkischen Shawl.)*

Hat sich der olle Knerjel wieder beschikkert wie ne Sackstrippe.

(Mit häßlichem Mienenausdruck):
Na, wart' du Lerge, du – dat soll dir sauer aufstoßen. Verbubanzt mich meene eenzige Schabracke.

(Der Shawl wird langsam lebendig.)[62]

Woman. Evenin'. *(Sniffs the alcohol-laden atmosphere. Goes to the rear, kicks angrily with her left foot at the Turkish shawl.)*

The ol' gal has decked herself out again like a stripper.

(Pulling a hateful face):

Na, jus' you wait you ol' bird you – that'll turn sour on your stomach. Play the very devil with my only horse-blanket, will you.

(The Shawl comes slowly to life.)

In the original "satiric fairytale", despite Decadentia's warm reception by the people, both contenders for the palm in the dramatic contest are ousted by a Stranger, who appears and declares that neither "alte Schönheit" – Epigo's aping of the old – nor "neue Schönheit" – Decadentia's claim to usher in a new era – is valid. Rather, there is only one Schönheit, one true beauty: himself. The Stranger is duly crowned, and the ugly twins fly away in the shape of "ein greuliches Zwitterwesen", a bizarre hybrid. It is clear, then, that Morgenstern's original judgement against both tradition-ridden and novel styles was decisively altered by his reworking of them for the cabaret, where the separation of the styles of "Decadence" (a label which disappears in the cabaret versions) from the context leaves them victorious, although in parodic form. This was typical of the effect of the "Schall und Rauch" cabaret, which parodied the whole range of the new drama that its founders sought in serious translations, adaptations, and productions to establish. The parody was a highly effective way of making the new styles comprehensible both to the actors who had to master and embody them and the audiences who had to absorb them.

It was, of course, the achievement of Reinhardt to stage a remarkable range of new drama, including, in the next three years alone, Oscar Wilde's **Salome**, Gorki's **The Lower Depths**, Hugo von Hofmannsthal's **Elektra**, Strindberg's **Crimes and Crimes, The Bond** and **Miss Julie,** Maeterlinck's **Pelleas and Melisande,** and Wedekind's **Erdgeist**, as well as to continue to perform Ibsen in contemporary styles. He opened his intimate theatre with a proto-Expressionist production of **Ghosts** with settings by Munch and the chiaroscuro lighting effects that were to influence the whole course of the cinema (see fig.3).[63] The aims of the serious productions were epitomized in the pointed deployment of parody of styles in the cabaret, with the effect that the new styles were acclimatized as our own idiom, and parody established as a mode of Modernist cognition. "Schall und Rauch" succeeded in banishing the traditional "twin" and making modernity a household word.

More interesting still, perhaps, is the further hint of the future suggested by the transformation of Morgenstern's first Decadentia piece for cabaret. If with hindsight we can see that Ibsen's family drama was the source of the original parody (providing the cast of characters of wife, husband and "Hausfreund" locked in demonic conflict), the intense brevity and defamiliarization through the use of the personal pronouns alone heralds a century of experiment with pronoun forms; to give just one closely allied example, the radio plays of the Viennese sound poet Ernst Jandl employ pronouns as characters who speak only in the subjunctive. It is again Morgenstern's poetic gift that gives his sketches this uncanny, prophetically innovative quality. A "Kleine Szene" published in the volume **Egon und Emilie** uses the same technique, and offers, in comic vein, a hermeneutic schema of the nature of time in modern drama akin to Dilthey's, which may have been known to him.[64]

Kleine Szene:

Unter Zeiten

Das Perfekt und das Imperfekt
tranken Sekt.
Sie stießen aufs Futurum an
(was man wohl gelten lassen kann).
Plusquamper und Exaktfutur
grinsten nur.[65]

Little scene:

Among the Tenses

The Perfect and the Imperfect
drank champers.
Cheers and here's to the Future
(which indeed one rightly pampers).
But Pluper and Second Future
only sneer.

There were times when Morgenstern, struggling to write a grand historical drama about Savonarola and instead triumphing in the cabaret, or finding his serious poetry neglected in favour of his serio-comic **Galgenlieder**, became profoundly depressed, recording, for example, "Ich bin Gelegenheitsdichter und **nichts** weiter",[66] "I am an occasional poet, and **nothing** more". But the "occasions" for which he wrote were the seminal occasions of twentieth-century poetry and drama.

It is not easy to establish a complete bibliography of Morgenstern's writings for the theatre. Again an historical accident has had the effect of concealing Morgenstern's contributions: it had been planned to publish several volumes of cabaret pieces from the "Schall und Rauch", but in the event only the first volume, which contained only Reinhardt's contributions, saw the light of day. Some of Morgenstern's sketches appeared in **Egon und Emilie** in 1907, but most waited for posthumous collection by Morgenstern's widow, in **Die Schallmühle** in 1927. Another collection appeared in 1938 under the title of another of his sketches, **Das Böhmische Jahrmarkt.** Others had been published earlier in different forms, often in periodicals, and were not republished; still others went missing, or remained in manuscript, as indeed have his attempts at more ambitious dramas.

If a genre considered ephemeral such as the cabaret sketch has not been well served by scholars, the record of performance in the various cabarets of Europe in his own time and since is even more difficult, perhaps impossible, to establish, although we know from a variety of incidental references that pieces by Morgenstern were performed not only in Berlin, but in Vienna, Munich, Leipzig, Zurich, and again in Berlin in the 1920s. Much cabaret is an oral lore handed down from one generation of performers to the next. Yet the problem of generic definition is finally more significant in concealing Morgenstern's dramatic contribution than any of the historical accidents to which he was subject, or even the accumulation of such accidents which has almost effaced all awareness of his work as a translator, writer, performer and publicist for the theatre. Defined as a "poet", Morgenstern was taken to be above the hurly-burly of the theatre. Yet the distinction, as so many of the examples show, does not hold.

Some recent German critics, developing Spitzer's and Kayser's classification of Morgenstern as "grotesque", have argued that in fact cabaret belongs to one of the three main types of modern lyric, namely, the "Lyrische Grotesken", lyric grotesques. This includes the "Angewandte Lyrik", "applied lyric", of Wedekind, Arno Holz, and Morgenstern, to Brecht, by the way of the black humour of van Hoddis and Lichtenstein, the "concrete poetry" of Stramm, and the Dada collages of Ball, Arp, Schwitters, and Mehring. This type of poetry constitutes the "Gesellschaftslyrik" of the twentieth century. As Clemens Heselhaus has written: "Die eigentliche lyrische

Groteske war zum musikalischen Vortrag im Kabarett bestimmt,"[67] "the genuine lyric grotesque was intended for musical recital in the cabaret". This interpretation of the significance of Morgenstern's contribution goes far towards registering the major shift that took place in poetry; but the dramatic elements, the sketches and plays themselves, are not adequately incorporated into this account, although certain theatrical "subtypes" are referred to in passing, for example, the mime (in Stramm) and the "Maskenspiel" in Brecht.

Morgenstern and **Das Theater**

On the success of the cabaret, and the improvement in his health, Morgenstern returned to Berlin, and immediately became actively engaged again in the theatre. He was invited to become a director, refused, but took the post of Dramaturg at Felix Bloch Erben. Shortly after, in 1903, he was asked to assume the editorship of a new periodical, **Das Theater**, which was intended as an extension of the new theatre enterprises, and he moved into the office of the publisher Bruno Cassirer. It was the first of Reinhardt's attempts to give literary support to the theatre.

The little bi-monthly was well-received, with its vivid accounts and reviews of current productions, essays by leading playwrights and directors, discussions of the acting methods of past and present, articles on foreign theatre ranging as far as Japan and Bali, and not least its profusion of illustrations, including photographs and designs of productions, portraits of artists and actors, depictions of theatrical devices such as masks, and a variety of **fin-de-siècle** ornament by, among others, Aubrey Beardsley. Morgenstern himself as editor contributed a number of pieces, ranging from brief notices, humorous news items, and topical sketches, to considered critical comment on playwrights such as Strindberg and Hugo von Hofmannsthal. The first issue, appearing on 1 October 1903, for example, contained an article on and a portrait of the famous Shakespearean actor of the early nineteenth century, Friedrich Ludwig Schröder, whose performances in A.W. Schlegel's translations marked a beginning of modern theatre in Germany; an important essay by Hofmannsthal, "Die Bühne als Traumbild", "The Stage as Dream-image"; an illustration of "John and Salome" by Beardsley; a discussion of Wilde's **Salome**; illustrations of Pompeian masks, an essay on "Naturtheater"; a striking print of a Japanese actor; and reviews of the Berlin theatres.[68]

Later issues continued these interests, giving house room to major productions like Hofmannsthal's **Elektra**, Tolstoi's **Fruits of Life**, Gorki's **Lower Depths**, Lessing's **Minna von Barnhelm** and Shakespeare's **A Midsummer Night's Dream.** The interest in Wilde continued; Strindberg receives considerable attention; Ibsen takes the lion's share of Heft 3 (20 October 1904), with several illustrations from the production of **The Pretenders** in which Max Reinhardt played Bishop Nicholas. English and French drama and stage design are well represented. In short, Morgenstern edited a timely, attractive, and committed theatre magazine, calculated to draw attention to the productions in Reinhardt's theatres, and extend understanding of the new styles and their application to the classics.

Morgenstern's attitude towards the magazine and his own function as editor is made very clear in a letter to Reinhardt in late 1904. He begins by making the pregnant suggestion that Reinhardt contribute part of his **Regiebuch** for the production of **A Midsummer Night's Dream**, in particular the section relating to scene iii. The publication of Reinhardt's **Regiebücher** have since that time contributed greatly to his reputation as a director. Morgenstern pointed out that it would take up the suggestion made by Gregori in the ninth issue that actors should try to describe the achievements of their colleagues in such a way as to "fix" them objectively, unlike the usual critical notice, which gives only a specific subjective image of the performance, in short, no description at all.

Morgenstern was not prepared, however, to become himself a mere "chronicler" of the two theatres, as Reinhardt had enjoined upon him in a recent conversation, in which Reinhardt had expressed his disappointment at a particular notice. Earlier, when they had had more resources, he had been able to call upon others to contribute and secure in that way a handsome coverage; but he could not do it single-handed, unless he were to spend all of his time at the theatres; and for that he must be more of an exclusively professional theatre man than he was:

> Wenn ich ein richtiger Chronist der zwei Theater sein sollte, so müßte ich eben im wesentlichen immer dort sein und die Sache nicht nur so par distance betreiben. So dann aber müßte ich auch innerlich mehr ausschließlicher Theatermensch, Fachmensch sein, als ich nun einmal bin.[69]

> If I were to be a proper chronicler of the two theatres, I should have to be there all the time and not conduct the matter from a distance. But then I would have to be inwardly a man more exclusively of the theatre, a professional, than I really am.

Morgenstern, moreover, is pleased to point out to the demanding Reinhardt that "Statt dessen habe ich selten mehr Verse gemacht als eben diesen Winter",[70] "instead of that I have rarely written more poetry than I have this winter".

These signs of tension were succeeded by signs of real disagreement, not over time or money, but over the development of the theatre itself. It is clear that as Reinhardt moved into the National Theatre and began his career of spectacular large-scale successes on the world's stages, Morgenstern began to part company with him artistically. Reinhardt's famous production of **A Midsummer Night's Dream**, with which he inaugurated his reign as Brahm's successor as Director of the Deutsches Theater, enthusiastically received on all sides, Morgenstern undertook to criticize in the very pages of **Das Theater** itself. This production featured the elaborate, detailed setting of the forest, making breathtaking use of the new technical device, the turntable stage, and all the available effects of the recently installed electric lighting (fig.4). Morgenstern tactfully but unmistakably signals his dissent:

> Mit der Neueinstudierung von Shakespeares "Sommernachtstraum" hat Max Reinhardt die Klassikervorstellungen des vergangenen Winters womöglich noch in den Schatten gestellt. Man wird nicht anstehen, diese Aufführung in ihrer Art vollendet zu nennen. Und man kann persönlich ganz ruhig anderen Prinzipien huldigen und doch seine reine Freude haben an diesem außerordentlichen Aufwand von Fleiß, Erfindung und Bildnerlust, diesen Einfällen einer naiven und unerschöpflichen Laune – denn naiver Optimismus und nicht (wie offenbarlich bei Beerbohm-Tree) Raffiniertheit ist der Grundzug all dieses heiteren Spiels –, diesem liebenswürdigen Gewirk verschiedener Künste,

liebenswurdig, eben weil kein Bayreuther Katholizismus dahinter steckt, sondern nichts als einfache blühende Sinnenfreude, diesem glücklichen und übermütigen Humor, diesem sicheren Gefühl für alles Theatralische im allerbesten Sinne.

Es ist wahrlich nichts Kleines, was hier hervorgebracht wurde: das muß gesagt werden – trotz des großen äußeren Erfolges und trotz der Einwände, die von anderen künstlerischen Standpunkten aus dagegen erhoben werden mochten. Wir dürfen stolz sein auf eine solche Vorstellung. Denn sie überragt das gemeine Maß in jedem Fall.[71]

With the new production of Shakespeare's **A Midsummer Night's Dream**, Max Reinhardt has put last winter's productions of the classics in the shade, if that is possible. No one will hesitate to call this production perfect in its way. And one can personally go on quietly reverencing quite different principles and still take an unmixed pleasure in this extraordinary display of industry, invention, and decorative energy, these ingenious caprices of a naive and inexhaustible temper – for naive optimism and not (as obviously with Beerbohm-Tree) sophistication is the fundamental characteristic of all this lively theatre –, this charming effect of diverse arts, charming precisely because no Bayreuth religiosity lurks behind it, but rather nothing but straightforward, blooming, sensuous pleasure, this happy and confident humour, this sure instinct for everything theatrical in the best sense of the word.

It is truly no small achievement, what has here been produced: that must be said – in spite of the great external success, and in spite of the objections which from other artistic points of view might be raised against it. We may be proud of such a performance. For it towers above the average in any case.

Morgenstern's years of association with Reinhardt tell here, in the quiet assurance of his judgement. We know that the theatre to which he himself was committed, the anti-Naturalist theatre of the imagination he depicted in his short comic play, **Des Widerspenstigen Zähmung: ein Traum (The Taming of the Shrew: a Dream)**, was Shakespeare's own theatre. The place of the play is Hell, into which a living playwright falls, only to find it peopled with Shakespearean shades, who, led by Falstaff and Hal, decide to play a joke on him and pretend that he is Shakespeare. The playwright (who is in fact Hauptmann) is easily persuaded that he is indeed the great poet. A further group of Shakespearean characters from various plays address him: Hamlet, Lear, Petruchio. Katharine pretends to believe he is Shakespeare. Finally, the rude mechanicals from **A Midsummer Night's Dream** arrive, and the playwright proposes they do the play of Pyramus and Thisbe together. He will take on the role of Wall himself.

Wand: Ihr seid sehr gütig, gnädiger Herr.

Der versunkene Dichter (zu Wand): Also, losgelegt, schafft mir Steine zur Stelle!

Die Drei (Wand, Mondschein und Löwe): Steine?

Der versunkene Dichter: Oder Bretter oder Balken –, – zum Teufel, versteht ihr nicht, daß man eine Wand nicht aus nichts machen kann?

Wand: Ich bin auch durchaus nicht aus nichts gemacht. Wenn ich rechne, daß meine Eltern zusammen 42 Jahre alt waren, als sie sich heirateten, so sind 42 Jahre 9 Monate nötig gewesen, um mich auf die Welt zu bringen.

Heinz *(zu dem versunkenen Dichter):* Er selber ist die Wand, er selbst, Thoms Schnauz![72]

Wall: You are very gracious, great Lord.

The fallen Poet: All right, get going, fetch me stones, bring stones to this spot.

Wall, Moonshine and Lion: Stones?

Poet: Or planks or girders. – What the devil, don't you understand that one can't make a wall out of nothing?

Wall: I am most certainly not made out of nothing. When I think that my parents were 42 years old between them when they married, then 42 years and nine months were needed to bring me into the world.

Hal *(to the fallen poet):* He himself is the Wall, he himself, Thomas Snout!

The hapless Naturalist continues to undermine the play, and it needs the combined forces of Caesar, Romeo, Prospero, and finally Ariel, who embodies the poetic imagination, to persuade him that he is not Shakespeare. The lesson holds good for the hapless director, however successful, good-humoured, and ingenious: in the true theatre one does not need bricks to represent a wall, nor even to build one.

That lesson was incarnate in Morgenstern. As in the dictionary of an invented language of poetry he had conjured up as a boy, it runs like a fine line of gold through his labours for Ibsen the dramatic poet, for the seminal innovations of the cabaret, and for the pioneering wizardry of Reinhardt's intimate theatre. He carried it with him into his later poetry, and one dares to surmise he carried it with him beyond the grave, where, quite possibly, his voice registered above the chorus a graceful and witty protest against God's grandiose theatre, reminding Him that His best effects were achieved in the first week.

Notes

I should like to thank the Librarian of the Institute of Germanic Studies, London for his kind assistance. I should also like to thank Professor Dr Manfred Naumann of the Humboldt-Universität East Berlin for his generous help, Professor Richard Sheppard of the University of East Anglia for his informed advice, and Janet Garton of the University of East Anglia for her help with Ibsen's Norwegian. Most of all I should like to thank Dr Julian Hilton and the excellent cast of the University of East Anglia Drama Department's production in December 1983 of a literary and satirical cabaret in the style of turn-of-the-century Berlin, in which they showed that their inventiveness was equal to Morgenstern's best sketches. Another version of the cabaret was given at the Symposium on Max Reinhardt held at Oxford 27–29 March 1985 under the auspices of Oxford University, Oxford Polytechnic and the Austrian Institute, London.

1. Michael Bauer: **Christian Morgensterns Leben und Werk.** Vollendet von Margareta Morgenstern unter Mitarbeit von Rudolf Meyer (R. Piper & Co. Verlag München, 1933), pp.31–32.

2. All translations are my own unless otherwise noted.

3. **The Gallows Songs.** Christian Morgenstern's **Galgenlieder.** A Selection. Translated and with an Introduction by Max Knight (Berkeley, 1963), pp.92–93.

4. Ibid., pp.16–17.

5. Leo Spitzer: "Die groteske Gestaltungs– und Sprachkunst Chr. Morgensterns", **Motiv und Wort. Studien zur Literatur– und Sprachpsychologie** (Leipzig, 1918). See also Wolfgang Kayser: "Morgenstern und die Sprachgroteske", in **Das Groteske. Seine Gestaltung in Malerei und Dichtung.** (Hamburg, 1960), pp.162–69.

6. Alan Young: **Dada and After. Extremist Modernism and English Literature** (Manchester, 1981), p.20.

7. Christian Morgenstern: **Galgenlieder, Gingganz und Horatius Travestitus. Sämtliche Dichtungen I**, Band 6 (Zwinden Verlag Basel, 1972), p.20.

8. Young, p.13.

9. **The Gallows Songs**, pp.30–31. See Johan Wrede's discussion of this poem in "Reading as Experience: the aesthetic of interpretation", **Comparative Criticism**, ed. E.S. Shaffer, vol.5 (Cambridge, 1983), pp.3–20.

10. Bjørnstjerne Bjørnson: **Gedichte.** Übersetzt von Max Bamberger, Ludwig Fulds, Cläre Mjöen, Christian Morgenstern und Roman Woerner. Hg. von Julius Elias (München, Langen, 1908).

    B. Bjørnson: **Die Neuvermählten.** Übers. von Christian Morgenstern und Julius Elias (München, 1908).

    A useful bibliography containing a section [2. Werke, d) Morgensterns Übersetzungen] is included in Martin Beheim-Schwarzbach, **Christian Morgenstern** (Reinbek bei Hamburg, 1964), pp.160–61. It is, however, not complete, omitting, for example, mention of Bjørnson's play.

11. August Strindberg: **Inferno.** Autorisierte Übersetzung von Christian Morgenstern. Berlin: Georg Bondi and Stockholm: C. and E. Gernandt (1898). Erster Band, Skandinavische Bibliothek, hrsg. von Gustaf af Geijerstam.

    Morgenstern's translation has almost been forgotten, owing to the fact that Emil Schering substituted his own translation for Morgenstern's in the edition of Strindberg's works that he received Strindberg's permission to prepare in 1904. Thus the most recent

English translation of **Inferno** fails to mention Morgenstern, despite a lengthy and detailed introduction of nearly a hundred pages dealing with Strindberg in Berlin and Paris. (August Strindberg: **Inferno and From an Occult Diary**, translated with an introduction by Mary Sandbach. Harmondsworth, 1979). The Introduction (pp.7–94) mentions Schering twice (p.6 and p.7).

Scandinavian critics appear to be no better informed. A major book on **Inferno**, Gunnar Brandell, **Strindberg in *Inferno***, translated by Barry Jacobs (Harvard University Press, 1974), fails to mention Morgenstern's translation, and implies that Schering did it at the time of **Inferno**'s first publication:

> "Thus, one might think that Strindberg is being self-contradictory after the Inferno crisis when he explains in a letter to his German translator, Emil Schering, on June 19, 1898, that he did not cease to believe in an afterlife during this short period as an atheist." (Brandell, p.54)

Despite this forgetfulness on the part of critics, Morgenstern's translation is a more refined and subtle piece of work than Schering's.

12. Morgenstern's translations of Hamsun are listed in **Nordische Bibliographie**. Herausgegeben von dem Nordischen Institut der Universität Greifswald. Bearbeitet von Fritz Meyer. 3. Heft: Knut Hamsun (Verlag Georg Westermann/ Braunschweig/ Berlin/ Hamburg, 1931). The entries supply full publishing details, and itemize reviews and, in the case of plays, performances and reviews of performances.

The listings are as follows:

Abendröte. Schauspiel in drei Aufzügen. Autorisierte Übersetzung aus dem Norwegischen von **Christian Morgenstern.** (173 S. 8⁰). München, Albert Langen, 1904. [242]

Publication led to thirteen reviews; the first performance took place in the Neues Theater in Frankfurt in 1921, resulting in five reviews (pp.15–16).

Spiel des Lebens. Schauspiel in vier Aufzügen. Autorisierte Übersetzung aus dem Norwegischen von **Christian Morgenstern.** München, Albert Langen, 1910 (166 S. 8⁰) [508]

Twenty-one reviews are listed; the first performance took place in the Schauspielhaus, Dresden, followed by several other productions through 1926, and a number of reviews of them (pp.22–23).

13. In a letter to Clare Ostler from Berlin dated 23 November 1895, Morgenstern described Schlenther's publication of his articles on "Neueste Deutsche Lyrik" in the **Vossische Zeitung**, and spoke of his hope that he would be given a portion of the regular theatre reviewing. Christian Morgenstern: **Alles um des Menschen Willen. Gesammelte Briefe.** Auswahl und Nachwort von Margareta Morgenstern (München, 1962), p.62.

14. James Walter McFarlane: **Ibsen and the Temper of Norwegian Literature** (Oxford, 1960), p.55.

15. For an account of earlier translations into German, see William Henri Eller: **Ibsen in Germany 1870–1900** (Boston: Richard G. Badger. The Gorham Press, 1916).

16. On **Papa Hamlet** and pseudotranslation, see Gideon Toury: "Translation, literary translation and pseudotranslation", **Comparative Criticism**, ed. E.S. Shaffer, vol.6 (Cambridge, 1984), pp.51–54.

17. See Morgenstern's enthusiastic letter to Sudermann of 13 April 1892, **Briefe**, p.22.

18. See Appendix to this paper for translation of extracts from Morgenstern's Scandinavian

diaries, as published in Bauer, pp.95–98. Bauer evidently pieced out the diaries with letters; I have quoted somewhat more extensively than he from the letter to Marie Goettling (20 January 1899, **Briefe**, pp.85–87). The letter from Ibsen (2 January 1800) is cited in **Briefe**, pp.91–92. The original was in Norwegian.

19. Quoted in Bauer, p.98.

20. Henrik Ibsen: **Sämtliche Werke in deutscher Sprache**, eds. Georg Brandes, Julius Elias, and Paul Schlenther, Bd.I (Berlin, 1898), p.xvii.

21. **The Correspondence of Henrik Ibsen**, the translation edited by Mary Morison (London, 1905), pp.331–32.

22. Georg Brandes: **Einleitung** to Ibsen: **Sämtliche Werke**, Bd.I, p.ix.

23. Ibid., p.xxi.

24. Letter to Brandes, 23 July 1872. **The Correspondence of Henrik Ibsen**, p.242.

25. **Sämtliche Werke**, I, p.527.

26. **Peer Gynt**, translated by Morgenstern, appears in Band 4 of the **Sämtliche Werke**.

27. Henrik Ibsen: **Peer Gynt**. Hundreårsutgave, eds. Francis Bull, Halvdan Koht, Didrik Arup Seip, Vol.VI (Oslo, 1930).

28. **Peer Gynt** translated by R. Farquharson Sharp (London, 1906).

29. **Peer Gynt** translated by Christopher Fry (London, 1962).

30. **Peer Gynt** translated by Michael Meyer (London, 1963). This version was performed at the National Theatre.

31. **Peer Gynt** translated by David Rudkin. RSC Playtext. (London, 1983). This version was performed at The Other Place, Stratford.

32. I am indebted to Malcolm Griffiths for his discussion of this crux in recent English translations in "Troll Words, Troll World: Ibsen's **Peer Gynt** in translation", paper read at the British Comparative Literature Association Workshop Conference on "The Theory and Historical Study of Literary Translation", held at University College London 6–7 September 1984.

33. Meyer: "Note on the Translation", **Peer Gynt**, p.185.

34. In a recent treatment of Ibsen's reception in Germany, for example, David E.R. George: **Henrik Ibsen in Deutschland. Rezeption und Revision. Palaestra** (Göttingen, 1968), pp.1–104, Eckart's translation is treated at length, while Morgenstern's is simply not mentioned. In this case, Morgenstern has been sacrificed to the critic's imposition of a schema for reception which divides it into "Reception: Ibsen the Naturalist"; "The First Revision: Ibsen and the New Romanticism"; "The Second Revision: Ibsen and the New Classicism"; and "The Third Revision: Ibsen and Expressionism". Eckart's bad translation serves as a convenient vehicle for the critic's claims for an "Expressionist" phase. This procedure serves Ibsen and Expressionism as ill as it does Morgenstern.
On **Peer Gynt**, see especially pp.84–93.

35. Siegfried Jacobsohn's review of the opening is reprinted in **Ibsen auf der deutschen Bühne. Texte zur Rezeption.** Hrsg. von Wilhelm Friese (Tübingen, 1976). This quotation is on p.126.

36. Ibid. This collection also cites a post-war East German edition of Ibsen in which Morgenstern receives credit for his translation on the title page: Henrik Ibsen, **Dramen.** 2 Bde. (Rostock, 1965). Nachdichtung der Versdramen: Christian Morgenstern. Übers. der Prosadramen: Bernhard Schulze; Einleitung: Horst Bien. Unfortunately, I have been unable to locate a copy of this edition.

37. To Efraim Frisch, 24 February 1902, **Briefe**, p.108. The letter contains further comment on Ibsen, relating especially to **Catalina.**

38. Morgenstern: **Epigramme und Sprüche**, in **Sämtliche Dichtungen**, II, Bd.14 (Basel, 1976), p.64. The pun on 'roof over' and 'thought through' is untranslatable.

39. Morgenstern: **Sprüche**, in **Sämtliche Dichtungen**, I, Bd.7 (Basel, 1972), p.73f.

40. Walter Rösler: **Das Chanson im deutschen Kabarett 1901–1933** (Henschelverlag, Berlin, 1980), p.124.

41. Georg Hirschfeld, quoted in Morgenstern, **Galgenlieder, Gingganz, Horatius Travestitus. Sämtliche Dichtungen** I, Bd.6 (Basel, 1972), p.249. See also the excellent account given in Rudolph Meyer: **Christian Morgenstern in Berlin** (Stuttgart, 1959).
Meyer was a contemporary whose critical comments on Morgenstern's poems roused him to create the parodic figure of a critic, Dr Jeremias Müller, in whose name Morgenstern indited a series of mock commentaries on the **Gallows Songs.**

42. Morgenstern, quoted in **Sämtliche Dichtungen** I, Band 6, p.248.

43. Hirschfeld, ibid., p.249.

44. Ibid.

45. Letter from Max Reinhardt, in Morgenstern: **Briefe**, p.72.

46. Letter from Ernst von Wolzogen, in Morgenstern: **Briefe**, p.93. The Alfred Kerr parody on this occasion was most probably **Hundeschwanz**, "Drama in sieben Bildern von N.N. besprochen von Alfred Kerr (um 1896)", "Dog's Tail, Drama in seven scenes by N.N. reviewed by Alfred Kerr (c.1896)" reprinted in Morgenstern, **Die Schallmühle, Grotesken und Parodien, Sämtliche Dichtungen II**, Band 13 (Basel, 1976), pp.161–63. The editor identifies the piece as the one performed at the Überbrettl (p.164).

47. Morgenstern, **Das Mittagsmahl (Il pranzo)**: Gabriele d'Annunzio, **Die Schallmühle**, p.131f.

48. Christian Morgenstern: **Egon und Emilie** (**Kein Familiendrama**), in **Die Schallmühle**, pp.89–91. This short play was performed, in my translation, by students of the Drama Department of the University of East Anglia, 5–10 December 1983, as part of a Berlin cabaret production, under the direction of Dr Julian Hilton, and again on 29 March 1985 for the Symposium on Max Reinhardt held at Oxford 26–28 March under the auspices of Oxford University, Oxford Polytechnic, and the Austrian Institute, London.

49. "Notizen", **Das Theater.** Illustrierte Halbmonatsschrift redigiert von Christian Morgenstern, Heft 3, 7 November 1903 (Bruno Cassirer, Berlin), pp.45–46.

50. See Heinrich Braulich: **Max Reinhardt: Theater zwischen Traum und Wirklichkeit** (Heuschelverlag, Berlin, 1969), p.40.

51. For example, Lisa Appignanesi: **Cabaret** (London, 1984), p.34 mentions Morgenstern only as a beneficiary of the "Schall und Rauch".

52. Letter from Kayssler, in Morgenstern: **Briefe**, p.94.

53. Ibid.

54. The opening night of the "Schall und Rauch" is reported differently by different sources. It seems that there was a trial run, which included the Don Carlos parody, at the Künstlerhaus in der Bellevuestraße under the title "Schall und Rauch" (it is this performance that Appignanesi refers to as a "benefit" for Morgenstern); and an opening proper, "Eröffnungs-Vorstellung", on 9 October 1901 at Unter den Linden 44, the building normally described as the home of the "Schall und Rauch", when it had been decided to perform cabaret on a regular basis.

Heinrich Huesman, **Welt Theater Reinhardt. Bauten. Spielstätten. Inszenierungen** (München, 1983) gives the former as the opening. This useful reference work sets out to list all Reinhardt's productions, including programmes of cabaret evenings, and architects' plans of all Reinhardt's theatres; but it must be used with care, as it is not as complete or as accurate as it appears. It records only a handful of Morgenstern's sketches:
(a) **Galgenlieder**: performed 3 July 1901, 7 July 1901; and five times in the Carltheater, Vienna;
(b) **Die Jongleuse**: performed 8 and 11 October 1901; and three times at the "Schall und Rauch II" (1921);
(c) **Der Laubgraf**: announced for performance 22 October 1901, but banned; performed at the "Schall und Rauch II";
(d) **Glockenspiel**: announced for 10 April 1902, but not performed.

Poems of Morgenstern, probably **Galgenlieder** and other poems, are reported as performed by Helene von Sonnenthal at a special Festvorstellung in Berlin on 25 January 1930.

The programme for the opening night proper is given in Braulich: **Max Reinhardt**, p.40 (cf. note 50). It is that programme which we reproduce here.

55. Frank Wedekind: "Die Kaiserin von Neufundland", in **Gesammelte Werke**, 9 vols. (München 1919–20), VI, pp.335–75, translated by Anthony Vivis as "The Empress from Newfoundland", with an introduction by Julian Hilton, in **Comparative Criticism**, ed. E.S. Shaffer, vol.4 (Cambridge, 1982), pp.233–68.

56. Günther Rühle: "Was an uns ist noch Peer?" [review of Stein's production], **Theater Heute**, Jahressonderheft 1971, pp.29–31.

57. Michael Patterson: "The myth of bourgeois individualism – Ibsen's **Peer Gynt**" in **Peter Stein. Germany's Leading Theatre Director** (Cambridge, 1981) p.69.

58. Letter from Kayssler, in Morgenstern: **Briefe**, p.97.

59. Morgenstern: **Briefe**, p.101. The letter is to Ludwig Landshoff, a musician; "in einem Satz" may refer to a musical phrase as well as to a sentence.

60. This tale has been reprinted under 'Essays' in **Christian Morgensterns Werke in vier Bänden**, hrsg. von Clemens Heselhaus (München, 1982), I, pp.202–11.

The cabaret version of Decadentia's first entry was published as "Das neue Preislied",

Die Schallmühle, p.82. An English translation of that version, under the title "The New Prize Poem", appears in Christian Morgenstern: "'The End of the World' and pieces from **Literary History Illustrated**", trans. by Elinor Shaffer, **Comparative Criticism**, vol.6 (Cambridge, 1984), pp.265–68.

61. Max Reinhardt: **Schall und Rauch**, Bd.I (Schuster & Loeffler, Berlin, 1901), pp.76–77.

62. Morgenstern: **Knochenfraß, Die Schallmühle**, p.84.

63. Lotte Eisner: **The Haunted Screen: Expressionism in the German Cinema and the Influence of Max Reinhardt** (London, 1969), p.34.

64. For a brief account of Wilhelm Dilthey's analysis of dramatic time, see E.S. Shaffer: "Hermeneutic Approaches to Drama and Theatre", **New Approaches to Drama**, ed. Julian Hilton (Methuen, London, forthcoming).

65. Morgenstern: "Unter Zeiten", in **Egon und Emilie** (Munich, 1907).

66. Morgenstern: **In me Ipsum**, in **Stufen, Sämtliche Dichtungen** II, Bd. 15 (Basel, 1977), p.36.

67. Clemens Heselhaus: **Deutsche Lyrik der Moderne von Nietzsche bis Yvan Goll** (Düsseldorf, 1961), p.288.

68. The fullest account is Leonhard M. Fiedler: "Christian Morgenstern und 'Das Theater'", Einleitung to the facsimile edition of **Das Theater** (1903–5). Redigiert von Christian Morgenstern, pp.VII–XXXIV.

69. Morgenstern: Letter to Max Reinhardt, Berlin, December 1904, **Briefe**, p.135.

70. Ibid.

71. Morgenstern: "Notizen", **Das Theater**, Heft 8 (15 February 1905), p.96.

72. Morgenstern: **Des Widerspenstigen Zähmung (Ein Traum), Die Schallmühle**, p.151.

Appendix

Morgenstern's Norwegian Diaries: Encounters with Ibsen

On 8 May 1898 Morgenstern set off on his journey to Norway, with the task of translating Ibsen before him. On 10 May his steamer landed in Christiania after a stormy voyage. In Fru Hansten's sanatorium in Nordstrand, a suburb of the city, he rented "a beautiful spacious room", sending his childhood friend Marie Goettling a description, and a sketch, of the surroundings:

> All round is tall fir forest; just in front of my window a stream rushes down and the view stretches out over . . . the distant fjord landscape. Before you lies the immense arm of the great Christiania fjord . . . The charms of this landscape are not easily describable in their constantly changing variety. At this moment for example everything lies stark in snow; it is all as if incised in a silver plate and engraved; the fjord in lighter-toned silver . . .
>
> The sunsets and moonlit nights are beyond anything. I can contemplate leaving here only with sorrow . . .
>
> About three times a week I travel to the city, a quarter of an hour on the train. There I often go to the University library, the art gallery, the theatre, a concert, or to someone's house. Often too I go to the harbour, a passionate observer, my whole happiness in pure perceiving.

On 1 July 1898 he met Henrik Ibsen for the first time, in the reading room of the Grand Hotel. After several such meetings he noted:

> 22 October 1898. Telegram from Elias [one of the editors of **The Complete Works of Ibsen in German**] asking whether "Stüber" is an actuary or a secretary. I go to meet Ibsen in the Reading Room of the Grand Hotel at noon. We decide in favour of "actuary". Ibsen replies to my question about professors and Germanists: "Yes, yes, Herr Dr Elias always wants everything so frightfully academic. I have never made any effort to write 'correctly', but have deliberately taken words and turns of phrase from colloquial speech, and tried to enrich the written language with them. I've gone out of my way to write 'correctly' for him."
>
> We talked again of the other translations and he said he would certainly read mine, when he received them. He questioned me with great solicitude as to whether I was warmly dressed, and in general was again very friendly and encouraged me, as always, to visit him again, to which I replied that I would take the liberty very soon of bringing him my new book [a volume of poetry, **Ich und die Welt, The World and I**, which was just then being printed.] Ibsen asked, "And did you come to the city specially on account of this telegram?" – I tell him that I have already begun translating **Brand**.
>
> "Well, well, you'll have your work cut out for you."
>
> "I have allowed myself ten months." He was delighted with everything.
>
> Before Sinding's concert I met Ibsen at Blomquist's. He was sitting at a table in coat and top hat leafing through "Studio". He asked me to join him. He was as always very friendly. I told him I was on my way to the concert. He wanted to go too, he said, although he was completely unmusical:
>
> "This piece pleases me, and that one doesn't, but I have no idea why. Unfortunately, I have absolutely no understanding of music." When I replied that I too was only an amateur in musical matters, he answered:
>
> "No, no, you actually learnt to play the piano; all that was denied me." He went there only on account of Miss Hildburg [Hildur] Andersen, an interesting woman and a pianist, a friend of his. – In the evening he sat in front in the second row with his beautiful white head visible and stayed manfully right to the end. Afterwards he looked for his coat, took me by the hand, and led me with him part of the way; I complied cheerfully, but a bit nervously.
>
> 14 January. Together with Ibsen in the Reading Room of the Grand. Noon. (He was wearing a brown coat with silk lapels.) He soon began to talk about my translation:

"Yes, I find it extraordinarily successful, the verses are in a fluent German such as I never would have thought possible in a translation." And as he departed he said:

"I thank you again for your splendid work." He thanked me also for the 'Scenes from **Brand**' that I had given him in manuscript as a Christmas present, and declared that as I had succeeded so well with **The Comedy of Love**, which certainly wasn't easy, I would be just as successful with the rest. He inquired after the state of my work and my situation in Nordstrand in the friendliest way . . . On my saying I wanted to visit Romsdalen in the spring, he advised me to go especially to Molde, Hardanger, etc. He described for me Molde's lovely sheltered falls with Jötenheim in the background, and the route by train to Trondheim and by coastal steamer to the south, in all about 26 hours.

18 Feb. I meet Ibsen in front of Cammermeyer's. He approaches me, makes the usual inquiries, is in a good mood.

"I have finally begun to work rather more seriously on my new play. It's always like that about this time of year. I hope to finish some time in the late autumn." [He was working on **When We Dead Awaken**, which Morgenstern would translate.]

I wish him joy of the work, and good luck. And he thanks me with great good cheer, and shakes my hand for a long time. (I think of the "deviltries" that had been predicted from him.) I had told him earlier that I am now almost finished with the third act of **Brand**, but how hard it was.

"Yes, I can believe that; but you are so clever, you'll soon manage it!" At the end he asked me where I was going: "To the library?" Yes. – When Ibsen is so serene, he seems to me touchingly amiable.

20 March 1899. An hour and a half with Ibsen. He comes towards me from the dining room through the drawing room; is extremely cordial.

"Today we can speak Norwegian." He insisted I come into the dining room, where his wife stood by the table. He introduced me. Two other guests are there . . . – Ibsen sits at the head of the table, not wearing his glasses, very happy, pours me a glass of port, clinks glasses, thanks me. His wife, very friendly, directs various questions at me, half in Norwegian, half in German. Ibsen tells a story (in Norwegian) with great animation about a hat maker he had met in a railway carriage while on a journey through Saxony, and who took his profession with immense seriousness:

"Det var ham en store hellige **livsopgave**." ("To him it was a great and holy life's work.") The hatter had expatiated on all that a hat conceals beneath it. And how a thinker must have a different hat from a manual worker, and so on. Ibsen's wife added: "In the end, Ibsen embraced him as a colleague, for he was such a precise connoisseur of hats."

Ibsen asked me about **Emperor and Galilean** and said that Elias had written to him with 56 questions, which he Ibsen was sure that I could answer. As we were saying our farewells he threw his head back and irradiated me with the piercing blue light of his gaze – a moment like a lion.

11 June. Evening. Together with Henrik Ibsen in the Reading Room of the Grand Hotel. We talk eagerly about the productions of his plays: Zacconi, Duse, Kainz, Reinhardt, etc. He asked about having a German ensemble here. I told him about the Berlin theatres, the production of **Brand** in the Schillertheater, of **Emperor and Galilean** in the Belle Alliance Theatre; it was put on without his permission. We talked of Zacconi and his just recently created interpretation of the role of Borkmann in Trieste. Ibsen was very concerned about whether he also had a good translation, so that nothing alien to the play crept in.

In July Morgenstern wrote to Marie Goettling from Bergen to describe his tour:

From right next to this old Norwegian church at Hop near Bergen I send you my best greetings. I have been out of Christiania since May and was until the beginning of July in Molde south of Trondheim, and then I made a gorgeous tour in several grand fjords and now I've settled again near Bergen in the above-named highly idyllic place, probably until the end of August. I am hard at it trying to finish **Brand**. I've stood on the spot where Ibsen first got the idea for the poem.

Later, after the completion of the last play, **When We Dead Awaken** , Ibsen wrote his thanks to Morgenstern (the original letter is in Norwegian):

Christiania 2 January 1900

Dear Mr Morgenstern,

I should have written to you long ago to thank you for your masterly, refined translation of my new play into German. Forgive me for writing only now. I have read the whole translation carefully and cannot understand how you could have done it in such a short time. And you have rendered every phrase so fully! I thank you from my innermost heart! Be assured, that I understand very well how great a share you have contributed to the friendly reception the book has had in Germany.

Dear friend – I have so much to thank you for. First for your warm, kind telegram, when you brought your work to a conclusion. This was the first news of it that I received from afar, which made it doubly welcome.

And then you sent my wife and me your lovely, high-spirited Summer poems, from which I can see that you have lived a summer in true poetic fashion.

And when shall I have the pleasure of seeing you up here again? Until then be well and accept my grateful greetings and thanks.

Yours faithfully,

Henrik Ibsen

John Millington Synge: Transforming Myths of Ireland

Simon Williams

There is much to distinguish the drama of turn-of-the-century Modernists from that of their predecessors and their contemporaries in the commercial theatre. An especially notable feature is the Modernists' view of disjunction between the individual and his/her social environment. While the conventional theatre of the nineteenth century was devoted largely to presenting reassuring fictions of the benefits of progress and of the individual's function as initiator or agent of progress, the Modernists revealed its fictitiousness. This revelation was achieved primarily by disclosing how little correlation there was between the sustaining fictions of society and the individuals these fictions were assumed to include. But few of the characters by whose experience this revelation is achieved are totally isolated from the social world, few even wish to be. Most oscillate between their desire to be part of society and its fictions and their instinct or perception that by nature they are ill-suited to participate in social life. Often they emulate that which is socially admirable, striving towards achievement that can be little short of heroic, but almost invariably they will fail due to lack of inner capacity. This arises, variously, from lack of self-confidence, a profoundly ironic view of themselves, or from too clear an insight into the fictiveness of the fiction. In their failure such characters seem diminished in stature, even absurd, yet in every case a residue of the value of the fiction they have attempted to fulfil remains. We, as the characters' audience, feel disconcertingly divided in our response to their failure. On the one hand we laugh at their pretensions and recognize the fallaciousness of the fiction, on the other, acknowledging the strength of the fiction's appeal, we feel warmly, sometimes admiringly towards their need to strive. As Modernist characters are the essence of contradiction, so too are our responses to them.

Modernist playwrights had difficulty in finding theatres to produce their plays. Most were first seen not on commercial stages nor in the subsidized theatres of Europe, but in small, independent theatres, which led a fitful existence in the larger cities. Among these theatres, the Irish National Theatre[1] seems initially to have been an exception as the founders of the movement, especially W.B. Yeats and Lady Gregory, were bent on maintaining a distinctly unmodernist singularity of viewpoint in their audiences. Although they were determined to introduce plays that had none of the triteness, stock characters, and gaudy spectacle they considered typical of the commercial theatre – and most theatre in Dublin was little more than an offshoot of London – they clearly intended to nurture a drama that argued for wholeness rather than disjunction in the human condition, one that helped rather than hindered the creation of a fiction of Irish society. Whatever their disclaimers about being chained to the various nationalist causes of their time, Yeats and Lady Gregory's purpose was to regenerate in the eyes of Irishmen and the world at large an image of the Irish as a cohesive, Gaelic race.

Of all European countries in the late nineteenth century, Ireland was probably most given to creating fictions, or myths, about itself. This was due mainly to the Irish perception of itself as a country occupied by an alien race, the English. The origins of the popular myth of Ireland that fuelled the nationalist causes at the end of the nineteenth century can be traced to the writings of the Young Ireland movement of the 1840s, to the stridently nationalistic poetry of Thomas Davis and the belligerently anti-English essays of **The Nation**. Later this was given a softer, more lyrical aura in the poems of Thomas Moore, in the popular novels of Irish life, and in several highly successful melodramas. The popular myth presented the Irish as a race distinguished by moral purity and natural piety, enshrined in its devotion to the Catholic church. The Irish, so the myth went, were distinguished by their capacity for suffering, strengthened by their unremitting hostility to exploitation by the materialistic, rapacious English. In contrast to the English, the Irish were highly idealistic, untroubled by the need to lay up things in this world. They lived in the loveliest of lands, and this loveliness served mainly to highlight their plight, as while by nature the Irish were stoical and indifferent to the material world, nonetheless they were being unjustly deprived of their natural inheritance. Ireland came to be seen as a lost paradise, a violated Eden – Thomas Moore especially made from the landscape images both of the mutability of human life and of a poignantly unattainable ideal world. Implicit in this myth of Ireland was the assumption that while the Golden Age had passed with the coming of the English, it would return once they had left Irish shores for good.

Associated with this popular myth, though of English rather than Irish or Anglo-Irish origin, was the perception of the Irish as grand talkers with fertile imaginations and an unusual capacity for drink. In the theatre, this was encapsulated in the stock figure of the Stage Irishman, a harlequin-like figure who combined "typical" Irish traits with an ability to manipulate ingeniously those around him, though always with an amorally innocent intent.[2] Though such an image was an English creation, it was, as the popularity of the novels of Charles Lever and Samuel Lover and the melodramas of Boucicault attest, acquiesced in not only by the Anglo-Irish but also by those Catholic Irish who read or attended the theatre. Taken together, these popular myths of Ireland portrayed the Irish as a passive race, as a people more sinned against than sinning, stalwart, even heroic sufferers in public, genial nonentities in private.

It was in reaction to fictions such as these that many of the Modernists wrote. Yeats, in his manifesto for the Irish Literary Theatre, declared as much. "We will show", he wrote, with the Stage Irishman in mind, "that Ireland is not the home of buffoonery and of easy sentiment, as it has been reported". But before he had even finished the sentence, he acquiesced, at least in part, to another aspect of the popular myth, for he wished to show Ireland to be "the home of an ancient idealism".[3] Such idealism was part of his conception of the "Celtic Twilight", most succinctly explained in his essay "The Celtic Element in Literature". In this, drawing upon the ideas of Matthew Arnold and Ernest Renan, Yeats idealized the Celts as the European race closest in spirit to "the lower creation",[4] by which he meant they were still partially in the animist phase of human development, at one with nature. As a result, in contrast to technologically more developed societies, above all the English, the Irish longed not for finite ends but for the infinite, for a perfection of being that can never be attained in life. This was suggested to them by the sounds of the Irish countryside and the lineaments of the landscape. Such longing for the infinite ennobled them and gave their sufferings a distinctly heroic timbre. Suffering, Yeats claimed, informed the most characteristic examples of Celtic art. Melancholy was inherent to the Irish poet and his laments. These laments were rarely caused by the deprivations of social life, rather they recorded a loss beyond that of the individual, expressing a state of being rather than a particular injustice or private calamity. "Men did not mourn merely because their beloved was married to another, or because learning was bitter in the mouth, for such mourning believes that life might be happy were it different, and is therefore the less mourning, but because they had been born and must die with their great thirst unslaked".[5] All such poetry, Yeats concluded, should properly be clothed in the language of excess.

It was in the service of his own myth of Ireland that Yeats founded the Irish Literary Theatre. On its stage he wished to see plays that were "remote, spiritual, and ideal",[6] ones that did not arouse "nervous tremors" like the commercially produced drama did. He called for plays that gave audiences a sense of their past and of their common community as Irish people, above all works based upon the national sagas. He envisioned an integrative theatre in which a bond was established between the stage and the audience, in which the spirit of the sagas and the relatively untouched purity of the contemporary Irish peasant would be seen to have an identity. As for his audience, it was to be composed not of the overeducated cynics of the modern city, but of "a few simple people who understand from sheer simplicity what we [the playwrights] understand from scholarship and thought",[7] as if the auditorium were to be filled with those quintessentially "Irish" figures, saints and scholars. The purpose of the drama, as of all culture, Yeats wrote, is "to bring again the simplicity of the first ages",[8] an ambition he felt possible as Ireland combined both a rural society still in the animist phase of development and, in the city of Dublin, a more advanced society that was able to meditate upon the world around it, yet was not wholly corrupted by modern life. Such a conjunction of circumstances was, Yeats argued with possibly questionable historical accuracy, ideal for the generation of great drama, as the examples of Periclean Athens and Elizabethan London show. This drama would appeal to the Irish love of oratory, to that supposedly unique delight of the Irish people in the excessive in speech and expression. So as to allow that excessiveness to stand forth in all its glory, scenery should be spare, a background to rather than an environment for the action. Yeats's distinctly classical conception of theatre included the minimum in actorial gesture and movement, so that the audience's attention was directed towards language by which the inner life of the character could be palpably felt. In this severe theatre, there should be none of the distracting trappings and stage business characteristic of the commercial theatre. The Irish theatre, as envisioned by Yeats, was to be highly abstract in all but language. True to his perception of the idealism of the race, the world of appearance was to be put aside in order to realize truths not discoverable by the eye.

Yeats was never to realize the theatre outlined in his theoretical writings of the 1890s. This was due to many causes, to the sheer lack of overt theatrical energy in his own plays, to fundamental questioning by many in the Irish National Theatre movement of the authenticity of his vision of Ireland, and to the evolution, especially under the auspices of the Fay brothers, of a style of acting better suited to more realistic modes of drama.[9] But while the ideals proved inadequate, the Irish National Theatre did not. While in the early, stormy days of the enterprise many left the company because of differences with its policies, Yeats himself stayed on. He adapted his views at least partially to the realities of the stage. In the process he guided the theatre away from the narrowly nationalist causes with which it had initially been identified. Instead, in its most important and controversial offerings, it came to produce work more closely aligned to that of the European Modernist playwrights, in which the national myth no longer went unquestioned. This was not an easy passage. As the theatre's repertoire expanded to include plays often critical of Irish society, it quickly lost the moral support of nationalist parties and the integrative function of the stage seemed to be transformed into one that was disintegrative. Few theatres can have been subject to such a relentlessly hostile critical barrage; none, at least in the early twentieth century, had such combative elements within its audience, elements that made themselves nationally conspicuous in the series of riots following the first performance of Synge's **Playboy of the Western World** in January 1907.

The plays of Synge and Yeats's uncompromising championship of them were undoubtedly the chief cause for the defection of nationalist support. But to regard Synge, as many of his contemporaries did, as unremittingly hostile to Ireland and to the nationalist myths that sustained it, is to misrepresent his attitude. Like his fellow playwrights in the Irish National Theatre, Synge took cognisance of the political and social life of his times. Unlike most of them, however, he avoided identifying himself with any specific cause or particular viewpoint. Ireland was his subject matter, myths of Ireland partially his concern, but they did not dominate his vision. Instead the ideals contained within the myths were incorporated into the action in a manner paralleling the treatment by many European Modernists of social fictions. While Synge rarely portrayed characters fighting to be free of such fictions, concern with these fictions was clearly implied by the action. While the action of the play led to radical questioning of the validity of the fictions, the conclusion did not represent a total rejection of them. Rather the fictions – the myths of Ireland, both popular and Yeatsian – are transformed and regenerated in the course of the action. In a characteristically Modernist way, Synge has his audience recognize both the value and the fallacies contained within the myths of Ireland.

That Synge was deeply attached to these myths, the Yeatsian in particular, is demonstrated by the first of his plays to be written, the second to be performed by the Irish National Theatre, **Riders to the Sea**. The Aran Islands, where the play is set, were an area of considerable importance to Synge as to Yeats. Here Gaelic was spoken, the original language of the Irish peasant. The harsh climate of the islands and the constantly turbulent seas surrounding them meant that life for the islanders was a never-ending battle with the elements. Natural forces exercised such a formidable determining influence over them that the islanders might justifiably be regarded as being closer to the animist phase of being, more in touch with what Yeats had called "the lower creation", than any other of the Irish coastal-folk or peasantry. This was reflected in the islanders' belief in non-Christian supernatural forces and in the residual survival of pagan ritual practices, both of which were more marked in Aran than elsewhere. As a consequence, while the islands were not untouched by the presence of the Catholic church, the priesthood had less hold over the islanders' spiritual life than elsewhere. All these factors are included in **Riders to the Sea**; they can be felt in the omnipresence of the sea, in the wildness of the weather, in references to the observation of Samhain, a pagan festival, in the inefficacy of the priest's prayers for the safety of Bartley, and, above all, in the presence of supernatural forces that, in the course of the play, grow to be active agents.

When the play was staged at the Molesworth Hall in February 1904, Synge was careful to ensure that all costumes and props were as faithful as possible to the clothes and furniture of the Aran cottages. So concerned was Synge for naturalistic authenticity, that he even went to the trouble of having certain artifacts brought to Dublin from Aran to be used in the production.[10] Day-to-day living was to be the medium through which the islanders' tragedy was to be perceived; therefore the stage and its cottage setting become a landscape of portents, the events of the plays transpiring not through overtly theatrical gestures or sharply delineated reversals of action, but through the revelation offered by the tiniest of details. From the very start, for example, we are certain that Michael has met his death by drowning in the north. The hushed, urgent voices of the girls and the violence of the storm outside create an atmosphere that leads us to expect the worst. When that worst comes, it is not made known through any dramatically delivered statement, but through Cathleen and Nora recognising the dropped stitches on the stocking they find in the bundle of clothes. In the same manner, a few moments earlier, we have recognized that Bartley is going to his death when we hear that he has left wearing Michael's shirt. Through such disclosures, the staging operates on what might be called "animist" principles. Although we never see the natural environment, objects of the human world take on, as it were, natural life. Through them abstract forces are made concrete, the fate of human beings realized.

There is a distinctly lyrical quality in **Riders to the Sea**, as everything moves towards coherence, towards a peculiarly sombre harmony. In the course of the play the three women of the family grow in heroic stature. There are tensions between them in the first ten of the play's twenty or so minutes, and these give the action a certain momentum. Maurya is testy and demanding, but her daughters' reaction to this is not submissiveness and acceptance; they are impatient with her, preoccupied as they are with the practicalities of living. During Bartley's brief appearance, Maurya becomes protective and self-pityingly protesting, while her son seems impervious to her pleas, thinking exclusively about his journey to the mainland and of how the farm will be run in his absence. But these passages of friction between family members do not reduce them in our sight, nor do they allow us to view them ironically. This may be because such tensions are not at all abnormal. There is little animus between mother and children, rather a familiarity between them at their difference. Also they articulate themselves in a language less specific than in those of Synge's plays with a more comic tone. They do not speak with the peculiar, occasionally contorted idiom and phraseology that is so often a mark of Synge's characters. In their exchanges, they do not attempt to engage in competition with each other or even try to acquire temporary dominance. Instead an identity gathers between them, a common bond against the angry forces of nature. This lends them a degree of impersonality which has led several critics to compare the play to Greek tragedy.[11]

The heroic stature of the family is augmented by their being victims of supernatural forces. **Riders to the Sea** is the only one of Synge's plays in which the supernatural has a dominant and entirely determining presence. It is immanent and is referred to by characters with a directness that is almost prosaic, though all the more penetrating for being that. When Cathleen refers to "the black hags that do be flying on the sea"[12] keening Michael, we have no difficulty is accepting these presences as part of the world of the play. While we might account for them as a particularly apt way of describing the sensation of being controlled by nature, Synge does not encourage that view. Though the style of representation may be naturalistic, the perspective adopted towards the supernatural does not invite us to analyse it in the quasi-scientific way advocated by the Naturalists. The supernatural is neither explored nor explained, it just gains in credibility to the point where we unquestioningly accept the reality of Maurya's vision of Bartley being followed by Michael on the grey pony. Equally unquestioningly, we accept the fact of Bartley's death as a result of this pursuit.[13] The ghost rider Michael, therefore, becomes the antagonist of the play, and the central conflict grows to be not only man against nature, but also man against the supernatural. Through an unnerving collusion between nature and the dead, the island family appear to have placed upon them an ancestral curse. As victims of this curse, they rise yet more in stature, becoming in essence aristocrats of the pagan world, suffering and ennobled personages, close to the mythic figures of Yeats's imagination and not entirely alien to the ideal figures of the popular Irish myth.

As the play draws to its conclusion, it moves from the dramatic to the lyric mode. This creates a rich tension, as while we witness the final extinction of the male line of the family, we also experience an unusual sense of completion. Maurya's threnody consists primarily of her recalling the deaths by drowning of the men in her family. In strongly repetitive rhythms she re-enacts the past. First the women enter to keen the body of Bartley, a few minutes later the men come in carrying the body itself. Language and physical action form a unity. But the most notable aspect of the final lamentation is its tonal quality, which corresponds to one of Yeats's key definitions of that which is uniquely Celtic. Throughout this passage there is a lack of personal anguish. As Nora sees Bartley's body being carried to the cottage, she refers to it as inanimate. "They're carrying a thing among them", she says, "and there's water dripping out of it and leaving a track by the big stones" (III, p.23). The impersonality suggested by these lines is amplified by Maurya who, in her lament, seems almost oblivious to the particular loss of Bartley, especially when we hear, "it's fonder she was of Michael" (III, p.25). Her words are accompanied by sprinkling holy water gathered during "the dark nights after Samhain" (III, p.25), a pagan not a Christian ritual. Accordingly her speech begins to lose the tone of protest, resolving itself in the final line of the play into a statement of acceptance: "No man at all can be living for ever, and we must be satisfied" (III, p.27). While it would be stretching the point to read into these lines a sense of celebration, the play comes to rest where reconciliation occurs between humans and the natural and supernatural forces against which they are set. The heroic image of the Aran islanders prevails, and a oneness is observed between human beings and their environment.

Riders to the Sea is arguably the most complete realization of the Yeatsian myth of Ireland staged by the Irish National Theatre, more complete than Yeats achieved in any of his own plays. Perhaps this is why those of Synge's critics who consistently faulted him for departing from his Irish sources saw in it his one abiding contribution to a purely Irish culture.[14] But Yeats, surprisingly, was not entirely won over by the play. He recognised its qualities, but had his doubts as to its vitality on stage. **Riders to the Sea**, he said, "seemed for all the nobility of its end, its mood of Greek tragedy, too passive in suffering".[15] He preferred Synge's more controversial play **The Shadow of the Glen**, which was produced some months before **Riders to the Sea** in October 1903.

This production was not an auspicious occasion for the Irish National Theatre Society. Incensed by the play, the two vice-presidents of the society most closely associated with nationalist movements, Maud Gonne and Douglas Hyde, resigned, and the sustained critical assault upon the theatre began. This was led by **The United Irishman**, a newspaper edited by the formidable journalist and politician Arthur Griffith. That the nationalists should be offended by Synge's unflattering portrayal of the Wicklow peasantry was not surprising, but that Yeats should champion the play and continue to champion Synge to the extent of appointing him as a director of the Abbey Theatre was surprising in the extreme. It clearly indicated a shift in his own ideas on the function of the Irish National Theatre.

Yeats's support of Synge became readily apparent in a protracted correspondence he conducted with Arthur Griffith in the pages of **The United Irishman**, a correspondence to which others contributed. These letters centred mainly around two accusations made by Griffith against Synge. First, Griffith insisted it was wrong for the playwright to show any Irish woman as capable of leaving her husband – "Irish women", he claimed, "are the most virtuous women in the world".[16] Secondly he stated that the play had no right to masquerade as an authentic description of Irish life as it was taken from a foreign source – "The play has an Irish name, but it is no more Irish than **The Decameron**. It is a staging of a corrupt version of the old-world libel on women – 'The Widow of Ephesus'".[17] But, try as Yeats and a few of Synge's defenders might to point out that women in Ireland were not all as virtuous as the myth would have it and that Synge himself had first had the story from an Aran Islander, the playwright quickly came to be regarded as the bane of the nationalist cause. In fact, there were good reasons for this, though the issues debated in the press do not adequately identify them. They were red herrings hiding what we might speculate as being a more fundamental disquiet over Synge's play. It seemed aimed deliberately at subverting both the popular and the Yeatsian myths of Ireland.

As the curtain rises on Nora tidying the room in the presence of her husband's corpse, she is properly uneasy, but once she launches into her conversation with the Tramp, her unease is undercut by the normality, even the humour in her tone of voice and language. The reverence that should normally determine the behaviour of a wife faced with her dead husband's body is distinctly absent. Indeed it becomes apparent that his death is a release rather than a deprivation when we learn that before he died "he put a black curse" on her. The wake, surely one of the most definitive of Irish customs, is also an off-key affair, signified merely by "a couple of glasses on the table, and a bottle of whiskey . . . with two cups, a tea-pot and a home-made cake" (III, p.33). All this the tramp proceeds to enjoy. The plays opens with a distinct air of oddness, for the ceremonies normally expected at an important phase of family life are absent.

Although the stage setting is solely that of the cottage, the natural environment of the glen is always in the forefront of the characters' consciousness. Nora and the Tramp, who quickly strike up a comfortable relationship, talk at length of the countryside in which they live, but where they do not find themselves at ease. In their eyes it lacks all poetry; it is oppressive rather than beautiful, filled with gloom instead of the soft refulgence described in conventional lyric poetry. The landscape provides them not with images by which they can describe their longings for the infinite or unattainable; rather it is a world from which they would prefer to escape. The Tramp speaks of his fear "crossing the hills when the fog is on them" (III, p.37) while Nora, when Michael joins them, describes the view from her cottage door as nothing but a desolation that deadens her. As she sits looking out, she sees "nothing but the mists rolling down the bog, and the mists again, and they rolling up the bog, and hearing nothing but the wind crying out in the bits of broken trees were left from the great storm, and the streams roaring with the rain" (III, p.49). The very monotony of her language re-enacts the dreariness of mountain weather.

Most who inhabit this country seem to be ill at ease with it. The rural society Synge has his characters conjure up is far from the idealized society of popular myth, equally far from the Yeatsian vision of man living at one with nature, responsive to all its changes and stoical in the face of loss. Patch Darcy, possibly Nora's ex-lover, is the only person who seemed to be at home on the bare slopes of the hills, physically attuned to their rigours and to herding the sheep, which were as close to him as humans. He "would walk through five hundred sheep and miss one of them, and he not reckoning them at all" (III, p.47). However, early on we hear that Darcy unaccountably went mad, dying in a ditch, his body carrion for the crows. Too much closeness to nature must, one surmises, be dangerous to mental health. Those who do survive, such as Michael, a displaced sailor from the coast, are at peace neither with themselves nor with nature. Michael's shepherding is distinguished by his inability to control his sheep. As the action of the play discloses, his love for Nora is more than a little dependent on the money he thinks will come to her when he marries her. He is a greedy, craven person, one who contradicts the conception of the Irish as an idealistic race. Then, when Dan finally comes to life, in, it must be noted, a grotesque parody of the Resurrection, he turns out to be little more than a vindictive hooligan, confirming all of Nora's accusations against him.

In **The Shadow of the Glen**, in contrast to **Riders to the Sea**, Synge would seem to be violating myths of Ireland that had been propagated with fervour for several decades by nationalist interests. Furthermore, these myths had been confirmed rather than refuted in those plays of peasant or heroic life that had been staged during the Irish National Theatre's various seasons. Synge, understandably, appeared to many in his audience as an iconoclast. But his attitude in the play towards the myths of Ireland was not quite as negative as suggested so far. While he destroys the time-honoured view of Ireland as a lost paradise, he also recreates it in the minds of certain of his characters. In so doing he particularizes and reinvigorates it, at one and the same time encouraging us to distance ourselves from it yet leading us to feel fully its attractive force.

In this process the Tramp is a crucial character. Synge idealized tramps, possibly seeing in them a self-projection.[18] They were not bound by property, they had escaped the stifling forces of a settled existence, characteristic of any society. They were, in essence, anti-communal figures, dependent solely upon their own resources, masters of their own imaginative world. Nevertheless, the Tramp in **The Shadow of the Glen**, a seeming nay-sayer to social orthodoxy, is not himself an entirely unorthodox figure. He bears a distinct resemblance to the Stage Irishman, who, whatever Yeats's and Synge's reservations about him, was highly popular on the commercial stage of turn-of-the-century Dublin.[19] The Tramp, like the Stage Irishman, is no man of strict and upright virtue. Despite his choice to wander the roads, he is given to relishing his creature comforts when he can get them. He is remarkably adaptable to changing situations, skilled at playing both sides of an argument when his survival depends on it. This is apparent in the way he quickly accommodates himself to Dan's plan of action when the "dead" man comes to life while Nora is briefly out of the cottage. But, when all is said and done, his sympathies, like those of his generic type, veer spontaneously towards those whose impulses are similar to his own, to the undertrodden, to those who embody the values of warmth and kindness. Above all, he is a man of ready wit and a great talker. As played by William Fay at the première, the Tramp was no shabby, hirsute vagabond, but a gracious and attractive man whose charms worked with considerable ease on the rebellious Nora.

No doubt "loveless marriage" is, as Synge claimed, the central theme of the play. Nora's rebellion, first against her husband, then against Michael as he shows himself to be feckless and mercenary, is strong and ringing, framed with few of the ironies that surround the rebellion of Ibsen's more famous Nora. Her ability to articulate her disgust means that her departure from the misery of her life in the cottage, while seemingly forced by her husband's dictates, is an alternative she chooses freely. That she does so in the company of the Tramp is more debatable. He offers her a world where she is unconfined, specifically described to her in language redolent with much of the traditional poetry of the Irish countryside. Instead of staying in a landscape obscured by gloomy mists rising from the bog, she will go to kinder climes, embarking on a life in which the vagaries of the weather are invigorating rather than oppressive. Instead of hearing "the wind crying out in the bits of broken trees were left from the great storm", the Tramp tells her, "you'll be hearing the herons crying out over the black lakes, and you'll be hearing the grouse, and the owls with them, and the larks and the big thrushes when the days are warm" (III, p.57). He envisages a hedonistic engagement with nature that denies age and the settled life that aggravates the experience of aging. Of course, as she goes, Nora does not fully espouse the alternative. She knows she will be cold, knows that she may, as her husband has remarked, end up "stretched like a dead sheep with the frost on her, or the big spiders, maybe, and they putting webs on her, in the butt of a ditch" (III, p.55). She is also aware that the Tramp's benign view of nature is little more than fine speaking, is itself a myth, representing more a changed attitude towards the world than a condition that can actually be achieved. But she chooses him because, like the traditional Stage Irishman, he can spin a colourful tale – "you've a fine bit of talk, stranger, and it's with yourself I'll go" (III, p.57). As they leave, Nora and the Tramp provide a final image of a pastoral Ireland, invigorated by youth and a truculent, assertive individualism, in contrast to the two inactive men left behind supping on their whiskey.

The process of using aspects of the Irish myth to give vitality to individuals is not especially strong in **The Shadow of the Glen**. Any long coda of poetic outpouring would create a serious imbalance with the remainder of the play. Furthermore, overstatement would disrupt the finely ironic equilibrium through which we sense that the sedentariness of Dan and Michael is closer to the reality of Irish peasant life than a young couple swinging down sunlit country lanes. Nevertheless, the liberation this couple had achieved remained with Synge. In his first full-length play, **The Well of the Saints**, staged at the Abbey Theatre in February 1905, he subjected the particularly Irish penchant for myth-making to a more extended analysis.

Predictably Synge's tale, adapted from a medieval French source, of two beggars whose vision of their own beauty and of the beauty of the world around them is sorely tested by their sight being restored to them, aroused almost universally hostile responses. Arthur Griffith's might be taken as representative. "The atmosphere of the play is harsh, unsympathetic, and at the same time sensual. Its note of utter hopelessness evokes a feeling akin to compassion for the author. What there is 'Irish', 'national', or 'dramatic' about it even Oedipus might fail to solve. How is it that the Irish National Theatre, which started so well, can now only alternate a decadent wail with a Calvinistic groan?"[20] While we might question his religious judgement, Griffith was not wholly wrong in his description of the play's atmosphere. Yet again Synge seemed deliberately to be set upon destroying popular mythical preconceptions of Ireland. For a start, he sets **The Well of the Saints** in Ireland "one or more centuries ago" (III, p.69). This was an especially provocative time to choose, as it was the period out of which the most potent aspects of the popular myth were created, the seventeenth and eighteenth centuries, when Irish Catholics became increasingly a persecuted majority and the image of them as great sufferers full of piety evolved. The world Synge presents on stage, however, is populated by no such idealized figures. His two blind beggars, Martin and Mary Doul, are no picturesque adjuncts to any idyllic mountain community. Though conventionally beggars are objects of pity, we quickly learn to regard them with sympathy mixed with scepticism. Not that the Douls are extravagantly grotesque in any way, but their relationship is recognizably human. They are constantly crossing each other, their conversation arising more from friction than from amicable agreement. They arouse our laughter as we perceive the difference between their illusions of their great beauty and the ugliness, or at least plainness, of their actual appearance. Nevertheless they are not total butts for our humour, as the moment either one of them stops thinking solely of him or herself, they show a canny sense of what the world is really like. Martin, for example, half knows the truth about Mary's looks. As he observes, "I heard Molly Byrne saying at the fall of night it was little more than a fright you were" (III, p.73). Mary too is no simpleton, but is fully aware that the world is a rough place and that seeing might make it so: "there's a power of villainy walking the world, Martin Doul, among them that do be gadding around, with their gaping eyes, and their sweet words, and they with no sense in them at all" (III, p.75). When it comes to interacting with this world, they behave as if they are more a part of it than separate from it. Martin assumes that the "wonders" the Saint is spreading around him have more to do with "putting up a still behind in the rocks" (III, p.77), while Mary reckons "maybe they're hanging a thief, above at a bit of a tree" (III, p.77). The community of which they are a part is far from peaceful or conventionally pastoral, but is riven by egotistical drives and by a violence that is never far beneath the surface. Indeed, the most notable event that occurred at the crossroads where the Douls beg, next door it should be noted to a ruined church, is that there "they killed [an] old fellow going home with his gold . . . and threw down his corpse into the bog" (III, p.77).

Above it all stands, one might almost say hovers, the Saint. Though he has been described as an eminently noble figure, as one who embodies credibly some of the finer ideals of the Catholic church,[21] it is difficult to read him that way. To begin with, he is actually called "the Saint", an ironic soubriquet as saints only become saints well after they are dead. This makes him appear a rather questionable figure. Even before he enters we are prepared to regard him as something of an innocent, when Molly Byrne reports his remark that "young girls . . . are the cleanest holy people you'd see walking the world" (III, p.83). This elicits from Mary a suitably caustic response, "the Saint's a simple fellow, and it's no lie" (III, p.83). Whether he is or not, Molly has no faith in him, regarding the tale of the well as little more than a pious fiction to elevate him in the villagers' eyes. As an expression of their irreverent attitude towards the Saint, the villagers, led by Molly, drape his cloak around Martin, giving the beggar the bell and holy water as if in mock-sanctification, all this in an episode obviously contrived to let us see the Saint in a distinctly sardonic light. These elaborate proceedings before his entrance are a fitting prelude to what is to occur when he appears. The Saint, however worthy his cause and ingratiatingly mild his language, has little sense of the real experience of those to whom he ministers. This becomes abundantly clear as we witness the difference between his assumption of the consequences of curing the Douls' blindness – "it's the like of you who are brave in a bad time will make a fine use of the gift of sight the Almighty God will bring to you to-day" (III, p.89) – and the consequences themselves. Martin, despite being half-aware of Mary's ugliness, has still allowed his illusion of her beauty to dominate how he thinks of her. When he realizes the truth, in a moment of unusually brutal theatrical power, he rejects her with words filled with hatred and rancour: "there isn't a wisp on any grey mare on the ridge of the world isn't finer than the dirty twist on your head. There isn't two eyes in any starving sow, isn't finer than the eyes you were calling blue like the sea" (III, p.97). Meanwhile, the Saint, after a mild rebuke, leaves to continue his mission of healing elsewhere.

If Synge has resolutely pursued his purpose of destroying myths of Ireland in the first act, in the second he continues by providing as misanthropic a view of the human condition as any he wrote either in his prose or drama. Martin Doul, now he has sight, moves to the centre of the play. He discovers that the world is without pity, that power rather than charity is the prime operative force in human relationships, that the church is an indifferent rather than a benevolent institution, with no concern for the poor it is its avowed purpose to assist. In his subservience to Timmy the Smith, a brutal, sentimental fellow, Martin discovers work is no liberation or means of fulfilment, but a humiliating necessity. Through Timmy he discovers there is little coherence or consistency in human conduct. These realizations take place against a landscape that is far from the idyllic Ireland of nineteenth-century poetry. It is not sunny or mild or painted with the misty blues and greens of summer, but a cloudy, wintry landscape with mud-filled roads, bathed in raw air.

Martin becomes a creature of this world, but here, more strongly than in earlier plays by Synge, we begin to identify division in him and in our response to him. While he exists in a state of servile dependence, he grows to achieve renewed cohesion. As the victim of the villagers, he comes to learn the truth about his place in the community, so far hidden from him by his blindness. This realization reaches its most painful point at the start of Act 3 when we see him, not without a certain harshness in our laughter, for the first time terrified of every sound around him. But his experience while he has sight has also led to a growth in stature. His imagination has been redirected away from personal concerns towards the world around him. As the lowest in the social order of the village, he becomes the most articulate scourge of the corruption in the life he sees about him. This is accompanied by a growth in his awareness of the potential beauty that the world can realize. Crucial in this regard is his scene with Molly, the centrepiece of Act 2. In attempting to lure her away from the village to "lands beyond . . . with warm sun in them, and fine light in the sky" (III, p.115), his language grows in resonance and expressive power. Despite herself she is drawn towards him – "It's queer talk you have if it's a little, old, shabby stump of a man you are itself" (III, p.115). So marked is Martin's transformation, so eloquent the imagery of his speech – "Though it's shining you are, like a high lamp, would drag in the ships out of the sea" (III, p.117) – that the change has been likened to the growth from man to artist.[22] At the climactic point he reaches a poetic vision of Ireland similar to that of the Tramp in **The Shadow of the Glen**, though more richly and sensuously expressed: "Let you come on now, I'm saying, to the lands of Iveragh and the Reeks of Cork, where you won't set down the width of your two feet and not be crushing fine flowers, and making sweet smells in the air" (III, p.117). Molly, whose attraction to him is fleeting at best, will not go. Instead Martin receives his final humiliation from her, Timmy, and Mary, though this does not destroy the strength of his poetic vision, which remains with him into the last act.

In this act, Martin proceeds, with no little help from Mary, with whom he is reconciled, to rebuild an imaginative vision of the two of them and of the world they once again cannot see. The personal myth is suggested first by Mary; in this they substitute images of their eminence and gravity for ideas of beauty. Mary's hair "would be grey, or white" making "a great wonder" (III, p.129) of her face, while Martin would grow "a beautiful, long, white, silken, streamy beard, you wouldn't see the like of in the eastern world" (III, p.131). Both will acquire in their own minds grandeur and majesty. These compensating images of themselves occur in association with poetic images of the Irish landscape, which they knowingly cultivate as an antidote to their awareness of the harshness of the world. During his final confrontation with the Saint, as he attempts to prevent the second curing, Martin fights for the right to maintain his poetic vision. This has come to him not through the evidence of his eyes, nor has it been passed to him through the mediation of the Saint. It is the product of his own imagination, a purely individual world created for himself, a denial of the truth he knows and a defence against it, an earned denial and an earned defence. It is articulated in familiar Irish terms, as Martin describes "looking up in our own minds into a grand sky, and seeing lakes, and broadening rivers, and fine hills are waiting for the spade and plough" (III, p.141). As he fights the Saint, in whom we begin to detect a streak of vindictiveness, Martin acquires the quasi-heroic stature of a man striving to preserve what is his against the pressure of social conformity. He becomes a formidable, eventually superior opponent, both because of his greater intelligence and because, unlike the Saint, his vision has strength. It is not just a lame articulation of inherited ideas of the holiness and beauty of Ireland. However far from the objectively verifiable truth Martin's vision is, it is authentic as it expresses himself and defies the world as he knows it. He and Mary leave to journey south, to where they will hear "a soft wind turning round the little leaves of the spring and feeling the sun" (III, p.149), to where, Martin argues, "people will have kind voices maybe, and we won't know their bad looks or their villainy at all" (III, p.149). They leave as the Tramp and Nora did, outcasts from a hostile, enclosed society. As in the earlier play, the ending is ambiguous. Mary especially knows of the dangers of the road ahead and Timmy concludes with the ominous observation that "the two of them will be drowned together in a short while, surely" (III, p.151). Nevertheless, they go carrying the sympathies of the audience with them and a vision, tentative at best, of a renewed, imaginative realm that the individual can make out of the myths of Ireland.

No such tentativeness marks the ending of Synge's most famous play, **The Playboy of the Western World**. None of his plays caused such a public outcry as this when it was first produced at the Abbey Theatre in January 1907, and later when it was taken on tour down the eastern American seaboard. Ostensibly the trouble in Dublin was caused by Christy's line referring to "a drift of chosen females, standing in their shifts itself" (IV, p.167), but accounts of the first night suggest that the band of nationalist protesters had been made uneasy about the play long before Christy's "immoral" observation gave them an opportunity to break up the performance.[23] Their initial unease was undoubtedly due to Synge's reputation of being hostile to the nationalist cause, but his text did nothing to assuage their fears. Of all his plays, **The Playboy of the Western World** creates in its audience that divided viewpoint so characteristic of Modernist drama.

Structurally the play is puzzling. Initially it masquerades as a fairly conventional example of the traditional comedy with which Dublin audiences were familiar and comfortable. Christy and Pegeen are the young lovers, Shawn Keogh the familiar figure of the parasite, the Widow Quin the comic, middle-aged widow, a perennial standby in the commercial English theatre, Mahon the **senex iratus,** and Michael Flaherty the entertaining, buffoon-like father. But the play does not wear its conventional disguise for long. Characters quickly overspill the types in which they are contained, disclosing personalities evasive of definition. As if to reflect this, Synge, while maintaining the formal structure of traditional comedy, provides two endings, one conventional, the betrothal of the lovers crowned by the lines "Amen, O Lord!" (IV, p.157), the other highly unorthodox, in which the lovers are sundered, only one, Christy, appearing to have achieved completion. Pegeen, meanwhile, is cast back into the slough of Mayo peasant life. Synge reverses the expectations set up by the traditional comedy and in doing so violates once again the sensibilities of those who held fast to myths of Ireland.

His Mayo is a violent land, peopled by vagrants, peelers, and soldiers, who strike fear into the hearts of the settled peasantry. Its peasants are distinguished not by their oneness with nature, their piety, or ability to endure nobly, but by their addiction to alcohol, a theme that persists throughout the play. Meanwhile, the "holy-water hen"

Shawn Keogh, far from being the comic outsider, the traditional place for the type he represents, is, through his prostrate obeisance to Father Reilly, posited as characteristic rather than as exceptional in this rural community. But the uncertainties and denials so far implied by Synge's dramaturgy account only partially for the initial outcry against his play.

Perhaps the reason for this outcry lay in Synge's perception of the way in which personality is composed. His earlier plays are relatively traditional in that characters are self-contained, as if each has a hard core of identity that distinguishes him or her from others. In **The Playboy of the Western World** the action, centred as it is on Christy, is used to deny that identity. Christy, a half-articulate non-entity when he first comes on stage, is gradually built and builds himself into a fully articulate man, "a likely gaffer in the end of all" (IV, p.173). This he achieves mainly through his reaction to those who hear the tale of his fight with his father. Through Christy personality is seen to be a changing, flexible entity, not God-given, not even created by positive forces at work within the social or natural environment. It is the product of impulses that are worryingly ephemeral in nature. In accord with much European Modernist writing, and one thinks especially of the plays of Ibsen and the plays and theoretical writings of Strindberg, Synge challenges the conventional notion of man as a monolith. Such a notion was possibly most prevalent in a culture given, like Ireland's was, to making myths about itself. But, as if to aggravate the unease his elusive psychology might cause, Synge also exploits myths, and not only Irish ones, that seem to flaunt his reductiveness. In doing so they highlight it. But, while they cast Christy's career through the play into a mock-heroic light, at the end they still manage to shed an ennobling glow upon him. That these myths are more than just Irish in origin many critics have pointed out. Christy's progress in the Mayo peasant community has been likened to that of Christ, as there are references to several elements of Christ's personal symbolism, such as the girls bringing gifts and the "crucifixion" at the end.[24] He can also be seen as a latter-day Oedipus who has killed, in his imagination at least, his father and, in his resistance to the Widow Quin, is avoiding marriage to his mother.[25] There is also a touch of Don Quixote about his wanderings through the west of Ireland,[26] and, to Irish audiences, Christy can well seem to be a modern-day Cuchulain.[27] In his growth parallels have also been detected to Synge's own development as an artist.[28] In all cases, and the play is rich enough to bear these multiple interpretations, Christy's rise to adulthood is both mocked and nourished by the complex mythological associations.

It is in **The Playboy of the Western World** that Synge fully realizes his ambiguous attitude towards the sustaining myths of Ireland. He does so most completely and confusingly, for while in his earlier plays it is fairly easy to distinguish those passages in which he dismantles popular myth and those towards the end of the play in which he reconstructs it in changed form, in **Playboy** the contrary patterns evolve simultaneously. As the mythical view of Ireland degenerates, regeneration is already underway in Christy's awakening to the potential influence he has over the Mayo peasants. This is traced in greater detail than in the earlier plays. By the end Christy's status as a folk-hero and as a deliberate creator of myth is unmistakeable. After his first telling of the tale, Christy is more in control of his fortunes than characters in Synge's earlier plays, his growth of personality more self-conscious, more clearly a personal strategy, more actively used by Synge as an assault against the sensibilities of those members of the audience who wish to see their heroes invested with moral, and by implication national worth.

But Christy is not at the end divorced from his Irish context. His is not the tale of a rebel who casts off all ties in order to leave for that more distant "Western World", as Shawn Keogh would have him do. Instead, like Martin Doul, though with greater confidence, he moves from being an underprivileged, even exploited member of his society to one who is dominant. His rise is more spectacular, as he comes to articulate more clearly than others of Synge's heroes and heroines who go out into the byways of Ireland, a poetic vision of the country that does not sit ill with the popular myth. This is most obvious in the growth of his powers of language. From the beginning it is clear Christy has a natural gift for language. More succinctly than other characters in the play, whose language has a certain untidy flamboyance about it, Christy can capture well the quality of the world he has experienced or at least has imagined. He comes not from just another farming community, but from "a distant place . . . a windy corner of high distant hills" (IV, p.75); he does not see just ordinary human prettiness, but "young limber girls, and fine prancing women making laughter with the men" (IV, p.81), which leads Pegeen to compare him to the poets: "it's the poets are your like, fine fiery fellows with great rages when their temper's roused" (IV, p.81). Christy's powers of description develop with the growth in the story of his father's murder, becoming more extended, richer, though no less precise, suited well to describing particular emotional states, as when he speaks of the loneliness of the traveller: "it's a lonesome thing to be passing small towns with the lights shining sideways when the night is down, or going in strange places with a dog nosing before you and a dog nosing behind. . ." (IV, p.109). This amplification of suggestive power in his language reaches its climactic point in the final love scene with Pegeen where, unlike Martin Doul with Molly Byrne, his words make her oblivious of his diminutive body. He is able to use the most eloquent images of Ireland as a land of softness and beauty, as a living rather than a lost paradise, to win her over: "when the airs is warming in four months or five, it's then yourself and me should be pacing Neifin in the dews of night, the times sweet smells do be rising, and you'd see a little shiny new moon maybe sinking on the hills" (IV, p.147). It is the Ireland of Thomas Moore, not entirely purged of sentimentality perhaps, but more vibrant and clearly sketched in the imagination.

"**Riders to the Sea** . . . seemed for all the nobility of its end, its mood of Greek tragedy, too passive in suffering". Such was Yeats's judgement on Synge's play that accorded most completely with his own and the popular myth of Ireland. As Christy Mahon leaves the Flaherty shebeen to "go romancing through a romping lifetime from this hour to the dawning of the judgment day" (IV, p.173), the full implications of Synge's transformation of these myths become clear. He destroyed them, but in doing so reconstituted them. Admittedly his peasant heroes are distinguished neither by their moral purity nor by their piety; Synge has no time for such virtues, and, when they surface, as with Shawn Keogh, they are invariably cause for laughter. All the same, as his heroes leave, they do so as recognizable, Irish figures, peculiar idealists who have renounced the certainties of a settled world to engage in the less tangible pleasures of the imaginative life. They go not solely as dreamers but as ones who have chosen to remain aloof from the obligations and demands that hamper the lives of most people. These lone idealists maintain the image of Ireland as a land of particular beauty. Despite the muddiness and disarray of Irish country life, from it emerges a vision of its potential beauty, which, while never fully realized, is felt to have great power to nourish the imaginative life of the individual. Synge's departing heroes have also demonstrated a mighty capacity to suffer, not in the passive way identified by Yeats in **Riders to the Sea**, but in a manner that leads to rebellion, to a new sense of personal identity, and a gain in individual coherence. This does not lead towards constructive social action, that was never one of Synge's concerns, but it does lead to affirmation of the possibility of human growth and the assertion of individual values. These heroes always leave as magnificent talkers; no less than the Tramp in **The Shadow of the Glen**, Martin Doul and Christy Mahon are manifestly ancestors of the nineteenth-century Stage Irishman, though they are no longer the genial, ingenious, though ineffective servants of the **status quo** as their forebears were. Instead they leave as assertive, aggressive, spell-binding talkers whose very being is a protest against the constrictions that too often bear upon human behaviour. In Synge, that which was passive in Irish myth has been made active, and the paradise of Ireland, seen as so irretrievably lost in the nineteenth century, can be seen as a vital force in the imagination of his characters. But it becomes exclusively a condition of that imagination. This, no doubt, was cause for much of the nationalist suspicion of Synge. In his plays he had taken the fundamental underpinning that gave the myth legitimacy to his contemporaries, that is the qualitative difference between the idealistic Irish and the materialistic English, and transferred it wholly to Irish soil. It was now the Irish peasant who embodied many of the evils commonly associated with England. Irish idealism was presented as possible only in those who cast themselves off from social life. Irish society was as suspect as that of its nominal enemy. No wonder Synge's plays did not sit well with the nationalists.

The transference of the conflict between individualistic idealism and materialism to Ireland was highlighted in Synge's final play, **Deirdre of the Sorrows**. Here the Ireland ruled by Conchubor is peopled neither by mighty heroes, familiar from the sagas, nor by a nobly suffering peasantry. Instead it is a brutalized world, subject to the arbitrary dictates of a king who will stop at nothing, not even the destruction of his capital Emain Macha, in his frenzied attempts to gain possession of Deirdre. From the very start, Conchubor is a baleful presence in the play, not at once an actively malign figure, but a man whose failure to achieve his ends leads to a loneliness that compels him to destroy whatever he is excluded from. His understanding of how human affections can be won and held is woefully inadequate. In Act I, the only way he can approach Deirdre is to burden her with gold, silver, and massy hangings, as if he were merely the sum total of his possessions. By Act 3, the passive weight of matter has been transformed into active forces of oppression, Conchubor's "strange fighters", who speak words no one can understand and who fulfil their leader's commands mechanically.

In contrast, Synge invests in Deirdre all the more vital and attractive aspects of the Irish myth. This involved initially a reversal of contemporary audiences' expectations as Deirdre, a familiar figure from the sagas, stood primarily in their imagination as the epitome of unresisting suffering.[29] She is, of course, the opposite of this. Furthermore, unlike Synge's previous heroines, she does not grow into a state of ease with nature, nor does she become positively assertive; she is this from the beginning. Before she even enters, Lavarcham and the old woman speak of her as a child of nature, unaware of her beauty, "straying the hills" (IV, p.183), so entirely at one with the natural world that she is indestructible: "the lightning itself wouldn't let down its flame to singe the beauty of her like" (IV, p.185). Her isolation from society, though initially imposed by Conchubor, has, by her late adolescence, become her choice. Deirdre is no pitiful victim of circumstances. She has an acute sense of her individuality, is adamant against Conchubor's demands upon her, and is completely aware of her unsuitability to be his queen. Synge is not, however, content to have her be merely a self-possessed young woman. Despite her innocence of Conchubor's world of authority and political power, on her the trappings of royalty acquire a renewed splendour. As she appears before Naisi, "royally dressed and very beautiful" (IV, p.207), she wears the robes with ease, using them not for the power they symbolize, but to highlight her own glory. To give this glory a vibrant colouring, in the first act the two women compare Deirdre to the mythological queen Maeve, who was for an Irish audience a woman of powerful assertiveness, a staunch, even violent defender of her own rights. In the conflict between the oppressive materialism of Conchubor and the idealistic individualism represented by Deirdre, Synge's values are placed unmistakeably on Deirdre.

Naisi is a fitting companion for her, though he is not given the driving, heroic qualities normally associated with him in the frequent retellings of the Deirdre saga. Like her he is at one with nature, blithely exercising his physical mastery over it. Like the hares he and his brother are constantly chasing, he demonstrates an easy freedom from the restraints of the body. But this freedom is accompanied by a corresponding volatility of will. While Deirdre, always precisely aware of her physical responses, acts with certainty and self-knowledge, Naisi is easily cowed and equally easily inflamed. His high spirits are instantly quenched when he sees Conchubor's mark on the golden mug, though his defiance of the king grows rapidly as he responds to the initiatives of Deirdre during their love scene at the end of Act 1. Throughout she remains dominant, especially as she demonstrates how clear-sighted she is about the prophecy over her and Naisi's mutual fate. Rather than fill her with fear, the prophecy serves to instil her with vigour, the very brevity of life it offers giving that life a piquancy and strength it otherwise might not have had: ". . .for it's a sweet life you and I could have Naisi. . . It should be a sweet thing to have what is best and richest if it's for a short space only" (IV, p.209). Accompanying this heightened awareness of the potential in life is Deirdre's sense that she and Naisi will themselves become paragons, figures of mythical status. As she begins the love scene she speaks of herself of whom "a story will be told for ever" (IV, p.209), continues by seeing in Naisi not just a spirited young man but a symbolic figure, one who with his "brothers [is] called the flower of Ireland" (IV, p.209), and then conceives of her coming death as making "the sun red with envy and he going up the heavens, and the moon pale and lonesome and she wasting away" (IV, p.211). As they prepare to leave the house of her childhood on Slieve Fuadh, Deirdre and Naisi, to a far more intense degree than other of Synge's heroes, are bent upon fulfilling a powerful betrothal through nature that has dimensions close to the superhuman. To achieve this, however, they must take a step none of Synge's heroes have so far done; they must leave Ireland to take refuge in Alban – Scotland. Ireland under Conchubor gives them no freedom; it offers only destruction.

At the end of Act 1, Deirdre and Naisi are in the same position as Synge's earlier departing wanderers at the end of their plays. Their sequestration in the forests of Alban therefore gives him the opportunity to explore the viability of the mythical life and to confront his dominant theme. The result is, inevitably, a recognition of the eventual fictitiousness of the possibility of living constantly at the pitch of ecstasy in the embrace of nature. Humanity cannot sustain it, satiation and change challenge its durability. The result is a feeling of rootlessness that chafes at happiness and a distrust of the future that erodes companionship. "I've a dread going or staying", Deirdre says to Lavarcham. "It's lonesome this place having happiness like ours till I'm asking each day, will this day match yesterday, and will to-morrow take a good place beside the same day in the year that's gone . . ." (IV, p.219). Naisi too has experienced the mutability of feelings; the moment the possibility of their waning occurs to him, the process to a certain degree has begun. "I've a dread upon me the day'd come I'd weary of her voice", he tells Fergus. ". . .and Deirdre'd see I'd wearied" (IV, p.227). On hearing this sentiment, Deirdre recognizes the end has come. With characteristic decisiveness and prompted by a graphic description of aging by the crazed Owen, she coaxes Naisi to abandon the thought of living out their lives in dull acquiescence to the decay of vital feeling. Hence they return to Ireland, not to fulfil themselves, but to face whatever Conchubor has in store for them. In Ireland they will meet their death rather than a renewed life.

Despite the darkness associated in the play with Ireland, the traditional, poetic image has been maintained as a motif in the second act. Fergus, trusting in the honour of Conchubor, tries to woo Deirdre and Naisi back with language reminiscent of descriptions of landscapes from earlier plays. "To this day", he tells them, "the old men have nothing so heavy as knowing it's in a short while they'll lose the high skies are over Ireland, and the lonesome mornings with birds crying on the bogs" (IV, p.225). But the Ireland the lovers return to is far from this. In place of well-appointed lodgings to receive them there is a tent "with shabby skins and benches" (IV, p.241) set not on the open hillside but in a gloomy wood that harbours the "strange fighters" who will eventually kill Naisi and his brothers. Synge's depiction of Ireland as oppressive and dirty is possibly nowhere more complete than here.

The action of the final act initially complements the dreariness of the setting. Synge does not follow the traditional accounts of the battles fought by the sons of Usna against the overwhelming odds of Conchubor's troops. Rather their deaths occur off-stage, a result of treacherous scheming, not open confrontation. Furthermore, Conchubor does not turn out to be the rigidly determined tyrant he promised to be, but a broken man on the point of reconciliation, but still too resentful to act on it with determination. The dejecting atmosphere is further intensified by signs of the first quarrel between Deirdre and Naisi, as she holds him back when he runs out to help his brothers. Their parting occurs not on a final avowal of their unity, but at a moment when it appears that they have crossed each other. Not only has Synge undermined the splendour of the Ireland of the sagas, he has also denied the viability of the endurance of the regenerated myth within his central characters. That this can survive not as a living force but only as a memory becomes clear through Deirdre's long death speech, which, in contrast to the rest of the play, has an almost operatic formality to it, as if it has little to do with the actual business of life. At this point, Deirdre is dominated by an awareness that her life will itself become mythical, due to the intensity of its quality. Far from being passive in defeat, she speaks of everything that is happening as if it is already far in the past, as "a story told of a ruined city and a raving king and a woman will be young for ever" (IV, p.267). At the same time, in language and imagery that is strikingly simple and concrete – "I have put away sorrow like a shoe that is worn out and muddy" (IV, p.267) – she removes herself and all concerned from the squalor and violence of the events just passed. Conchubor she describes as wise, Naisi as one who "had no match for bravery" (IV, p.267), and herself as one who "had a life that will be envied by great companies" (IV, p.267). Devoid of personal rancour, Deirdre, like the earlier Maurya, protests not against temporary deprivation, but against the very conditions of life that made the continuation of her union with Naisi impossible. As the action has demonstrated, this impossibility had not come about through the exercise of arbitrary power by Conchubar: Deirdre's and Naisi's decision to return was an act of free-will with foreknowledge of the consequences. That power, despite the destruction it has caused, has little significance. The importance of the myth that survives is not the story itself but the idea of a woman unprepared to live anything but the most complete and fulfilling life. Consequently her death is "a thing will be a joy and triumph to the ends of life and time" (IV, p.269).

Despite the high drama and effectively simple rhetoric of this final scene, the play ends on an ambivalent note. Deirdre's death seems admirable, but it is also useless. She dies to avoid the inevitable decay that comes with aging, dies too in a refusal to bow to coercive forces. But all she achieves is the effect of a fine example; she invigorates no one. Those who are left are broken, Conchubor speaking now "with the voice of an old man" (IV, p.269). We are left with nothing but desolation. In **Riders to the Sea** Synge seemed to have given credence to popular myths of Ireland, in his comedies he explored how they could be used to give the individual renewed strength and cohesion. In **Deirdre of the Sorrows** the enquiry is taken further. Here, centring upon the most idealistic of all his characters, Synge demonstrates how, taken to the furthest limit, living out such myths can lead only to death. It is only through death that myth can be created and survive.

Synge's constant discourse on the nature of myth, conducted within an almost exclusively Irish setting, naturally aroused the ire of the nationalists. The particular strength of his plays lies in the characteristically Modernist manner in which he maintains whatever is most attractive in the past while questioning the values upon which it is built. This was, no doubt, the cause of Yeats's vigorous defence of his plays. That Yeats's own essays on the Irish Drama, published in **Samhain** between 1902 and 1908, were strongly influenced by Synge has long been recognized.[30] In these Yeats writes of a theatre radically different from the "Celtic Twilight" theatre he had described in the 1890s. Now theatre is not solely given to generating a rather vaguely conceived sense of national and racial identity. Instead it must be devoted to shattering the "idol-houses" of dogma and political doctrine; in some ways it must be active against social cohesion. It must appeal not to audiences' moral senses, as these are an aspect of their social conditioning, but to their imagination. This is released through the representation on stage not of the "personified averages" of the commercial theatre, but of unique characters, whose newness of vision will arouse the audience's sense of the limitations and compromises of social life. At the same time, these characters, through their sheer uniqueness, will create a sense of whatever is unique in the life of Ireland. National identity, therefore, no longer comes through the repetition of stereotypical myths, but is to be found in whatever is fresh, extravagant in language and defiant in stance. Most importantly, Yeats sees performing in his theatre artists who are not aloof disdainers of the materialistic world, but, like Synge's heroes, are aggressive combatters of it, full of scorn, spilling over with words and imaginative visions that arouse the awe of their audiences. These artists, of whom Synge's characters seem to be exemplars, – minstrels, singers, actors – appeal as much through the strength of their personality as through what they have to say. But above all, Yeats prizes the "reciter", a figure possibly closer to Synge's characters in their final apotheoses than any other. "The reciter cannot be a player, for that is a different art; but he must be a messenger, and he should be as interesting, as exciting, as are all that carry great news. He comes from far off, and he speaks of far-off things with his own peculiar animation, and instead of lessening the ideal and beautiful elements of speech he may, if he has a mind to, increase them".[31]

In contrast to his European contemporaries, Synge's drama is unusually optimistic. Ibsen's characters, for example, almost invariably founder in the gap that lies between their perception of the true nature of fictions and their attempt, despite their insight, to fulfil in spirit those fictions. Synge's, however, show no such failure. **Riders to the Sea** tends to authenticate nationalist myths, his comic drama denies them. But while denying them, he reinvigorates them, shifting them from the realm of social to that of individual experience. In **Deirdre of the Sorrows**, the viability of their survival in this new realm is questioned. While Deirdre's suicide marks their inevitable failure, they continue as ideas though their vitalizing power is questioned.

Notes

1. I use this term to cover the various theatres directed by Yeats and Lady Gregory from the founding of the Irish Literary Theatre in 1897 onwards.

2. The most recent of several surveys on the history of the Stage Irishman is Robert Graves: "The Stage Irishman Among the Irish", **Theatre History Studies** I (1981), pp.29–38.

3. Quoted in Lady Gregory: **Our Irish Theatre** (New York, 1965) p.9.

4. W.B. Yeats: "The Celtic Element in Literature", **Essays and Introductions** (New York, 1961), p.173.

5. Ibid., p.182.

6. "The Theatre", **Essays and Introductions**, p.166.

7. Ibid., p.166.

8. Ibid., p.167.

9. See Malcolm Kelsall: "Makers of a Modern Theatre: Frank and William Fay", **Theatre Research International** III, 3 (May 1978), pp.188–99.

10. David H. Grene & Edward M. Stephens: **J.M. Synge** (New York, 1959), p.158.

11. Robin Skelton: **The Writings of J.M. Synge** (London, 1971), pp.49–51.

12. J.M. Synge: **Collected Works**, Vol.III, **Plays**, Book 1, ed. Ann Saddlemyer (Gerards Cross and Washington D.C., 1982), p.17. All subsequent quotations from Synge's plays are from this edition and references to them are included in the text.

13. This has led some critics to question the success of the play. See especially Malcolm Pittock: **"Riders to the Sea", English Studies** 49 (1968), pp.445–49.

14. Daniel Corkery: **Synge and Anglo-Irish Literature** (Dublin and Cork, 1931).

15. "J.M. Synge and his World", **Essays and Introductions**, p.336.

16. Robert Hogan & James Kilroy: **Laying the Foundations, 1902–1904**, The Modern Irish Drama, A Documentary History II (Dublin, 1974), p.80.

17. Hogan & Kilroy, p.78.

18. "For Synge – indeed for many Irish painters and writers – the vagrant is the personification of a romantic element in Irish life and an antidote to the devouring concern for land that has dominated Irish life for centuries. Either through envy or self-pity Synge began to see the tramp as a shadow of his own mood". David H. Greene & Edward M. Stephens: **J.M. Synge**, pp.91–92.

19. See the reviews of Frank Fay in **Towards a National Theatre**, ed. Robert Hogan (Dublin, 1970).

20. Robert Hogan & James Kilroy: **The Abbey Theatre: The Years of Synge, 1905–1909**, The Modern Irish Drama: A Documentary History III (Dublin, 1978), p.20.

21. Nicholas Grene: **Synge: A Critical Study of the Plays** (London, 1975), p.114.

22. Alan Price: **Synge and Anglo-Irish Drama** (London, 1961), pp.144–51.

23. See James Kilroy: **The Playboy Riots** (Dublin, 1971) for a thorough documentation of the demonstrations occurring during the play's first run of a week at the Abbey Theatre.

24. Howard D. Pearce: "Synge's Playboy as Mock Christ", **Modern Drama** VIII (December, 1965), pp.303–10. Reprinted in **Twentieth Century Interpretations of The Playboy of the Western World**, ed. Thomas R. Whitaker (Englewood Cliffs, 1969), pp.88–97.

25. Mary Rose Sullivan: "Synge, Sophocles, and the Unmaking of Myth", **Modern Drama** XII (1969).

26. Skelton, p.123.

27. Toni O'Brien Johnson: **Synge: The Medieval and the Grotesque**, Irish Literary Studies II (Gerrards Cross, 1982).

28. James F. Kilroy: "The Playboy as Poet", **PMLA**, 83 (1968), pp.439–42.

29. See afternote to **Grania** in Lady Gregory: **Selected Plays**, ed. Elizabeth Coxhead (London, 1975), p.216.

30. Suheil Badi Bushrui: "Synge and Yeats", in **A Centenary Tribute to John Millington Synge, 1871–1909: Sunshine and The Moon's Delight**, ed. S.B. Bushrui (New York, 1972), pp.189–203.

31. W.B. Yeats: **Explorations** (New York, 1962), p.215.

Edvard Munch and Modernism in the Berlin Art World 1892–1903

Carla Lathe

The battle for exhibition space

One of the results of the contemporary focus on Modernism is that some of the leading figures have been identified with the movement on the basis of work which forms only part of their total production. The portion of their work which is considered Modernist may be highly valued by some, but rejected by others who have different preferences. It has been said that "the modern movement arose from a confusion of the aims of painting with poetry (and perhaps also with music). It disintegrated as a result of the separation of the arts, perhaps due to the reassertion of the difference intrinsic to each".[1] When one examines the point when the confusion of the arts became apparent in the work of a particular artist or writer, it sometimes seems to have arisen from reciprocation in a stimulating environment. This can be seen in the case of Munch and the development of Modernism in Berlin 1892–1903.

Berlin became capital of Germany in 1871 after the Prussian military successes in the wars between 1864 and 1871. The last decades of the century were a time of change and rapid expansion in the city. Some of the people in authority were quite young. The Emperor, Wilhelm II, a grandson of Queen Victoria and Prince Albert, succeeded to the throne in 1888 when he was twenty-nine. Probably the most influential person in the Berlin art world was also relatively young. Anton von Werner became director of the Academy of Arts in 1875, when he was thirty-two. In 1887 he became leader of the **Verein Berliner Künstler**, the most powerful organization for painters, sculptors and architects in Berlin. Von Werner had spent the winter of 1870–71 at the Prussian military headquarters during the Franco-Prussian war. He was well-known for his genre scenes illustrating contemporary Prussian history and was considered a court painter. He reinforced the tastes and distastes of the Emperor, who took an active interest in art, patronized the **Verein Berliner Künstler** and was an amateur painter himself. Wilhelm II hoped to see the development of a German national art. Although he and the people he appointed to hold responsible positions in the arts were willing to import samples of international culture, they believed that contemporary German art should be patriotic, a reflection of the authoritarian and militarist system which had united Germany.

In spite of the nationalist aspirations of the Emperor, a large proportion of the painters working in Berlin were internationally orientated. Some were foreigners, others had spent years abroad, keeping friends in France, Holland, Scandinavia, Switzerland. This led to difficulties over the issue of patriotism. The Prussians, having just conquered the French, were hardly eager for French-inspired art to dominate their own. Von Werner apparently considered the French Impressionists to be eccentrics and is reported to have said in a speech in 1890, "mit den Impressionisten . . . will ich mich hier nicht beschäftigen, da ich sonst vielleicht auch auf andre Kuriosa verfallen könnte". ("I will not concern myself here with the Impressionists . . . lest I succumb to other curiosities").[2] He was hostile to those members of the **Verein Berliner Künstler** whose art was influenced by developments in France and Holland, and he was suspicious of the naturalist depiction of life among poorer people as shown by Max Liebermann and the Munich Impressionist Fritz Uhde. The members who resented von Werner, in turn, suggested that he attached more importance to diplomacy than to the quality of art and that under him the artists' association was guided by commercial concerns.[3]

While the leaders of Prussian society in the 1890s were still the traditional landowners and officers in the army, there was in Berlin an expanding middle class of industrialists, doctors, educationalists, to name but a few. Some of the art buyers in these circles were not interested in the paintings of German history encouraged by the Emperor. One of them was Julius Elias, an editor of annual reports on contemporary German literature **(Jahresberichte für neuere deutsche Literaturgeschichte)**. Elias was sympathetic to the Naturalist movement in literature and was a friend and admirer of Ibsen. Although his main subject was German literature, Elias showed great interest in modern art and had met Monet, Pissarro and Cézanne while he was in Paris in 1890. According to Kenworth Moffett, Elias arranged for the Paris art dealer Durand-Ruel to exhibit ninety-five paintings in the Hotel Kaiserhof in Berlin in 1892.[4] It was not an event which attracted much press publicity, but Elias began to interest other Jewish collectors in modern French art. Elias also became an influence on Hugo von Tschudi, the director of the Berlin National Gallery 1896–1908, who was dismissed in 1909 because he had not only taken an interest in the unfashionable German Romantics but had also smuggled a collection of modern French pictures into the loft of the museum.

A prime objective of many people interested in modern art in the Berlin of the 1890s was the opportunity to exhibit it. Apart from the private collections, Pächter's small gallery in the Dessauerstrasse showed some French Impressionists and Neo-Impressionists as well as Japanese art. Otherwise only Fritz Gurlitt occasionally exhibited French and modern German art. On Unter den Linden there was a gallery owned by Eduard Schulte which showed paintings by Germans wanting to exhibit their work independently of the **Verein Berliner Künstler**. Early in 1892 Walther Leistikow, Ludwig von Hofmann, Max Klinger, Franz Skarbina and others began to exhibit there together as a group of eleven, "Die Elf". This group embraced the interest in Naturalism, Impressionism and the modern style in the applied arts which began to emerge in Berlin in the 1890s. Their exhibitions encountered fierce criticism.

Apart from the group "Die Elf", a number of members of the **Verein Berliner Künstler** wanted to have exhibitions showing different art styles to the National Realism approved by the establishment. In 1892 there was a new exhibition committee in the **Verein**, consisting largely of members who wanted to show selections of foreign art. To a greater or lesser degree, they all supported the modern movement. A member of the exhibition committee was Adelsten Normann (1848–1918), a Norwegian painter living in Berlin. While in Norway in the summer of 1892, Normann had seen an exhibition of paintings by Edvard Munch which had largely favourable reviews there. At Normann's suggestion, and according to the newspaper **Die Freisinnige Zeitung** (13 November 1892) with a recommendation from Fritz Uhde, the exhibition committee invited Munch to bring to Berlin the paintings he had shown in Kristiania that summer.

For Munch it was an honour to hold an exhibition under the auspices of the **Verein Berliner Künstler**. He was then twenty-eight and had exhibited paintings regularly in

Kristiania since 1883, also in Copenhagen, Paris and Munich. He had been taught in 1881 at the Drawing School (Tegneskolen) in Kristiania, then by the Norwegian Impressionist painters Christian Krohg and Frits Thaulow, and in 1889 by the French painter Bonnat. In Norway Munch was considered a radical artist and was known to be a friend of the anarchist writer Hans Jæger, notorious for his novel **Fra Kristiania-Bohêmen** (from the Kristiania-Bohême, 1885). Jæger wrote a study of Kant and recommended in his publications free love, self-analysis and a personal perspective. A portrait of Jæger was included in the exhibition Munch brought to Berlin. His other paintings included scenes of figures in a landscape and showed an inclination to focus on moods, changes in light and weather. At least twelve of the fifty-five pictures showed evening light and had titles such as **Sonnenuntergang** (Sunset), **Der Abend** (Evening), **Dämmerung** (Dusk), **Nacht** (Night) or **Mondschein** (Moonlight). Munch was curious about the relationship of sense impressions caused by different moods, light or weather and he sought to convey subjective perceptions in his art. In Berlin he discussed his pictures with the Swedish writer Ola Hansson who quoted him as saying about the painting **Sonnenuntergang**, a forerunner of **The Scream**:

> er male nicht das Naturbild selbst, sondern das Erinnerungsbild, nicht die Szenerie direkt und aus erster Hand, wie sie in der Aussenwelt dasteht, sondern das subjektive Abbild davon, das sich für längere oder kürzere Zeit auf seine Netzhaut und in seine Seele eingeätzt und eingebrannt hat und das immer in grellen Farben hervorspringt aus dem Schwarzen unter den Augenlidern, sobald man die Augen schliesst.

> he does not paint the image of nature itself but the image in his memory, not scenery directly and at first hand, as it stands there in the outer world, but its subjective likeness which for longer or shorter periods of time is etched and burnt onto his retina and into his soul and which constantly springs in garish colours out of the darkness under his eyelids as soon as he shuts his eyes.[5]

Hansson was among the many critics who remarked that Munch's procedure was more characteristic of literature than of painting and he compared Munch with modern poets like Dauthendey who wished to reveal the unconscious through memories. In his article Hansson observed that Munch's search for images which expressed a synthesis of psychology and art was new and experimental.

Munch's pictures of fleeting impressions and moody people provided the greatest possible contrast to the predominantly static representation of people by von Werner. A critic wrote of von Werner's paintings: "unendlich trocken und steif stehen meistens zwölf bis sechzig uniformierte, auffallend ausdruckslose Herren herum. Man denkt, ein Modebild für Militärschneider, eine Illustration zur Kleideordnung" ("generally twelve to sixty endlessly dry and stiff gentlemen in uniform stand around, remarkable for their lack of expression. You might think it a fashion picture for military tailors, an illustration for regulations regarding dress").[6] The exhibition committee probably wanted to provoke an argument and must have known the contempt that Munch's pictures would receive from von Werner's faction for the unfamiliar handling both of figures and of paint. In the event, Munch's exhibition brought into the open the conflict between opposing groups of artists in Berlin. It was recognized as a test case and its aftermath helped to create the opportunity for further displays of Modernism in the Berlin art world.

When von Werner's supporters first saw Munch's pictures hanging on their walls on 5 November 1892, they were horrified. It was not the subject matter which alarmed them but Munch's technique which he had learnt partly in France and with which the artists in Berlin were unfamiliar. They thought that his paintings were unbelievably badly painted. A marine painter, Hermann Eschke (1823–1900), drew up a petition that the paintings should not be shown to the public out of respect for art. An extraordinary meeting of the **Verein** was called for 11 November to debate the issue. By a slim majority of fifteen votes, it was decided to close Munch's exhibition at once, only six days after its opening. Considering that von Werner's overwhelming concern is reputed to have been with diplomacy, it is not surprising that the opposing faction made most of the issue of etiquette, whether it was good manners to close an exhibition by a foreign guest. The meeting developed into an angry, noisy riot and subsequently the controversy was taken up by the press, with supporters on both sides. According to the **Freisinnige Zeitung** (7, no.276, 13 November 1892), "als die Abstimmung über den 'Fall Munch' geendet hatte, da trat der berühmte Radirer Prof. Köpping auf und brach in die empörten Worte aus: 'Nun kann kein anständiger Mensch mehr dem Künstlerverein angehören'. Mit etwa 80 Herren verliess er den Versammlungssaal. Damit war die Sezession entstanden . . .". ("when the voting about the 'Munch case' had ended, the famous engraver Prof. Köpping came forward and exclaimed in disgust, 'now no respectable person can continue to belong to the Art Association'. Together with about 80 gentlemen he left the assembly hall. With that the Secession came into being . . ."). The sculptor Max Kruse, who had been on the exhibition committee, remembered that the scene was quite violent. Amidst yelling and whistling, the so-called secessionists fought their way out past the other members who tried to prevent them from leaving.[7] Those who did make their exit, decided to form a "Freie Vereinigung Berliner Künstler".

This splitting of the association was often reported as the division between old and young members, and Munch, too, in his letters home explained that those who wanted to close his exhibition and remove the exhibition committee were old, while those who supported him were young.[8] It is therefore surprising to discover that the artists who spoke in favour of keeping this exhibition open were mainly elderly or middle aged and that their art can hardly be called revolutionary. One of them, August von Heyden (1827–97) taught history of costume at the Berlin Art Academy and his pictures of Germanic mythological figures were in keeping with the Emperor's own heroic idealism. Another speaker, Ludwig Knaus (1829–1910), devoted himself to social realism in genre scenes, was popular for his pictures of children and became a professor and member of the Academy. Karl Köpping (1848–1914) was famous for his engraved copies of old master paintings, particularly of Rembrandt. Hugo Vogel (1855–1934), a professor of painting at the Academy and member of the group "Die Elf", did genre and history paintings, including large frescoes with scenes from Prussian history. Apart from Vogel, the men who protested at Munch's treatment spanned the same age groups as Eschke and von Werner in their sixties and forties, so it is clearly inaccurate to divide the factions according to age into young versus old. Those who were referred to as "young" were simply more tolerant of artistic innovation and variety than those who were labelled "old". It was important for Munch and for the development of modern art in Berlin that there was a body of older, well-established painters who were sympathetic to the exhibitions of new art from abroad. They made it possible for disparate points of view to co-exist in the same place.

In retrospect, the precise nature of what happened to both Munch and the Berlin art world as a result of his exhibition is not well known. At the time, it was reported in the press as a secession and many have continued to trace the formation of the Berlin Secession to Munch's exhibition. The American art historian Reinhold Heller has more recently presented a different interpretation of the events and come to the conclusion that the closure of Munch's exhibition in 1892 cannot be linked with the founding of the Berlin Secession in 1898.[9] Most frequently, the split in the **Verein Berliner Künstler** after Munch's exhibition is presented in art history as a progression of the **avant garde**, the young against the old, the radicals against the conservatives. Artists like Max Liebermann, who were to become prominent in the Berlin Secession at the end of the decade, are given credit for having supported Munch against the members who wanted to close his exhibition.[10] The pattern of names in newspaper reports suggests a different story. Munch meanwhile showed some business sense in that he quickly allowed Schulte to show his exhibition in other cities in Germany, in Düsseldorf and Cologne, before he re-opened it independently in Berlin. The fees from this tour provided him with an income.

The eighty or so members of the **Verein Berliner Künstler** who were determined to make a stand for artistic freedom over the issue of Munch's exhibition were a broad collection of painters, engravers, sculptors and architects. They tried to oppose the older association from within. In January 1893, three professors at the Berlin Academy, August von Heyden, Hugo Vogel and Franz Skarbina (1849–1910) who were referred to as "Secessionists" in the press,[11] had to resign their teaching positions on account of the hostility from von Werner and other members of the Academy. In June 1893, the "Freie Vereinigung Berliner Künstler" had an alternative exhibition to the large one arranged by the Berlin Art Academy at exhibition premises near the Lehrter Bahnhof. The rival exhibition included works which had been rejected by the Academy's jury, for example by Munch, Strindberg and Käthe Kollwitz. Julius Elias mentioned Kollwitz's work in a review and wrote that he thought that she was influenced by Munch. Although it did not have the funds to start a secession until 1898, this jury-free exhibition and the small ones held by the group "Die Elf" every spring between 1892 and 1897 constituted a challenge to the Berlin art establishment.

Opposition to the large annual exhibition arranged by the Berlin Art Academy, "die Grosse Berliner Kunstausstellung" appears to have been the chief aim of those who established the Berlin Secession in 1898. The painter Walter Leistikow (1865–1908), who had belonged to the group "Die Elf" and had befriended Munch, was the driving force behind the founding of the Secession. When the jury of the "Grosse Berliner Kunstausstellung" refused Leistikow's picture of fir trees and a path along a bank, Richard Israel bought it and donated it to the National Gallery.[12] Leistikow and a group of fellow artists made the final break with the **Verein Berliner Künstler** and chose Liebermann to be president of the Berlin Secession. They acquired their own building and in the spring of 1899 opened their rival exhibition with works by Corinth, Slevogt, Liebermann, Trübner and Hodler among many others. By 1901 they showed the French Impressionists and then in 1902 Munch exhibited with them the paintings he later called "Livsfrisen".

In the first decades of the twentieth century, the intimate and subjective art which Munch brought to Berlin gradually found sympathetic response and German Expressionism became a firm alternative to the art originally approved of by the Prussian authorities. The latter suspected the Secessionists of being anarchists and traitors to their country. Nevertheless, **avant-garde** groups such as **Die Brücke** and

Der Sturm were able to exhibit in Berlin and it developed into an important international focal point for Modernism.

The beginning of the Munch myth

As Berlin was the centre of imperialist propaganda and the leadership of the **Verein Berliner Künstler** tried to stifle the development of modern art, why did painters like Munch and Leistikow stay there? One reason for Munch to stay was that he made many friends who adopted and promoted him. They were not of course the influential art critics who supported the leadership of the **Verein Berliner Künstler**, but largely unknown amateurs and entrepreneurs in the field of art. The purchasing power of the anti-imperialists could rival that of official patronage, and Munch received commissions to do portraits from people who loved modern art. With hindsight it may seem significant that some of those who first supported him were later to become part of the Modernist hierarchy. Julius Meier-Graefe (1867–1935), an aspiring writer in the early 1890s, wrote his first pieces of art criticism on Munch in 1894–95 and in the first decades of the twentieth century became one of the Expressionists' most revered art critics. Another young man who took an interest in Munch was Walther Rathenau (1867–1922), who was to become famous as Germany's Minister of Reconstruction in 1922. He had been an industrialist and later a politician strongly in favour of democracy rather than the absolute power of the Emperor, but he was assassinated by the right wing in 1922. In July 1893 he had bought Munch's painting **Regnveirsdag på Karl Johan** (Rainy Day on Karl Johan), and Munch in 1907 painted portraits of him. In 1895 Munch also did lithograph portraits of Harry Count Kessler (1868–1937) who became director of the Archducal Museum in Weimar in 1902 and was influential in promoting modern design. When these people first met Munch in the early 1890s, they were not only younger than he was but were also, in contrast to him, unknown. The columns written about the scandal Munch's exhibition had caused in the **Verein Berliner Künstler** had made him, unlike them, something of a celebrity among non-conformists.

Berlin was an important centre for literature, having excellent theatres and enterprising publishers. At the time when Munch arrived there, there was a great vogue for Scandinavian literature among Germans with a progressive outlook, and he made friends with the colony of Scandinavian writers and students in the city. Some writers of dissent like Ola Hansson actually found it easier to publish in Germany than in their own countries.[13] The contemporary popularity of Ibsen's plays was beneficial to other Scandinavians. They were helped by the Berlin drama society **Die freie Bühne** which was founded in 1889 and led by Otto Brahm, an admirer of Ibsen. This society hired premises in a theatre for its matinée performances of plays; by restricting the audience to its members, it hoped to escape the censor. **Die freie Bühne** had a sensational opening on 29 September 1889 with Ibsen's **Gengangere** (Ghosts) which was banned at the time. In 1890 it staged Strindberg's **Fadren** (The Father) and in 1892 **Fröken Julie**. Berlin was probably the first place outside Scandinavia to consider Strindberg the rival of Ibsen; according to Max Halbe, tea parties in West Berlin were divided between supporters of Ibsen and those of Strindberg.[14] Brahm in 1890 published the first issue of a journal attached to the **Freie Bühne** and again gave prominence to Scandinavian literature. He included in its first year translations from Kielland, Hansson, Garborg and an abridged version of Hamsun's **Sult** (Hunger). There was so much good will towards modern Scandinavian writers in Germany at the time, that Ola Hansson, who had settled in Berlin and was considered an expert on modern literature, could with the aid of the journals **Die freie Bühne** and **Die Zukunft** raise the money for Strindberg to travel to Berlin and receive a maintenance allowance. Strindberg arrived in September 1892. When Munch's exhibition caused an uproar in the Berlin art world two months later, he was soon adopted by the literary avant garde.

In the absence of the usual outlets for modern art, writers tried to foster it. There were no journals specifically for modern art in Berlin in the early 1890s. When Walter Leistikow wanted to publish an article on "Die Affaire Munch", he did so in December 1892 in **Die freie Bühne**. In 1894, under its new name **Die neue Rundschau**, the journal again published an article on Munch, this time by Stanislaw Przybyszewski. **Die Zukunft**, another literary journal, published a mildly sympathetic review of Munch's exhibition by Ola Hansson in May 1893 and Munch painted a portrait of the editor's wife, Frau Maximilian Harden, in 1894. Like Julius Elias, the editors of these journals were liberal and interested in fin-de-siècle Scandinavian Modernism. In a letter home on 26 November 1892, Munch mentioned that he had visited Julius Elias a few times, and Elias in December 1892 bought Munch's painting **Bal** (The Dance).

The literary critic who may have had most significance for Munch's development in Berlin was Ola Hansson (1860–1925). He befriended Munch, even invited him to spend New Year's Eve with him and his wife, but Munch could not go on account of illness.[15] Hansson had written articles about many modern writers in France, Scandinavia and Russia and also about some painters. In 1887 he discussed the French symbolists in his essay in **Framåt** on Huysman's **L'Art moderne** and other work; **Die freie Bühne** in 1890 included it in the series of Hansson's essays on "Das junge Frankreich". In 1892 Hansson published an essay on Klinger, in 1893 two articles on Böcklin.[16] His wife, Laura Marholm, translated his work from Swedish into German and the essays provided many German writers with an introduction to Modernist literature abroad as well as to Nietzsche at home. Nietzsche's publisher Fritzsch actually reprinted Hansson's two articles on the philosopher as a brochure in 1890. Hansson was also known for his short stories in the collections **Sensitiva amorosa** (German edition: **Sensitiva amorosa**. Neue Herzensprobleme, Berlin 1892) and **Tidens kvinnor** (German edition: **Alltagsfrauen**. Ein Stück moderner Liebesphysiologie, Berlin 1891). Under Hansson's influence, Max Dauthendey and Stanislaw Przybyszewski pursued an interest in expressing "psycho-physiological" and intimate revelations in art, which they were to apply to Munch when they published their Modernist aesthetic theories.

Several writers at the time thought that they were better equipped to explain the new art than art historians or critics who were specialists. They believed that it was primarily a question of interpreting the psyche and that it needed an understanding of the creative process, not accumulated knowledge. Franz Servaes, when defending Bierbaum's art criticism from the detraction of a professional, maintained that the temperament of the young artists was in greater need of explanation than their technique. In his estimation the aims of research and of creative art were different. Excessive deference to scholarly definitions should not in an age of art for art's sake prevent a creative writer from interpreting "die Malerpsyche aus seiner Poetenpsyche heraus mit eigenen Worten und unmittelbar" ("the painter's psyche from within the poet's psyche with his own words and literally").[17]

The value of the subjective art criticism published on Munch by Modernist writers is debatable. On the one hand they gave him publicity, but on the other his fame was established on a literary basis, and writers were responsible for starting a myth about him and his art. Modernist writers who were interested in the psyche made little attempt to be objective in their assessments of Munch. They often involved themselves with the emotional content of his pictures and felt at liberty to interpret the images of his fantasy in their own idiom. The more the official press rejected him, the more stridently the writers close to him tried to promote him and sell his pictures on their own terms, emphasizing their own interest in the psyche. Writers out of sympathy with the art favoured by the authorities made much of Munch's radical challenge to the art world. They generally compared him with writers whom they themselves admired, for example Nietzsche, Ola Hansson, Dehmel and the French Decadents. In this way, Munch's art became identified with literary preoccupations.

Munch met some of the many writers who were to publish articles on him in Strindberg's favourite wine bar "Zum schwarzen Ferkel". It was at the corner of the Neue Wilhelmstrasse and Unter den Linden. A blackened sheepskin was suspended over the entrance. Strindberg had dismissed the original name "Das Kloster" deriving from its Gothic windows, for the less sanctified "Zum schwarzen Ferkel". The proprietor allowed the author the liberty of transforming his sheep into a piglet. The thought of a black creature may have evoked associations with the **Chat Noir** in Paris which had a similar Gothic interior. The Berlin wine bar became a meeting place for people interested in modern literature, but was also a centre for bohemianism and drunkenness.[18] Gunnar Heiberg, who had known Munch in Norway in the 1880s, introduced him to the circle which gathered there.

The first painting which Munch did in Berlin was a portrait of Strindberg (fig.1). Among the other writers whom he could meet in "Zum schwarzen Ferkel" were the Pole Przybyszewski, the Germans Richard Dehmel, Julius Meier-Graefe, Paul Scheerbart and Peter Hille, the Swede Adolf Paul and the Dane Holger Drachmann. Apart from Strindberg, those closest to Munch were Przybyszewski (1868–1927) and Meier-Graefe (figs.2,3). Przybyszewski was a medical student who took a special interest in neurology and was attracted to the occult, liking to think of himself as a Satanist. He had published articles on Nietzsche, Chopin and Ola Hansson which were printed together as a book in 1892 with the title **Zur Psychologie des Individuums** (Concerning the Psychology of the Individual). Przybyszewski also edited the Polish workers' gazette, **Gazeta Robotnicza**. His series of literary works could, according to Julius Meier-Graefe's article on him in **Die Gesellschaft** (3–4, 1895, p.1040), have borne the subtitle "Naturgeschichte einer Menschheit unter dem Reich Nietzsches" ("Natural history of a people during Nietzsche's empire").

Julius Meier-Graefe was another student, who had come to Berlin in 1890 to study engineering. He started writing there and in 1893 published a first person narrative about a cruise up the Norwegian coast to the North Cape to see the midnight sun. According to the critic Franz Servaes, Meier-Graefe brought him this first novel, saying that he wanted to establish a literary position in Berlin.[19] Servaes in 1896 described Meier-Graefe as a young man of means with good connections and completely cosmopolitan bearing who was not a bad writer and had a happy, childlike sense of humour and unlimited enthusiasm. Servaes thought that Meier-Graefe had two failings: he treated literature and art a little like sport, and he deliberately made compromises from business considerations.[20] In his article on Przybyszewski in **Die Gesellschaft**, Meier-Graefe showed that he was impressed by Nietzsche and Dostoevsky, and that he approved of Przybyszewski's display of masks and of some "künstlichen Alkoholismus" ("artistic alcoholism").

Fig. 1. **August Strindberg** *1892, oil, National Museum, Stockholm*

A reaction to the current aristocratic paternalism in society and the arts was a defence of the individual, for which Nietzsche was a spokesman. Echoing Nietzsche, Munch's literary friends in Berlin cultivated the ideal of an intellectual aristocracy. Morality in the Jewish-Christian tradition had succeeded in setting the last slaves free in the nineteenth century, but Nietzsche had scorned it as the morality of slaves,

"Sklaven-Moral" (**Zur Geneologie der Moral**, chapter I, p.10). He used the word "slave" repeatedly, evidently giving no thought to the bestial commercial exploitation of human beings that slavery involved. Nietzsche had corresponded with Strindberg for six weeks in the winter of 1888–89 and had sent him copies of **Zur Genealogie der Moral** and **Götzendämmerung**. Nietzsche was admired by Strindberg and by other Modernist writers in Berlin who rated psychology and individual intuition higher than aesthetics or morality.

In their curiosity about unconscious layers of perception, the writers and artists influenced by Nietzsche came at times perilously close to losing their sense of the value of life. Wishing to impress others by their knowledge, they played with the illusion that people were an arena of conflicting powers, without any hope of stability. Strindberg and Munch had memories of extreme suffering but also searched their memories for

Fig.2. **Przybyszewski**, *1893–5, pastel, OKK M 134, Munch Museum, Oslo.*

Fig. 3. **Julius Meier-Graefe**, *c.1895, oil, National Gallery, Oslo.*

past happiness.[21] While brooding mainly on feelings of pain, loss and injustice, they used private experience to create a polemical art. They were at first more interested in expressing the daemonic than in healing, and not surprisingly, suffered from mental illness at some time or other. Strindberg, Munch and Przybyszewski in the course of the 1890s expressed notions of a dramatic struggle between evil and goodness, darkness and light which was a version of the ancient Manichean heresy. Although they had had a religious upbringing, their vanity and fondness for intellectual athletics gave them no peace of mind. Some of the work of the group "Zum schwarzen Ferkel" was callous and petty in its striving for effect. For example, in Strindberg's play **Fordringsägare** (The Creditors), which was performed in Berlin in January 1893, a man tells his ex-wife: "du har ingen själ för resten, det är bara en synvilla!" ("Anyhow, you have no soul. It's merely an illusion").[22] Przybyszewski in his articles and book on Vigeland wrote: "denn das Normale, das ist die Dummheit, und die 'Degeneration', das ist das Genie" ("For that which is normal is stupidity, and 'degeneration' is genius").[23]

Nietzsche influenced the group "Zum schwarzen Ferkel" particularly in the assumption that frenzy ("Rausch") was the physiological precondition of art.[24] Przybyszewski in his book on Nietzsche and Chopin demanded that art should not only spring from frenzy but also produce it.[25] When Przybyszewski played Chopin's music on a piano in the wine bar, he was accordingly technically inaccurate. His Polish friend Wysocki remembered that Przybyszewski at the piano whispered, prayed, murmured poetry to himself.[26] With a face expressing an agonized cramp, his fingers hit the keys with indescribable fury. The effect upon his audience was, according to Franz Servaes, "dass alle wie elektrisiert waren. Einige schrieen, andere warfen sich auf die Knie, manche liefen, wie von einem höheren Geist (oder einer höheren Narrheit) gepackt, in der Stube herum" ("that everyone was as if they had been electrified. Some screamed, others cast themselves onto their knees, some ran around the room as if seized by a higher spirit (or a higher folly)").[27] Munch, too, was impressed by Przybyszewski's rendering of Chopin and later wrote about it with uncharacteristic effusion.[28]

The appeal to frenzy encouraged creative licence to destroy not only art as it had been up to then but also people. Writers influenced by Nietzsche showed no less contempt for others than the ruling authorities in Berlin. There was apparently cruelty in the way Strindberg and Przybyszewski treated their wives. Strindberg blatantly exploited Ola Hansson and Laura Marholm. The wish to be different at all costs led to occasional pleasure in obscenities, blasphemy and brutality in manifestations of disease and unhappiness, for example in Przybyszewski's first-person narrative about the breakdown of a neurotic person, **Totenmesse** (Requiem Mass, 1893). There was an element of competition in demonstrating cases of psychological disturbance.

When Munch had associated with Hans Jæger's circle in the 1880s, he had encountered similar attitudes and the interest in psychology. He had begun to write fragments about his own life, which correspond with scenes in the pictures he produced in the 1890s. In Berlin he continued his literary activities and curiosity about psychology. The writers with whom he associated appear to have encouraged him to project mental frenzy and anguish which led to the series of paintings he developed in the 1890s, and in 1918 called **Livsfrisen** (The Frieze of Life). In a letter to the Danish painter and critic Johan Rohde at the end of March 1893 from Berlin, he made his first reference to his work in grouping studies into the series of pictures. Munch wrote that the series would be concerned with love and death and that several of his earlier pictures belonged to it, for example the man and woman on the beach, the red sky and the picture with the swan. He continued his letter:

> Så skit som kunsten i sin almindelighed står her i Tyskland – vil jeg dog sie en ting –den har den fordel hernede at den har frembragt enkelte kunstnere der rager så høit over alle andre og som står så alene – f. ex Böcklin som jeg næsten synes står over alle nutidens malere – Max Klinger – Thomas [sic] – Wagner blandt

musikerne – Nietsche [sic] blandt filosoferne Frankrige har en kunst der står over den tydske men ikke større kunstnere end de nævnte –

As bad as art in general is here in Germany, I want to say one thing: it has the advantage of having produced some artists who so surpass all the others and who are so alone – for example Böcklin – whom I almost rank above all contemporary painters – Max Klinger – Thomas [sic] – Wagner among the musicians – Nietsche [sic] among the philosophers. France has an art that ranks above the German, but no greater artists than those mentioned.[29]

Munch in 1893 therefore found Germany as stimulating as France. The names he mentioned were all favourites of his Berlin friends and the "artists" selected for praise in his letter show that he was attracted to philosophy and music as well as art.

In December 1893 Munch opened a new exhibition in Berlin. It was radically different from the exhibition which had caused the uproar a year earlier and showed a new focus on psychological distress. It included six paintings as a series on the theme of love, ending with **The Scream**. The exhibition again reaped a storm of abuse in the press. Some critics thought that Munch's art had gone from bad to worse, and that he must be ill. The Norwegian newspaper **Morgenbladet** reported on 7 December 1892 that a German newspaper had asked whether Munch, in contrast to other painters, painted with his feet instead of with his hands. The correspondent thought that Munch had never before painted in such a bizarre way, and found it sad to see a few pictures, especially portraits, which showed that he really had talent. The correspondent wrote that the large painting **Døden i sykeværelset** (Death in the Sick Room) faced the spectator as he entered, and he described **Ved dødssengen** (At the death bed), **Rose og Amelie** and **Skrik** (The Scream). He thought that people left the exhibition feeling sickened and that a few Berliners offered 50 Pfennig instead of the one Mark entry price, taking a quick look before leaving.

The new sombre and shocking pictures in Munch's exhibition were in part a reflection on his new friends. Apart from the images of death and disease, Munch now showed the picture of two ugly prostitutes which he first exhibited with the title **Interieur** and later as **Rose og Amelie**. In 1893–94 he developed more explicitly erotic images than before, showing reflections on stages of love and how they affect the psyche. There are parallels in the stories by Ola Hansson and Przybyszewski, as well as in the poems by Dehmel and the plays by Strindberg and Heiberg which were all receiving publicity at the time. In 1893–94 Munch painted versions of **Stemmen** (The Voice), **Piken og døden** (The Girl and Death), **Madonna, Vampyr, Løsrivelse** (Separation), **Pubertet, Rose og Amelie, Hendene** (The Hands), **Kvinnen i tre stadier** (The Woman in Three Stages). The catalyst for the display of eroticism appears to have been the writers in the group "Zum schwarzen Ferkel" and they were among the few to appreciate the change at the time. Przybyszewski wrote a highly enthusiastic review of the "Liebe" series and published it with the title "Psychischer Naturalismus" in **Die neue Rundschau** in February 1894. A few months later that year, he published in Berlin the first book on Munch, **Das Werke des Edvard Munch**, in which he reprinted his article and added contributions by Willy Pastor, Franz Servaes and Julius Meier-Graefe. Przybyszewski interpreted Munch's series as a daemonic, instinctive revelation of the unconscious mind. Meier-Graefe, who was persuaded by Przybyszewski to write an article for the book, described the paintings

Puberty, The Hands and **The Girl and Death**. He praised Munch for his psychology and for his instinctive reaction to women, not concealing his hatred. Meier-Graefe contrasted the coy mysticism in von Hofmann's pictures with the frankness in Munch's images, preferring the latter because they gave the mind something to think about.

When Meier-Graefe and Przybyszewski wrote about Munch's pictures in 1894, they overlooked the less sensational images. A glance at Munch's earlier portraits of women and girls could have shown them that he was not a misogynist when he came to Berlin. Apart from the conventional poses of women peering out of a window or combing their hair, Munch had exhibited sympathetic portraits of his sisters, as in **Inger on the Shore** (fig.4). Przybyszewski applied his own terms to Munch's new pictures and referred to the images of women as a vampire or madonna, although Munch had given more general titles. The painting exhibited in 1893–94 as "Liebe und Schmerz" (Love and Pain) thus became known as "Vampyr" after the publication of Przybyszewski's article (fig.5). Munch later regretted this poetic licence. As an older man, he was weary of hearing that his paintings were literary and blamed such interpretations on the climate of ideas in the 1890s. When he was asked why he had called the painting "Vampire", he replied that he had not intended it to be literary, it was only of a woman kissing a man on the back of the neck. He explained "men det var i Ibsentiden – og når folk endelig ville gasse seg i symbolsk uhygge og kalte idyllen for Vampyr, så hvorfor ikke"? ("it was in the time of Ibsen – and if people were really bent on revelling in symbolist eeriness and called the idyll 'vampire', why not?")[30]

However much Munch may later have distanced himself from literary aspirations, he became identified with his friends' form of Modernism and developed it as part of his self-image. The writers who lionized him and promoted his psychological studies were influenced by Nietzsche and inspired by Dostoevsky, and they cast him into a mould as an anarchist and exponent of Nordic anxiety and brooding. Przybyszewski and Meier-Graefe both loved Dostoevsky's novels and Meier-Graefe even wrote a book on him, **Dostojewski der Dichter** (Dostoevsky the writer) in 1926. Meier-Graefe later remembered that Munch's supporters had wondered whether the role of Dostoevsky could be repeated in the visual arts.[31] He and Przybyszewski praised Munch for expressing what they believed to be important areas of human awareness, and Munch appears to have approved of their articles. He published an extract from Przybyszewski's essay at the back of the catalogue of his exhibition at Stockholm in 1894, and said in the winter of 1908–9 that he thought that Meier-Graefe had written with more understanding about him than anyone else.[32] This remark was made when Munch was in a psychiatric clinic in Copenhagen. Meier-Graefe had actually written relatively little about the pictures. At first he had published essays on Munch in **Das Werk des Edvard Munch** in 1894 and in the Munch print portfolio known as "Die Meier-Graefe Mappe" in 1895. Kenworth Moffett wrote that "in both these two first critical efforts there is a highly literary approach and little concern with the works of art themselves" (**Meier-Graefe as art critic**, Munich, 1973, p.10). For the portfolio Meier-Graefe deliberately chose eight prints which he considered representational, not fantasy pictures, including **The Sick Child, Moonlight, The Lonely Ones, Christiania Bohême I** (figs.6–8). In view of these reflective, unassertive pictures, it was simply dishonest of Meier-Graefe in his introduction to project Munch as an abrasive artist: "er sucht Feindschaft" ("he seeks strife", p.18). In **Christiania Bohême I** Munch portrayed himself sitting on the left, smoking and watching the men in conversation opposite him. Nearest to himself, he placed a water carafe. While he indicated a distance between people, neither this

Fig. 4. Inger on the Shore, *1889, oil, Rasmus Meyer Collection, Bergen.*

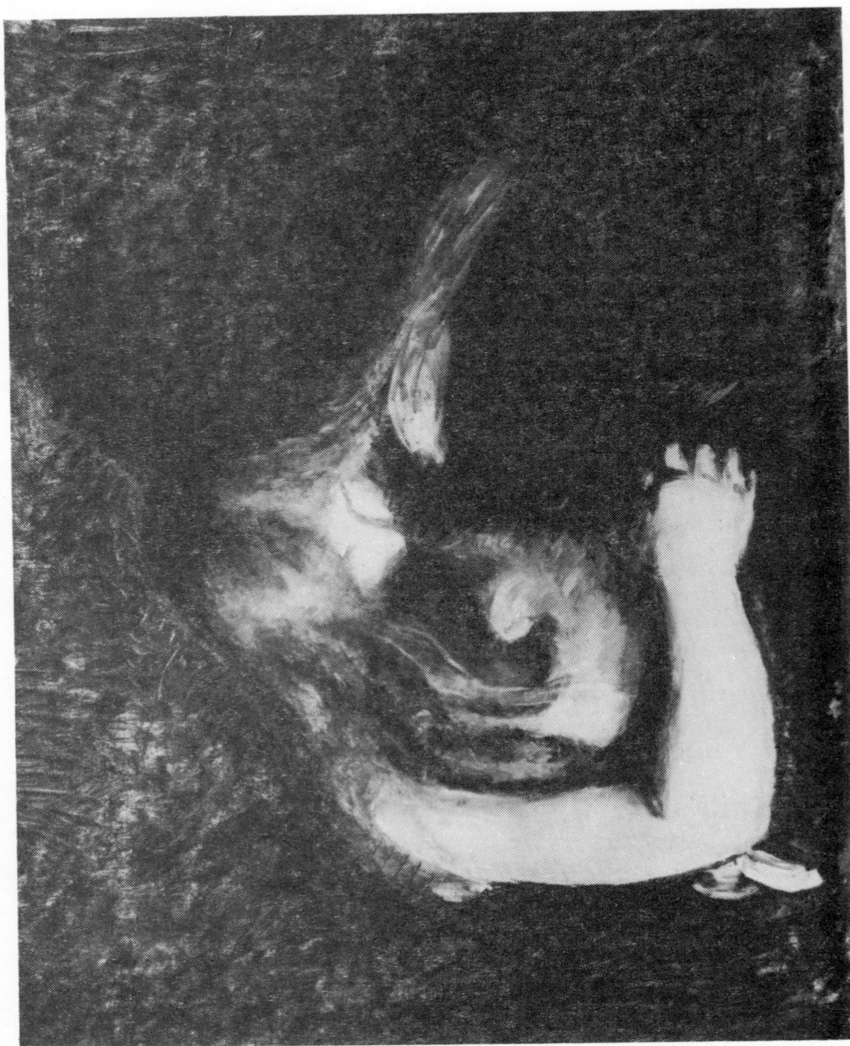

Fig.5. Vampire, *1893, oil, Konstmuseum, Göteborg.*

print nor any of the others in the collection can fairly be described as polemical. It seems that Meier-Graefe wanted to manipulate Munch into a figure who would shock. His concern was not for quality but for sensation. When Meier-Graefe was in Paris and hoped to sell some of Munch's pictures at Bing's gallery **L'Art nouveau**, he asked Munch in a letter on 12 December 1895 to send something like **The Scream**: "starke Sachen" ("strong stuff").[33]

Fig.6. **The Sick Child**, *1894, drypoint, OKK G/r 7, Munch Museum, Óslo.*

Munch's pictures changed after he met Hansson, Strindberg, Przybyszewski, Meier-Graefe, and from the 1890s on, there were critics who thought that his association with literature in Berlin was detrimental for his artistic development. The critics included Andreas Aubert in Norway and Thadée Natanson in Paris in the 1890s.[34] Even a contemporary writer, Arthur Holitscher, expressed his doubts as to the merit of Munch's reception by the literary Modernists. He wrote in **Die Zeit** (207, 17 September 1898, p.186) that he believed that Meier-Graefe, Przybyszewski, Pastor and others had done Munch and his art a disservice while he was in Berlin by praising him as a herald of a new cult: "sie fassten ihren Enthusiasmus mit beiden Fäusten und stiessen mit ihm das Publikum vor dem Kopf" ("They seized their enthusiasm with both fists and rammed him at the public's head"). Although Munch's art had improved

Fig. 7. **Moonlight**, *1895, drypoint and aquatint, OKK G/r 12, Munch Museum, Oslo*

Fig.8. Christiania Bohème I, *1895, etching and drypoint, OKK G/r 9, Munch Museum, Oslo.*

Fig.9 Arrival of the Mailboat, *1890, oil, Private Collection.*

greatly, according to Holitscher, people in 1898 no longer took any notice of him.

Interestingly, Meier-Graefe was to repeat his procedure of creating a legend about an artist and linking him with Dostoevsky. The art historian A.M. Hammacher writing on "Vincent and the Words" in J.B. de la Faille's standard volume on **The Works of Vincent van Gogh** (Amsterdam, 1970) thought that Meier-Graefe had done van Gogh's art a disservice in his novel on the painter, **Vincent**, published in 1921: "his (van Gogh's) works were now unrestrainedly associated with the melodrama of the torn, toiling, suffering artist". For Meier-Graefe, the words van Gogh wrote in his letters were more attractive than the pictures:

> when he (Meier-Graefe) sees the paintings as a substitute [Ersatz] for the words, we have arrived at a nadir of deadly solemn but false 'ethical-literary' appreciation ..... Fauvism in France – no less in debt to Van Gogh for its inspiration – did not experience a similar blending of literary and pictorial values nor did it whisk Van Gogh up, as German expressionism had done, into such a maelstrom of ecstasy and inner laceration (p.21).

Many of the Germans who were attracted to Munch's pictures were interested in spiritualism and Nietzsche, and they chose to ignore his more serene paintings. When there is stress on Munch's links with the **avant garde**, it is still usual to concentrate on his images of heightened emotions, and to pay little or no attention to his less dramatic work. This trend has gone so far that a myth has developed about Munch, and one recent book on his graphic art states that he "once accidentally killed a man in a brawl",[35] which is quite untrue. His art thus tends to be associated primarily with aggression and bad nerves, but this is not representative of his life and work as a whole. In 1892 he had brought to Berlin scenes of Norwegian life which showed no neurosis, for example the paintings **Inger on the Shore** or **'Jarlsberg' kommer (Fra Åsgårdstrand)** which was called in the catalogue **Der Dampfschiff kommt** (The Arrival of the Steamer) (see figs.4 and 9). He continued to create not only a series of pictures illustrating people's attitudes to living and dying, but also more direct images of nature, as in his landscapes and pictures of workers, of children, of women washing or bathing. It may have been with relief that he sometimes withdrew from the intellectual circles in the cities, and his work often showed a disillusionment with bohemianism. He liked to spend the summers in the resort and fishing village of Åsgårdstrand, where he found in the landscape and local people material for some of his most characteristic pictures, for example **Pikene på bryggen** (The girls on the jetty, 1899). It seems significant that he admitted to Albert Kollmann in a letter in 1904 that he felt well in Åsgårdstrand, ill in Berlin.[36] His images of good health, as of people swimming and sunbathing, received less critical attention than his images of figures who appear ill at ease in their environment. It is difficult to reconcile the peaceful and lyrical pictures which he had created from the beginning of his career with the myth about him which began as a result of his exhibitions and literary reception in the 1890s. His art of course affirmed a wide range of human experience, deprivation as well as fulfilment. Could it be a predilection for violence and sensation in the critic that places more value on Munch's images of distress than on those of survival and tranquillity?

Munch had to live with the myth and partly adopted it. He counted Dostoevsky among his favourite writers and was prone to mull over his own psyche. After his death in 1944, his letters and a large body of literary fragments were left together with his pictures to the city of Oslo, and he wrote in his will that it should be left to the discretion of the experts to decide to what extent they were to be published.[37] The words in his literary fragments have aroused considerable interest and, as in the case of van Gogh, some people choose to give them priority over the pictures. It would appear that Peter Watkins based a film about Munch on the unpublished notes, using a limited number of pictures as illustrations for words. Watkins ignored a substantial section of Munch's oeuvre including the last thirty-four years of his career which did not fit the image of the tortured artist. The fact that Munch became extremely successful and owned several properties was suppressed and the film made at least one viewer inquire whether the artist had ended his days in the psychiatric clinic.[38] Those who seek to popularize Munch's life like to dwell on the images of anguish which he created mainly as a result of his close association with Modernist writers from Hans Jæger onwards.[39] He however freely changed his style and his pictures can be appreciated without reference to the Munch myth.

Munch's breakthrough as a printmaker

Munch may have formulated his ideas on aesthetics and had nearly a decade of exhibition experience behind him when he came to Berlin, but one thing he had never done was to make a print. Several factors can have led him to learn graphic techniques in 1893–95. It appears that Norwegian students could not learn printing techniques at home in the 1890s. When Munch's later fiancée, Tulla Larsen, wanted to learn etching, she went to do so in Berlin.[40] It is not certain who taught Munch, but it may well have been Karl Köpping, the speaker who led the eighty or so members out of the meeting of the **Verein Berliner Künstler** which voted to close Munch's exhibition. Karl Köpping was director of the master studio for etching and engraving at the Berlin Art Academy and had an international reputation as an expert in graphic art. He supported the modern style in the applied arts, making delicate vases as well as original prints and reproductions of other painters. According to **The Studio**'s special summer number on "Modern Etching and Engraving" in 1902, "Köpping's etchings of Rembrandt, Frans Hals and Munckacsy have gained him world-wide fame. There is nothing to equal it" (p.1). Köpping taught among others Joh. Nordhagen, a well-known Norwegian etcher. As leader of the oppositional group in the **Verein Berliner Künstler**, and chairman of the "Freie Verein Berliner Künstler", Köpping was clearly sympathetic to new art.

Making prints is of course a slow, intricate procedure, and Munch needed instruction in the use of his tools, in the preparation of plates, the application of wax grounds and aquatints for etching, the different chemical solutions for different metals and qualities of line, as well as the calculation of the length of time required for the plate to be submersed in acid or mordant to produce the design he had in mind. In the case of drypoints, a line once made by an incision into a plate cannot easily be erased. The technicalities of printing obviously require patience and attention to detail and the end-product is known to be the greatest test of draughtsmanship. It was a recognition that Munch was beginning to master these skills which first earned him respect from people who appreciated fine art. As early as December 1894 Eberhard von Bodenhausen, who was chairman of the supervisory board of the elegant magazine **Pan**, wrote to Munch: "es scheint mir geradezu als ob die Radierung Ihr eigentliches Gebiet sei" ("It really seems to me as if etching is your primary domain").[41] When Munch in March 1895 exhibited his first prints, the critic Jaro Springer wrote in **Die Kunst für Alle**: "er bemüht sich hier um eine künstlerische Technik, und durch die Radierung wird Munch vielleicht wieder für die wirkliche Kunst zurückgewonnen" ("he here applies himself to an artistic technique, and perhaps through etching Munch will be won back for genuine art").[42]

Jaro Springer worked in the print room of Berlin's Altes Museum. He was a critic for the Munich based art journal **Die Kunst für Alle**, sometimes using the pseudonym "Dr Relling", and he there repeatedly chided the **Verein Berliner Künstler** for rejecting Munch's art. Munch's friend the art historian Jens Thiis was in Berlin in the winter of 1892–93 and 1894–95 and became an associate of Springer's when they

Fig. 10. **Dr Seidel**, *1895, drypoint, OKK G/r 42, Munch Museum, Oslo.*

studied in the museum print room, the "Kupferstichkabinett". They used to meet over a drink with fellow art historians and discuss questions of art, not least the Munch affair. There was an early appreciation of Munch's prints in this section of Berlin's museum. One of the art historians who associated with Thiis and Springer was Max Friedländer, who later became director of the Kupferstichkabinett and, as Thiis rightly observed, built up one of the best collections of Munch's prints in the world.[43] A later assistant of the Museum's print room, Curt Glaser, was the first to write a comprehensive biography of Munch in 1917.

Munch spent most of his time in Germany in 1894–95 doing portraits and graphic art. He began printmaking with drypoints on copperplates, for example the portrait of the surgeon Dr Hermann Seidel, father of the novelist Ina Seidel, whose home in

Fig.11. **The Berlin Tiergarten**, *1896, drypoint and aquatint, OKK G/r 42, Munch Museum, Oslo.*

Brunswick he visited (fig.10).[44] Munch had always been good at doing portraits and appears to have found little difficulty in making incisions in the copper where he wanted them. He sometimes sketched a view directly onto the metal, but in the case of portraits also used preliminary sketches and sometimes photographs. He appears to have approached printing processes with ease, confidence and pleasure. He sometimes took his plates to professional printers, but he also did some of his own printing.

Munch enjoyed the drypoint technique so much that he would carry a copperplate and burin with him in his pocket. If something caught his eye, he could stop and do an outline of his impression there and then. The drypoint and aquatint **Berlin Tiergarten** may have arisen in this way (fig.11). The white areas in this etching of the three women in the park were varnished before the powdered resin was applied for the aquatint, and the darkest lines were made by the drypoint burin. They show that Munch worked out a design from the interplay of light and shade. The print does not convey a social or psychological message, but an impression of transience and shifting light. It is understandable from delicate prints like this one and the portraits, that art lovers approved of Munch's etchings, not only because of the craftmanship, but also because of the mood they were able to convey.

Some of Munch's earlier paintings provided him with compositions for prints, and he liked to make parallel versions in different media, for example in **Moonlight** or **The Lonely Ones**. Jens Thiis observed that the prints were a natural transition from

Munch's "blue" paintings and inclination for monochrome in the early 1890s, as in **Night (Moonlight)** and the **Self-portrait with a cigarette**, both in the Oslo National Gallery.[45] The paintings influenced the prints and vice versa. Munch sometimes produced a hatchwork effect in his use of paint, or bold outlines and silhouettes. He also superimposed certain features in his composition, for example a line of trees in one colour over another line of trees, which enables the viewer to look through the tracery of the branches, and makes a decorative effect. The fact that Munch enjoyed making prints as well as painting pictures is overwhelmingly obvious from his vast and varied production. Elizabeth Prellinger in her catalogue **Edvard Munch, Master Printmaker** (New York, London, 1983, p.4) writes: "while the events of a sad life provided the material for Munch's often gloomy imagery, nevertheless shining through his graphic work is an undiluted joy in experimentation and creation . . . It is Munch the passionate technician who emerges in these remarkable works of art". Munch became a master printmaker particularly in his time in Paris 1896–98, where he learnt to do woodcuts and colour printing. Arne Eggum, the leading expert on Munch's art, observes that Munch crystallized much of the central imagery from his memories in his prints and that the strict but different requirements of each graphic medium he used may have gradually freed him from his previous themes.[46]

Munch's friends in Berlin could share his interest in printmaking as well as in the projection of individual feelings. They admired other painter-etchers, like Max Klinger and Félicien Rops. Ola Hansson had a print **Verführung** (Seduction) from Klinger's series of etchings **Ein Leben** on his wall at home. Klinger had been a close student friend of Munch's former teacher Christian Krohg and was one of the artists whom Munch praised in his letter to Johan Rohde in March 1893. Meanwhile, some of the artists Munch met in Berlin made prints and probably also encouraged him in his own work. The Germans included Walter Leistikow, Max Liebermann and Fidus (the pseudonym for Hugo Höppener). Leistikow taught at the Berlin Kunstschule 1890–93 and tried all the graphic arts: engraving, woodcuts, lithographs, designs for wallpaper. His stylized art may have appealed to Munch. In March 1895 Munch exhibited jointly with Axel Gallen-Kalléla who was also new to printmaking, which he learnt in Berlin. Berlin may not have been a promising place for modern painters, but modern printmakers did find appreciation for their work. The many writers and publishers in Berlin made it a good centre for book illustration and it was partly in this way that the Jugendstil could find an outlet.

The recognition of a need for a new inter-arts magazine, **Pan**, came predominantly from the leaders of modern literature in Berlin. The magazine became, according to the art historian Philippe Jullian, the most splendid and interesting review of the period.[47] Otto Julius Bierbaum, who had edited **Die freie Bühne** for six months in 1893–94 and had produced three volumes of modern poetry **(Moderne Dichteralmanacke)**, wanted to expand **Die freie Bühne** into an illustrated journal, a sample of modern book design. To attract subscribers to pay for illustrations for the new venture, he and his co-editors had to invite the support of museum directors and art collectors. The aim was to bring the new movement to the attention of people who wanted to promote German national art. Aristocrats, museum directors, collectors and historians joined the list of subscribers, perhaps believing that beautiful book design was inherently part of a German tradition.

The idea for **Pan** was discussed first in the home of Stanislaw and Dagny Przybyszewski in about February to March 1894, when Przybyszewski also organized the monograph on Munch, **Das Werk des Edvard Munch.** Dagny chose the name Pan.[48] The realization of the project was due to the industry and co-operation of their friends. Apart from Bierbaum and Meier-Graefe, the founders were Richard Dehmel and Eberhard von Bodenhausen. They were joined by Hartleben, Scheerbart and von Hofmann. At the first official meeting on 1 May 1894, Bierbaum and Meier-Graefe were elected editors and business executives by the advisory board. When Böcklin, who was made honorary president of **Pan**, visited Berlin that summer, there was a banquet in his honour. The aim of the first editors was to represent literature and art equally. **Pan** published the work of the artists and writers who had supported Munch in the conflict over his first exhibition in Berlin; it was therefore a further step in the direction of tolerance for artistic innovation.

The first editors of **Pan** actually tried to do too much at once and were responsible for only the first three issues, as they were dismissed in September 1895. Their financial mismanagement and Meier-Graefe's purchase of Lautrec's colour lithograph **Mademoiselle Marcelle Lender** without due consultation of the editorial committee, gave the art historians and artists on the supervisory board the opportunity to take over the magazine and make it a publication more specifically for art than literature. Under different management, **Pan** continued to be a very fine but mainly German Jugendstil publication. Hans Hofstätter in his **Geschichte der europäischen Jugendstilmalerei** (Köln: Du Mont Schauberg, 1969, p.176) writes that the journals **Pan** and its successor **Die Insel** encouraged the development of art produced for books and that the circles attached to these publications actually drew many artists away from Munich to Berlin. Przybyszewski and his friends continued to make contributions, but the vigour and variety of the early days was reduced. German book art could flourish in **Pan**, but several of the group which had met in "Zum schwarzen Ferkel" left Berlin for Paris, where their Modernism could thrive in greater freedom.

The first editors had hoped to help Munch sell prints through **Pan**, and he did contribute a drypoint portrait of Knut Hamsun to the first issue in 1896. Munch must have been stimulated by the wide range of modern printmaking presented by the magazine, for example by Vallotton's woodcut of Robert Schumann in **Pan, I.** His intaglio prints were different from the fine line work of Liebermann, Leistikow or Klinger, although there is a similarity between some of his and Liebermann's drypoint portraits. In 1894 he began to do lithographs in Berlin and this gave him the chance to explore a very expressive medium in which he could reduce the images of his paintings more freely and starkly than in his etchings or drypoints.

Munch's etchings in the Meier-Graefe portfolio, published in June 1895, were for sale in the **Pan** offices in Berlin and Paris, where there were also programmes for the Théâtre de l'Oeuvre, etchings by Klinger and Thoma, posters by Toulouse-Lautrec and Vallotton. Although sales of the "Meier-Graefe Mappe" were not high, one of Munch's influential patrons at the turn of the century, the businessman Albert Kollmann, is said to have been attracted to Munch's prints for the first time through seeing this portfolio.[49] Kollmann was a German art lover who advised collectors, dealers and museum directors as to what they should buy. He brought Munch's prints to the occulist Dr Max Linde who had a large collection of modern art and of Rodin's sculptures. In Berlin in 1902 Kollmann introduced Munch to Linde who bought a complete set of Munch's prints and the painting **Fertility**. Linde arranged for Munch to do a series of prints of his family, house and garden in November 1902. According to Linde, it was with Kollmann's intellectual co-operation and in the stimulating company of Munch that he produced a book, **Edvard Munch und die Kunst der Zukunft** (Edvard Munch and

Fig. 12. **Self-portrait**, *1895, lithograph, OKK G/1 192, Munch Museum, Oslo.*

the art of the future) which was published in Berlin in 1902.

Linde's idea of modern art implied a complete break with the classical ideal. In this he confirmed the ideas of Munch's first German friends like Paul Scheerbart, who had no time for Greek humanism. Linde praised Munch's prints in particular and wrote that people who found the paintings incomprehensible would be convinced of Munch's lasting significance as an artist by looking at his woodcuts. Contrasting the modern age with that of antiquity, Linde stated that Christianity had raised ethical standards, made people more sensitive to each other and compassionate to the weak. To Linde modern art seemed broader and richer than that of antiquity because it did not avoid ugliness in human nature. He wrote that Munch in his way of interpreting people's souls and emotions had only one parallel, namely Rodin. The subject matter of both artists aroused people's empathy and compassion.

By showing Munch's prints to collectors, Kollmann gradually fostered greater sympathy for Munch in the German art world. In 1902 Kollmann also showed Munch's prints to the county court judge Gustav Schiefler who was very knowledgeable about modern graphic art and who was to compile a catalogue of most of Munch's prints between 1894 and 1926. Kollmann brought Munch's etchings with him in 1902 when Schiefler went to Linde's house to see their collection of Impressionist art. Schiefler later remembered that he at once found Munch's prints exceptional in the powerful expression of inner experiences and in the handling of the material.[50]

In 1902 Munch was invited to show his paintings of love and death with the Berlin Secession, and this marked a turning-point in his career as a painter. In 1903 he exhibited his prints with the Secession and in that year the Berlin Museum's Print Room acquired its first two lithographs: the self-portrait of 1895 (fig.12) and the lithograph of **Madonna** (1902) which had the lower half of the image cut off where there is a foetus in the border. Therefore in little over a decade after his first rude rejection by the Berlin art establishment, Munch's pictures were being acquired for the Museum's collection. It is worth noting that it was his prints rather than his paintings which first met with official approval. Meier-Graefe through the print portfolio, Jaro Springer in **Die Kunst für Alle**, Linde and Schiefler in their books, the first lithographs in the Berlin Museum's Print Room, all point to an early conviction that the strength of Munch's art in the 1890s lay primarily in his skill as a printmaker. It was surely this that stimulated the next generation of German artists, while they may have influenced Munch in his paintings.[51] Although Munch's first reception in Berlin had been hostile, he stayed, made friends, learnt graphic techniques, and went on from there to establish his international success. The development of modern art in Berlin was not just a march of the **avant garde**. There were older artists who helped the younger ones, writers who promoted painters, and Munch was welcomed for his contribution to one of the Germans' favourite art forms, printmaking.

Notes

Professor James McFarlane gave me the subject of "The group 'Zum schwarzen Ferkel'" for postgraduate research, and I am most grateful to him for being my tutor in the German department of King's College, Newcastle upon Tyne, University of Durham, and in the School of European Studies at the University of East Anglia, Norwich. I first wrote about "The group 'Zum schwarzen Ferkel': an aspect of the literary life of Berlin in the 1890s" in an unpublished dissertation in partial fulfilment of the MA degree from the University of East Anglia, 1966. Parts of the article published here were used in my radiovision script on Munch for the BBC Open University's course A 315 on Modern Art and Modernism (1983), and I am grateful to the BBC for allowing me to reproduce the material. The consistently generous assistance I have received from the staff of the Munch Museum in Oslo, particularly from Arne Eggum and Gerd Woll, has made it possible for me to continue research. Being freelance since 1972, I have relied on relations and friends for support and should like to thank the librarians of the University of East Anglia, and Charlotte Carstairs, Mary Sandbach, Sally and Li Epstein.

1. Stephen Spender: **The Struggle of the Modern** (London, 1965), p.185.

2. Quoted by Harry Count Kessler: "Herr von Werner", **Kunst und Künstler**, 2 (1904), reprinted in **Kunst und Künstler. Aus 32 Jahrgängen einer deutschen Kunstzeitschrift**, edited by Günter Feist (with the assistance of Ursula Feist) (Mainz, 1971), pp.287–90.

3. See for example Walter Selber (pseudonym for Walter Leistikow): "Die Affaire Munch", **Die freie Bühne**, 3 (1982), pp.1296–1300.

4. Kenworth Moffett: **Meier-Graefe as art critic** (Munich, 1973), note 177, p.163.

5. Ola Hansson: "Vom künstlerischen Schaffen", **Die Zukunft**, 3 (1893), p.321.

6. See note 2 above.

7. Kruse's memories were published by Erich Büttner in his postscript "Der leibhaftige Munch" to the German translation of Jens Thiis: **Edvard Munch** (Berlin, 1934), p.85.

8. **Edvard Munchs brev: Familien**, selected by Inger Munch, edited by Johan Langaard, Munch-museets skrifter I (Oslo, 1949), nos.126, 128.

9. Reinhold Heller: "The Affaire Munch, Berlin, 1892–1893", Papers from the Tenth AICA-Congress at Munch-museet, Oslo, 29 August 1969, and "Affæren Munch, Berlin 1892–3", **Kunst og Kultur**, 52 (1969), pp.175–91.

10. See for example note 8 above, p.298.

11. **Weser Zeitung**, no.16560, Bremen (9 January 1893).

12. See Rudolf Pfefferkorn: **Die Berliner Secession. Eine Epoche deutscher Kunstgeschichte** (Berlin, 1972), p.31.

13. See Irmgard Günther: "Die Einwirkung des skandinavischen Romans auf den deutschen Naturalismus 1870–1900", dissertation (Greifswald, 1934), Nordische Studien, Band 14; and Arne Widell: **Ola Hansson i Tyskland, En studie i hans liv och diktning åren 1890–1893** (Uppsala, Skrifter utgivna av litteraturvetenskapliga institutionen vid Uppsala universitet, 9, 1979).

14. Extract from Halbe's **Jahrhundertwende** (Danzig, 1935) published in **Strindberg im Zeugnis der Zeitgenossen**, edited by Willy Haas (Bremen, 1963), p.221.

15. Max Dauthendey referred to Hansson's friendship with Munch in a letter of 19 January 1893, **Sieben Meere nahmen mich auf. Ein Lebensbild mit unveröffentlichten Dokumenten aus dem Nachlass** (Munich 1907). Hansson's invitation to Munch, 29 December 1892, is in the archive of Munch-museet, Oslo.

16. See Stellan Ahlström: "Ola Hansson som konstkritiker", **Konstrevy**, 5–6 (1958), pp.234–39.

17. "Kunstkritikk und Berufskritikk", **Neue deutsche Rundschau**, 5 (1894), p.84.

18. See J. Bab, "Die neuromantische Bohème", **Die Berliner Bohème, Grosstadt-Dokumente**, edited by Hans Ostwald, II (Berlin and Leipzig, 1904), and C. Lathe: "The group 'Zum schwarzen Ferkel': a study in early modernism", unpublished PhD thesis, University of East Anglia, 1972, p.36.

19. "Vom jungen Meier-Graefe", **Julius Meier-Graefe, Widmungen zu seinem 60. Geburtstag** (Munich, Berlin, Vienna, 1927).

20. "Der erste Jahrgang des 'Pan'", **Die Zeit** (Vienna), no.94 (18 July 1896), p.43.

21. See Arne Eggum's article "The theme of death" in the catalogue **Edvard Munch, Symbols and Images**, National Gallery of Art, Washington, 1978, pp.143–83.

22. **Samlade Skrifter** 23 (Stockholm, 1914), p.260.

23. **Auf den Wegen der Seele** (Berlin, 1897), p.47.

24. "Zur Psychologie des Künstlers", Streifzüge eines Unzeitgemässen, **Götzendämmerung** (1889), **Nietzsches Werke** 8, edited by Fritz Koegel, 12 volumes (Leipzig, 1896), pp.122–23.

25. **Zur Psychologie des Individuums**, I (Berlin, 1892), p.47.

26. Alfred Wysocki, **Sprzed Pół Wieku** (Kraków, 1956).

27. "Jung Berlin" III, **Die Zeit** (5 December 1896), p.155.

28. "Mein Freund Przybyszewski", **Pologne Littéraire** (15 December 1928), p.2.

29. Letter in the archive of Munch-museet, Oslo.

30. Quoted by C. Gierløff, "Kampår", **Edvard Munch som vi kjente ham. Vennene forteller** (Oslo, 1946), p.133.

31. "Munch", **Frankfurter Zeitung**, no.245 (1927), reprinted in Meier-Graefe's **Grundstoff der Bilder** (Munch, 1959), p.182.

32. See H.P. Rohde: "Edvard Munch på klinik i København", **Kunst og Kultur** 46 (1963), p.266.

33. Letter in archive of Munch-museet, Oslo.

34. Aubert in **Morgenbladet** (1 November 1895), and Natanson: "Correspondence de Kristiania", **La revue blanche**, 59 (November 1895).

35. Alfred Werner: **Graphic Works of Edvard Munch** (New York, 1979), p.vii.

36. Quoted by Peter Krieger: **Edvard Munch. Der Lebensfries.** Exhibition Catalogue (Berlin Nationalgalerie, 1978), p.11.

37. Karl Stenerud: "Edvard Munchs testamente", **Edvard Munch. Mennesket og kunstneren** (Oslo, 1946), p.2.

38. Fr. Alfred Gower-Jones, **Radio Times** (24 April 1976).

39. See Carla Lathe: catalogue to the exhibition **Edvard Munch and his Literary Associates**, Library Concourse, University of East Anglia (Norwich, 1979) and Carla Lathe: "Edvard Munch's Dramatic Images 1892–1909", **Journal of the Warburg and Courtauld Institutes**, 46 (1983), pp.191–206.

40. Jens Dedichen: **Tulla Larsen og Edvard Munch** (Oslo, 1981), p.17.

41. Letter dated 12 December 1894, Munch-museet archive.

42. "Ausstellungen und Sammlungen", signed "J.S.", **Die Kunst für Alle**, 15 April 1895.

43. Jens Thiis: **Edvard Munch og hans samtid: slekten, livet og kunsten, geniet** (Oslo, 1933), p.210. I am very grateful to Sally Epstein for taking me to see the Berlin art collections.

44. See **Edvard Munch. Graphik aus dem Kupferstichkabinett der Staatlichen Museen zu Berlin DDR**, catalogue edited by Hans Ebert, Brussels 1971, no.7.

45. Note 43 above, p.186.

46. Arne Eggum: **Edvard Munch. Malerier – skisser og studier** (Oslo, 1983), pp.141–42.

47. Philippe Jullian, **Dreamers of Decadence**, translated from the French **Esthètes et Magiciens** (1969) by Robert Baldick (London, 1971), p.210.

48. Franz Servaes, note 20 above.

49. Christian Gierløff, **Edvard Munch selv** (Oslo, 1953), p.139.

50. Gustav Schiefler: **Meine Graphiksammlung** (1927), new version edited by Gerhard Schack (Hamburg, 1974), p.30.

51. See Arne Eggum: "Brücke og Edvard Munch" in the catalogue **Die Brücke – Edvard Munch**, Malmö Konsthall, 1979 (text in Norwegian, Swedish and German), and A. Eggum: "'Children with Nature', The Landscapes of Edvard Munch" in the Munch exhibition catalogue, Newcastle upon Tyne Polytechnic Art Gallery, 1980.

Ulysses and The Magic Mountain: Two Terminal Novels and The Decline of the West

Michael Robinson

"Nu min undergång"
Det är hela världens sång.
– Birger Sjöberg

Of the numerous attempts to explain the condition of Europe after the First World War, Spengler's **The Decline of the West** had probably the most widespread if short-lived impact. The tone of Spengler's book suited the mood of post-war pessimism, and by situating the immediate crisis within an historical framework that appeared to demonstrate its inevitability, he offered both a description of what he termed a "late culture" that tallied with contemporary anxieties, and an explanation that partly alleviated these fears by an appeal to the "unalterable necessity of destiny" (I, p.39)[1] which lay, or so he claimed, behind the present situation. The first part of **The Decline of the West** was published in 1918, the second in 1922. It is therefore contemporary with **Ulysses** (1922) and **The Magic Mountain** (1924), both of which were several years in the writing, and all three books are similar in their attempt to sum up a whole culture in what was widely regarded as its crucial and possibly final phase.

Indeed, Spengler's analysis of contemporary civilisation, with its critique of liberalism, democracy, and the idea of progress, has many affinities with the ideologically conservative side of literary Modernism, both in England and Germany. His expectation of disciplined "hard metal natures" (I, p.38) who will shortly assume power is, for example, analogous with Yeats's anticipation of a "harsh, surgical, masculine" future in **On the Boiler** (1939),[2] while the historical morphology he employs, with its rigid paralleling of cultures and past events, has an evident consonance with the thinking and style of Pound's **Cantos**, as well as with the method used by Yeats in **A Vision** (1925) to reach certain general conclusions about the cyclical movement of history and the present crisis which were, as Yeats himself recognized, similar to those of Spengler.[3]

But the most significant similarities arise from Spengler's description of urban life and his judgement upon megapolitan culture. His account of "the cold intelligence that confounds the wisdom of the peasant" in a society ruled by a "conception of money as an inorganic and abstract magnitude, entirely disconnected from the notion of the fruitful earth" (I, p.33) is in keeping with the cultural criticism of Yeats, Pound and Eliot, and with the richer structures of their poetry, too, while his general vision of the city as a dessicated, traditionless "stone desert" (II, p.99), inhabited by rootless, neurotic and mechanised nomads, is clearly affined with another 1922 publication, **The Waste Land**. The essential terms of Spengler's analysis are present in the following definition, where they are associated with a further Modernist preoccupation, the imminent apocalypse. For the gradualism of Spengler's title belies the tenor of its content: its veneer of historical exactitude notwithstanding, **The Decline of the West** is also an elaborate fiction of the falling towers and a by no means reluctant anticipation of the barbarians who will shortly camp among the ruins. As Spengler writes:

> In place of a world, there is **a city, a point,** in which the whole life of broad regions is collecting while the rest dries up. In place of a type-true people, born of and grown on the soil, there is a new sort of nomad, cohering unstably in fluid masses, the parasitical city dweller, traditionless, utterly matter-of-fact, religionless, clever, unfruitful, deeply contemptuous of the countryman and especially that highest form of countryman, the country gentleman. This is a very great stride towards the inorganic, towards the end. . .
>
> (I, p.32)

It is this dual theme, the rootlessness of modern life and the terminal nature of the civilisation in which it is lived, which Mann and Joyce share with Spengler, and which they develop most fully in **Ulysses** and **The Magic Mountain**. The terms Spengler uses to describe the modern city dweller have often been applied to Joyce's hero, Bloom. Indeed, to several of Joyce's fellow Modernists, Wyndham Lewis, Eliot and Pound, Bloom was the incarnation of Spengler's "unanchored 'late' man of the megapolis" whose "matter-of-fact feeling and mechanizing thought" (II, p.112) was projected with monumental thoroughness in a novel that was itself organized mechanically through a network of linguistic clichés, in which Joyce, emulating and surpassing **Bouvard et Pécuchet**, pinned down the triviality of the urban mind. Of course, the novel also depicts Stephen Dedalus as rootless and alone, but he stands aside from Dublin life by choice, having denied his church and the nationalism and language of his country in order to adhere to a broader tradition which is present in his mind. Bloom, on the other hand, is immersed in a society he doesn't consider leaving. Thus for Eliot, in his seminal essay "Ulysses, Order and Myth" (1922), he was at the heart of "the immense panorama of futility and anarchy which is contemporary history",[4] and Pound saw **Ulysses** as "a summary of pre-war Europe, the blackness and mess and muddle of a 'civilisation' led by disguised forces and a bought press, the general sloppiness, the plight of the individual intelligence in that mess! Bloom very much is the mess".[5]

It is easy to assemble evidence in support of this reading. In **Ulysses** Joyce certainly continued the dissection of a city which he had already depicted as a centre of emotional and intellectual paralysis in **Dubliners** (1912). "I call the series Dubliners", he wrote to Curran, in 1904, "to betray the soul of that hemiplegia or paralysis which many consider a city",[6] and in the "Wandering Rocks" episode of the novel, for example, he goes on to portray the fragmentation and mechanical nature of urban life by his use of a montage technique that brings nineteen separate episodes in different parts of Dublin into gratuitous conjunction. The juxtapositions are designedly meaningless ("Corny Kelleher sped a silent jet of hayjuice arching from his mouth while a generous white arm from a window in Eccles Street flung forth a coin"),[7] in order to convey a fundamental absence of relationship between the simultaneous but discrete particles of city life, and while the paths of the characters may intersect, they do not intermingle: typically, Bloom has left the bookstall before Stephen enters. In fact, throughout **Ulysses** the streets of the city offer a scene of general movement which conceals an underlying lack of community. One of the few remaining enclaves of apparent fellowship is the group of idlers who gather in the Ormond bar to sentimentalize over the past and retreat from the present in the singing of old songs. Elsewhere, in the newspaper office, the library or the cab men's shelter, associations are temporary, and throughout the novel the life of the city is bound together not by human contact or co-operation but by the coincidental presence of external details cast up by the dynamo of urban life – a three-master making for port, a newspaper Bloom was going to throw away, or a crumpled handbill announcing the arrival of Alexander J. Dowie. At one moment there is a sudden stasis, suggesting the paralysis below the surface:

> At various points along the eight lines tramcars with motionless trolleys stood in their tracks, bound for or from Rathmines, Rathfarnham, Blackrock, Kingstown and Dalkey, Sandymount Green, Ringsend and Sandymount Tower, Donnybrook, Palmerston Park and Upper Rathmines, all still, becalmed in short circuit. (p.188)

But otherwise the urban machine, as Bloom notes, keeps "pegging away" (p.150), indifferent to the individual citizen and never transforming an aggregate of atoms into an integrated whole.

From the moment Bloom is first introduced it is his consciousness that filters the flow of urban life depicted in **Ulysses**. And the social significance of this consciousness seems perfectly clear: it embodies the commercialism, pervasive materialism, dissonance, subtle impotence, fragmentation and vague ideals of the common man Ortega y Gasset dubbed "the spoiled child of human history",[8] with his belief in material comfort, popular science, and progress. He is "l'homme qui croit ce qu'il lit dans les journaux",[9] his mind an urban bustle and miscellany, a mass of **idées recues** which retail the **muflisme** of the age. Joyce satirizes this microcosm of the public world both in detail (as when the whore's query, "How's the nuts?" provokes the earnest Bloom to reply "Off side. Curiously they are on the right. Heavier I suppose. One in a million my tailor, Mesias, says" (p.599)), and in breadth, as in the catalogue of Bloom's library (p.832), the contents of his bureau drawers (p.848), or his schemes to get rich quick, buy and furnish a dream home or initiate an age of universal brotherhood in "the new Bloomusalem in the Nova Hibernia of the future" (p.606), all of which reveal a mind occupied by the inflated discourse of the estate agent and the illustrated magazine.

But Bloom is urban in other respects. Above all, he is lonely, rootless and, to all appearances, passive. For one brief instant his life was touched by history, when he picked up Parnell's hat, knocked off in a riot (and he is again on hand to perform the same service for Stephen after the fight with Private Carr: "history repeating itself with a difference" (p.762)), but normally his role is more modest. Continually imposed upon, pushed around, assaulted by irate nationalists or mimicked by urchins, he suffers windy rhetoric in "Aeolus", noise in "Sirens", and political violence in "Cyclops", always seeking and yet never finding the human contact for which he yearns. Cuckolded by Molly, with whom he sleeps head to toe, his encounters with Gerty MacDowell, Richie Goulding, or Martha Clifford (who doesn't even know his real name) are unvaryingly sterile. His father's suicide, Rudy's death, and Milly's leaving home have broken up the family and, for all the superficial gregariousness of Dublin life, he has known no close friendship since the loss of Apjohn and Meredith. Even his colleague, Hynes, has to ask his christian name, and the crowning snub to a difficult day is to see himself recorded as "L. Boom" in the list of mourners at Dignam's funeral. No one, it proves, really knows Bloom, although several, notably Nosey Flynn and

Lenehan, single him out as a man apart: "He's not one of your common or garden" (p.302).

What makes the greatest contribution to the impression of Bloom's loneliness, however, is Joyce's extended use of the interior monologue whereby the fragmented quality of his felt experience is rendered uniquely his own and untranslatable into another's discourse. Moreover, use of the internal monologue also emphasizes a disparity between Bloom's spoken language and the far richer discourse of his private thoughts. When he begins to speak it is often in the formal, tired phrases of polite conversation which disappoint after his preceding reflections. For example:

> There he is, sure enough, my bold Larry, leaning against the sugarbin in his shirtsleeves watching the aproned curate swab up with mop and bucket. Simon Dedalus takes him off to a tee with his eyes screwed up. Do you know what I'm going to tell you? What's that, Mr O'Rourke? Do you know what? The Russians, they'd only be an eight o'clock breakfast for the Japanese.
>
> Stop and say a word: about the funeral perhaps. Sad thing about poor Dignam, Mr O'Rourke.
>
> Turning into Dorset Street he said freshly in greeting through the doorway:
> – Good day, Mr O'Rourke.
> – Good day to you.
> – Lovely weather, sir.
> – 'Tis all that.
>
> (p.69)

As Budgen remarks, "Bloom can see and be seen, but he can never be touched, and that despite all the apparent amiabilities of intercourse."[10]

It is, however, through his race that Bloom is quintessentially urban. His rootlessness is inherited:

> What first reminiscence had he of Rudolph Bloom (deceased)?
>
> Rudolph Bloom (deceased) narrated to his son Leopold Bloom (aged 6) a retrospective arrangement of migrations and settlements in and between Dublin, London, Florence, Milan, Vienna, Budapest, Szombathely . . .
>
> (p.854)

He is thus, like his creator, traditionally "a metropolitan type, neither a native nor a foreigner, a denizen of the megapolis, a wanderer of the diaspora, equally at home and ill at ease in any city of the world".[11] Mulligan calls him the wandering Jew, the Patriot, Ahasuerus, and he is not only isolated from the community in which he finds himself; he is also identified as different and obscurely threatening. He has no religion, and Budgen's comment is apposite: "Stephen's irreligion would shock them [his fellow Dubliners] less than Bloom's agnostic indifference".[12] Such "jews", Mr Deasy remarks, "are the signs of a nation's decay" (p.41), materialists, cosmopolitans, freethinkers, who bear with them the insidious forces of dissolution spreading out from the cities and eroding the old order, their intellectuality, money and egalitarian thinking being, as Spengler among others asserted, important factors in the final destruction of an integrated community. A number of Modernists subscribed to this view, among them Eliot, with his desire to see a limit placed on the number of free thinking Jews in any community. "My house is a decayed house", he writes, and implies the cause, the Jew who "squats upon the window sill" (like Mr Deasy, Eliot used to use a lower case "j"). Nothing coheres for

> The rats are underneath the piles.
> The Jew is underneath the lot.

and the rootless Bleistein ("Chicago Semite Viennese") stalks with sagging knees uncomprehendingly through what emerges as the once stable and harmonious cultural heritage of Europe. Or as Pound commented more succinctly: "The details of the street map are local but Leopold Bloom (né Virag) is ubiquitous".[13]

However, in both his portrait of Bloom and his treatment of urban life, Joyce distances himself from many modern prejudices. That Bloom is lonely and rootless is something of which he is himself aware: "I, too, last my race. Milly young student. Well, my fault perhaps. No son. Rudy. Too late now. . . . soon I am old" (pp.367–8: compare Spengler's comment on the city dweller: "The continuance of the blood relation in the visible world is no longer a duty of the blood, and the destiny of being the last of the line is no longer felt as a doom" (II, p.104)). But the very fact that he feels and thinks differently, adhering to values that are not those of his fellow Dubliners, means that he frequently occupies a critical distance from his surroundings. And since it is through Bloom's mind that Joyce conducts much of the irony in the novel, his consciousness is not reducible to a disordered succession of clichés. It has a distinguishable mode of expression which discriminates between experiences as well as merely passively recording impressions. His ideals may be confused but his personal virtues – good will, tolerance, fortitude, humour, self-knowledge, and a certain resilient intelligence – are evident, and his perspective as an outsider permits an objectivity that fits him for the role of commentator. Indeed, Bloom is exceptional rather than average. "As the day wears on Bloom should overshadow them all", Joyce told Budgen,[14] and even Hugh Kenner, who writes of him as if he were a walking cliché, is forced to admit that ". . . when Joyce makes Bloom suddenly ask 'Do fish ever get sea sick?' we are in the presence not of an exercise in nineteenth-century pessimism but of a tribute to the unpredictable creative leaps of the human soul".[15] If Bloom is religionless, traditionless, matter-of-fact, and sterile, in the Spenglerian sense, he is also perceptive, compassionate and creative. The "Lestrygonians" episode, which is sometimes cited in evidence of his limitations, in fact shows him ordering and controlling the "mess" with considerable skill. His thoughts repeatedly cut deftly through appearances, and his discourse frequently traps phenomena with an apposite, often witty, phrase. He recognizes the dangers of hollow rhetoric – "Flapdoodle to feed fools on" (p.204) – and is shrewdly perceptive of the world about him. In the proximity of Thomas Moore's statue and a urinal he observes an appropriate "meeting of the waters" (p.205); in Evangelism he recognizes a "paying game" (p.190); and Mrs Purefoy's numerous children are, he notes, "hardy annuals" (p.203). His characteristic discourse is in fact very much a making strange of ordinary clichés rather than their indiscriminate use, and several observations in "Lestrygonians" actively transform and adapt common usage with a revitalizing effect, as for example in his comment on Mrs Purefoy's Methodist husband, "Method in his madness" (p.203) or his incisive adaptation, "The harp that once did starve us all" (p.213) with its neat deflation of a sentimental national romanticism.

Moreover, Bloom's thoughts frequently indicate an innate pessimism that belies the facile optimism often attributed to him. The melancholy of his relationship with Molly fuses with his general knowledge to translate a sense of urban atomization into a vision of a future end: "Gas-balls spinning about, crossing each other, passing. Same old dingdong always. Gas, then solid, then world, then cold, then dead shell drifting around, frozen rock like that pineapple rock" (p.212). And the thrust of this passage also informs his most extended meditation on urban futility. As a cloud casts its shadow over Trinity's "surly front", Bloom's mood darkens, too, and he dwells upon the peculiar balance between stasis and movement, permanence and flux, which is gathered up in a single city:

> Trams passed one another, ingoing, outgoing, clanging. Useless words. Things go on the same; day after day: squads of police marching out, back: trams in, out. Those two loonies mooching about. Dignam carried off. Mina Purefoy swollen belly on a bed groaning to have a child tugged out of her. One born every second somewhere. Other dying every second. Since I fed the birds five minutes. Three hundred kicked the bucket. Other three hundred born, washing the blood off, all are washed in the blood of the lamb, bawling maaaaaa.
>
> Cityful passing away, other cityful coming, passing away too: other coming on, passing on. Houses, lines of houses, streets, miles of pavements, piledup bricks, stones. Changing hands. This owner, that. Landlord never dies they say. Other steps into his shoes when he gets his notice to quit. They buy the place up with gold and still they have all the gold. Swindle in it somewhere. Piled up in cities, worn away age after age. Pyramids in sand. Built on bread and onions. Slaves. Chinese wall. Babylon. Big stones left. Round towers. Rest rubble, sprawling suburbs, jerrybuilt, Kerwan's mushroom houses, built of breeze. Shelter for the night.
>
> (p.208)

As his thoughts move from the particular to the general, from Dignam and Mina Purefoy to the multitude of living and dead, Bloom's vision stretches out to embrace the apocalyptic end of the city. Everything passes, or remains to pass eventually. But significantly Bloom does not linger in exultation over the idea, and the critical self-awareness of his next thoughts place this vision in perspective: "This is the very worst hour of the day. Vitality. Dull, gloomy: hate this hour. Feel as if I had been eaten and spewed" (p.208).

And so it is throughout Ulysses. The many intimations of an apocalypse which the urban world casts up, as if in keeping with the notions of Spengler or of Eliot, are subordinate to their context. The "Agendath is a waste land, a home of screech owls", from "Oxen of the Sun", with its suggestion of an end in infertility and chaos, arises from the drunken excitement of the medical students, and the whole "Circe" episode, which is recalled as "Armageddon" in the summary of Bloom's day (p.860), is only one aspect, the night side of a city made vivid by fatigue, alcohol, and the lurid promiscuity of the quarter in which Stephen and Bloom find themselves. Both the ghost of Bloom's father and Alexander J. Dowie announce the Apocalypse (pp.612, 636); the whore, Florry, proclaims the latter day (p.623); and the Newsboys shout a stop press edition declaring the "Safe arrival of Antichrist" (p.623) before, with distant voices calling

"Dublin's burning", the earth trembles, the midnight sun darkens and the dead and the living celebrate Armageddon with a black mass (p.695). But Joyce's mode as he records these visions remains comic. The End of the World who appears on an "infinite invisible tightrope" is grotesque but not alarming, "a two-headed octopus in gillie's kilts, busby and tartan filibegs" singing "Wha'll dance the keel row, the keel row, the keel row?" (p.624).

This balanced treatment of Bloom and of the Apocalypse is typical of Joyce's portrait of the city in general. Neither urban nightmare nor drab wilderness, it is the essential element in which the characters live. Joyce, too, always elected to live in cities. His sensibility was supremely urban and **Ulysses** is, of course, resonant with the intensity of his identification with a Dublin he wished to preserve, not destroy. As he informed Budgen, "I want to give a picture of Dublin so complete that if the city one day should suddenly disappear from the face of the earth it could be reconstructed out of my book".[16] "The Dublin of **Ulysses**", Edmund Wilson noted, "is a city of voices",[17] and within and behind the slang, shop talk, catch phrases, advertising slogans, nicknames and topical jokes, the miscellany of lyrics from music hall and opera, romantic novels, trade catalogues, newspapers and pantomime, the city is constantly present, the substantial, various reality alive in the citizen's mind and interacting with those who live in it, a customary habitat both vital **and** sterile which emerges through the thoughts and language of its inhabitants who are as familiar with its customs and idiosyncracies as the countrymen of an earlier literature were with the intimate details of the landscape in which they lived: "Bloom crossed to the bright side, avoiding the loose cellarflap of number seventyfive. The sun was nearing the steeple of George's church. Be a warm day I fancy" (p.67). It is clear that this nomad at least is at home.

Joyce confronts urban society directly. In **The Magic Mountain**, Mann takes up many of the same preoccupations but obliquely, translating them from the industrial and commercial cities of central Europe to the rarified air of a sanitorium whose inhabitants are seemingly cut off from everyday concerns. To the newcomer to the International Sanatorium Berghof, the mountain seems a direct contrast to the world he or she has left behind, a timeless, isolated world with customs of its own. But on acquaintance it emerges as a reflection of the flatlands below, "a point", in Spengler's words, "in which the whole life of broad regions is collecting", intensified, abstracted and distilled in hermetic conditions.

According to Spengler, "final cities are **wholly** intellect" (II, p.99), and both in its abstraction and its mechanical organisation, the mountain society provides such a milieu. Moreover, as Ibn Hassan has remarked:

> Urbanism: Nature put in doubt, from Baudelaire's "cité" to Proust's Paris, Eliot's London, Joyce's Dublin. It is not a question of locale but of presence. The sanatorium of **The Magic Mountain** and the village of **The Castle** are "cities" still.[18]

Certainly the sanatorium displays a kinship with the urban landscape of **The Waste Land** or the Paris to which Marcel returns in **Le temps retrouvé**. The generally indifferent, unthinking, aimless mass of patients, heedlessly evading responsibility in fads and the automatism of the mountain's regime, recall both the Parisians whom Marcel discovers in the wartime capital, living "les derniers jours de notre Pompéi" as they await "le sort des villes du Vésuve . . . une génération d'intervalle, des intellectuels que toute idée nouvelle intéresse et des causeurs de qui aucun interrupteur ne peut obtenir le silence" as they delight in the aesthetic play of searchlights, planes and burning buildings which create "l'apocalypse dans le ciel",[19] and the sombre postwar crowd flowing over London Bridge under the brown fog of a winter dawn in Eliot's "Unreal city". An uneasy mixture of all the European nations, the Berghof's clientèle is cosmopolitan, traditionless and irresponsible ("In the mountains, there you feel free").[20] Feverish, neurotic, barren and afflicted by ennui, they play with their pistols or their cards as Eliot's Londoners play chess or the gramophone, waiting for something to happen or for death's knock. It is in fact a city of the dead and all the inhabitants are inwardly tainted. They can connect nothing with nothing and, cut off from fertility, indulge in casual affairs, vulgar sensuality, and sterile eroticism. It is a highly artificial society, with its own rhythm and time. The seasons there "don't keep to the calendar" (p.94)[21] but each day is unvaryingly punctuated by the same set meals and the weeks and months by regular lectures and entertainments. It has officials whose word is law, an aristocracy based on length of stay and the seriousness of disease, rules and customs relating, for example, to the wearing of hats or the catching of colds, and its own moral standards.

When Hans Castorp, a character who possesses "a certain native and lofty simplicity" (p.236), is introduced into this world, he is rapidly attracted to the life of the mountain. "A certain something sympathetic in the air" (p.238) appeals to him. "He was by nature and temperament passive", the narrator comments, "and loved . . . to see time spacious before him, and not to have the sense of its passing banished, wiped out or eaten up by prosaic activity" (p.103). He is easily assimilated into the daily routine, therefore, and what begins as a holiday adventure becomes a permanent way of life. But like Bloom, Castorp has qualities that distinguish him from the life about him. He possesses "a spiritual craving to take suffering and death seriously" (p.296), and in him the mountain awakens latent forces that are developed throughout his stay. Down in the flatland, he realizes, "he had actually been in a state of simple ignorance" (p.237), but up here he is afforded "glimpses into a world the existence of which one never dreamed" (p.410). His growth, however, is not gratuitous. Early on in his stay, Hofrat Behrens recognises his special talent for the place, and during a crucial conversation with Madame Chauchat he observes himself that to benefit from the "alchemistic-hermetic pedagogy" which the mountain affords, the individual "must have a little something in itself to start with" (p.596).

In fact Mann's early description of Castorp is profoundly ironic. This "simple personality" who "was thoroughly in his element in the atmosphere of this great seabord city" [Hamburg] whose sights and sounds awakened in him "only the agreeable, homely sensations of 'belonging'" (pp. 30–31) is, for all his "blond correctness", "adequate" ability at tennis, "sensible" talk and "monotonous" voice (p.29), not entirely the "legitimate and genuine product of the soil in which he flourished" (p.30) that he appears to be. The narrator suggests, but finally withdraws the word "mediocre" as an adequate description of Hans Castorp because "somehow or other [he] saw no positive reason for exertion" (p.32) in the society in which he lived. He was, the narrator remarks, "vaguely conscious of the deficiencies of his epoch" (p.32) and, when the features of the age in which Castorp lives are evoked, for once without irony, it is in terms that accord essentially with the rootless, unfruitful, inorganic and traditionless society of Spengler's historical account. However outwardly stimulating, the life around Castorp is seen "to be hopeless, viewless, helpless, opposing only a hollow silence to all the questions man puts, consciously or unconsciously . . . as to the final, absolute, and abstract meaning in all his efforts and activities" (p.32). It lames the personality, infecting it with "a sort of palsy which may even extend from his spiritual and moral over into his physical and organic part" (p.32). And yet if this paralysis explains the passivity in Castorp which responds to the timelessness of the mountain, it also distinguishes him as a man, again like Bloom, over and above the average, since in recognizing the deficiencies of the time he is able to accept the opportunity of knowledge and experience when it occurs.

On the mountain, therefore, the education of Castorp through his exposure to the conflicting pedagogy of Settembrini and Naphta, and to the example of Peeperkorn's personality, involves a coming to terms with his age, its failings and its future. And since, as the narrator suggests, a man lives not only his own personal life but also the life of his epoch, Castorp's experience is representative of something larger than his own individual destiny. Both Settembrini and Madame Chauchat speak of him as Germany, divided between Western and Eastern Europe, and as the novel comes increasingly to represent the condition of pre-war Europe as a whole, so Hans Castorp, who has absorbed, discussed, pondered and experienced the conflicting strains of the continent over the previous seven years, embodies it too.

This is especially so in the last section of the novel, where Castorp's response to the prevailing mood is seismic:

> It seemed to Hans Castorp that not only he himself had arrived at this point, but that all the world, "the whole show", as he said, had arrived there with him; he found it hard to differentiate his particular case from the general.
>
> (p.627)

The "Great God Dumps", as this mood is called, is indicative of "the pointlessness and lack of organic prospects of pre-1914 Europe and [of] the aggressive moods which purposeless existence fostered".[22] When Castorp looks about him at his fellow patients, he perceives their common rootlessness: "He saw on every side the uncanny and the malign, and he knew what it was he saw: life without time, life without care or hope, life as depravity, assiduous stagnation; life as dead" (p.627). This mood becomes increasingly apocalyptic. Although Castorp "was able to a certain extent, to free himself from embroilment with the prevailing temper" (p.698), seeing through it all as "hocus pocus", he is nevertheless aware that "all this could come to no good, that a catastrophe was impending, that long suffering nature would rebel, rise up in storm and whirlwind and break the great bond which held the world in thrall; snatch life beyond the 'dead point' and put an end to the 'small potatoes' in one terrible Last Day" (p.633). The language used to describe the patients' behaviour is resonant with the implications of the coming catastrophe. To facilitate the craze for photography that swept through the sanatorium "the bedroom windows and doors were draped with black cloth, and people busied themselves by dim red lights over chemical baths, until something caught fire" (p.628). The photographs revealed "groups of people with startled, staring eyes in livid faces dazed by the magnesium flare, resembling the corpses of the murdered set upright". Successive passions show the patients living beyond their means and pandering to jaded appetites, while the introduction of geometrical teasers "for a time consumed all the mental powers of the Berghof world, and even the last thoughts and energies of the dying" (p.628).

The prevailing atmosphere is thus a sinister combination of futility and fanaticism whose unbridled sway promises a universal and inescapable "end of horror" (p.635).

Even the humanist, Settembrini, is sucked in, his clear eye "dimmed by the prevailing spleen ... whose tool and underling Herr Settembrini's fine understanding had become" (pp.689, 700). Like the Man from Rome in Mann's later story, **Mario the Magician** (1930), Settembrini "was not the man to win free" (p.700) from the approaching intolerance. In the face of forces he comprehends only in part, his liberal humanism with its faith in reason and progress and the eventual elimination of "a past seething with superstition" (p.98) is ultimately shown to be impotent.

Meanwhile Castorp's other mentor, Naptha, is now in his element. "War, war! For his part, he was for it; the general hankering seemed to him comparatively creditable" (p.690). It is the outcome of all he has preached, the future he never doubted would come. "What I **do** see", he comments, several years earlier, "is the last feeble stirrings of the instinct of self-preservation, the last remnant at the command of a condemned world system. The catastrophe will and must come – it advances on every hand and in every way" (p.380). Naphta heralds the apocalypse. With his fur-lined cape, Gobelin tapestry, velvet carpet, baroque chairs, and esoteric works he is, in the first place, a post-Wagnerian decadent. Mann knew at first hand the **Kosmiker-Bund** which, in the intellectual **demi-monde** of pre-war Munich where Spengler also lived, had adopted apocalyptic modes of thought in an attempt to redeem a universe they believed stifled by intellectualism. To revitalize an exhausted culture this group, among them Ludwig Klages, Karl Wolfskehl, Alfred Schuler and Ludwig Derleth, sought a return to the primitive and instinctual. Derleth appears in the early story, **Beim Propheten** (1904), as well as in the later novel, **Doctor Faustus** (1947), where the narrator, Zeitblom, ponders upon "how near aestheticism and barbarism are to each other" (p.373),[23] and Mann explores the juxtaposition of bloody barbarism and bloodless intellectualism in greater detail. But Naphta also anticipates the absolutist and apocalyptic attitudes that are sometimes characteristic of Modernism. His admiration for the primitive fourteenth-century carving of the crucifixion, "so ugly and so beautiful" (p.393) is a modern taste in harmony with his general view of the "degradation of humanity" (p.396) as beginning with the Renaissance and continuing down to the present. In this, as in his political absolutism with its demand for "a single principle, which shall unify asceticism and domination" (p.402), he resembles T.E. Hulme, a fellow militarist, who held order to be "not merely negative but creative and liberating", who scorned the "sloppy thought of today", and in particular the nineteenth-century faith in progress, and who affirmed the superiority of what he perceived as the organic, hierarchical society of the Middle Ages to the movement of deterioration that succeeded it. His totalitarian demand for an austere, cold, hard, rigid social order and for art forms that embodied identical values as the nearest approach to "the Perfection that properly belongs to the non-human"[24] is analogous with the deadly formal perfection that Hans Castorp comes to identify with the network of **leitmotivs** involving militarism, Spanish discipline, and the icy regularity of the snow crystals he observes in the climactic chapter, "Snow", a network ultimately identified in the novel with Naphta's fanatical terrorism.

More pertinent to the present context, however, is Naphta's relationship with the supporters of the paradoxically named Conservative Revolution whose adherents, among them Klages, Langbehn, Moeller van den Bruck, and Spengler, "sought to destroy the despised present in order to recapture an idealised past in an imaginary future".[25] Hans Castorp observes this characteristic in Naphta: "To his mind, Naphta was as revolutionary as Settembrini, only in a conservative direction – a reactionary revolutionist" (p.461). His audacious paradoxes allow the reactionary to appear as its opposite: in his discourse reaction becomes progress and progress reaction, freedom bondage and bondage freedom, and his ruthless application of reason in the service of the irrational confounds the earnest objections of Settembrini. His ideal of a binding community, a **bindungsvolle Gemeinschaft** as in the "anonymous and communal" (p.393) Middle Ages, belongs to the vocabulary of German nationalism, but he presses its claims in a totally untraditional manner. A voluptuary of violence, his values and arguments are both Spenglerian and conservative-Modernist in substance and method, as for example when he contrasts what Eliot termed "the blood kinship of 'the same people living in the same place'"[26] with a life in cities divorced from the soil and under "the devilish domination of money and finance" (p.405). He asserts the primacy of faith, or soul, over intellect as a vehicle of knowledge, and yet supports his arguments with a refined intellectual casuistry. The only values he accepts are rural and military. Youth, he argues, no longer delights in freedom: "its deepest pleasure lies in obedience" and "what our age demands, what it needs, what it wrestles after, what it will create, is Terror" (p.400.)

Significantly the Jewish Jesuit who expounds these apocalyptic formulations is himself the **déraciné** intellectual typical of the period, indeed like Spengler who in 1910 abandoned teaching, settled in Munich, and during the war years "lodged in a dreary slum, took his meals in cheap working-class restaurants, and wrote much of the **Decline** by candle-light".[27] His dream of an organic community stems from his lack of integration, and is a compensation for the experience of acute rootlessness which leads him to identify the source of his alienation with the prevailing liberal ideology. In the words of one of Naphta's contemporaries, Moeller van den Bruck, liberalism is "the expression of a society which is no longer a community . . . Everyman who no longer feels a part of the community is somehow a liberal man . . . Liberalism has undermined cultures. It has annihilated religions. It has destroyed nations. It is the self-dissolution of man",[28] and in the aftermath of the war which Naphta heralded, the disaffection of the nomadic rootlessness such writers identified with urban society was mobilized by National Socialism in which many of the desires and speculations of such homeless intellectuals and **artistes manqués** were realised. The Caesars on whose appearance Spengler counted appeared on cue to provide the unstable and unfruitful late world so often described and disparaged by these thinkers, with the culmination of all these terminal theories, fictional or otherwise.

However, **Ulysses** and **The Magic Mountain** are not terminal novels merely in their subject matter; the adjective also applies to their nature as novels. In his description of the features of a culture in its final, megapolitan phase, Spengler includes a summary of the characteristics of its art. "All is pattern work", he claims, the surface embellishment of intricate, extended structures that reflect the tiredness of a culture moving from autumn to winter. There is a loss of inwardness, creativity and inspiration. "The self-evidence of aim, the unselfconsciousness of the execution, the unity of the art and the culture – all that is past and gone" (I, pp.295, 292). Writing of the late-comers, the Impressionists and Wagner, he points to the primacy of the labouring artisan over the effortless creator. Without the support of a living tradition, he asserts, creation becomes more difficult. Fluency and ease are unknown and, as he concludes, with typical, exultant pessimism, "we have to reckon with the hard cold facts of a **late** life . . . Of great painting or great music there can no longer be, for Western people, any question" (I, p.40).

Spengler's attitude has a certain congruence with Mann's speculations on the situation of the modern novel, an art form, incidentally, which goes virtually unmentioned in Spengler's book, except for one striking allusion to "the great Novel, the survey of all things human by the **emancipated** intellect [which] presupposes the world city" (**II**, p.93). Of **Doctor Faustus**, for example, Mann observed: "The book, as art, is something late, final, extreme, and its very boldness and honour consist in being extreme".[29] He remarked upon "the curious brand of reality that clings to it, which seen from one aspect is total artifice",[30] as a feature of a late culture, and in the novel itself he explores his own creative dilemmas through the medium of Adrian Leverkuhn's music. To Leverkuhn only parody seems to afford the possibility of a limited creative freedom in an age when art has become critique and no one knows any longer "what inspiration ... what genuine, old, primeval enthusiasm, insicklied critique, unparalysed by thought or by the mortal domination of reason" (p.237) is. Creation is threatened if only because "Every composer of the better sort carries within himself a canon of the forbidden, the self-forbidding, which by degrees includes all the possibilities of tonality, in other words all traditional music" (p.239).

Here, as throughout a novel in which Mann attempts to make his book "the thing it dealt with, namely constructivist music",[31] the word 'writer' may be substituted for 'composer' since the crisis of musical form and expression confronting Leverkuhn is a paradigm of the problems Mann faced during the same period. He was continually aware of a crisis which manifested itself in a "dissatisfaction with traditional forms, in a curbing of 'invention' by means of critical reflection and, finally, in a tendency toward experimentation with structure".[32] His essay, **Die Kunst des Romans** (1939), sees the novel as having reached the stage of "critique", of self-consciousness and intellectualism, and as early as **Bilse und Ich** (1906), in which he defended himself against accusations of writing a **roman à clef** in **Buddenbrooks** (1901), he shows himself aware of the relatively small part played by inspiration in his books. **Betrachtungen eines unpolitischen** (1918), moreover, reveals the deep impression which Pfitzner's opera, **Palestrina** (1917) had on Mann, for its treatment of the theme of creative paralysis and cultural exhaustion, an impression that was reinforced by the same composer's polemical essay, "Die neue Aesethetik der musikalische Impotenz" (1920). Thus during the period when he was at work on **The Magic Mountain**, Mann already observed that "the activity of the artist is highly problematical nowadays, when the decline of the entire Western culture seems to be in the offing",[33] and his identification of the threat of sterility as the most serious symptom of this cultural crisis relates his work to contemporary examinations of the same theme in **The Waste Land** (1922) and **Duineser Elegien** (1923), as well as to Spengler's cultural theories.

But the most instructive comparison remains the one with **Ulysses**. Mann's knowledge of Joyce's novel was delayed and second-hand, but when he chanced upon Harry Levin's monograph on Joyce in 1943, he was struck by the description of **Ulysses** as "a novel to end all novels", and promptly applied it to **The Magic Mountain**.[34] A number of similarities between the novels have already been suggested. Both were written over a period of years, dealt with pre-war Europe and were published in the 1920s. Both made extensive use of irony and parody. Both have heroes who are the object of this irony and at the same time sufficiently detached and distinguished from the assumptions of their age to be the vehicles of their authors' more general criticism. Both also speculate on time and intend their narratives to arrest its flow and gather in the whole of their society, whether for one day or over seven years. Finally both employ the **leitmotiv** as a technical device to achieve this so that the novel might be apprehended synchronically as well as diachronically. In Mann's words, **The Magic**

Mountain, "... while it portrays the hermetic enchantment of its young hero in a timeless realm ... endeavours itself through its artistic means to do away with time; to bestow upon the entire musical-conceptual world that it embraces total **presence** in every moment and to produce a magical **nunc stans**",[35] while in **Ulysses** the sense of movement is all on the surface. Beneath it the patterns of myth and language halt the city in its tracks. The material of both novels, in short, is organized to an exceptional degree and the recurring themes and fragments modify and accrete meanings which only fall into place in their total context when the books as a whole have been read.

But it is in the way they reflect the cultural crisis, and the predicament of the novel in particular, that their similarity is most pertinent. Their presence as completely intended and consciously executed books is one aspect of this. Paraphrasing Mann's own qualms, Gunilla Bergsten writes of the way in which "unfettered imagination, spontaneous invention of characters and plots is impeded by reflection and by the paralysing feeling that everything the conventional novel can express has already been said",[36] and Erich Kahler, in the course of an attempt to define the nature of such terminal books, extends this observation, pointing out that the "traditional art forms have grown problematic through external, social and cultural evolution, as well as through internal evolution, evolution of technique".[37] Modern novelists have not only to take into account a greater and more equivocal amount of available material; they also have to deal with an increase in the extent of knowledge at a time when the non-fictional often appears a more tempting medium. The sheer amount of knowledge both these books include – not necessarily felt knowledge in the Jamesian sense, not indeed necessarily profound knowledge, but the accumulated, inherited knowledge of a civilisation grown aware of itself – is obvious whether it takes the form of Hans Castorp's studies in the section entitled "Research", or Joyce's presentation of Gerty MacDowell as the sum of her reading in romantic fiction. The novelist, it seems, masters the growing complexity of the world by an increase in speculative analysis and exegesis and by a corresponding increase in the density and elaboration of the presentation. Indeed, in **Doctor Faustus** Mann has Leverkuhn ask "whether at the present stage of our consciousness, our knowledge, our sense of truth, this little game [art] is still permissible, still intellectually possible, still to be taken seriously; ... Pretence and play have the conscience of art against them today. Art would like to stop being pretence and play, it would like to become knowledge" (pp.180–82). In this situation Joyce's response was to continue to play, although aware, as he wrote to Harriet Weaver, that "it is no more than a game, but it is a game that I have learned to play in my own way. Children may just as well play as not. The ogre will come in any case".[38] Meanwhile Mann curtailed plot and action and emphasized the critical and reflective nature of the novel. And yet, in the end, both Mann and Joyce essayed a consciously constructed form of novel rather than an invented one, Joyce already asserting technique over invention in **Ulysses** and Mann continuing from the use of quotations in **The Magic Mountain** to the still greater constructivism of the Joseph tetralogy, **The Beloved Returns**, and **Doctor Faustus**, with their foundation in myth and history. In the work of both writers there is an increasing inclination "to look upon all life as a cultural product taking the form of mythic clichés and to prefer quotation to independent invention",[39] and yet, paradoxically, this adoption of previous structures, whether Homer's **Odyssey** or the Faust legend, does not restrict the later writer's freedom but proves to be the method by which the creative inhibitions of a late culture are transformed into the ability to produce a **summa** of this world – as is the case in both **Ulysses** and **The Magic Mountain**.

And it is precisely as multi-layered, multi-faceted accounts of the modern world that **The Magic Mountain** and **Ulysses** distinguish themselves from Spengler's equally compendious terminal fiction. Although at the outset all three writers may have shared certain preconceptions regarding the culture they inherited, in the case of Joyce and Mann the vigour of their art and its ability to apprehend and extend this culture demonstrates its continuing vitality.

It is not, however, that **Ulysses** and **The Magic Mountain** contradict the assumption of artistic decline merely by their existence, but it is the manner of their achievement which is decisive. In its organization of a kaleidoscopic welter of detail, of particles of knowledge, fragments of discrete fact, and shards of meaning into a unified fiction, their constructivism does not result in a fixed, rigid, petrified structure such as Spengler diagnosed and produced in **The Decline of the West**. Rather, it is the very incorporation of contemporary trivia and, in Joyce's case, the detritus of the streets, that endows their novels with something of the richness and variety as well as the complexity of the modern city.[40] This harvesting of trivia, moreover, is fundamental to the shift from the nineteenth-century Naturalism in which both writers commenced to write, to Modernism. In the former, the observed world is held together by a determined sequence of tightly drawn causal links; in the latter, the multiple and compacted causations of a world in which meaning is overdetermined and experience discontinuous and fragmentary are conveyed by a problematical combination of piecemeal association and extended narrative that is neither linear nor rectilinear but multidimensional and self-conscious, the vision of a writer who, as James McFarlane has observed, "saw the world not as an accumulation of categories, abstract concepts and general laws but as an infinitely complex lattice of relationships, personal to him, of which his mind was the centre and co-ordinator".[41] Such a narrative mode, which has its parallels in drama, music, and psycho-analysis, in Strindberg's Chamber Plays (1907), Schoenberg's **Erwartung** (1909), and Freud's Case History of "Dora" (1905) as well as **The Interpretation of Dreams** (1900) and **The Psychopathology of Everyday Life** (1901), is characterized by its simultaneous representation of many layers of meaning in a discourse that is both ambiguous and polyvalent, and which resists reduction to any such petrified and inhibiting schemata as Spengler's determinist morphology, which in its application to history of the biologist's conception of living forms through the metaphorical pattern of cultural birth, growth, maturity, and death, remains rooted in the organicist thinking of the nineteenth century. Unable to respond to the complexity of the modern world with the openness to experience of Joyce or Mann, Spengler forces his material into a premeditated scheme where every past event signifies a closed future. "The prelude of a future . . . with which the history of West-European mankind will be definitely **closed**" (I, p.38) is a typical formulation, as he dehumanizes history by transforming it into a sequence of natural processes and engulfs the particular and the individual in the totalitarian character of his categories. In Joyce and Mann, on the other hand, the work as a whole consists of significant, discrete details which are not petrified but animated by the shaping power of the imagination, and which also require the active participation of the reader for their eventual composition just as Schoenberg's music, as Adorno noted, "requires the listener spontaneously to compose its inner movement and demands of him not mere contemplation but praxis".[42] Like its musical and pictorial counterparts, the Modernist novel, even when most elaborately composed, accords its reader the freedom to extract from a cornucopia of material the lineaments of a narrative not readily apparent in its contiguous surface, in much the same way as that other compendium of the modern mind, **The Interpretation of**

Dreams, indicates a latent meaning beneath the manifest accumulation of surface detail.

Thus when Joyce exclaims "It all makes a pattern",[43] his excited realisation refers to a book (**Ulysses**) which is not mechanical and closed but allusive and full of loose ends, both intentionally and by accident since in Modernist art life, in the shape of **objets trouvés**, often abets art. And conversely, in certain Modernist works, art displays an ability to generate surplus meaning and reproduce life. For even the patterns, as they form and cohere, are not the end of the story – in any case, not for Joyce. In **Ulysses**, at least, the novel, notwithstanding its complex artistic organization, comes as close to accommodating the blooming confusion of life as it is perhaps possible for the novel to come, especially when, as Richard Ellmann has remarked, Joyce "introduces much material which he does not intend to explain, so that his book, like life, gives the impression of having many threads that one cannot follow".[44] Or to adopt, for a moment, the soil-bound imagery of Spengler's discourse, where culture "blooms on the soil of an exactly-definable landscape, to which plant-wise it remains bound" (I, p.106), quite simply, in the urban landscape of **Ulysses**, Bloom blooms.

Notes

1. All references to **The Decline of the West** are to the translation in two volumes by C.F. Atkinson (London, 1932) and will be included in the text between parentheses.

2. **Explorations** (London, 1962), p.434.

3. See **A Vision** (London, 1962, p.11) where Yeats describes how he and his wife "drew their first symbolical map . . . and marked upon it the principal years of crisis, early in June 1918, some days before the publication of Spengler's **Decline of the West**, which, though founded upon a different philosophy, gives the same years of crisis and draws the same general conclusions".

4. Reprinted in Seon Givens, ed.: **James Joyce: Two Decades of Criticism** (New York, 1948), p.200. For the relationship between **Ulysses** and **The Waste Land**, see Giorgio Melchiori: "**The Waste Land** and **Ulysses**", **English Studies** 35 (1954), pp.56–68, Robert Adams Day: "Joyce's Waste Land and Eliot's Unknown God", in **Literary Monographs**, vol.4, edited by Erich Rothstein (Madison, 1971), pp.137–210, and Stanley Sultan: **Ulysses, The Waste Land and Modernism** (Port Washington, 1977).

5. Ezra Pound: **The Pound-Joyce Letters** (London, 1968), p.251.

6. **Letters**, edited by Stuart Gilbert and Richard Ellmann, 3 vols. (New York, 1966), Vol.1, p.55.

7. All references to **Ulysses** are to the Bodley Head edition (London, 1960) and will be included in the text between parentheses.

8. **The Revolt of the Masses** (London, 1961 edition), p.75.

9. **Pound-Joyce Letters**, p.206.

10. **James Joyce and the Making of Ulysses** (Bloomington, 1967), p.274.

11. Harry Levin: **James Joyce** (London, 1960), p.79.

12. **James Joyce and the Making of Ulysses**, p.274.

13. T.S. Eliot: **Collected Poems and Plays** (London, 1969), pp.37, 40, and **Pound-Joyce Letters**, p.198.

14. **James Joyce and the Making of Ulysses**, p.116.

15. **Dublin's Joyce** (London, 1963), p.10.

16. **James Joyce and the Making of Ulysses**, pp.67–68.

17. **Axel's Castle** (London, Fontana edition, 1961), p.181.

18. "POSTmodernISM", **New Literary History**, Autumn 1971, p.19.

19. **A la recherche du temps perdu** (Paris, Pléiade edition, 1954), Vol.3, pp.806, 807, 762, 759.

20. "The Waste Land", **Collected Poems**, p.61.

21. All quotations from **The Magic Mountain** are from the translation by H.T. Lowe-Porter (Penguin edition, 1960), and will be included in the text between parentheses.

22. T.J. Read: **Thomas Mann: The Uses of Tradition** (Oxford, 1974), p.263.

23. References to **Doctor Faustus** are to the translation by H.T. Lowe-Porter (London, 1949) and will be included in the text between parentheses.

24. **Speculations** (London, 1936), pp.74, 55, 10.

25. Fritz Stern: **The Politics of Cultural Despair** (New York, 1965), p.222.

26. **After Strange Gods** (London, 1934), p.18. Compare Spengler: "This I call race. Tribes, spets, clans, families – all these are designations for the fact of a blood which circles, carried on by procreation in a narrow or a wide landscape" (II, p.113).

27. H. Stuart Hughes: **Oswald Spengler** (New York, 1952), p.5.

28. Quoted in Stern, pp.316–17.

29. Letter to Ernst Fischer, quoted in Gunilla Bergsten: **Thomas Mann's Doctor Faustus** (Chicago, 1969), p.179.

30. **Genesis of a Novel**, translated by R. and C. Winston (London, 1961), p.29.

31. **Genesis of a Novel**, p.55.

32. **Thomas Mann's Doctor Faustus**, p.107.

33. Quoted in **Thomas Mann's Doctor Faustus**, p.106.

34. **Genesis of a Novel**, p.76.

35. Quoted in Theodore Ziolkowski: **Dimensions of the Modern Novel** (Princeton, 1969), p.204. See also Mann's other description of the **leitmotiv** as "that magical formula which points forward and backwards and which is the means of bestowing present validity upon its inner totality at every moment" (p.207).

36. **Thomas Mann's Doctor Faustus**, pp.99–100.

37. **The Orbit of Thomas Mann** (Princeton, 1969), p.21.

38. Quoted in Richard Ellmann, **James Joyce** (Oxford, 1959), p.594.

39. **Genesis of a Novel**, p.125.

40. See Budgen's account of how Joyce could "collect in the space of a few short hours the oddest assortment of material", **James Joyce and the Making of Ulysses**, p.172.

41. "The Mind of Modernism", in **Modernism**, edited by Malcolm Bradbury and James McFarlane (Harmondsworth, 1976), p.83.

42. **Prisms** (London, 1967). Adorno's essay in this collection, "Spengler after the Decline", is an important attempt to place Spengler in relation to Modernism.

43. Quoted in Richard M. Kain: "Motif as Meaning: The Case of Leopold Bloom", in Thomas F. Staley and Bernard Benstock, eds.: **Approaches to Ulysses** (University of Pittsburgh Press, 1970), p.61.

44. **James Joyce**, p.377. See also Robert M. Adam's detailed study of the random and the constructed in the novel in **Surface and Symbol: The Consistency of James Joyce's Ulysses** (New York, 1962), and Frank Kermode's observation, in his analysis of the modern apocalypse in **The Sense of an Ending** (London, 1966), that **Ulysses** alone of the major texts of Anglo-American Modernism "studies and develops the tension between paradigm and reality, asserts the resistance of fact to fiction, human freedom and unpredictability against plot" (p.113).

Expressionism and Vorticism: An Analytical Comparison

Richard Sheppard

Writing in mid-1914, Ezra Pound indicated that he saw an affinity between Vorticism and Expressionism when he said: "A good vorticist painting is more likely to be mistaken for a good expressionist painting than for the work of Mr Collier" ("Edward Wadsworth, Vorticist", **TE**, 15 August 1914, p.306), and C.R.W. Nevinson, the English Futurist closely associated with the Vorticist circle, did the same when he referred, in a lecture of 12 June 1914, to "the Expressionists, such as Kandinsky, Wyndham-Lewis [sic], Wadsworth, etc., or Vorticists as I believe the latter now like to be called..." ("Vital English Art", **TNA**, 18 June 1914, p.160). Sixty years later, the art historian Richard Cork, in his monumental and exhaustive study, pointed out that the "urgency and harshness" of Vorticism were "akin to the excoriating art of the Expressionists",[2] and in an essay entitled "Vorticism: Expressionism English style",[3] the literary critic Ulrich Weisstein extended the comparison, drawing attention to typographical similarities (p.29), the importance of abstraction and primitivism for both movements (pp.31,33), and the concern of both movements to explore "the instincts and emotions which play around the dark core of life" (p.35).

Germany and the Vorticists

Much data legitimizes such comparisons. Even though French art and literature and Italian Futurism made a more dramatic and intensive impact on the Vorticists (belying Weisstein's description of Vorticism as "that Anglo-Saxon offshoot of Expressionism" (p.28)), and even though the Vorticists rarely used the term "Expressionism"[4] – a fact which is not surprising given the same reluctance on the part of the German **avant garde** during the pre-war years[5] – it is clear, in retrospect, that the English movement owed a certain amount to Germany and its German counterpart.

Several of the Vorticist circle had spent time in Germany. Lewis was in Munich in early 1906 and wrote at least one letter home from the Café Stephanie in the Amalienstrasse, the **venue** of the Munich artistic **bohème**; Edward Wadsworth's knowledge of German dated from 1906 when he too studied in Munich (Cork, 1, p.215); Gaudier-Brzeska had also been there in 1909;[6] Pound visited Giessen and Freiburg in Summer 1911;[7] and T.E. Hulme was in Berlin for nine months – probably November 1912 to July 1913 – and visited Marburg at least once during that period where he heard a lecture by Hermann Cohen, the foremost Neo-Kantian philosopher ("Erkenntniskritiker") of the time.[8]

From such contacts, their reading of philosophers such as Nietzsche (q.v.), Schopenhauer, Weininger and Stirner (who is referred to in Lewis's "Enemy of the Stars" (**B1**, pp.76–77) as Stirnir, the author of **Einige und Sein Eigenkeit** [!])[9] and various personal experiences, the Vorticists formed a double attitude towards Germany: on the one hand a profound antipathy to official, Wilhelmine Germany, and on the other, an ambivalent receptivity towards the German **avant garde** who were alienated from that system and of whom, for Pound at least, Heine was a worthy predecessor. The former attitude – a more violent version of which marks Expressionism – is evident throughout the Vorticist period and becomes more pronounced after August 1914. In "Enemy of the Stars", for example, Lewis referred to Berlin as the place of heavy, pestilential, oppressive materiality (**B1**, pp.73, 81), and **Tarr** (which Lewis wrote in the winter of 1914–15 and began serializing in **TE** on 1 April 1916) not only abounds in anti-German sentiment (see especially the Preface to the first edition), but has two of its main characters – Otto Kreisler and Bertha Lunken – stand respectively for German "melodramatic nihilism" and "the kind of Germanic culture encountered in Hauptmann and Sudermann" (**RA**, p.149). Pound openly confessed to being "not particularly fond of Germans" ("Through Alien Eyes I", **TNA**, 16 January 1913, p.252) and often attacked German **Kultur**, **Bildung** and **Wissenschaft** as a more insidious example of the inhuman tyranny of German militarism.[10] Indeed, in February 1917 he even went so far as to blame "the hell of contemporary Europe" on "the lack of representative Government in Germany, and . . . the non-existence of decent prose in the German language" ("James Joyce: At last the Novel Appears", **TE**, February 1917, p.22). And even Hulme, the least anti-German of the Vorticist circle, devoted a considerable amount of space in his essays in **TNA** and the **Cambridge Magazine** of 1915 and 1916 to attacking the German "objective-organic view of the state", according to which the state is a "metabiological, spiritual organism . . . in which the individual forms a part" ("War Notes", **TNA**, 30 December 1915, p.198).

At the same time, Lewis, in the "Editorial" to **B2**, also recognized an "unofficial Germany" which "has done more for the movement that this paper was founded to propagate, and for all branches of contemporary activity in Science and Art, than any other country" (p.5). Had Lewis wanted to acknowledge the Vorticists' debt more precisely, he might well have singled out the painter and theoretician Wassily Kandinsky (referred to by Pound as the "mother" of Vorticism (**B1**, p.154)) and the theoretician of abstraction Wilhelm Worringer. The Vorticists would have known Kandinsky's visual work from several sources: he had exhibited twelve engravings and two paintings at the Allied Artists' Association (AAA) salon in 1909; three paintings (including **Improvisation 6** (1909) and **Komposition 1** (1910) at the 1910 AAA salon; six woodcuts with an album and text at the 1911 AAA salon; three paintings (**Improvisation 29** (1912), **Landschaft mit zwei Pappeln** (1912) and **Improvisation 30 (Kanonen)** (1913)) at the 1913 salon; three paintings (**Kleines Bild mit Gelb** (1914), **Studie für Improvisation 7** (1910) and **Bild 1914**) at the 1914 AAA salon (see Cork, 1, pp.214–17), and **Sonntag** (c.1904–05) and **Zwei Vögel** (1907) at the exhibition of German woodcuts in the Twenty-One Gallery in Spring 1914.[11] At least one of the Vorticists, Wadsworth, was intimately acquainted with Kandinsky's treatise on abstraction, **Über das Geistige in der Kunst** (which had appeared at Christmas 1911), since he published seventeen translated extracts from it in **B1** (pp.119–25), sixteen of which came from the first half of the chapter "Formen- und Farbensprache". As Cork maintains (1, pp.215–16), Kandinsky was primarily important to several of the Vorticist circle because he helped them towards abstraction. Correspondingly, five of the fourteen passages **omitted** by Wadsworth from "Formen- und Farbensprache" either allow or advocate the use in painting of empirical objects and Wadsworth's development away from the "speeded-up Impressionism" of Futurism evident in his pictures **Radiation, March** and **Scherzo** (1913–14) may well have been connected with his study of Kandinsky's theory (Cork, 1, p.214). Similarly, although Hulme did not rate Kandinsky's work very highly ("Modern Art III", **TNA**, 26 March 1914, p.661), he approved of his abstractionism in principle; Nevinson, in "Vital English

Art", an article which implicitly used abstraction as the touchstone of modernity, called Kandinsky's three paintings at the 1914 AAA salon "three of the finest modern pictures I have ever seen" (p.160); and Lewis (who, according to Weisstein, "never sympathized with Kandinsky's art" (p.30)) not only praised him in an interview as "the chief apostle of absolute abstraction in painting in Europe today" (**Daily News and Leader**, 7 April 1914, p.4) but also, five years later, in **The Caliph's Design**, that "little vorticist bagatelle" (**WLoA**, p.133), called him "the most advanced artist in Europe ... according to the above criterion of 'modernness' [i.e. abstraction]" (**WLoA**, p.167).

There were, however, two other motives behind Vorticist interest in Kandinsky. Wadsworth's choice of extracts from "Formen- und Farbensprache" indicates that he was drawn to Kandinsky's theories of the mystical origins of the **innerer Klang**, the inner resonance of a work of art, as do his remarks accompanying his translations concerning "cosmic organisation" and "the deeper and more spiritual standpoint of the soul" (p.119). And Pound, that "ardent Kandinskyan" (Weisstein, p.30), having read Kandinsky's "chapter on the language of form and colour" ("Vorticism [1]", **The Fortnightly Review**, September 1914, p.465), found that it confirmed his ideas on the writing of verse. For Pound, Kandinsky's notion of the "innere Notwendigkeit" which generated a work of art corresponded exactly to his own thinking about "the creative power of the artist"[12] – that unconscious psychic drive which produced the completely appropriate image. In other words, Kandinsky's work contributed to the formulation of both sides of the Vorticist aesthetic – the advocacy of hard-edged, abstract form and the concern with primal energy.[13]

From mid-1909 until he went to Berlin in late 1912, Hulme had been an enthusiastic Bergsonian. He translated his **Introduction à la métaphysique** (which appeared in 1913) and commended him for liberating men from anthropomorphism, the absolute hold of logical reason ("Searchers after Reality. II. Haldane", **TNA**, 19 August 1909, pp.315–16) and a mechanical and deterministic view of the universe ("Mr Balfour, Bergson and Politics", **TNA**, 9 November 1911, pp.38–39). He also expressed his gratitude to him for giving him back a concept of "soul" ("Notes on Bergson III", **TNA**, 23 November 1911, pp.80–81) and a "spiritual view of the world" ("Notes on Bergson IV", **TNA**, 30 November 1911, p.111).[14] Hulme's experience of Berlin, the overheated world of its **avant garde** (described in "German Chronicle") and, most particularly, his discovery of Worringer through reading Paul Ernst's essay "Kunst und Religion" changed all that.[15] Hulme's letter to Marsh (see note 8) indicates that when he first went to Berlin, he knew only of "Einfühlungsästhetik" which, deriving from the work of Riegl, Lipps and Volkelt, assumed a harmonious relationship between man, the world and art-objects and legitimized a representational art which allowed the beholder to feel himself into the object and at home in the world. Worringer's work, however, (which Hulme, stimulated by Ernst's essay, seems to have got to know only in 1913 since it is not mentioned in the letter to Marsh as featuring in his conversations on aesthetics with Rupert Brooke in late 1912) criticized the Lippsian aesthetic for its anthropo- and ethnocentrism and proposed a different kind of aesthetic – that of "Abstraktion" – as a way of explaining non-representational, non-Western and pre-Renaissance art. According to Worringer – (see especially his **Abstraktion und Einfühlung** (1908), **Die altdeutsche Buchillustration** (1912) and **Formprobleme der Gotik** (1912)) – such art derived from a drastic sense of not being at home in the world, of being exposed to chthonic, daemonic powers, and represented man's attempt to defend himself against engulfment by means of stable, abstract forms. Worringer's revolutionary notion of "Abstraktion", encountered in the over-heated atmosphere of **avant-garde** Berlin, had four effects on Hulme. First, it connected with and intensified his sense, already well-developed by his reading of Bergson, that the world was in flux; second, it developed his sense that this flux was chaotic and destructive rather than harmonious and spiritual; third, it made him more open to abstract art; and fourth, it gave him the sense that the era which had produced and was legitimized by "Einfühlungsästhetik" – the liberal humanist epoch – was coming to an end. The shifts in Hulme's outlook are immediately evident in his publications after his return to England in mid- to late 1913. In "Mr Epstein and the Critics" (**TNA**, 25 December 1913, pp.251–53), Hulme, for the first time, announced the end of the post-Renaissance era and declared Epstein's abstract sculpture appropriate to the new age. In "Modern Art I. The Grafton Group" (**TNA**, 15 January 1914, pp.341–42), "Modern Art and its Philosophy" (a paper delivered to the Quest Society on 22 January 1914, **Speculations**, pp.75–109) and "Modern Art II" (**TNA**, 12 February 1914, pp.467–69), Hulme announced the same break-up of the Renaissance humanist attitude, acknowledged his debt to Worringer and proposed an austere, constructive, geometric art. And in "A Lecture on Modern Poetry" delivered in early 1914,[16] he summarized Worringer's views on abstraction (pp.70–71) and argued that the modern age, being one of impermanence, required a new verse which "resembles sculpture rather than music", which "appeals to the eye rather than to the ear", and which "has to mould images, a kind of spiritual clay, into definite shapes" (p.75). Thereafter, all Hulme's aesthetic and philosophical writings involved a critique of humanism: Worringer's art-historical distinction had become a polemical weapon.

Although Hulme did not consider himself a Vorticist and was at loggerheads with Lewis, his ideas had an undeniable effect upon the group. First, his insistence on hard, geometric art almost certainly reinforced that tendency to abstraction which was so prevalent among the Vorticists by early 1914; second, his thinking must have strengthened that interest in "primitive" art which was also present by the same date; and third, he must have begun to transmit the conviction – which is, to the best of my knowledge, never foregrounded in the title or substance of any work by any member of the Vorticist group before 1914 – that the history of the West was about to undergo a drastic change of direction. The effect of Hulme's reception of Worringer is most evident in the case of Pound. Hulme's demand for hard-edged art was, of course, nothing new to Pound (who had known Hulme since 1909 and who, in his Imagist theorizing of 1912–13, had made just such demands himself). Nevertheless, Pound's essay "The New Sculpture" (**TE**, 16 February 1914, pp.67–68) clearly indicates that he, as a direct result of hearing Hulme's lecture of 22 January 1914 (p.67), was becoming aware of the cultural-historical implications of those demands. Thus, when Pound wrote that "Mr Hulme was quite right in saying that the difference between the new art and the old was not a difference in degree but a difference in kind, a difference in intention" (p.68), he implied that he too was beginning to sense the passing of an era, and accordingly, the same essay went on to demand a neo-primitivism in art (which, for Pound, was to be found in the work of Epstein and Gaudier-Brzeska ("Exhibition at the Goupil Gallery", **TE**, 16 March 1914, p.109)). Whereas Futurism had made the Vorticist group more aware of the technologization of the world, but presented this process – reassuringly – as part of a positive, upward movement of history, Hulme's version of Worringer implied that a much more fundamental upheaval was in store for the modern world from which men would need to seek refuge in works of austere, hard-edged geometricity, not works which celebrated the flux of modern life.

Had war not broken out, the Vorticists would probably have become even more familiar with and positive about German Expressionism. The Twenty-One Gallery show of modern German art included twelve paintings by Moriz Melzer; two early woodcuts by Kandinsky (see above); one unidentifiable woodcut by Ernst Ludwig Kirchner; either a woodcut from **Die kleine Passion** (1913) or **Grosse Kreuzigung** (1912) by Wilhelm Morgner;[17] two woodcuts, two water-colours and a drawing by Max Pechstein; and the woodcuts **Ruhende Pferde** (1911–12), **Trinkendes Pferd** (1912), **Tierlegende** (1912), **Tiger** (1912) and **Schöpfungsgeschichte** (1914) by Franz Marc;[18] and Lewis, in the Foreword to its Catalogue, praised the exhibits for their disciplined, brutal austerity (i.e. their approximation to a major aspect of the Vorticist aesthetic) (**B**1, p.136). Furthermore, in "German Chronicle", Hulme drew his readers' attention to such Expressionist magazines as **Pan, Die weissen Blätter, Der Sturm,**[19] **Der lose Vogel** and **Die Aktion** (p.224); reported on a visit to Kurt Hiller's Cabaret GNU on 24 May 1913 (see note 8) at which items by Ernst Blass, Paul Boldt, Arthur Drey, Alfred Wolfenstein and Hiller himself were read out (pp.224–25); reviewed Hiller's **Der Kondor** (1912), the first and controversial anthology of Expressionist poetry (p.225–28), with particular reference to individual poems by Blass, Else Lasker-Schüler, Georg Heym, Drey and René Schickele;[20] mentioned Werfel's anthologies **Der Weltfreund** (1911) and **Wir sind** (1913), Max Brod's anthology **Tagebuch in Versen** (1910), Shickele's anthology **Weiss und Rot** (1910), Herbert Grossberger's anthology **Exhibitionen** (1913) and Alfred Lichtenstein's anthology **Dämmerung** (1913); and indicated that he had had at least one extensive conversation with Hiller's close friend, the psychiatrist Arthur Kronfeld (cf **DSdNC**, 2, pp.596–97). Overall, Hulme's article – which must have been the first ever to point English-speaking readers towards Expressionist poetry[21] – gives the impression that things are happening in Berlin which, even if not entirely comprehensible to the Englishman, are new, intelligent, aggressive and worth watching. If the Vorticists failed to follow Hulme's pointers, it was probably more because the War cut off their access to the sources[22] than because there was a quality in Expressionist poetry which made it inherently alien to the Vorticists (cf Weisstein, p.31). Had the Vorticists known that combination of formal discipline and apocalyptic violence which marks much of the poetry of, say, Jakob van Hoddis, Heym or Georg Trakl, they would have had no difficulty in assimilating this mode of writing to their own ambiguous aesthetic.

The Problems of a Comparative Study

Although Vorticist receptivity towards the German **avant garde** encourages one to take the initial comparative thoughts further, such an undertaking involves two methodological hazards. First, there is the danger that it will degenerate into a nominalistic exercise in which the critic attempts to define an abstracted concept (i.e. Vorticism or Expressionism) either by drawing up a list of doctrines and surface stylistic traits or by narrowing down the concept to one "essential feature". Where the former approach bedevils much of the copious secondary literature on Expressionism,[23] the latter makes itself felt in the much less numerous discussions of Vorticism.[24] Inevitably, both approaches produce artificial questions (such as those which ask how far individuals are representatives of movements); readings of texts, be they literary or visual, which sacrifice complexity to conformity with abstract definition; and the neglect of historical data. It has to be remembered that "Expressionism" was a label imposed by outsiders and accepted by practitioners (if at all) only relatively late,[25] and that the label "Vorticism" was invented by Pound for the Rebel Art Centre group only a few weeks before the appearance of **Blast** 1 on 15 July 1914 (Cork, 1, pp.232–35)[26] more as a publicistic slogan than, as was the case with the term "Futurism", the summation of a set of doctrines subscribed to by a closely-knit group (ibid., p.248). Second, there is the danger – which Weisstein did not entirely avoid – of presenting the two movements as static and self-contained. The two labels apply to phenomena which were both dynamic and diverse. Even Vorticism, which, unlike Expressionism, was small, geographically concentrated and relatively short-lived, underwent a change after the outbreak of war, and there was considerable stylistic diversity not only between but also within the work of the individuals who constituted the two movements.[27]

If then, the two movements are to be compared, it is first necessary to get beyond the reassuring sense of static unity which comes from a reductionist use of their labels, and then to overcome the scepticism about such a comparative project which inevitably arises when the internal diversity, previously concealed by those labels, is recognized. It then becomes possible to identify and compare the problematics which informed the two movements, and, by locating them in the cultural situations from which they arose, to compare the texts which were created as the diverse and even (self-) contradictory responses to those problematics.[28] By concentrating on the subliminal interplay between problematic and response, such an approach views the resultant texts not as autotelic aesthetic objects but as signifiers of the diverse possibilities generated by that interplay. Concomitantly therefore, the same approach, inasmuch as it concentrates on "libidinal apparatus"[29] rather than surface style, views the two movements not as phases in a linear history of art or literature, but as aspects of that cultural **brisure** from which European Modernism as a whole arose.

Methodological hazards notwithstanding, the Expressionists and Vorticists shared a very similar problematic. As Lewis said, reviewing the "-isms" of the pre-war years: "In every case the structural and philosophic rudiments of life were sought out. On all hands a return to first principles was witnessed" (**BaB**, p.257). Basic to that search was the rejection of the norms of bourgeois humanism and of classical or representational art (cf **BaB**, p.103). Gottfried Benn's **Morgue** poems (1912), one of which begins: "Die Krone der Schöpfung, der Mensch, das Schwein / geht doch mit anderen Tieren um"; Rob Cairn's statement in Lewis's "The French Poodle" that "Man is losing his significance" (**TE**, 1 March 1916, p.40); Alfred Döblin's "Ermordung einer Butterblume" (1911) which shows the impotence of human arrogance in the face of Nature; Carl Einstein's fantastic novel **Bebuquin** (1906–09) which is one long inversion of anthropomorphic thinking; Pound's censure of the humanist artist ("The New Sculpture", **TE**, 16 February 1914, pp.67–68) and polemic against the Renaissance ("Affirmations VII", **TNA**, 11 February 1915, p.410); the rejection of the anthropocentrism of the Marburg **Erkenntniskritiker** Hermann Cohen which is common to both Hulme (**Speculations**, p.19) and the early Expressionist Neuer Club (**DSdNC**, 2, pp.455–59); the scepticism vis-à-vis the capacities of human reason which characterizes Hulme's writings on Bergson and the irrationalist half of the Neuer Club; Hulme's writings from the months after his return from Germany (see above); Kandinsky's mystical view of art; the Vorticists' machine forms; Marc's paintings and woodcuts which placed animals at the centre of Creation; Gaudier-Brzeska's primitivism and rejection, in his letter of 24 October 1912, of "a badly understood tradition which has always taught blind adoration of the Greeks and Romans" (**Savage**

Messiah, p.46) – all, in their various ways, aim, like much of Lewis's major prose fiction from the Vorticist decade, at the subversion of "the humanistic paradigm, the received idea of a pre-existing human nature and the illusions of an autonomous, centred 'self' or formal identity" (Jameson, p.51; cf Wees, p.191).

Conversely, both Vorticists and Expressionists sought, through their artefacts, to envisage a new kind of being – and here, echoes of **Zarathustra** are audible – in whom the repressed powers of creativity – that "lost reality and . . . lost intensity" as Pound puts it ("Affirmations VI", **TNA**, 11 February 1915, p.411; see also **Gaudier-Brzeska**, p.114 and "Vorticism [2]", **TNA**, 14 January 1915, p.277) – are released; who thereby stands out from the masses and who, precisely because he is not the rationally ordered, harmoniously centred self of bourgeois humanism, is capable of living adequately amid the tumultuous, many-layered violence of the modern world.[30] And it was exactly this connection between art and life that Lewis was making when he said, in retrospect, that the "novel alphabet of shapes and colours" created by Vorticism, Cubism and Expressionism "presupposed" (i.e. was the expression of) a "new human ethos".[31]

At the same time as they presented a "creative personality" in print or on canvas, or made statements about "creativity" in their essays and manifestos, both Expressionists and Vorticists implicitly posed four linked questions: Is the irrational power of creativity spiritual/intellectual or natural/animal? Is that power only apparently creative and in reality destructive? Is it related to cosmic forces? And are those forces, assuming that they exist, ultimately patterned or destructive?

Not surprisingly, the possible answers to such questions are bewilderingly diverse. Not only is there no consensus about the answers within either movement, but individual artists will present a "creative personality" only simultaneously to deconstruct that presentation, or, in several texts from roughly the same period, offer answers to such questions which stand in stark contradiction to one another. In Expressionist literature, Walter Hasenclever's play **Der Sohn** (1913), Reinhard Sorge's play **Der Bettler** (1911), Georg Kaiser's play **Von Morgens bis Mitternachts** (1912) and Hanns Johst's play **Der Einsame** (1917) provide good examples of the former phenomenon. In all four, a hero is presented whose creativity is, at the outset, repressed by a real father, or, in the case of Kaiser's and Johst's plays, patriarchal authority (the bank and small-town philistinism). And in all four, the heroes seek to release that creativity by a desperate revolt. However, after what seems like initial success (episodes when all four heroes experience a moment of intense, unfettered release of their creative potential), the plays, with varying degrees of self-consciousness, deconstruct the ethos of creative vitalism. **Der Sohn** shows that ethos leading the son into the hands of politically suspect, right-wing anarchists; exposes it, in the scene with the prostitute, as nothing more than a dressed-up form of adolescent self-dramatization; and, in the final act, shows it bringing the son to the brink of murder (which is avoided only because the father has a convenient heart-attack when the son is about to pull the trigger). In **Der Bettler**, the same ethos leads the central character to a double murder, and in the other two plays, it brings about the death or ruin of several secondary characters and a state of totally disillusioned, emotional exhaustion in the two central characters (a conclusion which is avoided in the dizzily spiralling **Der Bettler** only because the action stops before its full implications can be realized). In all four cases, the forces of creativity are shown to be closely related with forces of destruction. One can see the same debate in the inner contradictions of the visual, literary and theoretical work of Kandinsky 1908–14,[32] the various strands of the poetry of Jakob van Hoddis (cf **DSdNC**, 2, pp.485–95) and the prose and poetry of Heym. Although critics have often imposed a unity on Heym's work, it actually points in several directions. Where his early poems and dramas (1908–10) point to the conclusion that the irrational powers driving human nature are basically bestial, destructive and linked with a hostile Fate (**DSdNS**, 2, pp.498–500), some of his stories and poems from 1911 involve a sense that behind the dark stratum of human experience, there lies a spiritual power which points beyond itself to a force in the cosmos that is basically good (**DSdNC**, 2, pp.504–7). In none of the cases cited is it a question of simple "development": various alternatives are juxtaposed – probably without the artist's awareness – and the reader is invited to consider and choose.

The abstract debate within Expressionism about the nature of creativity revolved around that untranslatable word **Geist**.[33] For Kandinsky, imbued as he was with theosophical ideas,[34] **Geist** was the creative, metaphysical power behind the cosmos ("das Ewig-Objektive") which also worked in the human personality ("das Zeitlich-Subjektive") to produce art. In contrast, Kurt Hiller, who disliked Kandinsky's mysticism (cf "Ausstellung der Pathetiker", **DA**, 27 November 1912, col.1514), regarded **Geist** as something purely human, designating a rational/moral faculty of perception, decision and will (cf **DSdNC**, 2, pp.470–71). Consequently, in 1918, he engaged in a violent, public polemic with his former friend Fritz Koffka over precisely this issue. Whereas Koffka described **Geist** in a religious fashion as "die grosse Liebe, die von ausserhalb her die Welt umfängt",[35] Hiller equated the same concept with "Ratio" and described it as that which imposes morally-directed, human control on the irrational, animal parts of the personality and the chaos of Nature.[36] A third position – one which was particularly characteristic of early Expressionism (cf Korte, passim) – was most clearly taken by Ludwig Rubiner who, in the immensely influential essay "Der Dichter greift in die Politik" (**DA**, 22 May and 5 June 1912, cols. 645–52 and 709–15), described **Geist** as the power of "Intensität", the "Wille zur Katastrophe" (col. 715) which produced "Feuersbrünste, Explosionen, Absprünge von hohen Türmen, Licht, Umsichschlagen, Amokschreien" (col. 646). Where, for Kandinsky, **Geist** was spiritual and creative, for the pre-war Rubiner it was chthonic and essentially destructive (even if it did provide the experience of "eine ewige Sättigung in einem einzigen Moment" (col. 647)); where, for Hiller, **Geist** was a purely human faculty, for the Rubiner of the pre-war years it was linked with the violent forces of untamed Nature.

The same debate went on among the Vorticists and is particularly evident in Lewis's early prose and drama. Here, shifting perspectives within and on the narratives, ironically detached modes of narration and impeccably Vorticist statements in the mouths of characters whose point of view is suspect or flawed combine to show that Lewis was experimenting with psychological and metaphysical attitudes rather than maintaining one dogmatically – a statement which applies to his work both during the narrowly Vorticist period and the decade 1909–20 as a whole. For example, it is clear that Lewis meant at first to celebrate the pre-modern characters of his early short stories (1909–11)[37] as "primitive creatures, immersed in life, as much as birds, or big, obsessed, sun-drunk insects" (**RA**, p.117). However, these stories became progressively darker over the two years until, in the last of them, "Brobdingnag" (**TNA**, 5 January 1911, pp.2–3), Lewis shows how easy it is for happy, primitive "naturalness" to tip over into murder and insanity, and the story (which, significantly perhaps, was Lewis's last piece of prose fiction to be published for three years) ends: "I felt, in quitting Kermanec, that the shadow of doom had fallen upon this roof".[38] Possibly as a result of this conclusion, Arghol, the central figure of "Enemy of the Stars" (**B**1, pp.51–85), is the complete antithesis of the early "primitives". In Arghol, Lewis has created a being whose creative principle is not an earthy vitality, but a cold, white, brutal, intellectual will. Arghol has set himself against the threat posed by chaotic Nature and deliberately expunged the (associated) female side of his personality. At first, it seems that Lewis is unambiguously celebrating this monster (who is so akin to the typically Vorticist man-machine), but the values that he stands for are called into question when Hanp, his "half-disciple" in whom there is still a "deep female strain" (p.65), murders him out of resentment at his massively male authority – whereupon the "relief of a grateful universe" (p.84) becomes audible (cf Materer, 1976, p.50). "Enemy of the Stars" is as much a critique as a celebration of Arghol (and, by implication, the notion of creativity as hard-edged, monumental will): the play shows the self-destructiveness of Arghol's way of life even while setting it up as an ideal.

If Lewis's early stories and Vorticist play provided the two poles of the problematic, his prose fiction of the first two war years complicated it. **Tarr**, written during the Vorticist period and before the Great War had made its impact, is, to some extent, a restatement of what Lewis had already said. Otto Kreisler, "the place of archaic regression" (Jameson, p.103) is a more extreme version of Lewis's early primitives,[39] whose self-destructiveness forms its own critique. And Tarr himself, whose very actions are heavy and machine-like, who finds the flesh and the female repugnant and who preaches a view of creativity based on the ascetic intellect and will, is similar in type to Arghol (cf Materer, 1976, p.64). And as with Arghol, Lewis offers an implicit critique of what Tarr stands for: despite his repugnance, he has an affair with Bertha, a heavily fleshly, Romantic German Maiden; he comes across as an "emotionally shallow" and "boorish young man" (Materer, 1976, pp.57, 65); he hardly ever seems to produce any art of note despite his claim to be an artist; his name, Sorbert [Sorbet] Tarr, with its implications of black stickiness and melting sweetness, fits ill with the icy clarity he professes and makes him more than slightly comic; and in the second half of the novel, he succumbs to the sensuality of Anastasya who completely overturns all the ideals he had earlier professed. Lewis, even while putting ideas into Tarr's mouth, deconstructs them through his presentation of the total character.[40] Consequently, within the context of Vorticism, **Tarr** can be read as a critique of the two extreme notions of creativity with which that movement is associated. On the one hand, Tarr is frequently depicted, in the first part of the novel, as an amalgam of machine-parts, a hard-shelled, mechanical automaton whose actions are not governed by a personal pronoun. As such, he is reminiscent of the inhuman beings to be found in Lewis's pictures of the same period[41] and the change he undergoes through the agency of Anastasya clearly implies the unacceptability of that ideal of personality. On the other hand, Kreisler's name derives from the German word for a spinning-top, "Kreisel",[42] an image which relates directly to the notion of the Vortex as that is depicted in **Blast** – "stable and self-contained, yet suggesting whirling concentrations of energy ... spinning in space on an unshakeable axis" (Wees, p.177). Clearly, the fact that Kreisler destroys himself indicates that Lewis had reservations about the Vorticist ideal of energy as well. Nevertheless, having shown the limitations of both hard-edged form and unconstrained energy, **Tarr** explores a third possibility in Anastasya (whose name comes from the Greek word for "resurrection"). In her, the extremes of intellect and energy – Apollo and Dionysos –[43] have been fused into a being who is whole, balanced and self-possessed without anarchy or egotism. Although Lewis offers no label for the creative drive which impels her and makes her so special, it is very different from the angular violence hymned in the pages of **Blast** and points beyond the "conflictual organization" (Jameson, p.48) of the rest of the novel and, indeed, of the Vorticist movement as a whole.

The same debate about the nature of creativity is continued and made more complex elsewhere. "The French Poodle" (**TE**, 1 March 1916, pp.39–41) is not certain whether men are driven by a power which is the same as or different from that which drives animals, whether the spontaneity of animal nature is higher or lower than that of the creative force behind human nature, and whether war is a product of the vital forces of Nature, the animal powers in man or a perverse destructiveness that is peculiar to man. "A Young Solider" (ibid., p.46) is uncertain whether to admire or condemn the vital urges in a young soldier glimpsed in the Tube, depicting him as a Nietzschean blond beast, "a born warrior, meant to kill other men as much as a woman is meant to bear children". Similar ambiguities are evident in the two narratives which involve Cantleman, another of Lewis's **personae** (**BaB**, pp.66, 84). In "The War-Crowds 1914" (part of an unpublished book written in July–August 1914, some of which appeared as a variant entitled "The Crowd Master" in **B**2, pp.94–102), Cantleman is presented as yet another, lesser Arghol who, despite his cerebral detachment, permits himself to experience the "female" enthusiasm which drives the crowds in Trafalgar Square at the outbreak of war (**BaB**, pp.78–80). This does nothing for him, however, and confirmed in his previous beliefs, he rejects the female even more emphatically for the superior, male, intellectual detachment of "the stone Nelson" on his column (p.80). In "Cantleman's Spring-Mate", however, written three years later (**TLR**, October 1917, pp.8–14), this version of the creative personality is deconstructed. After a vision of lush, natural fecundity (a passage which, in its sensuality and freedom from narrative irony, is unlike anything else in Lewis's early prose and in which the procreative urges in man are derived unequivocally from the powers of Nature), the previously aloof Cantleman makes a country girl pregnant. So far, as Materer says (1976, p.71), this is a straightforward case of "ironic defeat", but then, to complicate matters, Lewis links the sexual drive with the War, concluding: "And when [Cantleman] beat a German's brains out, it was with the same impartial malignity that he had displayed in the English night with his Springmate" (p.13): clearly, in terms of this story, to succumb to Dionysos is as dangerous as to ignore him. In none of these shorter pieces, however, is there a figure like Anastasya: their multiple ambiguities are presented and the reader is left to puzzle further.

A similar process is implicit in the three visual styles of the illustrations of **Blast** (Lipke and Rozran, p.202). Moving as they do between representationalism and abstraction; balance and imbalance; violently and less obtrusively imposed form, they are at one level visual attempts to get beyond anthropomorphism and, at another, visual responses to the question of how far rigid form needs to be imposed on natural energy. The same problematic underlies Gaudier-Brzeska's diverse sculptures of 1914. On the one hand, hard-edged Vorticist works like **Bird Swallowing a Fish** and **Toy** imply the necessity of subjecting chaotically violent Nature to humanly imposed form, but on the other hand, vitalistic works like **Stags** and **Birds Erect** imply that Nature, which may seem chaotic to the conventional eye, has its own inherent principle of organic form which the artist must learn to perceive and reproduce. The same applies to Ford Madox Hueffer's "The Saddest Story" (a chapter from his novel **The Good Soldier**) and Rebecca West's "Indissoluble Matrimony" in **Blast** 1. Neither Hueffer nor West were Vorticists in the reductionist or doctrinal sense, but Lewis must have perceived that both pieces bore on the problematic which exercised his circle. The former piece is a relatively straightforward investigation of the nature and effect of the passional, sexual energies on the excessively civilized, humanized world of polite society, but the latter piece is much more complex. Here, an enfeebled, excessively cerebral petit-bourgeois is seized by the violence of Nature (personified by his "over-sexed" (p.102), quarter-negro wife). As a result of swimming at night in the "Devil's Cauldron", they both turn into completely primitive beings who nearly murder each other. Clearly, "Indissoluble Matrimony" is both an implicit critique of the male who has done violence to the female in himself (and on whom, therefore, the female inevitably takes revenge), and a statement about the close relationship between the creative, sexual urge and the destructiveness of inhuman Nature. Like Lewis in his war-time stories, West shuns a simple resolution, leaving the reader to find his own way between a series of polar suggestions about the nature of creativity which are both antithetical and complementary.

The Vorticists' theoretical statements on the same subject are similarly complex. To take one detailed example only: throughout the years 1909–1918, Pound veered between an immanentist view of creativity which locates the source of that power in human nature or a human tradition, and a more mystical neo-Platonism (cf "The Approach to Paris VI", **TNA**, 9 October 1913, p.695). And in the more strictly defined Vorticist period, he veered between a view of creativity as an ordered, spiritual, pythagorean power (hence the mathematical imagery in "Vorticism [1]") and a violent, chthonic, barbarian power (cf "The New Sculpture"). Nor will one find Pound making any consistent statements about Nature during this period. Sometimes, like Lewis in "A Review of Contemporary Art" (**B2**, p.40), he writes as though Nature were inherently patterned, commends Chinese geomancers for their intuitive sense of that patterning (**B2**, p.138) and counsels the modern artist to seek it out and reproduce it abstractly in his work. Sometimes, however, he writes as though Nature were pure chaos and implies that the artist's task is to impose form upon that chaos. Pound is typical of the movement as a whole: like the Expressionists – and this is the major similarity between the two movements – the Vorticists were collectively agreed that a lost principle of creativity must be recovered, but differed widely over the nature of that power and the proper relationship between it and humankind. Accordingly, while the Vorticists' machine aesthetic of hard-edged forms is characteristic of many of their explicitly programmatic statements and foregrounded in many of their art-works, it is not the whole picture but simply one product of a more fundamental debate, the innermost terms of which have to be discovered at a much more subliminal level.

The Cultural-historical Situations of Vorticism and Expressionism

The above debate did not go on in abstraction. Rather, the terms in which it was conducted were closely bound up with the cultural-historical situations of the two movements. These differed in three important ways. To begin with, most Expressionists were born (in the 1870s and 1880s) into a society which was largely agrarian and semi-feudal; grew up in a society which was changing its nature at an unprecedented rate; and achieved maturity in a society which was centred on large, industrialized cities.[44] In contrast, the Vorticists were active in a society where the same process had been going on gradually, over the best part of a century, so that industry and machines seemed an accepted, "natural" part of the landscape (**B1**, p.40) rather than anything drastically new. As Lewis claimed to have told Marinetti: "We've had machines here in England for a donkey's years. They're no novelty to **us**" (**BaB**, p.34). Second, by 1914, the very nature of the emergent social and economic order in Germany stood in clear contradiction to the highly authoritarian, rigidly stratified institutions by which it had been uneasily, not to say forcibly, contained. In contrast, Liberal England did not suffer from the same sense of inner contradiction even if, in reality, that contradiction was there. Having come about more slowly, industrialization had been assimilated with greater ease, and the English ruling class, more adaptable than its German counterpart, had, to a markedly greater extent than in Germany, succeeded in taking the new monied classes into itself: despite the Feinians and Suffragettes, English society seemed to be in a state of harmonious evolution, not inner contradiction. Third, partly because of the rate of social change and partly because of the brevity of its existence as a nation, Wilhelmine Germany was haunted by a sense of historical impermanence, the paradoxical symptom of which was the exaggerated monumentality of so many of its institutions. English institutions, however, had never seemed so unselfconsciously secure, supported as they were by centuries of unbroken tradition and the wealth of a still submissive Empire.

As a result, the basic experience of the Vorticists differed from that of the Expressionists in several important respects. To begin with, the early Expressionists suffered from a threefold sense of oppression. At one and the same time, they felt cut off from a living past, oppressed by the huge weight of static, authoritarian institutions above their heads, and threatened by the violence which they perceived in the mushrooming cities. This threefold sense explains why so much of their most typical poetry consists in a collage of simultaneous impressions rather than a diachronic narrative; why the father (who, in their imaginations, was a hypostatized amalgam of the old authority of semi-feudal Prussia and the new authority of the successful capitalist) was such a major problem in their writings; why so many of their paintings and poems evince such a powerful sense of apocalyptic violence and why, in order to find roots, so many of them identified so readily with mythicized worlds, which were geographically or historically as far removed from the present as possible. In contrast, the Vorticists evinced a strong sense of standing within a well-grounded social continuum which had become stodgy and sterile rather than static and oppressive and whose modern manifestation – the machine age – was exciting rather than threatening. The whole of Pound's critical and poetic work during the Vorticist years (i.e. until he lost faith in England and moved to Paris)[45] was rooted in a confidence that English social institutions, although in a bad way, could be revitalized by the power of art. Accordingly, for Pound, the Vorticists were the radical inheritors of a tradition which was basically good but temporarily sterile and it was in this spirit that he proclaimed: "The futurists are evidently ignorant of tradition . . . We [the Vorticists] do not desire to cut ourselves off from the past" ("Wyndham Lewis", **TE**, 15 June 1914, p.234) and: "The vorticist has not this curious tic for destroying past glories" ("Vorticism [1]", p.468). Similarly, as late as **Blast** 2 (July 1915), Lewis could not envisage England losing her Empire which, in his view, was the "one thing that would have deeply changed her" (p.23) and could confidently assert that "life after the War will be the same brilliant life as it was before the War" (p.24). Accordingly, it is significant that of the Vorticist circle, only Hulme, **primarily as a result of his exposure to Berlin**, lost this sense of social continuity to any marked degree during the Vorticist period itself. Where his articles on Bergson from late 1911 proclaim the continuity of history, its "fixity and sameness" ("Notes on Bergson III", **TNA**, 23 November 1911, p.80), his post-Berlin articles imply that the present has somehow become detached from the past until, in late 1915, he could write quite explicitly: "One of the main achievements of the

Nineteenth Century was the elaboration and universal application of the principle of **continuity**. The destruction of this conception is . . . an urgent necessity of the present" ("A Notebook", **TNA**, 16 November 1915, p.158; **Speculations**, p.3).

In contrast, the early Expressionists had an ambiguous relationship with their society: although oppressed by and alienated from it, they were also, as good **Bürgersöhne**, dependent on and eager for recognition by it. And it was precisely this ambiguity which generated the violence of their social attitudes such as is to be found in Sorge's **Der Bettler** or Hasenclever's **Der Sohn**. This signified on the one hand a desire to smash the source of oppression, and, on the other, a resentment against a patriarchal society for failing to give them proper recognition. The Vorticist circle, however, had a much less polarized relationship with literary and artistic London and certainly did not feel so oppressed by English social institutions.[46] Indeed, some of them even gained the entrée for a while to the highest social circles. Lady Cunard wanted them to design little presents for the rich and influential guests attending a dinner in honour of George Moore, asked Lewis and Nevinson to lunch, invited Lewis to share her box at Covent Garden (**BaB**, p.89) and expressed her admiration for one of Cuthbert Hamilton's pictures. Lady Muriel Paget wanted the group around Lewis to design **avant-garde tableaux vivants** for a Picture Ball at the Albert Hall and Nevinson recalled being invited to dine by Lady Lavery and Lady Constance Hatch.[47] In late 1913, Lady Drogheda commissioned Lewis to decorate her dining-room (Cork, 1, pp.132–36) and he later recorded that, after the publication of **Blast** 1, coronetted envelopes showered into his letter-box and that, at one of Lady Ottoline Morrell's gatherings, he met the then Prime Minister, Mr Asquith, whom he was able to reassure about the a-political nature of Vorticism (Cork, 1, p.266; **BaB**, pp.46 and 50–51)! Even though the less socially acceptable members of the Vorticist circle – Epstein the American Jew, Pound the professional Bohemian, Bomberg the East End Jew and Gaudier-Brzeska the wild Frenchman – may well have disapproved of such contacts, none of them seems to have known that acute sense of social alienation which characterized German Expressionism. Conversely, one cannot imagine the German counterpart of English polite society extending the same kind of invitation to, say, Kurt Hiller, Emil Nolde, Herwarth Walden or Ludwig Meidner!

In consequence, where a prophetic or revolutionary stance came naturally to the Expressionists, the Vorticists, for all their apparent radicalism, rarely used the word "revolution". Affectionate if violent rebels, they existed much more within the given social institutions and did not feel the need to smash them because they did not feel trapped by them to anything like the same extent. Thus, in **Blast** 1, England is blasted **and** blessed (a series of texts for which there is no parallel in German Expressionist magazines), its institutions are attacked and enjoyed. Where the Expressionists looked for an apocalypse that would sweep everything away and initiate a society which was qualitatively different – an attitude encapsulated in Rubiner's "Der Dichter greift in die Politik"[48] – the Vorticists, while accusing English society of being dead (see, for example, Pound: **Letters**, pp.61–62), had a much greater faith in its ability to resurrect itself without violent upheaval. Lewis wrote, for instance: "Optimism is very permissible. England appears to be recovering" ("A Man of the Week – Marinetti", **The New Weekly**, 30 May 1914, p.329) and advocated a **modification** (not a revolutionizing) of the national temperament ("Kill John Bull with Art", **The Outlook**, 18 July 1914, p.74). Pound liked London, describing it on 18 March 1914 as "the only sane place for anyone to live if they've any pretence to letters" (Pound: **Letters**, p.72) and until he went to Paris, continually expressed his faith in "the power of tradition, of centuries of race consciousness, of agreement, of association" ("I gather the Limbs of Osiris IX", **TNA**, 25 January 1912, p.298; cf Materer, 1979, p.203) to renew the arts and society. Right in the middle of the Vorticist period, Pound even described what was happening in present-day England as a "renaissance, or awakening" (i.e. of what was dormant in the tradition) not as a cataclysmic irruption of powers from outside into that tradition ("Letter to the Editor", **TE**, 16 March 1914, p.117). And **Blast**, its radical clangour notwithstanding, presented England optimistically, as a "lump of compressed life" (**B**1, p.32), and the machine age as the contiuation rather than the antithesis of an older social tradition, in which the vitality that had moved past epochs was still active ("The Tradition", **Poetry**, February 1914, p.75). Although the Vorticists felt that violent movement was occurring beneath the placid surface of English society, they also felt, with the exception of Hulme after his return from Berlin, that that movement was taking English society in the same direction in which it had been moving before the sterility of the late Victorian epoch had intervened. In contrast, the Expressionists had an acute sense that violent forces were about to blow their society apart. As Heym remarked to Friedrich Schulze-Maizier in early 1910 as they walked home at night through the streets of Berlin: "Nun schauen Sie sich das einmal an. Wie gehetzt, wie hohl, wie gottverlassen! Das **kann** nicht bleiben, das muss zugrundegehen. Irgend etwas Ungeheures muss kommen, ein grosser Krieg, eine Revolution oder sonst etwas. Aber nur nicht so weiter!"[49] Accordingly, when Pound came, on 15 November 1918, to describe the events of the Vorticist years, he remarked: "As for the 'revolution', we have had one here during the war, **quite orderly** [my italics], in the extension of the franchise. Nobody much minds there being several more" (**Letters**, p.201). The double irony is evident: not only has a revolution not taken place, but Pound is actually more than a little pleased that this should have been so. There was a tacit collusion between English society and its aesthetic radicals: on the one hand, the Vorticists hurled ideas around that were revolutionary and subversive to a certain degree only while finding support from the stability of the very institutions they purported to be assailing, and on the other hand, established society took those ideas into itself from on high, proving, in the process, its liberalism and their harmlessness. What Lewis said of himself could apply to Vorticism as a whole: "'Kill John Bull' I shouted. And John and Mrs Bull leapt for joy, in a cynical convulsion. For they felt as safe as houses. So did I" (**BaB**, p.36) – an ambivalence which is also present in the contrast between the stable, realist setting of **Tarr** and the expressionistoid antics of its central figures. In Germany, however, there was not the same collusion: early Expressionism may have been as socially harmless as Vorticism, but its representatives were never so lionized by the social establishment and genuinely wanted violent social change which, as Korte has put it, was to be the "Inbegriff und Synthese aller Sehnsüchte des entfremdeten, den perhorreszierten Zwängen des Wilhelminismus ausgelieferten Subjekts nach Vitalität, exzeptionellen Erlebnissen, Erfüllung, Verwirklichung und Identität" (p.26).

Because of their differing cultural experiences, Nietzsche was far less important for the Vorticists than for the Expressionists. Whereas, on the whole, the Expressionists received Nietzsche positively, being particularly drawn by his apocalyptic cultural criticism and its counterpart, his ecstatic vitalism,[50] the Vorticists, rooted in an apparently reliable tradition, had less need of this. Although some of them were, for various reasons, drawn to Nietzsche before 1910 (cf T.E. Hulme, "The New Philosophy", **TNA**, 1 July 1909, p.198; Cork, 1, p.7; Materer, 1976, p.72),[51] their comments became guarded or ambiguous from 1910 to 1913 and hostile from 1914 onwards. Thus, in "Redondillas, or something of that Sort" (c.1910–11) (**Collected**

Early Poems, p.217), Pound said that he believed in "some parts of Nietzsche" but suspected him "of being the one modern christian"; Hulme, writing in mid-to-late 1913, associated Nietzsche with a linguistic experimentation with which he was not altogether happy ("German Chronicle", pp.224–25); Pound, writing in Autumn 1913, used the word "Nietzschean" pejoratively ("The Approach to Paris III", **TNA**, 25 September 1913, p.631); in **Blast** 1, Lewis associated Nietzsche with Marinetti's "war-talk, sententious elevation and much besides" (p.132); on Lewis's own admission, Nietzsche was "another and more immediate source of infection" for the ironically distanced **Tarr** in general and the negatively presented Kreisler in particular (**RA**, p.149); in **Blast** 2, Lewis connected Nietzsche with ecstatic war-fever (p.5) and the absurd Beresin of "The War Baby" (c.1916) (**Art and Letters**, Winter 1918, pp.14–41) is a caricature of the Nietzschean aristocrat. Precisely because the Vorticists were not haunted by a sense of imminent apocalypse, they could flirt selectively with aspects of Nietzsche's thought without, as so many Expressionists did, having to take his Dionysiac vision of chaos and rebirth seriously as a vitalist gospel of salvation. Thus, when they came to link that vision with Prussianism and the War, they could distance themselves from it with relative ease, as an unfortunate aberration which, as Pound said, was "all very well in conversation" ("What America has to live down VI", **TNA**, 19 September 1918, p.329) – but not, by implication, in practice.

Comparisons: The Texts

Given the above situation, Vorticist works differ from Expressionist ones in several major respects. First and foremost, the Dionysiac values – orgiastic sexuality, social apocalypse, natural violence and pan-demonism – are much more prominent in the German movement. In contrast, such elements are either totally absent from works by Vorticists, or present in a muted form, or controlled by strictly imposed form, or subject to a process of humanization. For example, most of Pound's poems from the Vorticist years do not foreground the demonic even when they deal with potentially demonic subjects,[52] and this is true even of those he published in the two **Blasts**. The (deleted) sexual reference of "Fratres Minores" and the "Goddam" of "Ancient Music" are innocuous compared with the sexuality and obscenity to be found, say, in the poems of Hugo Ball, Lichtenstein and Benn; the satire of "The Social Order" is mild compared with the Germans' vitriolic attacks on the **Bürger**; and "Et faim sallir le loup des boys" may be contemptuous of family life, but unlike Trakl's "Im Osten" (1914), in which wild wolves burst through the city gates, it contains, despite its title, no ravenous wolves! Apart from Pound's brief flirtation with primitivism in Spring 1914, it is the same with his criticism. Joyce is praised for not "ploughing the underworld for horror" and "presenting a macabre subjectivity" ("'Dubliners' and Mr James Joyce", **TE**, 15 July 1914, p.267) and Pound's version of the god Pan ("Arnold Dolmetsch", **TNA**, 7 January 1915, p.246) evoked a "bewildering and pervasive music moving from precision to precision within itself" – not the "panic terror" which afflicted so many of the German **avant garde**.[53] Analogously, although Eliot's poems (**B**2, pp.48–51) depict the surreal, empty surfaces of the modern city, they do not conjure up its demonic night-side as do the poems of Heym, van Hoddis and Lichtenstein.

The Vorticists' sense of the controllability of violence is particularly evident in their paintings, woodcuts and sculptures. Where, in the visual Expressionist work, a violent and anarchic background often appears to be about to burst through the lines which roughly and barely contain it, Vorticist visual works, with their thick geometric lines, transmit a much more secure sense that such violence can be contained. The same sense informs Pound's most Vorticist poem, "Dogmatic Statement on the Game and Play of Chess" (**B2**, p.19; cf Cork, 2, pp.293–94); Lewis's **Tarr**, the potential explosiveness of whose main characters is checked by the firm realism of its city setting and the easy, detached irony of the narrator;[54] and Hulme's vision of flux, which, after his return from Germany, was accompanied by a growing advocacy of rigid artistic, ethical and religious form. Even Hulme's translation of Sorel's **Réflexions sur la violence** (1916) commends not undirected, but carefully disciplined violence, used for precisely defined ends. Indeed, it was their attachment to form which led the Vorticists to bless the Hairdresser (**B1**, p.25) for making "systematic mercenary war" on the "wildness" of Mother Nature!

The Vorticists' tendency to humanize what is potentially demonic becomes more evident after 1914. In **Blast** 2, it is to be found in Hueffer's poem "The Old Houses of Flanders" (p.37) which offers a vision of genteel decay, not violent collapse; Jessie Dismorr's "London Notes" (p.66) which, despite its Cubist surface, is, apart from the last line, actually a very naturalized picture of London; and Helen Sanders's "A Vision of Mud" (pp.73–74) which, beginning as a terrifying vision of engulfment, loses its threat when we hear, at the end, that its subject is a health resort. Similarly, the "religious attitude" behind Hulme's theology of 1915–16, far from being akin to Rudolf Otto's sense of the numinous or Karl Barth's sense of demonic **krisis**, has been reduced to a much more manageable intellectual belief in original sin; and Part I of Lewis's "A Soldier of Humour" (**TLR**, December 1917, pp.32–46) evokes elemental and primitive powers only for these to be naturalized into a farce and rendered harmless in Part II (**TLR**, January 1918, pp.35–51).

By the same token, there is no equivalent in Vorticist works for the sense of imminent apocalypse to be found in Kandinsky's pre-1914 paintings and woodcuts, van Hoddis's "Weltende" (1910) or Heym's "Der Krieg" (1911) – and a comparison of Pound's "Meditatio" (c.1914) with Benn's "Der Arzt II" (1912) makes it quite clear that the Vorticists did not share the Expressionists' extreme sense of the animal in man. Consequently, when the Vorticists confronted Expressionist works, it was precisely such elements that they overlooked or played down. Kandinsky's paintings were appreciated for their abstraction rather than their sense of apocalyptic disorder; Lewis, appraising the woodcuts in the Twenty-One Gallery, saw "man and objects subject to him" and thick, blunt, brutal discipline (**B1**, p.136) – not the elemental suffering of Morgner's passion scenes, or the dormant animalism of Marc's **Ruhendes Pferd, Trinkendes Pferd** and **Tierlegende**, or the apocalyptic creativity of Marc's **Schöpfungsgeschichte** (see notes 17 and 18). Hulme remarked briefly on the "ferocity" of the Expressionist poetry that he heard in the Cabaret GNU ("German Chronicle", pp.224–25), only then to concentrate his account of it on its hard, cerebral and formal qualities. Only rarely do the Vorticists allow the dark, chaotic underworld of Nature and the Unconscious into the foreground of their work – one finds it in the natural violence of "Enemy of the Stars", the description of the Restaurant Lejeune in Part II, Chapter 5 of **Tarr**, the presentation of primal Nature in "Indissoluble Matrimony" and "Cantleman's Spring-Mate", Pound's single glimpse of the horrors of London's lower depths ("Through Alien Eyes II", **TNA**, 23 January 1913, pp.275–76) and Hulme's more developed sense of the chaos in Nature after his return from Berlin. However, such texts (which approach Expressionism in their intensity) are rare, not typical, and accordingly, the extremism of Vorticism is, to a certain extent, deceptive. Pound wrote of **Blast**: "The large type and the flaring cover are merely bright plumage. They are the gay petals which lure" ("Gaudier-Brzeska", **TNA**, 4 February 1915, p.381); and Lewis said in April 1919: "When you leap on to a new continent for the first time you are compelled to make a slight din to frighten away any savages that may be lurking in the neighbourhood" ("What Art Now?", in **WLoA**, p.114). The apocalyptic din of a world tearing itself apart which is to be heard among the Expressionists becomes, within Vorticism, a deliberately induced noise aimed at a world experienced as basically stable: the Vorticist knows of Dionysos and even approaches him, but only appears to let him get the upper hand.

Consequently, where early Expressionist works stress the unreality of the present, being situated in the vacant instant before things blow apart, Vorticism affirms the reality and plenitude of the present (**B1**, pp.7–8 and 147–48); where Expressionist works are torn by extremes, Vorticist works move much more confidently between those extremes (**B1**, pp.30–31); where the "Ich" of the Expressionist artist is continually attracted by mindless ecstasy or threatened by destructive violence, the Vorticist ego is confidently affirmed as the creator of form; where the "Reihungsstil" of early Expressionist poetry is the product of a desperate attempt to hold together an assemblage of fragments which is in danger of being exploded, the Poundian haiku is as centred, and therefore as secure as the circle-creating formula of analytical geometry with which Pound compared it (cf "Vorticism [1]", pp.467–68). Correspondingly, where Expressionist art involves a sense that objects are illusory, mere aspects of flux and hence in constant danger of breaking apart, the Vorticists have a much greater, though by no means unambiguous sense of the reality of objects. Thus, although the objects in their works are packed with or surrounded by energy, it is a propellant, not a destructive energy. The same attitude is visible in their theoretical work. Although Hulme could, in late 1911, agree with the proposition that "reality is a continuum" and "cannot be cut up into discrete objects" ("Bergsonism", **TNA**, 23 November 1911, p.94), by 1915, his essay "Cinders" (**Speculations**, pp.217–45) is based on the idea that the fundament of reality is not energy but hard, individualized objects. Similarly, although Pound's imagination was, thoughout the Vorticist period, engaged by Ernest Fenollosa's **The Chinese Written Character as a Medium for Poetry**,[55] with its basic notion that reality is flux, his own theoretical pronouncements, especially during his Imagist period, assumed the objectivity of things. And Lewis's statements on the same subject, consonant with his ambivalent statements on abstraction, veered between a sense of the object as having an irreducibly concrete structure and a sense of the object as a temporary constellation of energy (cf his "Note" for the Vorticist Exhibition of June 1915, **WLoA**, pp.96–97).

Correspondingly, the Vorticists' attitude to language is much more conservative than the Expressionists'. Only the early Hulme – interestingly enough under Nietzsche's influence – shows any marked sense that language is a system of arbitrary conventions which cannot do justice to reality ("Searchers after Reality II", **TNA**, 19 August 1909, pp.315–16). By 1915, however, even he is writing as though there were a necessary connection between words and things (cf "Romanticism and Classicism", **Speculations**, pp.134–35; "Bergson's Theory of Art", ibid., pp.158–59, 166). For the rest, the Vorticists' attitude to language is summarized in the quotation from Aquinas which Pound used in "Vorticism [1]": "Nomina sunt consequentia rerum" (p.470), and if they have any doubts in that proposition, they are evinced only obliquely, in the emphaticness with which Pound, for example, despite his familiarity with Fenollosa, consistently demands "the welding of word and thing" (**Letters**, pp.222–23). Consequently, Vorticism never produced experimental poetry of the order, say, of Kandinsky's **Klänge** or Stramm's **Sturm** publications (cf Weisstein, p.39) – indeed,

Hulme was actually a little disturbed by and even disapproving of the relatively unadventurous "moderne Dichtkunst" which he heard in GNU ("German Chronicle", pp.224–25). And despite Fenollosa's view that poetry, as an ideogram of a universe in flux, should be based on active verbs, Vorticist poetry is, on the whole, firmly noun-centred. In contrast, Expressionist poetry, deriving from a greater sense of instability, is marked by an inner conflict between superficially stable nouns and dynamic verbs. Thus, although Vorticist writing involves a robust sense of play, it does not have that irony towards language itself which one can find in the cynical rhymes, mixed registers and discordant use of classical form of early Expressionist poetry. For the Vorticists, ironic humour was a means of keeping primal violence within the control of language: for the Expressionists, irony was a more complex phenomenon – a means of dealing both with primal violence and with the fragility of that ultimate means of control. Because of their belief in the consonance of objects and language, grounded as it was in a more stable social experience, the Vorticists were that much farther away from the experience of "panic terror" which lies at the heart of continental Modernism.

The above distinctions explain the Vorticists' and Expressionists' differing attitudes to the machine and the city. The early Expressionists – like Heym, van Hoddis, Kirchner and Schmidt-Rottluff – saw the machine-city as a profoundly ambiguous irruption: although, on the surface, it seemed to be **the** quintessentially human context, in which rational control was most perfectly exercized and the range of human possibilities extended,[56] beneath that surface they perceived a demonic, violent night-side, coextensive with chaotic Nature and populated by semi- if not inhuman beings. The machine was an aspect of this ambivalence: apparently a monument to the human ability to systematize and control, but in reality a monster which, like the Golem of Paul Wegener's two films (1914 and 1920), was out of control and destroying its creator. For a while, the late Expressionists – like the Activists and the architectural theoretician Bruno Taut[57] – played with the utopian hope of restructuring this environment so that the machine could become the servant of man, but the German Revolution of 1918–20 demolished these exaggerated hopes with the result that after 1921, more than a few Expressionists turned their back on machine civilization or died by their own hand. Because Vorticism began from a much less drastic sense of cultural crisis, was not so intensely aware of the connection between Dionysos and the city and displayed greater confidence in man's ability to control, its representatives were able initially, to affirm machine civilisation to the extent that its artifacts could be transformed into "beautiful, painted forms" (Materer, 1976, p.56; cf **B1**, passim and Hulme: "Modern Art and its Philosophy", **Speculations**, pp.99–105). At the same time, they were also conscious of industrial civilization's "capacity for emotional brutality" (Cork, 1, pp.32–33),[58] and with time, this consciousness came to outweigh any impulse to celebrate the machine-city. Thus, Eliot's poems in **Blast** 2 present it as a "Waste Land"; Lewis's paintings **Workshop** and **The Crowd** (1914–15) depict, more clearly than ever before, the city as a dehumanizing prison (cf Cork, 2, pp.342–48); the history of Epstein's **Rock Drill** (1914–16) shows a clear movement away from "involvement with a mechanical culture" to "an indictment of a world that was rapidly becoming tyrannized by the machine" (Cork, 2, p.481); and Pound, once he had awoken to the reality of machine civilization – and of the Vorticists, he, living in the rarified atmosphere of literary London was slowest to do so – rejected it decisively in **Hugh Selwyn Mauberley** (1920) for an idealized past. This shift did not, however, involve those inflated visions of a machine utopia which marked late Expressionism,[59] and, because there was no revolution in England in 1918 onto which to project such fantasies, the possibilities for disillusion were not so great either.

Behind both developments lay the War, and, as with the machine-city, the Expressionists' attitude to the War underwent a dramatic change. Having, in their pre-war writings, either prophesied its coming with a fascinated dread (cf Heym's "Der Krieg" (1911) and Lichtenstein's "Prophezeiung" (1913)), or yearned for it in a romanticized form as a release from the tedium and repression of Wilhelmine society (cf Korte, passim; Ernst Stadler: "Der Aufbruch" (c.1912); Ernst Wilhelm Lotz: "Aufbruch der Jugend" (1914) and Heym's diary entries for 6 July 1910 and 15 September 1911, in Heym: **Dichtungen und Schriften**, 3, pp.138–39 and 164–65), more than a few, as Korte has shown, succumbed to the "Ideen von 1914" and greeted the War ecstatically, as soon as it broke out, as a means of spiritual and national renewal. Its reality was, however, shattering. Lotz, for example, who on 8 August 1914 had written an ecstatic letter to his wife, praising the sense of mystical unity he was experiencing in the army, wrote, on 21 August, after his experience of battle: ". . . in diesen Tagen ist mir der Krieg ein Greuel geworden".[60] Other Expressionists – like Oskar Kokoschka, Klabund, Paul Zech, Hugo Ball, Franz Marc, Rudolf Leonhard and Ludwig Rubiner, not to mention Friedrich, the hero of Ernst Toller's play **Die Wandlung** (1917–18) – experienced similar reversals. The powers of ecstatic unreason to which pre-war Expressionism had been particularly drawn turned, on the battle-field, when coupled with the technology of the machine-city, into horrific violence (cf Jameson, p.108), and it is probably true to say that by about mid-1915, almost no Expressionists were pro-war.[61] Consequently, from that date, one finds the Expressionists trying, like Franz Marc in "Das geheime Europa" and "Im Fegefeuer des Krieges",[62] to deal with the War by seeing it as a "Leidensweg", a purgatorial experience out of which a spiritually purified society would inevitably emerge. The Vorticists, in contrast, took longer to awaken to the reality of war and longer still to oppose it – indeed, of the Vorticist circle, only Nevinson (ironically enough, the self-styled Futurist) had turned against the War by Christmas 1914.[63] Pound rarely mentioned it in his letters, wrote only one or two war poems (one of which was a paraphrase of Hulme's war diary (**Early Poems**, p.286)), and when, from about Spring 1915, the War began to get into his consciousness (cf Stock, p.173) and essays, it was supported as a crusade against German **Kultur** ("This Super-Neutrality", **TNA**, 21 October 1915, p.595). Gaudier-Brzeska (killed on 5 June 1915) positively enjoyed battle (cf his letters to Pound in **Gaudier-Brzeska**, pp.59–71), calling it a "GREAT REMEDY" (**B2**, p.33) in the belief that it would complete the work the Vorticists had begun (cf Materer, 1979, p.31). Lewis's initial attitude, on his own admission, was "unsatisfactory" and "complex", being a mixture of moral crusading, intellectual curiosity and sheer romanticism (**BaB**, pp.7–8 and 85) from which a fascination for violence cannot be excluded;[64] and when, after Passchendaele (Summer 1917),[65] he turned against the War, he did so from an aesthetic feeling that it was "stupid" and a "nonsense" (**BaB**, pp.85, 151) rather than from moral or political conviction. And despite the privations of the trenches in early 1915 (**Further Speculations**, p.157) and his anger at the generals after the Dardanelles fiasco (Autumn/Winter 1915), Hulme too saw the War as a moral crusade against Prussianism and remained consistently pro-war until his death on 28 September 1917 – even if, by early 1916, he was "unable to name any great **positive** 'good'" for which he was fighting ("Why we are in favour of this War", **The Cambridge Magazine**, 12 February 1916, pp.304–05; **Further Speculations**, p.184). As with the Dionysiac powers in general, the Vorticists managed to shield themselves from the War in a way that the Expressionists could not.

If not physically, the Vorticists were, because of their protected cultural situation, less exposed psychically to its violence – which meant that they were less prone to ecstatic enthusiasm when it broke out, less overwhelmed by black disillusion and traumatic shock when its comforting justifications began to crumble, and less in need of millenarian interpretations when they had to find meaning in its continuation.

As a result of this distance and their growing antipathy to the machine civilization which seemed to have generated the War, Vorticist art and theory after about mid-1916 changed in two significant ways. On the one hand, the theory increasingly de-emphasized energy and gave greater weight to form and design,[66] and on the other hand, the art moved back from extreme abstraction and a fascination with the vitalist-primitive to more representational and recognizably human modes (cf **RA**, pp.128–29). Hence the humanism of Epstein's bronze **The Tin Hat** (1916), Pound's growing attraction to the humaneness of Chinese culture and advocacy of "clear, unexaggerated, realistic literature" ("James Joyce: At Last the Novel Appears", **TE**, February 1917, p.21). Hence, too, the civilized world of Pound's **Homage to Sextus Propertius** (1919) where love is a game, not a destructive passion, the formalism of Lewis's **The Caliph's Design** (1919), the relative realism of Lewis's "Guns" show (February 1919) (cf his Foreword to its Catalogue, in **WLoA**, p.104) and the move back to realism which marks the work of Bomberg, Etchells, Nevinson and Wadsworth around the end of the War (cf Cork, 2, pp.524–26). Having set out from a complex problematic and experimented with extreme notions of art and the creative personality, the Vorticists' experience of the War drove them back to a more moderate position which, despite their initially anti-humanist stance, one might describe as a "chastened, modernized humanism". In contrast, the Expressionists' experience of war and machine civilization, deriving from a more drastic sense of cultural crisis and even more extreme notions of art and the creative personality, led them, after 1915, to yet another extreme. Where the Vorticists could fall back on a sense of tradition, the Expressionists felt flung by the War into a void where any sense of meaning or order had to be created **ex nihilo**. Thus, late Expressionist art and literature are marked by a strident, even hysterical resolve to resituate the "Neuer Mensch",[67] purged of his violence and immoralism, in the centre of Creation, and, by utilizing his potential for "Menschlichkeit" and "Gemeinschaft", found a utopia in which his **Geist**, now understood predominantly as ethical potential, could be exercized to the full.[68] Such inflated, utopian hopes came to nothing after the failure of the German Revolution, and the subsequent disillusion is recorded in works like Toller's **Masse Mensch** (1920) and Kaiser's two **Gas** plays (1917–18). Faced with an even more apocalyptically perceived problematic than were the Vorticists, and having committed themselves, with an intensity and single-mindedness from which the Vorticists drew back, to even more extreme resolutions, the Expressionists' situation was, when these failed, that much more desperate than that of their English counterparts. Consequently, one finds no suicides among the Vorticists and nothing so extreme as the Gnostic Catholicism to which Hugo Ball committed himself in 1920. None of the Vorticists became, as did Johannes R. Becher, a leading ideologue of an authoritarian Marxist state; Lewis, fascist though he was for a while, never matched Hanns Johst's achievement in becoming an SS Brigadier General; and Pound's espousal of Mussolini's Italy as a modern version of the corporate, mediaeval state had more to do with literary fantasies than existential desperation.

Inasmuch as both movements are aspects of European Modernism, the preceding discussion involves four assumptions about that broader phenomenon: first, Modernism was not a uniform phenomenon throughout Europe; second, Modernism was a problematic to which there were several inter-related aspects and levels; third, any given individual or group of individuals could perceive that problematic in a more or less complex way and experience it in a more or less intense way; and fourth, there were various ways in which that problematic might be resolved. While it is true that Modernism was "a break with the traditions of the past",[69] that "break" was a much more cataclysmic experience for the German than for the English **avant garde** and provoked a "response" which was both more "conservative" than Eliot's and more "radical" even than D.H. Lawrence's.[70] Accordingly, a comparison of Expressionism and Vorticism inevitably reminds one of the un-Englishness of Modernism: several of the major "English" Modernists – Conrad, Pound, Eliot, Joyce, Yeats, Gaudier-Brzeska and Epstein – were not English at all; Lawrence detested England and lived outside it as much as he could; and the major formative experiences behind the work of Hulme and Lewis were as continental as they were English. That massive sense of institutional stability and historical continuity generated a feeling, not unknown today, that **anomie** begins at Calais,[71] and created a cultural context which tempered the radicalism and experimentation which characterized continental Modernism. Given which, it is not surprising that England should have produced a Modernist movement which combined a will to explore with a fundamental and durable sense of security, but it **is** surprising that England should have produced a version of Modernism at all.

Notes

1. I would like to thank the Alexander von Humboldt-Stiftung, whose generosity during Summer 1983 made it possible for me to research and write this article. The following abbreviations of book and periodical titles will be used throughout: **B1** = **Blast** 1; **B2** = **Blast** 2; **BaB** = P. Wyndham Lewis, **Blasting and Bombardiering** (1937) (London, 1967); **DA** = **Die Aktion; DSdNC** = **Die Schriften des Neuen Clubs**, 2 vols, edited by Richard Sheppard (Hildesheim, 1980–83); **P** = **Poetry**; **RA** = **P. Wyndham Lewis: Rude Assignment** (1947) (London, [1950]); **TE** = **The Egoist; TNA** = **The New Age; WLoA** = **Wyndham Lewis on Art – Collected Writings 1913–56**, edited by Walter Michel and C.J. Fox (London, 1969).

2. Richard Cork: **Vorticism and Abstract Art in the First Machine Age**, 2 vols (London and the University of California, 1976), 1, p.258.

3. Ulrich Weisstein: "Vorticism: Expressionism English Style", **Yearbook of Comparative and General Literature**, 13 (1964), pp.28–40; reprinted in **Expressionism as an International Literary Phenomenon**, edited by Ulrich Weisstein (Paris and Budapest, 1973), pp.167–80.

4. Wyndham Lewis clearly did not like the word. He described the Expressionists as "ethereal, lyrical and cloud-like", having a "fluidity" which is "that of the Blavatskyish soul" ("A Review of Contemporary Art", B2, p.40); regretted that Kandinsky had not found "a better word than 'Expressionist'" ("The Melodrama of Modernity", **B1**, p.143) and avoided the term when writing the foreword to the catalogue of the exhibition of German woodcuts in the Twenty-One Gallery in Spring 1914 (**B1**, p.136). Pound, despite his remark quoted at the beginning of this essay, wrote in a letter of 17 March 1915: "We

[the Vorticists] like Cubism and some Expressionism, but these schools are not our school" (**The Letters of Ezra Pound 1907–1941**, edited by D.D. Paige (London, 1951), p.101); and T.E. Hulme, the one member of the Vorticist circle who came into active contact with Expressionist groups in Berlin, notably that around Kurt Hiller, never used the word once in the extensive article that he published on the **avant-garde** scene there ("German Chronicle", **Poetry and Drama**, June 1914, pp.221–28). Indeed, he even went so far as to describe **Der Sturm** as "Futurist" (p.226) – a sure sign, incidentally, that the label "Expressionist" was not then current among the groups to whom it is now applied.

5. Cf Armin Arnold: **Die Literatur des Expressionismus** (Stuttgart, 1971^2), pp.9–15; **DSdNC**, 2, p.553 and note 4. The recently published **Briefwechsel** between Wassily Kandinsky and Franz Marc, edited by Klaus Lankheit (Munich and Zurich, 1983), throws more light on the same question. Although it covers the years 1911–1914, the terms "Expressionismus"/"expressionistisch" are used only twice (pp.120 and 163), and then deprecatingly.

6. H.S. Ede: **Savage Messiah** (1931) (London, 1971), p.25.

7. Noel Stock: **The Life of Ezra Pound** (London, 1970), p.102.

8. An undated letter to Edward Marsh in the Brynmor Jones Library at the University of Hull which, from internal evidence, was written in mid-1915, indicates that Hulme went to Berlin in November 1912 and he was certainly still there in May 1913 since his article in **Poetry and Drama** (see note 4) indicates that he was present at the evening of Kurt Hiller's Cabaret GNU at which Nietzsche's "Was den Deutschen abgeht" was read out (cf Richard W. Sheppard: "The Expressionist Cabaret GNU (1911–1914)", **DVjs**, 56 (1982), p.444). For the reference to Cohen see T.E. Hulme: "Humanism and the Religious Attitude", in **Speculations**, edited by Herbert Read (London, 1924), p.19. The latter essay was first published as "A Notebook" in **TNA** between 16 November 1915 and 10 February 1916.

9. Cf E.W.F. Tomlin: "The Philosophical Influences", in **Wyndham Lewis: A Revaluation**, edited by Jeffrey Meyers (London, 1980), pp.29–46.

10. See, for instance, "The Logical Conclusion" – a poem written "against the 'germanic' system of graduate study and insane specialization in the Inanities" (in **The Collected Early Poems of Ezra Pound**, edited by Michael John King (London, 1976), p.274). Also "This Super-Neutrality", **TNA**, 21 October 1915, p.595 and "Provincialism the Enemy I", **TNA**, 12 July 1917, p.245.

11. For reproductions of these paintings and woodcuts see: Hans K. Roethel and Jean K. Benjamin: **Kandinsky: Catalogue Raisonné of the Oil Paintings** (London, 1982), Vol.1 and Hans K. Roethel: **Kandinsky: Das graphische Werk** (Cologne, 1970).

12. Ezra Pound: **Gaudier-Brzeska: A Memoir** (London and New York, 1916), pp.113, 114.

13. Of the Vorticists, only Gaudier-Brzeska was totally disparaging about Kandinsky ("Allied Artists' Association Ltd.", **TE**, 15 June 1914, p.228). Hulme, while approving of his abstractionism, regretted the absence from his work of severe form ("Modern Art III", **TNA**, 26 March 1914, p.661) and Lewis censured his art for leaving "fields of discord untouched" (**B**1, p.142), for his "wandering and slack" sense of form (**B**2, p.40) and for his transcendentalism (**B**2, pp.43–44).

14. And in this respect, Hulme was typical of many Modernist intellectuals in the two decades

before the Great War. For a discussion of the more general revolt against "positivism" and "iron determinism", see H. Stuart Hughes: **Consciousness and Society: The Reorientation of European Social Thought**, revised edition (New York, 1977), pp.33–42.

15. Cf W.C. Wees: **Vorticism and the English Avant-garde** (Toronto and Manchester, 1972), p.78. Paul Ernst's essay is to be found in **Ein Credo**, 2 vols (Berlin, 1912), 2, pp.146–52 and the reference to Worringer is on p.147.

16. In **Further Speculations**, edited by Sam Hynes (Minneapolis, 1955), pp.67–76.

17. Depicted in **Wilhelm Morgner** (catalogue) (Münster, 1967), figs 194 and 199–204.

18. Depicted in Klaus Lankheit: **Franz Marc: Katalog der Werke** (Köln, 1970), figs 825, 831–33, 842–43.

19. One finds advertisements for **Der Sturm** in **Poetry and Drama** (and vice versa) as early as Spring/Summer 1913.

20. Cf Richard W. Sheppard: "The Early Reception of the Expressionist Anthology **Der Kondor**", **Literaturwissenschaftliches Jahrbuch**, 24 (1983), pp.209–34.

21. Jethro Bithell's **Contemporary German Poetry** (London and New York, 1909) contained no translations of Expressionist poetry and Hulme's article (which is not listed by Hynes in the Bibliography of **Further Speculations**) ante-dates Reginald H. Wilenski's two articles on modern German poetry which appeared in **Poetry** in January and February 1915, A.W.G. Randall's eight articles on the same subject which were scattered through **TE** between 1 June 1915 and August 1916, and Edward O'Brien's essay on August Stramm which appeared in **Poetry** in July 1916. Nevertheless, from the point of view of the reception of Expressionism in Anglo-Saxony, it is worth noting that the first of Wilenski's articles reviewed **Der Kondor**; that Randall, at various places, mentioned Werfel and Morgenstern, published a translation of Kandinsky's poem "Fagott" and Schickele's poem "Lobspruch" and discussed **Der Sturm** and **Die weissen Blätter**; and that O'Brien referred to translations of Stramm's plays **Sancta Susanna** and **Die Haidebraut** which had appeared in **Poet-Lore** in 1914.

22. And it was almost certainly for the same reason that Vorticism made, as far as I know, no impact on Expressionism.

23. Cf Richard Brinkmann: **Expressionismus: Internationale Forschung zu einem internationalen Problem** (Stuttgart, 1980), pp.1–4.

24. Cf William C. Lipke and Bernard W. Rozran: "Ezra Pound and Vorticism: A Polite Blast", **Wisconsin Studies in Contemporary Literature**, 7 (1966), pp.201–10; Cork, 1, p.12 where three essential characteristics of Vorticism are listed and Timothy Materer: **Vortex: Pound, Eliot and Lewis** (Cornell, 1979), p.87 where the "use of total abstraction" is said to be Vorticism's "distinctive feature".

25. Arnold, pp.9–15; see also note 4.

26. Pound's pre-Vorticist use of the word "Vortex" in his letter to W.C. Williams of 19 December 1913 is well known. Attention has, however, never been drawn to two earlier instances. The first stanza of his poem "Plotinus", first published in **A Lume Spento** (1908) reads: "As one that would draw thru the node of things,/ Back sweeping to the vortex of the cone,/ Cloistered about with memories, alone/ In chaos, while the waiting

silence sings:" (**Collected Early Poems**, p.36). And in "Through Alien Eyes III" (**TNA**, 30 January 1913, p.300) we read: "London . . . is like Rome of the decadence, so far, at least, as letters are concerned. She is a main and vortex drawing strength from the periphery".

27. Cf, for example, the discussions of the inner contradictions of Georg Heym's poetry in **DSdNC**, 2, pp.495–510, of those of Ernst Wilhelm Lotz's poetry in Hermann Korte: **Der Krieg in der Lyrik des Expressionismus** (Bonn, 1981), p.84, of Gaudier-Brzeska's three distinct sculptural styles in 1914 in Materer, 1979, p.86, and of the three distinct visual styles in **Blast** in Lipke and Rozran, p.202.

28. Cf the discussions of this whole problem in Pound: **Gaudier-Brzeska**, pp.5 and 15–16 and **DSdNC**, 2, pp.421–25.

29. Cf Fredric Jameson: **Fables of Aggression: Wyndham Lewis, the Modernist as Fascist** (Berkeley, Los Angeles and London, 1979), pp.10–11.

30. Cf Hughes, pp.33–42 and 105–60 where the philosophical background of this most typically Modernist concern is discussed. See also John Burt Foster jr: **Heirs to Dionysos: A Nietzschean Current in Literary Modernism** (Princeton, 1981), p.3.

31. P. Wyndham Lewis: **Wyndham Lewis the Artist** (London, 1939), p.18.

32. Cf Richard W. Sheppard: "Kandinsky's Early Aesthetic Theory: Some Examples of its Influence and some Implications for the Theory and Practice of Abstract Poetry", **Journal of European Studies**, 5 (1975), pp.19–40; "Kandinsky's Abstract Drama **Der gelbe Klang**: An Interpretation, **FMLS**, 11 (1975), pp.165–76 and "Kandinsky's **Klänge**: An Interpretation", **GLL**, 33 (1980), pp.135–46.

33. Cf Lewis D. Wurgaft: **The Activists: Kurt Hiller and the Politics of Action on the German Left 1914–1933** (Philadelphia, 1977); **Transactions of the American Philosophical Society**, 67, Part 8 (1977).

34. Sixten Ringbom: **The Sounding Cosmos** (Åbo, 1970).

35. Fritz Koffka: "Vom 'tätigen' und vom lebendigen Geist", **Das junge Deutschland,** 1 (1918), p.156.

36. Kurt Hiller: "Neben dem System", **Das junge Deutschland,** 1 (1918), p.222; cf Wurgaft, pp.29–31.

37. For a discussion of these see Bernard Lafourcade: "The Taming of the Wild Body", in Meyers (note 9), pp.68–84.

38. Cf Timothy Materer: **Wyndham Lewis the Novelist** (Detroit, 1976), p.31.

39. According to Materer (1976, p.173), the novel has its roots in an unpublished short story of 1909 entitled "Otto Kreisler" and Kreisler is clearly pre-figured by the pathological German of "The Pole" – a title in which there is, perhaps, an unconscious pun (**The English Review**, May 1909, pp.255–65).

40. Cf his letter of [March 1916] to Harriet Shaw Weaver, the editor of **TE**: "But I will admit that Tarr has just a trifle too many of my ideas to be wholly himself, as I conceived him. . . . if the book has a moral, it is that it describes a man's revolt or reaction against his reason" (**The Letters of Wyndham Lewis**, edited by W.K. Rose (London, 1963), p.76).

41. Cf the unpublished letter from Harriet Shaw Weaver to Lewis of 10 January 1916 (which is to be found in the Wyndham Lewis Collection in Cornell University Library) and T.S. Eliot: 'Tarr', **TE**, September 1918, pp.105–06 where the same kind of comments were made.

42. Lewis was clearly aware of this derivation since in Part V, Chapter 5 of **Tarr**, Tarr asks Bertha what "Kreisler" means and in the mad dance scene of Part III, Chapter 2, Kreisler behaves like a whirling spinning-top.

43. Cf Alistair Davies: "**Tarr**: A Nietzschean Novel", in Meyers, pp.107–19.

44. Cf Roy Pascal: **From Naturalism to Expressionism** (London, 1973), pp.124–26.

45. A process which is recorded poetically in **Hugh Selwyn Mauberley**.

46. In this connection, it is interesting to notice that the centre of the Vorticists' operations was Bloomsbury, right in the heart of established, polite London, whereas the Expressionists operated in the new areas of Berlin's West End. It is also interesting to contrast the anti-parental attitudes of so many of the Expressionists with the good relationships which the Vorticists seem to have had with their parents.

47. C.R.W. Nevinson: **Paint and Prejudice** (New York, 1938), p.58. Much of the information in this paragraph comes from unpublished letters from C.R.W. Nevinson to Wyndham Lewis of late 1913–early 1914 (see note 41).

48. There is a remarkable passage in Hulme's early writings, too long to quote here, in which he very accurately depicts and criticizes such revolutionary enthusiasm even though, at that date, he could not have been thinking about Expressionism ("Notes on Bergson II", **TNA**, 26 October 1911, p.610).

49. Georg Heym: **Dichtungen und Schriften**, 6 vols, edited by Karl Ludwig Schneider et al. (Hamburg, 1960–68), 6, p.15.

50. Cf Korte, passim; Gunter Martens: **Expressionismus und Vitalismus** (Berlin/Cologne/Mainz, 1971) and "Im Aufbruch das Ziel. Nietzsches Wirkung im Expressionismus", in **Nietzsche: Werk und Wirkungen**, edited by Hans Steffen (Göttingen, 1974), pp.115–66.

51. Cf Patrick Bridgwater: **Nietzsche in Anglo-Saxony** (Leicester, 1972), pp.135–37 where it is pointed out that Nietzsche was particularly important for **The New Age** – a periodical to which several of the Vorticist circle contributed during the years 1907–10.

52. Cf "Und Drang" (1911), "Sub Mare" (1912) (in **Collected Early Poems**, pp.167–68 and 194), "Coitus" (1914) and "The Spring" (1915) (in Ezra Pound, **Selected Poems**, edited by T.S. Eliot (London, 1968), pp.114, 95) which deal with elemental subjects in a very restrained, non-elemental way. Or compare the gentle stylization of "Effects of Music upon a Company of People" (**Collected Early Poems**, p.199) with the wild chaos of the best poems in the Expressionist **Ballhaus** anthology, published in Berlin in the same year (1912). And the highly civilized Chinese world evoked in **Cathay** (London, 1915) is marked by great empty spaces and a nostalgia for a lost world of ideal beauty – not by savage exoticism.

53. Cf. William J. Brazill jr.: 'Art and 'the Panic Terror'", in **The Turn of the Century: German Literature and Art, 1890–1915**, edited by Gerald Chapple and Hans H. Schulte (Bonn, 1981), pp.529–39.

54. In Part I, Chapter 4, Tarr, for example, is said to be undergoing a "comic Armageddon" – i.e. one that is relatively harmless.

55. Pound first got to know Fenollosa's writings in the second half of 1913. The essay on the Chinese written character was first published in instalments in **TLR** in Autumn 1919.

56. Cf Karlheinz Daniels: "Expressionismus und Technik", in **Expressionismus als Literatur**, edited by Wolfgang Rothe (Berne and Munich, 1969), pp.171–93.

57. See especially Bruno Taut: **Die Stadtkrone** (Jena, 1919).

58. Of the Vorticists, Gaudier-Brzeska was probably the most consistently anti-machine – cf his letter to Dr Uhlemeyer of 4 October 1910, in Ede, p.28–29.

59. A statement which is well illustrated by a comparison of the very subdued architectural proposals of the first twenty pages of Lewis's **The Caliph's Design** (London, 1919) and the ecstatic architectural utopianism of Taut's **Die Stadtkrone**.

60. Ernst Wilhelm Lotz: **Prosaversuche und Feldpostbriefe**, edited by Hellmut Draws-Tychen (Diessen vor München, 1955), pp.64–72.

61. Korte, whose research is very thorough, identifies only three Expressionist writers – Alfred Döblin, Fritz von Unruh and Paul Zech – who were still allowing pro-war material to be published after about mid-1915 (pp.116, 119, 134).

62. Franz Marc: "Das geheime Europa", **Das Forum**, December 1915, pp.632–38; "Im Fegefeuer des Krieges", **Der Sturm**, April 1916, p.2. It emerges from the Kandinsky/Marc **Briefwechsel** (see note 5) that the former essay was written in November 1914 (p.263).

63. C.W.R. Nevinson: "Painting War as a Soldier Sees It", **New York Times Magazine**, 25 May 1919, p.13.

64. This emerges very clearly from Lewis's attitude to the young soldier of "A Young Soldier", **TE**, 1 March 1916, p.46.

65. In **Wyndham Lewis the Artist** (p.78), this battle is identified as the turning-point in Lewis's attitude to the War.

66. See especially Ezra Pound: "Vorticism [2]", **TNA**, 14 January 1915, pp.277–78; Wyndham Lewis, "Prevalent Design", **The Athenaeum**, 21 September 1919, pp.1230–31; 12 December 1919, p.1343; 26 December 1919, p.1404; 16 January 1920, pp.84–85.

67. Cf Walter Reidel: **Der neue Mensch: Mythos und Wirklichkeit** (Bonn, 1970) and B.D. Webb: **The Demise of the "New Man"** (Göppingen, 1973).

68. Wurgaft gives the most comprehensive account of the late Expressionists' failure to translate their utopian hopes into real political terms.

69. Foster, p.3.

70. Cf Stoddard Martin: **Wagner to The Waste Land** (London, 1982), p.208 where such an approach to Modernism is suggested.

71. It is this kind of unspoken attitude, deriving from the English cultural experience, which often prevents English critics from empathizing with the European cultural experience. A recent example of this is provided by Alan Young's **Dada and After** (Manchester, 1981) whose central thesis is how sensible the English were to take no notice of the radical Modernist nonsense emanating from across the Channel.

The Modern(ist) One-Act Play

Egil Törnqvist

Although the one-act play can be traced back at least to Molière (**Les Précieuses ridicules**) and became a flourishing form of drama after 1740 (Pazarkaya), its function in those days was rather different from what we now associate with this subgenre. Sometimes used as a curtain raiser to whet the appetite of the audience and allow for late-comers to settle in, sometimes used as an after-piece to mitigate the horrors of the preceding tragedy, it was usually a comedy or a farce intended to cheer up the audience.

Around 1890 a major mutation took place. With the arrival of the little theatre movement, the one-act play almost overnight became recognized as a serious and independent art form; it now became customary to let a group of one-act plays fill an evening in the theatre. One of the few scholarly studies of the modern one-act play to date states unambiguously: "Seit Strindbergs theoretischem Debüt von 1889 muss der Einakter als eigenständige Gattung gelten" (Schnetz, p.24).

Strindberg had, in fact, already commented on the one-act form a year earlier, in his Foreword to **Fröken Julie** (**Miss Julie**):

> Vad det tekniska i kompositionen angår, har jag på försök strukit aktindelningen. Detta emedan jag trott mig finna, att vår avtagande förmåga av illusion möjligen skulle störas av mellanakter, under vilka åskådaren får tid att reflektera och därigenom undandrages författaren-magnetisörens suggestiva inflytande. Mitt stycke varar troligen sex kvart, och när man kan höra en föreläsning, en predikan eller en kongressförhandling like länge eller längre, har jag inbillat mig att ett teaterstycke icke skulle trötta under en och en halv timme . . . Min mening vore framdeles få en publik så uppfostrad, att den kunde sitta ut ett helaftonsspektakel i en enda akt. Men detta fordrar undersökningar först.
>
> (Strindberg, 1964, p.306f.)

> As far as the technical side of the work is concerned, I have made the experiment of abolishing the division into acts. This is because I have come to the conclusion that our capacity for illusion is disturbed by the intervals, during which the audience has time to reflect and escape from the suggestive influence of the author-hypnotist. My play will probably take an hour and a half, and as one can listen to a lecture, a sermon, or a parliamentary debate for as long as that or longer, I do not think a theatrical performance will be fatiguing in the same length of time. . . My hope is one day to have an audience educated enough to sit through a whole evening's entertainment in one act, but one would have to try this out to see.
>
> (Cole, p.178f.)

As this statement clarifies, Strindberg's interest in the one-act form was directly related to his (Naturalistic) ambition, as a dramatist, to create maximal illusion. But besides this, and more interesting in view of later developments, is his awareness that this type of drama could effectively appeal to the deeper emotions of the audience. Strindberg's "one-act psychodrama" (Jacobs/Strindberg, p.xvi), which was intended to keep an audience spell-bound from beginning to end, was born out of his decision to abolish the illusion-breaking intervals. The length of the one-acter would be determined by what an audience can consume in one sitting. The mere fact that Strindberg plays with the idea of making a one-act play as long as a full-length drama indicates that what concerns him is not the magnitude of the play in itself but the absence of intermissions; much later his dream of a continuous performance which could keep the audience in its grip was to be realized in another medium: the film.

Strindberg's concern for the one-act play returns a year later in his important essay "Om modernt drama och modern teater" ("On Modern Drama and Modern Theatre"). Commenting on the situation in those Paris theatres that catered for the "new", that is, the Naturalistic drama, Strindberg notes that in this kind of drama there is an emphasis on psychological character description rather than plot, an adherence to the unities of time and place, and a predilection for the one-act form. He continues:

> I det nya naturalistdramat märktes strax en strävan till det betydelsefulla motivets uppsökande. Därför rörde det sig helst om livets två poler, liv och död, födelseakten och dödsakten, kampen om makan, om existensmedlen, om äran, alla dessa strider, med deras slagfält, jämmerskri, sårade och döde, varunder man hörde den nya världsåskådningen om livet såsom kamp blåsa sina befruktande sunnanvindar.
>
> Det var tragedier, sådana man icke sett förr; men de unga författarne. . . tycktes själva rygga för att påtruga sina lidanden på andra mer än nödigt var, och därför göra de pinan så kort som möjligt, låta smärtan rasa ut i en akt, stundom i en enda scen.
>
> (Strindberg, 1913, p.298f.)

> In the new naturalistic drama a striving for the significant motif was felt at once. Therefore, the action was usually centered around life's two poles, life and death, the act of birth and the act of death, the fight for the spouse, for the means of subsistence, for honor, all these struggles – with their battlefield cries of woe, wounded and dead – during which one heard a new philosophy of life conceived as a struggle, blow its fertile winds from the south.
>
> These were tragedies such as had not been seen before. The young authors. . . seemed reluctant to impose their suffering on others more than was absolutely necessary. Therefore, they made the suffering as brief as possible, let the pain pour forth in one act, sometimes in a single scene.
>
> (Cole, p.18f.)

Strindberg then goes on to sketch the history of the **quart d'heure**, "typen för nutidsmänniskors teaterstycke" ("the type of play preferred by modern theatregoers", Strindberg, 1913, p.301). Tracing it back to Carmontelle, he notes that:

> Arten utvecklas sedan av Leclerq, vinner sin högsta fullkomning i Mussets och Feuillets kända mästerstycken för att nu sist i Henri Becque's **La Navette** bilda

övergången till den utförda enaktaren, som kanske blir det kommande dramats **formule**.

I proverbet fick man sakens kärna, hela utredningen, själarnes strid, hos Musset stundom närmande sig tragedien, utan att man behövde störas av vapenlarm eller statistprocessioner. Med hjälp av ett bord och två stolar kunde man få framställda de starkaste konflikter livet bjuder; och i den konstarten kunde först alla den moderna psykologiens upptäckter användas i populär utspädning.

(Strindberg, 1913, p.301.)

The genre was later developed by Leclerq, attained its highest perfection in Musset's and Feuillet's well-known masterpieces – and more recently in Henry Becque's **La Navette** to form the transition to the fully executed one-act play, which may become the formula for the drama to come.

In the proverb one got the gist of the matter, the whole dénouement, the battle of the souls, sometimes approaching tragedy in Musset, without having to be bothered by the clanging of arms or processions or supernumeraries. By means of a table and two chairs one could present the most powerful conflicts life has to offer; and in this type of art all the discoveries of modern psychology could, for the first time, be applied in popularized form.

(Cole, p.20f.)

Summing up his main points, we might say that Strindberg welcomes the one-acter because in its concentration on "the gist of the matter" and in its lack of illusion-breaking intervals, it creates optimal possibilities for empathy on the part of the audience. Being theme-centred rather than plot-centred, the one-acter also comes closer to being a **tranche de vie** than the artificial well-made play – especially since it tends to adhere to the unities of time, place and action. As an exponent of the Naturalistic tradition, the one-act play is also suitable for the dramatization of "the discoveries of modern psychology", notably what Strindberg around this time termed "the battle of the brains". Finally, there are the practical considerations – simple décor, small cast, etc. – which make the one-act play an attractive, because inexpensive, form for the small experimental stages soon mushrooming all over Europe.

While most of these statements are wholly sensible, the view that the one-acter lends itself to psychological characterization would be disputed by most theoreticians (Höllerer, p.550), who would rather argue that this drama form is too short to allow for any nuances in characterization; even the main figures tend to remain flat: "Zwei oder drei Eigenschaften, das ist alles, was sichtbar wird" (Schnetz, p.89). What matters is not so much the characters as the situation in which they find themselves.

If Strindberg, writing in 1889 when the modern one-act form was originating, regards this subgenre as the adequate Naturalistic form of drama, Peter Szondi seventy-five years later sees the one-acter as a means by which playwrights at the end of the nineteenth century tried to save the dramatic element in drama. According to Szondi, modern drama is characterized by a development from essentially dramatic, interhuman relations (man versus man) to essentially epic ones: extrahuman (man versus fate) or intrahuman (consciousness versus subconsciousness). To meet this crisis in modern drama, brought about by various ideologies undermining the belief in free will so essential to drama, a number of "Rettungsversuche" have been attempted.

These attempts to retain as much as possible of the dramatic element have been followed by a number of "Lösungsversuche", demonstrating various ways of dramatizing the epic ingredients, by this time recognized as indispensable. The one-act play falls under the category "Rettungsversuche"; the dramatic suspense is retained but it is transposed from the interhuman to the extrahuman sphere:

> Weil der Einakter die Spannung nicht mehr aus dem zwischenmenschlichen Geschehen bezieht, muss sie bereits in der Situation verankert sein. . . Deshalb wählt sie der Einakter, wenn er auf Spannung nicht ganz verzichtet, immer als Grenzsituation, als Situation vor der Katastrophe, die schon bevorsteht, wenn der Vorhang sich hebt, und im folgenden nicht mehr abgewendet werden kann. Die Katastrophe ist futurische Gegebenheit: es kommt nicht mehr zum tragischen Kampf des Menschen gegen das Schicksal, dessen Objektivität er . . . seine subjektive Freiheit entgegensetzen könnte. Was ihm von Untergang trennt, ist die leere Zeit, die durch keine Handlung mehr auszufüllen ist, in deren reinem, auf die Katastrophe hin gespanntem Raum er zu leben verurteilt wurde. So bestätigt sich der Einakter auch in diesem formalen Punkt als das Drama des unfreien Menschen. Die Zeit, in der er aufkam, war die Epoche des Determinismus, und dieser verbindet die Dramatiker, die ihn ergriffen, jenseits der stilistischen und thematischen Unterschiede: den Symbolisten Maeterlinck mit dem Naturalisten Strindberg.
>
> (Szondi, p.92f.)

When Szondi emphasizes the importance of the **situation** in the one-acter, he mentions a characteristic about which there seems to be general agreement:

> Usually it [the one act play] is rather short because it presents but a single dramatic situation or crisis and because it aims at a singleness of effect in comparatively short compass.
>
> (Lewis, p.18f.)

> Unity [in the one-act play] implies . . . a single major situation and its corollary, a single dominant impression.
>
> (Wilde, p.34)

> Eine hervorragende Idee beherrscht das Stück, das im allgemeinen kurz ist, da es von vornherein den Leser oder Zuschauer nur vor einzige dramatische Situation oder Verwicklung stellt und eine ganz bestimmte Wirkung hervorbringen möchte.
>
> (Hartmann, p.11)

> Im Einakter . . . dominiert nicht mehr der Mensch, es dominiert die Situation.
>
> (Schnetz, p.31)

In a very general sense it is of course true that compared to the full-length drama, where the situation usually changes from act to act, the one-acter for obvious reasons – notably the adherence to unities – cannot demonstrate any radical change of situation. Yet when Schnetz specifically defines "situation" as maintenance of the same factual circumstances ("sobald sich ein Faktum ändert, ändert sich auch die Situation", p.28), it becomes exceedingly difficult to agree with her that in the one-acter we can speak of "Einheit der Situation" (p.28). We will return to this problem.

Outgoing from Höllerer's conviction that "der Einakter wurde zu einer Form, die sich innerhalb des Dramatischen ihre eigenen Gesetze schuf, wie die Kurzgeschichte inmitten der traditionellen Prosagattungen" (p.551), Schnetz declares:

> Der Einakter ist in seiner selbständigen dramatischen Form eine junge Gattung, diese stellt sich in einer strukturellen Einheit dar, die bei anderen traditionsreichen Gattungen nur gewaltsam hergeleitet werden können. Die relativ kurze Zeitspanne von 1890 bis zur Gegenwart . . . erlaubt und ermöglicht es, die Gattung in ihrer strukturellen Einheit zu sehen, wie andererseits diese formale Übereinstimmung dazu berechtigt, den Einakter als Gattungseinheit anzusprechen.
>
> (Schnetz, p.14)

The modern one-acter, in other words, is regarded as a rather homogeneous art form. Having declared this, Schnetz goes on to formulate a number of "laws" – the importance of the "situation" being one – that are supposed to govern the modern one-act play. As appears from her index, these rules have been induced primarily from the analysis of some fifteen one-act plays. According to Schnetz, the one-act subgenre takes its place between the lyrical genre, defined as "monologic representation of a situation" and the dramatic one, defined as "dialogic representation of an action". The formula for the one-acter, then, reads: "dialogic representation of a situation" (p.167). This placing of the one-acter between the lyrical and the dramatic genre agrees well with Szondi's view of it as a de-dramatized drama.

The problem facing Schnetz is clearly the problem which confronts all those who examine a (sub)genre: to what extent can we find constants in the various works that are assumed to belong to one and the same category and in what measure do we deal with variables? Although Schnetz is aware that "die Struktur einer Gattung nicht unabhängig von ihrer historischen Stellung existiert" (p.14), she considers the life span of the modern one-acter too short to give rise to any significant structural variables.

This is a questionable viewpoint. One might just as well argue that the multifarious and hybrid nature of modern drama should lead us to expect that there are very few constants which are applicable to the whole corpus of one-act plays and that the variables would be much more conspicuous. This would at least be true of the Modernist one-acters, since "Modernism is less a style than a search for a style in a highly individualistic sense" (Bradley/McFarlane, p.29). The logical procedure would then be to divide the whole corpus into various categories for which more specific criteria are valid. But Schnetz does not do this. Her tendency to pronounce generalizing statements leaves the reader with a disturbing feeling that the one-act subgenre has remained more or less static throughout eighty years, otherwise characterized by continuous change, pluralism, overlapping and fusion of the arts, as the multitude of-isms indicates.

With the aid of a few exemplary one-act dramas an attempt will be made here to question this idea of homogeneity, in support of the standpoint taken by Halbritter, who convincingly demonstrates the fundamental differences between the "symbolist" (Yeats), the "epic-didactic" (Wilder) and the "grotesque" (Pinter) one-act play (for his critique of Schnetz, see Halbritter pp.11–15).

The questions to be posed in the following are: what do the plays here under consideration have in common? In what respects do they differ from one another? What is the relationship between constants and variables? Has the one-act play changed over the years? Is the "modern" one-acter by definition also a "Modernist" one-acter? To what extent are Schnetz' overall criteria applicable to the selected one-acters? Questions of this kind will be related to six one-act dramas, selected so that each one represents a particular writer, period and literary movement/style.

If it is true, as Schnetz (following Szondi) claims, that in the one-act play "Konflikt und Spannung entstehen nicht mehr zwischen Individuen, sondern zwischen Individuum und Situation" (p.31), then Strindberg's **Paria** (**Pariah**, 1889) is not a representative one-acter. For here conflict is a "battle of the brains" fought out between two men, Mr X and Mr Y. The change that takes place concerns the relationship between them: when the play opens they are friends; when it closes they have become enemies. The reason for this change is that hidden crimes have been revealed during the course of the play. A new situation has been created. The reactions of the characters to this new situation establish a new, negative, relationship.

As is made clear toward the end of the play, the two men are actually playing an intellectual – and a moral – game of chess with one another. Mr Y says: "Jag står själv i schack, men i nästa drag kan du vara matt – likafullt." ("You may have put me in check, but by the next move you may be check-mated – despite your cleverness!") Actually the opposite happens. The chess imagery is indicated visually throughout the play:

> **Mitt på golvet ett stort matbord med böcker, skrivdon, fornsaker på ena sidan; mikroskop, insektslådor, spritburkar på den andra.**
>
> **In the centre of the room, a large dining table. Piled on one side of it are books, writing materials, and archaeological artifacts. On the opposite side are microscopes, boxes with insects, and alcohol jars.**

This is clearly a "chessboard" with contrasting "chess-pieces" at either side. Although it is not stated explicitly, the two men are apparently sitting opposite one another at the table, like two chess players.

Both Mr X and Mr Y have committed crimes which have never been discovered and for which they have never been legally punished. In the case of Mr X it concerns accidental murder, in the case of Mr Y, forgery. The punishment for both crimes is a two-year sentence.

However, both men plead innocent. Mr X argues that he could not possibly know how fatal his blow would be to an elderly person; his ignorance of this caused the death of the old man, for which he thus cannot be held responsible. Mr Y, similarly, claims that he was not aware of committing forgery; he did it subconsciously and can therefore not be held responsible. If Mr X's reasoning seems more convincing, it is because it is evident that he could not benefit from the death of the old man, whereas Mr Y could clearly gain certain advantages from his crime. Besides, Mr X apparently acted on the spur of the moment, while Mr Y had time to ponder his action. Finally, the idea of ignorance seems more acceptable than that of subconscious impulses, since the latter would invalidate all ethical (legal) norms. Whereas Mr X seems to believe in the homogeneity of the (developed) personality and in man's individual responsibility for his actions – he takes an existentialist attitude – Mr Y argues that man is only responsible for the conscious part of his self, not for his subconscious drives.

Another major difference between the men is that Mr X gives a true version of his crime, while Mr Y presents a false one, borrowed from "Bernheims avhandling om ingivelser" ("Bernheim's treatise on subconscious desires and impulses"). While Mr X quite voluntarily confesses his crime, Mr Y tries to hide his; not until he is pressed on the matter does he reveal it and then, as we have noted, only in an embellished form. Moreover, Mr Y pretends that he has been punished for his crime, while in fact he has not. He has indeed spent some time in prison but this he had done as punishment for another, unspecified crime. The very location of the play, close to the prison in Malmö, where Mr Y would have landed had he been found out, is determined by his guilt feelings.

Another striking difference between the two men is that Mr X never shows any inclination to report Mr Y's crime to the sheriff (while he is willing to report his own), whereas Mr Y indicates that he is prepared to report on Mr X unless the latter gives him six thousand crowns. But Mr X refuses to let himself be blackmailed, especially since this would have involved stealing on his part; for as he himself says, he is incapable of stealing.

What all this demonstrates is that in the case of Mr Y, crimes in the past (prescenic action) are repeated in the present (scenic action), while in Mr X's case a crime in the past is undone, as it were, by his behaviour in the present. As a result of this the impression is conveyed that Mr Y is a born criminal or at least a recidivist, while Mr X is not.

Before the law, as we have already noted, their crimes are comparable. Yet already at the beginning of the play the justice of official law is questioned. A thief could be exonerated, it is stated, if it can be proved that he had stolen out of scientific interest but not if he had stolen out of need: "och likafullt", says Mr X, "skulle nöden vara den starkare, den enda ursäkten" ("despite the fact that need should be the stronger – as a matter of fact, the **only** – excuse".) The law, in other words, does not agree with a sound conception of justice; it cannot be trusted. This being the case, Mr X quite logically has taken the law into his own hands; on very rational grounds he has exonerated himself for his accidental murder.

At first sight he seems very consistent in his Nietzschean beyond-good-and-evil attitude. He himself is incapable of stealing, others cannot resist doing so. But these circumstances are to him merely psychological data, not ethical norms justifying evaluation in terms of virtues and vices. Similarly, he is of the opinion that a criminal, like a child, should be morally unaccountable for his actions. And at the end of the play he states that the question whether Mr Y is more or less criminal than himself does not concern him.

It is usually said that Mr X is the superman of the play, Mr Y the pariah referred to in the title. But if this were so, the struggle would be rather uninteresting. It is true, of course, that Strindberg strongly supports Mr X; even a perusal of the acting directions for the two men confirms that. Yet our antipathy for Mr Y does not necessarily lead to a feeling of sympathy for Mr X, who substitutes intellectual norms for ethical ones:

> Du är en annan slags människa än jag – om starkare eller svagare – det vet jag inte – brottsligare eller icke – rör mig inte! men att du är dummare, det är avgjort.

> You are an entirely different person from what I am. . . I don't know whether you are stronger or weaker. And whether you are more or less of a criminal is none of my business. . . But one thing is certain: you are more stupid!

Mr Y, in other words, is condemned not on moral but on intellectual grounds.

Mr X's extremely rational attitude, his tendency to see himself as an **Übermensch** creating his own laws and Mr Y as an irresponsible child – this "racist" attitude, I would suggest, is equivalent to the ethical (!) error of the classical hero: over-confidence, hybris. What is surprising and new in Strindberg's one-acter is that his hybris is never punished. Mr X is clearly the intelligent chess player who wins the game when at the end he forces his opponent to leave.

Alternatively, it could be argued that ethically speaking, the audience is left with an open ending and that it may well wish also to "punish" Mr X. It is interesting to note in this context that Mr X's penultimate speech, in which he repeatedly insists on Mr Y's stupidity, hardly adds to his stature. After all, a world ruled by Mr X's cerebral norms would be even more inhuman than the imperfect one this side of good and evil.

Besides, Mr X no less than Mr Y appears to delude himself. As a Naturalist, he believes that he has "done away with the idea of guilt, as well as God" ("Skulden har naturalisten utstrukit med Gud", Foreword to **Fröken Julie,** Strindberg, 1964, p.304); yet he demands penal retribution "for the sake of restoring equilibrium", that is, equilibrium between crime (guilt) and punishment. Similarly, although he feels guiltless, he has dreamt "many a night" of being in prison and is ready to report his crime to the sheriff. Apparently Mr X is not so free from guilt-feelings as he himself likes to think and not so different from Mr Y as he may first appear.

Actually, in the last instance both men are representative human beings. For are we not all unpunished criminals trying to exonerate ourselves for the disguised sins we have committed? Strindberg seems to hint at this when he has Mr X ask himself whether his former friend Stråman was ever "duly punished" – although he does not even know if he has committed a crime! And when he has Mr Y remark that the most painful thought to a prisoner is the awareness that all those "who go unpunished" are not also behind bars. The implication is that mankind should not be divided into guilty and innocent – we are all guilty – but into punished and unpunished. Viewed in this light, the absolute unity of time, place and action adhered to in the one-acter takes on thematic, imprisoning qualities, further emphasized by the stifling heat foreboding the approaching thunderstorm, announcing, it would seem, the punishment that clears the air and restores equilibrium.

If **Paria** takes its dramatic power from the battle of brains fought between two people, Maeterlinck's **Intérieur** (1894) deals with an altogether different kind of conflict: that between man and his fate. Instead of pitting one man against another, Maeterlinck pits a collective protagonist representing mankind against inexorable death. Whereas in **Paria** we can, theoretically at least, choose to identify ourselves or empathize with either of the two men (or with neither of them), in **Intérieur** there is no such choice, since the antagonist here is not a human being but an ontological agency. Moreover, unlike Strindberg's antagonist who, being human is in principle changeable, Maeterlinck's, being metaphysical, is static. It is therefore debatable in fact whether we can speak of any conflict in the proper sense in **Intérieur**. Rather, we are faced with an existential situation which we, the audience, share with the characters. It is this existential bond between stage and auditorium that above all secures our interest in the dramatized events.

It is in this light we must view Maeterlinck's own suggestive term "drame statique"; what he meant by this appears from the following often quoted passage from "Le Tragique Quotidien", which reads like a comment on the situation in **Intérieur**:

> Il m'est arrivé de croire qu'un vieillard assis dans son fauteuil, attendant simplement sous la lampe, écoutant sous sa conscience toutes les lois éternelles qui règnent autour de sa maison, interprétant sans le comprendre ce qu'il y a dans le silence des portes et des fenêtres et dans la petite voix de la lumière, subissant la présence de son âme et de sa destinée, inclinant un peu la tête, sans se douter que toutes les puissances de ce monde interviennent et veillent dans la chambre comme des servantes attentives, ignorant que le soleil lui-même soutient au-dessus de l'abîme la petite table sur laquelle il s'accoude, et qu'il y a pas un astre du ciel ni une force de l'âme qui soient indifférents au mouvement d'une paupière qui retombe ou d'une pensée qui s'élève, – il m'est arrivé de croire que ce vieillard immobile vivait, en réalité, d'une vie plus profonde, plus humaine et plus générale que l'amant qui étrangle sa maîtresse, le capitaine qui remporte une victoire ou "l'époux qui venge son honneur".
>
> (**Le Trésor des humbles**, p.233ff.)

Maeterlinck's old man may very well live a profound life but the problem is, of course, how his inner world and his position in the universe can be communicated **dramatically**; the subject seems epic (interior monologue) or lyrical rather than dramatic; not surprisingly, it has also been said that Maeterlinck's plays are not dramas in the proper sense of the word, that they constitute a new kind (Szondi, p.57).

On the realistic level **Intérieur** deals with a family that is about to receive a message that one of its members has just died. One of the daughters has left in the morning to visit her grandmother on the other side of the river. But in fact she had been wandering aimlessly on the beach all day until she finally drowned herself in the river. Having been found there, she is now being carried home.

To dramatize this simple story Maeterlinck divides the stage into two areas; an interior and an exterior. At the back of the stage we see the family inside their house, at the front of the stage we see two people talking to each other in the garden behind the house: the Old Man who knows the family well and the Stranger who, as his designation indicates, does not. After a while the exterior group is supplemented by the Old Man's granddaughters, who announce the arrival of the crowd that finally appears on the stage. We thus deal with three distinct groups of people: an interior onstage group, an exterior onstage group, and an exterior offstage group. At the end of the play the three groups unite.

To begin with we are only aware of two groups. Pitted against the backstage, interior, silent, ignorant group is the frontstage, exterior, speaking, knowledgeable group. The Stranger serves as an excuse for the Old Man to inform the audience about the situation. Leave out the Stranger and we are left with a (Brechtian) narrator!

The play is essentially about waiting. We are waiting for the knowledgeable group to inform the ignorant group about what has happened. The ignorant group, in other words, is waiting for a message without realizing it. But the knowledgeable group delays informing the ignorant one; not until the dead girl is brought close to the house is information given.

Already in the beginning the Stranger wants to inform the family. But the Old Man is hesitant; he points to the fact that the parents are sickly, that the sisters are still very young and that the sad message has to be given carefully. After a while he suggests that he and the Stranger should enter the house together but the latter is unwilling to do so. The Old Man then decides to wait for his granddaughter Marie; he will enter the house with her. But like her grandfather, Marie is soon seized with compassion for the family and asks him to postpone the whole matter until the following day, when it is light. With the arrival of her sister Marthe, the situation seems to take a new turn. Marthe reproaches her grandfather for not having informed the family and decides to do so herself. Yet having regarded the interior group for a while, she too loses the courage to take action.

It is evident that the hesitation on the part of the exterior group to inform the interior one (cf. the messenger in classical drama) has the simple dramatic purpose of extending the play into a normal one-acter. Yet out of this necessity Maeterlinck makes a thematic virtue: the hesitation becomes an expression of compassion for the family, an inclination to let them remain happy in their ignorance for yet a little while. In their hesitation and empathy the exterior group actually functions as a kind of chorus, voicing the feelings of the audience vis-à-vis the interior group.

The approaching crowd is the dynamic element in the play. As soon as Marie enters, she informs us that the crowd is coming. Next the characters report that they see the offstage crowd approaching silently, then that they can hear them mumbling prayers; Maeterlinck resorts here to the old device of **teichoskopía**, "looking from the walls". The audience can soon also hear the screaming of the children. Finally, the murmuring crowd appears on the stage, the children screaming. There is a definite crescendo in this arrangement, expressing how (the message of) death approaches the family.

However, **Intérieur** is not primarily a description of an individual family awaiting the message of death. Rather, this situation is a concretization, a theatrical metaphor, of a universal situation: man confronted with his own mortality. The Old Man makes this quite clear in some generalizing statements:

> Regarde, mon enfant, regarde: tu verras quelque chose de la vie. . .
>
> J'ai près de quatre-vingt-trois ans et c'est la première fois que la vue de la vie m'ait frappé. Je ne sais pas pourquoi tout ce qu'ils font m'apparaît si étrange et si grave. . . Ils attendent la nuit, simplement, sous leur lampe, comme nous l'aurions attendue sous la nôtre;
>
> Il faut ajouter quelque chose à la vie ordinaire avant de pouvoir la comprendre. . .

What must be added is precisely the awareness of death. Only when we take death into account can we really view life properly. The exterior group – especially the Old Man – standing in the darkness watching the lighted house has this overall perspective, but the interior group lacks it. The warm (note the fireplace) and harmonious interior showing "**une famille qui fait la veillée sous la lampe**" is a picture of man's attempt to create an idyllic life for himself by forgetting that day passes into night as life into death; in the word "veillée" meaning both "evening gathering" and "wake", the two aspects are fused. The illuminated house, sealed off from the surrounding dark world, is an image of man's existential fear, his vain attempt to protect himself against (the idea of) death. At the end of the play the doors stand open as a token of the fact that death has invaded man's life, and through the doors a starlit sky can be seen – eternity – contrasting with the clock inside and the fountain outside the house, symbols of the passing of time, of life.

Synchronized with the approaching crowd is a growing uneasiness on the part of the people inside the house; in this way Maeterlinck indicates that they intuitively begin to sense what has happened or – applying the parabolic variant – are gradually made aware of the arrival of death. Only the child is too small to sense anything of this; it remains calmly asleep in the deserted house; says the Stranger: "L'enfant ne s'est pas réveillé!" This final line clearly bears a reference both to the initial "**veillée**" of the family and to the dead girl who, Marthe has earlier said, "a l'air de dormir". A mystical note is struck in this link between the sleeping child and the dead girl. Is the latter, too, just asleep? And will she soon wake up to another life?

It is significant that this final line is spoken by the Stranger, whose mere designation sets him off from the other characters. Early in the play he notes that the family in the house has never met him. "Je ne suis qu'un passant; je suis un étranger". It is he who first discovers the dead girl. When the Old Man says that her hands were folded (as though she were praying), the Stranger corrects him by stating that her arms were hanging limp along her body. Towards the end he is left alone in the darkness at the rear of the house, while all the other characters gather in front of it to form one large crowd of humanity. His separateness from the rest is thus emphasized in various ways. These circumstances seem to justify the view that in the figure of the Stranger Maeterlinck has mysteriously indicated the presence of death.

There is an obvious kinship between Maeterlinck's Symbolist drama and Lagerkvist's Expressionist one-acter **Himlens hemlighet (The Secret of Heaven)** published in the collection **Kaos (Chaos**, 1919). As Lagerkvist himself clarifies in his manifesto **Modern teater. Synpunkter och angrepp (Modern Theatre: Points of View and Attack**, 1918), there is also a direct link between Strindberg's (pre)Expressionist dramas and his own one-acter; in Strindberg's chamber plays, he writes:

> Här är allt inriktat på ett enda. På att frigöra en enda stämning, en enda känsla, vars intensitet oavlåtligt växer och växer. Allt ovidkommande uteslutet, om det också skulle vara för sammanhanget och trovärdigheten ganska väsentligt. Allt som sker av betydelse, av lika stor betydelse. Inga bipersoner, alla likaberättigade i dramat, lika nödvändiga för att det skall bli till vad det är avsett att vara. Och i själva verket inga "personer" i vanlig vedertagen mening, ingen analys, ingen psykologisk apparat, ingen teckning av "karaktärer". Och dock inga abstraktioner – men bilder av mänskan sådan hon är då hon är ond, då hon är god, då hon har en sorg, då hon har en glädje.
>
> Förenkling. Och likväl rikedom. Rikedom också i själva formen: genom att allting spelar med, ingenting är dött, allt förandligat och insatt i dramat som en levande del av detta, och genom att motivet ideligen förskjutes, klipps av – för att fullföljas på ett annat plan. Virrvarr, men ett virrvarr med mening och reda.
>
> (Lagerkvist, p.35f.)

Everything is directed to one purpose – the liberation of a single mood, a single

> feeling whose intensity unceasingly grows and grows. Everything irrelevant is excluded even if rather important to the continuity or to the faithfulness of representation. Everything which occurs is meaningful and of equal weight. No minor roles, but all having an equal right to a place in the drama, and all equally necessary in order that the play will become what it is intended to be. And actually no "persons" in the usual, accepted meaning, no analysis, no psychological apparatus, no drawing of "characters". And yet, no abstractions, but images of man when he is evil, when he is good, when in sorrow, when joyful.
>
> Simplification. And, nevertheless, richness. Richness too in the form itself, because of the fact that everything plays its part, nothing is lifeless, all is inspired and put into the drama as a living part of it, and because the theme is always shifting, and is clipped off, to be pursued on another plane. Confusion, but a confusion with meaning and order.
>
> (Sprinchorn, p.626)

This description fits Lagerkvist's own early plays even better than Strindberg's chamber plays.

Himlens hemlighet deals essentially with such existential questions as the meaning of life and death, the identity of man, the conflict between good and evil, the function of love. Like Strindberg, in **Spöksonaten (The Ghost Sonata)**, Lagerkvist demonstrates how a good man entering the world gradually discovers that it is evil; how he tries to see love as an exception to the sad rule and a means of rescue; how he is disillusioned; and how he accepts the consequence of his negative discovery by voluntarily leaving the world. While Strindberg sets his play in a recognizable, albeit grotesque neighbourhood – an apartment house and its immediate environment – Lagerkvist settles for an explicitly allegorical one: "**ett mäktigt, blåsvart klot**" ("**a giant blue-black sphere**"). On this miniature model of Earth he places two characters, a Woodcutter and a Man in flesh-coloured tights, representing God and Death. They never utter a word and never look up from their symbolic activities: cutting wood and beheading marionettes respectively. Between these two metaphysical agencies seven characters are placed, representing mankind. By means of this imagery Lagerkvist very explicitly demonstrates how humanity finds itself in an existential dilemma, torn between the certainty of death and the hope of a benevolent metaphysical instance; "det inre uttryckt i något yttre", as Lagerkvist says in **Modern Theater** ("an inner condition expressed in something external and tangible", Lagerkvist, p.27f; Sprinchorn, p.620).

The central Expressionist idea that the staged reality is just a projection or image of an inner reality actually pervades the play. We find it expressed most strikingly in the outward appearance of the characters, referred to as the Dwarf, the Blind man, the Man on crutches, the Man with the iron hook, etc. As in Maeterlinck's **Les Aveugles**, physical shortcomings stand for spiritual ones. But unlike the situation in Maeterlinck's play, where all the characters as the title indicates suffer from the same defect, Lagerkvist varies the physical shortcomings; as a result of this, the characters can interact more vividly and the dramatic potential is increased.

Even so, **Himlens hemlighet** remains a fairly static play in which the protagonist, as is usual in Expressionist drama, "serves as an existential example, a paragon, very much like Christ in the passion plays" (Sokel, p.xx). The young Man's quest for knowledge or truth constituting the thin thread of action, the play illustrates a pilgrimage of sorts. But since it is a one-acter, where unity of place is adhered to, the different locales can only be indicated in a rudimentary way. Instead of moving from one place to another as in the full-length pilgrimage drama, the Young Man moves from one subsidiary character to another, each of them holding his own stage position and each of them confronting him with an attitude that is thematically and structurally effective at precisely the point where it is introduced.

It should be noticed in this context that **Himlens hemlighet** is no outright subjectivist play, no **Ich-Drama**, no modern psychological version of the medieval morality play. The subsidiary (evil) characters do not represent drives within the protagonist, who is indeed Christ-like. The major proof that they do not, is that they are on the stage – in the world – before he makes his entrance and after he disappears. Rather, the play is a parable in which the subsidiary characters incarnate the "human" qualities – indifference, egotism, cruelty – against which the protagonist reacts. Thus from the very beginning, before his appearance, it is demonstrated how the characters are either unable to communicate with one another or else only able to do so in a negative or primitive (sexual) way. The Dwarf, the Young Man's rival, comes closest to being his antagonist. There is a rudimentary triangle drama here, showing the Girl turning first to the Dwarf, then to the Young Man, then back to the Dwarf. But again this is merely a metaphorization of the pull within her – within man(kind) – between earthly and heavenly love.

Morally inferior to the protagonist and in this sense contrasting with him, the subsidiary characters are nevertheless his counterparts by the mere fact that they find themselves in the same existential dilemma, that of mankind. Thus the "open" quest of the Young Man has its equivalents in the more specific quests on the part of the minor characters. The Man with the skullcap seeks a rational answer to the meaning of life, the Blind man seeks a religious answer, the Girl an emotional one in love, and the Man with an iron hook a materialistic one by looking for worms in the ground.

Contrasting with the bare mundane environment that is lit by a sickly green light, are the visions of a pastoral paradise verbalized by the Girl and the Young Man. These visions are linked with the missing golden string on the Girl's guitar, symbolizing higher love. In vain she seeks for this string and for the "heavenly" tone it produces. The Dwarf with his phallic cane denies the existence of the string and admonishes her to play on all the others. The Young Man, by contrast, once he has fallen in love with the Girl, can hear her playing on it and he now envisions the wonderful pastoral scenery she has earlier told him about. Yet the Girl at this point does not play on her guitar at all, nor does she share his vision. What he hears and sees, in other words, is completely imaginary, a result of his being in love. "The secret of heaven" – this is the implication – can be revealed only in our imagination, in our dreams. It belongs to an inner reality sharply contrasting with the ones we have around us.

Expressionist drama is theme-centred rather than plot- or conflict-centred. This is especially true of the Expressionist one-act drama, since here the characters by definition find themselves in a relatively static situation, sharing the same plight. A closer look at the play demonstrates that it is built up of a number of thematic fragments, which are intertwined and counter-pointed to secure a certain amount of variation and dramatic rhythm. It is a "musical" structure, very characteristic of Expressionist drama, in which all the theatrical sign systems are brought into interplay.

To what extent does the epic theatre lend itself to the one-act form? The question poses itself when we take part of Bertolt Brecht's **Die Ausnahme und die Regel** (written in 1930). The drama has been summarized as follows:

> This short didactic play tells the story of a merchant who is trying to cross a desert in Asia at great speed in order to beat a competitor. He ruthlessly drives his coolie porter. In the waterless desert, when their supplies are running low, the kindly coolie offers the merchant some water he has secretly hoarded in his flask. The merchant mistakes the gesture for an attack upon his life and kills the coolie. At the subsequent trial it is established that the coolie had every reason to hate the merchant, so that the latter could not expect an act of kindness from him and was justified in interpreting the coolie's gesture as an attack. The merchant is acquitted as having acted in legitimate self-defense. In our world an act of kindness is an exception, hatred and violence the rule, by which alone we can regulate our conduct.
>
> (Esslin, 1961a, p.294 f.)

The play is divided into nine scenes, framed by a prologue and an epilogue. Each scene (except the last two) represents a separate locale. Dramatizing an expedition, the play has neither unity of place nor of time. In this respect it differs from the normal one-acter.

The narrative titles of the scenes are very characteristic of the epic theatre. Thus Scene 4 is entitled "Gespräch in einer gefährlichen Gegend". This title can obviously not be visualized in terms of stage décor; rather, it is meant to be projected onto the curtain or onto a screen. By indicating the locales in this verbal way, the playwright constantly reminds the audience that what it witnesses is theatre, not reality. It is one of the ways in which Brecht applies his **Verfremdungseffekt.**

Another way is the manner in which the characters fall out of their roles and address the audience directly from time to time. Already in the opening of the play we have a good example:

> DER KAUFMANN **zu seinen zwei Begleitern, dem Führer und einem Kuli, der das Gepäck trägt**: Beeilt euch, ihr Faultiere, heute über zwei Tage müssen wir bis zur Station Han gekommen sein, denn wir müssen einen ganzen Tag Vorsprung herausquetschen. **Zum Publikum**: Ich bin der Kaufman Karl Langmann und reise nach Urga, um die Schlussverhandlungen über eine Konzession zu führen.

Here the initial realistic illusion is suddenly broken when the Merchant – now a narrator addressing the audience – reminds us that we are watching a play.

A third manner resorted to are the songs that break the flow of action and point to what is thematically and parabolically essential to this "Lehrstück".

The **Verfremdungseffekt** also makes itself felt in the prologue and epilogue, where all the actors, now forming a chorus, express a moral altogether at odds with that of some of the characters; here the actors who are playing the parts of the Merchant, the Judge, etc., clearly fall out of their roles.

The Merchant's hunger for profit determines his recklessness against the Coolie, but this in turn gives rise to his fear of the Coolie's class hatred. The more he suppresses the Coolie, the more he fears for his own life. When the Coolie finally offers him his flask of water, the Merchant's fear has grown to such an extent that he mistakes it for a stone, a murderous weapon.

In the concluding court scene – usually inserted in a Brechtian play – the true criminal, the Merchant, is acquitted and his victims, the Wife and the Child of the dead

Coolie, are "condemned" to a life of misery. The final chorus amounts to a protest against this unjust verdict with a plea to the audience that it change the ways of the world and turn the rule (hatred) into an exception, and the exception (love) into a rule. With the didactic and activist message the play ends.

The central question of the drama is: why did the Coolie offer the Merchant water? The Guide believes that he did it out of humanity; when he is pressed for an answer by the Judges he nervously suggests another reason, which obviously does not make sense: the Coolie acted out of stupidity. The chief Judge, by contrast, assumes that the Coolie intended to kill the Merchant with the water flask, since as a representative of a suppressed class he had every reason to do so. The final Chorus, as we have seen, repeats the Guide's first view. A belief in altruism (love) is thus pitted against a belief in egotism (hatred). But there is also a third opinion, more relevant in fact than the ones yet mentioned, that of the Coolie himself: shortly before he is killed he soliloquizes:

> Ich muss ihm die Flasche aushändigen, die mir der Führer auf der Station gegeben hat. Sonst, wenn sie uns finden, und ich lebe noch, er aber ist halb verschmachtet, machen sie mir den Prozess.

In other words, neither the Judge nor the Chorus is right. The Coolie did not act out of hatred nor out of love but out of fear. The fear of the suppressor has its counterpart in that of the suppressed.

Viewed in this light the final moral, however noble it is, seems highly ironical. The Chorus asks the audience to turn the exceptional act of love it has just witnessed into a rule. But the audience, being better informed, knows that it has witnessed an act of fear, not of love. The message brought home to it is therefore: there is no exception, only a rule, the rule of fear. And yet it is hard to accept so negative a conclusion. Perhaps it is more legitimate to say that the Coolie's own motivation highly relativizes the positive view of the Chorus; as an audience we are left with the hope that if the exception to the rule has not been convincingly demonstrated on the stage, it could be so outside it, in life. The Coolie's failure to live up to the expectations of the Chorus becomes in the last instance a provocation to the audience. Rather than act as a jury – the normal kind of audience participation in a Brechtian play – we are told a lesson and are asked to apply it to our lives. In that sense **Die Ausnahme und die Regel** well deserves its subtitle "Lehrstück".

Unlike Brecht's epic one-acter, Sartre's **Huis clos** (1944) represents in a double sense an attempt to save the dramatic element in drama. As a one-act play it substitutes to a great extent situational for relational suspense. In addition to this, it exemplifies how a "Situation der Enge" (Szondi, p.96) can force people whose natural language is silence or soliloquy to dialogue and communication.

From another point of view, the narrow space serves to illustrate man's existential dilemma, his feeling of being unfree. It is no coincidence that many one-acters are set in isolated, imprisoning environments. But while most of these plays depict situations in life, **Huis clos** deals with a situation beyond life. Three people, a man and two women, find themselves together in a drawing-room furnished in the style of the (French) 1860s. They all realize that they are dead and that they have landed in hell. They begin questioning the justice of the verdict. Is it perhaps by mistake or by chance that they have come here? As they tell their life stories to one another, both they and we realize that they are not in hell by accident but that they are themselves responsible for their present misery.

The three have led far from blameless lives. One has killed her own child and caused the suicide of her lover, another has indirectly caused the death of the husband of her lesbian friend, a third has been killed as a deserter. We may therefore conclude that we are confronted with three criminals who suffer their justly deserved punishment. But this is obviously a very superficial interpretation. More relevant is the view that we are faced with three cases of false living (Verhoeff, p.78f.) and that the three are being punished not so much for what they have done as for what they have refrained from doing, for being parasites on their fellows rather than independent human beings taking responsibility for their own actions. If we adopt this view, the three characters come to represent a much larger group of people. The third alternative – arguing that the inability to take full responsibility for their own actions is an inherent human weakness – is that the three are representative human beings and that their crimes are merely variants of human shortcomings, introduced to increase the dramatic potential of the play (cf. **Paria**). But if this is true, everyone is predestined to end up in hell whichever way he/she has lived. It should be clear from this that only the second alternative is truly satisfactory.

Tied up with the question of how representative the three characters are is the question of how we should view their present environment. Again, we may choose between three alternatives. Along with many commentators we may simply regard it as a modern, secularized version of hell, as a place where physical torture has been replaced by mental suffering, fit for people who have lost faith in traditional Christian concepts of inferno.

More interesting is the idea that Sartre's hell actually stands for life on earth:

> Sartre will in der säkularisierten Wendung sagen, das gesellschaftliche Leben sei die Hölle; kehrt aber die Prädikation um und zeigt die Hölle als "salon style Second Empire", in dem sein Held, kurz bevor der Vorhang fällt, das Schlüsselwort spricht: "L'enfer, c'est les Autres." Durch diese Inversion wird ein problematisch gewordenes Existential, das Mitmensch-Sein, welches das gesellschaftliche Leben, die Möglichkeit eines Salons erst begründet, verfremdet und in der 'transzendentalen' Situation der Hölle als ein Neues erfahren.
>
> (Szondi, p.102)

Indeed, the step from Strindberg's **Dödsdansen (The Dance of Death)**, depicting hell on earth, to **Huis clos** is a short one. Yet Szondi overstates his point when he regards the choice of a transcendent locale as merely an alienation effect.

As a matter of fact – and this is the third interpretative alternative – the setting of the play seems primarily determined by the existentialist conviction that Sartre via his mouthpiece Inès expresses in the play:

> Seuls les actes décident de ce qu'on a voulu.
> Tu n'es rien d'autre que ta vie.

In other words, as long as man is alive, he can add something to or deduct something from his spiritual nature, a stature which is based solely on his actions, not on his ideas or desires. Thus Garcin's view that given another day of life, he could have lived up to the ideology he has betrayed is not of any value, since it is merely a view that cannot be tested in action – and has very little convincing power at that. While people always tend to think that they die "toujours trop tôt – ou trop tard", that is, either before they have performed enough good deeds or after they have performed too many bad ones, the fact is that they simply die when they have performed – or refrained from performing – a certain number of deeds. And since man's inherent value according to existentialist doctrine depends on the sum of his deeds, it follows that the final evaluation can only take place when there is a sum total, that is, when life is over. The choice of locale in **Huis clos** is, in other words, primarily determined by the need to find a point from which the **whole of life** can ethically and metaphysically be viewed. It has nothing to do with a belief in a life hereafter.

What then is the relationship between the three characters on the stage and the audience? With Szondi we may see it as a shared experience: life is an inferno to them as it is to us, and all human beings act alternately as tormentors and as victims to one another. But we may also see their situation as essentially differing from ours. They are dead, we are alive. Their life record is complete, ours is not. Unlike the three characters we can still do something with our lives, from their failure we can learn something.

With Szondi we may find that the reason why the hell in **Huis clos** is so similar to life is that it actually represents life. More valid, I believe, is the view that the similarity serves to emphasize the essential difference just mentioned. Much of the dramatic power of the play depends, for example, on the fact that words are uttered and actions are performed in a context that is utterly different from the one both we and the characters are used to. Thus an expression like "nous resterons jusqu'au bout seuls ensemble", which makes sense in life, is meaningless when uttered in a place where there is no end. Throughout the play Sartre stresses the fact that change is not possible in hell: the light burns forever, eyelids cannot be closed, murder and suicide are not possible, etc. As they themselves surmise in the closing lines, the characters are condemned to be together forever. If it is true that "l'enfer, c'est les Autres", there is in life at least the consolation that the others may vary. In Sartre's hell this is not so. By implication the playwright states that "l'enfer, c'est l'Inaltérabilité".

The dramatically valid equivalent of this emotional experience would be an extremely long one-acter full of repetitive elements, continuously forcing a sense of tedium onto the audience. But since this would clash with our primary need to be stimulated by the play we are witnessing, Sartre could do not better than provide us with an uninterrupted, imprisoning "slice of death", which we may expand upon in our own imagination; as the closing line reads: "Eh bien, continuons".

With Absurdism the one-act play becomes a dominant form of drama. The reason may possibly be sought in the fact that in a nuclear age the fate of mankind has become a burning issue; and as we have seen, the one-acter especially lends itself to a parabolic depiction of man's existential situation. Or it might be sought in the fact that the Absurdists try to make the audience **experience**, not just witness, modern man's anguish, bewilderment, loneliness and sense of emptiness. In their attempt to establish contact with deep emotional layers within the recipient, the Absurdists often resort to the device of intensification. This can best be done in a one-act play, since a full-length drama would include intermissions which necessarily break the theatrical spell and counteract any possible rapport with the subconscious part of the spectator. Just imagine an absorbing film cut into pieces by intermissions, or Ravel's **Bolero** divided into movements.

Although Absurdist drama shares certain characteristics with epic drama – critical detachment from the flat characters, comic ingredients, parabolic presentation – it is actually closer to Strindbergian "psychodrama" in its striving to work on the emotions of the audience. Admittedly, the difference is that while Strindberg strives to create empathy for his characters, the Absurdists seek to convey empathy for their situation, because this mirrors our own. In the case of his one-acter **Les Chaises**, written in 1951, Ionesco has himself indicated how important the continuity of the action is when stating that:

> The theme of the play is **nothingness** . . . the invisible elements must be more and more clearly present, more and more real . . . until the point is reached, – inadmissible, unacceptable to the reasoning mind – when the unreal elements speak and move . . . and nothingness can be heard, is mâde concrete . . .
> (Esslin, 1961b, p.100)

To the Absurdists the world is unintelligible and so a play which is intended to be a synthetic picture of (our experience of) the world should be shaped in such a way that it too seems unintelligible to the audience. Ionesco makes this clear in his Foreword to **Les Chaises**, when he states that he cannot understand his own play, since he cannot understand the world (Schnetz, p.117).

However, conflicting with the aim of creating a chaotic situation grotesquely reflecting our experience of the world, there is a need to structure the play in such a way that an emotional impact on the audience is secured. Thus on closer inspection a number of devices – the climactic build-up of the play being the most obvious one – can be found in **Les Chaises**.

Some of these devices, such as the emphatic reliance on visual imagery, can be traced back to Expressionist drama. Others, such as the constant setting aside of everyday logic, would appear to be largely a novel characteristic of Absurdist drama. An obvious example is the following: says the Old Man to the (imaginary) Belle: "Il y a en vous un tel changement . . . Il n'y a en vous aucun changement". This contradictory statement may be viewed in different ways. It may be seen as an indication of the emptiness of language. It may be regarded as a sign of the subjective nature of reality: we are unable to tell whether the lady in question has indeed changed or not; possibly the same goes for the speaker. But it may also be seen as a laconic satire on the clash between spontaneous reaction and socially conditioned, polite after-thought. Just as at another point in the play the playwright had the Old Woman perform a pantomime "**qui doit révéler une personnalité cachée de la Vieille**", from which she immediately returns to her role-playing, so here a subconscious outburst is immediately corrected by the super-ego. This brief example may be sufficient to indicate how complex and pregnant Ionesco's lapidaric dialogue often is.

The themes in **Les Chaises**, Ionesco has said, deal

> with emptiness, with frustration, with this world, at once fleeting and crushing, with despair and death. The characters I have used are not fully conscious of their spiritual rootlessness, but they feel it instinctively and emotionally. They feel "lost" in the world, something is missing which they cannot, to their grief, supply.
> (Cole, p.284)

What is missing are not least – "les Autres": people of flesh and blood with whom they can have a sense of communion. The empty chairs are a pathetic symbol of the absence of those who should sit on them. And as the chairs proliferate and are brought into the room in an increasingly rapid tempo, we are made painfully aware of the growing despair of the old couple, who remain as lonely on stage as they were in the beginning, before the room was "peopled" by chairs.

Instead of serving as consoling fellow-men replacing their dead parents, the invisible guests separate the Old Man from his wife: "Mon chéri, j'ai peur, il y a trop de monde . . . nous sommes bien loin l'un de l'autre". Finally there seems to be no room at all left for the couple. Having witnessed the arrival of the Emperor and presumably afraid to be present when the Speaker presents their message to the world, they jump out of the windows on either side of the room, voluntarily seeking death by water. The message is never communicated. The Speaker does indeed appear but he can neither speak nor write. The artist (the writer) – this seems to be a valid interpretation – cannot communicate the significance of the life the old couple has led. The meaning of life remains enigmatic. The explanation is handed over to God, "ADIEU" being the only intelligible and ambiguously ironic part of the Speaker's written message.

Throughout the play the theme of loneliness is stressed. The Old Woman is a mother substitute for her husband, just as the invited, wholly imaginary guests, as we have noted, "remplacent les papas et les mamans". Communion being denied them in life, the old couple dream of finding it in death "dans un même tombeau", but alas even this will be denied them: "Nos cadavres tomberont loin de l'autre, nous pourrirons dans la solitude aquatique". The way in which the double suicide at the end is performed testifies to this separateness even in death.

Before the Speaker appears, the chairs are turned so that their fronts are facing him and their backs are turned to the audience. By this arrangement Ionesco indicates that the invisible audience on the stage is identical with the factual one in the auditorium. The world represented by the invisible guests on the stage is suddenly extended to include ourselves. Stage and auditorium unite to form one **theatrum mundi**. The link between the two audiences is explicitly made at the end of the play when "**on entend pour la première fois les bruits humains de la foule invisible**", an ironical sound effect since it means that we are suddenly forced to accept the presence of characters whose existence we have until now denied. In one sense **we** are now in the position of the old couple, witnessing what they have witnessed, while in another sense – since the noises are those of an ordinary theatre audience at the end of a performance – we are the object of their longing for contact: the invisible crowd. The play thus ends on a note of role-switching, suggesting that life is not only enigmatic but also unreal. We might also say that the play ends with an ultimate provocation, questioning that our existence is any more real than that of the imaginary guests. As Ionesco put it: "The theme of the play is **nothingness**".

As we have seen, each of the six one-acters has its own characteristics and differs in significant ways from the others. The reason is partly to be found in the fact that each is representative of a particular dramatic style or movement: Naturalism (**Paria**), Symbolism (**Intérieur**), Expressionism (**Himlens hemlighet**), Epic theatre (**Die Ausnahme und die Regel**), Existentialism (**Huis clos**), and Absurdism (**Les Chaises**). Had we examined, say six Absurdist plays, the divergences would undoubtedly have been fewer. On the other hand, an examination of a large corpus of one-acters would inevitably have resulted in a much greater variety than is now the case.

It now rests with us to compare the six plays more systematically and relate them to some of Schnetz's overall criteria. Beginning with the most obvious characteristic, we may note that there is a considerable difference in magnitude between the shortest one, **Paria** (20 pages), and the longest one, **Les Chaises** (52 pages). Since quantity affects the structural and thematic aspects of a play, this difference may well be of significance; it might, for example, be argued that the crescendo technique employed in Ionesco's one-acter presupposes a play of a certain magnitude.

More interesting, perhaps, is the relationship between playing time and implied time of (scenic) action, **Spielzeit** and **gespielte Zeit**. In **Paria** the two are identical – around thirty minutes; also in this respect Strindberg adheres to the Naturalist demand for slice-of-life illusion. The same is true of **Huis clos** but here the final line – "Eh bien, continuons" – combined with the place of action makes us aware that what we have just witnessed will be repeated endlessly and that the concept of time, in fact, no longer applies. On the realistic level, both **Intérieur** and **Les Chaises** cover a few hours, **Himlens hemlighet** a few days, weeks, months, or years; on the parabolic level the three plays cover a life-time (that of the family, those of the Old Man and the Old Woman and that of the Young Man respectively). The scenic time-span in **Die Ausnahme und die Regel** is a few days.

The prescenic action, i.e. the action preceding the staged events, is more or less non-existent in **Himlens hemlighet** and **Die Ausnahme**, sparse in **Intérieur** (the story of the girl who drowned herself) and **Les Chaises** (the story of the Old Man's parents and of the couple's son) and fairly extensive in **Paria** (the past crimes of the two men, the story about Stråman) and **Huis Clos** (the past crimes of the three characters). Since the amount of prescenic information is central to Klotz' familiar distinction between "offen" and "geschlossen" drama, this means that **Himlens hemlighet** and **Die Ausnahme** approach the former category, while the remainder approach the latter. But while Lagerkvist adheres to a unity of place, which secures a certain unity of effect, Brecht does not. It is in fact debatable whether **Die Ausnahme** with its nine scenes and constant changes of locale could be regarded as a proper one-act play; if so, it belongs to what Schnetz terms "episodic one-acters". Alternatively, we might regard it as a full-length play **in petto**, a miniature drama. The very concept of alienation is inimical to one of the greatest assets of the one-acter: the possibility of stirring the audience emotionally.

With the single exception of **Die Ausnahme**, the unity of place is adhered to in all the one-acters. In some cases (**Paria, Intérieur, Les Chaises**) it concerns an environment familiar to the characters, which however takes on a new quality in the course of the play. In other cases (**Himlens hemlighet, Die Ausnahme, Huis clos**), the characters find themselves in a new and hostile environment (the world, the desert, hell) which they must come to terms with.

The central conflict in **Paria** concerns the contrasting ethics of the two men, in **Himlens hemlighet** the contrasting ethical behaviour of the Young Man and the rest of the characters, in **Die Ausnahme** the social struggle between the Merchant and the Coolie, in **Intérieur** man in the shadow of death, in **Huis clos** the eternal tormentor-victim triangle. **Les Chaises** falls outside the general pattern; here the discrepancy between what the characters and the audience experience replaces a conflict between the characters themselves; the audience becomes directly involved in the action.

Although the one-act form does not allow for any detailed character description, we may note that the characters in **Paria** and **Huis clos** are drawn more in the round than are those in the other plays. Yet even with Strindberg and Sartre it is obvious that the characters are less individuals than representatives of ethical principles, Kierkegaardian stages on life's way. In **Die Ausnahme** the **dramatis personae** are clearly typified to bring out the fact that they represent particular social groups or group interests. In **Intérieur, Himlens hemlighet** and **Les Chaises**, the typification helps to underline the universal nature of the characters, so that we can more easily see that their situation is ours, that it is the situation of "Everyman". If the flatness of the characters prevents empathy for them as human beings, it helps us on the other hand to empathize with their situation.

Of fundamental importance, as we have noted earlier, is the view that "die Situation im Einakter unabänderlich ist" (Schnetz, p.89) and that the characters are also unable to change "denn sie sind mit ihrer Situation identisch" (ibid.). It is true that the one-acter allows for little flexibility in this latter respect, but we may note that the Young Man in **Himlens hemlighet** undergoes a very definite change from initial hopefulness to final anguish resulting in suicide.

The basic question, however, is whether it is true that in the one-acter the situation remains the same from beginning to end. It is evident that new information is continually provided in the course of any play and with this new information, events, environments, ideologies, and characters are gradually transformed and appear in a new light. In **Paria**, Mr X and Mr Y discover that they have both gone unpunished for crimes committed in the past. The family in **Intérieur** discovers that one of its members has died. The Young Man in **Himlens hemlighet** discovers that the world is not paradise but hell. The Merchant in **Die Ausnahme** (erroneously) discovers that the Coolie is not to be trusted and acts accordingly. The trio in **Huis clos** discover that they are doomed to be each other's eternal executioners. The old couple in **Les Chaises** discover that, having seen the Emperor, they want to die "en pleine gloire". Unlike the other discoveries, this last one comes as a complete surprise to the audience; again Ionesco upsets the logic of drama, **l'art de bien préparer**.

Also in other, more factual respects the situation at the end of the plays is different from the one at the beginning. Mr X and Mr Y have turned into enemies. The family has lost a member. The Young Man has committed suicide. The Coolie has been murdered. The Old Couple have drowned themselves. **Huis clos**, where both murder and suicide prove in vain, falls outside the general pattern; here indeed the outward situation remains the same as in the beginning, for in hell no change is possible.

Our conclusion must be that the term "situation" is exceedingly vague. When it has been traditionally held that the one-acter deals with a situation that does not significantly change, the term has been used in a wide sense. Regarded as parables, most of the one-acters we have considered seem indeed to describe a major static situation: the plight of mankind. Yet since in any drama a dynamic element is necessary, and since this element is brought about by constant changes, it follows that even the one-acter must resort to several minor situations; or at least there must be a change from one situation to another – or we have no drama. We are confronted here with two different ways of describing the same object; compare the way in which the action of a drama may be referred to as a triangular situation (static) or as an A-leaves-B-for-C situation (dynamic). Unlike the full-length play, where a change of situation would normally be connected with a change of time and/or place, the one-acter would have to establish it within the given time-place setting. As a result of this, the interaction between the characters and their environment is even more important in the one-acter than in the full-length play.

Schnetz' claim that "im Einakter fallen Höhepunkt, Katastrophe und Schluss zusammen" (p.74) cannot be borne out by any of the plays under consideration. Her views that "das Geschehen des Einakters . . . kommt ohne Protagonisten aus" (p.91) and that "der Einakter kennt keinen persönlichen Gegenspieler" (p.108) are equally dubious. In **Paria**, we have noted, Mr X functions as a protagonist and Mr Y as an antagonist; the same functions are held in **Himlens hemlighet** by the Young Man and the Dwarf respectively, and in **Die Ausnahme** by the Merchant and the Coolie. In **Huis clos** all three characters function both as protagonists and antagonists in accordance with the credo "l'enfer, c'est les Autres". In **Les Chaises** there is a double protagonist, and in **Intérieur** a collective one – unless we regard the Old Man, the narrator, as the protagonist of the play.

If the one-act subgenre is thus much more protean than Schnetz would have us believe and, like all other (sub)genres, conditioned by the fluctuations of ideologies, media etc., it may nevertheless be meaningful to distinguish between two types, relating to the two main streams of drama: "the illusionistic one-acter" and "the non-illusionistic one-acter". Of the six plays selected, **Paria** belongs to the former category, **Himlens hemlighet** and **Les Chaises** to the latter one. **Intérieur, Die Ausnahme** and **Huis clos** are borderline cases, combining an illusionistic aspect with a non-illusionistic one. In many respects **Les Chaises** differs from the rest of the one-acters; in a number of ways Ionesco radically breaks with what had until then been regarded as fundamental dramaturgic rules.

The very brevity of the art form means that the number of "empty spaces" to be filled in by an audience is much higher than in a full-length play. The writer of one-acters must count on a very active audience participation. But this participation, as we have seen, can be largely rational (**Die Ausnahme**) or largely emotional (**Intérieur**). It can stress the similarity between the situation of stage characters and the situation of the audience; or it can stress the difference between the two. Usually we are dealing with a parallel-by-contrast, according to the rule that not until we see our own situation distorted or alienated in one way or another do we really see it. Surely, the Russian Formalist concept of **ostranenie**, carried over into the Brechtian **Verfremdungseffekt**, is the most fundamental and convincing proof of the inadequacy of what Strindberg termed the "little naturalism" yet formulated.

If we tend to think nowadays of one-act plays in terms of non-illusionistic drama, it is because most significant one-acters have been written in this vein – as appears from Höllerer's and Holm's one-act play anthologies. This is not surprising, since the general trend, at least since the 1920s, has led away from illusionism. Yet we must not forget that the illusionistic, "exoteric" one-acter is still the most frequent type.

This brings us to the ultimate question: to what extent can the one-act form be regarded as a manifestation of a Modernist trend in European drama? If we agree with Bradbury and McFarlane that the term "Modernism" has been used "to cover a variety of movements subversive of the realist or the romantic impulse and disposed towards abstraction" (p.23), then we must conclude that the initiator of the modern one-act play, August Strindberg, can be regarded as only partly Modernist in his short pieces. The matter is complicated by the fact that within the theatre, non-illusionism has been the rule and illusionism the exception. In this sense the theatricalist approaches of this century, Esslin has pointed out, actually mean a "return to an age-old tradition of theatre in which naturalism was merely one brief episode" (Bradbury/McFarlane, p.560). However, since realism is still with us – and with the arrival of new media (film, radio, television) in fact more so than ever – it seems reasonable to regard illusionism as the mainstream of drama (the word taken in a wide sense that includes the new media) and non-illusionism as a Modernist, admittedly very vital tributary. Gassner has remarked that playwrights of the last hundred years have been

> engaged in two kinds of theatre – the **modern** and the **modernistic**. The first sought realism of content, style, and form; the second aspired toward poetic and imaginative art. The first began to expel romantic and pseudo-realistic drama from the theatre by the 1870s, the second to challenge, modify and supplant realism by the 1890s.
>
> (Cole, p.xii)

This distinction seems useful. Transposed to our field of study it means that modern one-act drama, once realism gives way to various non-illusionistic -isms, or is taken care of by media outside the theatre, tends to turn into Modernist drama, all the more so since the brevity of the one-act form makes it "disposed towards abstraction". As a Modernist drama, the greatest asset of the one-act play would consist of its power to appeal to and even arouse hidden emotional drives within the spectator (the tradition launched by the Strindbergian "psychodrama" is perpetuated here), its power to depict a parabolic situation, and its power to catch the eternal in the momentary. The question may indeed be posed whether there is not, in principle, more genuine poetry of the theatre in the non-illusionistic one-acter than in the corresponding full-length play. If this is so, this type of one-act play may be regarded not only as a modern, but also as a Modernist phenomenon.

Literature

Bradbury, Malcolm and James McFarlane (eds.): **Modernism 1890–1930.** Harmondsworth, 1976.
Brecht, Bertolt: **Lehrstücke**. Hamburg, 1966. (**Die Ausnahme und die Regel**, pp.49–71.)
Cole, Toby (ed.): **Playwrights on Playwriting**. New York, (1960), 1964.
Esslin, Martin: **Brecht. The Man and His Work.** New York, (1959) 1961(a).
Esslin, Martin: **The Theatre of the Absurd**. Garden City, N.Y., 1961(b).
Halbritter, Rudolf: **Konzeptionsformen des modernen angloamerikanischen Kurzdramas**. Göttingen, 1975.
Hartmann, Alfons, **Der moderne englische Einakter**. Leipzig, 1936.
Holm, Ingvar (ed.): **I en akt**. Stockholm, 1966.
Höllerer, Walter (ed.): **Spiele in einem Akt**. Frankfurt am Main, 1961.
Ionesco, Eugène: **Théâtre, I**. Paris, 1954. (**Les Chaises**, pp.129–81.)
Klotz, Volker: **Geschlossene und offene Form im Drama**. München, (1969) 1978.
Lagerkvist, Pär: **Dramatik, I**. Stockholm, 1956. (**Himlens hemlighet**, pp.133–57.)
Lewis, Benjamin Roland: **The Technique of the One-Act Play**. Boston, 1918.
Maeterlinck, Maurice: **Le Trésor des humbles. Œuvres, I**. Paris, n.d.
Maeterlinck, Maurice: **Théâtre, II**. Paris, 1922. (**Intérieur**, pp.231–65.)
Pazarkaya, Yüksel: **Die Dramaturgie des Einakters. Der Einakter als eine besondere Erscheinungsform im deutschen Drama des achtzehnten Jahrhunderts**. Göppingen, 1973.
Sartre, Jean-Paul: **Théâtre**. Paris, 1947. (**Huis clos**, pp.111–69.)
Schnetz, Diemut: **Der moderne Einakter. Eine poetologische Untersuchung**. Bern, 1967.
Sokel, Walter H. (ed.): **An Anthology of German Expressionist Drama**. New York, 1963.
Sprinchorn, Evert (ed.): **The Genius of the Scandinavian Theater**. New York, 1964.
Strindberg, August: **Samlade skrifter, XVII**. Ed. J. Landquist. Stockholm, 1913.
Strindberg, August: **August Strindbergs dramer, III**. Ed. C.R. Smedmark. Stockholm, 1964.
Strindberg, August: **Strindberg's One-Act Plays**. Tr. Arvid Paulson. Introd. Barry Jacobs. New York, 1969. (**Pariah**, pp.151–71.)

Strindberg, August: **August Strindbergs dramer, IV**. Ed. C.R. Smedmark. Stockholm, 1970. (**Paria**, pp.25–44.)
Szondi, Peter: **Theorie des modernen Dramas (1880–1950)**. Frankfurt am Main, (1956) 1970.
Verhoeff, J.P.: **Sartre als toneelschrijver**. Groningen, 1962.
Wilde, Percival: **The Craftsmanship of the One-Act Play**. Boston, 1928.

Modernism and Samuel Beckett

John Fletcher

Samuel Beckett is a crucial figure in late Modernism and early Postmodernism. The novels **Murphy** (1938) and **Molloy** (1951), and the play **Waiting for Godot** (1953), are as central to the Postmodern aesthetic as **Ficciones, La Jalousie** or **Lolita**. Together with Borges, Robbe-Grillet and Nabokov, the authors of these other key works, he dominates the Postmodern landscape; and, also like them, he plunges his artistic roots deep in Modernism. In his case, indeed, Modernism – especially the work of James Joyce – offered not just a challenge to be taken up or a fertile soil to grow tall in, but represented aesthetic and sexual liberation, a turning point not only so far as art was concerned, but also a complete reorientation of life's pattern, a fundamental reappraisal and reordering of priorities which had previously remained unquestioned.

Beckett between Ireland and France

After all, he was very young at the time and his background was extremely provincial. He was born in 1906 into a comfortably-off Protestant family in Dublin. Apart from short holiday visits he did not go abroad until he was twenty-two. And then he went straight from backward Ireland to **avant-garde** Paris. He had done very well in his BA examinations at Trinity College, Dublin, and the lectorship in English at the Ecole Normale Supérieure which he took up in 1928 was meant to be the natural prelude to a conventional academic career on his return to Trinity.

Dublin had by then become the capital of a small newly-independent state, but was even more provincial than it had been when Ireland was part of the United Kingdom. In the days of the ill-fated Union, Dublin had been a major regional centre enjoying close ties with London, and through London with the rest of the British Empire (on which, as we know, the sun never set) and with the wider world. After independence the city stood, in international terms, a bit higher than Monrovia, not so high as Copenhagen, and at about the same level as Bogotà. The young Irish republic embraced neutrality (it would now be called non-alignment), and turned firmly in upon itself. The church, which had for so long been identified with the independence movement, was rewarded handsomely for its fidelity, and a theocratic regime was set up which today is proving difficult to dismantle. Censorship of books and periodicals was instituted, showing Beckett that ignorance was going to be officially condoned as being more conducive to godliness than knowledge, and that philistinism in all things to do with the arts had become the order of the day. When he appeared as a witness for the plaintiff in a Dublin libel action in 1937, counsel for the defence made a particular point of mispronouncing the name of Marcel Proust as "Prowst", well aware than in correcting him Beckett would strengthen the jury's already hostile reaction to one whom the barrister could, with impunity, dismiss as a "bawd and blasphemer from Paris".[1]

This crassly philistine and smugly inward-looking environment was the one from which Beckett escaped, in October 1928, initially for a period of two years; but when his contract came to an end he returned only briefly to Dublin and to the assistant lectureship at Trinity which had been created for him. He resigned the post after barely four terms in office, and left his native city, never to reside there again. In 1937, after several years of wandering, including long stints in London and in Hitler's Germany, he finally settled in Paris, where he has lived ever since. "If Beckett had any lingering doubts about the wisdom of moving to Paris", writes Deirdre Bair of this time, the libel case took good care of them: "Paris represented all that was good, pleasant and intelligent" and Dublin the opposite (Bair, p.269). Moreover, in Ireland all forms of contraception were banned; in Paris, sexual freedom and discretion about private matters were taken for granted. Small wonder that one of Beckett's earliest published works, a skit in the Trinity College undergraduate newspaper, was inspired by the embargo on the import of condoms into the Irish Free State.[2] From the safe distance of Paris he could but marvel in this piece, "Che Sciagura", at the puritanical outlook of his mother country, and pour nervous derision upon its absurdities; later, he was able to hone his wit more sharply:

> For the State, taking as usual the law into its own hands, and duly indifferent to the sufferings of thousands of men, and tens of thousands of women, all over the country, has seen fit to place an embargo on this admirable article, from which joy could stream, at a moderate cost, into homes, and other places of rendez-vous, now desolate. It cannot enter our ports, nor cross our northern frontier, if not in the form of a casual, hasardous and surreptitious dribble, I mean piecemeal in ladies' underclothing, for example, or gentlemen's golfbags, or the hollow missal of a broadminded priest, where on discovery it is immediately seized, and confiscated, by some gross customs official half crazed with seminal intoxication and sold, at ten and even fifteen times its advertised value, to exhausted commercial travellers on their way home after an unprofitable circuit.[3]

This passage comes from his second great novel, **Watt**, the last he wrote in English, some dozen or so years after dabbling in the naive experimentalism of "Che Sciagura", but the tone is similar, and the sense of relief at liberation from the repressions of Ireland just as palpable. Paris, the "supra-city of Modernism", offered "the climate, the appropriately fluid but semi-permanent cultural institutions, which young writers needed". For the youthful Samuel Beckett, it was the "ideal cosmopolitan city, cultured, tolerant, feverish and active, radical but contained".[4] Above all, it was the temporary home of the Anglo-American **avant garde**, to which the newly-arrived Trinity man felt a natural affinity, especially to its most characteristic organ, the little magazine **Transition**.

Beckett and the Anglo-American Avant Garde

Avant gardes are notoriously impermanent, and yet the phenomenon of the **avant garde** as such has shown, since about the turn of the century, surprising permanence and durability. There are, as Yves Navarre has pointed out, everywhere two kinds of **avant garde**, "la première, apparente, fracassante, phénomène de surface et de mode, anticonformisme qui devient un conformisme, sans tarder", and "la seconde, profonde, solitaire. . . Les vraies contestations", he declares, "ne sont pas apparentes. Elles ne se parent pas de thèses".[5] The greatest writers the Anglo-American **avant garde** has produced in our century – James Joyce, T.S. Eliot, D.H. Lawrence, Virginia Woolf,

Samuel Beckett – were either not **avant garde** personalities at all, or only marginally and for a short time during their careers. It is lesser figures like Gertrude Stein, Ezra Pound or Wyndham Lewis whom we find associated with, even leading, **avant-garde** movements of one kind or another.

As elsewhere, too, the Anglo-American **avant garde** cannot be clearly understood outside the wider context of Modernism in general, that "artistic and spiritual impulse which, at the start, looked radical but now impresses us with its tenacious conservatism, with its determination to preserve the Classic heritage and to get the museum in good order before closing-time".[6]

The first **avant gardes** began to emerge about 1890. It happened a little later in Britain and America than in other countries; as Geoffrey Thurley perceives, "England produced numerous Bohemian wavelets in the later nineteenth century, but no true **avant garde**".[7] (The same was even more the case in the United States due to the time-lag which did not cease to be a feature of cultural life in that country until after the Second World War.) But by 1908–9 there was a marked development of **avant-garde** activity, "a fresh move against realism, and a new phase in which the novelties of several arts – literature, music and painting – in several nations compounded into an eclectic modern fusion",[8] and it was not long before this began to make an impact on cultural life in London and New York. Ian Dunlop has documented, in a book entitled appropriately **The Shock of the New**,[9] two watershed art exhibitions which caused a scandal, that of the Post-Impressionists in London in 1910, and the Armory Show in New York (1913). Most Americans, Dunlop points out, had little contact with the Paris **avant garde**, and the Armory Show fulfilled a historic function in revealing to them a representative sample of what was going on in the fine arts in the European centre. This preparation of the ground, in London at least, was to make possible the birth of Vorticism, the only true home-grown **avant garde** the English have produced.

Although Vorticism was a largely English phenomenon, in the other countries of the British Isles there were movements which can perhaps qualify as **avant gardes**, most notably that associated with W.B. Yeats, Lady Gregory and Maud Gonne involving the promotion of a Celtic revival in Ireland, or possibly even Hugh Macdiarmid's more recent attempts to restore Scots to its ancient glory as a literary language in its own right. In this connection, too, the work of the London Welshman David Jones in furtherance of aesthetic self-consciousness for Wales ought not to go unmentioned, along with post-Poundian Subjectivism centring around Charles Reznikoff, Louis Zukofsky and William Carlos Williams in New York in the early 1930s. But the major development of the post-war period in Anglo-American **avant gardism** was undoubtedly the magazine **Transition**.

One of the most famous and influential of all "little magazines", **Transition** arose in 1927 in the American expatriate community of Paris. The American novelist Elliot Paul was closely associated with the review for the first two years, and its chief agent was Sylvia Beach, whose bookshop on the Left Bank was the favourite meeting-ground of Anglo-Saxon intellectuals in exile. The moment was unique. American writers, fleeing the land of prohibition, which seemed to them a cultural desert of continental proportions, benefited from a favourable exchange-rate which clinched for them the attractiveness of the French capital as a temporary refuge. British and Colonial writers came too, following in the footsteps of Moore, Symonds and Wilde, for whom Paris was not only a haven from British philistinism and prudery, but also the undisputed cultural capital of the world. Stuart Gilbert came there on his retirement from service in the East as one of His Majesty's colonial officials. And Samuel Beckett escaped there, as we have seen, from the stifling theocratic atmosphere of Eire, and to avoid London, because of what he called its "rules . . . the silly rules". A few native intellectuals, not suffering from the French malady of arrogant insularity and exclusiveness, were also drawn in: Valery Larbaud was the chief of these. Bi-cultural Alsatians like Hans Arp and Ivan Goll obviously felt at home, too, in a circle which was dominated – most appropriately – by a "Eur-American" devoted to intercontinental values, Eugene Jolas. And, most appositely of all, this church elected as its pope a writer of international stature and of universalist sympathies: James Joyce.

The doctors of the church were the two widely-read and cultivated men, Eugene Jolas and Stuart Gilbert. Gilbert was the more pragmatic and donnish; Jolas was the more quixotic and radical, thinking of his readers "as a homogeneous group of friends, united by a common appreciation of the beautiful" – the idealistic, anti-commercial tone was characteristic of Jolas.[10] But since both men were supremely intelligent and possessed fine critical minds, they complemented each other. It was they who laid down the guide-lines that the magazine was to follow in its eleven years of active life.

From the outset, **Transition** (the famous initial small "t" was adopted "to bait the critics") was defiantly, even truculently, Modernist. Indeed, it might well be viewed as Modernism's last vivid flowering. Jolas himself traced its spirit back to Hölderlin, Jean Paul, and to Novalis, whose **Hymns to the Night** he translated in 1929. Jolas indeed was fascinated by what he called the "preoccupation with the nocturnal" in some of the early Romantics, for whom "the dream and the daydream", he said, "the fairy-tale and the fable, constituted sources of a future literature", and to whom "poetry and life were identical"; above all, he admired what he called their "attempt to demolish the dualism of spirit and nature, of the I and the non-I". Among English poets, Blake was **Transition**'s supreme cult-hero, and Wordsworth the great betrayer of true poetry ("the trouble", it was said, "began with Wordsworth"). As for Realism and Naturalism, these were unfortunate aberrations, about which the least said the better; fortunately Rimbaud and the Symbolists had set matters to rights again. Maeterlinck's dream-monologues had provided the transition – it is difficult to avoid the word "transition" when discussing the review – to the neo-romantic Expressionists and to Dada, from which of course sprang Surrealism. **Transition**'s relations with Surrealism in "its heroic period", before it "discovered the Marxist ideology" and hardened into a "rigid dogmatism", were cordial enough: Artaud, Breton, Eluard, Leiris, Péret and others were all translated in its pages. Indeed, the two movements were in many ways very close, in spite of the fact that the Surrealists were criticized for not having transcended Freud and Dada. Jolas, not unlike the Surrealists, conceived **Transition** as a "mantic laboratory that will examine the new personality", as he puts it, "particularly with relation to the irrational forces dominating it, and combat all rationalist dogmas that stand in the way of a metaphysical universe", by championing, he went on, "the hallucinative forces now trodden under foot". But notwithstanding its "spirit of integral pessimism", **Transition** was basically a humanistic and liberal organ. Jolas's admiration for what was best in the American way of life was an immigrant's genuine and heartfelt admiration: "I had at the time, and I have still", he wrote in 1949, "an almost mystic concept of an ideal America, and I wanted to make of **Transition** a continuous manifestation of this concept". A section of a poetic contribution of his to the twenty-sixth number was revealingly entitled "America Mystica"; "We dream", it ends, "a new race visionary with the logos of God". But Jolas felt the "totalitarian menace" too acutely to be able to follow the Surrealists in their political flirtations, any more than he could accept that their exclusiveness was aesthetically justified. Stuart

Gilbert recalls proudly that the review "kept open house", being always on the look-out for the promising manuscript signed by an unknown name. Indeed, we could object that in spite of its hermetic manifestos, **Transition** was too eclectic: Ernest Hemingway and Hugo Ball make rather odd bedfellows.

The Surrealists were, therefore, seen as cousins: the family likeness was there, even if you did not always feel like agreeing with them. And in any case, Jolas viewed Surrealism as only the most recent landmark in the voyage which led from Jean Paul, and which he saw as continuing to his own -**ism**, Verticalism. The precise meaning of this term, Verticalism, is not easy to discover. It is variously defined by Jolas himself as "cosmological imagination", or the "attempt to liberate the human personality from the possession of nihilism":

> It stressed [he said] the creative urge towards a liturgical renascence by reconstructing the myth of voyage, migration, flight, and particularly ascent, in all its romantic-mystic manifestations. It sought the "marvellous of the skies" in the poetry of aeronautical flight, in the conquest of the law of gravitation, and in an aspiration towards aerial perspectives. It also developed the poetry of cosmic or sidereal flight, tried to sing of the stellar spaces, and accentuated the vision of the "third eye". In the poetry of mystic flight it sought a transcendental reality. This new poetry of ascent wanted to express its vision in a language that would make possible a hymnic vocabulary.

This definition would seem to make Verticalism a sort of neo-Futurism, and Jolas the Marinetti of the space age. That this was not exactly intended is shown by Jolas's long prose poem "The Third Eye", which ends with "America Mystica" mentioned earlier. The inchoate mysticism of this poem illustrates Stuart Gilbert's remark that in the "angry thirties **Transition** turned, under the guidance of its editor, more and more towards mysticism", so much so, in fact, that Gilbert claims as one of the lasting achievements of the review its "deflection of the trend of modern literature towards a visionary plane", of which the key word was "vertigral", a hybrid of "vertical" and another Jolas favourite, "integral".

The word "vertical", with its "four-dimensional" overtones, was borrowed from Léon-Paul Fargue, who wrote "on a été trop horizontal, j'ai envie d'être vertical". This saying heads a collective manifesto (to which the young Beckett lent his signature also) published in **Transition** in 1932. The declaration is clearly influenced by Jung's theory of the collective unconscious, although Jung himself is not named. It is significant, though, that Jung's essay on "Psychology and Poetry" first appeared in English in **Transition**. The "disintegration of the I" is advocated so that the "illumination of a collective reality" can become possible, leading, it is hoped, to "the synthesis of a true collectivism", which will naturally have nothing in common with the Soviet "materialistic" kind. Once again we are fascinatingly close to and yet distant from the Surrealists. But we are no nearer an understanding of what Verticalism really meant to Jolas, or for that matter, to anyone else, Beckett included (Gilbert is respectful about it, but hardly enlightening). It seems a classic instance of the attempt to create a literary movement by thinking up a name for it: Verticalism is clearly, like Vorticism in the fine arts, one of the non-starters of cultural history.

It is, in fact, much easier to situate and evaluate **Transition** as an artistic manifestation if we leave Verticalism out of account altogether. As a movement,

Transition was by no means free of inconsistencies. Particularly striking is the contradiction between the call for a return to content and the stress laid throughout the review on new, experimental forms; furthermore, words like "romanticism" and "classicism" were to be "retired from active service", and yet Jolas managed to find a use for them in the retrospective essay he wrote about the magazine in 1949. Nevertheless, in spite of inconsistencies, **Transition**'s main features can be summarized. It based itself on three cardinal tenets: Modernism, internationalism, and the "revolution of the word".

The "modernity" of the **Transition** standpoint is continually emphasized. The very title is indicative: the sponsors feel themselves in an "age of transition" from a largely repudiated past towards a glorious "cosmic" future. An early number announces that the review "will attempt to present the quintessence of the modern spirit in evolution". The reader is persuaded that "we need new words, new abstractions, new hieroglyphics, new symbols, new myths". **Transition**'s brand of Modernism was in fact in direct reaction to the world of Henry Ford, to what was called the "naive optimism of progress" and "machine-mammonism": "materialism", like "positivism", was a term of abuse in **Transition**'s hands.

The second plank of its platform was internationalism, and it did succeed in publishing work by writers from some twenty countries. The spirit was, however, more than simply international: it was internationalist. No frontiers were admitted in the world of the cultural consciousness: all intellectuals were brothers and sisters. Inspired by Joyce's example, the review sought to be "interlingual" (the term was Gilbert's). Of course, it began as an American expatriate magazine in which, it was claimed, American writers, gagged at home, could express themselves freely. One number announced that "the King's English is dying – long live the great American language"; American was preferred because of what was called "its greater richness and pliancy and nearness to life". And it is true that a concession to Anglo-Saxon readership was made, in that foreign texts were published in translations by Jolas, his wife Maria, Gilbert and others; but Jolas's verse incorporated fragments of French and German, and Hugo Ball's poem "Clouds" was written in a kind of cosmopolitan pidgin. The aim, in fact, was to "bring about a sort of poetic '**Internationale**'", as the review's subtitle – "An International Workshop for Orphic Creation" – made clear.

A third ambition followed from this urge to internationalism. **Transition** was, above all else, concerned to bring about the birth of a new literary language cleansed of all the tired, sullied vocabulary of the old. Language, it was felt, was infected by the malady of civilisation as a whole, and could no longer serve as an orphic instrument. This theory, derived from Joyce and Gertrude Stein, was supported by the practice, in the pages of the review, of what were called "sonorist iconoclasts" and "pure neologists", and of experiments in dream-writing. Language, it was said, was "aspiring to transcend the norm of speech and to retrieve the poetic form of its beginning"; Gilbert wrote admiringly of the sensuous suppleness of Old English, and Beckett of Dante's composite vernacular. Metaphors were employed to convey this complex idea: words were seen as "a fluid medium of vision", as "verbal sculpture", and Rimbaud's "hallucination of the Word" is admiringly quoted in an early collective manifesto, which goes on: "The literary creator has the right to disintegrate the primal matter of words imposed on him by textbooks and dictionaries, and to use words of his own fashioning and to disregard existing grammatical and syntactical laws". How far **Transition**'s clear stand on this has influenced what Gilbert later called the "contemporary recognition of the plastic element in language as a means of expression transcending the scope of mere communication and sufficient to itself", is of course something that is open to question. It seems that **Transition** here had the **Zeitgeist** on its side rather than against it, and the triumph must be attributed to that amorphous force rather than to **Transition**'s efforts.

These were the principal items in **Transition**'s programme. For all its excess of jargon, it was a programme not lacking in nobility and sense. It had further to commend it an openness to developments in the visual arts: certain of its covers were signed by Picasso, Léger, Miro, Kandinsky, Arp, Duchamp, Man Ray and Schwitters, and the work of such artists as Braque, Klee and Giacometti was reproduced in its pages. This in itself is no mean indication of the taste of its editorial staff, which did not always, alas, extend to the lay-out, which was often chaotic, with items thrown haphazardly together.

Transition was necessarily an élitist publication. "The plain reader to be damned" was one of its more truculent assertions. It refused to make concessions, and if it occasionally published the spuriously esoteric, or the would-be obscure, or the modishly unreadable, it must on the other hand be given credit for its valuable championing and regular publishing of Joyce's last work. It must also be congratulated for combating the "notion of delimiting prose and poetry"; it rightly saw verse and "imaginative prose" as one complex entity.

The twenty-seventh number (May, 1938) was the last; but that is not quite the end of the story. There was a partial post-war resurrection. In January 1948 the French art-critic, Georges Dethuit, launched a review appropriately entitled **Transition Forty-Eight**. Advisory editors were Georges Bataille, René Char, Douglas Cooper, Max-Pol Fouchet, Stuart Gilbert, Eugene Jolas, Jean-Paul Sartre and Jean Wahl. Although the two animators of the pre-war periodical were represented, and Samuel Beckett contributed to it and did some translating for it, it was hardly the same review.

The preamble to the first issue makes this clear: "The object of **Transition Forty-Eight**", it said, "is to assemble for the English-speaking world the best of French art and thought, whatever the style and whatever the application". And indeed the review consists entirely of translations from the French. This could not be disguised by the brave words, reminiscent of pre-war **Transition**, with which the preamble continues:

> These contributors are united by a common will to be true to truth, and a common awareness of a new age already kicking in the womb. That age, they hold, will utter a simplification, an astonishing simplification: whereby science and divination, metaphysics and the arts, all the lusty incompatibles, will no longer seem apart or out of joint, but fused and re-minted into a wise wholeness.
>
> It is their aim, and the ambition of this paper to recover somehow the virtue that has gone out of life: to unseal the spirit of festivity; to find again the adjustment, togetherness, at-one-ment of the tavern; to return to the sense of rapture.

In a Paris dominated by the very **littérature engagée** which pre-war **Transition** would have no truck with, the post-war paper was an anachronism. Of course, it published valuable things, but these were replicas of originals and not the originals themselves – and even some of the replicas, like those in pre-war **Transition**, were rather lame. It ceased publication definitively six numbers and two years later.

It is not easy to determine what was the net achievement of **Transition**'s "high, imaginative endeavour", as Stuart Gilbert put it. In so far as the review was in harmony with its time, it advanced causes that probably would have advanced anyway, if a little more slowly. Where it found itself out of sympathy with its age, it could not triumph. And in any case, world events caught up with it, and its internationalistic dream suffered the fate of all such dreams. The expatriate community on which it depended was dispersed, and now most of the names of those associated with it are forgotten. Yet it did champion Joyce, Kafka, Faulkner, Hemingway, early Beckett, Artaud, and the Surrealists; and it did find an audience for some of the neglected Romantics. In that way it has left a mark; and this is no mean achievement for any literary review. That such an uncompromising – and much vilified – paper should survive in spite of financial problems for over ten years, and all the while maintain a high standard and produce on occasion quite bulky issues, is a measure of its success. Perhaps this can be accounted for by the fact that it fulfilled a need. Its jargon and esotericism notwithstanding, it offered work that was often excellent, and its pages were free of the political and ideological wrangling which disfigured those of other periodicals at the time. And it was often shrewd in its appraisals, and not so far out in some of its predicitions; witness this one, from Eugene Jolas:

> The literature of the future will have no interest in competing with the possibilities for photographic and acoustic realism offered by the cinema, the radio, television, and similar mechanical inventions. I believe, therefore, that the literature of the future will tend towards the presentation of the spirit inherent in the magic tale and poetry, towards the poet's exploration of heretofore hidden strata of the human personality. It will probably express the irruption of the supernatural, the phantastic, the eternal, into quotidian life.

It is perhaps not stretching things too far to say that the "epic wonder tale giving an organic synthesis of the individual and universal unconscious", of which Jolas spoke, is precisely what Robbe-Grillet and other contemporaries offer us in their novels. Similarly, it could be argued that Claude Simon's fiction, or Nabokov's writing, involuntarily obey the injunction trumpeted in **Transition**'s notorious "Revolution of the Word" manifesto: "Time is a tyranny to be abolished". After all, it was **Transition** which said "The novel of the future will be a plastic encyclopaedia of the fusion of subjective and objective reality".

It can therefore be claimed with some justice that **Transition** formulated for the first time, or in an unprecedentedly forceful manner, some aesthetic tenets which are now common coin. The literary tempest it raised may seem a storm in a teacup, and the quarrels it engaged in are now forgotten. But it is difficult, when one thumbs back through the files of what Frank Kermode has called this "apocalyptic magazine", not to be excited by the epoch it reflects: a time in which the living masters were James Joyce and Paul Eluard, and the young hopefuls were called William Faulkner, Ernest Hemingway and Samuel Beckett.

Beckett and Joyce

The "living master" for whom Beckett felt the greatest kinship was, and always has been, James Joyce. As recently as 1980 he wrote in honour of the great Modernist: "I welcome this occasion to bow once again, before I go, deep down, before his heroic work, heroic being".[11] In the early phase of his own career his respect for Joyce was, not unexpectedly, shown in imitation. As Melvin J. Friedman has pointed out, "echoes of **Dubliners** resound through the pages of **More Pricks than Kicks**", Beckett's own collection of Irish stories, first published in 1934;[12] before that, in **Dream of Fair to Middling Women**, his first and still unpublished novel of 1932, he modelled a description of his hero Belacqua falling asleep on Joyce's Sinbad passage in **Ulysses**, and elsewhere in the book "tries his hand at a kind of post-**Ulysses** pastiche"[13] which lent itself directly (and predictably) to publication in **Transition**. The passages from **Dream of Fair to Middling Women** which the avant-garde magazine selected for publication – perhaps unfortunately, since they suggest that the whole work is written in a sub-Joycean manner – are "in some ways more obscure, because less disciplined, than even the knottiest passages of late Joyce, and there is no organizing principle which will make all things grist to the mill in the way Joyce almost miraculously can".[14]

The most detailed, as well as one of the most balanced, examinations of the artistic relationship between Joyce and the early Beckett has been carried out by S.E. Gontarski. He reminds us that Beckett was Joyce's "illstarred punster", and argues that in spite of a deep admiration for the master he early realised that he would need to pursue his own independent artistic course. **Dream of Fair to Middling Women**, Gontarski concedes, may represent Beckett's "first faltering steps along that path", but he suggests that Beckett probably did not write the novel which was to stand as his own truly independent statement until **Molloy**.[15]

Gontarski's conclusion – that Beckett may have written his most genuinely Joycean and yet most characteristically original novel in **Molloy** – is borne out by a close reading of that work. **Molloy** is Beckett's own, somewhat burlesque, version of Homer's **Odyssey**; although it is less systematic than Joyce's **Ulysses**, it must be considered as a great Postmodern adaptation of the legend, just as **Ulysses** is the great Modernist adaptation, assertive where Beckett's is diffident, each characteristic of the early and later phases of the modern movement. I would not claim that the parallels between **Molloy** and the **Odyssey** are observable at the structural level to the degree that they are in **Ulysses**; rather, I would argue that the alert reader soon becomes aware of a kind of subterranean parallel, even if the original and the imitation touch literally at only a few points. Certain passages in **Molloy**, indeed, do invite us to read them as Postmodern transpositions of the Ulysses legend. Molloy's stay at the police station, for instance, has affinities with Odysseus's encounter with the Cyclops, and the young woman who approaches Molloy on the beach suggests Nausicaa. A particularly striking example is the return of Moran-Odysseus. Although he finds no Penelope and slaughters no suitors (his servant Martha has left him and his bees have died) he wipes the slate clean anyway ("all there was to sell I have sold"),[16] and can receive Jacques-Telemachus back under the paternal roof. And we may certainly see in Edith a new Calypso and in Lousse the witch Circe, for Lousse puts a drug in Molloy's beer and holds him, he believes, by a spell; although she stops short of turning him into a pig, she does try to make him take the place of the dead dog which he ran over with his bicycle and which she had loved like her only child (p.33). It is entertaining to speculate why Beckett felt inclined to suggest these and other parallels between his story of Molloy/Moran and that of Odysseus, and the reason is clear enough. His feelings of admiration for Joyce have always been very strong (he is reputed, as recently as the award of the Nobel Prize in 1969, to have said that although he himself did not deserve it, why had Joyce never been similarly honoured?). He knew both the **Odyssey** and **Ulysses** well; perhaps not fully consciously, he wove allusions to the former, under the influence of the latter, into his own central masterpiece.

To digress briefly, I attempted to show in a recent note how Iris Murdoch's eminently Postmodern novel **A Severed Head** (1961) is a similarly oblique adaptation of a great classic, in this case Racine's tragedy of 1667, **Andromaque.**[17] The famous **Andromaque** formula – A loves B who loves C who loves D unrequitedly, leading to a tragic outcome – is closely followed in **A Severed Head**, but with a difference that the tone in Iris Murdoch's novel is burlesque whereas in Racine it is lofty. The difference is crucial because in the contemporary world it can be taken for granted that tragedy of the Racinian kind is no longer viable. Iris Murdoch's burlesque is not of the seventeenth-century kind, the "Virgile travesti" dear to poets nurtured on the classics. In its own distinctive way it is as serious a work as Racine's, since it argues a moral point of some importance: that we must be mature in our love of others, and that immature love destroys the lover.

The term which best fits this kind of writing is, to my mind, "necessary frivolity". Such "necessary frivolity" is characteristic of Postmodernism. In Beckett's **Molloy** we find, at one and the same time, a serious story of how one man (a sort of Telemachus-figure) goes in search of another (a sort of Odysseus-figure) and returns transformed into the man he has been seeking, and a dourly comic analysis of the entire human condition. In other words, we have a tale which, in its first part, reflects the wanderings of Odysseus, and in the second part Telemachus's search for his father and Odysseus's return; in this manner **Molloy**, like **A Severed Head**, illustrates and exemplifies a contemporary – and very characteristic – use of ancient mythology.

In another previous essay,[18] I attempted a psychoanalytical interpretation of **Molloy** which I based on Gilles Deleuze's exposition of the sado-masochistic syndrome, in his introduction to the French translation of **Venus in Furs** by Sacher-Masoch. My basic premise was that Molloy and Moran are not, as have often been claimed, a single persona, but two distinct characters. The basis of my argument was that Molloy is Moran's father, by way of the "chambermaid" whom Molloy mentions on p.7 and who later on becomes Moran's housekeeper, known under the name of Martha. The key to the relationship between Molloy, Martha and Moran – respectively father, mother and son – lies in the following revealing passage:

> Then . . . seeing her so old . . . I carried this sudden cordiality so far as to shake her by the hand, which she hastily wiped, as soon as she grasped my intention, on her apron . . . She must have wondered if I was not on the point of making an attempt on her virtue (p.120).

Martha is embarrassed by Moran's sentimental effusions because she knows what Moran does not: that she is his mother. "It's a wise child that knows its own father" says Telemachus in Book I of the **Odyssey**; Beckett's characteristic twist on this notion is that it is a wise child that knows who its mother is. But then Moran does not know either, except perhaps obscurely, that Molloy stands in a closer relationship to him than that of quarry to hunter.

The story, for all that, resolves itself in essentials to this: a man called Moran goes in search of a man called Molloy who is, in fact, his father; but he fails to find him. Indeed in a bizarre way he **becomes** his father, so in a manner can be said to have "found" him. Certainly – as the French might put it – he has "reintegrated" his father, becoming, through his wanderings, Odysseus in his turn. The first part of the novel, narrated by Molloy, thus becomes the story of Molloy's "wily-ness" (to use an

Odyssean expression). The second part, narrated by Moran, becomes the story of Moran's Odyssean journey and Telemachus-like quest.

In the present case, however, the myth is systematically debunked by the narrator: the phrase "I don't know" is a characteristic and repeated expression of lack of conviction in the business of narration. Nevertheless, the novel preserves the firm framework of myth; hence the continual stress on the necessity of writing the "report" which is imposed as an ineluctable duty on both writers, father and son:

> There's this man who comes every week . . . He gives me money and takes away the pages . . . When I've done nothing he gives me nothing, he scolds me. Yet I don't work for money. For what then? I don't know. (p.7; Molloy)

> A letter from Youdi, in the third person, asking for the report. He will get his report . . . One day I received a visit from Gaber. He wanted the report. (p.175; Moran)

These reports – which externalize the impulse to write which is internalized in Homer and Joyce – contain the record of the Telemachean quest in Part II for the Odyssean wanderer in Part I. This man, wily like Odysseus, does not hesitate, for instance, to throw sand in the eyes of the local police:

> Your papers! he cried. Ah my papers. Now the only papers I carry with me are bits of newspaper to wipe myself, you understand, when I have a stool. . . . In a panic I took this paper from my pocket and thrust it under his nose (p.20).

As this quotation makes clear, it is all very (if rather coarsely) funny. It could of course be capped by many a similar passage in **Ulysses**. What has happened is that Beckett, the Postmodern, has rewritten for our age the ancient masterpiece which Joyce rewrote in his Modernist age and for his Modernist age: the Homeric story of Odysseus the wanderer. And Beckett, like Joyce – but occasionally like Homer too, since the blind poet enjoyed a joke and savoured a comic situation – invites the reader to connive in the simultaneous debunking and exaltation of a noble myth.

It is in this sense that **Molloy** can be considered Beckett's **Ulysses**. Perhaps it can be considered so in another sense too. I refer to the centrality of **Molloy** in Beckett's overall achievement. Beckett's career, like Joyce's, divides very roughly into three phases; perhaps any great artist's does. The first is one of early experimentation when, strongly influenced by a few powerful older writers (in Beckett's case, Joyce himself and to a lesser degree Proust), the beginner tries to find and establish his own voice. The second is the period of maturity, in which one or more fully original works are produced; this tends to be the phase of greatest notoriety and growing reputation. In Beckett's case these works are **Molloy** and the play **Waiting for Godot; Murphy** and **Watt** are fine works too, but they stand, in relation to **Molloy** and **Godot**, in much the same relation as **Dubliners** and the **Portrait** stand to **Ulysses**: as mature, or almost mature, creations which provide the transition to the masterpiece(s). The third and final phase is one which few artists are capable of: that of vigorous, and frequently controversial self-renewal in the period following the work or works which establish them. Joyce, of course, went on from **Ulysses** to **Finnegans Wake**; and Beckett has gone on to produce a large number of relatively short pieces in both prose and drama which radically press on from the achievement of **Molloy** and **Waiting for Godot**. Like Joyce, he has been unable and unwilling to stand still; and he has by now lived considerably longer than Joyce did. Since **Molloy** and **Waiting for Godot** he has produced a whole new opus, and a radically different one, almost as different as **Finnegans Wake** is from **Ulysses**; so much so that it is tempting (for scholars and critics especially) to value the late work more highly than the achievements of the "middle years" which, after all, drew the attention of such scholars and critics to the writer in the first place. But usually with the passage of time a more normal perspective reasserts itself. The **Molloy** trilogy is Beckett's most discussed work of fiction, as **Waiting for Godot** is his most frequently performed play. Likewise Joyce will always be remembered primarily for **Ulysses**; he would be a very different artist if that work, alone of his writings, were absent from the canon. Beckett, likewise, would seem strangely deficient without **Molloy** to his credit. It is the cornerstone, the central loadbearing pillar: choose your own architectural metaphor as you will. To revert to literary terms, such works have an authority, a completeness, which marks them out, especially after the passage of time, as masterpieces in the strict sense of the word. Before long we wonder what life would be like without their existence. Thus, for myself, the closing words of **Molloy** seem as necessary, as inevitable, and as moving as Molly Bloom's conclusion "and yes I said yes I will Yes". They are very different in tone, of course, but this brings us back to the starting point: it is the difference between Modernism, with its confidence (in spite of all) in life and in art, and Postmodernism with its much greater diffidence. Here are Moran's final words, the words which close his report on his abortive (or was it?) Telemachia; words which perversely undermine the beginnings of his narrative, written after his return, but while he still felt "literary". Having relived his ordeal, through the act of recording it, he cannot any longer subscribe to the values which dictated his beginning. So this is how he sweeps it all away, and his book with it. But something survives, and every reader knows what it is, even if he or she has to find his or her own description for it – something like honesty, pride or resilience; the very heart of Modernism, and the very essence of Samuel Beckett:

> I went back into the house and wrote, It is midnight. The rain is beating on the windows. It was not midnight. It was not raining.

Searching for the Lost Ones

In common with Joyce and other Modernist writers, Beckett shows a marked preoccupation with sex in his fiction. No one can fail to note it; the only question is, what is it doing there?

The very first novel, **Dream of Fair to Middling Women**, written as we have seen in 1932, starts like this:

> Belacqua sat on the stanchion at the end of the Carlyle Pier in the mizzle in love from the girdle up with . . . Smeraldina . . . So now he sagged on the stanchion in the grateful mizzle after the supreme adieu, his hands in a jelly in his lap, his head drooped over his hands, pumping up the little blirt.

Belacqua is, clearly, manipulating the organ of his grief, "working himself up to the little gush of tears that would exonerate him. When he felt them coming he switched off his mind and let them settle". He rapidly becomes adept at "working himself up to the little teary ejaculation, choking it back in the very act of emission", and does it so often that the stimulus, through being continually thwarted, refuses to "work".

We also find (sparing ourselves the details) that this quite breathtakingly obscene imagination also gives us voyeurism in **More Pricks Than Kicks** (in addition to the indecent pun of the title), oyster kisses ("the osmosis of love's spittle") in **Murphy**, petting in **Watt** (Mrs Gorman and the hero being careful not to "trail, in the cloaca of clonic gratification, a flower so fair, so rare, so sweet, so frail"), a sordid sexual initiation in the sardonically-entitled **nouvelle** "First Love" (how Turgenev and D.H. Lawrence, who both used that title before Beckett did, would wince at this version), prostitution in **Mercier et Camier**, a man kept for immoral purposes in **Molloy** (as a result of which Molloy sourly concludes that "'twixt finger and thumb 'tis heaven in comparison"), senile attempts at sexual intercourse in **Malone Dies**, homoerotic sadism in **How It Is**, gross disparities of age between sexual partners in **Enough**, and so on. Peter Murphy has gone so far as to say that "the artist becomes a kind of vivisector-cum-pornographer" in **All Strange Away.**[19]

It would be easy to say that Beckett is not really interested in sex as such, but uses it as a metaphor for literary creation. This is a comforting explanation for a disturbing phenomenon, but unfortunately the evidence will not support it. Beckett – I refer of course to the writer, not the living man, about whose private life it would be impertinent to speculate – is fascinated by the sexual activity of the human animal, and rather like a zoologist examining the mating habits of marsupials, chronicles with gleeful fascination his and her behaviour. There is a clinical precision in Beckett's approach which is best exemplified by this passage from **Malone Dies**:

> There sprang up gradually between them a kind of intimacy which, at a given moment, led them to lie together and copulate as best they could. For given their age and scant experience of carnal love, it was only natural they should not succeed, at the first shot, in giving each other the impression they were made for each other. The spectacle was then offered of Macmann trying to bundle his sex into his partner's like a pillow into a pillow-slip, folding it in two, and stuffing it in with his fingers. But far from losing heart they warmed to their work. And though both were completely impotent they finally succeeded, summoning to their aid all the resources of the skin, the mucus and the imagination, in striking from their dry and feeble clips a kind of sombre gratification. (p.260)

Does the author give the impression of being disgusted by what he sees and describes, or is he merely fascinated by it? To help in answering that question, here is a fuller account of the abortive romance between Watt and Mrs Gorman:

> Mrs Gorman called [every] Thursday. Then he would have her in the kitchen, and open for her a bottle of stout, and set her on his knee, and wrap his right arm about her waist, and lean his head upon her right breast (the left having unhappily been removed in the heat of a surgical operation), and in this position remain, without stirring, or stirring the least possible, forgetful of his troubles, for as long as ten minutes, or a quarter of an hour. And Mrs Gorman too, as with her left hand she stirred the grey-pink tufts and with her right at studied intervals raised the bottle to her lips, was in her own small way at peace too, for a time.

> From time to time, hoisting his weary head, from waist to neck his weary hold transferring, Watt would kiss, in a despairing manner, Mrs Gorman on or about the mouth, before crumpling back into his post-crucified position. And these kisses, when their first feverish force began to fail, that is to say very shortly following their application, it was Mrs Gorman's invariable habit to catch up, as it were, upon her own lips, and return, with tranquil civility, as one picks up a glove, or newspaper, let fall in some public place, and restores it with a smile, if not a bow, to its rightful proprietor. So that each kiss was in reality two kisses, first Watt's kiss, velleitary, anxious, and then Mrs Gorman's, unctuous and urbane. (pp.153–4)

Once one gets over the outrageous nature of the subject-matter, one realises that this is both funny and – perhaps rather unexpectedly – touching. Touching, too, is the relationship between the young person and the old man in **Enough**; here too, once one gets over the shock at the "explicit" nature of the subject matter – as the sex shops' euphemism has it – one realises that this is, as always in Beckett, generalizing out from a coarse centre to an almost elegiac statement about loss: loss of hope through loss of love. That is why I suggest in my subtitle that sex in Beckett is searching for the lost ones: I am punning on the title of one of his more recent, beautifully intense prose texts, **The Lost Ones**, a haunting evocation of an "abode where lost bodies roam each searching for its lost one", that search, of course, being "in vain". We remember that in **Krapp's Last Tape** old, decrepit Krapp recalls with infinite sadness, crudely masked by sarcasm, the end of the affair with another Smeraldina, another "green one" to quote Joe's accuser in the television play **Eh Joe**, the "girl in a shabby green coat, on a railway-station platform"; what remains of all that misery, Krapp wonders. What remains is the literary statement, the evocation of a moment of sad happiness, as of the shade of an aspen in **Company**:

> You are on your back at the foot of an aspen. In its trembling shade. She at right angles propped on her elbows head between her hands. Your eyes opened and closed have looked in hers looking in yours. In your dark you look in them again. Still. You feel on your face the fringe of her long black hair stirring in the still air. Within the tent of hair your faces are hidden from view. She murmurs, Listen to the leaves. Eyes in each other's eyes you listen to the leaves. In their trembling shade.[20]

Company is the work of an old man who is recalling how he invented characters – the famous series with initials in M or W – "devising it all himself included for company". The elegiac tone is therefore overwhelming, the poignant sadness at lost things which survive, however, in the sharpness of memory. But Beckett is never sentimental, and if indecency can undercut a tendency in that direction, then he uses it. In other words, obscenity is an important literary device for him: as when old Krapp, agog at the recollection of a sexual encounter in a punt which concludes with his earlier self admitting that "it was hopeless and no good going on", checks his strong emotion at this reminder with a coarse remark about his medicinal copulations with another girlfriend who still comes to see him occasionally. For the treatment of sex in Beckett is really no different from anything else: if it was not so laughable it would make you weep. "Nothing is funnier than unhappiness" says Nell in **Endgame**, because if you do not make light of it it will destroy you. Hence the grave wit with which Beckett concludes his account of the hesitant lovemaking of Watt and Mrs Gorman:

> If Watt had had a little more vigour Mrs Gorman would have just had the time, and if Mrs Gorman had had a little more time Watt could very likely have developed, with a careful nursing of his languid tides, a breaker not unworthy of the occasion. Whereas as things stood, with Watt's strength, and Mrs Gorman's time, limited as they were, it is difficult to see what more they could have done than what they did, than sit on each other, turn about, kissing, resting, kissing again and resting again, until it was time for Mrs Gorman to resume her circuit. (pp.155–6)

Ruins, True Refuge

Melvin J. Friedman observes that in **The Implied Reader** Wolfgang Iser shows how the Modernist novel makes special demands on its reader, who must find his or her own keys and often turn them in stubbornly resistant locks. Discussing the problems raised for the reader by Faulkner's novel **The Sound and the Fury** and Ivy Compton-Burnett's **A Heritage and Its History**, Iser turns to Beckett's fiction and pinpoints the extreme demands made by Beckett's Postmodern texts. He argues that, unlike Faulkner's and Ivy Compton-Burnett's Modernist fiction, "Beckett's trilogy deprives the reader not temporarily but totally of his usual privileged seat in the grandstand. . . Such texts act as irritants, for they refuse to give the reader any bearing by means of which he might move far enough away to judge them. The text forces him to make his own way around, provoking questions to which he must supply his own answers".[21] Or as Iser's pupil Manfred Smuda has observed, "In this way [Beckett's] reader participates in the process of creation".

One notes here, perhaps, a certain divergence of view: Iser emphasizes the intractability of Beckett's prose, it rebarbative, off-putting quality; whereas Smuda shows, I think, greater sympathy with the texts in his stress – which I endorse – on the way Beckett's prose envelops one, so to speak, inveigles one into its coils, almost mesmerizes and bewitches one into sharing its subterfuges, As Smuda says, "The effect of Beckett's texts on the reader is to make him try to understand the technique itself, and to anticipate the direction in which these experiments with metalanguage will lead". This is certainly true of the very short piece – it runs to less than one thousand words – entitled **Still**. Written in 1972, this is Beckett's first prose text written in English since **From an Abandoned Work,** which dates from the early 1950s.

Going back even further, to the late 1930s, I am reminded that a student once wrote in an essay: "[**Murphy**] could easily have been Beckett's last work, the perfection of a stylistic development". It was not, of course, but the overt (if clearly parodistic) appeals to the reader in the earliest fiction – in **More Pricks than Kicks**, too, as well as in **Murphy** – diminish as the works progress but never entirely disappear. Taking my lead from the valuable work of Iser and Smuda, I shall look, in this concluding section, at some of the ways in which the reader is, as it were, "grappled" into the text by Beckett's verbal devices in a typically Postmodern fashion.

Still is a continuous unparagraphed piece of prose. It consists of sentences of normal length, but these are entirely unpunctuated, and as the syntax is elliptical, it is not easy for the reader, at least initially, to know how to pace a reading of the text. But read with natural breath pauses the piece is not difficult to understand; it is easier, for instance, than **Ping**, written some six years earlier. It returns to the familiar theme of "ruins true refuge" which runs through so much of Beckett's work, and not merely in the most recent fiction and drama. For if **The Lost Ones** of 1966 can be seen as a report from inside the gas chamber – that hideously modern refinement of Dante's torture rooms – its antecedents lie at the very origins of the **oeuvre.** In **Endgame,** for instance, the refuge that Hamm, Clov, Nagg and Nell occupy – sheltering from terrors which the play does not particularize, but which it is natural for us to think of as nuclear fall-out – is the setting for the story Hamm tells us about a madman he once knew. Visiting him at the asylum, Hamm would take him by the hand and drag him to the window. "Look! There!" he would exclaim. "All that rising corn! And there! Look! The sails of the herring fleet! All that loveliness!" The madman's reaction surprised Hamm at first: he would snatch away his hand and go back to his corner. All he had seen was ashes, Hamm realized; he alone had been spared, forgotten. Hamm comments: "It appears the case is . . . was not so . . . so unusual".[22] The story of the madman obviously has particular significance for Hamm: his vision has come to resemble the lunatic's, but unfortunately for him it is reality and not illusion. That is why he changes the tense "is" to "was"; the insane hallucinations of the past have become painful realities in the present.

The madman's attitude to his refuge becomes increasingly that of all Beckett heroes as the **oeuvre** progresses in time. Like him, they retreat appalled into their corner, shrinking away from a reality which terrifies them but appears, mercifully, to have forgotten them. They are (as Beckett said of the artist as long ago as the essay on Proust) "negatively active"; they shrink from the "nullity of extracircumferential phenomena, drawn in to the core of the eddy".[23] Theirs is an existence (it would glorify it to call it a life) of renunciation and retreat; their only experience (it would be too strong to use the term pleasure) is that of measuring the dimensions of their prison which, unlike Dante's damned, whom they otherwise resemble so closely, they espouse as a welcome refuge. The hero of **That Time** recalls nostalgically the ruin (an architectural "folly") where he hid as a child, and more recently the public buildings, libraries or art galleries, where he slipped in "off the street out of the cold and rain".[24]

This brings us back again, like so much else in Beckett, to **Murphy**. Murphy is a connoisseur of refuges, from his own beloved rocking chair to the cockpit in Hyde Park. His mind consists of three zones, "light, half light, dark, each with its speciality".[25] The first two need not detain us, but the third possessed neither

> elements nor states, nothing but forms becoming and crumbling into the fragments of a new becoming, without love or hate or any intelligible principle of change. Here there was nothing but commotion and the pure forms of commotion. Here he was not free, but a mote in the dark of absolute freedom. He did not move, he was a point in the ceaseless unconditioned generation and passing away of line.

This zone, the most favoured of all by Murphy, of course, is the paradigm of all "true refuges". The hero of "The End" reproduces it in his shell within a shell, the boat in which he makes his bed inside the shed on the overgrown and abandoned estate. In that enclosed, warm space he was, he has to admit, "very snug"[26] and subject, like

Murphy, to trance-like visions which protect him against the realities of a continuing existence, "without the courage to end or the strength to go on".

Similarly, Molloy's room and Malone's death chamber are two stations in the trilogy hero's calvary, which ends for the Unnamable "within the building, circular in form as already stated, its ground floor consisting of a single room flush with the arena" in which he churns the remains of his nearest and dearest into a revolting mush (p.323). From the Unnamable's pavilion it is but a short step to the rotunda of **Imagination Dead Imagine** and the cylinder of the "lost ones". But even these are not the "true refuge": that can only be sought in the elusive, even illusory silence of which, Moran says, "the universe is made" (p.121). Ruins, then, are perhaps not the true refuge which **Lessness** at first indicates, but rather, as its exquisite cadences express it, at the end of this most beautiful of all Beckett texts:

> True refuge long last issueless scattered down four walls over backwards no sound. Blank planes sheer white eye calm long last all gone from mind. He will curse God again as in the blessed days face to the open sky the passing deluge.[27]

Such defiance is not to be found in **Still**, which is more quietistic in tone; indeed, as we shall see, the word "quiet" occurs a couple of times, and "still" a couple of dozen times in the course of the text,not unexpectedly, given the title of the whole piece; Beckett is in the habit of taking as title a keyword from the text: another example is the use of the word "enough" in **Enough**.

The theme of refuge, however, lies at the heart of **Still**, as in so many other recent texts. The character is seen seated in a small upright wicker chair with armrests, staring out through the open window of his room at the valley opposite. Sometimes he looks towards the east through the eastern window at the beech on a hillside, and sometimes he looks out through the western window at the setting sun. To do so, he has to turn his head ninety degrees. The action is extremely limited, even given the brevity of the text. There are only twenty-eight definite articles in a total of thirty sentences. Most of these occur, as one would expect, towards the end of the piece, where the action tends to be concentrated on the movements of the character's head and hands. The movement of these parallels in miniature the movement of the sun which the character has been observing in the first two-thirds of the piece: the word Beckett uses is "deasil" which means, in Gaelic, right handwise, or motion as in the apparent course of the sun. The text itself moves from stress on light and sunshine (the opening word is "bright") to silent darkness (the closing words being "listening for a sound").

The text contains a number of verbal devices which, in Iserian terms, serve as "grapples" drawing the reader into the text. These are expressions like "apparently", "actually", "which to anticipate", "namely", "leave it so", "or try", and so on. These "grapples" lead the reader to notice a number of other verbal features of the text; the fact, for instance, that the word "still" occurs twenty times as an adjective and four times as an adverb, and the adjective "quiet" twice and the adverb "quite" twenty times. Moreover, the word "close" occurs ten times in its substantival or adjectival forms, and the same applies to "open". The reader quickly discovers that the whole text is based on elaborate combinations, which are mainly verbal and provide the basic structure of the piece, as in **Lessness**, with its structure based on repetition of sentences. (Earlier in his career Beckett preferred thematic combinations, such as the variations played on Murphy's biscuits, Watt's self-inspecting committee, or Molloy's sucking stones.) The reader then perceives further combinations within combinations, for instance that "quite still" occurs fourteen times, "not still" three times, and "dead still", "all still" and "still while" once each, making the total of twenty mentioned above. Beckett is of course not unique among the Postmoderns in constructing texts to elaborate formulas: the novels of Claude Simon and of other **nouveaux romanciers** are based on even more intricate schemes.[28] The devices in **Still** however consitute elaborate complicities, and invitations rather than irritants; that is, they are, in Smuda's terms, seductions rather than rebuffs.

Manfred Smuda also points out that Beckett "creates his own tradition [on the basis of a] store of relics from his previous [texts]", so that he builds consciously on what has gone before and expects the reader to pick up the echoes, both verbal and thematic, with which he builds up his **oeuvre**. Thus, the first line of **Still** ("Bright at last close of a dark day") recalls, in **From an Abandoned Work**, the opposite formula, "bright too early as so often". Moreover, the wicker chair recalls Murphy's rocking chair, and looks forward to the "mother rocker" of the 1981 play **Rockaby**. Indeed, the whole piece reads like a sketch by Beckett for television: the witness who observes the character from behind is like a television camera, and the phrase "when discovered" has this association also; likewise, "here back a little way" sounds like playback. In ways like these Beckett draws the reader of **Still** into another "true refuge", into yet one more of his characteristically intricate webs of allusion, echo, and verbal play. In old age but still at the height of his powers, he reminds one of a similarly deft, consummate artist, the eighty-year old Matisse of the late collages. Like Matisse in the 1950s, Beckett stands dominant today as one of Modernism's great survivors, postmodernly modern to the last.

Notes

1. Deirdre Bair: **Samuel Beckett: A Biography** (London, 1978), p.268. A subsequent reference to this book is indicated by the keyword "Bair". For Beckett's attitude to his country's prohibition of "unwholesome" literature, see "Censorship in the Saorstat", in **Disjecta** (London, 1983), pp.84–88.

2. Raymond Federman and John Fletcher: **Samuel Beckett: His Works and His Critics** (Berkeley, Los Angeles and London, 1970), p.5.

3. Samuel Beckett: **Watt** (Paris, 1958), pp.186–87. A subsequent reference to **Watt** is to this edition.

4. **Modernism 1890–1930**, edited by Malcolm Bradbury and James McFarlane (Harmondsworth, 1976), p.103. On the other hand, it has become easier in the last decade or so to see how deep Beckett's Irish roots go, how much he shares with Yeats and Synge "the complex fate of being Anglo-Irish" (**Beckett the Shape Changer**, edited by Katherine Worth (London, 1975), p.4.)

5. **Le Monde**, 14 November 1975, p.16.

6. George Steiner: "1973", **The Listener**, 3 January 1974, p.14.

7. **The Ironic Harvest: English poetry in the Twentieth Century** (London, 1974), p.29.

8. Malcolm Bradbury: "London 1890–1920". **Modernism 1890–1930**, p.185.

9. London, 1972.

10. All quotations are taken from issues of the magazine, which has been reissued in facsimile and can be found in university libraries, although copies of the original set are now hard to come by.

11. **International Fiction Review**, 11 (1984), p.59.

12. Melvin J. Friedman: "Prefatory Note", **The Seventh of Joyce**, edited by Bernard Benstock (Bloomington, 1982), p.28.

13. James Knowlson and John Pilling: **Frescoes of the Skull** (London, 1979), p.14.

14. Ibid., p.22, n.8.

15. S.E. Gontarski: "Samuel Beckett, James Joyce's 'Illstarred Punster', in **The Seventh of Joyce**, pp.29–36.

16. **Three Novels by Samuel Beckett: Molloy, Malone Dies, The Unnameable** (New York, 1965), p.175; all other references to the Trilogy are to this edition.

17. "Cheating the Dark Gods: Iris Murdoch and Racine", **International Fiction Review**, 6 (1979), pp.75–76.

18. "Interpreting **Molloy**" in **Samuel Beckett Now**, edited by Melvin J. Friedman (Chicago, 1970), pp. 157–70.

19. **Language and Being in the Prose Works of Samuel Beckett** (University of Toronto Press, forthcoming).

20. **Company** (London, 1980), pp.66–67.

21. **Studies in the Novel** (Summer 1975), pp.309–10. Quotations from Manfred Smuda come from **English and American Studies in German**, edited by Werner Habicht (Tübingen, 1970), pp.85–86. **Still** is published in **For to End yet Again and Other Fizzles** (London, 1976), pp.19–21.

22. **Endgame** (London, 1958), p.32.

23. **Proust** (London, 1931), p.48.

24. **That Time** (London, 1976), p.9.

25. **Murphy** (London, 1938), pp.111, 112.

26. **No's Knife** (London, 1967), pp.64, 67.

27. **Lessness** (London, 1970), p.20.

28. See "La Fiction mot à mot", by Claude Simon, in **Nouveau roman: hier, aujourd'hui, II**, edited by Jean Ricardou and Françoise van Rossum-Guyon (Paris, 1972), pp. 73–97.

The Scandinavian Ideology

Towards a mythology of Modernism

Göran Printz-Påhlson

It is a step of enormous importance for the conceptualization, if not for the content, of a formation of a Scandinavian mythology or ideology, when, during the eighteenth century, empirical considerations start to enter into the arguments of legitimization and affiliation which dominate the ethnological scene throughout the centuries. The famous picture of Montesquieu as conjured up by himself in the sustained discussion of climate in the XIVth and XVth books of **De l'esprit des lois**,[1] bent over his microscope, studying a lamb's tongue at different temperatures and noticing the variations of size of the **mamelons** and the **pyramides**, is a suitable emblem for the change that is taking place. It is anthropology coming of age, assuming the rigours of natural science and physiology, giving grounds for hypotheses however crude of the influence of material conditions or of observable variations of mankind.

> Cette observation confirme ce que j'ai dit, que, dans les pays froids, les houppes nerveuses sont moins épanouies: elles s'enfoncent dans leur gaines, ou elles sont à couvert de l'action des objets extérieurs. Les sensations sont donc moins vives.
>
> Dans les pays froids on aura peu de sensibilité pour les plaîsirs; elle sera plus grande dans les pays tempérés: dans les pays chauds elle sera extrême. Comme on distingue les climats par les degrées de latitude, on pourrait les distinguer, pour ainsi dire, par les degrées de sensibilité.[2]

The clinical terminology with the "bundle of nerves" and the typical eighteenth-century reduction of physiology to sensibility, place this text as central for the interpretation of a "Scandinavian sensibility" or Ideology. Not that the observations are in any sense new or original, nor that the conclusions are hitherto unheard of: they belong to the moralistic and propagandistic framework for ethnographic argument that Tacitus – one of the main sources for Montesquieu's observations of the people of the North – imposed on subsequent history writing. It is not in its substance but in its method of reasoning – in providing for what have been traditionally taken as simple truths, a Cartesian or Newtonian world – that Montesquieu's theory becomes so powerful.

A century before Montesquieu, Robert Burton (who was indeed, like his colleague Sir Thomas Browne,[3] much better informed about the Scandinavian people, having read both Saxo and Olaus Magnus), had ascribed the abundance of evil spirits, trolls and fairies in the far north to the foul air and miasmas of that region, ending his diatribe with a slightly anachronistic blast to what we now (with a venerable word) call pollution:

> But let the site of such places be as it may, how can they be excused that have a delicious seat, a pleasant air, and all that nature can afford, and yet through their own nastiness and sluttishness, immund and sordid manner of life, suffer the air to putrefy, and themselves to be choked up.[4]

No such blame for the poor inhabitants of climes not naturally blest with nature's gifts:

> Cold air, in the other extreme, is almost as bad as hot, and so doth Montaltus esteem of it, if it be dry withal. In those Northern Countries the people are therefore generally dull, heavy, and many witches, which (as I have before quoted) Saxo Grammaticus, Olaus, Baptista Porta, ascribe to melancholy. But these cold climes are more subject to natural melancholy (not this artificial) which is cold and dry: for which cause Mercurius Britannicus, belike, puts melancholy men to inhabit just under the Pole. The worst of the three is a thick, cloudy, misty, foggy air, or such as comes from fens, moorish grounds, lakes, muckhills, draughts, sinks, where any carcasses or carrion lies, or from whence any stinking fulsome smell comes.[5]

This is another classical account of the interrelations of climate, meteorology and ethnic characteristics, in method, although hardly in substance, quite different from Montesquieu's. It is not difficult to see how much has remained of classical Hippocratic humoral pathology and meteorology in the latter, although his etiological framework has been radically changed: he has entered into a different **episteme** (to borrow a useful term from Foucault).[6] The observations in **The Anatomy** (and this is the only one of many possible ones) are helpful in showing the pedigree of this kind of primitive ethnological reasoning in a long tradition of antique speculation, popular belief and superstition. The very lack of what we today would regard as logical causation, which may appear baffling to the scientific mind, can be extremely instructive to the student of the origin and survival of ideological phenomena.

Burton's assumption that cold or foul air, and in particular a combination of the two, cause all the pathological, psychological and to some extent supernatural phenomena which he associates with melancholy (taken in a much wider sense than the one now common) is in no way, as we would assume, incompatible with other causes, or explanations of a completely different nature, nor does it preclude contradictory observations.[7]

It is to some extent no doubt a temperamental quirk of Burton's that he is so happy-go-lucky in accepting any (or preferably all) ad hoc explanations that offer themselves. But this is in perfect accord with explanatory systems handed down from antiquity and accepted on a very wide basis in folk belief.[8]

As such beliefs have been part of an ideology or mythology of primitive ethnological observations for centuries, it does in no way appear strange to Burton to accept the Nordic races as prone to sickly melancholia even in its dire propensity for witchcraft, magic and demonology and at the same time give the climate its due for their longevity and excellent health (in this particular case with some help from an excellent diet):

> Damianus A-goes, Saxo Grammaticus, Aubanus Bohemus say the like of them that live in Norway, Lapland, Finmark, Biarmia, Corelia, all over Scandia and those Northern Countries, they are most healthful and very long-lived, in which places there is no use at all of Physick. Dithmarus Bleskenius, in his accurate description of Iceland, 1607, makes mention amongst other matters of the inhabitants and their manner of living, which is dried fish instead of bread, butter

and cheese, and saltmeats, most parts they drink water and whey, and yet without Physick and Physician they live many of them 250 years.[9]

No wonder that in such harsh regions and with such austere diet a little bending of the rules of normal Christian conduct must be allowed for, as is obvious in the example of Erik Väderhatt, whom Burton no doubt had encountered in Olaus Magnus's **Historia:**[10]

Erricus, King of Sweden, had an enchanted Cap, by virtue of which, and some magical murmur and whispering terms, he could command spirits, trouble the air, and make the wind stand which way he would; insomuch that when there was any great wind or storm, the common people were wont to say, the King now had on his conjuring Cap.[11]

Robert Burton's enormously erudite and entertaining presentation of traditional folk beliefs constitutes in itself an excellent corrective to simplifications and misunderstandings of man's early attempts to make sense of encounters with the foreign, the strange, and the distant in space and time, with what is nowadays sometimes in Existentialist terminology called "The Other". But the history of skepsis and relativism in anthropological observation goes back a long way, in Greek philosophy at least as far as Xenophanes (as the name indicates predominantly an observer of strangers)[12] who in a celebrated two-liner, quoted by Clement of Alexandria in Stromatos[13] traces relativism in religious conceptualization:

The Ethiopians say that their gods are snub-nosed and black, the Thracians that theirs have light blue eyes and red hair.

In a Hippocratic treatise, **Airs, waters and places**, we can find the very foundation of Classical climatology, already presented with a pluralism of causation which one may be excused for identifying with present-day structuralism or overdetermination, albeit anachronistically. This makes for a very rich combinatory matrix – in between elements of air and water, and qualities of wet and dry, hot and cold, which, on principle, can accommodate any (or preferably all) anthropological and physiological observations.[14]

The author of the Hippocratic treatise offers, as an example of the influences of life in Northern climate, the Scythians, who are described as pot-bellied from drinking waters from the marshes, fat and hairless, sluggish and timorous, emasculated from too much horse-back riding, in short a pretty despicable lot. It is mainly and with depressing consistency blamed on the weather. "For these reasons their bodies are heavy and fleshy, their joints are covered, they are watery and relaxed. The cavities of their bodies are extremely moist, especially the belly, since, in a country of such a nature and under such climatic conditions, the bowels cannot be dry. All the men are fat and hairless and likewise all the women, and the two sexes resemble one another".[15]

For anthropological-minded historians, like Herodotus in his description of the Scythians,[16] or Caesar's and Tacitus's canonical portrayals of the **Germani**, the climatological explanations of ethnic differences are never far away. It is not difficult to see why. When confronted with the stranger, with the "altérité" of foreign mores or habitus, the modes of explanation are limited: to physiological causes, and to material circumstances, to religious observances and to political organization. Of these, the first two categories are by far the most accessible for the casual observer or the compiler of hear-say accounts of far-off regions. It has often been maintained that the Classical world regarded everything outside its own domain as barbaric, quaint and incomprehensible: it seems to me, considering the lack of basic information at their disposal, that they did not do much worse than we do today in misunderstanding our close or distant neighbours.

A typical sweeping statement to this effect, and transposing it to current conditions, can be found in Fredric Jameson's **The Political Unconscious**, an interesting book, although supporting itself on a rather uncomfortable intermarriage of genre typology and Althusserian **Ideologiekritik** which is, in part, very pertinent to the present argument:

> /. . ./ in the shrinking world of the present day, with its gradual leveling of class and national and racial differences and its imminent abolition of Nature (as some ultimate term of Otherness or difference) it ought to be less difficult to understand to what degree it is a positional one that coincides with categories of Otherness. Evil thus, as Nietzsche told us, continues to characterize whatever is radically different from me, whatever by virtue of precisely that difference seems to constitute a real and urgent threat to my own existence.
>
> So from the earliest times, the stranger from another tribe, the "barbarian" who speaks an incomprehensible language and follows "outlandish" customs, but also the woman, whose biological difference stimulates fantasies of devoration and castration, or in our own time, the avenger of accumulated resentments from some oppressed class or race, or else that alien being, Jew or Communist, behind whose apparently human features a malignant and preternatural intelligence is thought to lurk: these are some of the archetypal figures of the Other, about whom the essential point to be made is not so much that he is feared because he is evil; rather he is evil **because** he is Other, alien, different, strange, unclean and unfamiliar.[17]

The idea that "Hell is the others" is a fundamental Existentialist contention which has a strong basis in anthropological speculation.[18] Furthermore, one should keep in mind that the classical concept of the stranger, **xenos** or **hospes/hostis** is an ambivalent one,[19] including the meaning "guest" as well as "stranger" and "enemy" for a society which counted hospitality among the sacred duties but at the same time was highly aware of the dangers incurred in exercising this duty. Following Jameson's terminology, one could maintain that there is, in addition and contradistinction to the ideological content of "The Other", also a utopian content, which posits a source of moral rectitude, esoteric wisdom or preternatural practices, horrifying perhaps, but also useful in ameliorating inclement weather conditions, in distant tribes. Examples abound: we can remind ourselves of Herodotus's description of the Hyperboreans, or of the Pythagorean content of the Salmoxis cult, of Plato's account of the Atlantides, of Caesar's sympathetic descriptions of the Gallic druidic organisation, or Tacitus's moral exempla of republican virtues, culled from the **Germani**.

As Francois Hartog has pointed out regarding Herodotus, the definition of "altérité" very often becomes a question of recognizing frontiers or differences, within the pagan world.[21] The Judaeo-Christian world, on the other hand, could not and would not be limited in such a way, when the **kerygma** of the Gospels had been imbued with a world-wide generality: it could be limited by the extent of the known world only. This is clearly indicated in Bernard Groethuysen's great work on the origins of the bourgeoisie in France and its posthumous sequels:[22]

> L'image que le chrétien se faisait du monde historique avait des limites bien marquées. Jérusalem et Rome formaient les centres de ce monde; en s'éloignant de ces deux centres de l'univers, le chrétien ne rencontrait plus que des peuples qui vivaient en dehors des grands courants de l'histoire. Or, voici que l'horizon s'ouvre. Les peuples de l'Asie, de l'Afrique, de l'Amérique réclament une place dans l'histoire de l'humanité.[23]

This is equally and earlier applicable to the Scandinavian countries. The opening up, in a very literal and unequivocal sense of the Christian **Civitas** which since Augustine had been populated by saints and sinners alike, still excluded the marginal heathens, be they ever so virtuous, while the traditions of Rome had to be to some extent sanctified by its later prominence.

At the same time, the Judaean tradition, as far as it was incorporated in the Christian one, had never had the easy-going pluralism in anthropological observations which the classical world had engendered. The Old Testament could not sanction any arcane or hidden knowledge among far-away tribes, nor any moral exempla among the Philistines or in Egypt: it could only recognize the Covenant which Jehova had made with his chosen people. It is the transfer of this covenant in Christian terms to the locus of Rome and her traditions and history which accounts for the centristic bias of European history.

> Pour le chrétien, le peuple romain avait eu la grande mission de préparer par ces conquêtes la domination universelle de l'Église. C'était là le point de vue sous lequel le chrétien devait envisager les grands faits de l'histoire romaine.[24]

There is thus a built-in bias in what later became known as the **translatio imperii**: the transference of the Divine succession to a secular one in the Roman empire,[25] as there was a built-in imperialist bias in the pagan **interpretatio Romana**: the translation of barbaric pantheons into familiar Roman deities.[26] St Augustine (and other patristic writers) had with great ingenuity relegated all these pantheons to the realms of popular demonology or, in some cases, to euhemeristic explanations. The enormous increase of ethnological information had to cause an explosion of traditional beliefs: it had to come, as it did, in the eighteenth century, underpinned to a large extent by anthropological theories of a very different nature than the traditional ones.

This is, of course, a very familiar story which has been given in many versions, most often concentrating on the rediscovery of classical learning or the discovery of non-European traditions and beliefs.[27] What is not so familiar, or not so sharply focussed, is the peculiar position of some of the marginal peoples in Europe, e.g. those who had not been included in the original **translatio Romana**.

Robert Burton found the demonology of his times irresistible, and was, at the same time, only too happy to assume the local traditions at work. The Nordic character's involvement with melancholy and the supernatural – as explained by traditional Hippocratic theories or any other means – may seem far-fetched to us, but was undoubtedly quite natural to him and his contemporaries (and indeed survived in slightly altered shape for centuries, as we shall see).

In Shakespeare, however, we find much more intriguing and subtle examples of cultural transgression and ethnological Otherness. Let us just remind ourselves of some extremely well-known passages.

In **The Tempest**, when Miranda – who has previously only been conversant with her imperious father, the subhuman Caliban, and the various airy spirits of the island, and just recently acquainted with Ferdinand whom she at first mistakes for a spirit (though "it carries a brave form", I,2, 414) – becomes aware of the variations and accomplishment of mankind, in the shape of the ship-wrecked lords, she exclaims:

O wonder!
How many godly creatures are there here!
How beauteous mankind is! O brave new world,
That has such people in't! (V,1, 182–4).[28]

This could be, and has been, taken as a celebration of the newly opened world of geographic discovery.[29] But Prospero's sour remark "'Tis new to thee" and Alonzo's (entirely conventional)[30] disbelief in **her** human status wholly redresses the balance in giving the difference between gods and mortals, rather than between man and man, as the salient transgression:

Alon. What is this maid with whom thou wast at play?
– Is she the goddess that hath sever'd us,
And brought us thus together? **Fer.** Sir, she is mortal;
But by immortal Providence she's mine:

Similar transgressions of boundaries are as central, although quite differently construed, in **Coriolanus** where Shakespeare often hauntingly anticipates the Marxian view of the classical city state in isolating the clash of interests between town and country.[31] The organicist metaphor of the State, so eloquently defended by Menenius Agrippa in his fable of the rebelling parts of the body, does not accommodate any distinctions between tribes or nations, but reinforces the pathological imagery of the play. "Contagion" is clearly a key word throughout; when Coriolanus is ready to leave Rome after his banishment, his standard vituperations take on the Hippocratic flavour of the miasmas of corrupted air surrounding him there:

You common cry of curs, whose breath I hate
As reek o' th' rotten fens, whose loves I prize
As the dead carcasses of unburied men
That do corrupt my air, I banish you! (III,3, 121–24).[32]

Such corruption Coriolanus found in the breathing air in Rome – which also is consistently echoed in Menenius's harangues against the plebeians: "You that stood so much/ upon the voice of occupation and/ The breath of garlic-eaters!" (IV,6, 97–99) and: "You are they that made the air unwholesome" (ibid., 130–31) and which he would change for a seemingly more salubrious climate:

Despising
For you, the city, thus I turn my back.
There is a world elsewhere. (III,3, 134–36).

This corruption is ubiquitous and inescapable. As Aufidius, the Volscian general, remarks at the end, Coriolanus has "for certain drops of salt" (indeed a preservative: his mother's tears), betrayed his assumed loyalties to his adopted city and broken "his oath and resolution like/ A twist of rotten silk"; (V,6, 94–95).

For Shakespeare or Coriolanus, their city state was obviously like any other city state. The destiny of Rome is conspicuously absent from this naturalist and foul-tempered essay in war and economics. In **Hamlet**, another play about corruption politics, there is not much more emphasis on national characteristics or national destiny: although Hamlet speaks often enough of corruption, "Hell's foul contagion" etc, and Marcellus of the King's Guard is given that most famous line: "Something is rotten in the state of Denmark", there is no attempt to link the corruption to anything but the illegitimacy of Claudius's reign. It has been suggested that the "fishmonger" imagery in Hamlet's scene with Polonius makes a conventional connection between salt as a preservative, like in Coriolanus's use of his mother's tears, and salt as an aid to fertility.[33] It could be added that Polonius entreats Hamlet to "walk out of the air" (which was supposed to have a bad influence on his mental afflictions) – here picking up the thread from Hamlet's earlier ramblings about Ophelia, touched with a most disagreeable pun on conception and corruption: "For if the sun breed maggots in a dead dog, being a good kissing carrion – Have you a daughter? – Let her not walk i'th' sun." (II,2, 181–84).

However, the sources of corruption are never related to political behaviour or institutions. As little as in **Coriolanus** is there any distinguishing between the nations involved, be they Poland (here perhaps substituting for Sweden with whom the Poles had shared a king until 1599),[34] or Norway, or Denmark, more than in terms of their ruling monarchs – who are, of course, most often referred to when the countries are mentioned, according to the custom of the day. Not are any general national characteristics being invoked as distinguishing factors, although the Frenchified ways of Osric or Laertes are perhaps meant to be contrasted with the simple demeanour of students from Wittenberg. The only sustained meditation on national character (and it occurs in a passage of somewhat doubtful authenticity)[35] is the well-known one on the Danes' tendency to drunkenness and revelry:

"Is it a custom?" Horatio asks about the carousal at the court, and Hamlet answers (obviously forgetting that he is talking to a compatriot):

Ay marry is't,
But to my mind, though I am native here
And to the manner born, it is a custom
More honour'd in the breach than the observance.
This heavy-headed revel east and west
Makes us traduc'd and tax'd of other nations –
They clepe us drunkards, and with swinish phrase
Soil our addition; (I,4, 12–20).

It was indeed the case that Danes had gained a reputation for intemperance and "swinish" habits.[36]

Hamlet continues in the somewhat uncharacteristic discursive mode of this speech to develop the idea in terms of individual fate or disposition, still touching on the terminology of humoral pathology ("complexion"):

So, oft it chances in particular men
That for some vicious mole of nature in them,
As in their birth, wherein they are not guilty
(Since nature cannot choose his origin),
By their o'ergrowth of some complexion,
Oft breaking down the pales and forts of reason,
Or by some habit, that too much o'erleavens
The form of plausive manners – that these men,
Carrying, I say, the stamp of one defect,
Being Nature's livery or Fortune's star,
– – – –
Shall in the general censure take corruption
From this particular fault. (ibid., 23–31).

The imagery here which reappears partly in the final appeal to the Queen about her chastity (III,4, 163–67), tends to represent **custom** as a frock, or livery to be put on at will, whether it is good or bad, thus counteracting the determinism in the explanations of climate and physical influence.

Let me briefly recapitulate the ideological insights gained in these three plays. The "brave, new world" of Miranda invokes the opening up of the known world of the Renaissance, but the traditional limits of humanity as well. The "World elsewhere" of Coriolanus is a Machiavellian reply to the internal economic exigencies of the City state. This note is also often heard in **Hamlet**, perhaps most clearly in the dramatically abstruse and rarely performed scene (IV,4) where Hamlet encounters Fortinbras's Norwegian army setting out on foot for its Polish campaign (with Hamlet on his way to England, from Elsinore! There is no need to labour the point: Shakespeare's Scandinavian geography is exceedingly weak).[37] For Shakespeare "custom" is, even for those who are "to the manner born", an existentialist, not an anthropological category: it is an individual repetition of acts, or (more often) abstentions from acts (as for Gertrude, not going to bed with the King; or for Hamlet, not getting drunk with the revellers).

What is missing from the picture is obvious: it is tradition, or history – what is so eminently present in the plays on English history. Coriolanus's Rome is a proto-Rome, brimming with ethnic excitement but bereft of the past: Rome has not yet been invented. What is missing in Hamlet's Denmark is the same, history and tradition. Scandinavia has not yet been invented, in a sense it has not even been discovered. There is no difference between the Danes and the Norwegians, or the Poles or the Swedes; no distinction. No wonder the only custom worth mentioning is drinking and carousal – unless it be the constant pointless tramping of armies along the foul marshes in order to

gain a little patch of ground
that hath in it no profit but the name (IV,4, 18–19).

No wonder Marcellus notices the stench of corruption in Denmark, which is to be taken, not in the modern sense of a metaphor for bad government, but as a very literal fetid emanation from the ghost-ridden and polluted air.

The preceding might have been a somewhat roundabout way of saying what could be stated much more directly, i.e. that the Scandinavians are in this period, to the Europeans, as to Hamlet, an "invisible event", not unlike the changelings so beloved by Elizabethan dramatists, who were "misshapen naturals, substituted by the fairies".[38] As an invisible race they have from this perspective of course no ideology of their own. So far I have been using "ideology" in an entirely tentative way, in order to denote a body of belief or speculation on intercultural phenomena, how men in history have regarded themselves in relation and reaction to other groups of men, in this particular case differentiated by geographical location and material conditions. It is obvious that the conceptualization of such an "ideology" is an entirely relative one, in so far as the "ideologist" must occupy some "middle ground" from which to evaluate the variations in ethnic character as being to "the North" or "the South" of himself (or "East" or "West", as the case may be).[39] This relativism seems to have been quite clearly formulated already by Xenophanes to the extent that his remarks on the Greek gods tally with his observations of Thracians and Ethiopians.[40] The centristic tendencies of the Greco-Roman and, later, the Christian World view tended to obscure this early relativism, which was replaced by "Hippocratic" explanations of physical causation.

If the eighteenth century had to "confront the Gods", in F.E. Manuel's succinct formula, it also had to confront the whole information explosion of ethnic variability. The great syntheses of anthropological ideas in Vico, Montesquieu and Herder (however we regard their relations to each other) have irrevocably changed the views of mankind on itself to a degree that makes a certain amount of ethnological relativism inevitable: the variations in the history of the human race enforce the acceptance of a progressivist scheme which must countenance the disconcerting spectacle of coming face-to-face with one's own ancestors in their brute and barbaric state of nature. At a time when Europe (in their salons) lionised the Noble Savage and shuddered exquisitely with Gothick horror, the actual opinions of contemporary Scandinavians could hardly have been lower. Many examples could be adduced: let me limit myself to two, from France.

In 1800, Mme de Stael in her **De la littérature considerée dans ses rapports avec les institutions sociales**, one of the earliest examples of comparative or transcultural sociology of art and literature, makes a famous distinction between **Littérature du Nord** and **Littérature du Midi**. Although she has stated her methodological commitment to an analysis of social institutions, she has absolutely nothing to say on the politics or institutions of Scandinavia of her own times (although she had been placed in a better position than most for observing these at close quarters).[41] Instead she writes, not entirely surprisingly: "Le climat est certainement l'une des raisons principales des différences qui existent entre les images qui plaisent dans le nord, et celles qu'on aime à se rappeler dans le midi".[42] And about the "nations of the North", she adds: "Le spectacle de la nature agit fortement sur eux; elle agit, comme elle se montre dans leur climats, toujours sombre et nébuleuse. Sans doute les diverses circonstances de la vie peuvent varier cette disposition à la mélancolie; mais elle porte seule l'empreinte de l'esprit national".[43] However, she avoids completely any references to contemporary Scandinavian literature and culture; her conception of **la Littérature du Nord** is a strange conglomeration of German and English literature, added to a body of "Bardes Écossais, les Fables Islandaises, et les Poésies Scandinaves".[44]

This admittedly widespread confusion about Celtic and Scandinavian reappears in **De l'Allemagne**, ten years later,[45] where she finally, in Chapter XXV, mentions a few names of Danish poets, Baggesen and Oehlenschläger, singling out the latter for particular praise as representing "d'une manière à la fois poétique et vraie l'histoire et les fables des pays habités jadis par les Scandinaves".[46]

She returns, however, very rapidly to climatological explanations which elicit her most ardent rhetorical effusions: "Les Héros, dans la fiction de la poésie du Nord, ont quelque chose de gigantesque. La superstition est réunie, dans leur caractère, à la force, tandis que partout ailleurs, elle semble le partage de la faiblesse. Des images tirées de la rigueur du climat caractérisent la poésie des Scandinaves".[47]

The year before the publication of **De la Littérature**, in France the illustrious **l'an VIII**, had seen the second performance, at Versailles, of a play of negligible merit by the later so notorious D.A.F. de Sade. It was also printed the same year.[48] It was called **Oxtiern ou les malheurs du libertinage** and is of great interest in this connection. Its setting is an inn barely a league from "Stokolm" and its villain-hero is the Don Giovanni-like Oxtiern, a Swedish **libertin** nobleman, who, thwarted in his designs on the virtue of young Ernestine, daughter of the Comte de Falkenstein, "le petit neveu du favori de Charles XII",[49] tries to engineer in a most diabolical way a duel between father and daughter(!) but is himself assassinated by an intended victim. As can be guessed from such a **résumé**, this is a jejune melodrama which offers no information about the country in question short of a few place names, and – in spite of the insistence on local colour in the quite respectable study of the novel which Sade had published the same year,[50] – no exotic atmosphere. Oxtiern is supposed to be modelled on Johan Turesson Oxenstierna (1666–1733), a peripatetic scion of the famous Swedish family, whose **Pensées** (1720–22) had enjoyed quite an international reputation. J.G. Oxenstierna, the delicate Swedish nature poet and author of **Skördarne,** was still alive at the time and may have regarded this parading of his family name with some indignation (if he ever was informed of the play).

Being well aware of the prevailing literary climate, Sade was careful in expressing both the required sentiments and the expected revolutionary zeal in castigating the immoral aristocracy. He has Oxtiern express his contempt for the moral scruples of his friend Derbac: "parce que tu es un être subalterne, plein de prejugés gothiques"[51] and not versed in modern philosophy. But to Sade's feverish imagination, the Scandinavian is no doubt the prototype of the Other, the dangerous, ferocious wild beast, beyond the pale of humanity and living only for bestial pleasures, which of course incur his secret admiration and applause (much more openly expressed in his clandestine works).[52] For Mme de Stael, the Scandinavian is the descendant of ancient bards and vikings, still wandering lonely on the moors in the mists, reciting ancient lays, prone to magic and incantation. In a different context, speaking of the background of English philosophy, she proffers with her customary neatness a distinction regarding the difference in attitude to religious phenomena of the North and South: "Dans le midi, le paganisme divinisait les phenomènes physiques, dans le Nord, on était enclin à la magie, parce qu'elle attribue une puissance sans borne sur le monde materiél".[53] The melancholy

Northerner, as Shakespeare or Burton had seen him, did not change very quickly from his stereotype image. How did he become the practical man, adept at handling the forces of nature?

If the "Otherness" of the Scandinavian character was still prevalent in the beginning of the nineteenth century, it was soon to be modified by the philosophical historicism that dominated this period. The fascination with the unique, the character, **esprit, Geist** etc. of every corner of the world led to a peculiar diachronism which tended to isolate the past as a separate entity, **illud tempus**, detached from any causal connection with present-day conditions. The Ancient Constitution, The Ancient Law, the Ancient agrarian communalism (or individualism)[54] came to be seen as absolutes, invested with unassailable authority, but also divested, in a mythology of a fall from a pastoral past, of any direct filiation with the present. Scandinavian Romanticism of the internal kind could only re-enact this fall, as in the most salient myths of its predicament (which also happened to be the two most widely appreciated instances of it outside Scandinavia – with the possible exception of the popular romance of atonement in **Frithiofs saga**): Oehlenschläger's **Guldhornene** and Atterbom's **Lycksalighetens ö**. The idealist philosophy of Germany, and in particular Hegel, created an impenetrable buffer for the Scandinavian ideology which became, as it were, effectively mummified in its own past.

When Marx and Engels started to formulate their doubts and insight about German idealist historicism in the 1840s, intent on confronting it with their own nascent materialist interpretation of history, they had as little use for Scandinavia as Hegel had had in his Lectures on Philosophy of History. As they were striving to lay the foundation of a "positive science" of history, based on division of labour and ownership, they found that it necessitated a study of the more advanced industrial nations on the one hand and of more primitive modes of production on the other; such a cosmopolitan "Geschichte der Menschheit" must always be studied in relation to the history of industry and exchange.

> Es ist aber auch klar, wie es in Deutschland unmöglich ist, solche Geschichte zu schreiben, da den Deutschen dazu nicht nur die Auffassungsfähigkeit und das Material, sondern auch "sinnlige Gewissheit" abgeht und man jenseits des Rheins über diese Dinge keine Erfahrungen machen kann, weil da doch keine Geschichte mehr vorgeht.[55]

This from **The German Ideology**, finished in the summer of 1846 (but not published until much later, in its entirety not until 1932). The backward, basically agrarian economy of the Scandinavian countries would be of even less theoretical interest for Marx and Engels, almost an embarassment, as it indicated an even more stagnant backwater, where the "real" forces of production could not be observed, where history had come to a stop, perhaps for ever. In a long letter from Engels to Marx in December 1846, which indeed seems to deserve a longish excerpt, this crude **Bauernwirtschaft** is given an energetic, if not absolutely serious interpretation:

> Als unschuldiges Nebenvergnügen hab' ich in der letzten schlechten Zeit ausser den Mädeln noch einigen Umgang mit Dänemark und dem übrigen Norden getrieben. Das ist dir eine Sauerei. Lieber der kleinste Deutsche als der grösste

> Däne! So ein Klimax von Moralitäts-, Zunft- und Ständemisere existiert nirgends mehr. Der Däne hält Deutschland für ein Land, wohin man geht, um "sich Mätressen zu halten und sein Vermögen mit ihnen durchzubringen" (imedens at han reiste i Tydskland, havde han en Maîtresse, som fortärede ham den bedste del af hans Midler, heisst es in einem Dänischen Schulbuch!) – er nennt den Deutschen einen Tydsk Windbeutel und hält sich für den rechten Repräsentanten des Germanischen Wesens – der Schwede verachtet wieder Dänen als "verdeutscht" und ausgeartet, schwatzhaft und verweichlicht – der Norweger sieht auf den verfranzösierten Schweden und seinen Adel hinab und freut sich, dass bei ihm in Norwegen noch grade dieselbe stupide Bauernwirtschaft herrscht wie zur Zeit des edlen Kanut, und dafür wird er wieder vom Isländer en canaille behandelt, der noch ganz dieselbe Sprache spricht wie die schmierigen Wikinger von Anno 900, Tran säuft, in einer Erdhütte wohnt und in jeder Atmosfäre kaputtgeht, die nicht nach faulen Fischen riecht. Ich bin mehrere Male in Versuchung gewesen, stolz darauf zu werden, dass ich wenigstens kein Däne oder gar Isländer, sondern nur ein Deutscher bin. Der Redakteur des avanciertesten schwedischen Blatts, des "Aftonblad", ist hier zweimal in Paris gewesen, um über die Organisation der Arbeit ins klare zu kommen, hat sich jahrelang den "Bon Sens" und die "Democratie pacifique" gehalten, mit Louis Blanc und Considérant feierlich unterhalten, aber er hat nichts kapieren können und ist so klug zurückgekommen, wie er wegging. Jetzt paukt er nach für die freie Konkurrenz, oder wie das auf Schwedisch heisst, **Nahrungs**freiheit oder auch självförsöjningsfrihet, Selbstversorgungsfreiheit (das ist doch noch schöner als **Gewerb**freiheit). Natürlich, die sitzen noch im Zunftdreck bis über die Ohren, und auf den Reichstagen sind grade die Bürger die wütendsten Konservativen. Im ganzen Land nur 2 ordentliche Städte, à 80 000 und 40 000 Einwohner resp., die dritte Norrköping, hat nur 12 000, alles übrige so 1 000, 2000, 3000. Alle Post-stationen wohnt ein Mensch. In Dänemark ist's kaum besser, da haben sie nur eine einzige Stadt, wo die Gottvollsten Zunftprozesse vorfallen... Das einzige, wozu diese Länder gut sind, ist, dass man an ihnen sehen kann, was die Deutschen tun würden, wenn sie Pressefreiheit hätten, nämlich wie Dänen wirklich getan haben, sogleich eine "Gesellschaft für den wahren Gebrauch der freien Presse" stiften und christlich-wohlmeinende Kalender drucken lassen. Das schwedische "Aftonblad" ist so zahm wie die "Kölner Zeitung", hält sich aber für "demokratisch im wahren Sinne des Worts". Dafür haben die Schweden die Romane von Fröken Bremer und die Dänen Herrn Etatsraad Oehlenschläger, Commandör af Dannebrogsordenen. Auch gibt es schrecklich viel Hegelianer dort, und die Sprache, in der jedes dritte Wort aus dem Deutschen gestohlen ist, passt famos für die Spekulation.[56]

Even if we try to disregard what can pass for prejudice or jokes in this diatribe – and we have little difficulty is recognizing some familiar complaints about Scandinavia – the drift of it is well worth taking seriously. Where Burton had praised the diet of the Icelanders and attributed to it their putative longevity, Engels is apt to take a more jaundiced view of such regimen. The sham liberalism of Lars Johan Hierta and his

"Aftonblad" is denounced, and the internal rivalry between the Scandinavian nations accurately and viciously described. The "freedom of the Press" is debunked in terms virtually anticipating Marcuse's "repressive tolerance": the Germans can only expect the same from this overrated privilege as the Scandinavians, i.e. the right to publish "Christian-wellmeaning chapbooks". Wherever he turns, Engels sees in the Scandinavians a kind of fun-house mirror-image of his own countrymen, a distortion of all their false pretences and short-comings: they are vying with the Germans in Teutonic pride, as "true representatives of Germanic essence". They have exhausted their heritage from the "greasy Vikings" and truly deserve the culture and literature they have got: the novels of Miss Bremer and the poetry of the **Herrn Etatsraad** Oehlenschläger.

However, there are no vestiges of traditional climatological explanations in Engels's account. The "stupid peasant economy" of the countries is exclusively blamed, with the obsolete institutions, and the facetious snide remark on the languages at the end. This should be seen in the light of ideas on the development of productive forces expressed in **The German Ideology**, this rich but loose-jointed book Marx and Engels had just completed:

> Die Beziehungen verschiedener Nationen untereinander hängen davon ab wie weit jede von ihnen ihre Produktivkräfte, die Teilung der Arbeit und den innern Verkehr entwickelt hat. . . [. . .] Die Teilung der Arbeit innerhalb einer Nation führt zunächst die Trennung der industriellen und kommerziellen von der ackerbauenden Arbeit und damit die Trennung von **Stadt** und **Land** und den Gegensatz der Intressen Beider herbei.[57]

The lack of cities of any respectable size or of any true metropolitanism in Scandinavia relegates the possible cultural life, the **Bewusstseinsproduktion** to a more primitive level.[58] This makes the criticism of Hegelian language in Scandinavia so pertinent in spite of its facetious tone: it is seen as a direct result of the economic backwardness. The German ideology, with its predilection for lofty abstractions, is here spilling over in areas which have even less control of their own forces of production. Even the very endeavour to avoid natural prejudice becomes a vain effort and a further enticement to idealism and false consciousness:

> Diese hochtrabenden und hochfahrenden Gedankenkrämer, die unendlich weit über alle nationalen Vorurteile erhaben zu sein glauben, sind also in der Praxis noch viel nationaler als die Bierphilister. . .[59]

In their book collaboration, Marx and Engels never got round to a formal definition of "ideology", but most of it, and indeed most of their writings in this period, is concerned with the images which are collectives imprinted on the national consciousness, images of their own being and origin, and of others' – classes or peoples (**Vorstellungen über sich selbst**; as **Schein** or **Illusion**) – which are seen as by necessity falsifying the true conditions of human intercourse. They have not yet found a materialist position strong enough to support their often heavily sarcastic and disjointed attacks on left-Hegelian or radical thinkers of other persuasions (Feuerbach, Stirner, Grün). What is made admirably clear, though, is their unambiguous identification of a national consciousness with the ruling class of this nation: "Die Gedanken der herrschenden Klasse sind in jeder Epoch die herrschenden Gedanken. . .".[60]

The answer to the inevitable entrenchment of ideas in the hegemony of the ruling class is, as with the forces of production, international interaction and competition – cosmopolitanism in other words. Only in world-wide interaction can the proletariat throw off its dependence on the false consciousness imposed by the ruling class. This is, needless to say, the main objective behind the **Communist Manifesto**, published two years after the completion of **The German Ideology**.

This cosmopolitan perspective, in spite of its strong emphasis on praxis, is in need of a comparative approach to ideologies. The Marxian re-interpretation of history, which is a radical one insofar that it assumes a world-wide perspective and challenges ruling ideas, must concentrate its analytic energies on the advanced nations of Europe and their victims, oppressed in colonialism. Scandinavia cannot offer any interesting development in its "stupid peasant economy". But the method used is not without relevance, as Marx and Engels were indeed studying the transference of ideas from one national or cultural context to another. As S.S. Prawer has pointed out in a brilliant series of chapters in his book **Karl Marx and World Literature**,[61] the concept of cosmopolitanism and ideology are closely linked, and can be seen as transcultural reflexes of each other in interaction: behind the analyses can be seen the **palimpsest** method Marx has described in another text:[62]

> It is well-known how the monks write silly lines of Catholic saints **over** the manuscripts on which the classical works of ancient heathendom had been written. The German literati reversed this process with profane French literature. They wrote their philosophical nonsense beneath the French original.

If the concept of ideology is seen in this light, as borrowed or reciprocal reflexes of conceptions formed at other times or in other localities, it becomes obvious that cosmopolitanism of a wide-ranging kind offers the only remedy, the only secure foundation of a science of sociology, as it is for the proletarian revolution: "Die Arbeiter haben kein Vaterland".[63] Only through the emancipation of the proletariat can the local refractions of social knowledge be restored to transparency: this is the creation of a **world literature**.[64]

I have dwelt for so long on the question of cosmopolitanism[65] in the development of Marxist theory in this (pre-**Capital**) phase, not because it can be said to have any immediate influence on the formation of ideological self-images in Scandinavia in the second half of the century, but because in itself it mirrors the mechanisms of rejection and renunciation which are constitutive for these images. These mechanisms can with great advantage be studied in Scandinavian writers from Almqvist to Strindberg, from Ibsen to Hamsun. What these cannot explain, however, is the rehabilitation of the Scandinavian ideology which occurs at the tail end of the nineteenth century in various and indeed opposed contexts: as a marginal, but powerful ingredient in the formation of a brand-new mythology of Modernism, and also as a component of a more sinister nexus of speculations on race and nationalism, eventually culminating in what one of its founders called: "Der Sehnsucht der nordischen Rassenseele in Zeichen des Volksmythos".[66]

Engels had in later years very little to say about Scandinavian literature: a translation and some remarks on the medieval Danish ballad of Herr Tidman (1865)[67] and much later some comments on Eddic poetry in opposition to Wagner, in **The**

Origin of the Family (1884).[68] But the way he described Scandinavian culture as reflections of the habits of other nations or of their own past, establishes a palimpsest view of their national identities.

Stanley Rosen has, in a thoughtful essay on philosophical nihilism which he sees, somewhat surprisingly, both as an extension of Cartesian physics and as a form of decadence, pointed to the similarities between Marx and Nietzsche, not only as to their shared background of ideas, but also to the final solutions they reach:

> The Cartesian revolution may be said to terminate in two nineteenth-century programs for a radically more direct and violent enterprise – Marx's revolution of the proletariat and Nietzsche's radicalisation of nihilism in preparation for the superman.[69]

And much later on in the book: "Each [of them] labored to free the spirit by advocating a return to the body as the locus of generative power".[70] This I find an unacceptable simplification of Marx's position, but undoubtedly striking when applied to Nietzsche.

One might have expected Nietzsche to look to the North or other marginal cultures for fuelling his Aryan hypothesis, like Gobineau had done before him.[71] However, this is not the case; indeed he seems as uninterested or even inimical to Northern culture as Marx and Engels had been. Nonetheless, his arguments about the relations of "modernity" to Northern climes are of perpetual interest.

Nietzsche begins his final onslaught on modernity in **Der Antichrist** with a quote from Pindar (X Pyth. 30) which summarizes his contention that the Germans themselves are sufficiently marginal:

> -Sehen wir uns ins Gesicht. Wir sind Hyperboreer – wir wissen gut genug, wie abseits wir leben. "Weder zu Lande noch zu Wasser wirst du den Weg zu den Hyperboreern finden": das hat schon Pindar von uns gewusst. Jenseits des Nordens, des Eises, des Todes – **unser** Leben, **unser** Glück. . .[72]

The cultural isolation of the North – as signified by the mythical Hyperboreans – is to be seen in a familiar perspective, but somehow turned upside down – threatened by southerly winds, by the scirocco. "Lieber im Eise leben als unter modernen Tugenden und andern Südwinden!"

The sustained attack on Christian morality in **Der Antichrist**, which is closely connected with the argument in the earlier **Genealogy of Morals**, in particular Section II, is also, and perhaps as much, an attack on the Judaeo-Christian conception of history, where secular history is seen as a direct descendant of sacred history and the **translatio Romana** warrants the continuity of the German Empire.[73] Nietzsche goes, as always, straight for the jugular:

> Und noch einmal verübte der Priester-Instinkt des Juden das gleiche grosse Verbrechen an der Historie – er strich das Gestern, das Vorgestern des Christentums einfach durch, er **erfand sich eine Geschichte des ersten Christentums.** Mehr noch: er fälschte die Geschichte Israels nochmals um, um als Vorgeschichte für **seine** Tat zu erscheinen: alle Propheten haben von **seinem** Erlöse geredet. . .[74]

In this account of St Paul's mission to the Gentiles it could have made some sense to appeal to the last bastions of heathendom in Europe; but Nietzsche has no need to extrapolate any **Germanentum** outside Germany. True enough, he is willing to include die **Skandinavische Wikinger** among the examples of **Blonde Bestie** in **Genealogy** (I:xi) although this is hardly the eulogy it is sometimes assumed to be, rather an explanation of the suspicion (Mistrauen) the Nordic race has inspired in the rest of Europe (and, as he wisely adds, the modern Germans are barely related to the old Teutons, either by blood or by concept: **Genealogy** I:ii).

It is impossible fully to appreciate Nietzsche's attitude to the North without taking into consideration his relations to Richard Wagner. After his early, quite enthusiastic response to Wagner in **Unzeitgemässe Betrachtungen** (4), he turned against his former friend and mentor in **Der Fall Wagner**, one of his most brilliant and exhilarating pamphlets from his last active year where he performs a joyful vivisection of the artist of **décadence**, this "Cagliostro of Modernity". Wagner's is a diseased art: "Wagner est une névrose". He is the epitome of decadent art, displaying "die drei grossen Stimulantia der Erschöpften, das **Brutale**, das **Kunstliche** und das **Unschuldige** (Idiotische)".[75] With gruesome prescience, he paints a picture of the German (or Nordic) youths under Wagner's spell, drunk on the Germanic myth, ending with a fugue-like paean to the opposed forces of the South:

> Sind sie doch samt und sonders, gleich Wagner selbst, **verwandt** mit dem schlechten Wetter, dem deutschen Wetter! Wotan ist ihr Gott: aber Wotan ist der Gott des schlechten Wetters. . . Sie haben recht, diese deutsche Jünglinge so wie sie nun einmal sind: wie **könnten** sie vermissen, was wir **andere**, was wir Halkyonier bei Wagner vermissen: **la gaya scienza**: die leichten Füsse; Witz, Feuer, Anmut; die grosse Logik; den Tanz der Sterne; die übermütige Geistigkeit; die Lichtschauder des Südens; das **glatte** Meer; – Vollkommenheit. . . .[76]

It is not always easy to follow Nietzsche in the late phase in his abrupt changes from multi-layered irony to dithyrambic frenzy; but it is nonetheless quite clear that his denunciation of the mists and miasmas of the North is complete and devastating. The vestiges of traditional Hippocratic concepts are there – and Nietzsche was of course very familiar with their sources – both in the stress on bad weather and on drunkenness (cf. in **Götzendämmerung** (3), the section on what the Germans lack, where he apostrophizes "the two great European narcotics, alcohol and Christianity"). But for Nietzsche, the whole Tacitean myth of the virtuous **Germani** and their love of liberty has to be deconstructed into its opposite: "Definition des Germanen: Gehorsam und lange Beine" (**Der Fall Wagner**, 11).[77] Finally, in the second Postscript, he complains about being misunderstood with a very topical and typical reference to the devastation of the German vineyards by Phylloxera:

> Seitdem aber in den Weinbergen des deutschen Geistes ein neues Tier haust, der Reichswurm, die berühmte **Rhinoxera**, wird kein Wort von mir mehr verstanden.

He has come a long way here from any übermensch-theory in the conventional and misunderstood sense. In his rejection of the Germanic myth, so immensely powerful in this period and later, Nietzsche ought to be freed of any charge of complicity with the

Myth of the twentieth century. He is, in fact, its earliest and fiercest critic. In linking it with the concept of "modernity", he has furthermore created a powerful instrument for interpreting the origins of Modernism.

This study of a particular case of ethnic Otherness or "altérité" has so far, at least in theoretical understanding, hardly advanced at all. The explanatory framework described in sundry observations from different countries and centuries is, on the material level, amazingly constant and depressingly jejune: dominated by what I have referred to as Hippocratic explanations, including a loose cluster of climatological and physiological speculation over a long period of time, it repeats with feeble monotony the same message: people who live to the north of "us" seem to be dull, sluggish, corrupt, inclined to drunkenness, melancholy, madness and witchcraft (or in some more modern versions Hegelian philosophy). At the same time, they also seem to be healthy, long-lived, hardy, vigorous and, when aroused, ferocious, in particular when living in mountain regions far away from the foul emanations of the northern marshes. Strange dietary habits and foul smells are also present,[78] but less distinctive traits, as these seem to be perpetual ingredients in descriptions of ethnic "otherness". But, on the whole, so are most of these characteristics, and many parallels can be found from confrontations with other cultures all over the world.

This has been an investigation of the anthropology of **exclusion**, and therefore the cluster of idealized qualities has hardly entered it, as it belongs to an anthropology of **emulation**. The negative picture must be supplemented with its positive counter-image which we could call The Scandinavian Mythology, in contradistinction to The Scandinavian Ideology. It would include the Gothic revival in the eighteenth century,[79] Montesquieu's derivation of democracy and liberty from ancient Germanic law, liberalism in nineteenth-century historiography[80] and the nationalism of the patriotic/ethnic variety in the same century, sustaining itself on Vico and Herder and eventually contributing to the confusion of racial theories, from Gobineau and Wagner to Rosenberg and Hitler. To unravel this is a very important task for the elucidation of the Scandinavian image.

Also, no consideration has been given to "real" or actual relationships between nations in Europe during this period, but only to the "falsche Vorstellungen" of ideology which Marx addressed in his preface to **The German Ideology.** Obviously, the brief expansion period of Scandinavian and in particular Swedish politics must have made an impact. Notice, however, that even the presentation of Charles XII is coloured in classical Tacitean moralism: Voltaire sees him as a noble but doomed exemplum straight out of Plutarch; Samuel Johnson as a substitute for Hannibal in his rendering of Juvenal's Xth satire in The Vanity of Human Wishes.

Even so, this merely accounts for the **external** view: the really interesting results cannot be obtained until this view has been confronted with the self-image produced in the countries concerned in accordance with, or in dialectical opposition to, the external images. To the Germans of the nineteenth century Scandinavia appeared as a tarnished mirror, to be despised and resented, perhaps also feared and envied. This had wide-ranging repercussions in Scandinavia, and **skandinavismen** which was the dominating cultural and political ideology between 1848 and 1864 can be seen as in part a reaction to German cultural expansion (before and independent of the political one). This is most noticeable in writers with a strong awareness of European consciousness, like Kierkegaard and Almqvist. Almqvist's **Svenska fattigdomens betydelse**, a long essay from **Törnrosens bok**,[81] bears witness to this in its insistence on the values of the

Swedish peasant economy and the homely pleasures of the Swedish landscape, its flora and fauna.

The Scandinavian writer of the nineteenth century was forced to re-invent Scandinavia for himself. He did that in opposition to the massive neglect and even mistrust he would encounter from the rest of Europe. For a long time he had been dazzled by the splendours of European culture and amazed, like Miranda, by a brave new world outside his native domain; towards the end of the nineteenth century, in the "modern breakthrough", he is for the first time able to exclaim, defiantly, with Coriolanus: There is a world elsewhere!

It is easy enough to explain the motivations behind the Scandinavian "modern breakthrough" at the tail end of the nineteenth century, but it is not easy to explain its tremendous impact, in particular in Germany, and the sudden, complete reversal of the Scandinavian image there. This present study can be read as a preface to James McFarlane's two brilliant essays in the volume **Modernism**:[82] "The Mind of Modernism" and "Berlin and the Rise of Modernism 1886–96", where for once the Scandinavian contribution to the formation of early Modernist doctrine and practice is judiciously evaluated. In the latter essay, he gives a comprehensive survey of the Scandinavian influences on German drama and literature in Berlin, placing Naturalism and Modernism as contiguous and to some extent overlapping phenomena: "Scandinavia enjoyed a particularly high esteem, partly because Ibsen (and, to a lesser extent, Bjørnson) had already left a deep impression on German and European theatre but also because, within the climate of opinion that had made a book like **Rembrandt als Erzieher** into a best-seller, the appeal of Scandinavia on emotively ethnic grounds was considerable. (When the – on first publication, anonymous – 'Rembrandt author' wrote to thank a Scandinavian critic for a particularly fulsome review, he advanced the notion that, on the analogy of Nietzsche's **Übermensch**, he might perhaps refer to the Scandinavians as **die Überdeutschen**.)"[83] Even if one has to assume a certain amount of irony in this statement, it is amazing to consider how far the Scandinavian image had travelled since the middle of the century.

Nietzsche, who had his earliest adulation among Scandinavians (Brandes's lectures on his work in Copenhagen in 1886 are rightly regarded as a watershed in his reputation, and Strindberg, Ola Hansson and Hamsun were among his devoted admirers), was with uncanny sharpness able to put his finger on the essential contribution to Modernism in his final reckoning with Wagner: "Diese **Unschuld** zwischen Gegensätze, dies 'gute Gewissen' in der Lüge ist vielmehr **modern par excellence**, man definiert beinahe damit die Modernität".[84] McFarlane highlights the same duplicity or ambivalence as the central tenet of early Modernism in "The Mind of Modernism", and quotes from Strindberg's **Till Damascus** III: "Be one-sided no more. Do not say 'either . . or', but instead 'both . . and'!"[85] This is a defiant clarion call, a declaration of independence from the stricter dialectics of Hegel, Kierkegaard, Nietzsche. But also, in its innocence, a declaration of independence from the oppression of the Scandinavian Ideology.

How was Ibsen possible? How were Strindberg, Jacobsen, Hamsun, Munch possible? The "innocence between contradictions" which gave its strength to the Scandinavian moment in European Modernism could not last long: by the time of the First World War it had spent its force and other elements were ready to dominate Modernism in its later phases. Scandinavia reverted to its invisible state, "traduc'd and tax'd of other nations", but more and more again dwelling, like the Hyperboreans in Pindar, in some blissful but ghostly existence beyond the North Wind: "Neither by ship nor land canst thou find the wondrous road to the trysting-place of the Hyperboreans". But this wondrous road (thaumatán hodón) is well worth looking for, not least if it leads to a trysting-place which is also a place of contest (agón).

Notes

1. **De l'esprit des lois**, edited by Gonzague Truc (Paris, 1961), vol.I.
2. ibid., vol.I, p.241.
3. See John Holloway: **Widening Horizons in English Verse** (London, 1966), p.16, mentioning that Browne used to have his daughter reading to him from Olaus Magnus.
4. **The Anatomy of Melancholy**, edited by Floyd Dell and Paul Jordan Smith (New York, 1927), p.209.
5. ibid., p.208.
6. As used in **Les mots et les choses** (Paris, 1966).
7. See G.E.R. Lloyd: **Science, Folklore and Ideology.** Studies in the Life Sciences in Ancient Greece (Cambridge, 1983); in particular on "dualisers" in Aristotle, pp.44–53.
8. See note 14, and above.
9. op.cit., p.558.
10. Olaus Magnus: **Historia de gentibus septentrionalibus**, edited by Mats Rehnberg (Stockholm, 1982), Book III, p.14.
11. op.cit., p.177.
12. Or: perhaps somebody shown to strangers. I owe this observation to Jesper Svenbro (in conversation).
13. Kirk-Raven: **The Presocratic Philosophers** (Cambridge, 1957), 171.
14. G.E.R. Lloyd (ed.): **Hippocratic Writings** (Harmondsworth, 1978). See Lloyd's introduction.
15. Translated by J. Chadwick and W.N. Mann. In Lloyd, op.cit., p.164.
16. See François Hartog: **Le miroir d'Herodote** (Paris, 1980) esp. pp.21–51.
17. (London, 1981), p.115.
18. See my essay "Helvetet är de andra" in **Slutna världar öppen rymd** (Lund, 1971).
19. See Emile Benveniste: **La vocabulaire des institutions indo-européennes** (Paris, 1969), Vol.I, Book I, Ch.7; Book III, Ch.5.
20. Hartog, op.cit., pp.80ff.

21. **Origines de l'Esprit bourgeois en France** (Paris, 1927), Vol.I.

22. **Philosophie de la Révolution française**, précédé de **Montesquieu** (Paris, 1956).

23. ibid., p.18.

24. ibid., p.19.

25. **translatio imperii** is used in the Renaissance about the transmission of authority from Rome to the German Empire. See J.W. Burrow: **A Liberal Descent** (Cambridge, 1981), p.187 and references there. A very ingenious use of the concept for wider cultural problems of dissemination can be found in Frank Kermode: **The Classic** (Cambridge, Mass., 1983), p.30ff.

26. See note by Maurice Hutton to his edition of Tacitus's **Germania** (Loeb Classical Library), p.347.

27. Among other works, see Jean Seznec: **The Survival of the Pagan Gods** (New York, 1953), Frank E. Manuel: **The Eighteenth Century confronts the Gods** (Cambridge, Mass. 1959), Frank E. Manuel: **The Changing of the Gods** (Hanover and London, 1983).

28. References are to Frank Kermode's edition of **The Tempest** (Arden), Harry Levin's edition of **Coriolanus** (American Pelican) and Harold Jenkins's edition of **Hamlet** (Arden).

29. See D.G. James: **The Dream of Prospero** (Oxford, 1967) and Frank Kermode's introduction, p.xxvff.

30. See Kermode's very full note, p.37.

31. See M.I. Finley: **Economy and Society in Ancient Greece** (London, 1981) for a critical discussion of Marx's views on the classical city state, p.19.

32. cf quotations from Burton, above.

33. See Jenkins's note, Longer notes, p.466.

34. Sigismund (Zygmunt) had finally been deposed from his Swedish throne in 1599 after long wrangling. If we accept 1601 as the date for **Hamlet**, it ought still to have been topical.

35. Omitted in both Folio and Quarto 1. See note in the text, p.209.

36. See Jenkins's note, Longer notes, p.448.

37. See Jenkins's note, Longer notes, pp.449–51.

38. Robert Burton, op.cit., passim.

39. The related problem of "orientalism" has been recently discussed in Edward W. Said: **Orientalism** (London, 1978) and in various essays by the same author in **The World, the Text, and the Critic** (London, 1984).

40. See Jesper Svenbro: **La Parole et le Marbre** (Lund, 1976), Ch.II:1, Xenophane: la critique des mythes.

41. She had, as the wife of the Swedish ambassador, Stael von Holstein, been staying in Stockholm for several long visits, and had also visited Denmark.

42. **De la Littérature,** édition critique par Paul Van Tieghem (Genève & Paris, 1959), Vol.I, p.181.

43. ibid, loc.cit.

44. ibid., p.178.

45. **De l'Allemagne**, edited by Simon Balayé (Paris, 1968), I-II.

46. op.cit., vol.II, p.14.

47. ibid., p.15.

48. Printed at Versailles, Chez Blaizot, An huitième; reprinted by J.J. Pauvert (Paris, 1957).

49. op.cit., p.102. In another scene, he is called "le petit fils du favori".

50. Idée sur les romans, published as preface to **Les crimes de l'amour** vol.I, reprinted by J.J. Pauvert (Paris, 1955). The third volume contains a prose version of **Oxtiern**, titled "Ernestine".

51. op.cit., p.123.

52. See **Histoire de Juliette** (1797), where he in fact has much more to say about Sweden in Vol.V, which contains Borchamps' narrative about his experiences in Sweden before the assassination of Gustavus III. In spite of Oxtiern, Sade seems to have been quite well-informed about the political situation there, although obviously regarding it as more proper for pornography than for melodrama.

53. op.cit., vol.II, p.93.

54. Both can be argued from evidence in Tacitus, e.g. **Germania,** 16 (about individual habitations) and **Germania,** 26 (about communal agriculture).

55. Karl Marx/Friedrich Engels: **Die Deutsche Ideologie** (Dietz Verlag: Berlin, 1960), pp.26–27.

56. Engels an Marx, Dezember 1846, in MEW vol.27, pp.71–72. It is thanks to Jan Myrdal that this important passage has been noticed. See his **Skriftställning** 4, p.160f. It is also quoted, with interesting comments, in Kaj Svensson's postscript to the new edition of Nils Herman Quiding: **Slutliquid med Sveriges lag** (Stockholm, 1978) an important contribution to social ideas in Sweden in the nineteenth century.

57. op.cit., pp.17–18.

58. ibid., passim.

59. ibid., p.36.

60. ibid., p.44.

61. Oxford University Press, 1978.

62. Quoted from Prawer, op.cit., p.139.

63. from **The Communist Manifesto.**

64. See Prawer, op.cit., Ch.7: World Literature and Class Conflict.

65. Cosmopolitanism as such has of course a much longer history. For an important discussion, see Alan D. McKillop: "Local attachment and Cosmopolitanism", in **From Sensibility to Romanticism** – Essays presented to Frederick A. Pottle, edited by Frederick W. Hilles and Harold Bloom (Oxford, 1966).

66. Alfred Rosenberg, quoted by Georg Lukacs: **Die Zerstörung der Vernunft,** Vol.9 of the **Gesamtausgabe** (Neuwied, 1962).

67. Perhaps most easily available in Marx/Engels: **Über Kunst und Litteratur** (Dietz Verlag: Berlin, 1967), vol.II, p.219. There is an interesting discussion of the ballad and Engels's interpretation in Folke Isaksson, **Gnistor under himlavalvet** (Stockholm, 1983), p.41 ff.

68. Marx/Engels, op.cit., vol.I, p.316 (MEW, vol.21, pp.43–44).

69. **Nihilism: A Philosophical Essay** (New Haven, 1969), p.75.

70. ibid., p.199.

71. See for example Gobineau's correspondence with de Tocqueville, as edited by John Lukacs: **Tocqueville : The European Revolution and The Correspondence with Gobineau** (New York, 1959).

72. Quotations from Nietzsche follow the three volume Schlechta edition. As many various reprints (and translations) exist, I refer to section only, not to pages.

73. See note 25.

74. **Der Antichrist,** section 42.

75. **Der Fall Wagner,** section 5.

76. ibid., section 10.

77. ibid., Second Postscript.

78. A short introductory discussion of the anthropology of smell is found in Dan Sperber: **Rethinking Symbolism** (Cambridge, 1975), p.115 ff.

79. The best discussion in English is probably still John Holloway's chapter in **Widening Horizons in English Verse** (London, 1966).

80. see J.W. Burrow, op.cit., note 25.

81. **Törnrosens bok,** edited by Fredrik Böök, vol. VIII-X (Stockholm, 1921), pp.297–341.

82. **Modernism 1890–1930** (Harmondsworth, 1976), edited by Malcolm Bradbury and James McFarlane.

83. Ibid., p.115.

84. **Der Fall Wagner**, Epilog.

85. op.cit., p.88.

The Concept of Modernism in Scandinavia

P.M. Mitchell

Modernism belongs to the – recent – past. It is no longer modern. While the word might seem to connote if not what is to come then the immediate present, as it once did, "Modernism" in literature both within and without Scandinavia has been succeeded by "Post-Modernism", a term that one comes upon frequently in journals and newspapers. We understand: that which once was new is no longer new. What was to generate the aesthetic of a new path and that offended the aesthetic predilections of the interested public no longer shocks or offends. Drawing upon many antecedents that were not consciously part of a movement or a school, literary Modernism did indeed materialize, but in so doing it acquired historical patina and became acceptable in the salon.

The American critic Virgil Thomson once said, in referring to Gertrude Stein, that no literary work was incomprehensible after twenty-five years – except for Gertrude Stein's **Tender Buttons**. Scandinavian Modernism produced no Gertrude Stein and has left no incomprehensible work in its wake. It is now well over a quarter of a century since the great debate about literary Modernism started in Scandinavia, a debate that reached its apex around 1960–62 and has a monument in a stimulating collection of essays entitled **Pejling mod modernisme**, published in Copenhagen in 1962 hard upon a provocative exhibition of "Modernist" sculpture by the Swiss artist Jean Tinguely at the Louisiana Museum of modern art on the coast of the Sound north of Copenhagen. Now what was meant by Modernism?

Save for those who are familiar with recent ecclesiastical history, most readers who may seek definitions in encyclopaedias or dictionaries may be disoriented and discomfited. If one reads the article on "modernism" in **Svensk uppslagsbok** from the year 1951, for example, one finds only the explanation that the phenomenon is "et försök att se de kristna grundsanningarna i den moderna forsknings ljus och göra den tillgängliga för nutidsmänniskan" ("an attempt to perceive the basic Christian truths in the light of modern research and to make it accessible to contemporary man"). Similarly, the 1974 edition of the **Encyclopaedia Britannica** knows only the ecclesiastical definition of the term. **Ordbog over det danske Sprog** (vol.14, 1933) provides comparable historical definition. After stating that **modernisme** is an "anskuelse, retning (bevægelse), tendens, der er stærkt præget af og lægger stærk vægt paa det moderne. . ." ("view, direction [movement], tendency, that is strongly influenced by and lays great stress on what is modern. . ."), the dictionary gives as primary evidence from the year 1934 a statement by the critic Julius Lange: "Under de to følgende Skoleaar skyllede Modernismens stigende Strømme de sidste Rester af Kristendom ud af hans unge Tanke" ("During the following two academic years, the rising current of Modernism washed away the last remnants of Christianity from his young mind"). Generally speaking, the term Modernism did refer principally to a reform movement within the Catholic Church and a tendency that was condemned – ultimately unsuccessfully – by both Pope Leo XIII and Pope Pius V. As unexpected and unfamiliar as the recent ecclesiastical significance may now seem to participants in discussions about modern literature today, there is nevertheless a parallel to be drawn between religious and secular Modernism. Both question traditional values and would temper standards and beliefs to correspond to the new insights born of scientific discoveries, social changes, and shifting mores.

There were contrary voices, however. Knudsen & Sommerfelt's **Norsk Riksmålordbok** from the year 1947 made a shift insofar as the first definition is secular: "tendens, bestrebelse for å stemme med tidens krav og smak (særl. på kunstens og åndslivets område)" ("tendency, effort to agree with the time's demands and taste [especially in the realm of art and intellectual activity]") and records a noteworthy advanced usage from the year 1927 by Nils Vogt: "der findes ikke forsök paa at lave modernisme enten i gloser eller sætningsbygning" ("there is no attempt at Modernism either in vocabulary or syntax"). That is to say, the relation of syntax to Modernism was suggested some twenty-five years before the term "Modernism" gained currency. Still more surprising is Östergren's **Nusvensk ordbok**, volume 4 (1934) that cites the Finland-Swedish poet and critic Rabbe Enckell to the effect that, "Den litterära riktning, some redan vunnit ett stadigt fotfäste i Finland under namnet 'modernism', torde tills vidare vara rätt okänd i Sverige" ("The literary movement that already gained a foothold in Finland under the term 'modernism' must as yet be termed little known in Sweden"). This quotation alone is sufficient to demonstrate the **avant-garde** nature of Swedish literature in Finland by the early 1930s and the Finland-Swedish origin of Modernism in the Nordic countries. Under "modernistisk" Elmer Diktonius was even then probably identified as a Modernist, while the explanatory quotation reads, "Den egoism, oklarhet och benägenhet för hastverk, som utmärka många modernister" ("The egoism, lack of clarity, and the inclination toward haste that characterizes many Modernists") – from the year 1922. An additional comment from the Swedish dictionary is worth citing. "Modernism" was identified as "(alltför) modärn ande (e)l(ler) riktning. . ." ("all too modern spirit or movement. . ."). One notes the tenor of this early quotation: Modernism is self-centred and all too advanced.

Modernism as a conscious phenomenon existed among writers of Swedish in Finland but few years after World War I, but its existence was insular. It is a remarkable fact that Elmer Diktonius published his most important work, **Min dikt**, in 1921, a year before T.S. Eliot published **The Waste Land**. Nevertheless, no attention was paid to the Modernism that was being practised in Finland, so that two standard works on Swedish literature, Alf Henriques **Svensk litteratur** (1944) and Alrik Gustafson's **History of Swedish Literature** (1961) fail to discuss Finland-Swedish poets at all. That this could be despite some awareness of Edith Södergran outside Finland, demands explanation – which probably is to be sought in the political unrest and social isolation of the country. Finland was undergoing such political chaos in the post-World War I years, years of a tragic civil war between "Whites" and "Reds" in a struggle for control of the new republic, that such matters as syntactical experimentation were overshadowed. The independence of literature could not be mentioned in the same breath as the independence of Finland. Despite the Finland-Swedish beginnings of Scandinavian Modernism, then, the eyes of post-war literature in the other Nordic countries were searching elsewhere for inspiration. The germ of a possible pan-Scandinavian literature was not nourished; it was, again, a Scandinavianism that might have been. Measured by the cultural yardstick, Finland was much farther removed than Britain or France or Germany or the United States.

In attempting to determine the recent history of the term "Modernism" in Northern Europe, it is instructive to examine collections of essays or documentary evidence that permit retrospective analysis of cultural change and of public debate which took place during a given period outside Finland prior to 1962. Two illuminating Danish works of this nature are the montage **Kulturdebat i 20'erne** (1976) edited by Olav Harsløf, and the earlier collection of essays entitled **Kulturdebat 1944–58** (1958) edited by Erik Knudsen and Ole Wivel. One can quickly identify the major concerns of the eras under scrutiny – and also draw some conclusions about the years intervening. In fine, Modernism **qua** Modernism did not exist in the consciousness of any of the critics and imaginative writers who are represented in the two collections. Social and political thought and demands for action and reform, with the demonstrable impact of Marxist theory, dominated the 1920s. Not only was the concept of Modernism only vaguely present, there seemed to be no interest in what might be classified as modern, at least not for the sake of modernity. Moreover, the aesthetic and formal nature of poetry and prose was scarcely mentioned. Of the most influential radical periodical of the 1920s, **Kritisk Revy** (which was, to be sure, orientated towards architecture), Olav Harsløf writes "Litteratur- og kunstartiklerne og siden de filosofisk-sociologiske debatter var et tegn på en svækkelse af tidsskriftets erklærede mål. . ." ("The articles on literature and art, and later the philosophical-sociological debates, were a sign of the weakening of the periodical's declared aim. . ."). The embryonic debate about the direction of new literature did not mesh with the preconceived programme of modern architecture.

In the anthology dealing with the years 1944–58, one recognizes that the leading questions of the day were existential-philosophical, for the book is dominated by essays such as that on human responsibility, by Hal Koch, the professor of ecclesiastical history in the University of Copenhagen, and on **Angst**, by Vilhelm Grønbech, late professor of the history of religion. Modernism was not a subject for discussion. The leading critic of the literary left, Sven Møller Kristensen, was represented by an essay on "Saglighed og anarki" that originally had been published in the periodical **Vindrosen** in 1956. He used the word "modernisme" in a general sense with reference to painting and music, but declared that "sværmeriet for kønslivet som nøglen til alle problemer" ("the mania for regarding sex life as the key to all problems") seemed more significant than a new direction in literature. The Danish writer Hans Christian Branner – also in the year 1956 – had championed "Kunstens uafhængighed" ("the independence of art"), but neither here nor elsewhere was there any awareness of the growth or desirability of "Modernism". Even the young philosopher who was to be identified with Scandinavian and specifically with Danish Modernism, Villy Sørensen, indicated no awareness of it in a literary essay that had first been published in a Copenhagen newspaper in July 1957.

Now it is true that one cannot expect to possess enough objectivity about one's own time to be able to identify it by the descriptive term by which it may come to be known to posterity. It is therefore not surprising that there is a paucity of occurrence of the word "Modernism" outside Finland in the early years of what subsequently not only came to be called Modernism by retrospective critics but became a divisive state of affairs. While Modernism suggested a spiritual rallying point for the progressive believer, it was a red flag for the reactionary traditionalist. A case can be made for labelling 1954 or 1955 or 1956 as the beginning of a consciousness of Modernism in all of Scandinavia, but there was a fairly lengthy "pré-modernisme" that provided the seed that was to flower – and then wilt by 1970. Too facile is the explanation that the roots of Modernism (or any other recognized phenomenon in literature) have always been with us and have needed only to be identified. Whether or not, as Torben Brostrøm writes (**Modernisme før og nu** 1983, p.88), the Chinese invented imagery "og dermed et stykke modernisme" ("and with that a piece of Modernism") is like "the flowers that bloom in the spring". One might as well apply the adage, the old order changeth, giving way to the new, or adapt and oversimplify Hegel's irrefutable principle of thesis, antithesis, and synthesis. There is an element of truth in such clichés, but to stress them instead of more precise historical detail is to belabour the obvious. The seventeenth-century quarrel between "les anciennes et les modernes" was important for the development of French literature in particular and marked a shift in emphasis in critical thought, but was not the first or last time that there was a confrontation between classical and modern ways of expressing oneself or between traditionalism and radicalism. Time and again since then a younger generation has discovered its own truth and cast aspersions on received truth. As frequently has been noted, however, the speed with which one truth supersedes another seems to have increased, so that literary "movements" and "schools" are nearly to be equated with generations while at the same time there is a strong tendency (and this is a twentieth-century peculiarity) to want to identify literature by decades, albeit decades that were punctuated by two World Wars in the first half of this century.

Critics agree that modern literature as we now perceive it dates from the eighteenth century and more particularly from the second half of that century – from the time that man lost much of his religious Christian faith or, as Vilhelm Grønbech wrote in 1922, the traditional god died and was buried when men discovered that there was no way of proving that a god did not exist.[2] "Modern" is a thoroughly acceptable term, but it is multifaceted and flexible: Europe since the Reformation is modern; Western man is modern since the eighteenth century; the electronic age is modern; and modern music is whatever sexagenarian hearers do not like. But "modern" is not to be equated with "Modernist", a term that is relatively narrow in application and that lets itself be confined to a limited number of years in Scandinavia. With its ecclesiastical denotation, the term already existed and had as a connotation the adaption of traditional convictions to recent scientific thought and discovery. As applied to literature in general "Modernism" gained sudden currency outside Finland and general acceptance of the term to denote a direction in art and literature around 1955. That is, by then there was the consciousness first, that literary developments, notably in Denmark and Sweden, were parallel to similar developments in other countries, and second, that the new tenor of literary endeavour among younger writers was sufficiently distinct or discrete to carry a label.

The literary antecedents of the writers who called themselves and came to be called Modernists are easy to identify: they are in the first instance figures who have dominated the international literary scene as pioneers in the creation of new imagery and a new metaphorical, poetic language since the beginning of the twentieth century – James Joyce, Rainer Maria Rilke, T.S. Eliot, Franz Kafka. One might mention other forerunners of the new literature of a so-called experimental nature that arose soon after a brief lull that followed the Second World War, but there is scarcely a Scandinavian writer who would not admit some debt to these four creative masters of untraditional diction, syntax, and imagery. That is to say, the principal sources of inspiration for a new direction in literature came chiefly from without Scandinavia, although the position and impact of Edith Södergran (1892–1923), herself a trilingual with a multi-national background (Swedish, Finnish, Russian), should not be overlooked. An older, Danish, forerunner of Scandinavian Modernism was Sophus Claussen (1865–1931), whose poetry grew to be appreciated more by the Modernists than it had been during his lifetime. The younger poet who provided a fresh impetus to poetry in Denmark, Gustaf Munch-Petersen (1911–38), was aware of Edith Södergran by 1930, but he was not merely a Danish but also a Swedish poet himself, for he sprang from a bilingual (and academic) background. The term that first was applied to Gustaf Munch-Petersen's writing was "Surrealist" but his work can equally well be termed Modernist. After his death in the Spanish Civil War, he became a source of inspiration and a guiding light not only for his contemporaries and a still younger generation but also for slightly older writers, notably Tom Kristensen, who recognized in Gustaf Munch-Petersen the bold experimentalist who had been lacking on the Danish Parnassus and whose ideal had not been met by the so-called radical writers who attracted attention after the First World War – whose artistic creativity did not generally transcend either the homely or the didactic and even propagandistic nature of their work.

If one takes the lodestars of European Modernism as seen from a Scandinavian vantage point – Baudelaire, Joyce, Kafka, Rilke, then Edith Södergran and still later Gustaf Munch-Petersen – as exemplars, then it is apparent that the new literature they represented was not subject to partisan demands and not subservient to social and political tenets, despite the fact that Gustaf Munch-Petersen sacrificed his life for the cause of freedom in Spain.

In the course of relatively few years, the term Modernism came to be employed about a large number of writers. The several stimulating studies that Torben Brostrøm has published about recent Danish literature all have "Modernism" as a key word if not the **basso continuo**. A useful overall discussion of Modernism within a European and not only a Northern context is Poul Borum: **Poetisk modernisme** (1966, Swedish trans. 1968). Incidentally, Borum identifies the writing of Jens Peter Jacobsen (who died in 1885) as the beginning of Modernist Danish poetry, whereas most other critics perceive a turning point and a break with the poetic traditions of the nineteenth century in Danish poetic vocabulary and usage either in Sophus Claussen's **Naturbørn** in 1887 or, more convincingly, in Johannes V. Jensen's **Digte** (1906) with Jensen's translations of Walt Whitman.

"Modernism", like many other literary classifications – and one could mention Expressionism, Impressionism, and even Biedermeier – is either interrelated with or borrowed from the other arts. New directions in the visual arts are recognized more easily and more quickly than through the medium of the printed word. Less application is required of the viewer than of the reader to pass a superficial judgement – and the visual arts are not dependent on a knowledge of foreign languages in order to be judged. While the identifiable antecedents of a new direction in painting may differ from those of new poetry, the new literature of a generation can be described by adjectives that are employed to describe, praise, or condemn contemporaneous painting. There are therefore some metaphysical characteristics shared by the several arts, as difficult as they may be to abstract at the time. Wölfflin's and Walzel's "gegenseitige Erhellung der Künste" is valid for the present as well as the past. **Zeitgeist**, the spirit of the times, are not arbitrary phrases. In the small cohesive societies of the Scandinavian capitals, there is easier access to displays of current artistic endeavour than in larger nations such as Great Britain, Germany, the Soviet Union, and the United States, where cultivation of the arts is more diffuse and the same critics do not write for the same few newspapers published in the nations' capitals – as is the case in the Scandinavian countries. Opinions of the best critical minds in New York, for example, may take a long time to penetrate to, say, the American Louisiana, whereas in the Nordic countries there is more likely to be a national awareness of what a critic said yesterday in the country's capital. The homogeneous and democratized nature of society in Denmark or Sweden, Norway, Finland or Iceland may also be in part responsible for this remarkable difference **vis-à-vis** the outside world.

While it is not difficult to identify ideas and authors from the beginning of the twentieth century until the post-Second World War period that have attributes of Modernism and indeed may even be revered as immediate forerunners by the spokesmen for the Modernist movements of the 1950s, the use of the term "Modernism" was casual and without partisan meaning until then. Matters other than poetic experimentation and radical syntax seemed so much more important after the first World War through the years of unstable peace until 1939 and then again in another global war, that one seeks in vain for earlier definitions of what became a matter of vigorous debate and poetic and critical activity between about 1950 and 1962. In Finland-Swedish literature, however, the home of the early, important Modernist writers, the term "Modernism" had already gained currency, as the quotation from **Nusvensk ordbok,** above, indicates. Unlike their later confrères in Denmark, Norway, and Sweden, the Finland-Swedish Modernists, with Rabbe Enckell as principal spokesman, could identify themselves as Modernist writers from the start. Judged from the standpoint of the history of the word in other Scandinavian but also English sources, this must be considered a noteworthy semantic phenomenon. If the term had currency in Swedish Finland, how could it have failed to come into use elsewhere in the North?

The impulse that generated Modernism in the Northern countries other than Finland came from without. That Denmark should be most open to the current of literary Modernism is not surprising. Denmark is the most international of the several Scandinavian countries – the country physically closest to Western Europe and traditionally a gateway for modern ideas to penetrate the North. The Danes may be considered more thinkers than doers as compared to the Swedes with regard to Modernism. There is a considerable literature of criticism on the subject in Danish. One critic in particular, Torben Brostrøm, became the principal speaker and interpreter of the movement in Scandinavia. It is of note, however, that the Danish poet Poul Borum's book, **Poetisk modernisme**, which in turn reflects a good deal of critical thought from abroad, chiefly from Germany and the United States, was translated into Swedish – a remarkable fact in view of the small number of books translated annually from Danish into Swedish. Since all Swedish critics could read the original Danish work without difficulty, the appearance of a Swedish translation suggests a broad interest in the reading public. Brostrøm made his first substantial contribution to the interpretation of Modernism with his **Poetisk kermesse** in 1962. Then in a series of other studies he shed light on various facets of Danish and European Modernism. The anthology of criticism entitled **Opgøret med modernismen** that Brostrøm edited in 1974 is of especial interest since it assembles several viewpoints, including strongly negative criticism, from a dozen years of critical pronouncements about Modernism. Several of the positions taken are worth noting. Writing in the journal **Kritik** (No.13) in 1970, Poul Behrendt repeated the truism that Modernism was as old as Baudelaire, but added, "(Gottfried) Benn var den første som gennemlevede den"[3] ("Gottfried Benn was the first one who lived it"), and thus suggested the close connection between Modernism abroad and the controversial German physician-poet Benn, who – possibly for political reasons – has received less attention than the early French and American representatives of twentieth-century Modernism. Behrendt also made the incisive observation that Modernism's "største værker er kunst over kunst" ("greatest works are art about art"). Much could be said to this very point in answering the sensitive question, whether Modernism is not too introspective and too little concerned with the problems of the so-called real world? Jørgen Elbek spoke of Modernist lyrics coming to the fore around 1960 and therewith occasioning a metaphysical break with the 1950s.

By 1966, however, he felt that the principal genres of Modernism already had reached a point of no return, or, as he put it, reached their own limits. While both Behrendt and Elbek may be interpreted as having expressed a modicum of scepticism about the intrinsic value and lasting quality of Modernism, Marxist critics in Scandinavia found literary Modernism to be problematical, just as modern painting has had an ambivalent fate in the Soviet Union. Hans Scherfig, a witty, rationalistic, ironic and sarcastic Danish novelist and critic, took a clear stand against Modernism in an article from the year 1965, reprinted in Brostrøm's **Opgøret med modernismen** in 1974. For Scherfig, Modernism "har en ærværdig tradition" ("partakes of an honourable tradition"); that is, it was reactionary and a return to the literature of the early nineteenth century that is often identified as "Romanticism". With inventive and hyperbolic humour, Scherfig claimed: "Det er en forsinket viderególrelse af et program, som blev vedtagen en måneskinsnat i Jena i 1799, hvor et antal germanske skribenter og deres hustruer påtog sig at ophæve virkeligheden . . . Deres tilhængere betegnes idag som **modernister**" ("It is a delayed extension of a programme that was promulgated in the light of the moon in Jena one night in 1799, when a number of Germanic writers and their spouses took it upon themselves to suspend reality . . . their adherents are today identified as Modernists").[4] Scherfig's statement needs some clarification: he is objecting to the introspection of Modernist writing that suggests the dictum **l'art pour l'art** that is anathema to the Marxist conviction, since such art does not assume a programmatic, didactic function for imaginative literature and therefore makes no effort to reach the social and economic goals of Communism. Moreover he assumes that whatever is not realistic in a rather narrow sense of the term is unreasonable and therewith unsupportable. He would not grant to poetry a reality that is not subjugate to some larger, overall plan. Finally, the connection with German poetry is suspect per se, although, curiously enough, the major antecedents of twentieth-century Modernism are only in part German. Kafka and Rilke were not tainted by the National Socialism which presumably was an undercurrent feeding Scherfig's prejudice, and which was re-enforced by the uncertainty surrounding Gottfried Benn, who, right or wrong, has been judged guilty by association. Although Scherfig's position is understandable considering his partisan commitment, not all Marxist critics have rejected Modernism out of hand and some have looked more kindly upon the new direction. Denmark's leading left-wing critic, Sven Møller Kristensen, viewed it as anti-industrialist and took the seemingly un-Marxist position that art simply does not lend itself to democratization. Thus Modernism's unorthodoxy could be excused or even welcomed; it represented a freedom from convention. Echoing György Lukacs, Ebbe Sønderriis attempted to sketch a larger picture in 1970 in an article in the journal **Vindrosen** entitled "Modernismens ideologi – og realisme" ("The Ideology of Modernism – and Realism"). He translated the English title of Lukacs' **The Meaning of Contemporary Realism** into Danish as "Modernismens ideologi" and saw in literary Modernism the reflection of social conditions of the day with concomitant social criticism understood. The political unrest of the 1960s, he pointed out, took place in those Western nations where Modernism was at home. In viewing the struggle between radicalism and "senkapitalistisk ideologi" ("the ideology of late Capitalism"), he concluded that "Modernismen kan ses som en sproglig protest imod disse tendenser" ("Modernism can be seen as a linguistic protest against these tendencies"). His foremost examples were from Danish literature: Svend Åge Madsen and Inger Christensen, two of the most original and influential writers of their generation, both of whom are indeed socially conscious but without a commitment to Marxism although they question certain aspects of contemporary society where the individual is the pawn of impersonal political and economic forces. Both Svend Åge Madsen and Inger Christensen gained much attention and praise for their experimentation with outward form – the former in prose, the latter in verse, the former because of the preponderance of the unexpected and the use of a **Verfremdungseffekt**, the latter by virtue both of a strict control of verse length and a kind of dense prose poetry coupled with a new perspective on contemporary (and mostly depressing) situations. Sønderriis concluded that these two writers actually had transcended Modernism and were moving towards a new Realism – which suggests a social as well as a literary programme.

In his recent book, **Modernisme før og nu** (1983) Torben Brostrøm is unwilling simply to perform an autopsy on post-war Modernism and would instead identify a resurgence of Modernism which has obtained in Denmark during recent years. To be sure, there is a parallel to be noted between the established Modernist poets such as Per Højholt and Svend Åge Madsen on the one hand and several young writers born after 1950 on the other; there are also sufficient differences between the generations that future literary historians will presumably put them into different categories. In particular, the association of the younger poets with the popular music of about 1980 seems to present a contrast with the "modern" music of Schönberg, Stravinsky, and other composers who have an association with literary "Modernism". This difference, although sensed by literary critics including Brostrøm, has not been specifically enunciated by them. Brostrøm has, however, made a commendable attempt to synthesize the literary experimentation of three decades and to bring it into an historical relationship with the antecedents of twentieth-century Modernism. Whether his synthesis will acquire historical validity time will tell. To judge by the proliferating tendency of twentieth-century criticism, a prognosis that his classification will be accepted is doubtful unless the now ubiquitous term "Post-Modernism" is dropped. One recalls that the term "Expressionism" became a replacement for "Post-Impressionism" around 1900. No matter the judgement of literary history to come, Brostrøm deserves acclaim for his delineation of literary interrelationships and parallels and his recognition of lines of development that are not independent of one another. His point is well taken, that most literary invention is a matter of rediscovery: "litterære fornyelser er så at sige altid genopdagelser".[5] That is, what seems novel is often something that has been superseded or forgotten. Brostrøm gives several examples of older verse that might well be classified as belonging among the newest efforts of younger Danish poets. The common – and striking – element is the experimentation with syntax, not infrequently visually and typographically. One aspect of Modernism comprises the concrete poetry which engaged in typographical playfulness which was also characteristic of some Baroque poetry of the seventeenth century – as has often been pointed out.

The number of Swedish writers who embraced Modernism as a doctrine was large and the number of distinguished Modernist poets in the Swedish language also large. Besides the two Finland-Swedish writers who were an early source of inspiration for proponents of Modernism, Edith Södergran and Elmer Diktonius (1896–1961), there were several of Sweden's best-known writers in the years since World War II. There is an indisputable bond between the Swedish literary movement identified as "40-tal" and postwar Modernism. The members of the "40-talister" were either to become writers labelled Modernist, in which their Modernism dates from 1940 or before, or they were to serve as sources of inspiration for younger Swedish poets of the postwar years. This fact becomes clear when one examines the collective volume **Kritiskt 40-**

tal that was issued under the editorship of two of the outstanding "40-talister", Karl Vennberg and Werner Aspenström. In the first essay (dating from the year 1945) in the collection, "Om ordkunstens kris" ("The Crisis of the Art of Writing"), Lars Ahlin puts the question, "Men modernism?" ("What about Modernism?") That is to say, not only was he conscious of the new experimentation but also of the term with which it was to be identified. An essay by Sven Alfons, first published in **BLM** in 1946, is entitled "Lyrisk modernisme". To be sure, the idea informing the essay is not identical with any discussion of "Modernism" ten or twenty years later, but withall, the basic insights are the same: there is a sense of dependency on such forerunners as Baudelaire and Rilke – names that are ubiquitous in later literature dealing with Modernism. Unlike Modernism in general, however, the Swedish "40-tal" was to a large extent self-nourishing. Several Swedish poets, notably Birger Sjöberg, Erik Lindefors, and Karl Vennberg evinced striking originality and had a strong impact on their Swedish contemporaries as far back as 1925. A score of years later, critics would pay homage to Sjöberg's **Kriser og kransar** from the year 1926, although today's reader is surprised to find the volume full of rhyming verse and strong rhythms. Sjöberg's poetry does not exemplify a radical treatment of syntax – while Erik Lindegren's **Mannen utan väg** from the year 1945 demonstrates those characteristics that would label it Modernist. Whether or not one should speak of "40-talism" or "modernism" is really a semantic problem. It should be borne in mind, however, that the Swedish authors – both critics and imaginative writers – of the twentieth century were aware of developments abroad and conscious of those forces that were the major determinants in the moulding of Western literature. Noteworthy is the fact that Lindegren and Vennberg translated T.S. Eliot in 1937, for Eliot is one of the half-dozen giants of twentieth-century literary Modernism. Theirs was nevertheless not the introduction of Eliot to the Swedish reading public, for Karin Boye and Erik Mesterton had translated Eliot's **The Waste Land** several years earlier.

Since Pär Lagerkvist belongs to an earlier generation, he has been given little consideration as a forerunner of Swedish Modernism, but only a superficial acquaintance with his earliest works such as **Ångest** suffices to demonstrate his affinity for the movement later identified as Modernism, although – if simply by virtue of his age – he was not one of "40-talisterna". It is no more possible to dismiss him than Edith Södergran as an antecedent of Swedish Modernism, and the less so since he found his **métier** in the drama, for drama is the least cultivated of the genres in Modernist literature.

A relatively early but remarkable assessment of Swedish Modernism is contained in Göran Printz-Påhlson's study **Solen i spegeln. Essäer om lyrisk modernism** from the year 1958. Printz-Påhlson's brilliant analyses of a series of Swedish Modernists – analyses that have retained their validity – permit us to draw a conclusion that he himself did not draw, **viz**, that the Finland-Swedish and Swedish Modernists are less dependent on foreign models than the Modernist poets of the other Scandinavian countries. Elmer Diktonius, Rabbe Enckell, Gunnar Ekelöf, Erik Lindegren, Werner Aspenström . . . these are poets that Printz-Påhlson adjudges so trenchantly that we still accept his conclusions about their precursors and interrelationships. His observations reinforce our opinion of the consanguinity of "40-tal" and Modernism as well as the impact the leading poets using the Swedish language (notably in Finland) have had on later writers. In speaking of Lindegren's **Mannen utan väg** (1942), he passes a judgement that may be applied to other Modernists: "läsarens tolkning blir fri så länge en viss allmän relation bevaras . . ." ("the reader's interpretation remains free as long as certain basic relationships are preserved"). Fundamental elements of recognition are "järnhårda struktur och symbolkunst . . ." ("iron-hard structure and symbolic art").[6] Lindegren's symbolism of which Printz-Påhlson is speaking is visual rather than abstract, and visual symbolism is characteristic of Modernist poetry that not infrequently is also classed – at least around 1950 – as **sensymbolism**.

At first glance, Norway offers a very different image. Norwegian as well as foreign critics have been in agreement that Modernism was slow in taking hold in Norway. Writing in **Norsk litterær årbok** in 1967, Odd Martin Mæland expressed the belief that, compared to Denmark and Sweden, Norway was isolated with respect to literary experimentalism, for Norwegian post-bellum literature remained chiefly traditional.[7] In 1966 Poul Borum could write of Norway, "på mange måder et litterært U-land" ("in many ways an underdeveloped country in literary terms").[8] That "Dikterens forhold til språket er blitt identisk med hans forhold til verden" ("The writer's relation to language has become identical with his relation to the world") suggested to Mæland a more conservative attitude in Norway than in the other Northern countries. In the periodical **Vinduet** in 1966, Willy Dahl mentioned en passant "den forsinkede modernist-debatten vi hadde i Norge i 1954" ("the delayed debate about Modernism that we had in Norway in 1954").[9] In the same periodical, the same year, however, Ole Langseth declared, "Uten å ta stilling til 'modernism' og eksperiment-diktning i sin alminnelighet må man ha lov til å slå fast at bevegelsen bort fra de tradisjonelle mønstre har bidradd til å skape en alvorlig splittelse i vårt kulturliv" ("Without taking a position on 'Modernism' and experimental poetry in general, one must admit that the movement away from the traditional patterns has contributed to bringing about a serious division in our cultural life").[10] If we accept this statement at face value, then Norway cannot be considered really to have been much behind the times, for there must have been a considerable infusion of Modernism into literary life if it could have had such a divisive effect prior to 1966. As early as 1954, Paal Brekke – himself a representative of Norwegian Modernism – wrote a counter-critique defending Modernism, in replying to an attack by the critic André Bjerke. Brekke stated, i.a., "Vår egen Wergeland var også modernist. Han konsentrerte seg til døde om å uttrykke enkle tanker på en innviklet måte" ("Our own Wergeland was also a Modernist. He concentrated himself to death on expressing simple thoughts in a complex way").[11] And Nils Brantzig, in reviewing recent poetry for **Vinduet** in 1960, could claim that "modernisme som formretning har det siste tiåret slått igjennom med full styrke også hos oss" ("Modernism as a formal movement has really come to the fore during the last decade also in our country").[12] He pointed out that Brekke's **Roerne fra Itaka** possesses elements of "modernistisk formspråk" – a formally Modernist language. Stein Mehren, who identified himself as a Modernist, made the somewhat curious remark – it verges on the oxymoron – that Modernism even then was confronting stagnation and renewal. "Idag", he maintained, "betrakter modernismen seg selv som tradisjon, mens den virkelige tradisjon nærmest betraktes som smittefarlig" ("Today Modernism views itself as a tradition, whereas the real tradition is looked upon almost as dangerously contagious").[13] The year before, in **Vinduet**, Willy Dahl had severely criticized contemporary Norwegian poetry for attempting to be Modernistic while lacking comprehension for the substance of Modernism. "Det er ikke 'modernisme' dette, dette sikter mot. Man kan sludre på rim også" ("It is not 'Modernism' that this has its sights on. One can also talk rhyming nonsense").[14] Dahl evoked an ironic reply from Paal Brekke, who noted that Modernism was of no interest to Norwegian criticism before Norwegian poets allied themselves with it: "Det ble møtt med uforstand, mer enn kritikk . . ." ("It was received more with a lack of comprehension than with criticism").[15] The debate about Modernism carried on in **Vinduet** led to a number of definitive statements by Brekke which belied Dahl's claims and gave evidence of parallelism between Modernist endeavour in Norway and abroad, particularly in Sweden, although quantitatively Modernist literary production was relatively less than in Sweden or in Denmark.

Most striking has been the shift to Modernist poetry in Iceland. Modernism meant the abandonment of traditional Icelandic verse with its commitment to strict alliterative patterns. For the Modernist, the rules for alliteration, repetition, and rhyme have been replaced by free verse. While there are poets who continue to write in the Icelandic tradition, the advent of Modernism meant in essence a break with the past and an internationalization of Icelandic poetry – that therewith has become less descriptive and more symbolic and, to a certain extent, more metaphorical, although the older poetry could be highly metaphorical in a different way. A dominant tradition once broken can scarcely be re-established as dominant. The disruptive nature of Modernist poetry met with considerable scepticism in Iceland, as might be expected, but it also served as the impulse for a new literature that might more easily become known and accepted in the orchestra of European poetry.

The break with tradition antedated the acceptance of literary Modernism in Iceland, however, for it can be dated from the publication of Steinn Steinarr's **Ljóð** in 1937. While his verse cannot be satisfactorily translated because of the inherent difficulty in reproducing in another language the original unity of diction, imagery, metaphors, and connotations, as well as the ethical substance of a poem, Steinn Steinarr and his successors make Icelandic poetry more accessible than before to the outside world, while Icelandic expository prose, which is less open to experimentation than verse, is also readily translated, as the partial translations of Þórbergur Þórðarson's **Íslenzkur aðall** into five languages – or translations of some stories by the younger Thor Vilhjálmsson into six or seven languages indicate. Icelandic Modernism really came into its own with the publication of Jón úr Vör's **Þorpið** in 1946, a work that in its conception vaguely reminds one of Edward Arlington Robinson or of Edgar Lee Masters' **Spoon River Anthology**.

As events in Southeast Asia tended to engage the conscience of intellectuals young and old in the old world and the new from about 1964 onward, there was a comparable decline in public deliberation and debate of such matters as "poetic Modernism", although numerous books and articles now appeared that attempted to give the movement recognizable contours. In Sweden the periodical **Ord och Bild** may be used to assess the times. While there had been a lively discussion of Modernism in the preceding few years, American intervention in Southeast Asia became a predominant issue during the 1960s and the pursuit of Modernism was left to be carried out by the literary historians. Following the controversy about Vietnam and the supposed overall threat of "Americanism", the matter of women's liberation took the Swedish spotlight to the extent of superseding the earlier, active argument about Modernism. Several other periodicals, notably the Norwegian **Profil**, show a similar turn to the left with concomitant interest in political and social issues as their contributors removed themselves from reflections on the kind of poetry and prose for which the Modernists stood.

The fading of the Modernist movement and in particular the attacks upon Modernist Scandinavian literature make it the easier to put Modernism into focus and to define it. Moreover, definitions are easier to generate in retrospect than when one is in mid-stream. Some striking observations by several Scandinavian critics may be fused with some general observations to answer the query, what was Modernism in Scandinavia? That is, what was the concept of Modernism shared by imaginative writers and critics that permitted the identification of some literary efforts, chiefly poetry, for better or for worse as Modernist? In the first instance, Modernism was understood to be a new direction, a break with tradition, but at the same time it had clear antecedents in the nineteenth and early twentieth century. To this extent it can be said to have shared a common trait with all attempts at the revitalization of belles-lettres at any time; there is a synthesis of certain old ideas and certain new ideas. No definition of Modernism can be given without at least naming Baudelaire as a point of origin and source of inspiration. Certain other writers – Eliot, Pound, Kafka, Rilke – were mentioned again and again by those Scandinavian authors who either called themselves Modernists or were so called by critics. Not all the impulses came from outside Scandinavia however. Among others, Sophus Claussen, Edith Södergran, Elmer Diktonius, and Gustaf Munch-Petersen provided models for young poets.

All the writers mentioned contributed to a freeing from linguistic and literary restraints – a tendency that necessarily would be viewed with scepticism by conservative stylists and by no means a guarantee that the literary production of writers who no longer felt themselves bound by convention **ipso facto** possessed substance and lasting quality. To compound the problem, the movement we call literary Modernism went hand-in-hand with Modernism in the other, and notably pictorial, arts but also including architecture. One Danish critic wrote in 1961 that "modernisme blev opfundet af Mies van der Rohe i 20'erne" ("Modernism was invented by Mies van der Rohe in the 1920s").[16] As art went to the forefront, public appreciation lagged behind. As Poul Henningsen has said, when art is at the forefront, it must offend.[17]

Modernism was offensive on at least three counts that were intrinsic to the movement. First, the creative act seemed to be accepted as a substitute for religion. That is, poetry assumed the role that the German writer Stefan George had wished to give it. Little attention has been paid to Stefan George among the Modernists, but Finn Stein Larsen in his significant chapter on poetry in Jørn Vosmar's **Modernismen i dansk litteratur** (1967) pointed out the parallelism: "at skabe en religion af den skabende proces" ("to create a religion from the creative process").[18]

Second, Modernist poetry suggested not merely experimentation but syntactic dissolution. It was as if words, creations of the human mind, could supersede human **ratio**, although, of course, the "dissolution" was the work of the poets themselves; words remained words and could be moved about in checkerboard fashion. Experimentation with poetic form and especially syntax was the essence of poetic Modernism. Torben Brostrøm has pointed out that, unlike the traditional poet, the Modernist reversed the creative process by putting words together and then deducing what their content was. This technique could also be called impressionistic.

Third, Modernist poetry was considered incomprehensible because of the concatenation of imagery that extended beyond the borders of bourgeois experience and contained no ethical message that might excuse poetic culpability if the end product fitted into some sort of pattern or expressed some grand moral idea. Instead, the Modernist's work smacked of **l'art pour l'art** and displeased both bourgeois and Marxist judges. It had no clear function or use in a material or utilitarian world.

Generally speaking, impartial critics saw in Modernism a step beyond the Symbolism that hitherto had predominated in the **avant-garde** literature of the twentieth century, but there was no agreement as to whether or not Modernism was a rejection of so-called late Symbolism or actually an extension of it. In 1967, Finn Stein

Larsen felt that Erik Knudsen, one of Denmark's early Modernist writers of the post-Second World War period, spoke in "opposition til den sensymbolske æstetik" ("opposition to the late Symbolist aesthetic")[19] despite the fact that Larsen could declare in the same essay that Modernism possessed an intimate connection with Symbolism. The same year in Norway, Odd Martin Mæland took the identical position; for him the beginnings of Modernism were to be found in late Symbolism, whereas the newer Modernists were "anti-symbolsk".[20]

The autonomous role of language seemed apparent to all critics. Mæland states, "Dikterens forhold til språket er blitt identisk med hans forhold til verden" ("The poet's relation to language has become identical with his relation to the world"), while the goal of the poet was "å strukterere meningsløshet og kaos i en estetik, dvs. meningsfull og ordnet språkform" ("to structure meaninglessness and chaos into an aesthetic, ie, meaningful and ordered linguistic form").[21] A defence of the concern with language is found in a single sentence in an essay by the Norwegian Modernist poet Stein Mehren in 1964: "For å kunne uttrykke oss selv, må vi snakke om oss selv, og for å kunne snakke om oss selv, må vi beskrive vårt språk mens vi bruker det! Dette er modernismens store dilemma . . ." ("In order to express ourselves, we must talk about ourselves, and in order to talk about ourselves, we must describe our language while we are using it! That is the great dilemma of Modernism . . .").[22]

In sum, Modernism in the Northern countries comprises parts of a larger European picture. Finland-Swedish writers were the **avant garde** of Modernism – as distinguishable from Impressionists and Symbolists by virtue of their freedom with syntax, their dependency on association, and their compelling imagery – but they were unallied with the mainstream of Scandinavian literature for over a decade. The ascendancy of Modernism in the other Northern nations followed the example of several literatures in the major Western nations – and its fall similarly reflected an international mutation. From early disregard or rejection, it moved into a central position in literary controversy, generated lengthy discussions as to its nature and relation to the other arts – only to acquire respectability and to lose its dynamism and caustic quality. Modernism must now experience either rejuvenation or replacement. In part this is but a matter of terminology. The new term "Post-Modernism" suggests a concept that is more chronological than programmatic.

Notes

1. **Kulturdebat i 20'erne,** edited by Olav Harsløf (Copenhagen, 1976), p.131.

2. Vilhelm Grønbech: **Religiøse strømninger i det nittende århundrede** (Copenhagen, 1922), p.1.

3. Poul Behrendt: "Den fængslede tiger", **Kritik** No. 13 (1970), p.31.

4. Hans Scherfig: "Modernismens tradition" (1965), repr. in Torben Brostrøm (ed.): **Opgøret med modernismen** (Copenhagen, 1974), p.100.

5. Torben Brostrøm: **Modernisme før og nu** (Copenhagen, 1983), p.134.

6. Göran Printz-Påhlson: **Solen i spegeln. Essäer om lyrisk modernism** (Stockholm, 1958), p.148.

7. Odd Martin Mæland: "Modernisme i Norge?" in **Norsk litterær årbok,** (Oslo, 1967), p.185ff.

8. Poul Borum: **Poetisk modernisme** (Copenhagen, 1966), p.9.

9. "Willy Dahl om Bengt Emil Johnsons lyddikt", **Vinduet** 20 (1966), p.248.

10. Ole Langseth: Review of Halldór Laxness: **Islands klokke, Vinduet** 20 (1966), p.177.

11. Paal Brekke, **Verdens Gang,** 13 October 1954.

12. Nils Brantzig: "Ny lyrikk 1960", **Vinduet** 14 (1960), p.283.

13. Stein Mehren: "Modernisme – stagnasjon og fornyelse", **Vinduet** 19 (1964), p.23.

14. Willy Dahl, **Vinduet** 17 (1963), p.308.

15. Paal Brekke: "Regnskapet revidert", **Vinduet** 17 (1963), p.310.

16. Poul Erik Skriver in **Pejling mod modernisme,** edited by Knud W. Jensen (Copenhagen, 1962), p.50.

17. Poul Henningsen, ibid., p.16.

18. Finn Stein Larsen: "Lyrik", **Modernismen i dansk litteratur,** edited by Jørn Vosmar (Copenhagen, 1967), p.27.

19. ibid., p.16.

20. Odd Martin Mæland, p.202.

21. ibid, p.167.

22. Stein Mehren, p.19.

Den hemliga glöden. An Episode in the History of the Reception of Finland-Swedish Modernism

Johan Wrede

Finland-Swedish Modernism played an important role in the invasion of Scandinavia by the international literary revolution in the 1910s and 1920s. It is true that neither Edith Södergran, Hagar Olsson, Elmer Diktonius nor Gunnar Björling, and still less the somewhat younger Rabbe Enckell or Henry Parland, could claim to have been the first Scandinavian Modernists to appear, but it may be said that Finland-Swedish Modernism was the first such movement in Scandinavia which really compelled its restricted cultural community to pay serious attention to a modern literary form of expression. For that reason, as the emergence of Finland-Swedish Modernism came to be recognized, they formed a kind of battering ram which was used to force an entry for Modernism in the other Scandinavian countries.

In 1922 the first generation of Finland-Swedish Modernists improvised its first attack in the bilingual journal **Ultra**. The Finnish contribution to the journal was weaker than the Swedish and when **Ultra** ceased publication after only a few months, Modernism made slow progress in Finnish-language cultural circles. The perspectives of literary Modernism were not strongly represented even among the well-known group of writers who took their name from the album **Tulenkantajat** (1924), where internationalism and cosmopolitanism were highly valued. In Swedish-language cultural circles, however, Modernism gained greater currency in the years which followed. In fact the discussion of Modernism and the divergence of opinion it aroused were so violent that the Modernists who wrote in Swedish felt they were being deliberately provoked. As a response to the culturally conservative attacks, they published the journal **Quosego**, which appeared in 1928–29. This marked the final establishment of Finland-Swedish Modernism.

The reasons for its success lay not only in the energy and the quality of the Finland-Swedish Modernists. The smallness of the cultural circle and the over-heated political and cultural climate during the first decades of the Finnish Republic also played a part. While the Modernist experiments in the rest of Scandinavia could be regarded as a curiosity, the Modernist revolt aroused powerful reactions in Finland. Culture in this former Swedish and – for one century – Russian dependency, which had only recently gained its political independence, naturally sought at the same time to express its own identity. This was calculated to increase the conflicts between competing ideals. Perhaps in part because of its cosmopolitan complexion and its dependence upon foreign models, Modernism was regarded as hostile to national ambitions. Finnish culture was awaiting its dawn while the Swedish feared its dusk. The Swedish-language minority, which had already lost its dominant political position through the electoral reform of 1905, felt a quite understandable anxiety regarding its cultural future, and this also contributed to the vehemence of the reaction directed against the advocates of Modernism. They were regarded as traitors and saboteurs who in a critical moment had chosen a foreign nihilism when they should have been fighting to defend their cultural inheritance. Indignation against the Modernists quite frequently assumed a political colouring. Among the invectives directed against them, "Bolshevism" was one.

In reality none of the Modernists expressed themselves in a markedly political way – not even Diktonius, who was a frequent contributor to **Arbetarbladet** – but the mere connection with the workers' press can have sufficed. That "vår svenska socialist-diktare" ("our Swedish socialist poet"), as Diktonius was called in an article in **Viborgs Posten** (24 October 1925), aggressively attacked Traditionalism and praised Modernism, can have been viewed in the light of the fact that in the Soviet Union the People's Commissar of Education, Anatoly Vasilyevich Lunacharsky, encouraged Modernist art with the expressed aim of undermining the old cultural values. How well the cultural situation in the Soviet Union was known in literary Finland is difficult to gauge. What is certain is that the giant to the East was widely regarded as a threat, and by the Establishment identified with barbarism itself.

Political attitudes also play a discernible role in the remarkable episode which drew attention to Modernism in the autumn of 1925, the sensation surrounding Åke Erikson's collection of poetry, **Den hemliga glöden** (The Hidden Fire). The main figure in this episode was Bertel Gripenberg (1878–1947). Apart from his patriotic verse, this celebrated poet had gained his literary reputation with his sensual epicurean poetry in a **fin-de-siècle** manner, poetry which had both perturbed and excited his bourgeois public. The collections **Rosenstaden** (The Rose City, 1907) and **Svarta sonetter** (Black Sonnets, 1908) were particularly renowned. In **Aftnar i Tavastland** (Evenings in Tavastland, 1911), Gripenberg plucked the strings of the national lyre in a manner which aroused unstinted admiration. He was not an intellectual poet. He was above all a master of artistic form and is still regarded with some justification as one of the great masters of the Swedish sonnet. However, his reactionary political views have made much of his poetry difficult to take, although at that time, during the nineteen-twenties, he was without doubt the most celebrated of the then active Finland-Swedish poets. The first edition of his collected works had appeared as early as 1918, and three years later it was followed by a new edition. As the years passed both the poems and the editions multiplied. His reputation was also high in Finnish-language Finland where he was looked upon as above all a devoted patriotic poet. In Sweden too he had friends and admirers in the literary world.

Nevertheless Gripenberg regarded his poetic career only as a substitute for other, more splendid ones, above all for military exploits. Politically, Gripenberg was a reactionary, and in order to understand his outlook properly it is necessary to see him as a product of the Russian Empire and of aristocratic family traditions. Only thirteen years before his birth, the ancient noble line to which he belonged had been elevated to the rank of a baronetcy. Without doubt, the milieu in which he grew up attached great importance to the significance of descent. His father, the Senator Johannes Gripenberg, had made a fine career as a civil servant. Bertel Gripenberg himself was born in St Petersburg where his father was then working in the chancellery of the Finnish Minister and Secretary of State. This proximity to the imperial milieu influenced Gripenberg's outlook and values throughout his life. He entirely accepted, apparently without reservation, aristocratic behaviour and ideals, both the bad and the good. He maintained an arrogant attitude regarding nobility of birth which became increasingly divorced from reality in a world where socialism and collectivism were advancing and imperial thrones and royal houses were being overthrown. He was not, of course, unaware of what was going on around him, though he was blind to the historical significance of it all; and in his poetry he delivered diatribes against the new age, its baseness, its mediocrity, and (worst of all) its democracy. But if Gripenberg was a Don Quixote, he was a vociferous Don Quixote, who kindled no sympathy for the oppressed and was without chivalry towards his enemies. Of course he had his admirers. The poet's son dedicated an affectionate and admiring portrait to his father,[1] and Nordenstreng, who reveals that the poet was not entirely lacking in personal charm, has bestowed an admiring panegyric upon his poetry.[2] Yet it has been difficult for more recent criticism to discover any traces of greatness in the pathetic poses of this author of the **ancien régime**. Apart from his gift for poetic form, he seems to have possessed no personal qualities likely to awaken sympathy and respect.

Gripenberg's own view of his achievement as a writer as being a surrogate for heroic deeds is revealing in so far as it underlines the role of writing as a compensatory phenomenon in his life. When young he had dreamt of becoming an officer, but delicate and as he himself says in his memoirs, "soft",[3] he had run away from cadet school, tormented by its bullying. He had begun to study law, but dropped his studies without ever obviously having greatly exerted himself. A troublesome eye disease gave him an excuse to ply his books with caution. He did not attain his financial ambitions either. He was compelled to pursue a kind of self-deception in order to obtain a place for himself in his own social group. Friends helped to find him posts as a private tutor or overseer on various estates and manor houses. This made it possible for him to live in the milieu which he always regarded as his own. In time he actually became a landowner himself, even though on a modest scale. It therefore seems natural to interpret the posturing arrogance in Gripenberg as a way of covering up a deep trauma, a profound sense of failure and inadequacy. In the volume of memoirs, **Det var de tiderna** (Those Were the Times), recollections of hunting, of the social esteem he enjoyed as an authority on dogs and horses, have an almost pathetically prominent role. However, it was the Civil War in 1918 which became "the great time" of his life.

In a general psychological sense, one might say that the war provided him with a release from being at odds with the times, a condition once and for all bestowed on him by an anachronistic childhood milieu. In the abnormal situation of the Civil War, and in the White cavalry unit with which Gripenberg served, albeit in the very prosaic duties of a subordinate officer in the supply service, his view of the social order and his highflown heroism could seem reasonable enough. And here he felt at home. In **Det var de tiderna**, he writes:

> Det är påfallande att det inom vårt kära regemente rådde en verklig kavallerianda av det slag som är en styggelse för demokrater och pacifister. Det är svårt att riktigt definiera denna anda, men man kan kanske säga att den bestod av en god portion pojkaktighet, av litet övermod och litet lättsinne. Litet fåfänga och mycket ambition. Den omfattade också en obetingad plikttrohet och ett omutligt allvar när det gällde tjänsten. I såkallade intellektuella kretsar är denna människotyp föraktad och icke populär, för mig är den sympatisk, mera sympatisk än någon annan människotyp. Det var lätt och roligt att umgås med alla dessa raska unga män och med dem slöt jag vänskapsband, vilka aldrig ha brustit. De ha gjort mitt liv rikare, ljusare och gladare och jag bevarar dem alla i vart och tacksamt minne.
>
> (p.244)

It is striking that within our regiment there reigned a true cavalry spirit of the kind that is an abomination for democrats and pacifists. It is difficult to define this spirit exactly, but one might perhaps say that it consisted of a considerable amount of boyishness, a little pride and a little rashness. A little vanity and a lot of ambition. It also encompassed an unquestioning loyalty to an uncompromising seriousness where duty was concerned. In so-called intellectual circles, this human type is not popular and is held in contempt, but for me it is attractive, more attractive than any other type of humanity. It was easy and amusing to live with all these hale young men and I formed bonds of friendship with them that have never been broken. They have made my life richer, brighter, and more cheerful, and I remember each one of them with gratitude.

Gripenberg performed no feats of heroism during the war. Even his prosaic tasks were not carried out with any very great success, as he candidly admits in **Det var de tiderna** (p.246). But in spite of this, for Gripenberg the war was an incomparable time:

När jag ser tillbaka på det korta fälttåget vårvintern 1918 och jämför denna tid såsom den lyckligaste och gladaste tid jag har upplevat. Den står fram i ett alldeles särskilt skimmer, i en underbar strålglans. Det var ett liv på gränsen mellan dröm och verklighet, det var en tid, då årtiondens drömmar faktiskt blevo verklighet. Sådant är en lycka, som det inte förunnas alla människor att uppleva. En sådan inre harmoni som då har jag aldrig förr eller senare erfarit. Jag gick liksom i ett inre rus, jag liksom svävade i högre rymder, trots alla mina prosaiska omsorger, och när det var slut kändes det liksom att stiga ned på marken igen. Sällsamma tid! Sällsamma tid av hopp och förtröstan, av ljusa drömmar, av självförglömmelse och mäktig vilja! Utan minsta tvekan kan jag säga att Frihetskriget för mig verkligen helt och fullt var DEN STORA TIDEN.

(p.252)

When I look back over the short campaign during the late winter of 1918, this period emerges as the happiest and most delightful time I have ever experienced. It stands out in an altogether special light, in a wonderful radiance. It was a life on the border between dream and reality, it was a time when the dreams of decades actually became a reality. Such happiness is not granted to everyone. Such an inner harmony as I then felt I have never experienced before or since. I lived as it were in an inner intoxication, as if I soared in higher regions, in spite of all my prosaic cares, and when it was over it felt like descending to the ground again. Rare time! Rare time of hope and comfort, of bright dreams, of self-forgetfulness and mighty will. Without the slightest hesitation I can say that the war of independence was for me really and truly THE GREAT TIME.

This was Bertel Gripenberg's view in 1943, but it was in no way a late rationalisation of old memories. The war had assumed this dimension in his poetry ever since 1918, in the collections **Under fanan** (Beneath the Banner, 1918), **Efter striden** (After the Battle, 1923), and **Den stora tiden** (The Great Time, 1928), and in the play, **Kanonernas röst** (The Canons' Voice), which appeared in 1922. In this war poetry from the immediate post-war period, Gripenberg also channelled the disappointment felt in conservative "White" circles over the unexpected political changes after the victory. Far from becoming a conservative monarchy in alliance with Germany, Finland became a fairly liberal republic which sought for political support in Great Britain and the USA.

In many respects the poem "När trumpeten ljöd" ("When the Trumpet Sounded") from the collection **Under fanan** may serve as a representative example of Bertel Gripenberg's poetry after 1918:

Det var som att bli ung på nytt
när krigstrumpeten ljöd.
det var som om allt mörker flytt
och mäktigt blodet sjöd.
Det var liksom att kasta av
allt tungt som själen tryckt
och dränka i ett vredgat hav
allt gammalt, fult och styggt.

Det kändes som att lägga bort
sin gamla, slitna själ
och tänka enkelt, klart och kort
och vara sund och hel.
Det var att vilja endast ett,
blott det som plikten bjöd.
Det var så enkelt, skönt och lätt,
när krigstrumpeten ljöd.

(p.48)

It was like being young again, when the trumpet
of war sounded. It was as if all darkness vanished
and mightily the blood seethed. It was like
throwing off everything which pressed heavily
upon the soul, and drowning in a frenzied sea
everything old, ugly, and repulsive.

It felt like putting aside one's old, threadbare
soul and thinking simply, clearly and to the
point, and being sound and whole. It was to will
only one thing, only what duty offered. It was so
simple, fine and easy, when the trumpet of war sounded.

This was the distinctive figure, a symbol of political reaction, who in 1925 played the main role in the debate over Finland-Swedish Modernism.

At the end of September 1925 there appeared from Holger Schildt, the same firm which had published Edith Södergran and Hagar Olsson, and from 1923 Diktonius as well, a volume of poetry comprising 117 pages, and entitled **Den hemliga glöden**, by an author who called himself Åke Erikson. All the 66 poems in the book were written in free verse and the collection was therefore regarded as Modernist. The content gave grounds for the conjecture that the author was a young man who had spent some time in the devastation and gloom of post-war Germany.

The book was first reviewed in **Hufvudstadsbladet** (29 September 1925) by the young critic, Olof Enckell. Enckell would of course later become known as one of Modernism's supporters, but in 1925 he had still not accepted the new poetry. His attitude to Åke Erikson was cautious but positive. He thought that in him one encountered a young poetic spirit who "visserligen ännu ej nått några förfärande djup eller en absolut fulländning" ("had certainly not yet attained any terrible depths or absolute perfection"), but with a turn of phrase which was typical of the period, he concluded by wishing the new poet "Välkommen till Finlands svenska dikt" ("Welcome to Finland's Swedish poetry"). The new critic obviously felt responsible for the continuance of Finland-Swedish culture. But some of Erikson's poems irritated him by a banal Berlin spleen, which had already been exhausted at its point of origin. He also conjectured that Erikson was influenced by Diktonius. In this he was certainly right.

Diktonius reviewed his young imitator the following day in **Arbetarbladet**. He also welcomed the collection, but he pointed out that this poet wrote as well as he could in a Modernist manner, without actually being a Modernist. Erikson had not realised the importance of "concentration" (**koncentration**) for modern poetry. "Det **är** mångt och mycket i hans dikter", Diktonius commented, "men **sker** ganska litet, och den modernistiske dikten är innerst just ett skeende". ("There **is** a great deal in his poetry, but not much **happens**, and the Modernist poem is deep down precisely a happening"). The poet's outlook on life was also "lite si och så" ("not up to much"). Åke Erikson did not realize the significance of what was taking place, he was an anti-bourgeois bourgeois. There was thus a slight but perceptible political element in Diktonius's critique.

Hagar Olsson, **Svenska Pressen**'s enterprising young critic, who in her role as editorial secretary for **Ultra** had been one of the leaders of Modernism, published an enthusiastic review of **Den hemliga glöden** on 3 October, with the title "Vår modernaste skald: Åke Erikson" ("Our most Modern Poet: Åke Erikson"). Her enthusiasm is easily understood. In spite of the recent misfortunes of Modernism, a new champion has suddenly emerged in the ranks. Naturally enough, she found it appropriate to see the new book as a sign that the earlier Modernist attempts had not been lone swallows. A whole generation was now prepared to use the resources of Modernist poetry! As to the nature of these resources, Hagar Olsson's review was not particularly enlightening.

But she found (as it proved with justification) sure signs of Edgar Lee Masters in the young adept to whom she extended a welcome. In his poetry she believed she found, as in all modern poetry (!), a kind of "**surréalisme**", an "over-realistic" ("**överrealistisk**") poetry. The quotation marks are Hagar Olsson's own, and are fully justified. She has not much to say about Erikson's formal qualities, but a good deal about his outlook on life. She considers that like Pär Lagerkvist, Erikson has been strongly influenced by the spiritual struggle which culminated in the World War and the inflamed atmosphere which succeeded it. But Erikson does not entirely fit into the pattern Hagar Olsson wishes to see. The young man is discontented with the world, which is all very well. But he lacks an aim, and that is not as it should be. He wants to destroy all gods "så att man får se att de gamla är bara stoft och de nya bara munväder" ("so that one may see that the old are only dust and the new only empty talk"), she quotes him as saying. "En ganska tröstlös attityd som säkert blir tråkig i längden" ("A pretty desperate attitude which will certainly become boring in the long run"), is her comment. Perhaps the Ultraist, Hagar Olsson, felt herself singled out since she writes "Han driver blodigt med de nya gudarna, som han påstår att man skriker om så förskräckligt. Han insinuerar att de aldrig infunnit sig. Det låter onekligen som ville han bekämpa sig själv" ("He makes cruel fun of the new gods, who he insists people are making such a frightful fuss about. He insinuates that they have never appeared. It certainly sounds as if it is himself he is attacking"). But, she concludes her review, it is precisely Erikson's poetry which is "beviset på att de nya gudarna börjat röra på sig" ("the proof that the new gods have begun to stir").

The difference in critical approach between Diktonius and Olsson is characteristic of the two critics. Diktonius comes with a series of objections and does not try to conceal them: Erikson is not a true Modernist. Hagar Olsson, who clearly sees faults and inconsistencies in the newcomer, tries to explain them away as well as she can. She wants to make the most of his debut for the Modernist cause. Of the numerous reviews which Åke Erikson's book received in the daily press, there are few, apart from the ones already mentioned, of any interest. They contain virtually nothing in the way of literary analysis, but from the point of view of reception history they seem to reveal a certain willingness to accept, if not Modernism in general, then at least this particular Modernist poet. This tolerant attitude may depend upon a view of Erikson as less challenging than Södergran and Diktonius, and in contrast to them, as actually reserved about the new ideals. A reviewer who signed himself "H-ström" in **Viborgs Nyheter** wrote that this volume of poetry was undeniably a work of art "som försvarar sin plats i varje hem, där icke beundran för det gamla hävdvunna utesluter intresset för det nya inom skaldekonsten" ("which deserves a place in every home, where an admiration for what is old and time-honoured does not preclude an interest in what is new in the art of poetry" – 6 October 1925). A reviewer with the initials H.J.W. in **Borgabladet** confessed openly that he could not fully appreciate "denna Södergranpoesi; just **poesien** är förborgad för mig" ("this Södergran-type poetry; it is precisely the **poetry** which is hidden from me" – 10 October 1925). Nevertheless he ends his review with a somewhat naive but positive judgement: "Erikson är en sympatisk diktare, som man läser med stort nöje. Han lovar mycket" ("Erickson is an attractive poet, whom one reads with great pleasure. He shows great promise"). The reviewer in **Vasabladet**, who signs his review "Gn", expresses alarm over the poet's negative attitude to life:

> Och denna inställning inger oro. Skall den unga diktaren, som onekligen intresserar oss, kunna övervinna den och nå en mera fruktbar syn på tingen. Den som har hunnit så långt att han även funnit de "nya gudarna" vara bara munväder tar ju onekligen på sig ett visst ansvar och ställer upp vissa mål för sitt framtida skapande. Alla vänner av den svenska dikten i Finland skulle bli mycket glada om han infriade dem.
>
> (21 October 1925)

> And this attitude gives rise to concern. Will the young poet who undeniably interests us be able to overcome it and attain a more fruitful view of things? Anyone who has come as far as to find that the "new gods" are only empty talk assuredly assumes a certain responsibility and sets up certain aims for his future creation. Every friend of Swedish poetry in Finland ought to be very pleased if he fulfilled them.

Erikson's "negativism" was associated by this conservative reviewer with radicalism, while the newcomer's lack of faith in the new ideals was taken to be a constructive sign.

The same day as this review was published, **Hufvudstadsbladet** contained a short informal article, "Den lovande skalden Åke Erikson" ("The Promising Poet Åke Erikson"). Åke Erikson's collection of poetry was immediately placed in an entirely new light. The article, which was written under the pseudonym of Jack Godeman (Egidius Ginström), revealed that the secretive Åke Erikson was the same person as Bertel Gripenberg. The ensuing laughter was hearty, as was the relief. Jack Godeman's own relief is unmistakable:

> Välkommen gamle mästare av den förnäma sonetten till vår härjade parnass, tack Erikson för att du kom till oss i vårt betryck! Litet skämtsamhet bland muserna sätter en liten i-prick också på vår gråa tillvaro. Välkommen Erikson! Kom till oss som Karlson som Person som Svenson, när gosselynnet åter kommer över Dig. Välkommen som Gripenberg då Du sjunger ur djupet av ett manligt hjärta!

> Welcome old master of the noble sonnet to our ravaged Parnassus, thank you Erikson for coming to us in our distress! A little humour among the muses dots the i of our grey existence as well. Welcome Erikson! Come to us as Karlson – as Person – as Svenson, when the boyish mood takes you. Welcome as Gripenberg when you sing from the depths of a manly heart!

This reference to dotting the "i" (**i-pricken**) is worth noting. Here Ginström takes malicious delight in alluding to Hagar Olsson's review of Erikson's book, where she declares: "Han är pricken på i:et – lika träffsäker och koncentrerad som en sådan bör vara" ("He is the dot on the 'i' – as sure of aim and concentrated as such a one ought to be"). What Ginström may not have observed, but which must have made his allusion particularly painful to Hagar Olsson, was that this formulation in her review contained a concealed polemic against Diktonius. The latter had commented on Erikson's lack of concentration; in its form modern poetry demanded concentration in every word, down to the last dot on the "i". But Hagar Olsson maintained polemically that there was nothing wrong with Erikson's form. On the contrary, it was "överraskande mogen" ("surprisingly mature"). It now emerged that Diktonius had been the more perceptive.

There were probably not many who noticed this particular ignominy. And when a columnist in **Hufvudstadsbladet** varied the theme with "Pricken på å ä ö" ("the dot on the å ä ö" – 23 October 1925), he undoubtedly only had Hagar Olsson's mistake in calling her arch enemy "the dot on the 'i'" in mind.

The dominant reaction among readers of Gripenberg's Modernist book seems to have been that the old master had unmasked both Modernist poetry and the Modernist critics. It was all too easy to write or imitate this kind of poetry. Anyone could do it. And the criticism which had not seen through the forgery was incompetent. That was the general opinion. But on the other hand, the admired poet Gripenberg was a skilful writer. In spite of everything, not just anybody could imitate what he had succeeded in doing.

This circumspect warning against drawing premature conclusions was expressed as early as 22 October 1925 in **Hufvudstadsbladet**. The paper's literary editor had launched an inquiry among a number of literary critics, Yrjö Hirn, Arvid Mörne, Erik Kihlman, Emil Hasselblatt, Bertel Appelberg and Hagar Olsson. With varying degrees of commitment, they explained that Gripenberg's attack, if indeed the book could in fact be regarded as such, was clever but not devastating. The editor had also interviewed Bertel Gripenberg himself by telephone. And even if the text printed in the newspaper does not necessarily reproduce his words exactly, Gripenberg's first public statement on Åke Erikson is of great interest.

In much later accounts of Bertel Gripenberg's coup, **Den hemliga glöden** is sometimes portrayed as nothing but a calculated attack on the new poetry. His own comments, insofar as they are correctly reproduced in **Hufvudstadsbladet**, do not support that impression.

> Idén fick jag i våras, när jag med Runar Schildt och Arvid Mörne besökte Sverige. Talet föll på den moderna dikten och vi kommo överens om att den var ganska lätt att imitera. Efter hemkomsten använde jag lediga stunder till skrivande av fri vers och på tre veckor var **Den hemliga glöden** färdig. Jag började det hela som ett skämt, men snart nog kom allvar med i spelet. Där finnas många strofer, som jag vidkännes såsom mina, i full och ärlig mening – där finnas naturligtvis också rent parodiska bitar, såsom t.ex. "Skrik" och de filosofiska utgjutelserna.
>
> En allvarlig avsikt med mitt försök var att visa, att man kan skriva modernt utan att skriva obegripligt. Den stora koncentrationen som Diktonius predikar, tror jag inte på. Med ord som bortlämnas följer alltid innehåll med. Så blir modernismen ofta obegriplig. Emellertid är jag övertygad om att modern, fri diktkonst kan leda till utmärkt dikt.
>
> Att jag utgav dikthäftet anonymt, berodde på att jag denna gång ville få alldeles ärliga omdömen. Och jag har knappast någonsin förut med större spänning motsett och med mera fröjd läst litterära kritiker än när det gällde den okände debutanten Åke Erikson.
>
> (22 October 1925)

I had the idea in the spring, when I visited Sweden together with Runar Schildt och Arvid Mörne. The new poetry cropped up in our conversation, and we agreed that it was fairly easy to imitate. After returning home, I devoted my spare time to the writing of free verse, and in three weeks I had completed **Den hemliga glöden**. I began it all as a joke, but soon enough an element of seriousness entered into it. There are many stanzas which I acknowledge as my own, with complete sincerity. Naturally, there are also pieces of pure parody, such as "Yell", and the philosophical outpourings.

One of the serious purposes behind my attempt was to show that it is possible to write in a modern fashion without writing incomprehensibly. I do not believe in the great concentration which Diktonius preaches. When words are left out, the content always goes with them. Thus Modernism often becomes impossible to understand. However, I am convinced that a modern, free verse can result in excellent poetry.

I published the volume anonymously because this time I wanted to receive a

> completely honest opinion. And I have hardly ever awaited the outcome with greater excitement, or read the literary reviews with more pleasure than when they concerned the unknown tyro, Åke Erikson.

Gripenberg clearly states here that alongside the element of parody in Erikson's collection, there is also a sincere attempt at employing modern poetic form. All the literary critics who were interviewed also expressed opinions on the same lines: Appelberg was perhaps the least articulate, but he, too, maintained that Gripenberg's experiment could certainly be regarded as having opened the way to modern poetry for the general public. All the others placed great stress on the fact that in the figure of Erikson, Gripenberg was obviously seeking a new form of poetic expression. Naturally enough, Hagar Olsson pointed out, quite correctly in fact, that the attempt had released new springs of creativity in Gripenberg's poetry.

The famous literary historian and aesthetician, Yrjö Hirn, explained that in his opinion Gripenberg did not reach up to the level of Diktonius as a Modernist poet. In so doing he also declared himself to be on the side of Modernism and against its detractors. Arvid Mörne's comments show that he feared a public reaction diametrically opposed to the one at which Appelberg hinted:

> Jag hör ej till dem som ställt mig [sic] avog mot vår ultradikt och jag finner det beklagligt, om skämtet skall leda till ökad oförståelse för den moderna strömningen. Men jag erkänner att så många utmanande ord ha fällts om den gamla dikten, att det är mer är begripligt att en av den gamla stammen en gång ger ordentligt ifrån sig. Gripenbergs gest var fräsch.

> I do not belong to those who have turned me [sic] against our ultra-poetry, and I find it a cause for regret if the joke leads to an increased lack of understanding for the modern current. But I confess that so many provocative words have been said about the old forms of poetry, that it is more than understandable if one of the old school should for once give as good as he got. Gripenberg's gesture was healthy!

There is here an explicit sympathy for Modernism. But one is also aware of Mörne's opinions that Gripenberg's prank was not unprovoked. The Modernists have themselves courted the conflict by their own comments on traditional poetry. It is quite probable that Mörne has Hagar Olsson's and Elmer Diktonius's rough treatment of Jarl Hemmer and Gripenberg himself in mind.

But let us return to Gripenberg's comments in the interview. There he admits to a genuine interest in the Modernist forms of expression, an admission which would not have been appropriate if he had really only had a negative attitude to the poetic resources of Modernism. The material evidence for this is also cogent. Several of the poems in **Den hemliga glöden** express attitudes and ideas which are without doubt Gripenberg's own. It is hardly likely that he intended to ridicule them.

Finally, it is not at all improbable that at the time when **Den hemliga glöden** was written, Gripenberg had already begun work on his translation of Edgar Lee Masters' **Spoon River Anthology** (which was to appear in 1927). Gripenberg would hardly have embarked upon this enterprise without a positive interest in modern poetry.

It is therefore incontrovertible that Gripenberg's attitude to Modernism was divided. During the autumn of 1925, Gripenberg made a couple of statements in connection with the debate about **Den hemliga glöden** which also contain a kind of political animosity towards the Modernists. As we shall see, in a statement from 1926, Gripenberg turns to a certain extent against Modernist forms of expression as well. How is this ambivalence to be explained? Let us first consider Gripenberg's statements.

In **Hufvudstadsbladet** (22 October 1925), Hagar Olsson had argued that in the role of Åke Erikson, Gripenberg had undergone an important poetic renewal, and in connection with this she mentioned the collection **Under fanan**, from which Åke Erikson's book diverges completely as regards both content and temper. "Även våra övriga skalder kunde ju – när de, liksom Gripenberg, tröttnat på de gamla gudarnas trista och desillusionerande sällskap – försöka sig på en liten Eriksoniad. Det kunde hända att även de bleve 'levande' på nytt" ("Our other poets might also try their hand at a little Eriksoniad – when, like Gripenberg, they have tired of the melancholy and disillusioning company of the old gods. It could be that they, too, might come to life again").

This induced Gripenberg to reply in **Hufvudstadsbladet** that he was by no means tired of the old gods:

> Däramot rör sig min av fröken Olsson så förkättrade diktsamling **Under fanan** just om den enda illusion som jag numera har kvar, nämligen den vita illusionen, kampen mot bolsjevismen. Och för denna illusion tänker jag, om jag lever, även framledes **kämpa med klingande meter och rim** (till den lilla kraft och verkan det hava kan), eftersom det sannolikt ej mera skall förunnas mig att kämpa för den med vapen i hand. (27 October 1925)

> On the contrary, my collection, **Under fanan**, which Miss Olsson so decries, is concerned with the only illusion I now have left, that is, the White illusion, the fight against bolshevism. And for this illusion I intend in future, too, if I live, **to fight with ringing metre and rhyme** (with what little effect it may have), since it will probably never again be granted me to fight for it with weapon in hand.

What lay behind this sudden attack? Perhaps it was only that Gripenberg wanted once and for all to stress that the ideals expressed in **Under fanan** had been not in the least affected by his Eriksoniad. But his comment also seems to imply that the modern form was not as ideologically pure as ringing metre and rhyme. Gripenberg drew a similar indefinite link between modern form and armed revolution not long afterwards in a short poem in imitation of Diktonius and containing allusions to his review of **Den hemliga glöden**, which was published in the humorous paper, **Garm**, 1 November 1925:

Tack.

Tack. Diktonius.
för era vänliga ord
om min unga son Åke.
Jo jo, det är kanske litet si och så med
  hans livsåskådning.
den lymmeln
men vad kan man också vänta
med en sådan far.

Men råkas vi nångång skall vi dricka
brorsskål
och ni skall få se
att jag kan vara glad och gemytlig.
Och råkas vi först på barrikaderna
så skall vi sikta på hjärtat
och inte på huvet,
ty det ser så otäckt ut när man skjuter
sönder käkarna
på varandra.
Det säger en som vet.

Thanks.

Thanks, Diktonius,
for your friendly words
about my young son Åke.
Oh yes, his outlook on life was perhaps
not up to much,
the rascal,
but what can one expect
with such a father.
But if we ever meet, we'll drop the
titles
and you will be able to see
that I can be gay and genial.
And if we meet first on the barricades
then we'll aim at the heart
and not the head,
for it looks so horrid when people shoot
each other's
jaws to pieces.
So says one who knows.

I have not been able to discover if something apart from Diktonius's review in **Arbetarbladet** gave rise to this otherwise unprovoked reaction. It appears, however, that when his parodies proved so successful with the public, Gripenberg was inspired to pursue the attack against the two Modernist critics – strictly speaking, the only ones in the country at this time. They had not made any secret of what they thought about Gripenberg's aesthetically and politically conservative poetry. Now he could get his own back. Whether or not there is a question of personal undertones here, these contributions are unequivocal expressions of Gripenberg's intention to distance himself from Modernism.

Precisely as Mörne had feared, **Den hemliga glöden** also gave rise to attacks on Modernism, and above all on Modernist criticism. It is probably a voice from the Christian-conservative phalanx which directed a violent missive against Modernism in **Församlingsbladet** (5 November 1925), using the pseudonym Laicus. On this occasion, Futurism in the Soviet Union was singled out as a parallel phenomenon or example to Finland-Swedish Modernism. Hagar Olsson attempted to refute the attack in the same paper (19 November 1925) by substituting the assailant's ideological and political labels and replacing them with their opposites:

> Reden sammanställningen "futurism, bolsjevism och ateism" faller på sin egen orimlighet. Att den litterära modernismen står i kontakt med tidens sociala strävanden är ett faktum, men det torde man även kunna säga om den moderna kristendomen. Hur oberoende den litterära futurismen däremot är av politiska meningsskiljaktigheter bevisas bäst därav, att den i sitt hemland, Italien, livligt understötts av fascismen och dess hövding Mussolini – vilken hyllats som "den store futuristen" – medan den samtidigt i det bolsjevistiska Ryssland vunnit rätt stor spridning bland poeterna (men ingalunda hyllats av myndigheterna, utan tvärtom av Trotskij utdömts med ungefär liknande ord som skribenten i "Församlingsbladet" använder). Och vad ateismen beträffar, är den beskyllningen så barock, att man knappast kan betrakta den som medveten förvrängning utan snarare som ett utslag av fullständig okunskap. Den individualism som behärskade poesien före "modernismen", den var ateistisk, och det är just mot denna negativa ateism, som den nya poesien vänt sig. Det religiösa inslaget i den moderna poesien torde knappast undgå någon som ens ytligt känner den. Även om detta är en sökande religiositet, som kanske inte godkännes av "Församlingsbladet", borde den dock i stort sett vara mera överensstämmande med kristendomens anda än den iskalla fanatismen hos en krigshetsare, som av politiska skäl skriver i "Församlingsbladets" spalter.

> The combination "Futurism, Bolshevism and Atheism" is bound to collapse under the weight of its own absurdity. That literary Modernism is in touch with the social aspirations of the age is a fact, but one ought to be able to say as much of modern Christianity, too. On the other hand, how free literary Futurism is of political adherence is best illustrated by the fact that in its homeland, Italy, it is vigorously supported by Fascism and its leader, Mussolini – who has been honoured as "the great Futurist" – while at the same time in Bolshevist Russia it has gained considerable circulation among the poets (but has been by no means honoured by the authorities there, and has rather been condemned by Trotsky in approximately the same words as are used by the contributor to **Församlingsbladet**). And so far as Atheism is concerned, the accusation is so baroque that one can hardly regard it as a deliberate misrepresentation, but rather as a manifestation of perfect ignorance. The individualism which dominated poetry before "Modernism" was atheistic, and it is precisely against this negative atheism that the new poetry has turned. The religious element in modern poetry ought hardly to escape anyone who is even superficially acquainted with it. Even if this is an inquiring religious outlook, which perhaps does not meet with the approval of **Församlingsbladet**, it seems nevertheless to be generally more in accordance with the spirit of Christianity than the icy fanaticism of a warmonger, who writes in the columns of **Församlingsbladet** for political reasons.

Församlingsbladet published Laicus's response alongside Hagar Olsson's reply. Somewhat lamely he explained the collaboration between Modernism and Futurism as an accident of history – a political debt of gratitude.

Another exchange which flared up in **Nya Argus** between Hagar Olsson and Hans Ruin might be described as a battle between two antagonistic critics. Ruin was then a rising star in the academic firmament, and had an important position as literary critic in **Nya Argus**. Under the heading "Modernitet och dikt" ("Modernity and Poetry", 1 November 1925), he mounted an attack on Hagar Olsson. He attempted to prove (and in this he was no doubt correct) that Hagar Olsson's opinion of Åke Erikson had been reached in part on the basis of preconceived and fashionable ideas, which she had not analysed in any great depth. Ruin concluded with the formulation: "Eriksönerna av i dag äro kanske i morgon – passerade. Så vida de icke föredraga att redan i dag avslöja sig som de gamla. Var blev förnyelsen, vad gällde skriket?" (" The Eriksons of today may be tomorrow – passé. As long as they do not prefer already today to reveal themselves as the old. What became of the renewal, to what did the outcry amount?") And Ruin quotes Erikson's poem "De nya gudarna" ("The New Gods", **Den hemliga glöden**, p.105f) where the new gods are declared meaningless.

This led Hagar Olsson to reply with an attempt to demonstrate the weakness of Jarl Hemmer's poetry. She took her cue for this association from Ruin himself. "Jag tror för min del", Hagar Olsson wrote, "att Eriksönerna av i dag kunna vara lugna även om de, som dr Ruin säger, skola vara passerade i morgon. Det är ändå bättre än att vara passerad redan i dag". ("For my part, I believe that the Eriksons of today can rest easy even if, as Dr Ruin says, they should be outmoded tomorrow. It is still better than being already passé today"). Her response was published in **Nya Argus** on November 16, accompanied by a reply from Ruin. Ruin makes it clear there that he had attacked Modernist criticism, not modern poetry, but he nevertheless subsequently intimates that modern poetry is more uncontrolled and easily tempts the writer "till förhastade alster" ("to over-hasty products"). This remarkable opinion seems not to have been confined to Ruin. Among the academic critics however Hirn and Mörne took a more favourable view of Modernism.

Den hemliga glöden also prompted numerous commentaries by professional literary critics in Sweden.[4] The reactions there were similar to those in Finland. It was considered obvious that Åke Erikson had not only been intent on making fun of Modernism. Many of his poems had to be regarded as having been written with total seriousness, and the new form had clearly extended the poet's range.

Discussion of **Den hemliga glöden** then gradually died down. But in spring 1926 the collection was awarded a prize by the state panel for literature. The Modernists took this as a deliberate provocation. Thus the collection gained a new topicality. See Olof Enckell's foreword to the facsimile edition of **Quosego** (1971, p.xvii).

It is likely that this award was partly responsible for the appearance of Rabbe Enkell's subsequently so well-known article, "Gammalt nytt och verkligt nytt i poesi" ("The Old New and the Really New in Poetry"), which he managed with his brother's help to have published in **Hufvudstadsbladet**, 5 December 1926. In his article Rabbe Enckell tried to show that Gripenberg had failed as a Modernist: "Erikson har trott sig skriva eller parodiera modernistisk vers. Men den modernistiska dikten har fullständigt undangått hans försök att efterbilda den till väsendet, har gjort det blott typografiskt" ("Erikson believed he was writing or parodying Modernist poetry. But the Modernist poem has completely eluded his attempt at imitating its essential nature, he has done so only as regards the typography"). The difference consists in Erikson only having attained the level of descriptions while a Modernist poem ought to lead the reader into an active participation "som gör sig sinnligt förnimbart i de tillspetsade uttrycken" ("which makes itself physically perceptible in the heightened expressions").

Diktonius had of course said something similar, but Gripenberg did not remember that. Rabbe Enckell's contribution stimulated Gripenberg to write a new article. Once again he said that the Modernistic poems in Erikson's collection were "till en del skämt men till en del allvar" ("in part a joke, but in part seriously intended"). This time Gripenberg himself pointed out that the change of form also gave his poetry a new content: "Jag fann under arbetets gång att jag med fördel kunde använda mig av den fria versen för behandling av vissa motiv, som jag inte hade kunnat eller velat använda i metrisk vers" ("In the course of my work I found that I could turn the use of free verse to my advantage for the treatment of certain motifs which I had not been able, or had not wished, to use in metrical verse"). This is a remarkable admission, and one which was fully justified. As a poet Gripenberg had previously been confined to a certain limited area of poetic expression, an artificial and ornate style, which also limited the scope of his subject matter. Now he was able to write plainly and to purge his heart of agonies and fears. Nevertheless, Gripenberg expressed in his reply more clearly than he had done before the same mistrust of free verse which Hans Ruin and many others had put forward: it was all too easily mastered, all too easy a source of humbug.

There are several remarks in Bertel Gripenberg's response to Rabbe Enckell which are of great interest in so far as reception history is concerned. He says that the book fulfilled a purpose by "på ett iögonfallande sätt påpeka den måttlösa överskattning, vilken tack vare en ensidig kritik kommit den modernistiska dikten till godo" ("calling attention in a striking manner to the excessive over-estimation which had been conferred on Modernist poetry thanks to a one-sided criticism"). He maintains that in both **Svenska Pressen** and **Hufvudstadsbladet**, literary criticism had been in the hands of confirmed apostles of the Modernist gospel. This "svåra missförhållande" ("most unsatisfactory state of affairs") is, he says:

> ägnat att hos vår fåtaliga svenska publik minska intresset för vår även annars med svårigheter kämpande svenska litteratur. En godtrogen publik som till äventyrs av dess kritikers ensidiga beröm låter locka sig att köpa en för vanlig sund människa onjutbar och obegriplig bok, reagerar helt naturligt mot en sådan besvikelse.

> calculated to diminish the interest among our small Swedish public for our Swedish literature, which also has to contend with many other difficulties. An unsuspecting public which perchance allows itself to be enticed by the one-sided praise of these critics into buying a book which is unpalatable and incomprehensible to a normal healthy person, quite naturally reacts against such a disappointment.

This situation, Gripenberg continues, is "för vår svenska kultur farligare än alla äktfinnars angrepp" ("more dangerous for our Swedish culture than all the attacks of Fennophiles").

Gripenberg was certainly correct that Hagar Olsson in **Svenska Pressen** was the mouthpiece of Modernism. That he also transformed Olof Enckell into a prophet of Modernism must have depended almost entirely upon the fact that his brother, Rabbe's, article had been taken by **Hufvudstadsbladet**. Diktonius had of course been immeasurably more active in **Arbetarbladet**, but Gripenberg presumably regarded the readers of this newspaper as in any case beyond the pale. There was a grain of truth in Gripenberg's account of the situation, in so far as Modernism received strong support in the most important organs of the press. But purely in terms of volume, Modernism was clearly at a disadvantage. Of the leading critics among those who were most unsympathetic to Modernism, the most distinguished was probably Hans Ruin, who also possessed an exceptionally good forum in **Nya Argus.** However, what the commotion over **Den hemliga glöden** does demonstrate is that in 1925 the critics were in general more inclined to accept a modern poetic form than at Edith Södergran's debut in 1916.

Gripenberg's reply to Rabbe Enckell's article is, however, a characteristic example of the ways of thinking and seeing which made Modernism so controversial in Swedish-language Finland, and which thereby paradoxically assisted the success of Modernism.

In the present context it is not possible to analyse the poems of **Den hemliga glöden** more closely. It should, however, be clear that the book consists in part of parodies, partly of poems which are seriously intended. In contrast to Hagar Olsson, Diktonius and Rabbe Enckell had seen the faults in Erikson's Modernist form. Erikson lacked "concentration"; in other words, his poetry was not sufficiently dynamic. To a certain extent, Gripenberg had himself given that accusation even more force by proclaiming that "concentration" was superfluous and deleterious to sense (see above). Many of the poems in **Den hemliga glöden** in fact appear mechanical and, as Diktonius and Rabbe Enckell argued, they are only descriptive. This is in general true of precisely those poems which are **not** parodies, for example "Råttkungens fångar" ("The Rat King's Prisoners") and even "Gammal historia" ("Ancient History"), which Ruin again admired.

One of the poems had been singled out by Gripenberg as unequivocally a parody, namely "Skrik" ("Yell", p.42). In conclusion, I wish to pay a little attention to this poem.

Om jag skriker på gatan
så tar mig polisen
och bötfäller mig.
Och om jag reser ut på bondlandet
och skriker i den tysta skogen,
så skrattar alla ekorrar och trastar
åt en sådan dåre.

Men på ett järnvägståg
som brusar fram med full fart
under jorden,
står jag på plattformen
mellan två vagnar.
Tåget dånar som en orkan,
dess dån dränker alla ljud –
där står jag och skriker
med fulla lungor.

If I yell out in the street, the police will
arrest me and fine me. And if I go out to the

country and yell in the silent forest, all the
squirrels and thrushes laugh at such a fool.

But on a railway train which rushes on at full
speed under the earth, I stand on the platform
between two carriages. The train roars like a
hurricane, its roar drowns every sound – there
I stand and yell with all my lungs.

In his article "Modernitet och dikt" ("Modernity and Poetry"), Hans Ruin sees this poem as a kind of telling and unintentional example of the weakness of Modernist poetry:

> Det är, om man vill, känsla så det förslår. Men denna känsla är absolut opersonlig, bara ett skrik. Och att bara konstatera känsla, rus eller vad man vill kalla det hos en konstnär, är som att hos en sångare konstatera röst i dess rent fysikaliska mening, ljud alltså. Någon konst är det ännu icke, all lyckad formulering till trots.
>
> Men det är sant – den nya poesin vill på många håll just slunga det personliga. Det är det kollektiva som skall fram, massans själ, alltså de förenklade, odifferentierade tonlägena. Men att vara som de andra är nu som förr det lättaste. Det förklarar mer än en gång framgången med Eriksons parodi.

> This is, if one likes, emotion with a vengeance. But this emotion is absolutely impersonal, only a cry. And only to notice emotion, intoxication or whatever one likes to call it in an artist, is like noticing the voice in its purely physical sense in a singer, simply as sound. It is not yet a question of art, irrespective of a few happy phrases.
>
> But it is true, the new poetry wants in many respects to throw the individual away. It is the collective which must emerge, the soul of the masses, therefore the simplified, undifferentiated tones. But to be like other people is now as always the easiest of things. It explains the success of Erikson's parody on more than one occasion.

Thus far Ruin. But "Skrik" is among the most frequently quoted and anthologized of these poems. It does not appear to have been thought a bad poem. For my part, I find it is possible to interpret it as an interesting psychological document. Ruin is very likely correct in seeing the poem as an attack on the inarticulateness which Gripenberg believed he had discovered in Modernism. There is no doubt that Gripenberg sincerely meant that anyone who cries out inarticulately is rightly fined and regarded as an idiot. But if one interprets the poem with a kind of hermeneutic of suspicion, the last verse concedes that the experience of inarticulateness is justified. When the "I" of the poem cries out in the roar of the hurricane, it is a liberation from constraint. Psychologically, "Skrik" seems to me a key poem in **Den hemliga glöden**. Here feelings which have been repressed in restricting forms really flare up. Here Gripenberg, who has grown up warped by outmoded conventions, finally breaks for a moment out of the prison which has ruined him. The inarticulate cry which drowns in the roar of the onrushing train – a true Futurist situation – is for once an unadorned expression of the hidden fire in the poet Bertel Gripenberg, the fire which he normally sought to make acceptable in the form of elegant sensualism, fanatical militarism, and an attitude of provocative reaction. It must have been a relief for Gripenberg to publish Åke Erikson's poems. This is where the seriousness of his Modernism is to be found. And it is psychologically interesting that this was the poem which Gripenberg singled out as a parody! For in this perspective, "Skrik" seems to be Åke Erikson/Bertel Gripenberg's most honest poem.

In that case, Hagar Olsson's reference to "surréalisme" hits the mark, although without her being aware of it. Bertel Gripenberg's intervention in the debate about **Den hemliga glöden** is from this point of view reminiscent of an attempt at concealing what has inadvertently been stated too clearly. The warlike gesture in the poem "Tack", and the grand flourish against Bolshevism in his reply to Hagar Olsson, can both be seen as the poet's attempts once more to close a rent in the military tunic covering the hidden fire which has momentarily shone out.

Thus I am inclined to interpret **Den hemliga glöden** as a very personal document; a document which the author would not have been able to produce, had not Modernist style – even in an imperfectly conceived form – come to his rescue. In return, and obviously at least in part against Gripenberg's own intentions, the stylistic experiment of the conservative Gripenberg seems also – far from having demonstrated the superficial facility of Modernist style – to have advanced public interest in Modernism itself. By placing the debate about Modernism at the centre of public concern over a long period, the collection played an important role in the history of the movement's reception.

Notes

1. Erwin Gripenberg: "Bertel Gripenberg" in **Min Far. Kända män skildrade av sina barn**, edited by Aili Lindfors (Helsingfors, 1948).

2. Rolf Nordenstreng: **Bertel Gripenberg och hans skaldskap** (Stockholm, 1921). Other works on Gripenberg are Magnus Björckenheim: **Bertel Gripenbergs ungdomsdiktning** (Helsingfors, 1950); Jarl Louija: **Symbolit ja kielikuvat Bertel Gripenbergin tuotannossa** (Helsinki, 1959). Of far greater interest than these works is the section on Gripenberg in Lauri Hyvämäki: **Sinistä ja mustaa** (Helsinki, 1971).

3. Bertel Gripenberg: **Det var de tiderna** (Helsingfors, 1943).

4. Among the reviewers of the work in Sweden were Nils Erdman (**Nya Dagligt Allehanda**), B. Bäckström (**Göteborgs Handels- och Sjöfartstidning**), Bo Bergman and Ruben G:son Berg (**Aftonbladet**). This material has not been available to me, and I base my discussion on accounts of their articles in **Hufvudstadsbladet**, 15, 23 November, 12, 16 December 1925.

Translated from Swedish by Michael Robinson.

Isak Dinesen v. Karen Blixen: Seven Gothic Tales (1934) and Syv fantastike Fortællinger (1935)

Elias Bredsdorff

On 10 April 1931 Karen Blixen wrote from Africa to her brother Thomas Dinesen that she had begun to write a book; she wrote it in English because then it might have a better chance of selling, but she feared that the language might present difficulties. An American publisher to whom she had sent part of the manuscript was very encouraging, however, and found the leisurely style and language "exceedingly attractive". When she had finished the first of the **Seven Gothic Tales**, her English friend in Kenya, Hugh Martin, vetted the manuscript.

Some early drafts were written in a mixture of Danish and English, however, and a draft for the beginning of "The Old Chevalier" (then entitled "Nocturne") is entirely in Danish.

After **Seven Gothic Tales** had been published first in America and then in England and praised also for its language by several critics (e.g. the **New York Herald Tribune Books**: "a masterpiece of English prose produced by one whose native tongue is not English", and the **Times Literary Supplement**: "she may be congratulated on her ability to write a foreign language with such easy fluency")[1] and after the Danish papers had discovered that the pen name of "Isak Dinesen" covered Baroness Karen Blixen, she said in an interview in the Danish paper **Politiken** that she did not think the book would have sold in Denmark, "otherwise it would, of course, have been easier for me to write it in Danish, even though I am capable of writing in English".[2]

When – after the fabulous success in the English-speaking world of **Seven Gothic Tales** – Karen Blixen decided to allow her book to appear in Danish she decided to rewrite the book herself after having first rejected an attempt by the poet Valdemar Rørdam to translate the tales into Danish: she also found it impossible to co-operate with the author Jesper Ewald in translating the English version into Danish. To the latter she wrote (22 February 1935) that she had arrived at the conviction, "at jeg kan dansk, –ikke alene lige saa godt som engelsk, men jeg vil næsten tillade mig at sige: saa godt som nogen dansk Skribent" ("that my command of Danish is not only as good as that of English, but I am almost prepared to say: as good as that of any Danish writer").[3]

In her brief introduction to the first edition of **Syv fantastiske Fortællinger** (dated September 1935) Karen Blixen wrote that she had not thought that her book would interest Danish readers, but now that it was being translated into other languages it seemed natural that it should also be published in her own country. "Jeg har da gerne villet, at den i Danmark skulde komme som en original dansk Bog og ikke i nogen, om end aldrig saa god Oversættelse" ("I have wanted it to appear in Denmark as an original Danish book and not in any kind of translation, however good").

Professor Knud Sørensen in an important essay entitled "Studier i Karen Blixens engelske og danske sprogform" has dealt with **Seven Gothic Tales** and **Syv fantastiske Fortællinger** from a philological and stylistic point of view and also with another of her main works in English and Danish, **Den afrikanske Farm** and **Out of**

Africa.[4] I quote from his concluding summary concerning Karen Blixen's first book:

> Den engelske sprogform i den amerikanske førsteudgave af **Seven Gothic Tales** er præget af arkaismer og af afvigelser fra standard-engelsk, herunder danismer. En del af afvigelserne er blevet fjernet i senere engelske udgaver. Den danske version, **Syv fantastiske Fortællinger**, er for adskillige passagers vedkommende fri fordanskning, med en hel del udvidelser og præciseringer, snarere end oversættelse. Mange passager i de dele af teksten, der kan betegnes som egentlig oversættelse, er præget af anglicismer. Hos Karen Blixen kan der således påvises en dobbeltvirkende interferens: når hun skriver på engelsk, optræder der danismer, og når hun oversætter sit engelske til dansk, er det til en vis grad præget af anglicismer. Tilbage står – fra en sproglig synsvinkel – billedet af en forfatter, der besidder en høj, men ikke fuldkommen, grad af tvesprogethed.

> In the American first edition of **Seven Gothic Tales** the English language form is characterized by archaisms and departures from standard English, including Danicisms. Some of the depártures have been removed in later English editions. The Danish version, **Syv fantastiske Fortællinger**, is a free Danish rendering as far as a number of passages are concerned, with a number of expansions and more precise formulations, rather than actual translation. Many passages in the part of the text that may be termed translation proper are characterized by Anglicisms. Thus it is possible to point to a double interference: when she writes in English, Danicisms occur, and when she translates her own English into Danish a certain number of Anglicisms occur. From a linguistic point of view one is left with the image of a writer possessed with a high degree of, but by no means perfect, bilingualism.

Knud Sørensen's approach is mainly a philological one, even when he gives examples of the liberties Karen Blixen took when she recreated **Seven Gothic Tales** in Danish.

While entirely agreeing with the conclusions drawn by Professor Knud Sørensen, my main task in this article is to examine the deliberate changes in words, sentences and paragraphs which Karen Blixen made when she rewrote her **Seven Gothic Tales** in Danish and the effect these changes have had on both style and content.

In the following I shall discuss these textual changes as falling into eight different categories.

1. Deliberate changes of dates, numbers, names, etc.

Most of these changes are unimportant for the understanding of the tales. It does not matter whether a certain episode took place in May 1823 or 1821. In the English text the highest wish of a young woman is to have nine children, but in the Danish version to have twelve children. "A man about fifty" is changed into "en Mand paa omkring tresindstyve Aar", and in another story a cardinal's age is changed from seventy to sixty. And it is irrelevant whether one must wait "a million years" (as in the English text) or "ti Millioner Aar" (as in the Danish version) for something to happen. Why Karen Blixen decided to change "toward spring" into "hen paa Efteraaret", or "eight years ago" into "for tretten Aar siden" we shall never know. It may be just a whim that "two old oaks" in Danish becomes "to store Elme", that a "large elm tree" becomes "et stort Akacietræ", and that "the grey and black horses" appear in Danish as "den brune og den skimlede Hest". In "The Monkey" she writes: "Again a verse from Euripides ran through his head", but in "Aben" the same line reads: "Igen randt et Par Linjer af Aeschylos ham i Tankerne". There are plenty of such unimportant changes, probably made simply for the sake of making a change.

2. Paragraphs without any counterpart in the English version

After the title character in "Den gamle vandrende Ridder" has given an account of the night he spent with the young, unknown girl, the Danish version continues:

> Ja, ser De, her er min Historie egentlig forbi. Der sker ikke mere i den, der skete ikke mere. Men jeg, som fortæller den for første Gang, jeg kan daarligt slutte af her, hvis De da har Taalmodighed til at høre paa mig længere. Jeg vilde gerne, for en Gangs Skyld, fortælle, hvordan det siden gik mig selv.
>
> For hvad hende angaar, kan jeg ikke give Dem nogen Forklaring.

There is nothing corresponding to these six lines in "The Old Chevalier".

"Et Familieselskab i Helsingør" contains various paragraphs to which there are no counterparts in the English text. In "The Supper at Elsinore" the two De Coninck sisters complain to Madam Bæk, the housekeeper, that there is so much lying, so much falsehood, in the world, and she comforts them by saying: "Well, what of it? It would be worse still if it were actually true, all that they tell us". Up to this point the Danish text follows the English text, but there is nothing in the English text corresponding to the following seven lines in the Danish text:

> Og naar de skreg op om alle unge Mænds Usselhed, gav hun dem et hvast Sideblik og sagde: "Ja, jeg tror dog nok, at de er tre Procent mere til at stole paa end Pigerne", – og dette kunde nu lyde som et ualmindelig fint Regnestykke, men Madam Bæk, der i det de Coninckske Hus havde hørt meget tale om Procenter, havde ikke klart for sig, hvad Ordet betød, men mente, at de var tre Gange saa paalidelige.

Occasionally an addition in the Danish text may be due to the fact that in her English original text Karen Blixen was forced to leave out an untranslatable Danish nursery rhyme. Thus it is only in the Danish text of the same tale that we find these lines:

> Til den helt unge Generation beskrev Frøken Eliza, med en yndefuld, lille Figureren, sig selv i to Linier af den gamle Dansevise:
>
> "Her er gamle Lisemor,
> hun er Dukke fra ifjor".

3. Sections of English text with no counterpart in the Danish version

Whereas there are many examples of essential additions in the Danish text, there are only few examples of the original text being longer than the Danish text. A fairly isolated example is the following paragraph from "The Supper at Elsinore", to which there is no counterpart in the Danish version: "A sailor, or a sailor's daughter, judges a person of the other sex as quickly and surely as a hunter judges a horse; a farmer, a head of cattle; and a soldier, a rifle".

After having mentioned the name of Struensee Karen Blixen found it necessary to inform her non-Danish readers: "This doctor was much in advance of his time". This information has been removed from the Danish version, presumably because she found it unnecessary for Danish readers.

4. Verse quotations in English and Danish

It seems obvious that when writing **Seven Gothic Tales** Karen Blixen often had Danish nursery rhymes or other verse lines in mind and tried to recreate them in English.

In "The Poet" the following lines occur:

Early at midsummer-dawn the cock was crowing,
Twenty-nine cradles had I set a-going,

which turn out to be her own translation of the Danish verse which is quoted in "Digteren":

Midsommernatten var ikke lang,
to og tyve Vugger satte jeg igang.[5]

Later in the same story there is what appears to be an incomplete nonsense verse, which runs like this:

Make ten of one
and two let be.
Make even three.
And nine is one,
and ten is none. . . .

Only in the Danish version entitled "Digteren" is full justice done to the stanza:

Find Mening i,
et Een er Ti.
Gør To'en fri
og Tre'en lig,
saa er Du rig.
At een er Ni
og Nul er Ti,
forstaar Du vel? –
Her har Du Heksens lille Tabel.[6]

A few lines later the following four verse lines are quoted:

My mother, the harlot
who put me to death,
My father the varlet
who eaten me hath. . . .

But the solution is found in the Danish version, where the original verse is quoted in its entirety:

Mor voldte min Død,
Min Fader mig nød,
Min Søster Malene
Tog alle mine Bene
Og lagde dem i en Silkeklud
Og bar dem under Enebærbusken ud,
Kvirrevit, da blev jeg en smuk, lille Fugl.[7]

It also happens that Karen Blixen was unable to find suitable rhymes in English and had to turn a Danish couplet into English prose. In "The Monkey" the Prioress says to Boris: "For where we have entered in, there also we withdraw". It is only in the Danish story, "Aben", that one realises that she had a Danish rhyme in mind:

Thi vi maa ind og ud ad samme Vej,
det første staar os frit. Det andet ej.[8]

And in "The Poet" she writes: "The Councillor remembered two lines of an old poem:

The gentle zephyrs cease to rock
Newly inslumbered Nature's cradle".

In "Digteren" she writes: "Justitsraaden mindedes to Linier af et gammelt Digt:

Zephyrer standse med at vugge
den nys indslumrede Natur. . . ."[9]

It seems fairly obvious that in all these cases the Danish poem or the Danish verse lines have been in Karen Blixen's mind when she wrote **Seven Gothic Tales**, and it is only in the Danish recreation of the story that the original quotations are revealed.

The following quotations, from "The Poet" and "Digteren" respectively, also illustrate the fact that the English verse lines are a translation of a Danish nursery rhyme:

He remembered the nursery tale of the thief who has stolen a fat sheep and is eating it in the moonlight.	Han mindedes Børnerimet om Tyven, der har stjaalet et fedt Faar og sidder og spiser det i Maaneskinnet. Spot-

Mockingly he holds up a bit of fat mutton to the moon, crying: See, my dear What I here Can with pleasure offer. And the moon replies: Thief! beware! Key, with care, Burn that stupid scoffer.	tende holder han en fed Bid op mod Maanen og raaber: Se, hvor fed, kom herned, tag den Bid i Munden, og Maanen svarer: Vogt Dig, Tyv, Nøgle flyv, til hans Kind er funden.

5. The Danish text expanded and changed

There are innumerable examples of the Danish text in **Syv fantastiske Fortællinger** having been radically changed in comparison with **Seven Gothic Tales**, and additions having been made to which no counterparts exist in the English text.

The following examples are based on a comparison between "The Roads Round Pisa" and "Vejene omkring Pisa":

She is jealous of the most absurd things.	Hun søger med Lys og Lygte efter Genstande for sin egen usalige Angst og Gru.
an enormous bed with red curtains	en mægtig Himmelseng med falmede, grønne Gardiner
Will you, as a man of noble birth and high mind, undertake to find her and bring her here?	Ved første Øjekast saa jeg, at De var en Mand af ædel Byrd og Tankegang, og forstod, at dette var et lykkeligt Møde. Vil De nu paatage Dem at finde hende og bringe hende til mig?
and I had liked him very much	og jeg selv havde ikke kunnet sige mig fri for en Svaghed for ham
I told the Prince that we must hurry up with the wedding, and I kept Rosina shut up in the house	Jeg forklarede Prinsen, at vi maatte fremskynde Brylluppet, men overfor ham fremstillede jeg med Omhu Rosinas Forelskelse i sin Fætter som en Flyvegrille, og jeg holdt Pigen under Opsigt i min Villa
To make Rosina happier...	For at opmuntre Rosina, som hang med Hovedet og mistede sit Huld og sin skønne Farve...

A faithful maid gave them away to me	Rosinas Kammerpige, som dog havde noget Begreb om Pligttroskab tilbage, kom grædende ind til mig og fortalte mig om deres Flugt
when the statue is finished in marble or bronze, he breaks us all up	naar endelig Statuen staar færdig i Marmor eller Bronze, hvad han nu vil have den i, da slaar han os alle i Stykker og fejer os tilside, og bedre er vi da heller ikke værd
God therefore likes us in the same way as we like our dogs: because when he is in high spirits, we are in high spirits; and when he is depressed, we are depressed	Derfor elsker Gud os, ligesom vi elsker vore Hunde, thi naar han er i højt Humør, da er vi straks lystige og logrer med Halen, men naar han er nedslaaet, fordi der har ramt ham en eller anden himmelsk Modgang, da er vi med det samme bedrøvelige til Mode og tænker paa Selvmord
I want you to take it with you.	. . . vil jeg bede Dem tage imod den. Gid den maatte styrke Dem i Troen paa Tilværelsens Mirakler, og Skæbnens hjælpende Haand.

The following examples are all taken from "The Old Chevalier" and "Den gamle vandrende Ridder":

(an old theme:) namely whether one is ever likely to get any real benefit, any lasting moral satisfaction, out of forsaking an inclination for the sake of principle	Det var selve den klassiske Konflikt mellem Lyst og Pligt, som Herkules ogsaa kom ud for paa Skillevejen, som den gamle Herre i fuld Alvor tog op til Behandling. Lønner det sig at forsage en Tilbøjelighed for at gøre det, der staar for os som det Rette?
this was enough, I imagine, to make her lie awake at night thinking out new methods of punishing me	at det iblandt fik hende til at være mere fortryllende imod mig end nogensinde, og iblandt ogsaa til at ligge vaagen om Natten for at udtænke nye Torturmetoder
The girl had not been afraid, but I had been afraid. I had asked: "What am I to pay for this?"	Thi Nathalie havde ikke været bange, men jeg havde været bange. Det er en frygtelig Ting at vide god Besked. Jeg havde vidst Besked med, at man

	her i Verden maa betale de Varer, man faar, noget over Værdien; jeg havde taget Lektioner i denne Regnekunst. I Nathalies Arme, med hendes friske Aandedrag imod min Skulder, havde jeg spurgt, med Tvivl i Hjertet: "Hvad skal jeg betale for dette?"

Here are some examples extracted from "The Deluge at Nordeney" and "Syndfloden over Nordeney":

In the fall of it the man Kasparson had been killed.	(de saa) at af de to, som havde boet der kun den ene var i Live. De faldt paa Knæ og græd af Glæde, da de hørte, at det var Kaspersen, Kardinalens Tjener, som var knust under det faldende Tag, og at han selv endnu var imellem dem.
For it is the consciousness of hidden power which gives courage.	Det er Bevidstheden om den skjulte Styrke, som giver os Mod. Eller hvad er vel Trumf-Es paa Bordet imod en lille, dulgt Trumf i vor egen Haand?
she had to create herself.	hun skulde skabe et Menneske, sig selv, og er det ikke meget forlangt af en ung Pige, at hun skal gøre det helt paa egen Haand?

The next examples are taken from "The Dreamers" and "Drømmerne":

If he ever found in himself any original taste at all, he made the most of it.	Hvis det nogensinde hændte, at han virkelig var i Besiddelse af en eller anden selvstændig Tilbøjelighed, gjorde han det mest mulige ud deraf, og stillede sandelig ikke sit Lys under en Skæppe.
Now he would by no means let me go in alone.	Nu var der ikke Tale om, at han vilde lade mig gaa videre alene. Det, jeg her efterstræbte, det var af alt for høj Værdi for mig, til at han kunde overlade mig det.

She meant Pelegrina to be, likewise, the most beautiful, elegant, and fashionable of women.	Hun vilde have, at Pelegrina stadig skulde være den smukkeste og eleganteste af alle Kvinder, en Modedukke, hvis Mage ikke fandtes fra Rom til Paris.

And here are a few examples from "The Poet" and "Digteren":

No beggar could look worse.	Ingen Slagsbroder, der var smidt ud af Kroen, ingen udbrudt Slave med Justitsraadens eget Navn under den Politiplakat, som satte en Pris paa hans Hoved, kunde se værre ud.
He is, surely, the type of human who ought to have a guardian angel, and it would be noble in you if you would assist me in saving him by reading him a little sermon.	Han er et Menneske, der burde have en Skytsengel, og det vilde være ædelmodigt af Dem, om De nu straks vilde give Deres ærbødige Tjener Bevis paa, at De i Fremtiden vil dele hans Interesser. Kør med mig til Hirschholm, min elskværdige Fransine, og hold en lille Straffeprædiken for den unge Mand.

6. The English and Danish text have totally different meanings

There are several cases where the Danish text expresses entirely different meanings from the English original text. Here are a few examples:

as in a second youth ("The Roads Round Pisa")	som en Mand, der lykkeligt har overstaaet en svær Sygdom ("Vejene omkring Pisa")
Now it did not enter my head any more that it ever has to alter my answers in church. When the priest says: "O God, make clean our hearts within us", I have never thought of telling him that it is not needed, or to answer anything whatever but, "And take not thy Holy Spirit from us". ("The Chevalier")	ligesaa lidt som det nogensinde er faldet mig ind at ændre mine Svar i Kirken, og naar Præsten siger: "O Herre, handl ikke med os efter vore Synder", da at svare andet end: "Og betal os ikke efter vore Misgerninger". Der var ikke noget i Verden, som jeg i det Øjeblik frygtede mere, som mindre var efter mit eget Hjertes Ønske, end at give hende tyve Francs, – men mit eget Hjertes Ønske, det var jeg nok

	færdig med her. Og det var jo det, som vi talte om, De og jeg, til at begynde med. ("Den gamle vandrende Ridder")
(Abelone was) of an extraordinary physical strength ("The Poet")	(Abelone var) særdeles net i Dragt og Væsen ("Digteren")
"Oh, I am tired of them", she exclaimed, passionately. ("The Poet")	"Ak, saadanne Mennesker, saadanne Dumme-Petere", sagde hun. ("Digteren")
He said, very slowly: "There the moon sits up high. You and I shall never die". ("The Poet")	Han fremstødte meget langsomt: "Der er Haab i Liv og Død. Vor Trøst er det, som vi betød. Og det har ingen Nød". ("Digteren")

7. The Danish text better than the English text

There are many examples of the Danish text being superior to the English text, from a linguistic, artistic and stylistic point of view. Here are some examples:

The Roads Round Pisa How much, he wondered, did this bravo of his, who had been so handsomely paid by him, make out of the affair from the other side?	**Vejene omkring Pisa** For hvilken Sum solgte min Skyldner mig?
a very gentle and sweet smile	et Smil saa værdigt som en Oldings, og blidt som et lille Barns
The Old Chevalier as if she herself had been another young woman of fashion, her rival, or as if she herself had been a young man who envied him his triumphs.	**Den gamle vandrende Ridder** som om han havde været en anden ung Skønhed og Løvinde i Paris, en Rivalinde, eller som om hun selv havde været en ung Don Juan, som hendes Mands Laurbær ikke havde tilladt at sove.
under laws of earthly reason	underlægge det den jammerlige mandlige Logiks Love
blending the deadly brew for his mistress, out of envy for her breasts	han er ude efter de Urter og Tyvsfingre, hvoraf han skal brygge Gift til

	sin Elskerinde, hvem han misunder hendes smalle Midje og Barm
your world does in reality look as if it had been made experimentally. But to us even the ideas of old Mr Darwin were new and strange.	at Deres Verden virkelig ser ud, som om den var blevet skabt forsøgsvis. Det er saaledes, at Nozdref's Kok lavede Suppe, og kom Peber, Salt og Urter deri, efter hvad han havde ved Haanden – "en eller anden Smag maa der vel komme ud deraf". – Men for os var selv gamle Herr Darwins Teorier nye, og højst problematiske.
in the course of this tale she imitated the monkey in the funniest and most gracefully inspired manner that one can imagine.	Hun begyndte sin Fortælling med et bedrøveligt lille Ansigt, men efterhaanden som hun selv blev revet med deraf, efterlignede hun Aben for mig med den mest fortryllende, yndefulde, genialt pudsige Mimik, man kan tænke sig.
The Monkey the golden bottle	**Aben** den dunkeltgyldne Flaske
had given her a shock	havde rystet hende og krænket hende som et frækt Overgreb
He had himself as a boy tried to run away from home to be a sailor.	Han havde selv som Dreng haft mange Drømme om Havet, ja, var engang løbet hjemmefra for at gaa tilsøs, var blevet hentet tilbage, og havde græmmet sig i lange Tider.
This maiden	Denne vildt jomfruelige Skabning
"What?" she asked. "Shall I have a child from that?"	"Et Barn?" sagde hun, "som kommer til at mangle to Fortænder? – Hvad er det, De vil bilde mig ind? Jeg har ikke været i Kapellet paa Hopballehus, og vor gode Pastor har ikke læst et Ord over hverken ham eller mig. Nej, Tante, kør nu smaat."

She was aware of him as a being outside herself.

Hun var sig ham bevidst som en selvstændig Skabning udenfor hende selv, hun erkendte ham som et Menneske, og dette greb ham paa den besynderligste Maade, som om ogsaa han erkendte sig som Menneske for første Gang i sit Liv.

The Deluge at Nordeney

Though not beautiful, she had the higher gift of seeming so

Syndfloden over Nordeney

Hun var vel ikke smuk, men hun førte, som man dengang sagde, en smuk Person

Why, he (God) knows it (the truth) already, and may even have found it a little dull.

Ak! Ak! Herren kender jo i Forvejen Sandheden, og hvis han har gabet en Smule over den, skal jeg ikke sige noget til det.

for it is the consciousness of hidden power which gives courage.

Det er Bevidstheden om den skjulte Styrke, som giver os Mod. Eller hvad er vel Trumf-Es paa Bordet imod en lille, dulgt Trumf i vor egen Haand?

tell me who you are, and recount to me your stories without restraint.

Fortæl mig da, hvem De er, og beret mig Deres Historie, frimodigt og uden Bagtanker, som om vi i Paradiset sad sammen og genopfriskede vort Jordeliv.

the deep vaults seemed to dig themselves down toward the pit.

de dybe Hvælvinger borede sig som rasende besatte Muldvarpe lige mod Helvede.

The Supper at Elsinore

a spiced odour of sanctity, which the young people remembered all their lives.

Et Familieselskab i Helsingør

en fin krydret Duft af Hellighed, en Odor sanctitatis, som sad de unge Mennesker lifligt i Næsen hele Livet igennem.

I could not have her without cheating law and order a little

jeg kunde ikke faa hende uden at gaa imod Loven og Profeterne

The Dreamers
I have never been able to get anything out of the orthodox love affairs of my country, which begin in the drawing-room with banalities, flatteries and giggles, and go through touches of hands and feet, to finish up in what is generally held to be the climáx, in the bed.

Drømmerne
Jeg har aldrig været istand til at faa noget ud af mit eget Lands Kærligheds-historier, der begynder omkring Dag-ligstuebordet med Komplimenter og Øjekast, for gennem en lang Række Visitter, Buketter og smaa Kys i Krogene at ende der, hvor de almindeligvis regnes for at opnaa deres Klimax, i Brudesengen.

moving and organizing things with her little hands

der med sine smaa Hænder rullede Laviner og satte dem i Gang

in all this splendour of woman's beauty, the magnificence of bosom and limb, and radiance of eye, or lip, and flesh

i al denne Legemspragt – Barmens og Lemmernes Herlighed, Haarets Rigdom, Læbernes Glød som en Skarlagens Snor, Øjnenes Glans under de lange Øjenhaar og Hudens fine Hvidhed

I have been told that lions, trapped and shut up in cages, grieve from shame more than from hunger.

Det er blevet mig fortalt, at fangne Løver i deres Bure lider langt mere af Skam end af Sorg.

The Poet
And in this still world there is a tremendous promise.

Digteren
Og denne farveløse Verden indeholder et mægtigt Løfte, en alvorsfuld, henrykkende Forjættelse.

Young Anders also confused the registers in the office

Den unge Anders Kube lagde sammen, hvor han skulde trække fra, i Protokollerne paa Kontoret

"But light", he said, "terrible as an army with banners".

"Men let er hun", sagde han, "let. Kong Salomon vidste, hvad han sagde: Forfærdelig som de, der er under Bannere".

and four bottles of communion wine would be no more to her than four bottles.

og fire Flasker Altervin var for hende ikke mere end fire Flasker anden god Vin til een Rigsdaler Flasken.

Hirschholm seems to have a little talent for scandal.

Hirschholms Kaffesøstre løber idag med en halv Vind.

(the principle) was plain dogma, indisputable.

det (princippet) var ikke Filosofi, det var Teologi, Modepynt, Kogekunst, den skinbarlige Trolddom.

The long wet grass was of a luminous green.

Det lange, vaade, dunkle Græs var lysende, livfuldt grønt, som Juveler i Skygge.

8. Entire long paragraphs totally rewritten

The Chevalier

Indeed, the haughtiness of the pretty young girl, or the old lady's majesty, existed no more on account of personal vanity, or on any personal account whatever, than did the pride of Michelangelo himself, or the Spanish Ambassador to France. However much greeted at the banks of the Styx by the indignation of his individual victims with flowing hair and naked breasts, Don Giovanni would have been acquitted by a board of women of my day, sitting in judgement on him, for the sake of his great faith in the idea of woman. But they would have agreed with the masters of Oxford in condemning Shelley as an atheist; and they managed to master Christ himself only by representing him forever as an infant in arms, dependent upon the Virgin.

Den gamle vandrende Ridder

Ikke hverken de unge, smukke Pigers Overmod, eller de gamle Damers nedladende Majestæt hvilede paa personlig Forfængelighed, de havde overhovedet ikke mere med det personlige Element at gøre end en Ambassadørs Pomp og Pragt, naar han overrækker sine Akkreditiver. Selve deres Yndigheder tilhørte dem, saa at sige, ikke personligt, de var Regalier, de var hellige Kar, som de vogtede og pudsede. Os dømte de efter vor Rettroenhed overfor Begrebet Kvinde, og saa overbærende som de hver for sig kunde være imod os, saa taalte de, i denne Egenskab, ikke det mindste Kætteri. Og lad det saa være rigtigt nok, at Don Juans Ofre, taget en for en, med flyvende Haar og blottet Barm, skriger deres Forbandelse imod ham fra den anden Bred af Styx, naar han skal sættes over, – et Nævningeraad af min Tids Kvinder, som skulde have siddet til Doms over ham, vilde have frikendt den Forfører, som til det sidste med Lyst satte tre Snese Aars Koketter paa sin Liste, for hans Tros Skyld, for hans urokkelige Troskab imod Kvindeligheden og Begrebet Kvinde. Og Kristus selv kunde de kun faa i den rette Harmoni med deres store Dogme, ved, med megen Snildhed, i Kunst og Poesi og from Børnelærdom bestandig at holde ham tilbage i den helt spæde Alder, i den hellige Jomfrus Arme.

The Poet

Anders had not been spoiled by fate. If he had been spoiled at all, it had been done by other powers. He had felt the common lot of his kind, that is: to be, as if he had been made out of some stuff essentially different from the rest of the world, invisible to other people. When he had met Fransine, she had seen him. Without any effort, her eyes had taken him all in. This sort of human non-existence of which he had at times been tired had come to an end, and he had promised himself much from his newly gained reality. If she was marrying the Councillor, and turning away her eyes, it was only reasonable that he himself should turn elsewhere.

Digteren

Anders var ikke blevet forkælet af Livet. Han havde som mange andre af sin Art følt, at han maatte være gjort af et helt andet Stof end andre Mennesker, og det af et Stof, som havde den Egenskab at være usynligt for dem. De kunne ikke se ham, selv om de vilde. Han havde lidt bittert, han havde ogsaa undertiden leet ad sin Ensomhed, i det lange Løb var den blevet ham tung at bære. Men da han havde truffet Fransine, havde hun ligestraks set ham. Uden ringeste Anstrengelse havde hendes klare Øjne opfattet ham helt og holdent. Han var henrykt blevet til foran dem, og hans Ikke-Tilværelse var forbi og helt glemt i samme Øjeblik. Han havde ventet sig meget af sin nyopdukkede Eksistens. Hvis hun nu vilde gifte sig med Justitsraaden og for evigt vende Blikket fra ham, kunde han lige saa godt gaa sin Vej af sig selv. Det, som Folk i Almindelighed kalder Døden, det var jo ikke af mere gennemgribende Betydning end en fornyet Usynlighed og Udstødthed, og det smertede mindre.

In order to understand the next extract from this tale it is necessary to know that in despair Anders has got drunk, something which Fransine has not discovered, however. But she is aware that there is something wrong, and she asks him, "her voice filled with laughter and tenderness: 'Anders, what is the matter?'" But here Karen Blixen's sense of English failed her, for she allows Anders to reply as if Fransine had asked him: "Anders, what is matter?" – a misunderstanding which would never occur in English. In the Danish version Fransine asks: "Anders, hvad gaar der af dig?"

And now follow the two entirely different continuations of the story in English and in Danish:

Anders was a long time in answering her, then he spoke very slowly: "Yes", he said, "you may well ask, Fransine. It is important. The spirit we need not talk about; it is not dangerous. But what is the matter? It has many strange things about it. It is the phlogiston of our bodies, being of negative weight, you might say. That is easy to understand, of course, but it gives you such great pain when it is demonstrated upon you. First we are treated by fire – burned, or roasted slowly, that comes to the same thing – and even then we cannot fly".

Anders var længe om at svare, og da han tilsidst talte, gik det kun langsomt for ham.

"Spørger Du om det, Fransine?" spurgte han. "Det skulde Du dog nødig gøre, det er jo det, Du ikke vil vide noget af. Der gaar meget af en Mand mellem Aar og Dag, – Sved, for Eksempel, og Taarer, for at regne saadanne Sager op, som man kan tale om i Fruentimmerselskab. Og jeg kunde fortælle Dig, hvis Du virkelig vilde vide Besked, – men det vil I jo ikke, – at det, som gaar af os, det er vort sande Væsen og Liv, langt mere end det, som bliver tilbage, og som I vil sætte i en Lænestol og trække broderede Morgensko paa. Det er jo ligesaadan med min Bøsse her", fortsatte han langsomt og stolt "det er jo det Skud, som gaar af, – siden Du taler om at gaa af, – og som rammer, der er dens sande Væsen og Sjæl, – og Kolben og Laasen og Løbet selv, de er alene til for Skuddets Skyld. Et Næveslag, hvis jeg engang, inden jeg dør, faar Lejlighed til at give et, det er mig, det er dog mit sande Væsen, mere end min Haand. Et Kys", – han sad længe ganske tavs, "et Kys, ser Du, det er mig mere end min Mund er det. Møget paa Møddingen, det skal I ikke rynke paa Næsen af, det er Køernes sande Væsen, og ved Gud noget af det bedste, de gør".

After a short paragraph, which is almost identical in English and Danish, the story continues:

Fransine smiled at the young man. Like many women, she did not recognize the symptoms of drunkenness in a man. "Oh, Anders", she said, "you do not know it, so I will tell you:

Fransine smilte til Anders; som mange Kvinder var hun ude af Stand til paa egen Haand at bedømme, om en Mand var beruset. "Ja, Anders", sagde hun, "tror Du, jeg har glemt, at

I can fly. Or nearly. Old ballet-master Basso said to me: 'The other girls I have to whip up, but I shall have to tie two stones to your legs soon, or you will fly away from me'".

Du har grædt for min Skyld? – Begge mine Hænder var vaade af Dine Taarer, da Du var gaaet i Formiddags, jeg holdt dem op til min Mund. Jeg ønskede ikke engang, at Du skulde holde op at græde. – Dumme Fransine, dumme dumme Anders. Og hvad skal jeg ønske nu? – Naar Du er glad, da har jeg ikke noget mere at ønske i Verden".

"Jo, for saa kommer der noget lige paa tværs af det hele, Fransine", sagde Anders, med eet dybt modfalden og fortvivlet, "og det er Naturloven om Phlogiston. Den er ikke just saa svær at forstaa, naar man læser om den, men den er svær at finde sig i, naar de praktiserer den paa os selv. For skulde man ikke mene, at et Menneske, som bliver brændt levende op for at fornøje Guderne, – enten det nu bliver i lys Lue eller paa en langsom Ild, det kan være lige meget, og en af Delene gør de i hvert Fald ved os, – at han i det mindste skulde have det at trøste sig paa, at nu bliver han lettere og lettere, og tilsidst kan han vel flyve. Men saadan gaar det ikke, Fransine, for Phlogiston, det Djævelskab, har negativ Vægt, og jo mere der brænder bort af os, jo tungere bliver vi. Ja, det er tungt, der er ikke andet at sige til det".

"Jo, men Anders", sagde Fransine, "Du ved det ikke, saa skal jeg fortælle Dig det. Jeg kan flyve, eller næsten flyve. Gamle Balletmester Basso sagde til mig: 'De andre Piger maa jeg piske op, men jeg bliver snart nødt til at binde to Sten til Dine Ben, ellers flyver Du jo fra mig'".

Conclusion

Karen Blixen was right when she said that her command of Danish was as good as that of any Danish writer, but she was wrong when she said that her command of Danish was as good as that of English; in fact her command of Danish was much better than that of English. And she was right when she stated that the Danish version of **Seven Gothic Tales** was going to be an original Danish book and not just a translation, however good.

Superficially the seven tales in the English and Danish versions are identical in the sense that the plot and the main structure correspond to one another in each of the seven tales. But the manner of telling the story, the language, the style, the artistic subtleties, differ in many respects. She was at home with the Danish language in a way she was not at home with English – in spite of the fact that her mastery of English has been praised by many. When Karen Blixen rewrote **Seven Gothic Tales** in her native language as **Syv fantastiske Fortællinger** it was not only a "Gendigtning" (to use her own expression) – it was an improvement of what had already been hailed as a literary masterpiece.

To English and American readers part of the fascination of **Seven Gothic Tales** may have been the suggestion of a foreign accent in the language, the fact that it was **almost** perfect English, in the same way as it has been pointed out time and again that one of the charms of Joseph Conrad's prose was that the reader was aware of the fact that English to him was an acquired language, not the author's native language. When a foreigner is praised for his or her good command of English, then there is behind the compliment a hidden suggestion that it is not English. Maurice Chevalier's French accent was a tremendous asset when he spoke or sang in English. Karen Blixen's Danish accent in her English prose may have been an extra advantage to a great writer.

In his diary for 19 December 1845, Hans Christian Andersen wrote that in Berlin he had heard Jenny Lind singing in the Opera, and he added, "She sings in German in the same way, I think, as when I read my fairy tales, the homely accent shines through, but, as they say about me, that's exactly what makes it interesting".

An English friend of mine, who is an experienced translator from Danish into English, pointed out a number of unidiomatic expressions, un-English phrases and word orders in **Seven Gothic Tales** and wondered why all such things had not been corrected by Karen Blixen's American publisher. He added, "Perhaps he thought that the bad English was part of the originality (le style est la dame!). Perhaps some critics did, too".

Karen Blixen was completely at ease when she wrote in her own language. That is why the original text sometimes looks more like a translation, and the translation like an original text.

Notes

The editions used for the above essay are the following: **Seven Gothic Tales**. By Isak Dinesen. Putham, London, 1934. Karen Blixen: **Syv fantastiske Fortællinger.** Gyldendal, Copenhagen, 1961 (reprint of first Danish edition, 1935).

1. **New York Herald Tribune Books**, 8 April 1934. **Times Literary Supplement**, 6 September 1934.

2. **Politiken**, 1 May 1934.

3. For the factual information contained in the first paragraphs I am indebted to an article by Grethe Rostbøll in **Blixeniana 1980** (pp.29–269), "Om 'Syv fantastiske Fortællinger'. Tilblivelsen, udgivelsen og modtagelsen af Karen Blixens første bog".

4. **Blixeniana 1982**, pp.263–308. The section concerning **Seven Gothic Tales** had originally been published in **Danske Studier**, 1981.

5. The Danish quotation is taken from a ballad, originally of Norwegian and Swedish origin.

6. Quotation from P. Hansen's Danish translation of Goethe's **Faust** (the Witches' Kitchen).

7. Quotation from the Danish translation of one of Grimm's **Märchen.**

8. Quotation from P. Hansen's Danish translation of Goethe's **Faust** (Mephisto's words to Faust).

9. Quotation from a paraphrase of the Danish ballad entitled "Aage og Else" by Niels Wivet.

Knut Hamsun's **Sult**: Psychological Deep Structures and Metapoetic Plot

Atle Kittang

It is generally agreed upon today that **Sult** belongs to those literary works from the end of the nineteenth century which mark a turning point in the history of the European novel. Knut Hamsun himself may have been well aware of this. In a letter to Georg Brandes, written shortly after the publication of **Sult**, he repeatedly insists that he has **not** wanted to write a conventional novel with "marriages and picnics and parties".[1] This antagonistic attitude towards the prevailing norms of narrative art is also a constant theme in those famous lectures from 1891, by means of which Hamsun confirmed his position as the **enfant terrible** of the Norwegian literary institution.[2]

But to describe **Sult** negatively as an early specimen of the "anti-novel" does not bring about any clearer understanding of the book's positive characteristics. What kind of literary work is **Sult**? What makes it such an original and astonishingly **modern** novel?

One answer, which has the advantage of being close to Hamsun's own general ideas of the novel during the early 1890s, is that **Sult** belongs to the tradition of psychological Naturalism. In his letter to Georg Brandes Hamsun compares his book not only with Dostojevsky's **Crime and Punishment**, but also with the **Germinie Lacerteux** of the Goncourt brothers, that is, with a kind of literature where conventional novelistic plots and characters have been replaced by documentary investigations into the peculiarities of physio-psychological cases. If we add to this all the years of starvation and misery which characterize Hamsun's own biography during the difficult years of the 1880s, we get the model from which so many interpretations of **Sult** have taken their general idea: **Sult** is a documentary study, based upon personal experience, of how starvation affects a sensible mind.

Such a reading may explain some of the links between the novel and its author, and thus shed some light upon that ambiguous space between fiction and autobiography from which so many of Hamsun's works seem to emerge. But it does not explain the structural aspects of the book, nor its deeper thematic purport. And consequently, the interpretation it offers of the main motif, of the novel's hero, and of its plot, is too narrow and even superficial.

Let me substantiate this claim by a couple of preliminary remarks touching upon some selected aspects of the novel.

First of all, there is no simple relationship between the hero's hunger and his peculiar destiny. Starvation is of course – as in "real life" – the sympton of a real physiological lack. But on the other hand, not all the strange behaviour and reactions of the hero can be explained as consequences of his hunger. Hamsun himself has emphasized this, in a letter from 1888, when the first fragment of what was to become the novel of **Sult** was published in the Danish review **Ny Jord**.[3] On the other hand, the motif of starvation goes far beyond the mere "Naturalistic" or physiological level of meaning. In Hamsun's book hunger is also a metaphor, signifying a more fundamental lack or emptiness, which is a central aspect of the psychological deep structures investigated by the writer.

Secondly, **Sult** is not only a meticulous **report** on the psychology and social situation of a starving young man. It is also a very complex **story** which takes us from early autumn to winter, from a situation of misery where (to a certain extent, at least) the starving hero nevertheless is able to write creatively, and into a deep crisis where he destroys his manuscripts and abandons his artistic vocation. But paradoxically enough, this disastrous course of events also brings our hero from a state of total **isolation**, living in a narrow shed of a room which is compared to a coffin (the meaning of this simile will be discussed later on), and to a kind of social **integration** within the grotesque family in the lodging house in Vaterland. On his way from isolation to integration, the hero has to pass through the tragi-comic love affair with Ylajali. The profound irony of the whole thing is, however, that our hero meets his Waterloo as an artist in a situation where starvation has ceased to be any problem, since food is regularly provided by the landlady. Thus, **Sult** appears as a kind of negative novel of education, or better: its plot is that of a true novel of disillusionment.

My third preliminary remark concerns the narrative form of the novel. **Sult** is in fact a first person novel of a rather peculiar kind. It starts in retrospect: "Det var i den tid jeg gik omkring og sultet i Kristiania, denne forunderlige by som ingen forlater før han har fåt mærker av den. . ." ("All of this happened while I was walking around starving in Christiania – that strange city no one escapes from until it has left its marks on him. . .").[4] But this narrative distance between the first person narrator and the "narrated I" is gradually abolished. Throughout the rest of the novel the narrative movement, that is, the totality of the text, is inseparable from the gradual development of a consciousness. This consciousness, without name and biographical antecedents, is nothing but a string of perceptions and fantasies, ambitions, desires and strange kinds of behaviour, kept together as a textual unity by two permanent traits only: its inner lack (symbolized by the hunger, but also specified as erotic desire) and its artistic drives.

This peculiar and productive connection between the textual movement of the novel and its all-dominating consciousness is seen very clearly in the opening sequence of the book, where the hero is presented in a state of awakening:

> Jeg ligger våken på min kvist og hører en klokke nedenunder mig slå seks slag; det var allerede ganske lyst og folk begyndte å færdes op og ned i trapperne. Nede ved døren hvor mit rum var tapetseret med gamle numre av "Morgenbladet" kunde jeg så tydelig se en bekjendtgjørelse fra fyrdirektøren, og litt tilvenstre derfra et fett, bugnende avertissement fra baker Fabian Olsen om nybakt brød. [. . .]
>
> Det lysnet mere og mere og jeg gav mig til å læse på avertissementerne nede ved døren; jeg kunde endog skjælne de magre, grinende bokstaver om "Liksvøp hos jomfru Andersen, tilhøire i porten". Det sysselsatte mig en lang stund [. . .]. (p.7)

> I was lying awake in my attic room; a clock struck six somewhere below; it was fairly light already and people were beginning to move up and down the stairs. Over near the door, where my wall was papered with old issues of the **Morning Times**, I could make out a message from the Chief of Lighthouses, and just to the left of that an advertisement for fresh bread, showing a big, fat loaf: Fabian Olsen's bakery. [. . .]

> It was getting lighter, and I concentrated on the advertisements by the door; I could even read the slim, mocking typeface declaring: "Shrouds available, Miss Andersen, Main Entrance, to the right". That satisfied me for a long time [. . .].
> (p.3f)

The sequence describes a transitional situation where light gradually replaces darkness. Out of this transition the text's own consciousness is born, a psychological being is created, so to speak, from the nothingness of the night, from the nothingness which marks the limits of the text's own life. Gradually we learn about his social situation as an unemployed writer with no money and with nothing to eat. But here, at the starting point, what is worth noticing is that when this mind comes to life, it is as a consciousness of symbols, and more precisely of linguistic symbols, of texts. What is grasped as the light gets clearer, are fragments of the **Morning Times**: letters, messages, information.

These textual fragments papering the walls of his coffin-like attic are certainly not chosen at random. They refer in fact to central themes and motifs in the novel. The baker's advertisement prefigures the dialectics of starvation and nourishment; later, when the hero wishes to mark his difference from the rest of humanity, he will envisage himself as a shining lighthouse, standing erect in the middle of an ocean of human misery. And the grim, mocking letters announcing "Shrouds available" are in fact the first signals of the death motif, pointing to one of the secret thematic centres of the novel. But what strikes us most strongly here in this opening sequence, is not so much the motifs as the textual character of their introduction. Let me put it this way: just as the reader's mind constitutes itself as a consciousness of the text called **Sult**, so the text's own consciousness is born as a consciousness-of-text. The passage from nothingness to being, symbolically expressed through the awakening of the hero, is in both cases mediated through the mode of textuality.

This interpretation may appear like pure sophistry, like a splitting of the hairs of Hamsun's text. However, my reason for insisting upon the initial scene of awakening the way I have done, is not only to exemplify how narration and story are closely interrelated right from the beginning of the novel. The awakening scene also offers the first indication of the basic psychological structures which form the main field of investigation in Hamsun's text. The story of a starving writer and his tribulations in the city of Christiania is, on a more profound level, a novelistic analysis of what a philosopher would have described as a phenomenology of consciousness. Instead of presenting us with a fully-fledged character, the text shows how a human subjectivity is beginning to take shape, in a dialectic interplay between the nothingness of pure consciousness and some exterior fragments of symbols, that is, of meaning. It is not a process where the outer world is firmly grasped by a mind already formed as an identity, nor is it a process where the mind seeks to identify with the outer world. It is rather a process where the mind's access to the world is mediated through an order of symbols which makes recognition possible and, simultaneously, separates consciousness from reality itself. Rephrased in the terms of Lacanian psychoanalysis (which has contributed essentially to my subsequent interpretation), what is at stake in the opening sequence of **Sult** is the constitution of the subject through the mediation of The Other – locus and carrier of the Symbolic Order.

Let us leave for a while the philosophical subtleties and take a brief look at some of the episodes following immediately after the awakening scene, describing the first of those aimless walks through the streets of Christiania which form the main substance of the book.

This first walk is characterized by a series of **meetings** which all make a strong impression on the hero. He meets an old woman in front of a butcher's shop; then he begins to follow an old cripple; the third meeting is with two women, one of whom will reappear later as Ylajali; and finally, on a bench in a park, he experiences a rather strange "meeting with himself".

There are considerable differences between these four meetings. The early glimpse of Ylajali introduces the thematics of desire in **Sult**, and triggers off what eventually will develop into a veritable "novel within the novel". The hero's meeting with himself is the first indication of a particular existential experience – a state of harmonious narcissism, sometimes with pantheistic shades – which never ceases to appear in Hamsun's work. Against the apparently positive characteristics of these episodes (– apparently, because all states of harmony in Hamsun are more or less brutally undercut by some hidden conflict), the two other meetings strike us as unambiguously negative.

However, the four meetings have at least two important traits in common. In some way or other, they all express what I would call "mirror experiences", and they all involve a curious tension between identification and aggression. It is as if the recognition implied in every specular experience is hampered by an irresistible impulse to split and separate.

Actually, both the old woman and the cripple embody in a rather grotesque way the hero's own existential condition. In the eyes of the old woman, "still full of sausage" (p.7), he finds a reflection of his own hunger. And the cripple, who by the way is compared with a "huge limping insect" (p.9), is not only as penniless and hungry and miserable as the hero himself. He also appears as a curious prefiguration of the hero's physical defect during the tragi-comic love game with Ylajali towards the end of the novel. Suffering from an injury in his leg after an accident in the street, the hero will in turn appear like a limping insect in his erotic pursuit of Ylajali around the family table in her apartment. Hamsun critics like Aasmund Brynildsen have recognized in such episodes the motif of the Double, so important in several of Hamsun's early novels.[5] (Another example would be the couple Nagel/Minutten in **Mysterier**). However, an adequate interpretation of this motif will have to consider its other face also, that is, the role played by aggression. The meeting with the old woman and her look "still full of sausage" fill the hero with disgust and nausea; and his reaction towards the cripple is aggressiveness pure and simple. In fact, if the two figures can be interpreted as grotesque mirror images of the hero's own condition, it is as if he needs to maintain a distance towards these exterior images of himself: as if the irresistible fascination has to be controlled by an act of mental separation.

This is even more striking in the park episode, where the hero "meets himself":

> Idet jeg ligger i denne stilling og later øinene løpe nedover mit bryst og mine ben lægger jeg mærke til den sprættende bevægelse min fot gjør hver gang pulsen slår. Jeg reiser mig halvt op og ser ned på mine føtter og jeg gjennemgår i denne stund en fantastisk og fremmed stemning som jeg aldrig tidligere hadde følt; det gav et fint, vidunderlig sæt gjennem mine nerver som om det gik ilinger av lys gjennem dem. Ved å kaste øinene på mine sko var det som jeg hadde truffet en god bekjendt eller fåt en løsreven part av mig selv tilbake; en gjenkjendelsesfølelse sitrer gjennem mine sanser, tårerne kommer mig i øinene, og jeg fornemmer mine

sko som en sagte susende tone imot mig. Svakhet! sa jeg hårdt til mig selv og jeg knyttet hænderne og sa svakhet. Jeg gjorde nar av mig selv for disse latterlige følelser, hadde mig tilbedste med fuld bevissthet; jeg talte meget strængt og forstandig og jeg knep øinene hæftig sammen for å få tårerne bort.

(p.19)

Lying in this position, letting my eyes float down over my chest and legs, I noticed the tiny leaping movement my feet made every time my heart beat. I sat up partway and gazed down at my feet. At that moment a strange and fantastic mood came over me which I had never felt before – a delicate and wonderful shock ran through all of my nerves as though a stream of light had flowed through them. As I stared at my shoes, I felt as if I had met an old friend, or got back some part of me that had been torn off: a feeling of recognition went through me, tears came to my eyes, and I experienced my shoes as a soft whispering sound coming up towards me. "Getting weak!" I said fiercely to myself and I closed my fists and said, "Getting weak." I was furious with myself for these ridiculous sensations which had overpowered me even though I was fully conscious of them. I spoke harsh and sensible phrases, and I closed my eyes tightly to get rid of the tears.

(pp.23–24)

What is described here is a profound experience of existential integrity: a unification in the Ego of something that hitherto only existed as "some part of me that had been torn off", a harmonious identity between mind and body which enables the hero to mirror himself in the separate parts of his body. But the feeling of integrity is triggered by an experience of alienation (the feet lead so to speak their own "leaping" life), and this initial splitting or separation is repeated at the peak of ecstasy, when the "I" turns aggressively against his own existential harmony, scolding himself as a father would scold an irresponsible child, driving as it were a wedge of language into the whispering and speechless communication between mind and body.

The meeting with the unknown ladies follows the same pattern. The moment of physical contact with Ylajali's arm, comparable to the hero's awareness of his own feet in the park, creates immediately a kind of erotic communication which is repeated as a specular communication between the two of them, across St Olaf's Place, when Ylajali has reached her apartment and looks down at her pursuer in the street: "Vi står og ser hverandre ind i øinene uten å røre os; det varer et minut; det skyter tanker mellem vinduet og gaten og ikke et ord sies" (p.15). ("We stood looking into each other's eyes without moving; this lasted a minute; thoughts shot between the window and the street, and not a word was said" (p.16)). But between those moments of erotic contact and specular identification a moment of aggression has already interfered: the hero's strange "lyst til å gjøre denne dame rædd, følge efter hende og fortrædige hende på en eller anden måte" (p.13) ("desire to frighten this woman, to follow her and hurt her in some way" (pp.13–14)), and to address her by means of meaningless phrases which strengthen her anxiety and unease.

In all these meetings, then, identification and separation, contact and aggressiveness, are woven into a complicated psychological pattern. The feeling of identity and wholeness which is created in the hero's mind, nevertheless originates outside him, in some other figure (be it his own feet) functioning as a mirror image. Into this specular experience some kind of separation is then invariably introduced, mostly in the shape of an aggressive impulse, splitting as it were the I away from a self-absorbing communication with his mirror image.

In this process, language and discourse act as a force of separation and aggression, as in the park episode and during the meeting with Ylajali. But language can also be a vehicle of the desire for harmonious wholeness and unity. This aspect is also most clearly seen in the meeting with Ylajali. In fact, the hero's fantasy name "Ylajali", with its "glidende, nervøse lyd" (p.13) ("smooth, nervous sound" (p.14)), emerges in order to fill **and** sustain the distance created between them by the hero's mocking aggression. The name is not only a symbolic substitute for the desired woman. It is also a symbol of **desire itself** – considered in the Lacanian sense of a drive sustained by lack, sliding from element to element in the chain of symbolic substitutes, and which can never be fulfilled without losing its character of being desire: Y-la-ja-li. . .

Before I continue my interpretative investigations into the text of **Sult**, I will present some more theoretical remarks on the psychological structure that I have analysed so far. My starting point will be the psychoanalytical theory of narcissism, and my aim is to establish a set of thematic categories which are sufficiently general to convert Hamsun's literary discourse into cognitive terms, and sufficiently flexible to secure this hermeneutical transformation without betraying the real complexities of Hamsun's text.

In the Freudian tradition, the theory of narcissism refers originally to the phenomenon of self-love or auto-eroticism, interpreted both as the first decisive step in the psychosexual development of the child, and as a structure of the Unconscious. Primal narcissism precedes any awareness of sexual difference; it is a kind of infantile (that means also prelinguistic) mirror experience where the child is able to organize the chaos of scattered sensual feelings into a unifying perception of its own body. Thus primary narcissism is the main condition of the foundation of an Ego. But as the French psychoanalyst Jacques Lacan has argued in his theory of the mirror stage, this crucial process presupposes an external image which the child may interiorize, and on which it can organize its growing self-awareness. Following Lacan, who builds his theory on clinical observations made by specialists like H. Wallon and M. Klein, the **infans**, still without language and bodily co-ordination, enters the mirror stage between the sixth and the eighteenth month of its life. By means of identifying with an equally formed body (in "pure" form its own mirror image), the child grasps the image of a total, unified form upon which the future Ego will be organized. Central in such a theory is the role played by The Other in the development from **infans** to **individuum**: The Other being this "place" outside of me where both my Self Image, "my" language and "my" desire originate.

This means, however, that narcissistic identification is not only the interiorization of an image. It is also the interiorization of a relation, that is, of the primary relation between Mother and Child. Since this relationship is essentially a sexualized relationship, narcissism means that an erotic structure is being implanted, originating, as Lacan puts it, in the desire of The Other (that is, of the Mother).

In **Sult**, the hero's "meeting with himself" in the park and the specular communication between Ylajali and himself illustrate these two basic aspects of narcissistic relationship. In the park episode, fragmentary sensual perceptions are unified into an experience of identity and wholeness, by way of which the hero is able to grasp himself as an Ego, and even finds confirmation of this Ego-identity in his surroundings. The mirror contact with Ylajali adds to this confirmation a promise of erotic communication which prefigures the hero's desire for reunification with a Mother figure, as I will try to show later.

However, these two episodes, together with the two other meetings in the first part of the novel, also indicate the other main aspect of the psychoanalytical theory of narcissism. In fact, the process of identification upon which my Ego is founded is already undermined by some splitting or separation. Birth itself, when I am physically separated from the symbiosis with the maternal body, is the first moment of splitting out of which, eventually, something like a human individual being develops. This complex process attains its most dramatic stage during the oedipal period, where the desire of a reunification with the Mother and the corresponding dream of an invulnerable and all-powerful Ego are shattered against socio-psychological laws and interdictions. Unconsciously, this crisis of narcissism is overcome by means of a castration fantasy, which eventually puts an end to the dangerous regressive wishes and sustains my further development into psychological independence and maturity. The unconscious message of castration teaches us that separation and lack are essential aspects of our psychological make-up, and that our existence as individual beings depends upon such an inner void or split in our existence. This profound message is, however, in permanent conflict with our infantile dreams of unity and reintegration, and also with our deepest convictions of being an autonomous Ego, a self-contained psychological entity.

The role played by language and symbols in the life of human beings is explained by psychoanalytical theory as a function of this primordial splitting. As Freud argued in **Beyond the Pleasure Principle**, and as Melanie Klein and Jacques Lacan have repeated in various ways, the acquisition and mastery of language and of symbolization in general are closely linked with our early experiences of absence and lack. Language and symbols represent both the absence of something (in Freud's famous "Fort! Da!" example: the absence of the Mother), and the desire to substitute something for this lack. They sustain the distance that separates me from the order of reality. They prevent me from any self-destroying fusion with the world surrounding me, as when the hero in **Sult** employs language as a means not only of aggression but also of self-defence. And they fill the inner and outer void with substitute representations, as when the hero invents the name of "Ylajali".

Not only the opening sequences, but in fact the whole text of **Sult** with its various plot elements, can be interpreted as a modulation upon this tension between narcissistic desire and splitting (or castration). This does not mean, of course, that Hamsun's novel is some kind of unconscious allegory about children's desire for their Mother, or about castration anxiety, etc. It is my contention, however, that in **Sult** Hamsun is approaching the same fundamental level of consciousness and the same psychological deep structures as Freud did some years later, along the paths of clinical experience and self-analysis. Here, in this astonishing correspondence between the novelist's investigations into the deep conflicts of subjective and intersubjective existence, and the future revolutions in psychology, lies perhaps the real modernity of Hamsun's early (and even later) works.

It can easily be shown how the tragi-comic love affair between Ylajali and the **Sult** hero reflects this pattern of conflict. The desire which eventually brings the hero into the bourgeois apartment of Ylajali is both a regressive oral desire for her breasts and lips (this is very neatly emphasized in the text), and a desire for recognition as an Ego. But all along the various scenes of seduction the hero is in multiple ways marked by the stigma of castration. During their second meeting, the hero is suffering from a sore finger – a self-inflicted wound which saved him from the dangerous lethargy of self-pity. His sore foot makes him limp like the old cripple when he is pursuing Ylajali around the family table. And the erotic spell is brutally broken when Ylajali notices, at the moment of sexual fulfillment, that he is even losing his hair – the third mark of castration on the hero's miserable body. Consequently, the love scene ends in frustration. The hero is ruthlessly expelled just as he is enjoying the prospect of being reunified with a maternal body.

It would be a simplification though, if this expulsion from the Paradise of the maternal body (which also happens to be a Paradise of the bourgeois Family) were construed as a negative experience only. It must also be interpreted as a salvation. From such a viewpoint, the signs of castration on the hero's body correspond to his moments of aggressiveness in those other narcissistic experiences that I have already analysed. Castration is so to speak his talisman which prevents him from being absorbed and dissolved in the erotic fusion with the (M)other.

This interpretation is sustained by the rather striking parallels between the erotic plot in **Sult** and the grotesque social integration within the family in the lodging house, which forms the hero's main temptation in the last part of the novel. What is described here is the fascinating effects upon the hero of a demonic family life to which he clings desperately, although it threatens both his pride, his self-respect, and his sense of individuality. In fact he is on the point of losing himself in a terrifying "family romance", and the magic centre of this romance, the landlady in the lodging house, is definitely a Mother figure (more so than Ylajali). Not only is she the one who feeds the hero, thus partly compensating for this inner lack of which the hunger is the main symbol. She is also pregnant with a child, and consequently a true symbol of maternity – of the biological symbiosis between Mother and Child which precedes any moment of splitting. The hero's experiences in the lodging house end, as does the Ylajali plot, with an act of expulsion. But this time its positive signification is unmistakable: it rescues the hero from the dangers of total regression.

The two secondary plots of **Sult** which I have mentioned briefly here, indicate two of the central thematic fields in the total novelistic universe of Hamsun: the conflicts and psychological mechanisms of love (e.g. **Mysterier, Pan, Victoria**, and the vagabond novels from the beginning of the twentieth century), and the inner and outer conflicts of social life (e.g. **Benoni, Rosa**, and **Konerne ved vandposten**). But **Sult** is above all a novel about the illusions and disillusions of an artist. For that reason I shall concentrate the following part of my interpretation upon the metapoetic plot of the book, trying to give some idea of how this principal theme is related to the structures that I have analysed so far.

To begin with, it is important to notice that what Hamsun offers in **Sult** is in fact a double portrait of an artist. On the one hand, he describes his hero as a **writer**, who has chosen this risky profession not only in order to earn a living, but also in order to gain recognition and fulfil some socially sanctioned ambitions. However, the hero's career as a writer brings him very little success and ends in total failure. On the other hand, the hero is furthermore presented through his powerful **force of imagination**, appearing as a breeding place of myriads of fantasies: erotic and sensual daydreams, exotic flights from reality, hallucinations of food, love, and music, visions of colours and forms, strange adventures and identities.

The innermost dream of the **writer** is to gain access to the Literary Establishment – to the Holy Family of Letters where the Almighty Editor (the Chief, as he is called in the novel) reigns as some sort of quasi-divine Father figure. To reach this aim the hero is willing to sacrifice his own individual talent on the altar of conformity and taste. He tries to write about the subjects and ideas that are most popular at the time, and at the Editor's request he attempts to remove from his articles and sketches all the traces of fever and intensity which come from his restless imagination. Behind this ambition it is easy to find a dream of social recognition and a narcissistic wish for self-realisation and integration which correspond to the erotic dreams and wishes that I have commented upon already. The dream of the writer is once more a mirror dream: a desire to recognize his own genius, his artistic Ego, in those signs of public recognition which arrive from The Other. Therefore, he has to conform to the images of success that Society keeps putting before him, like a mirror.

Why is this ambition never crowned with success? The hero himself seems to have a simple and straightforward answer to this question. It is because he always lacks the necessary material resources, such as paper and pencil when inspiration comes over him, or a place to work, or most importantly: enough food to eat. But underneath this simple answer the text hints at a more complex one, which puts the emphasis on the **ironic** aspects of the hero's situation as an artist. This complex answer focuses on the curious separation between the hero as a writer and his capacity of imagination – between the hero's ambitions and his creativity. In fact, on one occasion only do imagination, inspiration, and writing intermingle as productive forces in a successful creative process. This privileged moment is situated in the first part of the novel, and it marks at the same time its point of bifurcation: from now on, inspiration and writing, imagination and ambition will be definitively separated and will remain so throughout the rest of the novel.

As will be noticed from the following quotation, it is difficult to distinguish between Hamsun's description of poetic inspiration and those countless descriptions which can be found everywhere in the platonic-romantic tradition of aesthetics. Metaphors and motifs are in fact strikingly conventional:

> Jeg skriver som en besat og fylder den ene side efter den andre uten et øiebliks pause. Tankerne kommer så pludselig på mig og vedblir å strømme så rikelig at jeg mister en masse biting som jeg ikke hurtig nok får skrevet ned skjønt jeg arbeider av alle kræfter. Det fortsætter å trænge ind på mig, jeg er fyldt av mit stof og hvert ord jeg skriver blir lagt mig i munden.
>
> (pp.26–27)

> I wrote as if possessed, and filled one page after the other without a moment's pause. Thoughts poured in so abruptly, and kept on coming in such a stream, that I lost a number of them from not being able to write them down fast enough, even though I worked with all my energy. They continued to press themselves on me; I was deep into the subject, and every word I set down came from somewhere else.
>
> (p.36)

Of far greater importance is the setting of the scene. As in the opening sequence it is a scene of awakening, situated on the borderline between nothingness and being, in a room already presented by the text as a "gissen, uhyggelig likkiste" "hvis gulv gynget op og ned for hvert skritt jeg tok bortover det" (pp.7–8) ("This empty room whose floor gave a little with every step was like a badly put-together coffin" (p.4)). In this room, associated not only with death, but also with the image of the sea (the association is evident in the original, but almost imperceptible in the English translation), – in this no man's land the hero experiences poetic inspiration as an irresistible force, emerging from "somewhere else": from Otherness.

One of the consequences of this privileged moment will appear to be devastating: I am thinking of the hero's **hubris**, his self-deceptive arrogance which makes him leave the coffin-like attic room, although it appears later on to have been the only place where inspiration was found! Hamsun describes this arrogance with profound irony. But what is so special about such a miserable shed of a room? The answer can only be given by looking closer at its symbolic significance. As an image of death and nothingness it expresses exactly this fundamental lack or void which is the necessary condition of every act of imagination and symbolization; as an image of the sea it indicates this dynamic restlessness which characterises the forces of imagination. By treating such a symbolically loaded room with contempt, the hero is in fact alienating himself from the precondition of creativity. The rest of the novel is there to prove the disastrous nature of his decision.

This link between imagination and nothingness, enigmatic as it may seem, forms one of the central thematic points of the novel, which can be easily shown from the following two examples.

First of all, it is not accidental that the hero's most powerful fantasies are born not in the park or elsewhere in the city, but near the harbour, where the soft movements of the sea and the ships will act like a trigger on his imagination. However, the harbour is not only sea and ships and promises of exotic voyages. It is also, like the attic room, the image of a terrifying darkness inhabited by black monsters raising their bristles and waiting to pull him into the mortal void beneath the "heavy drowsiness" of its surface:

> Og sjøen vugget derute i tung ro, skibe og plumpe, brednæsede prammer rotet grave op i dens blyagtige flate, sprængte striper ut til høire og venstre og gled videre, mens røken væltet som dyner ut av skorstenene og maskinernes stempelslag trængte mat frem i den klamme luft.
>
> (p.33)

> Mørket var blit litt tykkere, en liten bris furet i sjøens perlemor. Skibene hvis master jeg så mot himlen så ut med sine sorte skrog som lydløse uhyrer som reiste bust og lå og ventet på mig.
>
> (p.44)

> In front of me, the sea rocked in its heavy drowsiness; ships and fat, broad-nosed barges dug up graves in the lead-coloured plain, shiny waves darted out to the right and left and kept going, and all the time the smoke poured like feathery quilts out of the smokestacks and the sound of pistons penetrated faintly through the heavy moist air.
>
> (p.46)

> The darkness was thicker now, a light breeze furrowed the pearl-grey sea. The

ships whose masts I could see outlined against the sky looked, with their black bodies, like silent monsters who had raised their bristles and were lying in wait for me.

(p.68)

But paradoxically, from this feeling of dissolution and submergence imagination begins its work, developing around the name of Ylajali a glittering erotic fairy-tale:

Fremdeles var det ikke en lyd som forstyrret mig; det milde mørke hadde skjult alverden for mine øine og begravet mig der i idel ro – bare stilhetens øde lyddulm tier mig monotont i ørene. Og de dunkle uhyrer derute vilde suge mig til sig når natten kom og de vilde bringe mig langt over hav og gjennem fremmede land hvor ikke mennesker bor. Og de vilde bringe mig til prinsesse Ylajalis slot, der en uanet herlighet venter mig, større end nogen menneskers er. Og hun selv vilde sitte i en strålende sal hvor alt er av ametyst, i en trone av gule roser, og række hånden ut mot mig når jeg stiger ind, hilse og rope velkommen når jeg nærmer mig og knæler: Velkommen, ridder, til mig og mit land!

(p.44)

Not a sound came to disturb me – the soft dark had hidden the whole world from me, and buried me in a wonderful peace – only the desolate voice of stillness sounded monotonously in my ear. And the dark monsters out there wanted to pull me to themselves as soon as night came, and they wanted to take me far over seas and through strange lands where no human being lives. And they wanted to bring me to Princess Ylajali's castle, where an undreamed-of happiness was waiting for me, greater than any person's! And she herself would be sitting in a blazing room all of whose walls were amethyst, on a throne of yellow roses, and she would reach her hands out to me when I entered, greet me, and cry "Welcome, O knight, to me and to my land!"

(p.69)

And the fantasy continues until it reaches the climax of an oral, erotic fusion: Ylajali's kiss.

My second example refers to a totally different episode, the hero's terrifying experience of darkness and anxiety at the police station. What this nightmare prefigures is the experience of individual death and dissolution: "Hvad om jeg selv var blit opløst til mørke, gjort til ett med det?" (p.49) ("What if I myself become dissolved into the dark, turned into it?" (p.77)). To begin with, the hero tries to defend himself by an imaginary act of regression: humming lullabies to himself like a Mother to her frightened Baby. Then another kind of salvation is introduced, so to speak, in the shape of symbolism itself: the invention of a new "word", **kuboå**, saves him from a complete breakdown. But this new combination of letters is not like the words of ordinary language. It has no meaning of its own, it can only be defined as a pure **difference**, and is in fact so described in the text: "Jeg hadde opgjort mig en mening om hvad det ikke skulde bety, men ikke fattet nogen bestemmelse om hvad det skulde bety" (p.50) ("I had formulated my opinion on what the word did not mean, but I had not yet come to a decision on what it **did** mean" (pp.78–79)). Such a decision will never be reached. As a hole – or gap – in language, the word **kuboå** signifies nothing more and nothing less than the void of emptiness which is the necessary condition for symbolism and meaning in general.

There are several connections between this nightmare episode and the hero's moments of inspiration and fantasy. On the one hand, we have some evident resemblances between the police cell and the coffin-like room of divine inspiration; these resemblances are also connected with the hero's experiences in the harbour. On the other hand, it is important to notice that the meditation upon the word **kuboå** leads directly on to a fantasy which is nothing less than a version in negative of the Ylajali fantasy from the harbour:

> Herregud hvor det var mørkt! Og jeg bringes igjen til å tænke på havnen, på skibene, de sorte uhyrer som lå og ventet på mig. De vilde suge mig til sig og holde mig fast og seile med mig over land og hav, gjennem mørke riker som ingen mennesker har set. Jeg føler mig ombord, trukket tilvands, svævende i skyerne, dalende, dalende. . .
>
> (p.51)

> God in heaven, how black it was! And I started again to think about the harbour, the shops, the dark monsters who lay waiting for me. They wanted to pull me to themselves and hold me fast and sail with me over land and sea, through dark kingdoms no man had ever seen. I felt myself on board ship, drawn on through waters, floating in clouds, going down, down. . .
>
> (p.80)

In this way the nightmare episode becomes a central clue to the understanding of the metapoetic theme in **Sult**. It expresses in a negative mode what the other episodes express more positively: namely, that fantasy, imagination, creativity and true writing are necessarily preconditioned by nothingness itself. Hunger, lack, emptiness and the principle of separation, by virtue of which individual consciousness, or Ego, is always already divided from the image of totality and fullness that constitutes the object of narcissistic desire: – those are the gaps and splits in human existence from which symbols, fictions, poetry and art emerge. This view of the nature of imagination is never absent from Hamsun's work, although it is often contradicted by more "positive", ideological conceptions of the artist and his functions. It is most clearly (and brutally) developed in the rather monstrous novel from 1920, **Konerne ved vandposten**, where the hero, Oliver Andersen, is not only an eunuch, but also a master of fiction, and thus a grotesque symbol of the Hamsunian artist: restless imagination drawing its force from a fundamental lack, and converting a self-sufficient world of fiction into an equally self-sufficient mode of existence. There can be no doubt about the sharpness of Hamsun's irony in **Konerne ved vandposten**. But irony, in Hamsun, is very seldom a rhetorical means of persuasion. On the contrary, it is the textual expression of deep insights into the existential truth of illusion: its central, and necessary, place in human life.

From this point of view, the failure of the **Sult** hero as a writer has to be interpreted as a consequence of his own arrogant blindness as to the real truth of his creative power. When he leaves his coffin-like attic room in order to seek public acceptance and social integration in the city of Christiania, he walks straight into the traps of narcissistic desire. However, he avoids being definitively trapped. Lack is so to speak his faithful talisman, it inhabits his being in different ways: as hunger, as signs of castration and incompleteness, and as a profound force of separation and division. In the final scene of the novel, when the hero is leaving Christiania and his scattered ambitions, all these forces of nothingness and separation are concentrated into an image not of defeat, but of victory:

> Ute i fjorden rettet jeg mig op engang, våt av feber og mathet, så ind mot land og sa farvel for denne gang til byen, til Kristiania hvor vinduerne lyste så blankt fra alle hjem.
>
> (p.140)

> When we were out on the fjord, I straightened up, wet from fever and exertion, looked in toward land and said goodbye for now to the city, to Christiania, where the windows of the homes all shone with such brightness.
>
> (p.232)

Pushed by the disastrous course of events, the hero separates himself not only from the city of disillusionment and misery, but first and foremost from his own erotic and social dreams and wishes. Logically, this final act of separation is imagined as a sea voyage – as a flight into the realm of death, emptiness and movement, the field of imagination itself. What is left behind is the symbolic image of narcissistic desire: the homes, shining with brightness, idyllic but treacherous promises of integration and "family romance".

However, this image of liberating separation is ambiguously permeated with nostalgia. And the goodbye is not a definitive one. Later in Hamsun's work there will always be a hero who returns from the sea, seeking the illusions of comfort and identity in some little town. We meet him again in Hamsun's next novel, where Johan Nilsen Nagel, passing by on the coastal steamer, is so fascinated by the sight of the small town that he spontaneously decides to go ashore. In **Mysterier** this proves to be a disastrous decision: trapped in the labyrinths of love and social life Nagel seeks his death by returning to the sea. But the ending of **Mysterier** is rather exceptional in Hamsun's work. As a rule, the typical Hamsun hero resists the temptations of narcissistic desire, clinging to his inner emptiness, his "hunger", as to his life. This is perhaps most clearly demonstrated in Hamsun's last novel, the enigmatic **Ringen sluttet**, whose main character, Abel Brodersen, bears such a strong resemblance to the **Sult** hero. The novel about Abel Brodersen is, fundamentally speaking, nothing but a repeated pattern of arrivals and departures, elaborated around an inner void: a human being devoid of any "character" or "identity". The **Sult** hero has no name; the hero of **Ringen sluttet** has a name filled with mythological connotations. But its etymological core reflects precisely the existential emptiness and restless movement around which Hamsun closes his ring of fiction: "air, wind, nothingness".[6]

Notes

1. Cf. Tore Hamsun (ed.): **Knut Hamsun som han var. Et utvalg av hans brev** (Oslo, 1956), p.75.

2. Tore Hamsun (ed.): **Paa Turné. Tre foredrag om litteratur** (Oslo, 1960).

3. **Knut Hamsun som han var**, p.53.

4. Quotations from **Sult** are taken from Knut Hamsun: **Samlede verker**, vol.1 (Oslo, 1954), and from Robert Bly's American translation, Knut Hamsun: **Hunger** (New York, 1967).

5. Cf. Aasmund Brynildsen: **Svermeren og hans demon. Fire essays om Knut Hamsun** (Oslo, 1973).

6. The main ideas of this article are developments of parts of the **Sult** chapter in my book **Luft, vind, ingenting. Hamsuns desillusjonsromanar frå Sult til Ringen sluttet** (Oslo, 1984).

Ringen sluttet: In Defence of Abel Brodersen

Harald Næss

Knut Hamsun's later work has been overshadowed by the achievement of his youth in the 1890s: though most of his twentieth century production has enjoyed widespread popular appeal, critics on the whole have concentrated their efforts on analyzing the early novels – **Sult** (1890, trans. **Hunger**, 1899), **Mysterier** (1892, trans. **Mysteries**, 1927), **Pan** (1894, trans. **Pan**, 1920) – which is natural, considering both their greater historical impact and the youthful exuberance of their style. On the other hand, one might have expected that James McFarlane's seminal essay from 1956, in which he placed these works in the forefront of European Modernism, would have led to a similar treatment of Hamsun's later work.[1] Until recently this has not been the case.* The following discussion of Abel Brodersen as a twentieth century "hero", is an attempt to show how the rarely read **Ringen sluttet** (1936, trans. **The Ring is Closed**, 1937), in addition to its distinction of being Hamsun's last novel, is one of his important books, containing the author's (as opposed to the politician's) latest wisdom and carrying still the stamp of his early Modernism.

This Modernism, which in his essay McFarlane referred to as "the whisper of the blood", and which is well illustrated in the novel **Sult**, involves both a revolt against bourgeois society – its beliefs, ideals, manners, style – and a lack of interest in its improvement through social reform. It demonstrates a total subjectivity, with a hero given to painstaking self-inspection and less intrigued by the objective world than by his own way of perceiving it. Furthermore it emphasizes the primal importance of art for its own sake, and explores art's anatomy and physiology, including the shock effects of abnormal fantasizing and perversity. **Sult**, as Hamsun claimed, was played on one string,[2] showing the Modernist way of saying the same things over and over again, each time differently, and this theme-and-variations technique applies to all his works, which are thematically much alike (the basic love triangle), though new dimensions are gradually added – Nagel's exploration of the demon within; Glahn's, and later Geissler's, primitivism; the preoccupation with cripples (already in **Sult**), disease, and uprootedness in the novels from the 1920s, etc.

It is Modernism's goal to avoid respectability and stagnation, and Hamsun's works show the author's attempt to keep his inspiration fresh by not repeating successes (like **Markens grøde**, 1917, trans. **Growth of the Soil**, 1920) and rather search for new ways of stating the old case. But for the modern, too, there is the altered perception of old age as well as the danger of routine, and, particularly, there is the tendency – not avoided by Hamsun – to adopt prophetic stances: politics entered his work after **Sult** and can be found in all his later books. Attempts have been made – and several times by Hamsun himself – to show that the opinions in his works are exclusively those of his characters, which is an argument easily refuted.[3] On the other hand, it is remarkable to what extent the politician – who inspired much of Hamsun's journalism – is absent from

* After submitting the first draft of this article I have seen Atle Kittang's impressive and exhaustive treatment of Hamsun's "novels of disillusionment", including **Ringen sluttet**, in his book **Luft, vind, ingenting** (1984).

his fiction. His form throughout his later production is dialectical. The statement of one person is countered by that of another – each of them, as Hamsun says, taken out of himself, though naturally he seems closer to some of his characters than to others.[4]

Ringen sluttet is a surprisingly youthful work from the hand of a seventy-seven-year-old writer. It has retained the young hero's (Tangen's, Nagel's, Glahn's) rejection of modern society as well as some of his obsession with the Self, and in its lack of direct doctrinal content, it shows once more the Modernist interest in art as form: saying the same things differently one final time. Those same things are, for instance, the feelings of a young boy hopelessly in love with an upperclass girl (like Johannes in **Victoria**, 1898, trans. **Victoria**, 1923). He spends years at sea and finally comes back different and disillusioned (like Oliver in **Konerne ved vandposten**, 1920, trans. **The Women at the Pump**, 1928). Later, as a gentleman-tramp, he finds himself surrounded by female friends and admirers (like Pedersen in **Vandrer**-trilogien, 1906–12, trans. **Wanderers,** 1922). He still does not seem acceptable to the woman he loves and dons his finest clothing (uniform) in the hope of impressing her (like Glahn in **Pan**). Finally he is paralyzed by inactivity (like Edevart in **Landstrykere**, 1927, trans. **Vagabonds**, 1930 and **August**, 1930, trans. **August**, 1931) and ends up living in a shack, with nothing to eat (like "Tangen" in **Sult**). Still, though there are unmistakable links with his other novels, including his early, Modernist, work, Hamsun's story of Abel Brodersen is unlike anything he had written earlier. More than most of Hamsun's work it is modern also in the sense of being based on very recent contemporary events and attitudes and having a "hero" who reflects the sentiments of later generations: Hamsun's prophetic gifts are nowhere more striking than here. Finally **Ringen sluttet** is a "good" book, as Hamsun himself assured his readers on the occasion of its publication: "**Ringen sluttet** er baade som Fantasi og som Tanke det bedste jeg har gjort" ("**The Ring is Closed** is, as fantasy and as thought, the best I have done").[5]

Ringen sluttet appeared on 10 October 1936, three years to the day after **Men livet lever** (1933, trans. **The Road Leads On,** 1934). These were eventful times for an eager newspaper reader like Hamsun. Adolf Hitler had come to power in 1933 and in April 1934 visited Norway onboard the cruiser **Deutschland**. The Norwegian pilot characterized the **Reichskanzler** as sympathetic, cheerful, modest, while later the same year Hamsun's former opponent in a newspaper debate, Dr Johan Scharffenberg, claimed Hitler was either crazy or a crook.[6] During the following year Leon Trotsky spent 18 months (9 June 1935 to 19 December 1936) among the Norwegians, until Soviet pressure forced them to withdraw his visa. His presence had been disturbing to many conservatives and a constant provocation to members of the new Norwegian nazi party. Hamsun's old sympathies for Germany were well known. "Jeg sender mine Børn et efter et til Tyskland. Der har de i Aarevis et andet Hjemsted, er i gode Hænder . . . hos dette ærlige og overlegent dygtige tyske Folk", he wrote in March 1934 ("I send my children, one after the other, to Germany. There they will have for years a second home, being in good hands . . . among the honest and remarkably able German people").[7] In June of the same year he appeared as one of the founding members of a new Norwegian-German society. His attitude to the new regime in Germany was best seen in the so-called Ossietzky Affair. Carl von Ossietzky, editor of **Die Weltbühne**, had been placed in a German concentration camp for his pacifist activities, and a number of prominent Norwegians, who wished to appeal to Hitler for Ossietzky's release, also turned to Knut Hamsun. Hamsun in a letter to Christopher Vibe, dated 18 June 1934, showed his support of the new Germany by refusing to sign the petition, which was submitted without his signature on 28 July.[8] More than a year later, on 22

November 1935, Hamsun published in **Aftenposten** a heartless and sarcastic attack upon Ossietzky and those who wished to nominate him for the Nobel Prize. It was followed on 14 December by a statement in **Arbeiderbladet**, in which thirty-three signed Norwegian authors deplored that Hamsun, "fri, velhavende og i enhver henseende betrygget" ("free, prosperous and in every respect secure"), attacked a person who had been placed in a concentration camp solely for the sake of his opinions.[9] Hamsun took his colleagues' reprimand much to heart. In February 1936 he wrote his friend Macody Lund, "jeg har ingensomhelst Ære eller Vet mere, jeg er bare at foragte, jeg er død. De bryr sig Fan om denne Narren i Koncentrasjonsleiren, de har Ordre til at gaa mot Tyskland 'med alle Midler'. Jeg har hørt si at nogen af Karerne understøttes av Moskva". ("I have no honour, no sense anymore, I am merely despicable, I am dead. They don't care a hoot about that fool in the concentration camp, they have orders to go against Germany 'with any means'. I have heard that some of those fellows are supported by Moscow").[10]

The international conflicts were similarly reflected in Norwegian domestic politics. The first Norwegian socialist government under Hornsrud had lasted for three weeks only (January 1928), and was followed by cabinets formed by the liberal and agrarian parties. While the agrarian party was in power (1931–33) – with Vidkun Quisling as Minister of Defence – there were serious labour conflicts (Menstad), and part of Greenland, which belonged to Denmark, was occupied by Norwegian nationalists. Quisling in those years formed his own national socialist party – Nasjonal Samling – which further provoked the socialists, who finally came into power on a more permanent basis in March 1935.

The post-war years had seen changes also of other kinds. Jazz, the new popular music, was heard for the first time in Norway. An American group, "The Orpheans", visiting at the Bristol Hotel in Oslo, even played Norway's national anthem in jazz rhythm, with the guests protesting (November 1928). One restaurant prohibited the dancing of the Charleston on its premises, and in hospitals patients deplored that the new vogue among women of cutting their hair short had also reached the nurses. In July 1928 Josephine Baker, a symbol of the new trends, visited Oslo, where newspaper photographs showed her dressed characteristically in "overalls".[11]

In the same year as **Men livet lever** (1933) two novels appeared, which brought a touch of "American" realism to Norwegian fiction, Gunnar Larsen's documentary treatment of the 1926 "lensmannsmord" ("the sheriff murders"), and Aksel Sandemose's account of love and murder, **En flyktning krysser sitt spor** (1933, trans. **A Fugitive Crosses His Tracks**, 1936). The following year, in Bergen, Hans Jacob Nilsen directed Lagerkvist's **Bödeln** (1933, trans. **The Hangman**, 1936). Einar Skavlan, who reviewed the piece, pointed to its clear anti-Hitler orientation: "Et høydepunkt er det da begeistrede selskapskledde damer geile av politisk henrykkelse plutselig roper 'Hill morderne!'" ("A highpoint is reached when enthusiastic ladies, dressed in fine clothes and roused by political ecstasy, suddenly shout 'hail to the murderers!'").[12] When the performance was repeated in Oslo, fascist members of **Fædrelandslaget** booed. In April 1933 a group of Russian writers, joined by Nordahl Grieg, sent a lacquered coffer to Hamsun, with the inscription "To the magnificent Knut Hamsun, who holds the mistaken opinion that the proletariat and the revolution do not know how to treasure and create art".[13] In his answer to Nordahl Grieg, Hamsun says he has never seen anything more beautiful: "Engang ved Leilighet vil jeg bede Dem forklare mig Miraklet" ("some time, when we have the occasion, I shall ask you to explain the miracle to me"). And he goes on to say, "Jeg vet ikke at jeg nogensinde har tvilet paa at

Proletariatet og Revolutionen kan skape Kunst . . . Men i ethvert Tilfælde er det ikke som Proletar og Revolutionær, men som **Kunstner** at Mesteren har skapt dette Skrin" ("I don't know that I have ever doubted that the prolеariat or the revolution can create art . . . At any rate, it is not as proletarian or revolutionary, but as **artist** that the master has created this coffer").[14] Two years later Nordahl Grieg's **Vår ære og vår makt** (1935, trans. **Our Power and Our Glory**, 1971) was performed at Den Nasjonale Scene. Hans Jacob Nilsen had struggled hard to produce this attack on Bergen shipowners, and the police were present on the opening night. Earlier the same year, in Oslo (Det Nye Teater), Agnes Mowinckel directed O'Neill's play **Desire under the Elms** – about greedy old Ephraim and Abbie, his third wife, who falls in love with his son Eben. Though less publicized than the Scandinavian plays mentioned above, the performance was characterized as truly remarkable ("kanskje den merkeligste forestilling i vårt århundredes teaterhistorie" ("perhaps the most remarkable performance in the history of the theatre during our century"))[15] and can hardly have escaped Hamsun's attention. All the more so because it describes the conflict of generations, which was his own problem at home: "det er ikke andet Marie og jeg gaar og grubler over end Børnene, saa ældgamle er vi blit" ("there is nothing else Marie and I worry about than our children, that's how ancient we have become").[16]

With his oldest daughter Victoria – married against her father's will in France – Hamsun had no contact, and he was fifty-three years older than his first-born son Tore. Many letters from the period 1933 to 1936 deal with his second daughter Ellinor, who wanted to be a film actress – her excessive slimming, use of makeup, dancing and café life are deplored again and again; on the other hand, Hamsun praised the brilliant style of her letters. The boys were seemingly less oppositional and adopted their parents' political views. However, to Hamsun they seemed extravagant, and in letters he castigated Tore (who studied to become a painter) for such trifles as using airmail stamps unnecessarily, not screwing the caps on his paint tubes, etc. When Tore was away from home (in Oslo, Munich) he was advised not to eat in restaurants, not to waste time and money on a Christmas vacation at home, not to worry about the quality of his living quarters: "jeg hadde ikke ovn om vinteren. Det er ikke det det kommer an paa hvorledes man bor, men at man har noget indi sig og vil ha det frem og op i dagen" ("I didn't have a stove in winter. It's not important how one lives, but that one has something inside and wants to get it out and up into the light").[17] The second son, Arild, was even worse off, trying to fight a depression. "Han synes ikke han har nogensomhelst ting i verden å gjøre", his mother wrote. "Jeg pines mer for hans skyld end for Ellinors. Hun har bare knekket bekkenet" ("He doesn't think he has anything whatsoever to do in this world. I suffer more for his sake than for Ellinor's. She has only broken her pelvis [in a bad motor accident]").[18] This is also the time when Henry Miller – Hamsun's great admirer and disciple in American literature – wrote to the old master, only to receive a cold and businesslike reply.[19]

Hamsun, who had no schooling of his own and always spoke ill of his wife's academic training, kept his children out of conventional and local career-oriented schools: the boys attended a school in Valdres, Ellinor a monastic school in Germany, etc. Instead they were permitted to satisfy their artistic ambitions, Tore as a painter, Arild as a writer, Ellinor a film actress, and Cecilia was interested in drawing. Naturally, they had difficulty emulating their famous father, and when they became depressed and inactive, he did little more than tell them that "Arbeide er en storartet Ting fremfor Lediggang" ("work is a magnificent thing compared to idleness"),[20] and Marie that she was too lenient in her educational methods. How well Hamsun nevertheless understood these problems can be seen from **Ringen sluttet**, a book in which his children may well have recognized themselves – despite endless changes in the original situations. In Tore Hamsun's novel **Mannen fra havet** (The Man from the Sea, 1984), the protagonist (born, like Tore Hamsun, on 6 March 1912, etc.) calls himself Abel Brodersen.

Ringen sluttet is the aging Hamsun's picture of his times, painted with the disinterested subjectivity of a great artist. International politics, for instance, in which Hamsun as journalist and private person found himself deeply involved on the side of the Germans, are barely discernible: the book's "villain" has an English-sounding name – Robertsen – and uses English expressions in his Norwegian. The political tensions within Norway are very much part of the novel's action, with its bankruptcies, strikes, unionized workers, etc., but, again, Norway's new socialist government is only obliquely referred to in the reckless manoeuvering which finally caused the wreckage of **S/S Spurven**: "Ja, ja det var da mandskapet førte skip på egen hånd" ("Yes, yes, so it went when the crew took over the ship" (p.199)).[21] Somewhat more directly the novel's tale of crime and murder adds a contemporary flavour to the story – Abel's sentimental relationship to his revolver, Lawrence who ended his days in the electric chair, Olga who cherished the memory of having slept twice with a real murderer, and similarly, the many references to negro jazz bands, young women with short hair dressed in men's clothing (overalls), or older women heavily made up. On the other hand, this modern small-town life only serves as background for a portrait of Abel: unlike a "social novel" such as **Segelfoss by** (1915, trans. **Segelfoss Town**, 1925), **Ringen sluttet** – like **Sult, Mysterier, Pan**, a.o. – is the story of its protagonist, a story of debilitating conflicts. The bankruptcies of the background – resulting in general unemployment and apathy – are concentrated in the account of Abel, whose hopeless struggle to please parents and peers produced in him a very special kind of passivity. Part Hamlet, part Oblomov, Abel is above all of the twentieth century.

Ringen sluttet was not well received by the critics, which cannot have been because of its form. If there are passages showing that Hamsun's hand is failing – particularly in some of the dialogues, the book has enough of Hamsun's best prose style to make it fascinating reading. Rather, then, the cool reception must have to do with the novel's seemingly lacking ideal, the way the protagonist progresses from what some readers would consider one defeat to another. Abel fails at school, though he is not unintelligent, he consorts with criminals, drunks, derelicts and becomes a murderer. He steals, squanders his inheritance, sires illegitimate children and messes up all his clothing. When he describes his life in Kentucky and Lolla comments "det er ikke godt å være vildt dyr" ("it can't be nice to live like a wild animal"), Abel answers "Jo, det var godt" ("Oh, yes, it was nice", p.49), and "Abel as animal" is Alf Larsen's theme in his review of the novel from 1937.

Larsen admired the style: "Han skriver som aldri før! Det er fullstendig uhyggelig så godt han skriver, ikke ett ord forbi, ikke den minste skjelven på hånden, og nu vandrer han dog mot sitt åttiende år! Alt er som en dans og en lek, ikke et dødt sted, ikke en tom setning, alt en eneste levende lett fullkommenhet – en lykke å lese" ("He writes like never before! It is altogether eerie how well he writes, not one word amiss, not the least shaking of his hand, and yet he is now approaching his eightieth year! Everything is like a dance and a game, no dead point, no empty sentence, everything one single graceful perfection – a joy to read"). And he adds, "men for en pine å medoppleve! En av de uhyggeligste bøker Hamsun noensinne har skrevet, og det vil si at det er en av de uhyggeligste bøker som noensinne er skrevet . . ." ("But, what a pain to experience!

One of the most frightening books Hamsun has ever written, which is to say, one of the most frightening books ever written . . .").[22] Larsen's article contains some of the dialectics that characterize Hamsun's own presentation – he deplores Hamsun's misanthropy here and elsewhere ("Han har gjort oss til rene negre og fantepakk alle sammen!") ("he has turned all of us into nothing but negroes and riffraff!"),[23] then admits that life in Norway is much the way Hamsun describes it. Or rather, that Hamsun, the ingenious writer, has shown his readers what this life is going to be like in the future, and if the future is grim, this is so because Hamsun and other great writers have betrayed their readers. What Larsen misses in Hamsun's work are above all words about eternity, words that would turn the readers' gaze upwards. Instead, Hamsun helps them turn it downwards, where they see man as something close to an animal.

Alf Larsen's exposure of Hamsun's nihilism is part of a series of periodic attacks on "literary treason", from Christen Collin's criticism of the older Ibsen (1894) to Kaj Skagen's exposure of the contemporary literary scene in Norway (1983). Eager to overcome his own pessimism, Larsen is searching for major messages and overlooks the dialectic mode, the small concessions, which make Hamsun both a fine realist and a writer of considerable warmth. Even though it could be said that, in Abel, Hamsun "tukter avgrunnsdriften i seg selv" ("chastizes the destructive urges within himself"), it is not true that "ethvert forsonende, ethvert positivt trekk er forsvunnet fra figuren" ("every redeeming, every positive feature has disappeared from the figure").[24] On the contrary, Abel is one of the more attractive of Hamsun's heroes. It is as though Hamsun, after prosecuting Abel, turns to Abel's defender and asks, like Peer Iversen in **Erasmus Montanus**, "Now, if you will take my proposition, I will defend yours". Harald Grieg must have sensed some of this ambivalence. After reading the manuscript he wrote to Hamsun: "Men trist er det trots alt sitt humør. D.v.s.: Sånne som jeg – med all verdens opdrift, blir uvilkårlig nedslått når Abel spør 'Hvorfor skal vi bli til noget?' Men andre – og kanskje de fleste – vil føle sig trøstet. Og det har kanskje vært litt av meningen med den?" ("But it is sad, despite all its humour. Viz: People like me – with all the ambition in the world – immediately become dejected when Abel asks 'Why must one strive to **be** something?' But others – and may be most people – will feel comforted. And that was perhaps the intention?").[25]

Composing a novel with more than thirty named characters demands considerable inventiveness and organizational skill, and Hamsun has used some of his earlier types. Oliver the eunuch with his many children (**Konerne ved vandposten**) is back as Tengvald; Fredrik Mensa, dead with a slice of bread in his hand (**Rosa**, 1908, trans. **Rosa**, 1925) is back as Fredriksen who, dying, clutches his last share in **S/S Spurven**; even the cake woman from **Sult** is back as Lili's mother. Otherwise many of the minor characters illustrate the vanity fair idea that nothing is as it seems – the dead man jumps to his feet when the police arrive (as in **Landstrykere**), the blind organ grinder is seen to have perfect eyesight when he needs it, and there are the old retired men who pretend to be sexually aroused by a clothesline full of women's underwear (a motif also in **På gjengrodde stier**, 1959, trans. **On Overgrown Paths**, 1967). Hamsun's irony is perhaps most biting in the case of Gregersen, whose cancer of the throat spreads to his back, so that he, who wished to "stå til jeg stuper" ("stand till I drop"), is finally driven away in a taxi – on his bended knees. Whoever is looking for ideals will find all of these characters to be caricatures; on the other hand, with the exception of Robertsen, they have all been drawn with some degree of sympathy.

The same is true of the three central women characters, Olga, Lolla, and Lili. John Hurt's Jungian pattern of "fascinating" and "gentle" women surrounding Ibsen's heroes[26] also applies in most of Hamsun's early love stories: Dagny/Martha, Edvarda/Eva, Victoria/Camilla, with more realistic and complicated variations throughout his later work. In **Landstrykere** Edevart loves Lovise Magrete and carries on an extra-marital relationship with Ragna, but there is also his sister Pauline, who watches her big brother with loving care. Abel's childhood friend Lili is somewhat gentler than Ragna, but as a married woman her situation is similar: for her friendship and sexual services the hero supplies her with money and other favours. Like Pauline in **Landstrykere**, Lolla is eager to protect her hero from exploiters of all kinds, and while Pauline develops a weakness for men of the cloth, Lolla studies the language and manners of fictional characters in order to become a lady. She is different from Pauline in being deep down a recklessly passionate woman: had she not got herself into the position of being Abel's stepmother, she could have become a new Angele, sinking with Abel slowly to the bottom.

Olga is a variation of Edvarda, though gifted with irony and a refreshing turn of phrase – "deilig og et troll" ("lovely and a troll", p.56). Like Edvarda she is withdrawn, unfree, lacking in generosity, but, again like Edvarda, she does as well as she can: "jeg prøver da på min måte å bli holdt på, sa hun stille" ("But I do try, in my own way, to be held onto, she said quietly", p.154). A typical Hamsun heroine, i.e. a hysterical woman with social ambitions, she is special in her tomboy excitement over Abel's daring and criminal tendencies. Still, like Ylajali of **Sult**, she is not prepared to accept the hero's unconventional life style, because she does not understand or appreciate its philosophic foundation. What drives her is simply sensationalism, one of her many kinds of "unatur" or artificiality.

Lili, Lolla, and Olga illustrate once more Hamsun's preoccupation with class. Like his other novels, **Ringen sluttet** is a study in social mobility. According to Hamsun, it takes three generations to produce a gentleman, and he also sees a woman's love in terms of class (cf. the poem "Hvad Kjærlighet er –?" ("What Love is –?")), the working class girl's concern about her future, the middle class wife's concern about what is proper, and the true Lady's indifference to everything but the few minutes of perfect love. Lili corresponds to Martha Ruud of "Hvad Kjærlighet er–?", Lolla aspires to the position of Fru Mignon, while Fyrstinnen is what Abel hoped to find in Olga, and didn't.

Against this backdrop of minor and secondary characters, Abel stands out as entirely different. Whether – on the surface – he seems better or worse than the others depends on the reader: what the anthroposophist Alf Larsen – Christian, conservative – saw as a reversion to the animal stage in 1937, a new generation, turning against the materialism of their parents, might well look to as a comrade-in-arms. Abel is described as "en frekk guttunge" ("a brazen little chap", p.8), "ikke noe for synet, men . . . hjelpsom" ("nothing much to look at, but . . . helpful", p.8). We hear that his father treated him miserably, but for Abel there was still the captain's collections of curiosities in the home and the nature wonders around the lighthouse – and, there was the never ending murmur of the sea. When he returns home after years abroad, he is still helpful, polite, well liked; he is also the only person at the sawmill with sufficient imagination and courage to rescue Alex from the mountain of jammed-up lumber. However, during his time in foreign countries some dramatic change has taken place within him, he tires easily of any job, the text speaks of his "forkvaklede hjerne" ("warped brain"), and he is even described as "denne tomsing, dette vrak fra Kentuckys jammerverden" ("this half-wit, this human wreck from Kentucky's valley of lost souls", p.108), though we are also told "han er ikke av dem som vil gjøre sig til" ("he isn't the kind to call attention to himself", p.110). After his third return from America – where he found that by not acting in time, he was guilty of his friend's death in the electric chair – he still looks rugged, with a proud bearing, and at the very end of the book, when both Lolla and Olga have lost interest in him, he still has the presence of mind to "set his house in order" before leaving once more for America: "han hadde sendt en barnesykkel op til Lili i Saggrenden og han hadde vært indom fotograf Smith og betalt ham" are the last lines ("he had ordered a child's bicycle sent to Lili's home in the mill district, and he had been to see photographer Smith and paid him", p.240). In **Børn av tiden** from 1913 (**Children of the Age**, 1924), Lieutenant Holmsen's final act was paying for his family portraits and ordering an organ for the church. Hamsun even permits himself the authorial comment, "redelig vilje til det siste, gylden vilje" ("steadfast and firm of purpose to the end"),[27] and he must have meant something by comparing Abel to his greatest hero, perhaps indicating to the reader that he/she should look at Abel with an open mind, take him seriously and listen to his message. One scholar has seen Abel's return to America as an act of atonement – a voluntary death for the sake of his sins and those of his times.[28] Tore Hamsun, on the other hand, tells of his father's plans for a second volume of **Ringen sluttet**: "Han gikk lenge og tenkte på å rette opp Abel noe. Han ville la ham ta straffen i Amerika og siden få ham hjem" ("For a long time he thought of rehabilitating Abel somewhat. He would let him take his punishment in America and then get him home").[29] Sin and atonement, though, is an alien motif in Hamsun's fictional universe, and **Ringen sluttet** is an unlikely **Bildungsroman**, with a hero gradually "rehabilitated". Actually, the following characterization of Abel, which seems to come from the author, is as complimentary as Hamsun ever allowed himself:

> Men i al hans ringhet var han ikke uten karakter. Det var noget. Han hadde en Guds likegyldighet for hvordan det gik. Det var noget. Han kunde tåle, kunde undvære. Han klænget sig ikke ind på nogen og søkte forsvar, for han var fordomsfrit kritikløs og syntes ikke han hadde noget som skulde forsvares. Hans svake opdrift og middelmåtige intelligens var hans eneste utrustning og senere hans rustning, men den var fast og fuldkommen, en suverænitet hos ham. Av det slaget den var; en suverænitet.
>
> (p.174)

> But in the depths of his obscurity, he was not lacking in character. This was something. He possessed a sublime indifference toward all conditions he encountered. And this was something. He could endure, he could do without. He did not cling to any living person for protection, for he was broad-minded and uncritical and did not feel that he himself had anything that needed to be shielded. His weak ambition and mediocre intelligence, these had been his sole equipment to start with; but together they had come later on to be a very bulwark of defense which, because it was both enduring and complete, rendered him independent – a sovereign in his own way.
>
> (1937 translation, pp.229–30)

Abel, drifter and escaped criminal, understands his predicament: "det begyndte i barndommen. Jeg var så uten alle chancer" ("it began way back in childhood. I was so utterly lacking in all chances", p.211). He has had friends and well-wishers all along, the principal at the naval academy was like a good father to him, but it was too late, his real father had betrayed him, and he had betrayed his father.[30] "Det er sjelden en søn kommer op mot far sin, vi hører det næsten aldri" ("It's seldom a son ever measures up to his father, we almost never hear of such a thing"), he tells the barber, and characterizes his own father as follows: "Far min kunde ikke ha levet en eneste dag slik som jeg lever år efter år. Det hadde han ikke emne i sig til. Han hadde emne i sig til å bli en aktet mand, det hadde ikke jeg. Han hadde emne i sig til å leve i veien for enhver anden som kunde ha røktet hans post på jorden akkurat på samme måten som han, om ikke bedre" ("My father couldn't have lived for a day as I have been living for years. He didn't have it in him for that. What he did have in him was the stuff to make himself a revered man – and that's something I lack entirely. He had the grand stuff in him to plant himself plumb in the way of every other person in the world who could have performed his appointed task exactly as well, if not better, than he", p.121). His father's ambitions for his son are not lost on him though. There is irony in his pleading with Lolla: "jeg sitter jo her og passer på som en smed for å bli noget" ("but I am keeping a sharp lookout for something I could be promoted to", p.107), but at the announcement that he will become a captain, "gik [det] som et blaf av glæde gjennem Abel og han sa som i forundring: Ja, sandelig lot det til at jeg kunde få prøve!" ("Abel must suddenly have felt a ripple of joy race through him, for he said, as though thoroughly amazed: Yes, it really does look as though they meant to give me a trial!" p.127). At this point he accepts the general attitude that trying to get ahead is natural for men, and he therefore describes himself and Angele as "freaks". In Kentucky they had walked out to watch the cacti because, as with Angele and himself, it was in their nature to be "vanskapt" ("freaks", p.204). Later he comes to formulate his philosophy differently:

> Hvorfor skal vi bli til noget? Det blir alle de andre og er allikevel ikke lykkeligere. De har hat strævet med å komme op, men de må se sig om efter lønnen. Deres ro er borte, deres nerver tyndslitte, nogen drikker for å greie sig og blir bare værre, de skal til hver tid gå på høie hæler, jeg som bor i en sjå ynker dem.
>
> (p.211)

> Why must one try to **be** something? All the others do that; but they aren't any happier, even so. They have had the struggle to come up, but they are compelled to look high and low for their reward. Their peace of mind is gone; their nerves are frayed; some take to drink in order to pull through and only find themselves even worse off. They insist upon high-heeled shoes for all occasions; and I, who live in a shed – I pity them.
>
> (1937 translation, p.281)

Then he goes on to describe his earthly paradise, different from Glahn's and different from Geissler's:

> Jeg har set i troperne hvorledes de lever der fra dag til dag, fra hånd til mund, lever av næsten ingenting og av solskin. Millioner lever slik. Der er det ikke noget som heter å komme op, de tænker ikke i penger og levebrød og indbo, deres liv er enkelt, de bruker blomster til smykker. Det var så pent for øinene å se på dem, så godt til øinene. Vi seilte ut til øerne og slog os til, vi hadde ikke noget i lommerne

> som de trængte, de vilde ikke kjøpe noget av os, og de tigget ikke. Vi gik op i landet, der danset de og lo, de var venlige og gav os frukt, de var vakre og brune, næsten uten klær.
>
> (pp.211–12)

> I have seen in the tropics how they live from day to day, from hand to mouth, live on almost nothing, except sunshine. Millions live like that. With them the thought of 'coming up' is meaningless; they do not think in terms of money and dining-room tables, their lives are simple, they wear flowers for their adornment. They were so beautiful to look at, such a pleasant sight for the eyes! We stopped at the Islands and got acquainted with them; they had no need of anything we might have had in our pockets; we had nothing they wanted to buy, and they didn't beg. We went up in the interior; they were dancing and laughing, they were friendly and gave us fruit, they have beautiful brown bodies, they wore almost no clothes.
>
> (1937 translation, p.282)

As always in Hamsun, the idyll is seasoned with irony: "Vi gik i skjorte, bukse og revolver der jeg kommer fra, Lolla, du skjønner ikke hvor meget naturligere det er end mange klær" ("All we wore where I come from was shirt and pants and a revolver. Lolla, you can't imagine how much more natural that is than to wear a whole lot of clothes", p.46). The peaceful paradise has its violence. As Cain killed Abel, so Abel killed Angele, his unborn child and, later, his friend Lawrence. In the work of Aksel Sandemose, the murderer-diarist condemns the jealousy that led to his **crime passionnel**, which Hamsun seems inclined to tolerate as "natural" – some of his attractive characters, like Inger in **Markens grøde**, Daniel in **Sidste kapitel** (1923, trans. **Chapter the Last**, 1929), Ane Maria in **Landstrykere** commit murder. In **Ringen sluttet**, however, the case is different in that criminality is associated with Abel throughout his life.

None of the major characters in Hamsun's later work are said to be artists, though many of them are associated with artistic production, which is certainly true of a storyteller and musician like August. Abel too is a storyteller, probably better than August, because he is more realistic and more sophisticated in his presentation. He is also more philosophically inclined – Clemens considers him charming and a pleasure to be with, the barber is confused to hear a common sailor use "such high talk", and Olga, on whom Abel tries out most of his wisdom, exclaims "du er blit så overstadig flink til å snakke at jeg har ikke hørt slikt" ("I've never heard anything like it how clever you've become at talking", p.211).[31] That Abel, like other Hamsun protagonists, is related to the artist is shown in the many uses of the word "hand", often associated with generative activities. Abel had "små hender, tyvefingre" ("small hands, the fingers of a thief", p.45), "hender rappe som en tyvs" ("hands, nimble as a thief's", p.9), "nette hender" ("deft hands", p.91), "hender som fløyel" ("hands like velvet", p.215). We are told that "han kunde gjøre alt med hendene" ("he could do whatever he wished with his hands", p.208), which includes making his **messingskrin** (brass coffer). . . "den merkeligste severdighet" ("the most remarkable attraction", pp.21–22), but it also cannot be denied that "hans merkelige håndlag, de myke fingrer" ("his remarkable hand, a set of nimble fingers") first and foremost belong to a professional burglar. Abel, we are told, gave no care to these hands of a thief, "han brukte å kline dem av på buksen" ("wiping them habitually on his trousers", p.45). In Hamsun, as elsewhere, social ambition is often symbolized by dress – Knud Sonnenfield's cap (**Den Gaadefulde** (The Enigmatic Man)), Nagel's yellow suit, Glahn's uniform, Lieutenant Holmsen's military cape, Geissler's lacquered boots, Edevart's gold rings, etc. Olga judges Abel by his dress, and Lolla keeps buying him new clothes in order that he can be judged according to his true worth. Abel, however, is a master at messing up his clothing. He has a special "gift" here – referred to throughout the novel and even inherited by his illegitimate offspring – which illustrates various aspects of his primtivism, his childlike carelessness, his sexual prowess, as well as his lack of respect for the law. Abel is the last of Hamsun's many criminals, and it is interesting to note that Otto Weininger (whose work Hamsun knew and admired) in his artistic typology uses "Verbrecher" to characterize the author.[32]

It is said of Abel that in America he had trained his hands to perform diverse tasks with wood and metal. It also says that his manner of telling a story followed the patterns of American colloquialisms, at times even borrowing a bit from cheap publications such as the **Police Gazette** (p.11). Later, when Olga listens to Abel's exhortations, she remarks: "svært så du kan si det fire – femdobbelt!" ("remarkable the way you can repeat things three or four times", (p.210)), which, fifty years earlier, had been Hamsun's criticism of Whitman: "Han siger en Ting fem Gange og altid paa samme storslagne, men betegnelsesløse Vis" ("He says a thing five times and always in the same magnificent, but non-descriptive manner").[33] But it is not necessary to **prove** Abel's Americanness, he had lived in the country and had his best friends and his wife there, he calls the black musicians "my fellow countrymen", (p.57) and he longs to get away from the snow of South Norway to the sunshine of Kentucky. Hamsun, as he sailed from America in the summer of 1888, left behind him "den stejle ustandselige Attraa: Formuen, Summen paa Kistebunden, det økonomiske Adelskab" ("the sheer, incessant greed: the property, the sum of money hidden at the bottom of the chest, the class system founded on economics"),[34] and his ambition was to travel to the Near East, to visit the Turk "som sitter utenfor sit lille hjem og hengir sig til langt på nat til lat hvile og til drømme" ("sitting outside his little home and giving himself up to relaxation and to dreams until far in the night").[35] Abel travels in the opposite direction, leaving behind him the materialism of his home to find "peace" in America.

One of the meanings of the expression "the ring is closed" must be that in Abel, "Tangen" of **Sult** has come back again. And his return is as shocking as his first appearance: if "Tangen" was the first "Russian" hero in Norwegian literature, Abel Brodersen is its first true hippie. Furthermore, "ringen sluttet" – from German "geschlossen" – could mean an early branching out and a final coming together. This fits the idea of two kinds of Hamsun heroes, an "Eastern" passive and pessimistic type, and, later, one that is "American", enterprising and optimistic. To the former category belong such characters as Pedersen, Lieutenant Holmsen, and Edevart; to the latter Benoni, Oliver, and August, with Holmsen and Oliver farthest apart. In Abel, August and Edevart have merged. With Edevart's childhood problems, love experience and general disillusionment, he also has some of August's good mood, friendliness, and ability to solve everyday problems.

McFarlane wrote of **Mysteries**: "Nagel's career is capable of being interpreted with equal validity as the reaction of a broad and generous mind to the stuffy restricting ways of a small and ingrowing community, and as the nervous, hectic projection of a lonely, unintegrated, divided mind. And it was surely the author's intention that it should be so".[36] In his demonstration of the Freudian deep structure within **Ringen**

sluttet, Atle Kittang, like Larsen before him, sees the negative aspect of this last Hamsun hero, using the Hebrew meaning of his name, "air, wind, nothing", to show the existential void in which the novel ends.[37] Perhaps, if we accept this poetic interpretation of Abel's name, we should also remember that on many occasions Hamsun claimed nothing to be more beautiful than the wind soughing in the trees.[38] What Larsen saw as an ugly picture of the future, modern readers will find at once more familiar and less shocking. Abel will always be a misfit among materialists, and may still be a stranger in his home country, but, as Henry Miller pointed out in an article on Hamsun, he is the stuff of which much modern literature is made:

> I dagens Amerika blir dessa motsträviga undantagsmänniskor allt vanligare, troligen på grund av det outhärdliga, förryckta levnadssatt som vi skapat åt oss. Att handla som om världen redan gått åt pipan er deras attityd. Att skapa ett eget liv mitt i död och fordärv, det er deras åstundan.[39]

> In present day America these rebellious exceptional people are becoming more common probably because of the intolerable, senseless way of life we have created for ourselves. To act as if the world had already gone to pot, that is their attitude. To create their own life in the midst of death and destruction, that is their wish.

Also, as Henry Miller has pointed out, and as most of Hamsun's readers will agree, it is possible to see a joy of life even in the bleakest of Hamsun's fictions: "It was from your Knut Hamsun that I derived much of my love of life, love of nature, love of man. All I have done, or hope I have, in relating the distressing story of my life, is to increase that love of life and all of God's creatures in those who read me".[40]

Finally, there is Abel's place in Hamsun's own tragic life story. As the poet at Nørholm – in style and opinions – grew more formal, doctrinaire, authoritarian, barren and bitter like Old Brodersen, so his heroes, with Abel at the end, moved towards the anarchy that characterized Hamsun's beginning career as vagabond and artist.[41] As a social and political person Hamsun had moved further and further away from this original home, though he could claim, with Ibsen, that "i natten og min digtning er jeg hjemme" ("during the night and in my writing I am at home"). Readers today will sense some of that nostalgia in Hamsun's later and darker work, even in Oliver, certainly in Abel, his most modern hero.

Notes

1. James McFarlane: "The Whisper of the Blood: a Study of Knut Hamsun's early novels", **PMLA** 71 (1956), pp.563–94.

2. "Der spilles blot paa en Stræng, men med Forsøg paa at faa Hundrede Toner ud af den" ("Only one string is being played upon, though with an attempt to get a hundred notes out of it"). Letter to Gustaf af Geijerstam (1890), in Tore Hamsun (ed.): **Knut Hamsun som han var** (Oslo, 1956), p.72.

3. On his negative statements about Switzerland, for instance, Hamsun wrote to Rene

Sonderegger: "Nu vil imidlertid KH bede Dem høistærede Hr. Redaktør, om at være saa venlig at formulere en Erklæring, som kan tilfredsstille den schweitsiske Læseverden, og som gaar ut paa at Forfatteren ikke selv hefter for Uttalelsen i hans Bok, men at han beklager den. KH. vil øieblikkelig underskrive en saadan Erklæring og sende Dem den til Publikation". ("Now, however, Knut Hamsun wishes to ask you, Mr Editor, to kindly formulate a declaration which will satisfy Swiss readers, and which says in effect that the author himself does not personally take responsibility for the statement in his book, but that he deplores it. KH. will immediately sign such a declaration and send it to you for publication"). Draft of letter to be written by Marie Hamsun, postmarked 4 February 1935. University Library, Oslo.

4. ". . . flere Hundrede forskjellige Skikkelser – hver især spundet ut av mig selv" (". . . several hundred different characters, each one of them spun out of myself"), in Tore Hamsun, **Knut Hamsun** (Oslo, 1959), p.281.

5. In **Gyldendal Norsk Forlag: Julekatalog 1936**, p.11.

6. In **Arbeiderbladet**, 18 August 1934. Information supplied in Odd Hølaas: **Norge under Haakon VII** (Oslo, 1946), p.346.

7. Letter to Wilhelm Rasmussen, quoted in **Extrabladet**, Copenhagen, 2 May 1934, and in **Aftenposten**, Oslo, 30 July 1981, p.5.

8. Letter to Vibe, in **Aftenposten**, 10 October 1978.

9. Full text in Helge Krog, **Meninger** (Oslo, 1947), pp.205–13.

10. University Library, Oslo, Brevsamling 130.

11. Odd Hølaas, op.cit., p.293.

12. Einar Skavlan: **Norsk teater 1930–1953** (Oslo, 1960), p.54.

13. **Living Age** (New York) 345 (1933–34), p.533.

14. Letter dated 20 September 1933. University Library, Oslo, Brevsamling 365b.

15. Paul Gjesdahl in **Norsk biografisk leksikon**, Vol.IX, p.374.

16. Letter to Erik Frydenlund dated 5 September 1934. **Edda** 1959, p.268.

17. In Tore Hamsun (ed.): **Knut Hamsun som han var** (Oslo, 1956), pp.169–71.

18. Letter to Albert Engström, 22 January 1936. Royal Library, Stockholm.

19. **Sexus/The Rosy Crucifixion** I/(New York, 1965), pp.368–69.

20. Letter to Cecilia, 6 November 1933. University Library, Oslo, Ms.fol.3195.

21. Page numbers for **Ringen sluttet** (given in parentheses after quotation) refer to **Samlede verker** (SV) vol.XIII (Oslo, 1964).

22. Alf Larsen: **I kunstens tjeneste** (Oslo, 1964), pp.116–17.

23. Ibid., p.112.

24. Ibid., p.114.

25. Letter to Hamsun, dated 7 July 1936. Gyldendal Norsk Forlag.

26. In **Catiline's Dream** (Urbana, 1972).

27. **SV** VI, p.188.

28. See Jan Marstrander: "Fra **Konerne ved Vandposten** til **Ringen sluttet**", in Arild Hamsun (ed.): **Om Knut Hamsun og Nørholm** (Oslo, 1960), pp.130–31.

29. Tore Hamsun: **Knut Hamsun** (Oslo, 1959), p.262.

30. The meaning of Brodersen ("his brother's son") could indicate that the Bible's Cain/Abel story is rendered here as a father/son relationship.

31. Atle Kittang claims that in Abel (and Gregersen) "[er] fråværet av språk . . . utforma som karakteriserande ledemotiv" ("the absence of language is worked out as a characterizing Leitmotiv") (**Luft, vind, ingenting**, pp.297–98.) However, though Abel (like Holmsen) is not a talker, he is nevertheless a master of language and in the important chapter XXVI argues his case with insight and eloquence.

32. **Über die letzten Dinge** (Wien, 1907), pp.vii, 124.

33. **Fra det moderne Amerikas Aandsliv** (Copenhagen, 1889), p.84.

34. Ibid., p.31.

35. In "Under Halvmaanen" from **Stridende liv** (1905). **SV** IV, p.272.

36. James McFarlane, **Ibsen and the Temper of Norwegian Literature** (London, 1960), p.141.

37. **Luft, vind, ingenting** (Oslo, 1984), p.303.

38. For instance in **En vandrer spiller med sordin** (**The Wanderer**, 1975) from 1909: "Det er ingen herlighet til som suset i skogen" ("There is no splendor like the soughing of the forest"). **SV** V, p.423.

39. **Dagens nyheter**, Stockholm, 3 August 1959.

40. Letter to his Norwegian lawyer, Trygve Hirsch, printed in Thomas H. Moore (ed.): **Henry Miller on Writing** (New York, 1964), p.209.

41. Hamsun and the Chicago anarchists of 1886: see Rasmus B. Anderson: **Life Story of Rasmus B. Anderson** (Madison, 1915), p.315. The concept of (Kierkegaard's) **Gentagelsen** (repetition of original poverty, youth, etc.) is a theme in several treatments of the old Hamsun, e.g. Thorkild Hansen's **Prosessen mot Hamsun** and Tankred Dorst's **Eiszeit**.

The Modes of Norwegian Modernism

Asbjørn Aarseth

On 9 October 1954, the Oslo newspaper **Verdens Gang** announced on its front page that in that Saturday issue readers would find a noteworthy article by one of the leading critics: "André Bjerke lashes out against Modernism in Norwegian Poetry". The article turned out to be a most unfriendly review of a slim collection of poems, **Drøm om havet** (Dream about the Sea), the first book by Erling Christie (b.1928). This was by no means the first public attack on the new wave in mid-century Norwegian literature. 1954 has been marked in the literary history of the country as the year of "the gibberish debate", following the accusations made by the poet laureate, Arnulf Øverland, on his lecture tour during the winter of 1953–54, speaking against the young poets of Scandinavia and their texts without meaning, "Tungetale fra Parnasset" (Gibberish from Parnassus). The printing of this lecture in **Arbeiderbladet** in April 1954 launched a series of contributions by critics who took sides for or against the new literary movement, with more or less balanced and well-informed arguments.[1]

As to the attitude of the general reading public at the time, there was probably little doubt that the overwhelming majority shared the traditional view of the nature of poetry. The way the book review in **Verdens Gang** was blown up as a special attraction, informs us about the assumptions of a newspaper editor as to the attitudes in his potential readership. The public flogging – in print that is – of a young Modernist writer who had dared to express his dream in obscure and irregular verse lines, and thus assume the name and dignity of a poet, was bound to arouse attention and satisfaction in postwar Norway.

If this is a reliable account of the literary climate in a small nation, not completely recovered from the effects of war and occupation, but with the best intentions of honouring its creative talents young and old, and of reconstructing its art and spiritual life, the question arises as to why the efforts to introduce a broader and more up-to-date concept of poetry should encounter such strong resistance. In Sweden the young poets of the 1940s, "fyrtiotalisterna", had made a considerable impact on the literary scene. They included important figures like Erik Lindegren, Karl Vennberg, and Werner Aspenström, writing poems of a more enigmatic kind and generally in a more sombre vein than Scandinavian readers had been exposed to earlier. And these modern poets were not regarded as particularly **avant-garde** in Sweden.

Also in Danish postwar literature Modernism was more or less taken for granted. The young writers who shared the idea of a spiritual reorientation in an age of materialist and technology-dominated thinking, gathered round the literary periodical **Heretica**, which was founded in 1948 and lasted for six years. This group included some of the most brilliant pens of the generation born around 1920, Thorkild Bjørnvig, Ole Sarvig, Ole Wivel, and Frank Jæger, and with Martin A. Hansen as a senior member. The heretics turned against Naturalism and Social Realism, expressing various degrees of belief in the value of poetry as a medium of reflection and cognition. The Modernist tradition to which they paid their tribute was of an international range, including among its leaders such names as Poe, Baudelaire, Rilke, and Eliot.

Literary historians and critics comparing the situation in Norway around 1950 to that of the neighbouring countries have been unanimous in describing Norway as an underdeveloped country with regard to Modernist poetry.[2] Somehow this verdict seems inevitable in the light of a comparative approach and with the concept of Modernism as a basis for the comparison. Maybe this is one reason for the relatively small interest on the part of Norwegian literary historians in giving surveys of the postwar period under the heading of literary Modernism. Such a survey is almost certainly bound to create the impression of a second or third rate nation.

Rather than add to the complaints regarding retarded literary development, we should analyse the conditions for creative writing in a country like Norway in the present century. And since the historical perspective for this attempt at a survey is defined by the idea of literary Modernism, it will be necessary to have a closer look at this period concept as a point of departure. So many critics and historians have asked the question: "What is (or was) Modernism?", and the answers provided seem to point in various directions. The concept of Modernism is sometimes regarded as the name of a historical fact, a substance which can be identified and dated. It is generally described as having a complex and many-sided nature, including so great a variety of trends, forms and ideologies that its delineation represents a major challenge for any historian of twentieth-century literature. It has also been argued that leading poets in the latter half of the nineteenth century, particularly among the French Symbolists, introduced this radically new kind of poetry.[3] Modernist writing would according to this view comprise a number of successive movements and programmes, Impressionism, Futurism, Surrealism and the like, all more or less opposed to the intellectual mainstream of Europe before and after the First World War, the belief in the progress of history and the potential of modern science.

As a period concept intended to designate the best parts of contemporary poetry, Modernism does not merely function as a historical label. It implies a positive evaluation and functions as a critical slogan, a signal of the will to be **avant-garde**. And because so many writers and literary schools over the years have reached for the honourable name of Modernism for their products in verse and prose, it has become increasingly difficult to capture the historical essence and common characteristics of all the known versions of so-called Modernist literature. Just as the concept of Realism was introduced around the middle of the nineteenth century mainly with the purpose of being a marketing device for the new kind of prose fiction, the concept of Modernism serves the purpose of arousing interest in the literary market-place of the twentieth century. To some extent it has been used as a glamorous wrapping aimed at exploiting the cult of the new experience as a value in itself. To be modern is as imperative for the artist of today as it was for Arthur Rimbaud more than 110 years ago: "Il faut être absolument moderne".[4] The modes, however, have not remained the same.

The fundamental changes in the recent history of literary communication are not easy to grasp, let alone explain in a convincing way. Most historians of European Modernism tend to turn to intellectual and social history when they are asked to throw light on the general conditions for the writing and reading of poems and narratives in the twentieth century. As an alternative source one might suggest the history of the introduction of the modern mass media. While not excluding intellectual and social conditions altogether from the picture, we might gain some advantage from a stronger focus on the changing situation of literary production in the context of the emerging multi-media society. Concerning the belated arrival of Modernism on the Norwegian literary scene, it can be argued that this is an effect as well as an aspect of the retarded development of the non-literary media on our sparsely populated and geographically speaking disconnected shores.

In terms of ideological orientation, Norwegian Modernism is probably best seen against the background of our recent political history. One of the dominant features of European Modernism is without doubt the pervasive internationalism of its most outstanding adherents. Comparing the main characteristics of the Romantic movement with those of Modernism, the most striking difference would seem to be related to the general attitude towards the idea of the nation. To the Romantic artist, individualist though he might be, the national spirit would in the last resort be the source of his sense of identity. The typical artist of the twentieth century is of a cosmopolitan bent. He is a dweller of the big city; his art reflects the throbbing life of urban civilization, where tribal concerns are practically non-existent.

Although a great many leading artists of Norway in the Romantic Age left the country for a shorter or a longer period of time and settled in various important cities on the continent, the painters in Dresden, Düsseldorf, and Paris, the writers mostly in Rome and Paris, their art did not leave their native land. There are very few exceptions to this general picture, the most noteworthy one being Sigbjørn Obstfelder (1866–1900). This **fin de siècle** poet, whose exquisite poems exploit the combination of exotic motifs and verbal musicality and whose mostly short prose pieces bear the mark of a restless and rootless mind cornered by a generally unsympathetic environment, is as close as one can get to a Norwegian Symbolist. If Rimbaud and Mallarmé are pioneers of European Modernist poetry, Obstfelder certainly can be regarded as an early bird in the context of Scandinavian Modernism.

During the years around the turn of the century, political activity as well as public attention in Norway was mostly directed at the problems caused by the union with Sweden. The strong national feelings aroused by the long struggle for complete independence, which actually brought the two countries to the brink of military confrontation, could not be expected to vanish as soon as the crisis was resolved through successful negotiations in 1905, and Norway was finally accepted on an equal footing with other independent states in the world community. The following years witnessed the ongoing process of nation building, in politics, in industry and shipping, in historiography and other fields of research, and, which is of particular interest in this connection, in literature and the arts. At the time when the European **avant garde** was being formed, and not only new ways of artistic expression were tried out, but elements of an entirely new concept of art, including literary art, were under investigation, the task set for Norwegian writers, poets and novelists alike, was to turn to the great traditional themes and forms of the nineteenth century and to cultivate the spiritual resources of a young and self-conscious nation. This did not leave much room for experimental minds. The common values of the people, joining forces under the slogan of "The New Working Day", were founded on the solid rocks of political and social stability.

The First World War only indirectly affected the Scandinavian countries, and consequently no significant moral crisis or ideological turmoil was created. In the 1920s both Denmark and Sweden had relatively close contacts with artistic currents on the continent. As a result elements from the theory and practice of new groups and movements like Dada, Surrealism and Expressionism were presented, debated, and to some extent integrated in these communities. In Norway, the most internationally orientated poet of the 1920s was Olaf Bull, but he was more interested in contemporary philosophy, primarily the ideas of Bergson, than in questions of poetics, although he was receptive to the artistic achievement of the French Symbolists. It has been argued that Kristofer Uppdal's poetry around 1920 shows the influence of German

Expressionism, and there is some evidence pointing in that direction.[5] However, due to his vigorous and prolific use of language in the unproblematic service of nature description, and also his basic interest in national and social themes, one hesitates to call Uppdal a Modernist poet, in spite of his occasional free verse and the cosmic range of his imagination. Kristofer Uppdal wrote a bold and powerful **nynorsk** (New Norwegian), frequently with a certain tinge of megalomania which made him a somewhat controversial figure in literary circles. Great acclaim was granted to the two major poets in the **nynorsk** tradition writing in the second and third decade of this century, Olav Nygard and Olav Aukrust. They were both firmly rooted in rural communities pervaded by genuine peasant culture. Instead of looking to contemporary European literature and art, they were concerned with the past, Nygard reading poems by the English Romantics, Keats in particular, and Aukrust studying the Christian mystical tradition and the Hebrew prophets. Their poetry is of a Romantic kind, including both the regional and the universal perspective, and they never felt the need to experiment with verse form. In the cultural climate of national revival, dominating entirely the first half of the twentieth century in Norway, the idealistic pathos of these two voices could not fail to be heard, although Nygard, who died early, did not enjoy much fame in his lifetime.

The **nynorsk** language movement, a product of National Romanticism in the nineteenth century, has remained a conservative cultural force for the greater part of the present century. This movement, cultivating a written language based on the common characteristics of genuinely Norwegian dialects as opposed to the originally Danish administrative language assimilated by the urban bourgeoisie and bureaucracy, had gained much ground during the early decades of this century, and thus provoked a countermovement which turned out to be equally conservative in its cultural orientation. This language conflict, focusing on literature as an important vehicle of national identity, tended to take away much of the attention that might otherwise have been given to contemporary Europe where questions about aesthetics and modern ways of creative writing were being debated.

Both sides in the conflict were concerned with the cultivation of national values, contributing to the ideological construction of the young state. Such conditions were no fertile ground for the seeds of Modernism. To most Norwegian writers and critics of the 1920s, language, regardless of which denomination, appeared as an organic part of the self. The aim was to keep it pure and immaculate, and if possible to reactivate its half-forgotten resources. This theory of language, antiquarian in nature, is widely different from the view concerning the ideal mission of the poet expressed by Stéphane Mallarmé in his poem to the memory of Edgar Allen Poe: "Donner un sens plus pur aux mots de la tribu".[6] In Mallarmé's case, purification does not suggest keeping out elements from the language of foreign tribes. Rather, it implies a Modernist programme of isolating the words from their conventional meaning by incorporating them in a new and unexpected verse context. Poetic language, according to this view, should not be regarded as an instrument of communication, a servant of ideas. It should function more as an invitation to focus on the expression as such.[7]

In the 1920s, when the **avant garde** moved with a lot of noise and much agility through most European circles of writers and artists, the various new movements were hardly able to establish a secure and lasting bridgehead on the northern shore across the Skagerak. Some efforts were made; a short introductory article written by Haakon Meyer on Franz Kafka together with a translation of Kafka's short story "The Murder", appeared in the leftist review **Mot Dag** in 1922,[8] a very early date for Kafka reception in any country outside Germany. This presentation does not seem to have had any traceable effect on Norwegian letters. Contemporary movements like Dada and Surrealism were not received at the time; the first comprehensive presentation of Surrealism as a literary movement to the Norwegian public appeared in 1980.[9]

The 1920s were not entirely without new signals, however. Emil Boyson (b.1897) started his literary career in 1927 as a prose writer; his first book was **Sommertørst** (Summer thirst), with the subtitle **A history**. The emphasis is not on the events recorded, but on the subtle nuances of the young mind under observation, a rootless and roaming mind, interpreted through an imagery of surprising complexity if not precision. This was prose written by a poet, a mode of narration which threatened to bury the narrative under a cascade of sensations, reflections and comparisons. Boyson had been studying the French Symbolists and other European poets of the nineteenth and twentieth centuries; his translations appeared over the years, mostly in the 1940s and 50s; a collection was published in 1965.[10] As early as before 1925 he had written poems in free verse, but at that time there was no publisher for such poetry in Norway, so when his first collection of poems was printed in 1934, he had resorted to a more traditional form. If we are looking for traces of European Modernism in the early work of Emil Boyson, the best place to look is probably his prose works; after **Sommertørst** he published **Yngre herre på besøk** (Young gentleman visiting) in 1936, not "A history", but "A fable" this time, and the year after **Vandring mot havet** (Journey towards the sea), which he classified as "Poetic prose" ("En prosa-diktning").

Boyson's prose style is in many ways unique in its often long-winded quest for some elusive and distant experience. He has not much to offer the common reader of fiction; the opening sentence of his last prose work is a warning to the reader instead of an invocation to the Muse: "I dette rum er intet at se for én som spør og speider og fort har tenkt sig videre". ("In this room there is nothing to see for somebody who asks and observes and intends to hasten on").[11] One is invited to stay in the room, to open the mind to the flow of images and meditations, as if in a poem:

> Nogen skimt, lik en øieblikkelig omskyvning som gir sjelens levende rum et annet utseende uten virkelig at ændre det – slik er kanskje barndommen for **den** som ser sig tilbake i pausen mellem søvn og næste søvn, eller kanskje er den ikke engang dét, kanskje bare gjenstanden for den vekeste hentydning, slik som klangen av fottrin forbi vinduet kan fortelle den blinde om det er dag eller sommernatt. For hvert minne som lar sig kalle og dukker op, mangfoldige som ikke når frem; minner som **er** der og ikke vekkes, men som likevel i de lydvareste stunder rører på sig, lik flaggermus rislende gjennem skumring, lik en sortnen for øinene **inne i** skumringens sortnen, lik et sildr av vellyst inne i en vågere vellyst; ingen griper dem, ingen kan tyde hvad de gjemmer.

> Some flashes, like a momentary alteration which gives to the living room of the soul a different appearance without really changing it – such may childhood seem to somebody who looks back in the break between sleep and the next sleep, or perhaps it is not even that, perhaps merely the object of the faintest hint, as the sound of footsteps past the window can tell the blind person if it is day or summer night. For each memory that is aroused and emerges, a great many that do not make it; memories that **are** there and are not revived, but that yet at the most sensitive moments stir, like bats rippling through the twilight, like having one's

> eyes grow dim **inside** the growing blackness of the twilight, like a trickle of delight inside a vaguer delight; nobody catches them, nobody can interpret what they hide.[12]

There is a certain Proustian quality in a passage like this. Boyson's wandering is a quest for lost identity and for reality, but it lacks the grand design of Marcel Proust's novel cycle about time and imagination. Proust's work has been studied with much admiration by French novelists of the 1950s and 1960s. Boyson has hardly had any followers in Norwegian fiction. Today he is chiefly known for his rather exclusive and aristocratic poetry. To view him as an early Modernist in this country is to accentuate his interest in the formal aspects of literary art, verse and prose, and his strong attachment to the great tradition of European Symbolism.

While the 1920s can be described as a decade of national consolidation, the 1930s did present some openings on the world at large. A series of modern novels in Norwegian translation, "The Yellow Series", with novelist and critic Sigurd Hoel as general editor, was started in 1929 and lasted till 1959. Among the European and American fiction writers introduced to the Norwegian public in this way, several can be said to represent Modernist kinds of writing, e.g. Faulkner (**Soldier's Pay**, 1933, and **Dark August**, 1934) and Kafka (**Der Prozess**, 1933). The series did not include such novelists as Proust, Joyce, Woolf and Céline, and Hoel's own novels were fairly traditional.

In the poetry of the 1930s there were occasional attempts at turning away from traditional poetic language and the subjects believed to be best suited for the lofty style of verse. An otherwise unknown poet, Halstein Sjølie, published in 1932 a book of poems, **Opgjør** (Reckoning). His poems are presented as pictures of the times, most of them dealing with social problems in an age of widespread unemployment, but a couple of them show a willingness to write about contemporary urban civilization and its mechanistic appearance in an affirmative way, reminiscent of poets like Walt Whitman and Carl Sandburg. The opening lines run like this:

Vi er barn av stålet og betongen.	We are children of the steel and the concrete.[13]

Less programme conscious in his modernity, more intensely bent on the whispered secrets of words and images is Rolf Jacobsen (b.1907), whose first collection of poems appeared in 1933 under the title **Jord og jern** (Earth and iron). The title may suggest some of the range of this poet, equally familiar with the countryside and the modern city. Jacobsen is frequently referred to as the first genuine Modernist in Norwegian poetry,[14] not only because he introduced the vocabulary of modern technology to the language of poems or because he wrote chiefly in free verse – this had been done before – but rather because in his work one will find a new attitude to the possibilities of language. He did not conceive of himself as a Modernist poet, although his publisher, Harald Grieg of Gyldendal, wanted to launch him as such.[15] One of the poems from his first book will serve to illustrate his way of combining elements from nature and civilization, animating the instruments of technology to create a metaphysics of modern existence:

Kraftledning

Under de stupende fjell stiger rungende mørke koraler:
Kirken dernede, den lave med hvelving av marmor
løfter sin messe i velde og maner de ville demoner,
åpner sin sorgfulle favn for det angrende hjerte.

Herdet i stålfont og døpt av de hese turbiner
stiger forløsningens hærtog med jubel mot lien og skogen,
skrider i heien med snehvite kniplingekjortler,
løfter de skinnende vinger av stål i forventningens skjelven.

Bort gjennem skogene, frem gjennem dager og netter
vandrer det skinnende tog med det levende budskap til jorden.

– Møt dem derinne ved natt på den grånende seter,
hør hvor de taler i tunger og strides med natten og Herren.

Lyn gjennem luften og sus av de skjærende vinger,
veiene møter, og dalen og solen med glede.
– Ned ifra bjerget de bærer med sanger mot landet
den hellige flamme fra himlen med dirrende hender.

Power Line

Under the plummeting mountain walls dark and resounding chorales rise:
Down there the low church, the one with the vaulting of marble
Lifts up the might of its service, and drives out, conjures the wild demons,
Opens its grief laden arms to the heart that's repentant.

Tempered in steel fonts, baptised by the husky-voiced turbines
Rises redemption's crusade with a cheer towards hillside and forest,
Strides through the uplands apparelled in snow-white lace tunics,
Lifts up its shining steel wings in the trembling of its expectation.

Out through the forests, away through both daytime and night-time
Wanders the shining crusade with its own living tidings for earth.

– Meet them in there when night falls on the darkening farmstead,
Hear as they speak in tongues, locked into strife with the night and the Saviour.

Lightning through air and the hum of the sharp, slashing wingbeats,
All the roads meet, and the valley, the sun meet in gladness.
– Down from the mountains with songs to the flatlands they carry
The holy flame out of the heavens, their hands are aquiver.[16]

In this poem Jacobsen is still exploiting the effects of a regular verse rhythm, and his form can hardly be called revolutionary. In his second collection, **Vrimmel** (Throng), published in 1935, there are also traditional poems, so the author is not limited to one particular mode. In his postwar poetry the traditional forms are exceptions.

To Rolf Jacobsen poetry is not the vehicle of ideas, although some of his poems can be interpreted as low-keyed warnings concerning the effects of modern civilization. He is not easily linked with political movements or religious creeds. To him a poem is an investigation into the nature and potentials of human language. Poetry is capable of improving our perception of reality; compared to prose it represents an expansion of language.[17] As a journalist, editor, and after the war employed in a bookstore, Jacobsen had professional experience of the printed media. This particular background is clearly visible in much of his mature poetry; the title of his 1969 collection is **Headlines.** This does not mean that his poems are dealing with the kind of news that is communicated by the mass media. On the contrary, one could say that his creative writing serves the function of counterbalance to the hectic and noisy world of the newspaper and other agents of prose communication. This contrast is manifest in a poem from 1965, really a piece of metapoetry, expressing an aspect of Rolf Jacobsen's poetics:

Stillheten efterpå

Prøv å bli ferdige nu
med provokasjonene og salgsstatistikkene,
søndagsfrokostene og forbrenningsovnene,
militærparadene, arkitektkonkurransene
og de tredobbelte rekkene med trafikklys.
Kom igjennem det og bli ferdige
med festforberedelser og markedsføringsanalyser
for det er sent,
det er altfor sent,
bli ferdige og kom hjem
til stillheten efterpå
som møter deg som et varmt blodsprøyt mot panden
og som tordenen underveis
og som slag av mektige klokker
som får trommehindene til å dirre
for ordene er ikke mere til,
det er ikke flere ord,
fra nu av skal alt tale
med stemmene til sten og trær.
[. . .]

The Silence After

It's time to be done
with these provocations and sales statistics,
Sunday breakfasts and combustion furnaces,
military parades, architecture competitions
and the triple rows of traffic lights.

Get through and be done
with the party preparations and market analyses
for it's late
it's far too late
be done and come home
to the silence after
which greets you like a splash of warm blood on your brow
and like the thunder en route
and like the strokes of mighty clocks
which make your ear-drums quiver
for the words no longer exist,
there are no more words,
from now on everything will speak
with the voices of stones and trees.
[. . .][18]

The demands on the reader made by a text like this are not excessive; Jacobsen's Modernism is never hermetic. His twelve collections of poems, of which ten are published after 1950, have been a major influence in the establishment of a Modernist tradition in contemporary Norwegian literature. He is also our most important poet in the international community. He has been translated into 18 foreign languages, and he was the only Norwegian poet included in Hans Magnus Enzensberger's **Museum der modernen Poesi** (1960), a book of poems by 96 poets of the twentieth century translated into German.

The complete poetry of Claes Gill (1910–1973) is made up of thirty-four mostly short poems. His art is aristocratic in many ways, choosy, sophisticated, often erudite, and while writers like Boyson and Jacobsen are of a definitely conservative bent in the question of language form, Claes Gill even preferred an old-fashioned spelling. He exploited the effects of archaism both on a verbal and on a mythological level. And yet there is general consensus about his position as one of the early Modernists in Norwegian poetry. He published two very slim collections of poems, and not only the poetic style, but even the binding of the books suggested an extremely conscious artist. The first book, **Fragment av et magisk liv** (Fragment of a Magical Life, 1939), was bound in plywood, whereas the second one, **Ord i jærn** (Words in Iron, 1942) had a cover made of blackout paper; both title and cover tacitly referring to the conditions imposed by the occupying forces.

Some years later Gill began a successful career as an actor and theatre director, and he was for many years a popular reciter of poems. The poseur is never far away in his poetry; the effects of sounds and images are carefully calculated, and the result has sometimes the character of verbal gesticulation. At a time when so many Norwegian poets took sides with the growing movement of national resistance, writing a defiant and clamorous kind of rhetoric to be distributed by the underground press or recited on the radio from unconquered territory, Claes Gill was paying his service to the art of poetry itself. He studied the French Symbolists and contemporary English poetry, particularly W.B. Yeats. Like these poets he cultivates the poetic resources of verbal musicality, so the visual aspect of his verse is not allowed to dominate as is the case in the work of many of the postwar Modernists. As in the case of Rolf Jacobsen, Claes Gill's poems are clearly composed with the effects of recital in mind. Occasionally he writes in the classical stanza metre or the sonnet form, but the attention to the sound patterns is also at work in his free verse.

In spite of a limited production, there is a wide range of subjects in these poems: "Byer, skog og marker glir forbi./ Et livs ideer står på sprang/ som mannskap fra et skib i brann". ("Cities, forest and fields drift by./ A Life's ideas are ready to jump/ like the crew from a ship afire").[19] They carry references to ancient Celtic Mythology (in a Yeatsian idiom), evoke impressions from Marseille, "Psyche's havn" ("The Harbour of Psyche"), pay homage to Emil Nolde (in German!) and to Nils Collett Vogt, paint the portraits of pale and distant ladies, pose the eternal questions about the purpose and mystery of life, and cherish sweet memories of the cool and green Summer of Western Norway. Many themes are touched upon and many frames of mind are called forth. One of them is the short duration of youth and the sense of the inevitable end:

Flyktende ungdom	*Fleeing Youth*

Flyktende ungdom!
    En hind
jagd av et kobbel
    halsende hunder.
	Fleeing youth!
	    A hind
	chased by a pack
	    of baying dogs.

Den store Jæger
    på post
mønstrer i kjølig
    ro sine hænder.
	The great Hunter
	    on guard
	examines coolly
	    and calmly his hands.[20]

The transience of life is a perennial theme in poetry, and several of Gill's poems represent this combination of ancient ideas and the modern technique of juxtaposing terse images. The result is frequently the effect of a chiseled artifact. With better reason than any other Norwegian poet of the twentieth century, Claes Gill can be characterised as an aesthete.[21]

In the mind of the reading public, the early 1940s was hardly a time for aestheticism. The situation called for verse in the heroic genre, and there was not much point in experimenting with form or studying the works of Symbolists and Imagists. If the 1930s had witnessed a certain faint trend away from national ideology and a more international orientation in Norwegian poetry, the war implied an immediate literary mobilization. The new medium of radio broadcasting had been in operation on a regional basis from 1925, and organized as one national system, Norsk Rikskringkasting, in 1933. The number of receivers was increasing fast in the late 1930s. Here was a new audience for poetry recitals as well as for other verbal communication and for music. When Nordahl Grieg on Constitution Day in 1940 recited his poem for that day on Tromsø radio,[22] the war was less than six weeks old, and the greater part of the country was conquered by the German invaders. Grieg's war-time poetry is written with a large audience in mind and has a strong national appeal. In order to have the desired effect, it had to be declamatory, emotional and easily understood. Nordahl Grieg had set the tune, and others followed in his wake: Arnulf Øverland, Gunnar Reiss-Andersen, Inger Hagerup. The five years of resistance against the occupying forces favoured extrovert poetry of a traditional kind. It meant a set-back to less patriotic ways of writing and to formal experiments. Modernism was temporarily out of the question in Norway.

The ideological situation with respect to the traditional national values was rather slow in changing after 1945. Poets could not go on writing in the pathetic style of the resistance. Most of them turned to nature, interpreting the life of plants and animals or the forms of landscape in terms of human experience. This had been done earlier, so the novelty had to be developed on the formal side. The advantage of a mode like this, traditional in theme and moderately experimental in poetic style, was that the result was not provocative; it could still be recognized as a poem. A representative of this trend of early postwar Modernist poetry is Tarjei Vesaas (1897–1970), an established prose fiction writer, who published his first collection of poems, **Kjeldene** (The Springs), in 1946, and the year after, in **Leiken og lynet** (The Game and the Lightning), ventured further into the semantic complexities of Modernist free verse without losing his foothold in his regional ground. One of the poems from the 1947 collection may illustrate his style:

Lomen går mot nord

Høgt som prikkar mot skyene
einsame endå dei er tvo,
går lomane nordover
og blir borte.

Berre eit kjølig skrik
når ned frå dei
dit vi står fast
i vårt store virrvarr.

Men ute av syne
styrer dei loddrett ned
i ein iskald sjø
som har vekt hemmeleg varme.

Slikt høyrer vi gjerne –
eit einsamt vilt hjarta
som i grenselaus fridom
endå søker ned til oss.

The Loons Fly North

High as specks against the clouds,
alone although they are two,
the loons fly north,
and disappear.

A single serene hoot
reaches us
standing below
in great confusion.

Once out of sight
they plummet down
toward an icy lake
that has stirred a secret warmth.

We like to hear such things –
a lonely wild heart
reaching down to us
out of its boundless freedom.[23]

The fact that an established writer of **nynorsk** decided to compose poems that deviated from, if not directly rebelled against the conventional norms of poetic expression, was bound to have its effect on literary circles in Norway. Vesaas, whose major prewar achievement had been fiction of the **Bildungsroman** genre in a solid rural setting, felt the need for developing new forms to express the modern sensibility and the increasing concern of the intellectual that seemed to emerge in the postwar era as the horrors of modern warfare were gradually revealed. He experimented with allegorical and symbolical techniques in his later novels with the aim of creating a more thought-provoking and disquieting effect than the everyday prose of psychological analysis would bring out. But Vesaas remained fundamentally true to his rural background, so his kind of Modernism never raised the question of identity in a more radical way; the confusion of man can be healed by the sympathetic voice of the wild loons passing on their way northward.

The poetry of Gunvor Hofmo (b.1921) is contemporary with that of Tarjei Vesaas, but her poetical quest is of a more uncompromising sort. Her poems focus on the sense of universal isolation, on suffering and on the notion of a more real world beyond the world of the senses. They are songs of desperation and longing, dealing with existential crises or contemplating the wordless countenance of God. To her poetry is a serious matter; it is the medium of an isolated soul facing emptiness or trying to sort out the silent signs of some distant secret. Occasionally she writes in a traditional form using rhyme and regular metre, but since her second collection, **Fra en annen virkelighet** (From Another Reality, 1948), free verse is equally important. Hofmo's Modernism is of a more abstract character than that of Vesaas; where his verses exploit the visual effects of nature imagery and thanks to the earthly dimensions of his **nynorsk** idiom are capable of conveying rather complex feelings without leaving the ground of real life, her work is less sensual and more in the intellectual vein. Her language is the Dano-Norwegian **bokmål** practised by the majority of Norwegian writers and traditionally linked with urban culture. Like several of the postwar Modernist poets in the **bokmål** tradition, she seems to pay less attention to poetry as a sound medium; her main concerns are with the expression of thoughts and emotions, frequently through nouns like "virkelighet" (reality), "tomhet" (emptiness), "ensomhet" (loneliness). This means that verbal musicality, still of considerable importance in the poetry of Jacobsen, Gill, and Vesaas, is losing ground in the poetry of free verse written in the late 1940s and 1950s. Poetry more and more becomes something written for the page, to be pondered in silence by the individual reader. The idea of poetry recital is not predominant in literary circles of this period.

In the atmosphere of enthusiasm which prevailed in the era immediately following the end of the German occupation, the young writers of prose and verse were acclaimed in a rather uncritical way; the literature of liberated Norway had a flying start. The war had meant isolation, but in 1945 the international community was available once more. The need was felt to counteract the tendency to provincialism and to repair the lack of critical tradition. In 1947 a literary periodical, **Vinduet** (The Window), was established by Gyldendal Press. Its purpose was to be a forum for critical debate and to inform its readers of trends and events in the international world of literature. **Vinduet** is still a leading periodical in its field, and it has played an important part over the years of changing literary modes. The need to open the window and let in fresh air from the world outside also led to efforts in the art of poetry translation, which had not been much cultivated previously. In 1947 Walt Whitman's "Song of Myself" was published in Norwegian by Per Arneberg, with an introductory essay. As one of the fathers of

American and European Modernist poetry in the second half of the nineteenth century, Whitman with his rich sensuality and his expanded and in some cases long-winded verse style might be expected to have a broadening effect on Norwegian poetry. The immediate effect was hardly noticeable, however; the poets of that time were heading in other directions.

In 1949 a selection of T.S. Eliot's poetry was published in Norwegian translation and with an introductory essay by Paal Brekke, **Det golde landet og andre dikt** (The Waste Land and other poems). Norwegian readers of poetry, accustomed to nature imagery and the rhetorical expression of national or moral issues, were hardly prepared for this kind of intellectually demanding and extremely erudite Modernism. The reception of Eliot as a poet and a critic was not without frustration and resistance in Norway. Paal Brekke (b.1923) had spent part of the war years in exile in Sweden, and had studied the contemporary Swedish poets as well as the leading figures of English Modernism. He had published poems in Sweden, and his first collection of poems to appear in Norway was **Jeg gikk så lange veier** (I Walked Such Long Ways, 1945), containing mostly poems of a conventional kind. The Modernist Paal Brekke dates from 1949 – the same year as his translation of Eliot poems was available; he published a book of poetry in a similar vein, **Skyggefektning** (Shadow-boxing). With much intellectual agility and with no respect for the logic and syntax of conventional poetic language, the poet turns against his bourgeois and trivial environment, eager to experience the reality of existence. Brekke introduced the long modern poem in Norwegian literature, not in the self-assertive, ponderous style of Whitman's "Song of Myself", but of a more questioning and analytical kind, fathoming the depths of postwar existence.

While Eliot had prefaced his "Love Song of J. Alfred Prufrock" with a quotation from Dante's **Inferno**, Brekke had chosen some lines from Milton's **Paradise Lost** as a motto for his long, fragmentary poem "Brokker av kaos" (Pieces of chaos), suggesting another hellish frame of reference. The speaker of the poem is investigating the effects of war and violence, his capacity for hatred and self-contempt and his attitude to violence. Poetry is no longer a language game with the purpose of creating meaningful and beautiful verbal harmonies; it is a weapon in some process of tearing down the façades of society. The struggle is metaphorical; it is shadow-boxing performed in secret between the four walls, but even so the speaker sees it as ". . . reflekser i et større spill/ av lys og angst og skygger –" ("reflections of a bigger game/ of light and fear and shadows –").[24] A poem reflects the spiritual conditions of its time; even its form is expressing or interpreting some aspect of contemporary existence.

Paal Brekke's poetic language is in many ways a shattering experience when it is compared to the regular stanzas of traditional poetry. He is not rejecting every kind of lyrical means of expression, however. His poems possess a rhythmical quality which clearly distinguishes them from prose, apart from the use of imagery and syntactical peculiarities. A short poem from his 1957 collection may serve to illustrate his verbal art. Here the speaker is not comparing himself to a tree, as the traditional Norwegian poet from Jørgen Moe to Tor Jonsson would do; he **is** a tree:

Tre ved stranden

Det mørke sus i blodets grener
Død, erindrende seg selv

erindrende i dette løv
sin vinges flukt mot lys, mot lys

mens natten langsomt, grå av lytten
reiser hodet under treets

røde grener, strakt mot himlen
speilet i et hav av blindhet –

Løft min krone, vind fra intet
søkende et tre ved stranden

løvet svarer når du roper
treet låner deg sin stemme.

Tree by the Shore

The dark roar in the branches of the blood
Death, remembering itself

remembering in this foliage
the flight of its wing towards light, towards light

while slowly the night, grey from listening
lifts its head under the tree's

red branches, reaching towards the sky
mirrored in a sea of blindness –

Lift my crown, you wind from nowhere
searching for a tree by the shore

the foliage answers when you call it
the tree lends you its voice.[25]

The kind of Modernism introduced and vigorously defended by Paal Brekke was regarded as rather hermetic. Both critics and poets were divided in their evaluation of this effort at catching up with the literary climate of contemporary Europe. The discord among the critics culminated in the gibberish debate in 1954. While there is reason to believe that the greater part of the reading public shared the negative attitude of Øverland and Bjerke, it soon became clear that most of the talented young writers sided with Brekke and Christie. If we look at the arguments set forth at the time, we find that the two sides in the controversy tend to focus on different aspects of the art of poetry. The traditionalists view poetic quality as a question of form. The function of a poem is to express some idea or attitude; the poet must create a form which is capable of communicating his idea to the audience. A mininum of logical or imagistic coherence is required to secure the desired effect. Modernist poems tend to ignore this basic condition, according to these critics, who frequently turn to the Swedish poets of the 1940s for examples.[26]

The Modernists' concept of form is a different one. Instead of regarding form as the appropriate vehicle of some identifiable emotion, they see it as a constant challenge to the artist. Poetic form is not something which can be inherited from the great works of the past; it is the object of investigation. A new experience of life implies a new literary form. In modern art form and content cannot be distinguished. And in the eyes of the young generation of poets in the 1950s, what was needed was a radical expansion of the range of poetic expression, not the limiting intervention of normative poetics.[27] To the Modernist poets during that decade verbal art was not the exercise of rhetoric with a view to popular taste; their poetic project was aiming at a fuller perception of reality. Poetry was a way of approaching the shattering experience of modern civilization; its deepest justification was that it had the power to heal the sundered mind of modern man. The poets of the 1950s had ambitions on behalf of their art. They conceived of themselves as therapists, not as entertainers.

Viewed in retrospect, this was the decade when European Modernism finally reached Norway and gained a foothold in the literature of the country as something more than an isolated instance. The attack launched against it by Øverland, Bjerke and others, had made the reading public aware of the new movement. Poets who had made their dėbut in the 1940s, Astrid Hjertenæs Andersen (1915–85), Olav H. Hauge (b.1908), Astrid Tollefsen (1897–1973), developed a freer kind of poetic language during the 1950s, the visual imagination gradually becoming more important. New poets entered the stage, eager to exploit the possibilities offered to the artist by the more open kind of poetics which had been introduced: Finn Bjørnseth (1924–73), Arnold Eidslott (b.1926), Peter R. Holm (b.1931). Their background was different, and they did not operate as a group or speak on behalf of a generation. They were individual voices in an age of heroic individualism. The young intellectuals read Sartre and Camus; Colin Wilson's **The Outsider** was translated into Norwegian in 1957, the year after it had been published in England; other favourite names were Kierkegaard and Kafka.

The new poets of this period did not write for large audiences. Their medium was primarily textual, i.e. the printed page with typographical arrangements as a means of expression. Many of them consciously renounced the aesthetic effects of verse musicality. This mode of communication demanded a great deal of attention from the reader; it was an exclusive, hermetic kind of art. For the general public a poem had always been a melodious and elegantly written piece of language, frequently with a touch of wit or humour, as in the work of Herman Wildenvey, or imbued with moral pathos and philosophical reflection, as in poems by Øverland and Reiss-Andersen. Such poetry had something for the ear as well as for the mind. Composers frequently turned to it for material, and choirs as well as concert singers would include it in their repertoire.

The new mode of poetry tended to turn away from this musical function, trying to compensate for the loss by appealing to the visual imagination and exploiting the sensual and semantic potentials of words in new combinations. Those who had hoped for a growing interest in poetry as a result of the increased European orientation and "modernization" of this art, were disappointed. The 1950s witnessed a steady growth in the sound media, those already well established, such as radio and gramophone, and a new instrument, the tape recorder. This development, favouring international popular music and song production, took away much of the attention traditionally reserved for literature, and poetry in particular, in a country like Norway. It has been suggested that the era of poetocracy, which had lasted for at least a hundred years in Norwegian history, vanished during the postwar period, and that philosophers and sociologists became the new leading figures of the public debate during the 1950s and after.[28] If this view has some validity, the decline in the authority of poetry is partly due to the literary development outlined above, the change in emphasis from sound to image patterns, a tendency to cultivate the conceptual rather than the tonal mode, although the art of verbal sonority still no doubt had a broad appeal. In an era of sound media expansion, the Modernists chose to approach their readers through inaudible means.

With their limited readership, poets risked rejection by the publishers. In Sweden, where the situation had been somewhat similar, one of the publishing companies organized a society with the purpose of promoting the distribution of books of poetry through club membership and price discount. This society, **Folket i Bilds Lyrikklubb**, established in 1954, was the model for a Norwegian society, **Lyrikklubben Diktets Venner**, organized by Paal Brekke in 1958. A periodical, **Diktets Venner**, edited by Brekke, was distributed to the members as part of the deal. The first issue opened with an article by Øverland followed by an article by Brekke, both commenting on the difficult situation for poetry due to limited demand. The time had come to join forces to save the poem, Modernist or not, from extinction. This society for the advancement and distribution of poetry lasted until 1962, when it was replaced by a more comprehensive society, **Den norske Bokklubben**, which developed a special branch for poetry.

If by 1960 the market situation was already changing, it was hardly due to new systems of distribution alone. The nature of the challenge presented by the new conceptual mode of Modernism that had taken over during the late 1950s and made Norwegian poetry difficult and to some extent hermetic, was primarily intellectual. It required a strong interest in language as a delicate instrument of communication and a minimum of literary education. From the years around 1960 and for almost two decades, Norwegian society, like the rest of the Western world, experienced a tremendous growth in the demand for higher education. The number of universities increased from one (before 1948) to four (after 1970), and the campuses gradually developed new fora for political and literary discussion. This meant among other things a greater potential audience for the young intellectual poet and at the same time an improved possibility for the new talents to join stimulating intellectual circles and gain self-confidence and artistic erudition.

Among the poets who emerged from student circles and made their way to success and nationwide fame during the early 1960s, two deserve more attention than the rest. Georg Johannesen (b.1931) had published a novel in 1957, but aroused greater interest with his first collection of poems two years later, **Dikt 1959** (Poems 1959). As the title suggests, this poet had the contemporary world in mind; his poems were not archaic or designed for a timeless public, they were comments on conditions and experiences of 1959. Georg Johannesen was immediately recognized for his radical position on political issues, but what makes him a poet is not his political engagement. Rather it is the temperature of expression, the eye for the paradoxical, the will to do away with clichés and conventional thinking:

Råd	*Advice*
om hvem som er verdt å høre på	on who is worth listening to

Du skal ikke høre på mennesker
som har overlevd to verdenskriger
De må ha små hjerter
og masse tålmodighet
De må ha regnet ut hva det koster
å slippe unna gratis
De må være veid på morderens vekt
Han sa: Dette blir ikke noe
La dem gå
[. . .][29]

You shall not listen to people
who have survived two world wars
They must have small hearts
and a lot of patience
They must have figured what it costs
to get away free of charge
They must have been weighed on the
scales of the murderer
He said: This amounts to nothing
Let them go
[. . .]

Johannesen published two more collections of poems in the 1960s, but in the following decade, when so many young writers used poetry to express their leftwing views on political issues, he turned to experimenting with allegorical prose in a style reminiscent of biblical narrative. To Georg Johannesen the art of poetry is not an intellectually challenging language game. It is an instrument designed to shake the philistine in his muddled thinking, to question views that are generally considered wise, to demolish the edifice of convention.

Ariadne hjalp meg ikke
Labyrinten ble revet innenfra
Slik fant jeg ut av den[30]

Ariadne did not help me
The labyrinth was torn down from within
That is how I got out of it

The other poet to appear from the student circles in the beginning of the 1960s was Stein Mehren (b.1935). His voice is entirely different; from his first book, **Gjennom stillheten en natt** (Through the Silence One Night, 1960), and all through the 1960s and 1970s, his poems philosophize on the self observing itself experiencing life and engaging in human relationships, reflecting on the transforming or destructive effect of reflection, regretting the loss of spontaneity as the curse of modern consciousness. And yet this extremely intellectual poetry is often intensely concrete in its rich imagery drawn from nature, from contemporary social life, or from ancient mythology.

Mehren studied modern philosophy, and in an essay of intellectual autobiography, "Femti – Seksti – Sytti: Åtti" ("Fifty – Sixty – Seventy: Eighty", published in 1980), he discusses the changing spiritual climate among young Norwegian intellectuals with special attention to the 1960s. He does not accept the label "an Existentialist with language problems", with which he has frequently been described.[31] There is definitely an element of Existentialism in his early poetry, a belief in the freedom of the self to perceive the nature of its relationship to other selves and to society and history. The ego can understand itself not as an isolated essence, but precisely as part of a greater whole, connected with a process of historical, or cosmological, or even mythical nature. A Romantic element can be traced in many of the poems; the quest for a lost innocence, the cult of unity and organic synthesis, the conscious use of archaisms. Still, it is a definitely Modernist version of Romanticism, a language-orientated kind of poetics, constantly questioning and investigating the possibilities of the image, requiring the reader to reflect and not to hurry on. For Mehren, the labyrinth is not a target to destroy, but rather an existential condition, something one must find one's way into, like a world of tangled signs which must be decoded.

Stein Mehren's poetry is not iconoclastic like that of Georg Johannesen; his style is more heartfelt and less ironic. Where Johannesen insists on reason as his sphere of influence, in his essays frequently referring to the age of Enlightenment, Mehren is more concerned with sentiment and imagination. He has also published a number of essays, commenting on contemporary issues in the arts and in the philosophy of culture, and generally adhering to the tradition from Schiller and the Romantics. These two poets, so different in tone and poetic method, illustrate the wide range of Norwegian Modernism, formally as well as ideologically, in the early 1960s.

By now several of the older poets, who had started their literary careers in the national tradition dominating the scene in the early postwar years, were beginning to investigate the expressive potentials of free verse and new kinds of metaphor. The senior among these, Gunnar Reiss-Andersen (1896–1964), had found the new style adequate for his mood in some poems as early as in 1949, but he hesitated to renounce the tonal effects of traditional poetry, as he had enjoyed considerable success with his poems in the conventional mode in the 1920s, the 1930s and particularly during the occupation. More wholehearted in its Modernist expression is the mature poetry of Astrid Hjertenæs Andersen. Her favourite genre is the verbal painting of landscape scenes, often with animals depicted with an underscored presence which creates a sculptural effect. This poet is an observing more than a reflecting mind; her project is to capture the configurations of an instant in a verbal image of lasting effect. There is a quality of classical composure in several of her poems in the 1950s and later. Her art focuses on the meaningful aspects of life, man and animal in harmony with the environment, and nature's green fields as the generous source of peace and nourishment. The idyll is the dominant mode in the poetry of Astrid Hjertenæs Andersen, as in "Frokost i det grønne" (Breakfast in the open air, 1964).

On the **nynorsk** side, the lyrical poets tended to be more faithful to the traditional verse form and the venerable national themes and motifs. Tarjei Vesaas had cleared the way for a more European concept of the poem, although he remained rooted in the soil of upper Telemark, and a number of writers followed in his steps, without turning their backs completely on tradition. Among these were his wife, Halldis Moren Vesaas (b.1907), who had published poems since 1929, Aslaug Våa (1889–1965), with her background in the same region as Vesaas, and two younger poets, Arnljot Eggen (b.1923) and Marie Takvam (b.1926).

It is a widespread opinion among Norwegian poetry readers that as a poetic language, **nynorsk** is generally more expressive and more suitable in conveying impressions and moods pertaining to landscape imagery than is the Dano-Norwegian idiom. The **nynorsk** poets are therefore believed to have an advantage over their **bokmål** colleagues. To settle for this view would imply endorsement of a traditional concept of poetry: a poem is basically an expression of a receptive mind experiencing and interpreting nature, preferably some rural or wilderness scene. It may be that **nynorsk** writers, because of their greater familiarity with some rural dialect and the countryside existence, can treat such subjects with a linguistic security their urban counterparts do not possess. It may also be that the **nynorsk** vocabulary because of the variations in regional dialects is richer when it comes to expressions for various natural phenomena. Dano-Norwegian can on the other side refer to a longer tradition as a literary language, and this probably means an advantage when it comes to more abstract reflection, whether in the direction of self analysis or criticism of civilization. Although such theories about language differences should not be overemphasized, this consideration may be appropriate in trying to account for the relative delay and formal moderation regarding the development of **nynorsk** Modernist poetry. European Modernism represents among other things an intellectual challenge, and if the **nynorsk** writers – of prose as well as of verse – hesitated to respond to it, part of the reason could be that their rurally based idiom was not ready for it.

Olav H. Hauge (b.1908) started in the idealist tradition of Aukrust and Nygard; his first book of poems was **Glør i oska** (Embers in the ashes, 1946). During the 1950s he developed a more earthly based kind of poetry, observing and meditating on the little things of everyday life without becoming trivial. He studied the work of other poets, in foreign languages as well as in Scandinavian, and he published translations of a wide range of poems, covering Romanticism, Symbolism, Expressionism, and Modernism. He never joined the literary circles in the capital, but preferred to remain true to his region, inner Hardanger, and to his experience of the landscape and culture of that part of Norway. And yet his poetry is not of a limited, regional appeal. During the 1960s he was acclaimed by the young generation of poets and critics as a true European. Like several among the younger poets, he is an admirer of Chinese poetry, and it can be assumed that the concentrated imagist quality of Hauge's short poems, the characteristic detail, the unexpected perspective illuminating an ordinary situation, is the result of that Eastern influence. With the exception of classical poets of the nineteenth century like A.O. Vinje and Arne Garborg, and two or three poems by Aukrust and Vesaas, the dominant tone of **nynorsk** poetry before Hauge's mature period has been grave, at times even pathetic, in the lofty style. Olav Hauge developed a different tuning fork. His poems frequently have wit, occasionally even self-irony, as in this one from the collection **Dropar i austavind** (Drops in the East Wind, 1966):

Gamal diktar prøver seg som modernist

Han med fekk hug å prøva
desse nye styltrone.
Han har kome seg upp,
og stig varsamt som ein stork.
Underleg, so vidsynt han vart.
Han kan endatil telja sauene til grannen.

Old Poet has a go at being a Modernist

He too had a mind to try
these new stilts.
He's got himself up,
steps warily like a stork.
Remarkable, how far sighted.
He can even count his neighbour's sheep.[32]

Poems like this one have given Hauge a relatively large audience during the last two decades. His Modernism is never hermetic and not weighed down by philosophical reflection. Its base is concise sensory perception, with the potential of semantic expansion. The prevailing mode of these poems is visual, but the vision is not fragmented beyond recognition; it is activating a kind of experience which is shared by the common reader in rural Norway.

The high esteem enjoyed by this lonely lyrical voice from Ulvik in Hardanger should not be interpreted as a come-back for Regional Romanticism, the cult of "hidden Norway" which had been a trend in some circles between the wars.[33] Rather it is an indirect symptom of the increased international orientation which characterized Norwegian Modernism in the 1960s. Another indication of this orientation is the amount of poetry (and fiction) translated from foreign languages. This was also a part of the picture in the 1950s when Arne Dørumsgaard (in 1950) started to publish his translations of classical Chinese poems, later on including Japanese and Korean poems, and Paal Brekke (in 1955 and 1957) translated Modernist poetry from Europe and the United States, while André Bjerke had concentrated his efforts on earlier periods of European poetry and published four collections of translations between 1947 and 1957. Others had also contributed. In the 1960s this activity continued, and a number of new translators, both **bokmål** and **nynorsk** writers, appeared, such as Sigmund Skard, Emil Boyson, Paal-Helge Haugen, Georg Johannesen, and Olav H. Hauge. A great variety of poets from many foreign countries and representing different periods and styles, were now available. In addition, the increased scope of higher education tended to reduce the effect of some language barriers.

The 1960s became a decade of literary experiments, in Norway as well as in the other Scandinavian countries. This was the case in the writing of prose as well as in verse. The Kafka reception in the 1950s did not result in any new school of writers. A couple of novels with some resemblance to a "kafkaesque" labyrinth world can be pointed out, both written by established authors: Johan Borgen's **"Jeg"** ("I", 1959) and Tarjei Vesaas' **Brannen** (The Fire, 1961). During the first half of the 1960s, another major Modernist writer was introduced to the Norwegian reading public: Samuel Beckett. His plays in particular received much attention, while his novels were considered less intelligible. This may indicate the force of tradition in postwar Norwegian fiction, but the last half of the 1960s witnessed a new generation of writers emerging, and among these the will to experiment with narrative form was manifest.

The literary situation in Norway underwent certain changes during these years, as a consequence of the development in mass communication. The new medium, television, was anticipated without much enthusiasm in conservative literary circles. In his 1954 essay, "Gibberish from Parnassus", Øverland had expressed his hope that Norway would be spared from television for some more years.[34] Two years later, one channel TV was established in Sweden (the second channel came in 1969), while regular TV transmission started in Norway in 1960, with a single channel, state monopoly and limited broadcasting time. Nevertheless, the book publishers and the writers' organization were concerned. Television in a small country like Norway meant increased tempo in the communication from the international world, producing a challenge and possibly a threat to the national culture. It was believed that certain measures would have to be taken by the authorities if one wanted the production of Norwegian literature to continue on the same scale as earlier. In his opening essay in the periodical **Diktets Venner** in 1958, Arnulf Øverland had suggested that if every one of the one thousand libraries in the country would buy one copy of every book of poetry published, the publishers would not risk losing money on this kind of books, and the poets would be free, if not rich people.[35] A similar idea was finally adopted by the

Storting, and a state purchasing programme for Norwegian poetry and fiction covering one thousand copies of each publication, intended for distribution to all public libraries, has been in operation since 1965. Two years later the government decided to exempt books from sales tax. As a parallel measure, financial support of talented writers in the form of scholarships of varying amounts escalated. This policy of literary protectionism is still effective in 1985, and there is no doubt about its positive effect regarding the conditions for literary experimenting over the last 20 years.

Traditionally an artist and especially a poet in Norway is regarded as a lonely individual with unique talents and considerable reluctance when it comes to joining the company of fellow human beings. During the 1950s, there had been no significant group of writers working together for a common purpose or sharing in a stimulating exchange of views, such as the Swedish "fyrtiotalisterna" or the literary circle around the periodical **Heretica** in Denmark. With the rapidly growing number of students on the different campuses and the general increase of educated people in the 1960s, the situation was bound to become more favourable for the forming of literary societies and political organizations among the young intellectuals. The image of the lonely genius was losing its basis correspondingly.

The most conspicuous group of young writers to emerge during these years was the people gathering around the editorial staff of the small but ambitious student periodical **Profil**, particularly during the years 1966–68. The critics were quick to focus on this group of talented writers, and much attention was aroused regarding their main project, to create a new tradition of Modernist fiction in Norway. Regarding poetry, they wanted to add momentum to the Modernist endeavour represented by some solitary poets of the preceding generation. This could best be done by a combination of creative and critical efforts.

The contribution of these young "profiles", Tor Obrestad (b.1938), Jan Erik Vold (b.1939), Einar Økland (b.1940), Dag Solstad (b.1941), Espen Haavardsholm (b.1945), and Paal-Helge Haugen (b.1945), to the literary history of the 1960s has been discussed by several critics and scholars from various viewpoints,[36] and I shall not give another survey here. One additional perspective, however, would be to focus for a moment on the character of this Modernist revival in its relations to the development of the modern media. The 1960s was an age of increased temperature in the field of experimental art in Scandinavia as well as elsewhere, and poetry had its full share. In Sweden the young poets had launched an anti-Symbolist rebellion on the basis of an uncommitted, relativist attitude to ideological or political issues. The image of the poet faithfully listening to his inner voice was felt to be antiquated in the age of social democracy. The trend was moving in the direction of the world of objects and relationships. "Concrete poetry", "the new simplicity", "everyday realism" – these were the slogans of the day, displaying the will among new poets to investigate alternative functions for verbal art.[37]

Similar ideas were on the agenda in Denmark. Hans-Jørgen Nielsen, poet, critic, and editor of the anthology **Eksempler** (Examples, 1968), coined the term "the third phase of Modernism" for the writings of his generation. He identified the common experience of identity crisis in the literature between the wars as the first phase, while the loss of faith in the healing power of the poetic image during the 1950s was seen as the second phase. In the third phase of Modernism Nielsen claims that poetry has lost its status as perception; the world has no fundamental nature to be perceived, and accordingly the poem is merely an example of a language game, something you do with words. Metaphorical complexity and lyrical analogies should be avoided, qualities which were criteria of value to the earlier generations. The result is metaphysical emptiness, and the role of the poet is secularized correspondingly. This "attitude relativism" was not a lasting trend, however. A change in the literary climate of opinion can be traced as early as 1965 in Sweden, when Göran Sonnevi published his poem on the Vietnam war, and towards the end of the 1960s a growing political engagement was manifesting itself among the poets in Denmark as well.[38]

Norwegian development took more or less the same course. The young prose writers in particular turned out to be susceptible to the leftist trend from around 1970, while most of the poets were less inclined to let their political sympathies affect their art. The change which took place in poetry during the 1960s does have ideological aspects, but basically it is a question of mode of expression. In an essay published in 1965 on the somewhat controversial issue of concrete poetry, Jan Erik Vold points to the many possibilities of new combinations of art forms open to investigation in the wake of technological development, with music, pictorial art, or theatrical elements of various kinds used together with verbal art forms. Concrete poetry, operating with letters or words on the page with the intention of creating visual effects rather than verbal communication, represents a violation of the borderlines between the art forms as traditionally conceived. Earlier generations of Modernists regarded communication through language as the basic concern of poetry; to the generation of the 1960s this was not as obvious as before. The possibility of complete understanding between human beings was questioned. A new kind of aesthetics was introduced in **avant-garde** circles, emphasizing the creation of emotional contact and personal experience.[39]

While the young Modernist poets of the 1950s, Brekke, Hjertenæs Andersen, and even Johannesen, had been writing mainly in the conceptual mode, only occasionally using sound effects, the poets of the 1960s slowly returned to the tonal mode. It was not a come-back of traditional verse forms, but a tribute to the recitability, i.e. the rhythmical and musical potentials of the lines as rendered by the human voice, preferably the voice of the poet. This mode of presentation was not uncommon among the Modernists of earlier generations; Jacobsen, Boyson and Gill are eminent readers and as writers highly conscious of the sound medium. After the war the typical Modernist poem had tended towards settling on the page, as a silent and cryptic challenge for the individual reader, leaving the song for the popular entertainer.

In the 1960s Stein Mehren was the first poet to include recital as an integrated aspect of poetic performance, and after him Jan Erik Vold, who published his first book of poems, **Mellom speil og speil** (Between mirror and mirror), in 1965, has developed a similar personal way of reciting his own poetry. Gramophone records with poets reading from their work have been produced, even if not all poets are prepared to perform in the grand oratorial style. Another way of exploiting the musical qualities of modern poetry is to arrange sessions of poetry and jazz. In these efforts at lifting the sphere of poetical effect from the book page to the sound medium where it once belonged, Vold has been a pioneer. Even if the bulk of poetry written and read in Norway in our time still adheres to the conceptual and visual mode introduced by the Modernist poets of the 1950s, the trend towards the tonal mode is a characteristic part of the present picture.

The mode of presentation is of fundamental importance to the principle of composition. Listening to a poem requires an "easier" style than a silent reading situation where the eye can move freely over the page and if necessary linger over a complex passage. The new "text poem" of the 1950s was an exclusive kind of art. This has changed somewhat during the late 1960s and 1970s; the poets are generally more intent on getting through to their audience. This increasing concern also led to a more active marketing: in 1968 Norsk Forfattersentrum (Norwegian Authors' Centre) was organized with the purpose of arranging visits and recitals by poets and fiction writers at schools and other institutions.

While the conceptual mode to some extent had favoured the short, semantically complex poem, the trend towards a more extrovert kind of poetry, frequently referred to as **nyenkelhet** (new simplicity), paved the way for lyrical expansion. The idea that a good poem is a short poem had been cherished in Modernist circles, and critics had voiced some reservations on this point.[40] In 1968 Jan Erik Vold published a bulky collection of mostly long poems, **Mor Godhjertas glade versjon. Ja** (Mother Goodheart's Happy Version. Yes), where the reader is invited to accompany the talkative speaker on his roaming about in the streets of central Oslo, his native town. Mainly on the humorous side, these poems reveal an unpretentious character with a keen eye for details and an understanding attitude towards his fellow men. The book was very favourably received by the readers, and was reprinted several times. Two LP records with the poet reciting were produced. A Modernist poet had found his audience. In his later work, including both short and long poems, Vold has remained a central figure.

Long poems of an entirely different kind were published in 1970 by Alfred Hauge (b.1915) in **Det evige sekund** (The eternal second). He is mainly known as a writer of historical and of fabulous novels. His poetic style is of an oratorial kind unlike anything written in Norway, but with some resemblance to Walt Whitman's poetry. The Modernist element is located in the poetic language more than in the orientation of ideas. Alfred Hauge combines elements from the national and idealist tradition of **nynorsk** poetry of the 1920s with an internationally coloured lyrical form, and the result is a singularly Modernist effect.

By 1970 free verse was by far the dominant form in Norwegian poetry, so in that sense Modernism was no longer fighting an uphill battle. Poets like Mehren, Økland, Vold, Paal-Helge Haugen, Olav H. Hauge and Arnold Eidslott continued to publish poems in their respective veins, and new poets appeared. It is not easy to perceive a significant change in the history of poetry over the last fifteen years. The various modes of Modernism seem to coexist peacefully in the poetry magazines and on the book market. Since the beginning of the 1970s prose fiction has received a much greater share of public attention than poetry, and the dominant novel form during that decade hardly deserves the name of Modernism. Writers like Solstad, Obrestad, Haavardsholm, Bjørg Vik (b.1935), Knut Faldbakken (b.1941), Liv Køltzow (b.1945), and Edvard Hoem (b.1950) have in various ways investigated the social conditions determining the mental habits and life of the modern individual. With some noteworthy exceptions recent Norwegian fiction has cultivated what might be called "blue denim prose" permeated by leftist and feminist ideologies. Modernist ideas about aesthetic effects and alternative ways of narrative discourse have not been at the centre of discussion.

The most important single factor to account for this development was the political debate concerning Norwegian membership of the European Common Market. Most intellectuals on the left found themselves joining forces with farmers and middle class national conservatives in opposing the Social Democratic government and the majority of the political parties which were in favour of membership. At the referendum on 25 September 1972, the electorate decided against full membership. The heated discussion on this issue had kindled a revival of the traditionally strong belief in self-determination, leading to a peculiar merger of socialist and nationalist ideologies.

Modernism as an internationally orientated movement was no longer a central agent in Norwegian fiction.

And yet formal experiments have been carried on, often with considerable success, by writers like Kjartan Fløgstad (b.1944), Cecilie Løveid (b.1951) and Jan Kjærstad (b.1953). With the exception of Løveid, the concept of Modernism does not seem altogether fitting for their contributions to the art of the novel. Fløgstad has tried to combine impulses from Latin American fiction, various kinds of popular literature and other mass media such as film, in presenting the world and ideas of young workers, sailors and intellectuals with their background in small industrial communities of Western Norway. The result is a literary form which reveals an artist consciously working on his medium and at the same time interpreting the existential conditions of his characters in political terms. An appropriate concept for the kind of writing practised in books like **Fangliner** (Painters, 1972), **Dalen Portland** (Portland Valley, 1977), and **Fyr og flamme** (Fire and flames, 1980) could be Social Modernism, as opposed to the general trend of Social Romanticism.

As a final comment it should be noted that for the young writers of the 1980s the concept of Modernism does not arouse much enthusiasm. It is not regarded as modern any more, and art must move on, whether a suitable critical concept can be found or not. In an interview regarding his 1984 novel **Homo Falsus**, Jan Kjærstad commented on his literary position by saying that it is a fundamentally realist novel:

> Det eneste merkelige ved fremstillingen er at ting gjentar seg i bestemte mønstre som røper konstruksjon. Sånn sett brytes realismen, og i spenningsfeltet mellom disse oppstår en dobbelteffekt som jeg ikke har noe navn på. Ett er imidlertid sikkert: Modernist er jeg ikke.

> The only odd thing about the account is that events are repeated in accordance with certain patterns revealing construction. In this way the realism is obstructed, and the field of tensions between these patterns engenders a double effect for which I have no name. One thing is for sure, though: I am not a Modernist.[41]

Notes

1. See Bjørn Nilsen: "En annen klode? Raskt tilbakeblikk på tungetaledebatten", **Profil** 2, 1968, pp.19–23.

2. E.g. Poul Borum: **Poetisk modernisme. En introduktion til moderne europæisk og amerikansk poesi fra Baudelaire til i dag** (Copenhagen, 1966), p.9; Odd Martin Mæland: "Modernisme i Norge?" **Norsk Litterær Årbok** (1967), p.189; Per Thomas Andersen: "Farvel til Europa? Om modernisme, provinsialisme – og post-modernisme", **Vinduet** 2, 1984, p.3.

3. This is the general view of scholars like Poul Borum: op.cit., Hugo Friedrich: **Die Struktur der modernen Lyrik. Von Baudelaire bis zur Gegenwart** (Hamburg, 1956), and Kjell Espmark: **Att översätta själen. En huvudlinje i modern poesi från Baudelaire till surrealismen** (Stockholm, 1975), while Malcolm Bradbury and James McFarlane in **Modernism** (Harmondsworth, 1976) suggest 1890 to 1930 as the most suitable dating.

4. "Une saison en enfer", **Œuvres complètes** (Paris, 1963), p.243.

5. See Vigdis Ystad: **Kristofer Uppdals lyrikk** (Oslo, 1978), pp.183–210, and Idar Stegane: "The New Norse Literary Tradition", **Review of National Literatures**, vol.12, **Norway** (New York, 1983), edited by Sverre Lyngstad, p.114.

6. Stéphane Mallarmé: **Œuvres complètes** (Paris, 1945), p.70.

7. See Arne Kjell Haugen: **Poesi, språk, latter. Fire essays om modernismen** (Oslo, 1982), p.29.

8. "Franz Kafka", **Mot Dag** (1922), pp.188f.

9. **Surrealisme. En antologi**, edited by Kjartan Fløgstad, Karin Gundersen, Kjell Heggelund, and Sissel Lie (Oslo, 1980).

10. **Europeisk poesi i norsk gjendiktning** ved Emil Boyson (Oslo, 1965).

11. **Vandring mot havet** (Oslo, 1974), p.7.

12. Ibid., pp.59f. Unless otherwise stated, the translations are my own.

13. Op.cit., p.7.

14. E.g. Sverre Lyngstad: "Modern Norwegian Literature: An Overview", in Lyngstad, op.cit., pp.44f, and H.M. Enzensberger (ed.): **Museum der modernen Poesie** (Frankfurt am Main, 1960, München, 1969), p.372.

15. See the interview in **Poesi Magasin** 2, 1984, p.9.

16. Translated by David McDuff, in T. Johanssen (ed.): **20 Contemporary Norwegian Poets** (Oslo etc., 1984), p.27.

17. See **Poesi Magasin** 2, 1984, p.9.

18. Translated by Paul Farmer, in Robin Fulton (ed.): **Five Norwegian Poets** (Lines Review, 55–56, Midlothian, 1976), pp.29f.

19. The lines are from "Rapsodi över et forfallent liv" (Rhapsody on a ruined life), Claes Gill: **Samlede dikt** (Oslo, 1967), p.18.

20. Ibid., p.54.

21. Cf. Harald Sverdrup: "Claes Gill og modernismen", **Vinduet** 4, 1950, p.477.

22. Nordahl Grieg: **Samlede dikt** (Oslo, 1947, 8th ed., 1976), p.154.

23. Translated by Kenneth G. Chapman, in Tarjei Vesaas: **30 Poems**, selected and translated by Kenneth G. Chapman (Oslo etc., 1971), pp.14f.

24. Paal Brekke: **Dikt 1949–1972** (Oslo, 1978), p.53.

25. Ibid., p.81.

26. E.g. Øverland: "Tungetale fra Parnasset", **I beundring og forargelse** (Oslo, 1954),

pp.228ff., and Carl Keilhau: "Poster i modernismens regnskap", **Vinduet** (1955), pp.229–39.

27. This view was expressed by Paal Brekke: "Om den nye lyrikken", **Samtiden** (1956), pp.85–103, Odd Solumsmoen: "Etter 'Tungetale' – striden", **Bokormens forsvarstale og andre essays** (Oslo, 1977), pp.85–92 (originally printed in **Samtiden** 1954), and Erling Christie: "Poesien og det virkelige", **Tendenser og profiler** (Oslo, 1955), pp.11–38.

28. See Gunnar Skirbekk: **Nymarxisme og kritisk dialektikk** (Oslo, 1970), pp.7f., and by the same author: "'I refleksjonens mangel. . .' Om vekslande intellektuelle elitar i norsk etterkrigstid", **Nytt Norsk Tidsskrift** 1, 1984, p.34.

29. Georg Johannesen: **Dikt** (Oslo, 1969), pp.25f.

30. Ibid., p.43.

31. **50 60 70 80** (Oslo, 1980), p.52.

32. Translated by Robin Fulton, in Robin Fulton, op.cit., p.46; also in T. Johanssen, op.cit., p.56f.

33. Cf. the interest aroused by the Danish critic Jørgen Bukdahl, whose books **Norsk national kunst** (1924) and **Det skjulte Norge** (1936) combined a national and a regional approach.

34. Cf. Øverland, op.cit., p.220.

35. Cf. "I tjeneste hos ordene", **Diktets Venner** 1, 1958, p.2.

36. Interesting comments and evaluations regarding the achievement of the **Profil** group during the late 1960s can be found in the following articles: Lars-Olof Franzén: "Svensk syn på norskt 60-tal", **Norsk Litterær Årbok** (1967), pp.176–84, Walter Baumgartner: "Die Dezentralisierung der norwegischen Poesie", **Scandinavica** 12 (1973), pp.77–105, Lars Mjøset: "'For faen, vi stikker'. Om profilkretsen fra sekstiåra", **Vinduet** (1973), pp.26–43, Odd Martin Mæland: "Reflections on Norwegian Literature", **The American Scandinavian Review** 62 (1974), pp.33–37, Erik Berge, Atle Kittang, Ivar Larssen-Aas, and Idar Stegane: "Dikting i oppbrot", **Kontrast** (1975), pp.5–25, Janet Garton: "New Directions in Norwegian Literature", Sverre Lyngstad, op.cit., pp.163–84, and Øystein Rottem: "Generasjoner og epoker. Litteraturhistoriske refleksjoner omkring 1960- og 1970-åra", **Norsk Litterær Årbok** (1983), pp.169–88.

37. Cf. Bjørn Håkanson: "Upproret mot symbolismen", **Vinduet** (1967), pp.69–75, and Lars Gustafsson: "Relativismen bakom sextiotalets svenska lyrik", **Skandinavische Lyrik der Gegenwart**, IX. Studienkonferenz der International Association for Scandinavian Studies, Kiel, 16–22 Juli 1972, hg. von Otto Oberholzer (Glückstadt, 1973), pp.11–19.

38. Cf. Hans-Jørgen Nielsen: "Efterskrift. Modernismens tredje fase: Fra erkendelse til eksempel", **Eksempler**, edited by Hans-Jørgen Nielsen (Copenhagen, 1968), pp.155–79, and by the same author: "'Attituderelativisme': En papirtiger på vejen til den rigtige tiger!" **Hvedekorn** 44 (1970), pp.166–69.

39. Cf. Jan Erik Vold: "Om kunst og konkret poesi", **Profil** 4, 1965, pp.26–32.

40. Cf. Bjørn Nilsen: "Hva er poetisk modernisme?" **Samtiden** (1966), p.281, and Olaf Bille: **Vår modernistiske lyrikk. En kritisk studie** (Oslo, 1973), p.49.

41. **Bergens Tidende**, 15 October 1984, p.38.

Dag Solstad and *Profil:* Norwegian Modernism in the 1960s

Janet Garton

In "En gjest" ("A Guest"), a short story from Dag Solstad's first published collection **Spiraler** (Spirals, 1965), the first-person narrator relates how an unexpected visitor arrives and stays with him for an unspecified time. It is immediately obvious that this is no ordinary guest – he had entered and settled into the narrator's chair whilst the latter was out – and he is welcomed in words with Biblical overtones which suggest that there is a particular significance about his visit: "Gyldne rundstykker ville jeg strø ut over bordet til ære for ham. Det skulle bli fest, for en gjest hadde sett til meg i nåde"(p.79). ("Golden bread-rolls I would strew over the table in honour of him. We would celebrate, for a guest had taken mercy upon me").[1] The visitor soon turns out to be a mixed blessing, however; he sits unmoving in the narrator's best chair, mocks and mimics him, and behaves in a more and more uninhibitedly destructive manner. After ripping up and threatening to burn some of the narrator's clothes in the stove, he takes out a knife and begins whittling away at the room, gouging holes in the wooden furniture and shredding the wallpaper, and finally sawing off the back of the very chair upon which the narrator is sitting. Although he is roused to physical protest by these actions, the narrator cannot influence the behaviour of his guest – until he capitulates and offers to hand over the keys of the flat. Immediately the guest departs, and the narrator locks the door in relief.

Now he can return to his dream: he has three small orange trees in plant pots, which he anticipates will one day provide him with all the warmth and ripeness of the South: "En gang vil appelsinene blomstre forundret som en oppadstigende sol i mitt værelse. Siden vil de modne, jeg vil fylle hendene med appelsiner og strekke dem mot lyset. Da vil tapetet blekne, alle sorger visne, jeg vil åpne vinduet og høre leende barn rope på solen" (p.80). ("One day the oranges will flower, amazed, like a rising sun in my room. Then they will ripen, I will fill my hands with oranges and stretch them towards the light. Then the wallpaper will fade, all cares will wither, I shall open the window and hear laughing children shouting at the sun".) The plants cannot endure being seen by anyone else, however; as long as the visitor is there, they must remain shut up in a dark cupboard. As soon as he is gone, the narrator takes them out and cares for them – but they have become sickly in the dark. And his joy at his freedom slowly turns into emptiness: "Dagen ble tom, lyset seg inn vinduet, det var gjennomsiktig og tomt. Jeg vandret fram og tilbake og betraktet gjenstandene" (p.93). ("The day grew empty, the light seeped in through the window, it was transparent and empty. I wandered to and fro looking at the objects"). He sits listening for sounds of his visitor returning – and he does return, to the narrator's joy, which is expressed in similar terms to his initial welcome. The power of the visitor is now boundless, and the narrator has no defences. Beneath the visitor's gaze he drops his precious plants on the floor and smashes them, in terms reminiscent of a religious sacrifice: "Jeg gjorde en bevegelse som om jeg velsignet dem . . ." (p.94). ("I made a gesture as if to bless them . . ."). The destructiveness of the visitor becomes more and more intimate; he cuts a hole in the narrator's coat, and finally attacks his soul: "Med taushet og latter river han store flenger i min sjel" (p.95). ("With silence and laughter he rips great gashes in my soul"). The narrator's protest is reduced to a pathetic gesture: once a week, when the refuse collectors come, he goes down to the dustbins and removes the shattered remains of his orange plants. He holds them in his hands as he recalls a fleeting glimpse of his former vision – but must then return them to the bin for another week, as he looks up defiantly to see the motionless figure of the visitor watching from the window of his flat.

The theme of this short story awakens echoes in the mind of any reader familiar with Modernist fiction from the earlier part of this century. The uninvited visitor who intrudes into one's life – indeed, who practically **becomes** one's life; the obscurely threatening, omniscient presence against which the hapless victim tries to marshall his defences without knowing how or even whether such a thing is possible; the total isolation, cut off from any support or meaningful response from another human being: all these are reminiscent of the parables of persecution and guilt told by Kafka in **Der Prozess** and **Das Schloss**. Reality is no longer to be relied upon, and personality itself is a fragile construct, liable to invasion by disturbing forces, which it fears and yet towards which it is irresistibly drawn. Dreams are shattered into potsherds as man realises the futility of rebellion and accepts the chaos and the unpredictability of an existence for which no logical explanation can be found.

Solstad's next book, **Svingstol** (Swivel Chair, 1967), was also a collection of short pieces. One of them, "Nærvær" ("Presence"), takes as its starting point a similar situation to that of "En gjest": the arrival of a visitor from outside and the development of the relationship between visitor and host. In this short story, however, we are in a totally different world.

The host in "Nærvær" is a landlady, and the visitor a lodger who takes a room in her flat. The story consists of a description of their everyday lives, particularly that of the landlady; the lodger is present mainly as a series of noises – doors opening, records playing, footsteps across the floor. The landlady's life is unremarkable in the extreme; she spends her time dusting the furniture, watering the flowers, sewing cushion covers for a charity stall at a bazaar. Life is safe, predictable, repetitious, and shorn of dramatic or disturbing events. The only interruptions to the smooth calmness of life come when the lodger asks if he may have a bath, and then – right at the end of the story – when the noises from his room suddenly cease for three days. When the landlady goes to investigate, any stirrings of excitement are immediately punctured by the prosaic discovery that he is in bed with 'flu; and the story ends with her making him a cup of tea.

Thus the visitor in this story is not an emissary from the subconscious or an embodiment of a destructive force, but an ordinary man, a Mr Bleaney of regular habits and retiring disposition.[2] The landlady is not undergoing a spiritual crisis, but placidly pursuing a way of life which is mapped out once and for all. The reader is not urged into exploring a deeper level of meaning beneath the surface narrative; the meaning is precisely on the surface, in the accumulation of trivia which make up a life.

The different intentions of the two short texts are further mirrored in the different narrative techniques employed, and in variations in language and syntax. "En gjest" has a first-person narrator, whose consciousness is the focus of attention; the narrative concentrates on his aspirations and fears. "Nærvær" is narrated in the third person, and with a point of view which is consistently external to the two figures in the action; thus we see nothing of what either is thinking, and are permitted only to watch their actions through the eyes of an external observer. "En gjest" alternates between dialogue and internal monologue, whereas there is no conversation to relieve the sameness of "Nærvær". The sentence structure in "En gjest" is also more complicated and varied, with frequent use of abstract and metaphysical vocabulary, reasonably long sentences and a number of subordinate clauses. In "Nærvær" the sentences are shorter, simpler and more concrete, often following a repetitive pattern and with a marked preference for main clauses and parataxis:

> Hun vanner blomstene, tørker støv, pusser sølv, skriver brev, går i syklubben.
> Han er høy.
> Han er mørk.
> Han er kraftig.
> Han går med frakkekraven oppslått.
> Plutselig står han inne i stuen og ber om å få låne badet.
> Litt senere hører hun badekranen fosse.
> Hun tørker støv av malerier, porselensfigurer, fotografier. Hun broderer mønstre til puter, hun trekker gardinene for vinduene.
>
> (p.164)

> She waters the flowers, dusts, polishes the silver, writes letters, goes to her sewing club.
> He is tall.
> He is dark.
> He is well-built.
> He wears his coat collar turned up.
> Suddenly he is in the room asking to use the bath.
> A little later she hears the bath water running.
> She dusts paintings, porcelain figures, photographs. She sews patterns for cushion covers, she draws the curtains across the windows.

The contrast between these two short stories is indicative of the contrast between the two collections from which they are taken; in just two years, Solstad's style and intentions had undergone a radical transformation. Furthermore, they are typical examples of two of the main trends within the wave of Modernist writing which dominated Norwegian literature in the mid-1960s, and in which Solstad himself played such a central role.

In a curious way, Norway was both an early and a very late arrival on the scene of European Modernism. Knut Hamsun, with his depictions of the "unconscious life of the soul" in novels like **Sult** (1890, trans. **Hunger**, 1899) and **Mysterier** (1892, trans. **Mysteries**, 1927), and other works of the 1890s, and Edvard Munch, with his stark and "unfinished" paintings of the late 1880s and 1890s, had been pioneers of change. They had begun the process of recording their disturbing visions of man's fragmented and irrational nature even whilst rationalism and "scientific" Naturalism were in their heyday. Both were misunderstood by their contemporaries, and both came to have a profound and continuing influence on twentieth-century literary and artistic movements, within Scandinavia and abroad. Even today, if the names of any Norwegian cultural figures since Ibsen can be said to be common currency in Europe, it is those of Hamsun and Munch.

However, despite the impact which Hamsun made on the literary world, he cannot be said to be the founder of a Modernist school in Norway. The most well-known Norwegian prose writers of the early twentieth century – Johan Falkberget, Kristofer Uppdal, Sigrid Undset – returned to a historical or social realism in their works which is more reminiscent of the 1880s. And Hamsun himself moved in that direction too, with works like the collective study of a community **Segelfoss By** (1915, trans. **Segelfoss Town,** 1925) and the didactic **Markens Grøde** (1917, trans. **The Growth of the Soil,** 1920). There are writers from slightly later in the century whose works can certainly be labelled Modernist: the poets Paal Brekke and Rolf Jacobsen, the novelist Johan Borgen, the poet and novelist Tarjei Vesaas; yet they cannot be said to be part of a cohesive tradition, rather isolated individuals with their own highly idiosyncratic portrayals of a tormented modern consciousness.

Thus it was that the sudden emergence of a group of young Norwegian writers in the mid-1960s with a common commitment to experimental and non-realistic writing seemed like the belated arrival in Norway of Modernism at last.[3] Norwegian prose was to be freed from the classical tradition in which it had with few exceptions remained frozen since the nineteenth century. The appearance of Dag Solstad's **Spiraler** in 1965 was one of the opening chords in what was very quickly to grow into a crescendo of literary and critical activity.

The literary historian who wishes to trace the growth of this new movement would do well to begin by looking at the literary magazine **Profil. Profil** developed from a student magazine founded in 1938, originally called **Filologen.** Since the war it had become a more specialized literary forum, and had changed its name to **Profil** in 1960. In the first issue of 1966, a new chief editor, Tor Obrestad (b.1938), took over, and a number of new names appeared on the editorial board: Noel Cobb (b.1938), Espen Haavardsholm (b.1945), Paal-Helge Haugen (b.1945), Dag Solstad (b.1941), Jan Erik Vold (b.1939). And it was this young generation, together with one or two others such as Einar Økland (b.1940), who was chief editor in 1964, and the slightly older Stein Mehren (b.1935), who contributed most of the articles and set the tone for the intense critical debate.

For these writers were not just producers of Literature between hard covers, but also critics and experimenters, who had a workshop attitude to creative writing; they set up a programme, criticized each other's contributions and provided a running commentary upon their own literary activity, its aims and problems. In an editorial article in the first issue of 1966, Tor Obrestad set out what they saw as the aim of the journal: to provide a focus for a Modernist movement. And he was at pains to demonstrate that Modernism and Norwegian literature had so far had little in common: "Vi vil gjerne presisere at dette omgrepet ikkje har så mykje med tid å gjere. Det har meir med ein annan måte å seie ting på, ein annan måte å skrive på enn den som har vore hevdvunnen her i landet sidan Snorre skreiv kongesogene. For oss er altså han som utforma **Draumkvedet** meir moderne enn ein Øverland, ein Skjæraasen".[4] ("We should like to make clear that this concept [Modernism] has very little to do with time. It has more to do with a different way of saying things, a different way of writing than has been officially approved in this country since Snorre wrote the Sagas of the Kings. In our eyes, the man who created **Draumkvedet** is more modern than an Øverland or a Skjæraasen").

"Ein annan måte å seie ting på" ("a different way of saying things") – Modernism implied not just a way of seeing the world, but also a style. This is a conviction which is repeated insistently in the pages of **Profil** in the writers' analyses of each other's work: Obrestad on Georg Johannesen, Vold on Stein Mehren (1, 1966), Økland on Johannesen (3, 1966), Økland on Cobb, Obrestad on Olav H. Hauge, Haavardsholm on Vesaas (4, 1966), Paal-Helge Haugen on Vold (5, 1966) – and so on.

Dag Solstad's own articles, of which the first is printed in **Profil** 1, 1966, also provide a constant accompaniment to his literary production, and can profitably be read alongside it; throughout his literary career so far, he has maintained the habit of investigating in article form the ideas he is at the same time transmuting into literary creation. The first article from 1966 entitled "Norsk prosa – europeisk modernisme" ("Norwegian Prose – European Modernism"), can be read as a pendant to his collection of short stories from 1965, **Spiraler**.[5] In his article he too takes up the problem of Modernist literature in Norway, or rather the lack of it. Norwegian prose has clung firmly to its traditions, refusing to experiment, and aiming at an illusion of reality rather than creating a dynamic world of its own: "I en vesentlig roman er kravet om objektiv sannsynlighet eliminert. Den kan være sannsynlig og den kan ikke være det, det spiller ingen rolle. I stedet kommer kravet om vesentlighet" (p.14). ("In a significant novel, the demand for objective probability is eliminated. It might obey the laws of probability or it might not, it makes no difference. In its place stands the demand for significance"). And it will not much help matters if Norwegian writers now attempt to produce a pale copy of European Modernism; they need to combine this "new way of saying things" with what is vital in their own native tradition. There is no inspiration to be derived from nineteenth-century realism; instead they must go further back to deeper sources, to the Nordic myths which are the incarnation of the people's dreams, and to the folk literature and folk tales which derive from them (compare Obrestad's recommendation of **Draumkvedet** as a model). The combination of a revitalizing of pre-modern myths with a modern experimental attitude to literature will result in a truly Norwegian Modernism.

The two criteria which Solstad here sets out as mandatory for the composition of Norwegian Modernist prose – the search for significance or "essentialness" of plot ("vesentlighet") rather than conformity with traditional standards of probability, and the centrality of mythical and dream-like elements – are met in the works of several of his fellow-writers at around this time. Einar Økland's collection of short stories **Svart i det grøne** (Black in the Green, 1967) depicts disturbing and irrational forces suddenly intruding upon everyday reality. Some of the stories in Tor Obrestad's **Vind** (Wind, 1966) have a nightmarish quality, a sense of impending catastrophe only partly accounted for by actual events. Espen Haavardsholm's first collection **Tidevann** (Tides, 1966) takes up the theme of the alienated individual and his relationship to an absurd and fantastic world, which is filtered through sequences of dream-like unreality. But before all these, Solstad's **Spiraler** itself had embarked upon a charting of the struggles of a consciousness to find its bearings in an unpredictable and hostile environment.

The isolated individual – and they are all ultimately alone in these short stories – is confronted in **Spiraler** with a world which is like a problem to be solved, but of which the solution is never revealed to him. He (the central character is always male) is playing a game of which he does not know the rules. "Klirring av tallerkener" ("The Rattling of Plates") describes a man settling into a discreet and comfortable hotel, which imperceptibly becomes a prison from which he cannot escape and where he is constantly confronted by situations in which he does not know how to behave. He has lost control of what happens, and fears that indeed anything may happen – silent women may suddenly explode, chandeliers may crash down and bury him. The people he meets are not real, but lifeless objects or figments of his own desires and fears. The end is defeat and withdrawal – he retreats to his own room, shuts out all outside sounds and asks to have his meals brought up. "En tomsekk og et tau" ("An Empty Sack and a Rope") also presents an image of an absurd existence: what one might call the archetypal existential experience of life as a station waiting room.[6] A man who has broken his mirror (ie lost all confirmation of his own identity) goes out with an empty sack to collect the scattered fragments of his self, "my bodies" as he calls them. He finds them all in the station waiting room, waiting for a train which will never stop for them as they have no luggage. It will not stop for him either – until he has the splendid idea of putting his bodies in his sack and using that as his luggage. At that the train stops; but the sack is too heavy and bursts before he can reach the train, tumbling his bodies over the platform. The train departs again, and as it departs he sees that it is entirely empty – no passenger has managed to board it. He walks off with his six bodies, no longer in charge – they have forced him to take off his shoes and walk barefoot like them.

The seven stories in this collection explore in various ways the dilemmas of an existence from which all safeguards are removed, in which the fragile identity is threatened on all sides, by invasion from an uninvited guest, or by an inability to control its separate and autonomous elements. The illusion of everyday reality has been replaced by the remorseless logic of a nightmare. Thus far Dag Solstad fulfils his own criteria, combining an internal structural coherence with fantastic, dream-like elements. However, it is difficult to perceive anything essentially Norwegian in this Modernism. Despite Solstad's assertion that it is to their own earlier tradition that Norwegian writers must look for inspiration, the tales he tells are far more reminiscent of writers like Kafka or Sartre than they are of Viking legends or folk tale. A couple of the stories are specifically linked to Norwegian experience: "Emigrantene" ("The Emigrants") must put a Norwegian in mind of the nineteenth-century emigrations to America, and "Herr Ps lørdag" ("Mr P's Saturday") is set in a small coastal town in which the arrival of the steamer on Saturdays is the high point of the week. Yet these settings serve as background to an essentially unlocalized crisis; the function of the steamer in Mr P's world, like that of the train in "En tomsekk og et tau", is that it allows him to invest his life's energy in planning a journey he knows he will never undertake. The stories in **Spiraler** would not betray their origin if translated into another European language; they take place in a landscape of the mind rather than in Norway. The most abstract of all the stories, "Det plutselige øyeblikk" ("The Sudden Moment"), describes the moment of the discovery of the meaninglessness, the gratuitousness of existence in terms which are unmistakably reminiscent of Sartre's descriptions in **La Nausée**:

> Han ble alene i butikken, igjen kom tingene over ham. Han visste så forbannet godt at de hadde navn, men det lyktes ikke å nøytralisere en eneste en av dem ved å mumle navnene sakte for seg selv. Stol, mumlet han. Gult lys, skruer, vindu. Men alt var som før.
>
> (p.25)

> He was left alone in the shop, and things overwhelmed him again. He was so damn certain that they had names, but he couldn't manage to neutralize a single one of them by muttering the names quietly to himself. Chair, he muttered. Yellow light, screws, window. But all was as before.

Compare this passage from **La Nausée**:

> Les choses se sont delivrées de leurs noms. Elles sont là, grotesques, têtues, géantes et ça paraît imbécile de les appeler des banquettes ou de dire quoi que ce

soit sur elles: je suis au milieu des Choses, les innommables. Seul, sans mots, sans défenses, elles m'environnent . . ."[7]

Despite his literary manifesto, then, Solstad's first book was more European Modernism than it was Norwegian prose. It was a phase, however, which was very quickly left behind. Early in 1966 Solstad published an article in **Arbeiderbladet** called "Språk og metafor" ("Language and Metaphor") – which must therefore have been composed very shortly after his first **Profil** article.[8] In a description of a seminar on modern poetry, he referred to a clash between the traditional view of poetry as a richly symbolic, metaphorical genre and a new kind of poetry presented by some of the Danish and Swedish authors, where metaphors were eschewed in favour of concretism and "ny-enkelhet" (a term for which there is no precise equivalent in English, suggesting a deliberate choice of simplicity, even naiveté, of form and expression). Solstad's reaction to the clash of views was, he admitted, an ambivalent one; he was reluctant to dispense with metaphor, which he regarded as an impoverishment of poetic language, and yet on the other hand confessed to being fascinated by the new concretism. A metaphorical world can so easily become entirely introspective, can cut its author off from contact with the real world – an experience which Solstad describes in a way which clearly refers to his work on **Spiraler**:

> Denne motviljen mot sinnets projiserte landskaper kan en som selv har arbeidet i denne formen godt forstå. Av egen erfaring vet jeg hvor lett man har for å virre rundt i sin egen tomgangsverden, og det muligens nettopp fordi den valgte form innbyr til det. Det kan komme en dag hvor det føles som en befrielse å kunne skrive kaldt og nøkternt: Det er en gate. Det er en sten. Det er en bil. Man føler seg da som en kylling som har knust skallet og plutselig er i verden.
>
> (**Artikler**, p.22)

> This aversion to the projected landscapes of the mind can easily be understood by one who has himself worked in this form. From my own experience I know how easy it is to spin around in one's own hollow world, and that is perhaps precisely because the form one has chosen leads one into doing so. One day it can come to seem like a liberation to be able to write coldly and soberly: That is a street. That is a stone. That is a car. One feels like a chick which has broken its shell and is suddenly there in the world.

Solstad is looking for a way out of the "landscapes of the mind"; but at the same time he warns that the new concretism can easily become sterile and tautologous, preoccupied with its own patterns and thus equally isolated from any points of reference outside itself. It can lead to an abdication of responsibility on the part of the writer: "Oppdagelsen av hverdagen . . . har ført til en ukritisk stilling til og devaluering av ansvaret for samfunnet" (**Artikler**, p.24). ("The discovery of the everyday world. . .has led to an uncritical attitude to and a devaluation of responsibility towards society". Here for the first time in his work Solstad takes up the theme of the author's responsibility to society – a problem which was to assume major importance for him by the end of the decade.

In 1966, however, it was the fascination with concretism and "ny-enkelhet" which gained the upper hand, in Solstad's essays and in his fiction. In essay after essay he repeated in almost identical terms the necessity for the author "å gå inn i hverdagen" ("to go out into the everyday world").[9] In "Tingene og verden" (**Profil**, 1967), he described his movement away from metaphor and symbol and towards an acceptance of things as concrete objects without deep levels of meaning: "Jeg begynte å se tingene, ikke som symbol-funksjoner av mitt indre univers, men som rent konkrete ting som ikke har noen annen mening enn at de er der og har en bestemt funksjon" (**Artikler**, p.34). ("I began to see things not as symbolic functions of my inner universe, but as purely concrete things which have no other meaning than that they are there and have a certain function").

With this recognition, Solstad makes the transition from an earlier phase of Modernism to a more recent one, from what has been called "sensymbolismen" ("late Symbolism") to "ny-modernismen" ("Neo-Modernism") – or even Post-Modernism.[10] In European terms, the marked similarity to Kafka and Sartre gives way to the acknowledged influence of the work of the contemporary Swiss-German writer, Peter Bichsel.[11] Or to take a parallel from closer to home, Solstad moves from what in Danish literary history is called the first phase of Modernism (of which the foremost representative is Martin A. Hansen, with his anguished exploration in works like **Midsommerfesten** ("The Midsummer Party", 1946) of the alienation and isolation of the writer) – to the second phase, exemplified in some of the early poetry of Klaus Rifbjerg. Rifbjerg's collection **Konfrontation** ("Confrontation", 1960) is – in part at least – a celebration of the everyday world and a debunking of the elitism of poetry and of the poet as seer:

Terminologi	Terminology
Ja, ja, ja nu kommer jeg ned til jer ord. Trompet: forblæst. Skov: vissen. Karyatide: antik. Kærlighed: løgn. Halleluja: ræb. Poesi: hvor er mit brokbind?[12]	Yes, yes, yes I'm coming down to you words. Trumpet: puffed. Forest: withered. Caryatid: antique. Love: lie. Halleluja: belch. Poetry: where's my truss?

It was in poetry that the "ny-enkel" movement was particularly successful in Scandinavia, with poets like the Swedish Sonja Åkeson and the Danish Jørgen Leth, who had been present at the poetry seminar Solstad attended. Several of Solstad's **Profil**-colleagues flirted with the genre – some of Tor Obrestad's poems in **Vårt daglige brød** (Our Daily Bread, 1968) and of Paal-Helge Haugen's in **Sangbok** (Song Book, 1969) show clear affinities. But it was Jan Erik Vold amongst Norwegian poets who most wholeheartedly embraced "ny-enkelhet" in his poetry, and in fact pioneered its introduction to the Norwegian cultural scene from 1965 onwards. In his happiest and most popular poems, from **Mor Godhjertas glade versjon. Ja** (Mother Goodheart's Happy Version. Yes, 1968) he demonstrates an easy familiarity with the world and with the rhythms of everyday language which provoke delighted recognition (eg "Tale for loffen" – "In Praise of White Bread"; "Kropper" – "Bodies").

In prose writing too, the "ny-enkel" tradition had consequences for literary form.

Short and concrete texts were an ideal vehicle for this way of writing – what Solstad in his essay "Spilleren" called "kortprosa" ("short fiction").[13] Here he defined two kinds of "kortprosa", the "mini-novel" and the "situational-descriptive" text. The "mini-novel", which he exemplified by means of a Peter Bichsel text, "Roman", is a novel reduced to a skeleton – containing the bare bones of a novel, but stripped of all the flesh, of all possibilities of interpretation or levels of "significance" so that it is entirely open:

> . . . personene er redusert til navnløse figurer som beveger seg, handlingen er redusert til brokket av mulig handling, intrigen eller intriger blir gitt i knappe informasjoner som forutsetter at man selv gjetter seg til den, eller dem, og enhver intrige som oppdages, lar seg med letthet dementere hvis man sier: dette er intrigen.
>
> (**Artikler**, p.72)

> . . . the characters are reduced to nameless figures which move, the plot is reduced to fragments of possible plot, the intrigue or intrigues are supplied in brief statements on the understanding that you yourself make guesses about it, or them, and every intrigue which is discovered can easily be denied the moment you have said: this is the intrigue.

The other kind of "kortprosa", the "situational-descriptive" text, is illustrated in Solstad's article by a couple of illustrations from Jan Erik Vold: a text which, as the name suggests, simply describes a situation in concrete, non-metaphorical language. It is often only a brief paragraph of seemingly banal content, which confirms that it is enough that things exist: they do not need explaining. Yet at the same time such a text can give us a sudden glimpse **behind** the surface stability of the world and into the precariousness of existence:

> Det er et **brudd** på det regelmessige og kan hvis vi er våkne, åpne, gi oss det bevissthetssjokk vi trenger for å konfronteres med en virkelighet som omgir oss. Denne situasjon frigjør oss og avslører enda en gang hvilken illusjon det er når vi etablerer vår verden som en trygg, regelmessig verden.
>
> (**Artikler**, p.75)

> It is a **break** with normality, and it can, if we are alert and open, provide the shock to our consciousness which we need in order to be confronted with the reality which surrounds us. This situation liberates us, and reveals yet again what an illusion it is when we establish our world as a safe, regular world.

Nowhere are these two kinds of "kortprosa" more clearly illustrated than in the collection of texts Solstad published in 1967, **Svingstol**. The prose text which I discussed at the beginning of this article, "Nærvær", is a good example of the first kind, the "mini-novel". In these two pages of story, the characters are nameless figures, the action happens in disconnected fragments and any hints of intrigue which are thrown out ultimately lead nowhere: a letter arrives from Finland – but the lodger just takes it in and no more is heard of it; he is suddenly standing in the room – but has only come to ask for a bath; he comes back to the flat in the middle of the night – but only to go to bed.

Things do not happen as we expect them to happen in novels; the text redirects our attention to what we expect from literature, and its relationship with reality. In **Spiraler** all actions were significant and stood in an essential relationship to each other and to the theme of the story; in **Svingstol** they seem lacking in significance and their relationship to be a fortuitous one.

The "situational-descriptive" texts seem equally lacking in significance. "Innganger" ("Entrances") describes the entrance to the narrator's block of flats and to the one next door, which is almost the same but just slightly different, and how he sometimes used to take the wrong one. "Oppsøkte en gang" ("Once visited") describes a visit to a friend and their conversation. Yet at the same time both texts are more than just descriptions; both contain that break with normality to which Solstad drew attention in "Spilleren", and which gives a glimpse of something beyond. "Oppsøkte en gang" is short enough to quote in its entirety:

> Oppsøkte en gang noen jeg kjente. Ble bedt inn og traktert med øl og smørbrød. Jeg forsøkte å fortelle noe, men fortalte alltid noe annet. Jeg lo mye og var vel støyende. Den jeg kjente lo også. Men mens jeg fortalte og lo og hele tiden forsøkte å fortelle det jeg skulle fortelle, oppdaget jeg at jeg ikke hadde noe annet å fortelle enn det jeg fortalte.
>
> (p.214)

> Once visited someone I knew. Was asked in and served with beer and sandwiches. I tried to talk about something, but kept talking about something else. I laughed a lot and probably made quite a lot of noise. The person I know laughed too. But as I talked and laughed and tried continually to talk about what I had intended to talk about, I discovered that I did not have anything else to talk about than what I was talking about.

By the end of the text, the "everyday" absentmindedness has acquired a sinister twist; there is an indication of panic at the discovery that the calm surface of reality has suddenly become opaque. One cannot get behind the conventional light-hearted veneer of a "friendly visit", though continually aware that there **is** something behind it; and as a result the text produces a feeling of claustrophobia. In similar fashion, the narrator discovers at the end of "Entrances" that he has gone in to the wrong entrance; but this simple discovery leaves him feeling "nesten forferdet" – "almost aghast". In a world where you know your entrances – and they are described in a most prosaic and concrete fashion – you can suddenly awaken "as if from a dream" and discover that you are in the wrong one.

Looked at in this light, these concrete texts reveal another facet and become in fact metaphorical – they are about something other than what they seem on the surface to be describing. And I do not think that to interpret them like this is to force their meaning. In an article about another of these ultra-short texts, "Telegram", Solstad has in fact explained that he was trying to say something on a metaphorical level, but felt that he had not made it clear enough.[14] Some of the texts in this volume do remain on an "everyday" level – "Nærvær" for example consistently resists interpretation as a metaphor – but there is lurking behind many of them a feeling of unease, at times of threat, which suggests that Solstad has not moved so far as one might at first think from the nervy, ominous world of **Spiraler.** His characters, his plots, even his style of writing have undergone a transformation, chaos seems to have retreated as the world becomes a safe and normal place again; yet the narrator is to be caught at times looking over his shoulder, as if aware that normality is itself yet another fragile construction, yet another landscape of the mind.

The problematic nature of normality and man's relationship to it continued to preoccupy Solstad in his fiction and in his essays. He was becoming increasingly fascinated at this time by the necessity of role-playing; the way in which everyone has to play a role in society, and particularly the role of the author, who was expected to behave as society's clown.[15] It was a role which the radical author had to use as a disguise, in order to function as a saboteur, to attack the accepted norms of his society from inside; and like a saboteur, he had to change disguises/roles constantly in order to avoid being identified, being pigeon-holed and rendered harmless by those forces which were resistant to change.[16] It is evident that Solstad's awareness of the responsibility of the author towards his society, which had previously been muted, was growing rapidly during this period. And he was acting out his own theories in constantly changing his authorial role; from one book to the next, it was impossible to know what narrative voice he would adopt.

In harmony with his theoretical statements, Solstad's fictional works at this time became increasingly a demonstration of society's powers of moulding the individual, and the way in which not just authors but all members of society are allotted a part which they have to play. His next work was a play, **Georg: Sit du godt?** (George: Are You Sitting Comfortably?), which was produced in 1968 in collaboration with his fellow-writer Einar Økland, and written in Økland's native **nynorsk.** It is the story of the life of Georg, but told backwards, beginning with his death on his fiftieth birthday and ending with his mother's screams at his birth – and the embarrassing discovery that he was in fact stillborn. The point made in the play is that he might just as well have been; all that he has done through the various stages of life has been what was expected of him – he has played his many parts in the approved fashion as described by the two narrators:

F.1 Georg har hittil synt seg som ein god nordmann, men ennå har han ikkje stilt seg på den mest alvorlege prøva. Å klare **ungdomen** slik den står skildra i litteraturen. Det er to krav han nå må oppfylle.

F.2 Krav 1: Hans første kjærleik må vere hans einaste kjærleik. Den han alltid vender tilbake til, og som brenn med eit overnaturleg lys.

F.1 Men det er ikkje nok. For at lyset skal brenne, må han oppfylle krav 2: Han må svike sin første kjærleik. Og svik han den, då svik han alt.[17]

N.1 George has so far behaved like a good Norwegian, but he has still not faced up to the most serious test. To cope with **youth** as it is described in literature. There are two requirements he must fulfil.

N.2 First requirement: His first love must be his only love. The one to which his thoughts always return, and which burns with a supernatural light.

N.1 But that's not enough. To keep the light burning, he must fulfil the second requirement: he must betray his first love. And if he betrays that, then he betrays everything.

The tone of the play is light and frequently comical, as these lines suggest, with their tongue-in-cheek allusion to Sigurd Hoel and his evangelism of love.[18] Solstad's next work, **Irr! Grønt!** (Verdi! Gris! 1969), which is his first novel (the form he has almost without exception preferred from then onwards), is a more serious attempt to investigate the chances of a successful revolt against the pressure to conform.

In 1968 Solstad published an article about the Polish author Witold Gombrowicz, "Nødvendigheten av å leve inautentisk" ("The Necessity of Living Inauthentically").[19] It is not a presentation of Gombrowicz, as Solstad makes clear at the start, but an account of what the author has meant to him personally; and in it he draws attention to the affinities between Gombrowicz's thinking and his own. He outlines Gombrowicz's theory of Form, ie the way in which a person behaves, and which is determined by outside pressures. No-one who has any awareness of his own situation can identify himself with his own Form, for that is to capitulate to the picture others have and to lose one's personal integrity: "Det betyr at de som virkelig identifiserer seg fullt ut med det de gjør, lever et liv uten innsikt og følgelig også et løgnaktig liv. Vår eneste mulighet til å leve et etter omstendighetene menneskeverdig liv ligger i å opprettholde en distanse til den måten vi opptrer på" (**Artikler**, p.94). ("Those who really identify completely with what they are doing are living a life without insight and in consequence a life of lies. Our only possibility of living a life which is relatively human and dignified lies in maintaining a distance to the way we behave"). Or, to use Solstad's vocabulary, man must be "en spiller" – a player who is continually aware of the fact that he is playing a role, and tries to demonstrate to others the falseness of the ideal of authenticity. To be identical with oneself – the ultimate heroic ideal of Western man – means in fact to be lacking in self-awareness; it is an ideal which is dangerously short-sighted because ultimately unattainable and self-destructive. The dream of Freedom is equally illusory, and can be held up only by those who lack insight or are deliberately trying to manipulate others; instead of "frihet", our only realistic goal must be "frigjøring" (a making-free, or liberation).

Irr! Grønt! is the fictional embodiment of Solstad's deliberations on inauthentic living; and even without his declared interest in Gombrowicz, the parallels with the latter's work would be clear. The young protagonist, Geir Brevik, tries like Johnnie in **Ferdydurke** to maintain a distance between himself and the roles he is playing, to be an observer and controller of his interaction with others – and like Johnnie, he continually fails.[20] The problem which faces both of them is that of being young, and of coping with other people's expectations of how they will fulfil their roles – "Å klare **ungdomen** slik den står skildra i litteraturen", as it is put in **Georg: Sit du godt?**

The clearest demonstration of the problem in **Irr! Grønt!** is in Geir's relationship with the old couple in whose house he lodges – a variation on the landlord/guest motif from "En gjest" and "Nærvær", but with a very different intention. Geir is invited for a meal by them, and as they watch him eat he realises that he is becoming in their eyes a representative of Youth. He cannot disappoint them, and becomes more and more caught in the role of "Youthful", fulfilling their expectations by being ravenous in his appetite, radical in his opinions, risqué in his language. He loses the distance he has been trying to maintain to his role – and after the meal he feels exhausted and depressed, and swears that he will never again be manipulated like that into fitting in to a conventional mould.

In order to break the mould of Youth, he decides, he must become the manipulator of a situation himself. And the way to do it is through a relationship with a "young" girl. Again the parallel with Gombrowicz is clearly evident: Johnnie uses Miss Youthful as a medium for his self-liberation, whilst Geir chooses another "modern girl", Benedikte Vik. The two girls play their roles as "modern girls" perfectly, whilst being fully aware that they are roles, in a way that Johnnie and Geir can only envy, and which threatens to trap them in return in the conventional role of "young admirers". Geir tries to break out of this enforced role by seeming to fulfil it (asking Benedikte to the cinema) and then refusing to act it out (not making a pass at her). But she is stronger; she draws him into seducing her as they sit in the dark, looking at slides of her on holiday, being "attractive" – and thus she reaffirms his lack of freedom:

> De hadde et samleie. Det gikk bra. Det var så deilig! Først da de var "nakne", lå hud mot hud, hår mot hår, utladet, nedtellet – etter å ha svevet i bildenes rom – meldte den bleke ettertanken seg. Da lå Benediktes ansikt nedenfor ham, han kjente henne igjen i mørket, den uavhengige, tilsynelatende Benedikte som hadde frigjort seg fra et bilde ved hjelp av en serie med bilder.[21]

> They had sex. It went well. It was great! Not until they were "naked", lay skin to skin, hair to hair, discharged, counted down – after having floated through picture-filled space – did pale after-thoughts begin to emerge. Benedikte's face lay there beneath him, he could make it out in the dark, the independent, seeming Benedikte who had freed herself from a picture by means of a series of pictures.

It has become a competition: each can only "free" themselves by means of the unfreedom of the other. Geir cannot win alone, he needs an accomplice – and turns to Brit Winkel, the mousy, self-effacing girl who is Benedikte's flat-mate and acts as a foil to her beauty and self-confidence. By taking her into his confidence, Geir persuades her to make the glass which she holds up to Benedikte into a distorting mirror. By effectively becoming a parody of Benedikte, Brit deprives her of her "faces", her perfectly assumed role – and Benedikte breaks down and flees. Geir, with Brit as his accomplice, has won.

But it is a hollow triumph, and a momentary one; Geir has freed himself from the role imposed by Benedikte only to feel immediately afterwards that he may have become trapped by Brit. And there is in any case something uneasily paradoxical about a liberation that can be attained only through the deprivation of others' freedom. Like Johnnie in **Ferdydurke**, Geir can only destroy or be destroyed by the girl who attracts him. There is a strong streak of misogyny in Gombrowicz's fiction;[22] and not a little of it is echoed in **Irr! Grønt!** Not only does Geir set out to render Benedikte's way of life impossible for her; he also uses Brit as his instrument, without stopping to think that he is interfering with her personality and picture of herself too – and nor is there any hint in the text that he should consider that. The central character is as isolated in this novel as he was in any of Solstad's earlier studies of the helpless figure cast adrift in a meaningless universe. Society exists for Geir Brevik, but it exists as a threat and a challenge; there is no suggestion of the possibility of real warmth, real contact. Other people, and especially women, are pawns or opponents in a power game in which cunning and daring are the requisite qualities, and the prize is a lonely victory.[23]

In less than five years, Solstad had experimented in his prose fiction with three widely differing authorial roles and narrative styles: from Kafkaesque fantasies of an absurd and alien universe, in a language rich in imagery and allusiveness, he moved to sketches of everyday normality, related in a spare and unadorned style reminiscent of Peter Bichsel – but where the calm stability of events could suddenly shift slightly and stir a lurking panic; and finally to a study in the style of Gombrowicz of an attempt to live with and gain control over the split between self and role which modern consciousness has inherited. Three phases which represent at the same time three trends in European Modernist fiction – or as Jan Erik Vold put it in an essay on Solstad in 1983:

> Trolig kan man si at Dag Solstad med sine tre prosabøker på 1960-tallet . . . skrev seg inn i og samtidig gjennom en nutidig europeisk prosatradisjon. Etter **Spiraler** . . ., **Svingstol** . . ., **Irr! Grønt!** . . . var forfatteren Solstads læretid hos fremmede mestre over, og han stod klar til å gå løs på sitt store hjemlige prosjekt: hvordan kunne det gå så galt med norsk sosialisme, kommunisme og fellesskapsfølelse fra 1930-årene og utover.[24]

> I think one may say that Dag Solstad with his three prose works from the 1960s . . . wrote his way into and through a contemporary European prose tradition. After **Spiraler** . . . , **Svingstol** . . . , **Irr! Grønt!** . . . Solstad's apprenticeship as an author with foreign masters was at an end, and he was ready to start work on his main home-grown project: to investigate how things could go so wrong with Norwegian socialism, communism and solidarity from the 1930s onwards.

It is quite probable that Dag Solstad, looking back from later developments at his early work, would agree with this assessment of it as a time of apprenticeship, a learning process before he settled down in earnest to his "real" work as an author. However, to dismiss his early writing as merely derivative, an adaptation and an imitation of European trends, is to do less than justice to his achievement in these works – and to the importance of Solstad's writing and that of the other members of the **Profil** circle for Norwegian literature in the 1960s. They brought about a revitalization of literary debate, and generated an excitement about and an interest in experimental literature which had been noticeably lacking before.

By the end of the decade, however, things were very different; and here again, Solstad's writings can be seen as symptomatic of a general shift in the literary climate. Already at the end of 1968 it is possible to detect both a generation change and a programmatic shift in the pages of **Profil**. Most of the Modernist authors had left the editorial board of the journal during the course of that year, and in the fifth and last issue of 1968 Hansmagnus Ystgaard, who took over as chief editor, published an editorial outlining the growing political commitment of contemporary Norwegian authors. They were not, he explained, intending to leave literature in order to enter politics, but to combine the two, to find new literary expression for ideas which were new to literature: "Det viktige ville være å skape nye, folkelige og politiske genrer som gjennom sine kunstneriske frembringelser kan formidle en ny forståelsesmodell av samfunnet".[25] ("The important thing will be to create new, popular and political genres which through their artistic achievements can convey a new model for the understanding of society"). Over the next few years, discussion of political literature and the political drift of literature was to be the dominant preoccupation of **Profil**. The Modernist wave of the 1960s was over.

For several of the authors who had been in the forefront of Modernist writing, the end of the decade was a time of decisive change. Their predominant concerns had been with literature as an end in itself, the possibilities and problems of form, and its effectiveness as a vehicle for conveying an existential experience of man's alienation. Now, although the interest in form was not abandoned, literature became for this group a vehicle for a much more precise and localized intention: to investigate the structure and conflicts of contemporary Norwegian society. Solstad himself and other members of the **Profil** group were to join the political organization which eventually became AKP (m-l) – the Marxist-Leninist Workers' Communist Party; and the creative literature they produced changed accordingly.[26] Tor Obrestad published the widely-discussed documentary novel **Sauda! Streik!** (Sauda! Strike!, 1972), which was based upon the facts of the strike at the Sauda aluminium works in 1970. Espen Haavardsholm wrote **Zink** (Zinc, 1971), a volume of seven "reading texts" investigating in semi-fictional form the Capitalist structure of society and particularly the effects of the system on those it exploits; and then in **Grip dagen** (Seize the Day, 1973) he provided a commentary in verse form on the political events in Norway in 1972–3, around the time of the Common Market referendum.

Solstad also changed his style of writing – yet again; and here too one can discern, on the surface at least, a movement away from the central concerns of Modernist literature. In his novels over the next decade, Solstad moved from a prime concern with form and a charting of human isolation and angst to a direct involvement with contemporary political conflict, expressed in a form which is much closer to the traditional realistic novel.[27] It was not a sudden or a complete change; in his next novel, the semi-autobiographical **Arild Asnes, 1970** (1971), the writer-protagonist is as isolated a figure as he has been in any of Solstad's previous works, and the attempts to discover a meaning in existence through commitment to a political cause are by no means unproblematic. The novel has been interpreted by some critics as an artist novel, obsessed with the dilemmas of the modern intellectual, rather than as a political novel about the direction of society's development and the need for commitment.[28] It is in my opinion ultimately both; Solstad never becomes a mere mouthpiece for the party line, but retains his own idiosyncratic and at times paradoxical stance, whilst remaining firm in his basic convictions. It is this which makes the investigation of his "political" period just as fascinating as that of his "Modernist" one; but it is an investigation which lies outside the scope of this essay.[29]

Not all members of the **Profil** Modernist group made the same decision as did Obrestad, Haavardsholm and Solstad; some, such as Einar Økland and Jan Erik Vold, changed much less radically, and could be said to have gone on writing in the Modernist tradition. Yet there is a remarkable consensus in the shift towards commitment as the sixties give way to the seventies. There is a combination of extraneous reasons for this: the heightened political awareness following the student riots of 1968 and the publicity about the Vietnam war in the late '60s; the growth of new left-wing political parties in Scandinavia; the increasing importance of the Common Market debate, which reached its climax in the Norwegian referendum of 1972. Society with its demands had broken into the writers' self-imposed isolation; and the writers responded by going out into their society and taking a political stance.

Notes

I should like to thank Dag Solstad's publishers for their help: Aschehoug forlag for providing me with reviews of the early novels from their archives, and Knut Johansen of Oktober forlag for supplying me with books, information and advice. Odd Martin Mæland ran to ground some elusive numbers of **Profil** for me and offered some helpful criticism of my article.

1. All quotations from **Spiraler** and **Svingstol** are taken from **Spiraler/Svingstol**, Aschehougs Fontenebøker (Oslo, 1980). All translations in this article are my own.

2. See Philip Larkin's poem "Mr Bleaney", **The Whitsun Weddings** (London, 1964), p.10.

3. See Odd Martin Mæland: "Modernisme i Norge?" **Norsk litterær** årbok 1967 (Oslo, 1967), pp.185–205.

4. Editorial commentary by Tor Obrestad, **Profil** Nr.1, 1966, p.2.

5. Most of Solstad's articles from this period have been collected and published in his **Artikler om litteratur 1966–1981** (Oslo, 1981). All quotations from his articles are taken from this volume unless otherwise stated.

6. Compare Johan Borgen's play from 1938, **Mens vi venter** (Whilst We Wait), and Martin A. Hansen's "Ventesalen" ("The Waiting Room"), from the anthology of short stories **Agerhønen** (The Partridge, 1947).

7. Jean-Paul Sartre: **La Nausée** (Paris, 1938), p.177.

8. "Språk og metafor", **Arbeiderbladet** 22 January 1966. Also published in **Artikler om litteratur 1966–1981**.

9. See "Språk og metafor"; "Tingene og verden" (**Profil** 2, 1967); "Det trivielle/det fantastiske – flukt/akseptasjon" (**Vinduet** 2, 1967).

10. These categories are used by Odd Martin Mæland in his article "Modernisme i Norge?" (see Note 3). "Postmodernist" is however a term which he would have reservations about using to describe this phase nowadays.

11. See Solstad's article "Spilleren", from Paal-Helge Haugen et al. (eds.): **Moderne prosa** (Oslo, 1968), pp.17–34. Reprinted in **Artikler**, pp.69–81.

12. Klaus Rifbjerg: **Konfrontation** (Copenhagen, 1972), p.9.

13. See my translation of "Spilleren" and of several short texts from **Svingstol** in "Dag Solstad: 'The Player'" etc., **Comparative Criticism** Vol.6, edited by E. Shaffer (Cambridge, 1984), pp.229–55.

14. "En kort prosatekst", **Vår samtid** 6, 1968. Reprinted in **Artikler**, pp.90–92.

15. "Om forfatterens rolle i samfunnet", **Profil** 4, 1967. Reprinted in **Artikler**, pp.58–60.

16. "Spilleren", **Artikler** pp.77–78.

17. **Georg: Sit du godt?** (Oslo, 1968), p.71.

18. The last line of the speech above is almost a direct quotation from Sigurd Hoel's **Møte ved milepelen** (1947, trans. **Meeting at the Milestone**, 1951): "svikter du kjærligheten, så svikter du alt" (Oslo, 1964), p.270.

19. Published in **Vinduet** 3, 1968; reprinted in **Artikler**, pp.93–102.

20. My references to **Ferdydurke** are to the translation by Eric Mosbacher (London, 1965).

21. **Irr! Grønt!** (Oslo, 1969), p.131.

22. See the chapter "Women and Other Trivia", in Ewa M. Thompson: **Witold Gombrowicz**, Twayne's World Authors Series (Boston USA, 1979), pp.118–21.

23. For an analysis of **Irr! Grønt!** which draws a more directly political conclusion from Geir's final isolation, see Knut Johansen: "Den gode spilleren", in Knut Johansen/Willy Dahl: **Konfrontasjoner** (Oslo, 1970), pp.102–29.

24. Jan Erik Vold: "NO BATHING CLUB 1962", from Dag Solstad: **Sleng på byen** (a collection of articles written by Solstad in 1962, when he was a journalist on the Arendal newspaper **Tiden**). (Oslo, 1983), pp.235–36.

25. Editorial commentary, Profil 5, 1968.

26. For an investigation of the socio-political background to the literary and political change of climate at the end of the 1960s, see Søren Matthiesen: **Dag Solstad. Kunst og politik** (Aarhus, 1981).

27. **Arild Asnes, 1970** (1971); **25.september-plassen** (25th of September Square, 1974); **Svik. Førkrigsår** (Betrayal – The Pre-War Years, 1977); **Krig. 1940** (War. 1940, 1978); **Brød og våpen** (Bread and Weapons, 1980).

28. See Erik Østerud: **Modernisme – partilitteratur – sosialrealisme** (Oslo, 1980).

29. Otto Hageberg charts the paradoxes and internal contradictions in some of Solstad's more recent work in "Politikk og eksistens. To røyster i Dag Solstads forfatterskap", printed in Otto Hageberg: **Frå Camilla Collett til Dag Solstad** (Oslo, 1980), pp.81–100; and in "Den store maskerade", **Vinduet** 1, 1983, pp.3–15.

James McFarlane: A Bibliography

Compiled by Charlotte Carstairs

This bibliography includes a listing of all of James McFarlane's books, translations and major articles in journals, books and newspapers. It was reluctantly decided to abandon the attempt to trace his prodigious output of reviews, as the resources for a properly exhaustive search were not available.

Books

Ibsen and the Temper of Norwegian Literature. London: Oxford University Press, 1960. Reissued, New York: Farrar, Strauss and Giroux, 1979.

The Oxford Ibsen. Edited and translated (except where otherwise indicated) by James W. McFarlane. 8 vols. London: Oxford University Press, 1960–77.

Vol.I. **Early Plays.** (With Graham Orton). 1970.

Vol.II. **The Vikings at Helgeland, Love's Comedy** (translated by Jens Arup), **The Pretenders** (translated by Evelyn Ramsden and Glynne Wickham). 1962.

Vol.III. **Brand** (translated by James Kirkup with the assistance of James W. McFarlane), **Peer Gynt** (translated by Christopher Fry with the assistance of Johan Fillinger). 1972.

Vol.IV. **The League of Youth, Emperor and Galilean.** (With Graham Orton). 1963.

Vol.V. **Pillars of Society, A Doll's House, Ghosts.** 1961.

Vol.VI. **An Enemy of the People, The Wild Duck, Rosmersholm.** 1960.

Vol.VII. **The Lady from the Sea, Hedda Gabler** (translated by Jens Arup), **The Master Builder.** 1966.

Vol.VIII. **Little Eyolf, John Gabriel Borkman, When We Dead Awaken.** 1977.

The Oxford Ibsen: reprints and reissues:

Ibsen: **An Enemy of the People, The Wild Duck, Rosmersholm.** Translated and edited by James W. McFarlane. New York: Oxford University Press, "Hesperides Book", 1961.

Ibsen: **The Pretenders.** Translated by Evelyn Ramsden and Glynne Wickham with Notes on Staging by Glynne Wickham. London: Oxford University Press (paperback), 1962.

Ibsen: **Peer Gynt.** Edited by James W. McFarlane. English version by Christopher Fry based on a literal translation by Johan Fillinger. (Text published in advance of Vol.III of **The Oxford Ibsen.**) London: Oxford University Press (paperback), 1970.

Ibsen: **Plays. Pillars of Society, A Doll's House, Ghosts.** Translated with an Introduction by James W. McFarlane. London: Oxford University Press paperback No.217, 1970.

Ibsen: **Plays. An Enemy of the People, The Wild Duck, Rosmersholm.** Translated with an Introduction by James W. McFarlane. London: Oxford University Press paperback No.254, 1971.

Henrik Ibsen: **Four Major Plays. A Doll's House, Ghosts, Hedda Gabler, The Master Builder.** Translated by James W. McFarlane and Jens Arup with an Introduction by James W. McFarlane. London: Oxford University Press, "The World's Classics" (paperback), 1981.

Discussions of Ibsen: essays by various hands. Edited with an Introduction by James W. McFarlane. Boston, Mass: D.C. Heath and Co., 1962.

Henrik Ibsen: A Critical Anthology. Edited with an Introduction by James W. McFarlane. Harmondsworth, Middlesex: Penguin Books, 1970.

Modernism 1890–1930. Pelican Guide to European literature. Edited with major contributions by Malcolm Bradbury and James W. McFarlane. Harmondsworth, Middlesex: Penguin Books, 1976. 2nd revised edition, Harmondsworth, Middlesex: Penguin Books, 1983. Includes:

"The Name and Nature of Modernism". Malcolm Bradbury and James W. McFarlane. pp.19–55.

"The Mind of Modernism". James W. McFarlane. pp.71–93.

"Berlin and the Rise of Modernism 1886–96". James W. McFarlane. pp.105–19.

"Movements, Magazines and Manifestos: the Succession from Naturalism". Malcolm Bradbury and James W. McFarlane. pp.192–205.

"Modernist Drama: Origins and Patterns". John Fletcher and James W. McFarlane. pp.499–513.

"Intimate Theatre: Maeterlinck to Strindberg". James W. McFarlane. pp.514–26.

"Neo-Modernist Drama: Yeats and Pirandello". James W. McFarlane. pp.561–70.

"Chronology of Events". Compiled by James W. McFarlane in collaboration with Robin Young. pp.571–612.

Translations

Knut Hamsun: **Pan.** London: Artemis Press; New York: Noonday Press, 1955. Reprinted, London: Souvenir Press, 1974.

(Co-translator Kathleen McFarlane) Thorkild Hansen: **Arabia Felix: The Danish Expedition of 1761–67**. London: Collins, 1964.

(Co-translator John Lynch) Thorkild Hansen: **North West to Hudson Bay: the life and times of Jens Munk**. London: Collins, 1970. As **The Way to Hudson Bay: the life and times of Jens Munk**. New York: Harcourt Brace, 1970.

Knut Hamsun: **Wayfarers**. New York: Farrar, Strauss and Giroux; London: Souvenir Press, 1980. Reprinted, London: Pan Books, 1982.

Slaves of Love and other Norwegian short stories. Selected and edited with an Introduction by James W. McFarlane. Translated by James W. McFarlane and Janet Garton. Oxford: Oxford University Press, 1982.

Articles

1949 "Arno Holz's **Die Sozialaristokraten**: a study in literary collaboration". In **Modern Language Review**, Vol.44, No.4, October 1949, pp.521–33.

1951 "An unpublished novel by Paul Ernst". In **Publications of the Modern Language Association of America**, Vol.66, No.3, March 1951, pp.96–106.

"An experiment with translation". In **Modern Languages**, Vol.32, No.3, September 1951, pp.88–95.

1952 "An academic experiment with translation". In **International P.E.N. Bulletin**, Vol.2, No.3, January 1952, pp.59–62.

1953 "Modes of Translation". In **Durham University Journal**, Vol.45, No.3, June 1953, pp.77–93.

"Goethe's **Faust**". In **Times Literary Supplement**, 25 September 1953, p.612.

1954 "Ludvig Holberg". In **Times Literary Supplement**, 29 January 1954, pp.65–67.

"Knut Hamsun in English translation". In **The Norseman**, Vol.12, No.5, September–October 1954, pp.340–44.

"Plasticity in language: some notes on the prose style of Ernst Barlach". In **Modern Language Review**, Vol.49, No.4, October 1954, pp.451–60.

1955 "Hans Christian Andersen". In **Times Literary Supplement, Children's Book Section**, 1 July 1955, pp.x–xi.

1956 "Translated into English". In **The Norseman,** Vol.14, No.2, March–April 1956, pp.114–15.

"The Heresies of Alexander Kielland". In **The Norseman**, Vol.14, No.2, March–April 1956, pp.116–20.

"The Essence of Ibsen". In **Times Literary Supplement**, 25 May 1956, pp.305–6.

"The Whisper of the Blood: a study of Knut Hamsun's early novels". In **Publications of the Modern Language Association of America**, Vol.71, No.4, September 1956, pp.563–94. Reprinted in German as "Das Flüstern des Blutes: Eine Studie über Knut Hamsuns frühe Romane". In **Auf alten und neuen Pfaden,** ed. Heiko Uecker. Frankfurt am Main: Peter Lang, 1983, pp.175–216.

"Sigbjørn Obstfelder: **En præsts dagbog**". In **Proceedings of the First International Conference in Scandinavian Studies.** Cambridge, 1956. pp.79–88.

1957 "The Tiresian Vision". In **Durham University Journal**, Vol.49, No.3, June 1957, pp.109–15.

1958 "The Bravura of Bjørnson". In **Times Literary Supplement**, 20 June 1958, p.344.

1959 "Back to the Land: August Strindberg". In **Times Literary Supplement**, 6 March 1959, p.128.

"A Note on Ibsen's draft manuscripts to **Vildanden** and **Rosmersholm**". In **Modern Language Review**, Vol.54, April 1959, pp.244–45.

1962 "Letters from Strindberg". In **Times Literary Supplement**, 18 May 1962, pp.349–50. Reprinted in **T.L.S.I: Essays and reviews from the Times Literary Supplement, 1962, London**: Oxford University Press, 1963, pp.27–35.

"Ibsen's **Kjærlighedens Komedie**: some corrections to the Centenary Edition". In **Scandinavica**, Vol.1, No.1, May 1962, pp.63–65.

1963 "Kjeld Abell: rebel of Danish drama". In **Times Literary Supplement**, 18 January 1963, p.40.

"Ibsen's Bildung". In **Times Literary Supplement**, 2 May 1963, p.456.

"Recent Trends in Ibsen Scholarship and Criticism". In **Scandinavica**, Vol.2, No.2, November 1963, pp.108–21.

1964 "Hauptmann, Ibsen and the Concept of Naturalism". In **Hauptmann Centenary Lectures**, ed. K.G. Knight and F. Norman. (Lectures delivered at the Institute of Germanic Studies, University of London in 1962.) London: University of London, 1964. pp.31–60.

1965 "Two Ibsen Dates". In **Scandinavica**, Vol.4, No.2, November 1965, pp.145–47.

1966 "Meaning and evidence in Ibsen's drama". In **Contemporary Approaches to Ibsen** No.1, ed. Daniel Haakonsen. (**Ibsen Årbok**, Vol.8.) Oslo: Universitetsforlaget, 1966. pp.35–50. Reprinted in German as "Sinn und Deutung von Ibsens Drama". In **Henrik Ibsen: Wege der Forschung**, ed. Fritz Paul. Darmstadt: Wissenschaftliche Buchgesellschaft, 1977. Vol.487, pp.277–93.

1967 "Bjørnstjerne Bjørnson". In **Encyclopaedia Britannica**. 14th edition. Chicago, London: William Benton, 1967. Vol.3, pp.737–38.

"Henrik Ibsen". In **Encyclopaedia Britannica**. 14th edition. Chicago, London: William Benton, 1967. Vol.11, p.1024.

"Norwegian Literature". In **Encyclopaedia Britannica**. 14th edition. Chicago, London: William Benton, 1967. Vol.16, pp.658–60.

"Sigrid Undset". In **Encyclopaedia Britannica**. 14th edition. Chicago, London: William Benton, 1967. Vol.22, p.489.

1974 "Henrik Ibsen". In **The New Encyclopaedia Britannica**. 15th edition. Chicago, London: Helen Hemingway, 1974–83. Vol.9, pp.151–3.

"Norwegian Literature". In **The New Encyclopaedia Britannica**. 15th edition. Chicago, London: Helen Hemingway, 1974–83. Vol.10, pp.1161, 1177, 1206, 1246.

1976 "Ibsen's 'I Billedgalleriet': a question of definition". In **Scandinavica**, Vol.15, No.1, May 1976, pp.39–41.

1977 "The Spoken Word of Literature". In **Scandinavica**, Vol.16, No.1, May 1977, pp.29–33.

"Ibsen Research and the Ibsen Year 1978". In **Contemporary Approaches to Ibsen** No.3, ed. Harald Noreng et al. (**Ibsen Årbok** 1975/76.) Oslo: Universitetsforlaget, 1977. pp.253–57.

1978 "Ibsen's poem-cycle 'I Billedgalleriet': a study". In **Scandinavica**, Vol.17, No.1, May 1978, pp.13–48.

1979 "Cultural Conspiracy and Civilizational Change: Henrik Ibsen, Georg Brandes and the Modern European Mind". In **Journal of European Studies**, Vol.9, Part 3, No.35, September 1979, pp.155–73.

"Ibsen – a dissenting view". In **Drama and Society** (**Themes in Drama** No.1), ed. J. Redmond, Cambridge: Cambridge University Press, September 1979, pp.299–311.

"A Note on Peer Gynt in Egypt". In **Studi per Mario Gabrieli**, ed. Ludovica Koch. Naples: Aion-n 1979, xxii, pp.261–64.

1980 "The Structured World of Ibsen's Late Dramas". In **Ibsen and the Theatre: The Dramatist in Production**, ed. Errol Durbach. (Papers presented at the "Ibsen and the Theatre" conference at the University of British Columbia, Vancouver, in May 1978 to celebrate the 150th anniversary of Ibsen's birth.) New York; London: New York University Press, 1980. And in **Ibsen and the Theatre: essays in celebration of the 150th anniversary of Henrik Ibsen's birth**, ed. Errol Durbach. London: Macmillan, 1980. pp.131–40.

1984 "Apostasy in Prose". In **Scandinavica**, vol.23, No.2, November 1984, pp.101–18.

Review Articles

In **Erasmus**
German Life and Letters
Modern Language Review
Modern Languages
The Norseman
Notes and Queries
Scandinavica
Times Literary Supplement